THE PRINCIPLE OF SUSPENSION (ASIDDHATVA) IN PĀṆINIAN GRAMMAR

CRITICAL STUDIES IN PĀṆINIAN SYSTEM

The series is intended to stem the dwindling concern towards, and to rekindle interest in Sanskrit grammar, which is an essential tool to unravel the richness of values enshrined in Sanskrit language. This would include studies which would provide insight into the technical aspects such as descriptive language of Pāṇini's Aṣṭādhyāyī (metalanguage), the metarules, the principle of suspension, the principle of *anuvṛtti,* its bearing on the elliptical nature of the aphorisms of Pāṇini's Aṣṭādhyayī and the like. We hope that studies in this series would help interpret correctly the principles sought to be explained by Pāṇini in his grammar.

THE PRINCIPLE OF SUSPENSION (ASIDDHATVA) IN PĀṆINIAN GRAMMAR

Translation and Analysis of the Mahābhāṣya section ad Tripādī (A. 8.2.1-8.4.68) in the *Aṣṭādhyāyī*

MAŁGORZATA SULICH-COWLEY

Motilal Banarsidass Publications

MOTILAL BANARSIDASS
PUBLICATIONS
4741/23, Ansari Road, Daryaganj, New Delhi - 110002 (India)
Email: *mlbd@mlbd.com* | *sales@mlbd.com* | *exports@mlbd.com*
Website: *www.mlbd.com*

The Principle of Suspension (Asiddhatva) in Pāṇinian Grammar
by
Małgorzata Sulich-Cowley

First Edition Published in 2022

Published in India by Motilal Banarsidass Publications

ISBN : 978-93-91759-47-6 (HB)

Printed and bound in India

FOREWORD

The present work mainly focuses on the portions of the Mahābhāṣya relating to the principle of *asiddhatva*. The author starts with an introduction to Pāṇini, the Aṣṭādhyāyī and its auxiliary texts. The structure of the Aṣṭādhyāyī itself evinces that it saw light after a long grammatical tradition. Pāṇini himself mentions ten predecessors whose influence can be estimated from the perusal of Aṣṭādhyāyī and other related works. This is undoubtedly a unique creation of human mind. Kātyāyana (4th century B.C.) wrote the vārttikas on the sūtras of Aṣṭādhyāyī and Patañjali (about 150 B. C.) wrote the Mahābhāṣya on both the Aṣṭādhyāyī and the vārttikas. The three grammatical works : Aṣṭādhyāyī, vārttikas and Mahābhāṣya have received the appellation, *trimuni vyākaraṇam.* It is due to the grammatical and hermeneutical complexities observed in the Mahābhāṣya that its serious and engaging study has been traditionally compared with the administration of a big empire (*mahābhāṣyaṁ vā paṭhanīyam mahārājyaṁ vā pālanīyam*). The Mahābhāṣya appears to be easy to comprehend but quite difficult to understand. It requires absorbing endeavour to arrive at the targetted meaning. This aspect is the significant area where the meaningful contribution of the author can be seen and appreciated. She also discusses the distinction between the *asiddhatva* of *ābhīya* section beginning with A. 6. 4. 22 and that of *tripādī* section that begins with A. 8. 2. 1.

The author discusses various aspects of the term *asiddha* in the fourth section. She gives the literal meaning of the word *asiddha* as 'that which has not been accomplished'. She rightly assigns the meaning 'suspended' to the term '*asiddha*', which effectively means that the grammatical operation or the aphorism which has prescribed that grammatical operation should be treated as if non-existent for a particular grammatical operation to take place. Then she moves on to take up the *tripādī* and *ābhīya* sections and presents a good exposition supported by illustrations. The discussion on the *kāryāsiddhatva* and *śāstrāsiddhatva* versus *asiddhavattva* is useful in understanding the issues involved. Her comparison between *siddhatva* and *asiddhatva* on the one hand and between *siddhatva* and *nityatva* on the other is also worth paying attention to. Taking up the problem of *sthānivadbhāva* she says that the traditional view of treating *sthānivadbhāva* and *asiddhatva* at par is highly unlikely since Pāṇini has used two different terms and apparently invokes the standpoint of S. D. Joshi in her support.

Besides discussing the relevant grammatical issues logically, the significant contribution of the author is the fifth section of the present work. In 5.1 she gives the analysis of *ṣatvatukorasiddhaḥ* A. 6. 1. 86 accompanied by an explanatory exposition of various grammatical issues that have come up while discussing the significance of the sūtra. In 5.2 (pp. 61-434) she presents the translation and analysis of the whole of *tripādī* with adequate illustrations showing grammatical structure. While discussing the sūtras, vārttikas and Mahābhāṣya in detail, the explanation of the grammatical structure of the illustrations helps the reader in comprehending the relevant grammatical issues in the right perspective. After a proper understanding of the import of the sūtra, one gains insight into the problem and thus is enabled to appreciate the significance of grammatical nuances.

The principle of suspenson (*asiddhatva-siddhānta*) is fascinatingly complex. The main issues of this principle are discussed with reference to the four sūtras of the Aṣṭādhyāyī, namely, *ṣatvatukorasiddhaḥ* A. 6. 1. 86, *asiddhavadatrābhāt* A. 6. 4. 22, *pūrvatrāsiddham* A. 8. 2. 1 and *sthānivadādeśo'nalvidhau* A. 1. 1. 56. Traditionally the concept of *asiddhatva* is delineated by Kātyāyana in his vārttika on the sūtra *ṣatvatukorasiddhaḥ* A. 6. 1. 86 : *ṣatvatukorasiddhavacanam-ādeśalakṣaṇapratiṣedhārthamutsargalakṣaṇabhāvārthaṁ ca*. The statement : *ādeśa-lakṣaṇapratiṣedhārtham* is purported to prohibit the grammatical operation conditioned by the substitute and the expression *utsargalakṣaṇabhāvārtham* consists in allowing the grammatical function based on the substituend. The word *utsarga* means 'substituend'. Its etymology may be understood like this: *utsṛjyate apasāryate ādeśena iti utsargaḥ*. It may be pertinent to point out here that according to the traditional interpretation *sthānivadbhāva* does not deviate from the interpretation of *asiddhatva*. However, S. D. Joshi's opinion differs. He holds the view that *sthānivadbhāva* has only positive function involved in a grammatical operation conditioned by the substituend since, according to him, it does not block the grammatical function occasioned by the substitute. Let me explain this point by referring to one of his papers published in Lokaprajñā[1]. Discussing the principle of *asiddhatva* in it he explains that the prohibition of the grammatical function conditioned by the substitute does not extend to the sphere of *sthānivadbhāva*.

In order to comprehend the view of S. D. Joshi in the right perspective, I reproduce his exposition of the principle under discussion from the paper mentioned above. While deriving the primary form *bhugna*, he says that after adding the primary suffix *kta* to *bhujo kautilye*, we have *bhuj + ta*. At this stage both *coḥ kuḥ* A. 8. 2. 30 and *oditaśca* A. 8. 2. 45 become applicable simultaneously. After the suffix *ta* has been replaced by *na* by *oditaśca* A. 8. 2. 45 in consonance with the grammatical requirement, the aphorism *coḥ kuḥ* A. 8. 2. 30 does not apply because *nakāra* is not a *jhal* consonant. By *pūrvatrāsiddham* A. 8. 2. 1, the substituted *nakāra* is treated as if non-existent and consequently *jhal* consonant *takāra* becomes available and *coḥ kuḥ* A. 8. 2. 30 applies. We have the form *bhugna* after replacing *j* by *g*. Here both the aspects *ādeśalakṣaṇaprati-ṣedha* and *utsargalakṣaṇabhāva* of the principle of suspension have applied. The other similar example which he gives is *rājabhiḥ*. Here the elision of *nakāra* takes place by *nalopaḥ prātipadikāntasya* A. 8. 2. 7 and as such the aphorism *ato bhisa ais* A. 7. 1. 9 becomes applicable. Since the latter sūtra belongs to *sapādasaptādhyāyī* and the former to the *tripādī*, the elision of *nakāra* is treated as if non-existent and *ato bhisa ais* A. 7. 1. 9 does not apply and we have the form *rājabhiḥ*.

According to S. D. Joshi only *utsargalakṣaṇabhāva* is seen to function in *sthānivadbhāva*. The prohibition based on the substitute (*ādeśalakṣaṇapratiṣedha*)

---

[1] *manmate tadvailakṣaṇyamevaṁ vartate - sthānivadbhāvena utsargalakṣaṇaṁ kāryaṁ kriyate. ādeśalakṣaṇaṁ na pratiṣidhyate. asiddhasiddhāntena tu utsargalakṣaṇaṁ kāryaṁ kriyate ādeśalakṣaṇaṁ ca pratiṣidhyate.* Lokaprajñā, volume 2, P. 273 (Lokabhashaprachara-samiti, Bada Odiya Matha, Puri, 1988). This was the felicitation volume dedicated to Shri N. S. Tatacharya.

does extend there. To explain this, he gives an example of *aijyata*: *yaj* + *ya* + *ta*. In this grammatical situation, the sūtra *luṅlaṅlṛṅkṣvaḍudāttaḥ* A. 6. 4. 71 prescribes the augment *aḍ* and *vacisvapiyajādīnāṁ kiti* A. 6. 1. 15 enjoins *samprasāraṇa*. Being *nitya*, if *samprasāraṇa* takes place, *yakāra* is replaced by *ikāra*. Then the condition of *aḍāgama* does not remain in force. But the augment *āḍ* becomes available by *āḍajādīnām* A. 6. 4. 72 since the base now begins with a vowel. Here the augment *aḍ* which is conditioned by the substituend does not take place but *āḍ-āgama* comes which is conditioned by the substitute. But the *sthāniuvat*-sūtra *acaḥ parasmin pūrvavidhau* A. 1. 1. 57 brings about the grammatical operation conditioned by the substituend. Obviously, he says, it does not prohibit the grammatical function based on the substitute[2]. He bases his view on Pāṇini's use of two different terms and hence opposes the traditional view which generally sees no difference between *sthānivadbhāva* and *asiddhatva*. So, according to him, there must be difference in their grammatical functions also. In this way his view logically culminates in holding that the sūtra *na padāntadvirvacanavareyalopasvarasavarṇānusvāradīrgha-jaścarvidhiṣu* A. 1. 1. 58 is an interpolation. On the other hand if we accept that this is the genuine sūtra of the Aṣṭādhyāyī, then by implication (*jñāpana*) we arrive at the conclusion that the *ādeśalakṣaṇapratiṣedha* does extend even to the sphere of *sthānivadbhāva*. It is clear that only terming A. 1. 1. 58 an interpolation becomes the raison d'etre for the point of view that *ādeśalakṣaṇapratiṣedha* does not have any role to play in *sthānivadbhāva*. The tenor of S. D. Joshi's view seems to be sweeping in the following manner. There are two parts of the

---

[2] *aijyata ityatra yaj ya ta ityasyāvasthāyām luṅlaṅlṛṅkṣvaḍudāttaḥ ityanena aḍāgamaḥ prāptaḥ. vacisvapiyajādīnaṁ kiti ityanena samprasāraṇaṁ prāptam. samprasāraṇam aḍāgamanimittaṁ vihanti. yataḥ samprasāraṇe kṛte ajāditvāt āḍajādīnām ityanena āḍāgamaḥ prāpnoti. na tu tatra āḍāgamaḥ iṣṭaḥ. atra samprasāraṇaṁ nityam. yataḥ samprasāraṇm aḍāgamanimittaṁ vihanti param āḍāgamaḥ samprasāraṇanimittaṁ na vihanti ityataḥ samprasāraṇasya nityatvam. atra ca sthānilakṣaṇaḥ utsargalakṣaṇo vā aḍāgamaḥ na bhavati. ādeśalakṣaṇa āḍāgamaśca bhavati. sthānivatsūtreṇa acaḥ parasmin pūrvavidhau ityanena utsargalakṣaṇabhāvaḥ sampādyate na tu ādeśalakṣaṇapratiṣedhaḥ*. Ibid., p. 271

sūtra *sthānivadādeśo'nalvidhau* A. 1. 1. 56: 1. *sthānivadādeśaḥ* and 2. *analvidhau*. So far as the first part is concerned, his view that *ādeśalakṣaṇapratiṣedha* does not extend here seems to be acceptable. But it is the second part which renders his view unacceptable. The part *analvidhau* necessitates the following two sūtras and also shows that *ādeśalakṣaṇapratiṣedha* does have a role to play in *sthānivadbhāva*. The compound *alvidhiḥ* has four kinds of *tatpurṣsa* in it. Let us take *alvidhiḥ* as a sixth case-ending *tatpurṣa*. In *avadhīt*, the elision of *akāra* of *vadha* takes place by *ato lopaḥ* A. 6. 4. 48. It is *alvidhi*. So, the substitue elision is not treated as the substituend. As such the sūtra *ato halāderlaghoḥ* A. 7. 2. 7 prescribes *vṛddhi* in place of the penultimate short *akāra*. To ward off this undesirable situation the rule *acaḥ parasmin pūrvavidhau* A. 1. 1. 57 applies and the elision is treated as the substituend and *vṛddhi* is prohibited. In this case both *ādeśalakṣaṇa-pratiṣedha* and *utsargalakṣaṇabhāva* are seen to take place. The grammatical operation which is conditioned by the substitute elision is prohibited by virtue of *acaḥ parasmin pūrvavidhau* A. 1. 1. 57. It may be understood that the substituend-induced absence of *vṛddhi* becomes a reality. The other illustrations *kāni santi* and *kau staḥ* show that the sūtra *na padāntadvir-vacanavareyalopasvarasavarṇānusvāradīrghajaścarvidhiṣu* A. 1. 1. 58 is required to dispense with the defect of overpervasion of the rule *acaḥ parasmin pūrva-vidhau* A. 1. 1. 57. Otherwise *iko yaṇaci* A. 6. 1. 77 in the first illustration and *eco'yavāyāvaḥ* A. 6. 1. 78 in the second would become applicable. So, the view that A. 1. 1. 57 is an interpolation needs to be examined logically.

However author's critical observations on Patañjali may be understood as inspirational in order that the young scholars are exhorted to dive deep into the grammar of Pāṇini along with the vārttikas and the Mahābhāṣya. Nevertheless this should be borne in mind that freedom of thought is attractively inviting to subscribe to such points of view which do not toe the line of traditionally accepted views. It is not that the final word has been pronounced in the system but to take a view which is critical of the tradition should be based on logical grounds and ought to be adequately exemplified.

Finally I take this opportunity to congratulate the author for the present work which will definitely arouse interest in the grammar of Paṇini and allied works.

Kanshi Ram

To Robin and my Mum, Ewa, for sharing my constant suspension in life

Contents

Preface

The present work is my slightly revised PhD dissertation which I defended in 2013 at the Oriental Faculty of the University of Warsaw. It is a result of my interest in the development of the Sanskrit linguistic tradition, which started many years ago at the time whilst I was still an undergraduate student in Warsaw, and continued during my studies in Pune.

The present volume concentrates on the early period of the development of the Indian Sanskrit grammatical tradition. It analyses the so-called suspension principle (*asiddhatva*) employed by Pāṇini in his *Aṣṭādhyāyī* and presents the interpretation of the phenomenon adopted by Patañjali, the most renowned commentator of Pāṇini and author of the *Mahābhāṣya*. The work focuses on the *Tripādī* section of the *Aṣṭādhyāyī*, namely the last three sub-chapters of the treatise, and the relevant excerpts from the *Mahābhāṣya* commentary. The principle of suspension was a unique device employed by Pāṇini in his system that allowed for the temporary omission of certain rules in the process of grammatical analysis. Its interpretation is, however, by no means uniform and agreed upon even within the school of Sanskrit linguistics. The aim of my research was to demonstrate the solutions Patañjali proposes to the problem of suspended rules in grammar, less to analyse whether these solutions were actually in accord with Pāṇini's intentions.

The work is divided into six chapters the first two of which form a brief introduction to the system of Sanskrit grammar and present the historical background of the Sanskrit linguistic tradition. Chapter 1 concentrates on a description of crucial elements of the Pāṇinian system, which have been chosen to enable the reader to follow the analysis of the *asiddhatva* section. Reference is also made to a number of relevant auxiliary texts such as the *Dhātupāṭha*, *Gaṇapāṭha*, *Uṇādisūtra*s and *Phiṭsūtra*s. Chapter 2 introduces the background of Patañjali and the *Mahābhāṣya*, gathering information regarding the time and place where the text was composed. Further, it presents a brief outline of some of the philosophical issues Patañjali raises. Chapter 3 explains the structure that was adopted in the translation of respective sections of the *Mahābhāṣya*. The translation follows a three-fold pattern: Pāṇini's *sūtra*, Patañjali's commentary and explanations with references to other grammatical and, occasionally, philosophical treatises. The adoption of such a structure aims to facilitate the understanding of the *Mahābhāṣya*, a text deceitfully succinct yet surprisingly complex in nature.

The latter three chapters concentrate on the principle of *asiddhatva*. Chapter 4 forms the theoretical background for the translation that follows. The first part of the chapter explains the terminological issues related to the semantic range of *asiddhatva* which Pāṇini never defined. The second part of the chapter discusses the *Aṣṭādhyāyī* chapters where *asiddhatva* operates with a particular focus on the *Tripādī* section, whose contents are presented in detail. In addition, I also discuss some crucial aspects of the way the *Tripādī* functions, such as the role and application of technical terms (*saṃjñā*) and rules of interpretation (*paribhāṣā*), or the subject of suspension. Chapter 4 also includes the state of research on the *asiddhatva* topic focusing on its interpretation in Pāṇini's *Aṣṭādhyāyī*. It also presents an outline of the *siddhatva* principle advanced by Joshi and Kiparsky; the proposition of one unified governing principle operating throughout the *Aṣṭādhyāyī* with the exclusion of the last three sub-chapters. This principle was never mentioned by either Pāṇini or any of his commentators but seems to be implied by the very use of *asiddhatva*.

The greatest part of the volume comprises Chapter 5, which contains the translation of *sūtra* A. 6.1.86 and section A. 8.2.1-8.4.68 of the *Aṣṭādhyāyī*, along with the *Mahābhāṣya* commentary and extensive additional explanations. The main focus of the present volume is the latter section; the former individual rule is often referred to due to its relevance for the *asiddhatva* concept. This is the first rule in which the term *asiddha* appears and its interpretation by early commentators influenced all the other instances of suspension in the *Aṣṭādhyāyī*. The summary of Patañjali's comprehension of the rules belonging to the *Tripādī* section, including the solutions he proposes with particular reference to those that go against Pāṇini's own treatise, is presented in Chapter 6.

There are a number of people who have supported me over the years and without whom this volume would never have been published; people who have been a constant inspiration and motivation along the way. Firstly, I would like to thank Prof. Piotr Balcerowicz, my MA and PhD dissertations supervisor, who has been my mentor for many years. He has taught me the importance of critical thinking in linguistic and philosophical research, and encouraged to think outside the box. I am extremely indebted to Prof. Johannes Bronkhorst who was always willing to discuss my ideas with me and whose expertise in the field of Sanskrit linguistics proved invaluable. Their often unorthodox approach to Sanskrit linguistics and philosophy allowed me to look at the Indian tradition from an entirely different angle. I would like to extend my gratitude to Prof. Marek Mejor who, as the only expert in Poland on Pāṇinian grammar, was an invaluable source of information. His attention to detail and extremely useful comments made it possible for me to appreciate the work of Sanskrit grammarians. This work would never have been written were it not for Prof. Saroja Bhate, whom I met during my stay in Pune all those years ago and who planted the seed of interest in the topic in question. I have benefited greatly from her immense knowledge combined with her critical approach. I would also like to express my gratitude to the Motilal Banarsidass Publications, who enabled me the publication of my work and for their patience throughout the process.

Last but not least, I would like to thank my mum, Ewa, and my husband, Robin, who have been extremely supportive over the years and persevered despite numerous crises along the way. And to them I dedicate this book.

Abbreviations

A – *Aṣṭādhyāyī*
abl. – *ablativus*
acc. - *accusativus*
aor. – *aorist*
AB – *Aitareya Brāhmaṇa*
AV – *Atharvaveda Saṃhitā*
AVP – *Atharvaveda Paippalāda Saṃhitā*
AVŚ – *Atharvaveda Śaunaka Saṃhitā*
ā3 – prolated vowel *a*
ṚgV – *Ṛgveda Saṃhitā*
ṚgVKh - *Ṛgveda Khilāni*
caus. – *causativum*
dat. – *dativus*
desid. – *desiderativum*
du. – *dualis*
f. – *femininum*
fut. – *futurum*
gen. – *genetivus*
impf. – *imperfectum*
impv. – *imperativus*
instr. – *instrumentalis*
intens. – *intensivum*
KS – *Kaṭhaka Saṃhitā*
KV – *Kāśikāvṛtti*
loc. – *locativus*
m. – *masculinum*
MPV – *Mahābhāṣyapradīpavyākhyānāni*
MS – *Maitrāyaṇī Saṃhitā*
MW – Monier Williams Dictionary
n. - *neutrum*
Nir – *Nirukta*
nom. – *nominativus*
perf. – *perfectum*
pl. – *pluralis*
pot. – *potentialis*
praes. ind. – *praesens indicativi*
prec. – *precativus*
PŚ – *Paribhāṣenduśekhara*

PhS – *Phiṭsūtra*s
ŚB – *Śatapatha Brāhmaṇa*
sg. – *singularis*
subj. – *subjunctivus*
TS – *Taittirīya Saṃhitā*
UN – *Uṇādisūtra*s
VMBh_1 – *Mahābhāṣya*, Kielhorn's edition
VMBh_2 – *Mahābhāṣya*, Rohtak edition
voc. – *vocativus*
VS – *Vājasaneyī Saṃhitā*

1 Sanskrit grammatical tradition before Patañjali

Language, speech, words and sounds have always been important for the Indian tradition; they already played a very important role in Vedic literature (1200-500 BCE). As the language of the four *Veda*s, namely the *Ṛgveda*, *Sāmaveda*, *Yajurveda* and *Atharvaveda*, became difficult to understand with time, it became of crucial importance to preserve them in an unaltered form for the proper performance of rituals. Any deviation from the original form of incantations might have rendered the ritual invalid. This attitude towards the *Veda*s led, firstly, to the development of the science of phonetics, and consequently grammar. Every school of Vedic tradition produced texts devoted to correct pronunciation called *prātiśākhya*s and *śikṣā*s. The former focused on the analysis of the text of the *Veda*s (*padapāṭha*) and their undivided form (*saṃhitāpāṭha*); they also discussed some general phonetic issues. The latter, on the other hand, were connected with a particular branch of Vedic texts. Most of the *śikṣā*s available to us are post-Pāṇinian.[1] The work known as *Pāṇiniyaśikṣā*, composed both in verse and in prose (or rather two versions of the same work), was attributed to Pāṇini but he was most probably not the author of either.[2] As for the *prātiśākhya*s, there are five texts available to us: *Ṛkprātiśākhya* composed by Śaunaka, *Taittirīyaprātiśākhya* belonging to the *Yajurveda*, *Vājasaneyiprātiśākhya* composed by Kātyāyana[3] belonging to the *Śukla Yajurveda*, *Atharvaprātiśākhya* (or *Caturadhyāyika*) by Śaunaka and *Sāmaprātiśākhya*. The former three are considered the oldest[4] but their precise chronology is very difficult to determine, as is their relation to Pāṇini.[5]

As the main focus of this work is Patañjali's *Mahābhāṣya*, only an outline of the earlier grammatical tradition will be presented here.

1.1 Pāṇini

Pāṇini, known also as Dākṣīputra Pāṇini[6] lived c. 5th-4th century BCE. He came from Śalātura in the north-western part of the Indian Subcontinent (probably near modern Lahore in Pakistan).[7] Pāṇini's work was preceded, as mentioned earlier, by a long tradition of phonetics and phonology. However, there must have also existed a grammatical tradition as one cannot expect the

---

1 SCHARFE 1977:176, CARDONA&JAIN 2017:105-107

2 CARDONA 1997a:182.

3 SCHARFE 1977:134. This Kātyāyana is most probably the author of the *vārttika*s in the *Mahābhāṣya* according to Scharfe.

4 WIELIŃSKA 1998:111, CARDONA1997(a):356 fn. 428.

5 WIELIŃSKA 1998:111-112.

6 VMBh_1 I:75.13, III:251.12. SCHARFE 1977:88.

7 SCHARFE 1977:88, CARDONA1997a:260-261, 268.

work such as Pāṇini's to appear without any prior and less sophisticated linguistic thought. As a matter of fact, Pāṇini in his own treatise mentions ten names: Āpiśali, Kāśyapa, Gārgya, Gālava, Cakravarman, Bhāradvāja, Śākaṭāyana, Śākalya, Senaka and Sphoṭāyana. These names of his predecessors serve as a technical device in the *Aṣṭāḍhyāyī* but they also imply the existence of a growing grammatical tradition in the centuries preceding Pāṇini.

1.2 *Aṣṭādhyāyī*

Pāṇini was the author of the *Aṣṭādhyāyī*; a work consisting of almost 4000 rules called *sūtra*s[8] divided into eight chapters (*adhyāya*) and further into four sub-chapters (*pāda*) each. The organization of the work is subject to the basic principle governing Pāṇinian grammar which was brevity (*lāghava*). The first chapter describes technical terms (*saṃjñā*) and rules of interpretation (*paribhāṣā*) which serve as metarules and help to interpret remaining rules of the treatise. The second chapter focuses on compounds (*samāsa*), *kāraka*s, nominal and verbal endings. Chapters three, four and five describe affixes (*pratyaya*),[9] such as feminine, primary (*kṛt*) and secondary (*taddhita*) suffixes. These chapters were by some considered analytical, contrary to chapters 6 to 8, which were referred to as syntactic because they describe operations on elements being parts of a sentence.[10] In the sixth chapter we find the rules prescribing accent, reduplication of morphemes and infixes, which continue into the seventh *adhyāya*. The last chapter of the *Aṣṭādhyāyī* focuses on operations pertaining to a *pada*, that is, usually, a finite word form, such as accent, reduplication of the whole word and consonantal sandhi.[11]

The *Aṣṭādhyāyī* can also be seen as composed of two parts, which are crucial for the understanding of *asiddhatva*, namely *Sapādasaptādhyāyī* – seven chapters and one sub-chapter, and *Tripādī* (or *pūrvatrāsiddha*) – the last three sub-chapters of the eighth chapter.[12] This division is made by the *sūtra* A. 8.2.1

---

[8] The number of rules differs in different commentaries: 3996 or 3981 in the *Kāśikāvṛtti* to which the *Śivasūtra*s and the opening stanza *atha śabdānuśāsanam* ("Here it is the instruction about words.") are added. The *Siddhāntakaumudī* of Bhaṭṭoji Dīkṣita presents 3976 rules. These differences are due to some of the *sūtra*s being divided in later commentaries, some being rejected and some being considered *vārttika*s. See SHARMA 2002:3, SCHARFE 1977:89.

[9] The opening *sūtra* of the third chapter uses the term *pratyaya*, which is translated here as 'a suffix' (also because the following rule in the *Aṣṭādhyāyī* establishes that a *pratyaya* is added 'after' a stem), even though it would probably be better to say 'an affix', as it allows a wider meaning.

[10] BUISKOOL 1939:15-16. Buiskool presents the division based on analysis (chapters 1-5) versus synthesis (chapters 6-8).

[11] RAY 2004:18.

[12] BUISKOOL 1939:19. Taking into consideration the division into analytical and synthetical parts, the former concentrating on the analysis of the word and the latter on building the word up

pūrvatrāsiddham || ("[All the subsequent rules up to A. 8.4.68 are considered] suspended with respect to the previous [rules]"). This work concentrates on this last section and the suspension principle (*asiddhatva*) as understood by Patañjali, the commentator of Pāṇini. A more detailed description of this section will be presented in chapter 4.

A brief outline of the devices employed by Pāṇini in his grammar will enable the reader to follow the structure and meaning of *sūtra*s, and will make discussion in Patañjali's *Mahābhāṣya* clearer. The *sūtra*s in the *Aṣṭādhyāyī* are of different types. The first two have already been mentioned, that is the *saṃjñā* and *paribhāṣā* rules; sometimes collectively called metarules because they form the foundation for proper understanding of other rules. The former introduce technical terms and can refer to linguistic elements, particular meanings of terms or describe their properties. *Saṃjñā*s constitute of common Sanskrit words assigned a technical meaning as well as artificial terms invented for the purpose of a grammatical system. The *paribhāṣā*s serve as rules of interpretation and could also be divided into different types. Some of them are explicitly stated in the *Aṣṭādhyāyī*, some are implied and later gathered in separate treatises; yet some are everyday maxims that commentators employ in grammar. The next class of *sūtra*s is governing rules (*adhikāra*). They introduce the topic and recur in following rules until another *adhikāra* stops them. Pāṇini uses governing rules for the sake of brevity together with the technique of *anuvṛtti* ('continuation'). The *niyama* and *atideśa* rules are restrictive and extending *sūtra*s respectively. Their purpose is to exclude elements from a given operation or include elements in an operation that was prescribed by a general rule. Pāṇini also employs optional (*vibhāṣā*) and negative (*pratiṣedha*/*niṣedha*) rules. The former can be three-fold: *prāpta* – making the previously mentioned operation optional; *aprāpta* – optional permission of an operation that without such permission would not take place, and *ubhayatra* – when *prāpta* and *aprāpta* occur simultaneously. There is also *vyavasthitavibhāṣā* where the option is fixed only for enlisted elements. Optionality is expressed in various ways by Pāṇini (*vā*, *vibhāṣā* and *anyatarasyām*), which, as Kiparsky showed,[13] suggests its varying aspects and which should be manifested in adopted translation ('usually, preferably', 'rarely' and 'optionally' respectively). Negative *sūtra*s can again be two-fold: *paryudāsa*, which excludes certain elements from the prescribed operation (term negation), and *prasajya*, which negates the operation itself (predicate negation). There are also words with irregular, or too complex,

again, Buiskool divides the second further part into two (which, of course, corresponds to the *Sapādasaptādhyāyī* and *Tripādī* sections) based on respective operating principles. These are *sarvatra siddham* and *pūrvatrāsiddham* respectively.

[13] KIPARSKY 1980:1.

formation process and these are gathered in *nipātana sūtra*s – rules where ready-made forms are presented. Lastly, we have *vidhi* rules – operational rules that prescribe operations such as substitution (*ādeśa*), addition of suffixes (*pratyaya*) or augments (*āgama*) and finally, deletion (*lopa*).

The *Aṣṭādhyāyī* codified Sanskrit to an extent, which prompted the composition of numerous commentaries within the Pāṇinian school. The first commentator whose work was preserved was Kātyāyana, living probably c. 250 BCE,[14] who was considered to have been a southerner.[15] His commentary takes the form of *vārttika*s, the statements explaining, elaborating on or modifying Pāṇini's rules. They were preserved in Patañjali's *Mahābhāṣya*, which will be discussed in detail in Chapter 2. There are *vārttika*s concerning only one third of the *Aṣṭādhyāyī* in Patañjali's work; we find them in 1245 *sūtra*s.[16] It is impossible to determine whether Kātyāyana commented on all the *sūtra*s, and the remaining part of his commentary was lost as it did not prove useful to Patañjali, or if he just chose to comment on only some of the rules. The latter is, however, less probable.[17] Kielhorn in his edition of the *Mahābhāṣya* identifies Kātyāyana's work based on repetitions and paraphrases he finds in Patañjali's text.[18] It has been suggested that Kātyāyana tried to find faults in Pāṇini's grammar but this view seems untenable. He rather, as Sharma concludes,[19] tried to show a different perspective from which *sūtra*s could be analysed.

Joshi was one of the scholars to have suggested that Kātyāyana was a follower of a different school of grammar and that contrary to Pāṇini, who represented a structural and formal approach to grammar, Kātyāyana's school represented a functional and semantic one.[20] However, these views did not gain wider acceptance.[21]

---

[14] RAY 2004:30-31.

[15] CARDONA 1997a:269, JOSHI 1968:i. This statement is argued for a couple of reasons based on the constructions Kātyāyana uses. One of them is his preference for *taddhita* formations over corresponding sentences (see fn 36) and the other the acceptance for negative compounds with finite verbs (such as *apacasi* – "You don't cook [right], you fool!"). With reference to the latter, SCHARFE (1977:139) referring to BLOCH (1961:65) claims that such constructions are characteristic to Dravidian languages, which is supposed to serve as an evidence for Kātyāyana's origin in the south of India.

[16] SHARMA 2002:6.

[17] One can only assume of course but it stands to reason that if other *vārttika*s had been available to Patañjali, he would have commented on them. Patañjali does not always elaborate on the *vārttika*s but he usually acknowledges their existence. Whether Kātyāyana composed only a partial commentary or it had already been lost by the time of the *Mahābhāṣya* is impossible to determine.

[18] CARDONA 1997a:247.

[19] SHARMA 2002:9.

[20] JOSHI 1968:iii.

[21] CARDONA 1997a:251.

The first full commentary analysing all the *sūtra*s of the *Aṣṭādhyāyī* that has been preserved is the *Kāśikāvṛtti*, composed by Jayāditya and Vāmana in the 7th century CE. It is an example of a running commentary, where its authors did not change the order of rules of Pāṇini's treatise. Not only does the commentary explain the rules, but it also provides them with examples of derivatives. It includes the *vārttika*s that we can find in the *Mahābhāṣya* but it proposes others as well.[22] This treatise was further commented upon and we have two commentaries: the *Kāśikāvivaraṇapañjikā* (*Nyāsa*) composed by Jinendrabuddhi, a Buddhist, in the 8th-9th centuries and the *Padamañjarī* composed at the end of the 9th century by Haradatta.[23]

One further commentary deserves to be mentioned, even though it was by no means the only one. In the 16th-17th centuries CE Bhaṭṭoji Dīkṣita composed the *Siddhāntakaumudī*, the best and most famous of *prakriyā* commentaries.[24] The *prakrīya* type of texts are no longer running commentaries; they concentrate on derivative and inflectional aspects of the Pāṇinian system and rearrange *sūtra*s thematically. An integral part of his work Bhaṭṭoji Dīkṣita made the *Uṇādi* and *Phiṭsūtra*s, auxiliary grammatical texts discussed below.

1.3 Auxiliary texts

There are a number of texts associated with Pāṇini's *Aṣṭādhyāyī*, which are indispensable to understand the treatise and apply rules correctly. It has not been determined whether Pāṇini can be considered the author of all the following works but he definitely made use of them explicitly or implicitly throughout his grammar. Some of them will also be referred to in the present work.

1.3.1 *Śivasūtra*s

This collection of sounds presented by Pāṇini is also known as *pratyāhārasūtra*s (the rules serving to form abbreviations), *varṇasamāmnyāya* (or *akṣarasamāmnāya* – both meaning a collection of sounds) or finally *maheśvarasūtra*s. The last name (as well as the name *śivasūtra*s) is connected to the idea that the mythical author could be Lord Śiva. They are fourteen short aphorisms composed by Pāṇini himself.[25] The sounds collected in these *sūtra*s represent the sounds of Sanskrit, with the exception of long and prolated vowels, the *jīhvāmūlīya* and *upadhmānīya* variations of the *visarjanīya* (as well as the

---

[22] SHARMA 2002:18-19, BELVALKAR 1997:30-31, SCHARFE 1977:174.
[23] CARDONA 1997a:279, SCHARFE 1977:174, SHARMA 2002:21-22.
[24] SCHARFE 1977:174, SHARMA 2002:26.
[25] CARDONA 1997a:160-161.

visarjanīya itself), and the *anusvāra* and *anunāsika*. The sounds are not arranged according to the place of articulation, as they are often presented in Sanskrit grammar, including by Pāṇini himself. On the other hand, their composition serves the *Aṣṭādhyāyī* perfectly. Each *sūtra* is closed with a marker (*anubandha*), called IT. Pāṇini forms the abbreviations, *pratyāhāras*, hence the name of *sūtras*, beginning with a sound and ending in a particular marker. The sounds included in such an abbreviation are subject to an operation prescribed by the *sūtra* where this particular abbreviation was used. Thus, he saves himself the effort of enlisting all the sounds important for operations and conforms to the principle of brevity.

1.3.2 *Dhātupāṭha*

The *Dhātupāṭha* is a compilation of verbal roots divided into ten classes: *bhvādi*, *adādi*, *juhotyādi*, *divādi*, *svādi*, *tudādi*, *rudhādi*, *tanādi*, *kryādi* and *curādi*. These roots are further divided into groups depending on shared properties such as accent and the personal endings they accept, i.e., *parasmaipada* and *ātmanepada*. Each one of about 2000 roots is accompanied by its meaning. Whether such was the original version, however, is an open question; there is the possibility of two existing versions of the *Dhātupāṭha*, one inclusive and one exclusive of root meanings. There is some evidence in the *Mahābhāṣya* that, at least at the time of Patañjali, the verbal roots were devoid of meaning.[26] Some scholars think, however, that the *Dhātupāṭha* always contained the meaning entries and the relevant passages in the *Mahābhāṣya* cannot be considered conclusive.[27] The authorship of this list has not been determined.

1.3.3 *Gaṇapāṭha*

The *Gaṇapāṭha* contains lists of nominal stems, which are of two types: closed (*parigaṇa*) with a fixed number of stems, and open (*ākṛtigaṇa*). The latter gives the possibility to include other stems not directly enlisted in the group but sharing similar properties. There is some evidence supporting the view that *gaṇa*s had existed before Pāṇini composed his treatise. It would be difficult, however, to assume that one of those could be entirely compatible with the highly technical system he created. It seems than we can safely assume that Pāṇini was the author of the *Gaṇapāṭha* he used.[28]

1.3.4 *Uṇādisūtras*

---

[26] For the summary of the discussion see CARDONA 1997a:161-162.

[27] For the discussion see BRONKHORST 1981.

[28] SHARMA 2002:39, CARDONA 1997a:165.

These *sūtra*s do not constitute a part of the *Aṣṭādhyāyī* but are often referred to by Pāṇini. They introduce suffixes added to verbal roots to form nominal stems.[29] Their name derives from the first suffix *uṆ* (=*u*). We know of two versions of the *uṇādi* suffixes: one divided into five chapters (*pañcapādī*) and another divided into ten (*daśapādī*), of later date.[30] Their authorship has not been determined with certainty. Śākaṭāyana is said to have been the author of the view that all the nominal stems derive from verbal roots,[31] but it is not certain whether Pāṇini shared this opinion. He introduces these suffixes in the *sūtra* A. 3.3.1 *uṇādayo bahulam* || ("[The suffixes] *uṆ* etc. [are] variously [added to verbal roots when the action refers to present time to form names]"). The term 'variously' (*bahulam*) suggests optionality in their application. Moreover, in following commentaries we often find an opinion that nominal stems formed with the help of *uṇādi* suffixes are treated as underived (*avyutpanna*).

1.3.5 *Phiṭsūtras*

This set of rules, prescribing accent for nominal stems, is considered to have been composed by Śāntanava or Śantanu.[32] Pāṇini does not refrain from discussing accent in his work but the contexts differ. He does not concentrate on the accent of single stems but prescribes its changes in the process of declension/conjugation or word-formation.

1.3.6 *Liṅgānuśāsana*

This treatise describes gender of nominal stems; subject matter not discussed in Pāṇini's *Aṣṭādhyāyī*. It is accepted that gender is known from usage (*lokāśrayāt*) and does not need to be taught. The text is divided into sections: feminine (*strīliṅga*), masculine (*puṃlliṅga*), neuter (*napuṃsaka*), feminine-masculine (*strīpuṃsaka*), masculine-neuter (*puṃnapuṃsaka*) and without determined gender (*aviśiṣṭaliṅga*).[33]

---

[29] CARDONA 1997a:170.
[30] SHARMA 2002:39.
[31] For the summary of the discussion see CARDONA 1997a:147.
[32] CARDONA 1997a:174, SHARMA 2002:40.
[33] SHARMA 2002:41.

2 *Mahābhāṣya* tradition

Pāṇini and the *Aṣṭādhyāyī* mark the beginning of the centuries-long tradition of Sanskrit grammar, whose development was not stopped by Pāṇini's codification of Sanskrit. The centuries following the emergence of Pāṇini's work saw two earliest commentators, Kātyāyana and Patañjali, and the three of them became the core of Sanskrit linguistic tradition, known as *munitraya* ('the trio of sages'). Their works became the point of reference for many other commentators in the following centuries. Patañjali, the latest of the three, is still considered to be the most authoritative figure in the Indian grammatical tradition.

2.1 Patañjali and the *Mahābhāṣya*

2.1.1 Patañjali

There has been extensive research trying to determine the place of origin and the time when Patañjali lived. It has been established, and is commonly accepted, that he must have lived about 150 BCE.[34] Patañjali's date is established on the basis of a number of expressions he used in his text amongst which we find: *aruṇad yavanaḥ sāketam* ("The Yavana besieged Sāketa") and *aruṇad yavano madhyamikām* ("The Yavana besieged Madhyamikā"). The Yavana refers to the Greek king Menander, who is considered to have lived between 140-120 BCE, and these sentences serve as examples for the rule introducing the aorist suffix *lAṄ* to express a past event that is widely known but was not necessarily witnessed by the speaker.[35] This indicates that Patañjali might have lived around that time, provided we accept the examples being of his authorship.

A more complex issue regards Patañjali's whereabouts. It seems reasonable to think that he must have come from the north. A hint might be provided by the expression used in the first *vārttika* in the *Mahābhāṣya*: *yathā laukikavaidikeṣu* ("As in worldly [usage] and Vedic [forms]").[36] As the *vārttika*

---

[34] For the review of the opinions of different scholars see MISHRA 2004:144-152, CARDONA 1997a:263-266.

[35] BRONKHORST 1987:43-44, CARDONA 1997a:263, SCHARFE 1977:153. Cp. A. 3.2.111 *anadyatane laṅ* | ("[When an action refers to the general past tense] excluding the current day [the l-substitutes of] lAṄ are introduced [after a verbal stem].")

[36] VMBh_2: I.33.5. The *vārttika* is longer and reads: *siddhe śabdārthasambandhe lokato 'rthaprayukte śabdaprayoge śāstreṇa dharmaniyamaḥ yathā laukikavaidikeṣu* | ("Since speech, its object, and the relationship between the two are established (and are known) from ordinary usage, and since one uses speech prompted by meanings in accordance with ordinary usage, the science (of grammar) restricts (usage of correct speech forms) for the sake of *dharma* just as (other sciences restrict behaviour) in ordinary and Vedic affairs."), see JOSHI&ROODBERGEN 1986:ix. Patañjali divides it into three parts for the purpose of his explanations.

is supposedly Kātyāyana's, it has been assumed that Kātyāyana must have been a southerner because, as Patañjali puts it, *priyataddhitā dākṣiṇātyāḥ* ("The southerners are fond of the *taddhita* suffixes"), and the forms *laukika* and *vaidika* are formed with the help of *taddhita* suffixes. It cannot, of course, be assumed that he lived in the south of India as we would understand it nowadays; more likely he had lived to the south of where Patañjali lived. Many scholars have dealt with the issue of Patañjali's place of origin.[37] According to the legendary account, Patañjali was the incarnation of the divine serpent Śeṣa[38] that fell into the hands of a woman called Goṇikā; hence Patañjali's name (*patat* – 'falling', *añjali* – 'hands').

This mythological account, together with some evidence from the *Mahābhāṣya* itself, led scholars to different, often mutually contradictory conclusions. Scharfe[39] claimed that Patañjali might have come from Mathurā, while others considered him an easterner; both interpretations, however, have been refuted.[40] Recently Aklujkar has analysed the possibility of Patañjali being a Kashmirian. In one of his articles he discusses three terms that could have referred to Patañjali, namely Gonardīya, Goṇikāputra and Gonandīya. Although these epithets could prove useful while determining Patañjali's area of residence, most scholars rejected the idea that they could refer to Patañjali. Aklujkar, however, analyses different commentaries on the *Mahābhāṣya* and works of other authors which do, or do not, identify Patañjali with all or some of the above names.[41] He concludes that Patañjali and Gonardīya were probably the same person, as was Goṇikāputra, but in this case the evidence is scarcer.[42]

The name Goṇikāputra does not pose problems with interpretation, especially in view of the mythological story of Patañjali's birth. The name Gonardīya, however, creates some difficulties. As Aklujkar points out, many scholars consider it to be a secondary derivative from the word Gonarda, which supposedly referred to a place.[43] He believes, however, that the word Gonarda was misspelled for Gonanda, which was a common name for the rulers of Kashmir; which also indicates that Kashmir itself might, by extension, have been referred to in such a way as well.[44] Therefore, Aklujkar sides with the opinion that Patañjali came from Kashmir, particularly when one takes into account extensive *Mahābhāṣya* tradition in that region in the centuries following Patañjali. He stresses Patañjali's acquaintance with the *Paippalāda Saṃhitā* of the *Atharva-*

---

[37] For the literature see CARDONA 1997a:269, CARDONA 2004:221.
[38] BHATE 2004:128-129.
[39] SCHARFE 1977:153.
[40] For different views and literature see CARDONA 1997a:270.
[41] For the arguments and the analyses of the sources see AKLUJKAR 2008b.
[42] AKLUJKAR 2008b:171.
[43] AKLUJKAR 2008b:162-163.
[44] AKLUJKAR 2008b:170.

veda, which is prevalent in Kashmir.[45] Moreover, the close association of Patañjali with the Nāgas, who were also, albeit not exclusively, connected with Kashmir, strengthens the claim.[46]

2.1.2 *Mahābhāṣya*

The *Mahābhāṣya*, while discussing Pāṇini's *Aṣṭādhyāyī*, also commented on the *vārttika*s usually attributed to Kātyāyana. Apart from these, we also find in the *Mahābhāṣya ślokavārttika*s, which are analysed and discussed by Patañjali in a similar fashion. Research has shown that in most cases they cannot be attributed to either Kātyāyana or to Patañjali himself.[47] They often served as the so-called *pratīka* – the point of reference for explanations of Pāṇinian rules. Patañjali's aim is to explain (*vyākhyāna*) the rules and not to paraphrase the *sūtra*s and *vārttika*s. The *Mahābhāṣya* is constructed as a dialogue between the teacher (*ācārya*), the student (*śiṣya*) and the teacher's assistant (*ācāryadeśīya*); we also meet a person with only partial knowledge of the problem or possessing partial answers (*ekadeśin*) and one who settles the final standpoint (*siddhāntin*).[48] Patañjali constructed his treatise in the form of 'question – objection – answer'. This particular scheme was not merely a literary procedure but also reflected the real methods of teaching in ancient India. The author asked questions, challenged the *sūtra*s and during his argumentation refuted the hypotheses one by one. Not only did he give examples (*udāharaṇa*) and counter-examples (*pratyudāharaṇa*) but also showed examples from everyday life (*dṛṣṭānta*) because Patañjali emphasised practical usage (*lokataḥ pramāṇam* – "the use amongst the people"), which he valued above a purely theoretical construction. Analysing the *vārttika*s, partly accepted and partly refuted, led to the conclusion (*siddhānta*).[49] The *Mahābhāṣya* consists of 85 parts called *āhnika,* which suggests that each of them was to be absorbed in one day (*ahan*). The first is called *Paspaśā* – the introductory lesson, which discusses matters of more general and philosophical nature. What Patañjali explores, for example, is the definition of the word, its character (*nitya* / *anitya* – if it is eternal or not), and the problem of a meaning carrier (whether it is a single phoneme or a whole word). Further, he also touches upon the purposes and means of studying grammar. Patañjali commented upon 1713

---

[45] AKLUJKAR 2008c:181.
[46] AKLUJKAR 2008a:80-81.
[47] For details regarding the work of different scholars see CARDONA 1997a:247.
[48] Joshi in his introduction to Patañjali's *samarthāhnika* distinguishes three main speakers: *pūrvapakṣin* (who raises doubts and finds faults in Pāṇini's or Kātyāyana's statements), *siddhāntyekadeśin* (who refutes the objections) and *siddhāntin* (who gives the final solution, disagreeing or agreeing with Kātyāyana and sometimes even rejecting the *sūtra* itself). JOSHI 1968:ii.
[49] CARDONA 1997a:253.

Pāṇinian rules and 8 *śivasūtra*s, not changing their order in the *Aṣṭādhyāyī*. It has been suggested that Patañjali was influenced by Buddhist philosophy, which was to be implied by his concepts of *padasaṃghāta* (lit. "assemblage of words") and *varṇasaṃghāta* (lit. "assemblage of letters"). Bronkhorst claims that these were inspired by the Buddhist concept of *nāmakāya* ("body of word"), *padakāya* ("body of sentence") and *vyañjanakāya* ("body of sound").[50]

2.1.2.1 Editions and translations of the *Mahābhāṣya*

The first critical edition of the *Mahābhāṣya* so far was prepared by Kielhorn and published in Mumbai between 1880-1885 (vol. I: 1880, II: 1883, III: 1885).[51] Almost a century later K. V. Abhyankar published a revised edition furnished with additional readings (vol. I: 1962, II: 1965, III: 1972); this edition was published by the Bhandarkar Oriental Research Institute in Pune. Similarly, only one complete translation of Patañjali's text into Marathi was made by V. S. Abhyankar (1938-1954) and edited by his son K. V. Abhyankar. In the years 1951-1962 P. S. Subramanya Shastri started preparing an English translation but only 28 *āhnika*s were finished.

As for other editions (presented here in chronological order), the earliest, together with a translation of a small part of Patañjali's text, is the translation of the first nine *āhnika*s of the commentary prepared by James Ballantyne in collaboration with pandits from Benares. The text is accompanied by the *Mahābhāṣyapradīpa* of Kaiyaṭa and *Mahābhāṣyapradīpoddyota* of Nāgeśa.

In 1912 Śivadatta Kudāla edited a section from the second *pāda* of the first *adhyāya* to the second *adhyāya* of the *Mahābhāṣya* together with the *Pradīpa* and *Uddyota*.

In 1937 Raghunātha Śāstrī and Śivadatta Kudāla edited the third *adhyāya* as commented on by Patañjali together with the *Pradīpa*, *Uddyota* and included footnotes collected from the *Chāyā*, *Padamañjarī* and *Śabdakaustubha*.

Guruprasāda Śāstri edited the text of Patañjali together with the commentaries of Kaiyaṭa and Nāgeśa, which was published in 1938.

In 1938 Mārulkara Śaṅkara Śāstrī edited the *aṅga* section of the *Mahābhāṣya* together with Kaiyaṭa's and Nāgeśa's commentaries. Part 1 contains the rules A. 6.4.1-7.2.35, while Part 2 continues to the end of the seventh chapter (A. 7.2.36-7.4.93).

Bhārgavaśāstrī Bhikājī Jośī edited the fourth and fifth *adhyāya*s with Kaiyaṭa's and Nāgeśa's commentaries in 1942; and three years later he added the

---

[50] A detailed account of the argumentation presented by Bronkhorst is outside the scope of the present work. For examples and conclusions see BRONKHORST 1987:43-71 and BRONKHORST 2002b.

[51] It was further edited and published also in Mumbai a few years later; I: 1892, II: 1906, III: 1909.

sixth *adhyāya*. In 1951 the first *pāda* of the first *adhyāya* was published as well. Collectively, they are known as the Nirnaya-Sagar Press edition.

Rudradhara Jhā Śarmā edited the first nine *āhnika*s of the *Mahābhāṣya* in 1954. This edition is accompanied by the *Pradīpa*, *Uddyota* and the author's own commentary *Tattvāvaloka*.

During 1962-1963 Vedavrata edited the whole text of the *Mahābhāṣya* together with Kaiyaṭa's *Pradīpa* and Nāgeśa's *Uddyota*. This edition, known as the Rohtak edition, was published in 5 volumes.

Bal Śāstri revised the text of the *Mahābhāṣya* edited by Śrī Guru Prasad Śāstri with both commentaries, and published them in eight volumes in 1987. Additionally, in 1988 first nine *āhnika*s were published by the same scholar with the following commentaries: *Śabdakaustubha* of Bhaṭṭoji Dīkṣita, Nāgeśa's *Uddyota* and Kaiyaṭa's *Pradīpa*.

In 1979 Veda Prakāśa edited the first two *āhnika*s and added a Hindi explanation.

In 1988 Dadhiram Sharma published Chapters 7 and 8 of the *Mahābhāṣya* with the *Pradīpa* and *Uddyota*.

In 1991 Surendranatha Dasgupta published the *āhnika*s 1-4 with annotations edited by Sibajiban Bhattacharya.

The most thorough translation of certain sections of the *Mahābhāṣya* into English was prepared by S. D. Joshi in cooperation with J. A. F. Roodbergen, which was published in several volumes. This translation was completed with extensive explanations of the text. The *Samarthāhnika* (P. 2.1.1) was published in 1968 by Joshi alone; in 1969 the *Avyayībhāvāhnika* (P. 2.1.2-2.1.49); in 1971 the *Karmadhārayāhnika* (P. 2.1.51-2.1.72); in 1973 the *Tatpuruṣāhnika* (P. 2.2.2-2.2.23); in 1974 the *Bahuvrīhidvandvāhnika* (P. 2.2.23-2.2.38); in 1975 the *Kārakāhnika* (P. 1.4.23-1.4.55); in 1976 the *Anabhihitāhnika* (P. 2.3.1-2.3.7); in 1980 the *Vibhaktyāhnika* (P. 2.3.18-2.3.45); in 1981 the *Prātipadikārthaśeṣāhnika* (P. 2.3.46-2.3.71); in 1986 the *Paspaśāhnika* and in 1989 the *Sthānivadbhāvāhnika*.

In 1957 Chatterji Kshitish published the *Paspaśā* chapter of the *Mahābhāṣya* together with an English translation and notes.

Another translation, into French, of the *Mahābhāṣya* together with the commentaries of *Pradīpa* and *Uddyota* was prepared by Pierre-Sylvain Filliozat. His *Le Mahābhāṣya de Patañjali avec le Pradīpa de Kaiyaṭa et l'Uddyota de Nāgeśa* was published by Institut Français d'Indologie in Pondicherry in India between 1975 and 1986. The following parts were translated: 1975: *adhyāya* 1, *pāda* 1, *āhnika* 1-4; 1976: *adhyāya* 1, *pāda* 1, *āhnika* 5-7; 1976: *adhyāya* 1, *pāda* 1, *āhnika* 8-9; 1980: *adhyāya* 1, *pāda* 2 and 1986: *adhyāya* 1, *pāda* 3. Toru Yagi concentrated on the *asiddhavat* section of the *Mahābhāṣya* and in five essays published between 1986-1994 he translated the commentary on Pāṇinian *sūtra*s A. 6.4.22-57 into French.

There have also been a few translations into Hindi, but also only partial ones. Yudhiṣṭhira Mīmāṃsaka translated the following passages: in 1972 the *adhyāya* 1, *pāda*s 2-4; in 1974 the *adhyāya* 2; in 1979 the *adhyāya* 1, *pāda* 1.

Charudeva Śāstri translated the first nine *āhnika*s into Hindi and published them in 1968.

In 1991 yet another Hindi translation appeared of the first two *āhnika*s together with Kaiyaṭa's commentary prepared by Śivanārāyana Śāstri.

2.1.2.2 Commentaries

There are a number of commentaries on Patañjali's *Mahābhāṣya* and on its further commentaries available to us; some of them on the entirety of the treatise and some only partial. The first text known to us is Bhartṛhari's *Mahābhāṣyadīpikā*.

Between 1973-1983 the commentaries of Kaiyaṭa's *Pradīpa* were edited by M. S. Narasimhacharya and published in ten volumes by the Institut Français d'Indologie in Pondicherry.

2.1.2.2.1 *Mahābhāṣyadīpikā*

This work, also known as *Ṭika*, was composed by Bhartṛhari in the 5th century CE.[52] The author did not comment upon the whole text or if he did, it has not survived. It comprises only the first 3 *pāda*s, explaining its other name – *Tripādī/Tripadī*. The commentary contains linguistic as well as philosophical considerations and it is best read together with another work by the same author, the *Vākyapadīya*. There is some evidence indicating that Bhartṛhari lived in the area of Gujarat or northern Maharashtra.[53]

K. V. Abhyankar, together with V. P. Limaye, edited the *Mahābhāṣyadīpikā* between 1965-1967.

In 1980 a fascimile edition of the extant manuscript of Bhartṛhari's commentary was published anonymously by the Bhandarkar Oriental Research Institute in Pune.

Some *āhnika*s were also critically edited by various scholars. In 1986 V. B. Bhagavat and Saroja Bhate edited *āhnika* 6 part 1 and in 1990 part 2. Johannes Bronkhorst edited the first *āhnika* of the text in 1987. In 1988 G. B. Palsule edited the *āhnika* 2; in 1989 together with G. V. Devasthali he edited the *āhnika* 4 and in 1991 the *āhnika* 7 with V. B. Bhagavat.

---

[52] FILLIOZAT 1991:9, CARDONA 1997a:244-245, 298.

[53] BRONKHORST 1983:397, BRONKHORST 1987:32.

2.1.2.2.2 *Mahābhāṣyapradīpa* (*Pradīpa*)

This first full commentary on the *Mahābhāṣya* was written in the 11th century CE by Kaiyaṭa, the son of Jayaṭa. The name of its author indicates that he could have come from Kashmir, where the tradition of Patañjali's treatise was highly developed.[54] The *Pradīpa* began the period in Sanskrit grammatical thought centred on the *Mahābhāṣya*. It should be noted that Kaiyaṭa was heavily influenced both by Bhartṛhari and the authors of the *Kāśikāvṛtti*. He was the one to establish the highest authority of Patañjali among the three *muni*s by saying: *yathottaraṃ munīnāṃ prāmāṇyam* ("The authority of *muni*s follows the order"), which meant that the tradition started with Pāṇini but the following commentators each should be considered more authoritative, with Patañjali assuming the throne.[55]

2.1.2.2.3 *Mahābhāṣyapradīpoddyota* (*Uddyota*)

This text, written by Nāgeśa (Nāgeśa Bhaṭṭa) in the 17th-18th centuries CE, is theoretically a commentary on the *Pradīpa* but it very often comments upon the *Mahābhāṣya* itself.[56] Nāgeśa was a student of Hari Dīkṣita, the grandson of Bhaṭṭoji Dīkṣita – the author of the *Siddhāntakaumudī*, which was a commentary on the *Aṣṭādhyāyī*. Nāgeśa came from Maharashtra, his father being Śiva Bhaṭṭa and his mother Satī of the Kale family. He was an extremely active scholar in different fields of grammar and composed such texts as the *Paribhāṣenduśekhara*, a collection of the *paribhāṣā*s accepted by the Pāṇinīyas, a treatise on the philosophy of language entitled *Mañjūṣā* (including its two abbreviated versions), and many others.[57] The school of grammar that was inaugurated by Nāgeśa still continues to develop to this day.[58]

Other commentaries that are worth mentioning are primarily the commentaries on Kaiyaṭa's *Pradīpa*. However, they do sometimes refer to the *Mahābhāṣya* itself. Only parts of them are available to us; the only commentary that was preserved for all the *āhnika*s of the *Mahābhāṣya* is the *Uddyotana* by Annaṃbhaṭṭa.

2.1.2.2.4 *Laghuvivaraṇa* and *Bṛhadvivaraṇa*

---

[54] FILLIOZAT 1991:12, CARDONA 1997a:245 with a fn. 344.

[55] EIP 2001:204.

[56] BELVARKAR 1997:34-35, CARDONA 1997a:245.

[57] EIP 2001:323.

[58] FILLIOZAT 1991:29, 31.

These works can be easily confused, as they both bear the title *Vivaraṇa*. They were composed by Rāmacandra Sarasvatī and Īśvarānanda respectively and it was Bhaṭṭoji Dīkṣita who distinguished them in his work *Śabdakaustubha*.[59] The *Laghuvivaraṇa* comments on the *āhnika*s 3-9 of the first *pāda* of the first *adhyāya*, the second *adhyāya* (without the second *āhnika* of the first *pāda*), the fourth, fifth and sixth *adhyāya*s (with the second *āhnika* of the fourth *pāda* missing). The *Bṛhadvivaraṇa*, on the other hand, comments only on the first nine *āhnika*s of the first *pāda* of the first *adhyāya*.[60] From the names of the authors and the colophons in the manuscripts it can be deduced that they were both *saṃnyāsin*s. Rāmacandra Sarasvatī is considered to have belonged to a Śaṅkarian order, connected perhaps with Kāmakoṭipīṭha in Kāñcīpuram.[61] According to EIP,[62] he was the father of Īśvarānanda, dated to the late 16th century CE, which allows for the dating of Rāmacandra to the beginning of the 16th century CE.

2.1.2.2.5 *Uddyotana*

This is the only complete commentary on the *Pradīpa* of Kaiyaṭa, which was composed by Annaṃbhaṭṭa, son of Tirumala Ācārya, who lived about 1560 CE. He came from Andhra but studied in Varanasi with Śeṣa Vīreśvara, son of Śeṣa Kṛṣna.[63] His area of expertise included not only grammar but also the fields of philosophy such as *nyāya* and *advaita*. Annaṃbhaṭṭa was heavily influenced by both *Vivaraṇa* commentaries. In his *Uddyotana* he makes references to the *Mahābhāṣya* commentary *Prakāśa* that was composed by Pravartakopādhyāya. It was not quoted or referred to in any other text.[64] The edition of the first two *adhyāya*s of the *Prakāśa* was published in Pondicherry in 1986 by M. S. Narasimhacharya.

2.1.2.2.6 *Ratnaprakāśa*

This commentary was composed by Śivarāmendra Sarasvatī whose whereabouts and date are unknown, except that he can be placed later than Annaṃbhaṭṭa and earlier than Nāgeśa, who, most probably, was familiar with his work. The only piece of information we have is that he was familiar with Telugu.[65] The full title of this commentary is *Mahābhāṣyasiddhāntaratnaprakāśa*

---

[59] MPV X.xiii, FILLIOZAT 1991:14.
[60] MPV X.ix.
[61] FILLIOZAT 1991:14.
[62] EIP 2001:219.
[63] EIP 2001:237, FILLIOZAT 1991:22, MPV X.xv.
[64] FILLIOZAT 1991:16-17, MPV X.xv.
[65] FILLIOZAT 1991:24.

and it is a commentary on the *Mahābhāṣya* itself, even though it is greatly indebted to Kaiyaṭa's *Pradīpa*. Śivarāmendra comments on the first four *adhyāya*s (with the exception of the final parts of the second *āhnika* of the *pāda*s 1 and 2 of the second *adhyāya*).[66] His theory of language was closer to that of the *nyāya* school than that of the grammarians.

2.1.2.2.7 *Nārāyaṇīya* (1)

There are two commentaries bearing this name. The author of the first, Nārāyaṇa, was a disciple of Dharmarāja Yajvan. The piece of commentary available refers only to the first nine *āhnika*s of the first *pāda* of the first *adhyāya*. It is also known as the *Kaiyaṭaṭīkā*. Nārāyaṇa is estimated to have lived about 1640 CE.[67] According to Yudhiṣṭhira Mīmāṃsaka, his dates are 1660-1710 CE.[68]

2.1.2.2.8 *Nārāyaṇīya* (2)

This *Nārāyaṇīya* was composed by Nārāyaṇa, a son of Devaśarman. The text comments on the *adhyāyas* 3 to 8.[69] It is sometimes called *Vivaraṇa* in the colophons. Nārāyaṇa came from Kerala and was probably a Nambudiri Brahmin belonging to the Ṛgvedic family. He should most probably be considered prior to Nāgeśa, living perhaps as early as 1597 CE.[70]

2.1.2.3 *Mahābhāṣya* text

There has long been a debate over the history of the *Mahābhāṣya* text and its tradition. Witzel in his article[71] discussed one archetype from which the text we possess today was supposed to derive and which Kielhorn considered to be the original text of Patañjali's work.[72] This view has been rejected, however; one of the reasons being the Vedic quotations in the *Mahābhāṣya* that appeared to be corrupted.[73] Bronkhorst draws the conclusion that the manuscripts that were used by Kielhorn in preparing his edition of the *Mahābhāṣya* could have derived from a common source that was not, however, the original text.[74] By analysing

---

[66] MPV X.ix.
[67] EIP 2001:253, FILLIOZAT 1991:25-26, MPV X.ix.
[68] MPV X.xvi.
[69] MPV X.ix.
[70] FILLIOZAT 1991:28, MPV X.xvi.
[71] WITZEL 1986.
[72] BRONKHORST 1987.
[73] RAU 1985:98-101.
[74] BRONKHORST 1987:15.

differences in the types of scripts used and tracing their historical changes, Witzel reached the conclusion that the archetype of the *Mahābhāṣya* that served the manuscripts we have nowadays dates to c. 1000 CE and comes from northern or western India.[75] Aklujkar is of the opinion that the manuscript in question derives from Kashmir.[76] Bronkhorst demonstrates that in the development of history of the *Mahābhāṣya* text we can distinguish one more branch of manuscripts that served Bhartṛhari while commenting on Patañjali's text.[77] This claim is further supported by variant readings that we find in Kaiyaṭa's commentary which otherwise do not deviate from these manuscripts on which Kielhorn's edition was based.[78]

The *Mahābhāṣya* text was considered lost at some point in history and revived by Candra. Aklujkar in his article,[79] after thorough analysis of the Kashmirian tradition of the *Mahābhāṣya*, stresses the importance of Patañjali's text in that region, extensively quoting from medieval sources. He also points out that none of the sources speak of the loss of the tradition, which stands in contradiction with what was traditionally held before.[80] The loss of the text and its apparent presence in the south has been established on the basis of the final verses of the second *kāṇḍa* of Bhartṛhari's *Vākyapadīya*. Of particular interest are verses 2.485-486: *yaḥ patañjaliśiṣyebhyo bhraṣṭo vyākaraṇāgamaḥ* I *kālena dākṣīṇātyeṣu granthamātre vyavasthitaḥ* II *parvatād āgamaṃ labdhvā bhāṣyabījānusāribhiḥ* I *sa nīto bahuśākhatvaṃ candrācāryādibhiḥ punaḥ* II ("The traditional knowledge of grammar – which, in the course of time, in the south had fallen from the pupils of Patañjali, [and] existed [there] only in the form of the book (i.e., the *Mahābhāṣya*) – was made by Candrācārya and others, who followed the seed-like *Bhāṣya*, into a many-branched [tree] again, after they had obtained the [correct] traditional knowledge from the mountain-range (Himālaya?)"), which has been analysed and discussed by many scholars.[81] Bronkhorst, in his interpretation of the above verses, obviously disagrees with the idea that it was Candra who revived the supposedly lost tradition of the *Mahābhāṣya*; tradition that meant to have preserved only in the south in a single book. Bronkhorst claims[82] that the situation was reversed; the *Mahābhāṣya* existed and was studied in the north and was taken south by Candra. He further stresses that it does not mean the loss of the tradition at all, but rather a different approach to it; before the time of Bhartṛhari, Patañjali was not as esteemed as later gramma-

[75] WITZEL 1986:252, BRONKHORST 2002a:194.
[76] AKLUJKAR 2008b:166.
[77] BRONKHORST 1987:30.
[78] BRONKHORST 1987:41.
[79] AKLUJKAR 2008a.
[80] AKLUJKAR 2008a:55.
[81] For the list of references see BRONKHORST 1983:392, the translation is Bronkhorst's.
[82] BRONKHORST 1983:396-397.

tical tradition claimed. The oral tradition disappeared in the south and was preserved only in manuscripts. Cardona interprets the loss of oral tradition in the above passage as referring to the entirety of grammatical tradition, including the *Aṣṭādhyāyī*.[83]

Bronkhorst's research has demonstrated not only that the *Mahābhāṣya* tradition pertained in the north whilst at the same time disappearing from the south, but also that Patañjali's authority as a commentator of Pāṇini was not established before the time of Bhartṛhari. The area of Kashmir, where the *Mahābhāṣya* was for centuries venerated, deserves particular interest. According to Aklujkar's analysis of Kashmirian sources belonging to the period between the 11th to 14th centuries, the *Mahābhāṣya* was not only extensively studied but also highly esteemed.[84] It was viewed as a source of well-being in the area and royalty in particular, a phenomenon known not exclusively in Kashmir at the time.[85]

---

[83] CARDONA 1978:98. For earlier Aklujkar's analysis see also AKLUJKAR 1978 and AKLUJKAR 1991.
[84] AKLUJKAR 2008a:57.
[85] AKLUJKAR 2008a:74.

3 Sources and the structure of the present work

Some issues regarding the structure of the present work as well as the employed sources require clarification. The main focus in the translation is the *Mahābhāṣya* and all the other elements included in the translation serve as auxiliary texts, without which Patañjali's commentary would be very difficult, if not impossible, to understand. The translation is comprised of three layers for the most effective and clear explanation of the text; it is organized according to the *Aṣṭādhyāyī sūtra*s, those which Patañjali chose to comment upon. The structure of the translation is, therefore, the following.

3.1 *Aṣṭādhyāyī*

The first level presents the *Aṣṭādhyāyī sūtra*s, both in Sanskrit original as well as in translation, which also includes these Pāṇinian rules which were omitted by Patañjali in his commentary. The reason behind such an approach is the nature of the *Tripādī* section, in which the order of rules is of crucial importance. The Sanskrit version of the *sūtra*s is provided to make Patañjali's comments clearer as he occasionally refers to original wording.

3.2 *Mahābhāṣya*

The next layer is the translation of the commentary divided into sections. Patañjali's commentary seems to be quite approachable but this can be very misleading. Patañjali adopted the form of a discussion for his composition, where different points of view are either accepted or rejected in the course of discussion. I have made an attempt to present this structure of 'question-objection-answer' in my translation. Such a structure also allows for further explanations of the basics behind Patañjali's discussions, which he himself does not offer in abundance.

3.3 Author's commentary

The last level consists of the explanation of the *Mahābhāṣya* text and provides detailed grammatical procedures for the examples given by Patañjali illustrating the *sūtra*s. The *sūtra*s in Pāṇini's grammar always apply sequentially, never simultaneously. However, in the formations that are examined, particularly at the first stage, different operations are shown as if they applied at the same time. This is not the case; this method has been adopted merely to facilitate the perception of the process and to focus on its most important stages. On the one hand, additional information is supposed to explain Patañjali's point of view; on the other, though, it is often impossible without reference to Pāṇini's *sūtra* itself and the actual operation the rule describes. In the case of *asiddhatva*, where the order of rule application may drastically influence the output, it is vital to show how the *sūtras* are actually applied and what their possible misinterpretation might cause. The *sūtras* used in the procedures are referred to in an index with the exception of those which are included in the *Tripādī* section.

This section can be also considered twofold in itself. Apart from proper explanation, reference is often made to the commentators of the *Mahābhāṣya*, such as Kaiyaṭa and Nāgeśa with their respective commentators Annaṃbhaṭṭa and Nārāyaṇa, the authors of the *Mahābhāṣyapradīpa*, *Mahābhāṣya-pradipoddyota*, *Uddyotana* and *Nārayaṇīya* respectively. Occasionally the *Kāśikāvṛtti*, composed by Jayāditya and Vāmana, is referred to as well. Their viewpoints are presented, although relevant passages are not directly translated not being the focus of this work. These later commentaries are used to help the reader understand Patañjali's ideas that can at times differ from the interpretation of later tradition; or rather that despite Patañjali's legendary status of authority, grammarians living in later centuries sometimes went against his interpretation of Pāṇini's *Aṣṭādhyāyī*.

A much later text, the *Paribhāṣenduśekhara* composed by Nāgeśa in the 17th century CE, is also employed. Patañjali refers to a number of *paribhāṣās* that were gathered by Nāgeśa. Occasional reference is also made to the *Vyāḍi-paribhāṣāvṛtti*, edited and translated by Wujastyk, which contains a few *paribhāṣās* that were not included by Nāgeśa.

3.4 Terminology

The most problematic issue concerning terminology has been the term *asiddha* itself, which Pāṇini never defined. This was not uncommon because technical terms that were borrowed from everyday usage were often left unexplained. It could, I believe, lead to the conclusion that *asiddha* should be read in its literal, or closest to its literal, meaning, namely 'that which has not been accomplished, effected'. It does, however, imply that the rule which has not taken effect was, in fact, applied and this is most definitely not the case in the *Tripādī* section. I have, therefore, opted for the translation 'suspended', which could easily be employed in all the instances of *asiddhatva* (which also include *asiddhavattva*, more on which below).

Pāṇinian linguistic terminology is not always compatible with the one adopted and developed by Western linguistics; we often find that Sanskrit terms have a wider scope. Therefore, some of the crucial terms have not been translated into English but I have decided to refer the reader to Pāṇini's own definition as that makes the translation clearer. Patañjali and later commentators, when they refer to sounds undergoing an operation, use the term *kāra* or sometimes *varṇa*.

In view of the topic of the *Tripādī* section, which deals with phonological operation, I have decided to use the term 'sound' in these cases and any others that require a reference to individual sounds. In some cases, however, the term 'word' was chosen when the context made it clear that it could not refer to any phonological/phonetic unit. I have decided not to apply the term 'phoneme' because not all the sounds undergoing particular operations are actually phonemes in Sanskrit, and the term 'sound' seemed a more neutral solution. The term *saṃhitāyām* is often translated as 'in close proximity' or 'in continuous utterance'. I have chosen the former as it agrees with Pāṇini's own definition described in the *sūtra* A. 1.4.109 *paraḥ saṃnikarṣaḥ saṃhitā* ("[The technical term] *saṃhitā* denotes the maximum proximity [of sounds]"). The terms referring to an option are translated differently in Pāṇinian *sūtras*: *vibhāṣā* ('rarely'), *vā* ('usually') and *anyatarasyām* ('optionally'). In the commentaries, however, they are all translated as 'optionally'.

The accent in Vedic quotations has not been marked. On the other hand, in the examples for the *sūtras* describing the accent *svarita* and *udātta* have been marked as '`' and '´' respectively above the vowels (e.g. à means an *udātta* accented vowel *a*, and á means the vowel *a svarita* accented).

3.5 Sources

The following translations and original texts were used.

3.5.1 *Aṣṭādhyāyī*

Three translations of the *Aṣṭādhyāyī* have been used including two providing the translation of the *Kāśikāvṛtti*:

3.5.1.1 *Aṣṭādhyāyī of Pāṇini*, Tr. Sumitra M. Katre, Motilal Banarsidass, New Delhi, 1989.

3.5.1.2 *The Aṣṭādhyāyī of Pāṇini*, Ed. and tr. Śrīśa Chandra Vasu, vol. I&II, Motilal Banarsidass, New Delhi, 1997 (1st edition: Allahabad, 1891).

3.5.1.3 *The Aṣṭādhyāyī of Pāṇini*, Tr. Rama Nath Sharma, vol. I-VI, Munshiram Manoharlal, New Delhi, 2002 (1st edition: New Delhi, 1987).

3.5.2 *Mahābhāṣya* and its commentaries

The following editions of the *Mahābhāṣya* and its commentaries have been used:

3.5.2.1 *The Vyākaraṇa-mahābhāṣya of Patañjali*, Ed. F. Kielhorn, vol. I, II&III, Bhandarkar Oriental Research Institute, Pune, 1986 (1st edition: Pune, 1880).

3.5.2.2 *Vyākaraṇa-mahābhāṣya of Patañjali with the commentary Bhāṣya-pradīpa of Kaiyaṭa and the super commentary Bhāṣya-pradīpoddyota of Nāgeśa Bhaṭṭa*, Ed. Vedavrata, vol. I-V, Haryāṇā Sāhitya Saṃsthāna, Gurukula Jhajjar (Rohtak), 1962-63.

3.5.2.3 *Mahābhāṣya-pradīpa-vyākhyānāni*, Ed. M. S. Narasimhacharya, vol. X, Institut Français d'Indologie, Pondichéry, 1983.

3.5.3 Auxiliary sources

Apart from the primary texts mentioned above, I have occasionally referred to other auxiliary sources, including later commentaries and treatises focusing on *paribhāṣās*, accent of nominal stems and *uṇādi* suffixes:

3.5.3.1 *Kāśikā-vṛtti of Jayāditya-Vāmana along with Commentaries Vivaraṇa-pañcikā – Nyāsa of Jinendrabuddhi and Padamañjarī of Haradatta Miśra*, Ed. Śrīnārāyaṇa Miśra, vol. I-VI, Ratna Publications, Varanasi, 1985.

3.5.3.2 *The Uṇādi affixes*, in *The Siddhānta-Kaumudī*, Ed. and tr. Śrīśa Chandra Vasu, vol. II pp. 147-333, Motilal Banarsidass, Delhi, 1995 (1st edition: Allahabad, 1906).

3.5.3.3 *The Phiṭ-sūtras*, in *The Siddhānta-Kaumudī*, Ed. and tr. Śrīśa Chandra Vasu, vol. III pp. 112-125, Motilal Banarsidass, Delhi, 1995 (1st edition: Allahabad, 1906).

3.5.3.4 *The Paribhāṣenduśekhara of Nāgojibhaṭṭa*, Ed. and exp. F. Kielhorn, vol. I-II, Indu-Prakash Press, Mumbai, 1868.

3.5.3.5 *Metarules of Pāṇinian Grammar; Vyāḍi's Paribhāṣā-vṛtti*, Ed. and tr. Dominik Wujastyk, vol. I-II, Egbert Forsten, Groningen, 1993.

4 The *asiddhatva* principle

The *Aṣṭādhyāyī* of Pāṇini, as was mentioned in Chapter 1, consists of 8 chapters (*adhyāya*), further divided into 4 parts (*pāda*) each, and is traditionally divided into two parts, the first of which combines the chapters 1.1-8.1 while the second part combines the last three *pāda*s (8.2-8.4), hence the name *Tripādī*. This latter part is the subject of this analysis. It is also called 'the *asiddha* section' (A. 8.2.1-8.4.68) as the first rule A. 8.2.1[86] *pūrvatrāsiddham* introduces the *asiddhatva* principle – suspension of following rules with respect to prior ones.

4.1 Terminology

As mentioned earlier, the very term *asiddha* poses certain difficulties while translating, which arise from the lack of definition provided by Pāṇini. It is a negated past passive participle of the verb √*sidh* – 'to be accomplished, fulfilled, effected, succeeded' and therefore it may mean 'that which has not been accomplished, has not taken effect, has not been accomplished' or, as I have chosen to translate it in the present work, 'suspended'. Having no suggestions from the author of the *Aṣṭādhyāyī*, we can assume that the term should be taken in its basic, literal (as much as possible) meaning. The aforementioned rule A. 8.2.1 is an *adhikāra* – a governing rule, thus referring to all the subsequent *sūtra*s until its scope has been stopped by another rule at the same level, that is, another *adhikāra*. In this case, however, the *asiddhatva* principle introduced in the rule governs all the *sūtra*s until the end of the *Aṣṭādhyāyī*. The *sūtra* means that the operations described in sub-chapters 8.2-8.4 are not visible, are suspended with respect to the previous rules in the treatise. The same principle works <u>within</u> the section as well, making each subsequent rule suspended with respect to the preceding rule in the *Tripādī*. We can say that within this particular section each *sūtra* is, in a way, the last, closing one in the *Aṣṭādhyāyī*.

4.2 The sections governed by *asiddhatva*

4.2.1 Rule A. 6.1.86

The first rule in chronological order where the term *asiddha* was used is a single *sūtra* A. 6.1.86 *ṣatvatukor asiddhaḥ* || ("[The single substitute of preceding and following sounds is considered] suspended with respect to the infix

[86] A. stands for *Aṣṭādhyāyī*, the first number stands for the chapter, the second for the sub-chapter and the last is the number of a rule. Therefore A. 8.2.1 means the 1st *sūtra* of the 2nd *pāda* of the 8th *adhyāya*.

tUK and the *ṣ*-substitution"). The detailed translation of this *sūtra* with examples and explanation is given in Chapter 5.

4.2.2 *Tripādī* section

The second case of the term *asiddha* is found in the section beginning with A. 8.2.1 *pūrvatrāsiddham* mentioned above. Operations described in this section refer to an item termed *pada*,[87] as the whole section is governed by the *adhikāra* A. 8.1.16 *padasya*.[88] *Tripādī* rules can describe operations referring either to a *pada*, to the interior of a *pada* or to the environment between two *pada*s. Below, I have gathered the details of operations to present the structure and summary of their contents.[89]

A. 8.2.

1. *adhikāra* sutra
2. the final *n* deletion
3. negation of *da* → *mu* before the suffix *nā*
4-6. accent *sūtra*s
7. *n* deletion at the end of a *prātipadika*
    8. negation of the deletion
9-14. *matUP*
    9-11. *m* → *v* of *matUP*
    12-14. *nipātana sūtra*s
15-17. *chandasi*
    15. *m* → *v* of *matUP*
    16-17. *nuṬ* before the suffixes *matUP* and *gha* (i.e., *taraP* / *tamaP*)
18-22. *r* → *l* (A. 8.2.21-22 – option)
23-30. deletion at the end of a *pada*
    24-28. *s* deletion
31-35. *h* substitution

---

[87] The term *pada* is defined in the following *sūtra*s: A. 1.4.14 *suptiṅantaṃ padam* ॥ ("[The technical term] *pada* denotes [an item] ending in nominal (*suP*) or verbal (*tiṄ*) endings"), A. 1.4.15 *naḥ kye* ॥ ("[The technical term *pada* denotes an item ending in the sound] *n* before [the affix] *Kya* (=KyaṄ, KyaC, KyaṢ)"), A. 1.4.16 *siti ca* ॥ ("[The technical term *pada*] also [denotes an item] before [an affix] with the marker *S*"), A. 1.4.17 *svādiṣv asarvanāmasthāne* ॥ ("[The technical term *pada* denotes an item] before [the class of affixes] whose first member is *sUP* (A. 4.1.2) excluding those denoted by [the technical term] *sarvanāmasthāna*"). Due to its semantic range the term *pada* is not translated into English.

[88] A. 8.1.16 *padasya* ॥ ("[In the section beginning here and extending up to and inclusive of A. 8.3.54 below, all operations introduced are] of a *pada*.")

[89] The sign '→' stands for 'substitution', the term which was avoided to make the presented structure more schematic and clearer.

31. *h* → *ḍh*
32-33. *h* → *gh* (A. 8.2.33 – option)
34. *h* → *dh*
35. *h* → *th*
36. *ṣ* substitution of final consonants
37. *baŚ* → *bhaṢ*
38. *d* → *dh*
39. *jhaL* → *jaŚ*
40. *t* / *th* → *dh*
41. *ṣ* / *ḍh* → *k*
42-61. substitution within the *niṣṭhā* suffixes (i.e., *Kta*, *KtavatU*)
42-49. *t* → *n*
50. *nipātana sūtra*
51. *t* → *k*
52. *t* → *v*
53-54. *t* → *m* (A. 8.2.54 – option)
55. *nipātana sūtra*
56. *t* → *n* (option)
57. negation of *t* → *n*
58-61. *nipātana sūtra*s
62-63. *KviN* → *kU* (A. 8.2.63 – option)
64-65. *n* substitution
66-71. *r* substitution
72-73. *d* substitution
74. *r* substitution (instead of *d* – option)
75. *r* / *d* substitution
76-78. vowel lengthening
79. negation
80. *da* → *mu* of *adas*
81. *ī* → *e* in plural
82. *adhikāra sūtra* – at the end of an utterance *Ṭi* is substituted by a prolated *udātta* vowel
83-86. types of utterances under consideration
87-92. prolation in a sacrificial utterance (*om* / *praṇava* etc.)
93. question (option)
94. reproach
95-96. threat
97-98. deliberation of choice
99. agreement or promise
100. question or praise
101. comparison (with *cit*)
102. *nipātana sūtra*

103. substituted prolated vowel is *svarita* – envy, praise, blame or anger
104. offence against custom, benediction or command
105. question or a narration
106-108. substitution of single vowels by a prolated vowel

A. 8.3.

1. final sounds of *matUP* and *KvasU* → *rU*
2. *adhikāra sūtra* – a nasalized vowel optionally replaces a sound which precedes a sound being replaced by *rU* in close proximity (up to A. 8.3.12)
3. *ā* → nasalized vowel (obligatory)
4. *anusvāra*
5. *m* (of *sam-*) → *rU*
6. *m* (of *pum*) → *rU*
7-12. *n* → *rU*
13. *ḍh* deletion
14. *r* deletion
15-16. *visarjanīya* substitution
17. *rU* → *y*
18. pronunciation of *v* and *y* (being a result of A. 6.1.78)
19-21. deletion of *v* and *y*
20. deletion of *y* after *oT*
22. *y* deletion
23-24. *m* → *anusvāra*
25-26. *m* (of *sam-*)→ *m* (A. 8.3.26 – option)
27. *m* → *n* (option)
28. *kUK* and *ṭUK*
29-30. *dhUṬ* (option)
31. *tUK* (option)
32. *ṅaMUṬ*
33. *uÑ* → *v*
34. *visarjanīya* → *s*
35-36. *visarjanīya* → *visarjanīya* (different contexts, A. 8.3.36 - option)
37. *jihvamūlīya* and *upadhmānīya* substitutions
38. *visarjanīya* → *s*
39-45. *ṣ* substitution (A. 8.3.42-43 – option)
46-47. *s* substitution
48. *s* and *ṣ* substitution
49-54. substitution *s* in Vedic literature
55. *adhikāra sūtra* – the sound *ṣ* replaces a non *pada* final in a close proximity (up to A. 8.3.119)

56. *s* → *ṣ*
57-119. *adhikāra sūtra* –*s* → *ṣ* after *iṆ* and *kU* (up to A. 8.3.119)
62. *ṣ* (of A. 8.3.59) → *s*
   63-70. exceptions (mostly in verbal stems)
   65-79. substitution in verbal stems
   78-79. *dh* → *ḍh* (A. 8.3.79 – option)
   80-85. substitution in nominal stems
   86-90. substitution in verbal stems
   91-94. *nipātana sūtra*s
   105-109. *chandasi*
   110-119. negative *sūtra*s

A. 8.4.

1-39. *n* → *ṇ* (A. 8.4.10-11 – option)
   12-13. in compounds
   14-24. in verbal stems (A. 8.4.23 – option)
   25-27. *chandasi*
   29-32. in *kṛt* suffixes (A. 8.4.30-31 – option)
   34-39. negative *sūtra*s
40. *s* → *ś* and *tU* → *cU*
41. *s* → *ṣ* and *tU* → *ṭU*
   42-44. negative *sūtra*s
45. *yaR* → nasal stop (option)
46-47. gemination of *yaR*
   48-52. negative *sūtra*s
53. *jhaL* → *jaŚ*
54. *jhaL* → *jaŚ* / *caR*
55-56. *jhaL* → *caR* (A. 8.4.56 – option)
57. *aṆ* → *anunāsika* (option)
58-59. *anusvāra* → a nasal stop homophonous with a following *yaY* (A. 8.4.59 – option)
60. *t* → *l*
61-62. substitution in initial sounds of verbal stems (A. 8.4.62 – option)
63. *ś* → *ch* (option)
64. *yaM* deletion (option)
65. *jhaR* deletion (option)
66. *anudātta* → *svarita*
   67. negative *sūtra*
68. *vivṛta a* → *saṃvṛta a*

4.2.3 *Ābhīya* section

In the sixth *adhyāya* we find the rule A. 6.4.22 *asiddhavad atrā bhāt* ‖ ("[From this *sūtra* to the *sūtra*] A. 6.4.129[90] [the rules to be applied are] as if suspended [with respect to each other]"), which opens the section governed by the principle of *asiddhavattva*. The views of various scholars regarding both terms *asiddha* and *asiddhavat* are discussed and summarised below. As the present work does not concentrate on this section, only a brief description will be provided here.

The *Ābhīya* section describes operations on other types of stems than the *Tripādī*; rules apply when a stem gets the designation either *aṅga* (in an earlier section) or *bha*. An *aṅga* is defined as an element to which a suffix is attached (A. 1.4.13 *yasmāt pratyayavidhis tadādi pratyaye 'ṅgam*); it is, therefore, a changing element in the same grammatical process, which is defined with respect to the suffix that follows. The *sūtra* A. 6.4.129 *bhasya*[91] introduces another domain; that of the stem termed *bha*. Similarly to the term *pada*, *bha* is also variously defined. Firstly, it denotes an item preceding an affix beginning with a vowel or the semivowel *y* (A. 1.4.18 *yaci bham*). It may also refer to an element ending in the sounds *t* or *s* before the suffix *matUP* (A. 1.4.19 *tasau matvarthe*). Finally, in Vedic it refers to a class of words before any following suffix (A. 1.4.20 *ayasmayādīni chandasi*).

The difference between the *Tripādī* and *Ābhīya* sections does not lie only in the types of stems the operations prescribed therein apply to, but also in the kinds of operations themselves. The main difference, however, is that the *sūtra*s in *Ābhīya* are suspended with respect to one another. They are not applied according to the order of their occurrence but, similarly to the remaining part of the *Aṣṭādhyāyī*, according to the conditions of application and general principles. Establishing the manner of rule application met with some difficulty due to problems with interpretation of A. 6.4.22 wording, namely, the expressions *atra* and *ā bhāt*. There are two possible interpretations of the latter: the first, which states that the scope of this governing rule extends up to the rule A. 6.4.129 *bhasya*, which introduces a new *adhikāra* and this is where it stops. The second interpretation states that the scope of the governing rule A. 6.4.22 includes the term *bha* as well; so all the *sūtra*s that fall within the scope of the governing rule A. 6.4.129 are subject to the *asiddhavattva* principle. The term *ā bhāt* is absolutely necessary because otherwise the principle of suspension would extend outside

[90] The expression *ā bhāt* means "until (*ā*) the [term] *bha*", which is precisely the *sūtra* A. 6.4.129 *bhasya*.

[91] A. 6.4.129 *bhasya* ‖ ("[The operations introduced hereafter, up to the end of this chapter apply] to [the pre-affixal stem designated by the technical term] *bha*.")

the domain of *bha* which ends in the fourth *pāda* of the sixth chapter. It would thus also apply to the rules that lie outside it, for example in the seventh chapter and such a situation is not desired.

An additional condition for *asiddhavattva* to work is that both of the rules in question belong to the *Ābhīya* section, otherwise the suspension does not work at all. The form *abhāji* ('it was broken', aor. pass.) will illustrate this condition:

(1) *bhañj* + *lUṄ*
(2) *bhañj* + *Cli* + *ta* (A. 3.1.43 *cli luṅi*,[92] A. 3.4.78 *tiptasjhisipthasthamibvasmas-tātāmjhathāsāthāmdhvamiḍvahimahiṅ*[93])
(3) *bhañj* + *CiṆ* + *ta* (A. 3.1.66 *ciṇ bhāvakarmaṇoḥ*[94])
(4) *aṬ* + *bhañj* + *CiṆ* + *ta* (A. 6.4.71 *luṅlaṅlṛṅkṣv aḍudāttaḥ*[95])
(5) *a* + *bhañj* + *i* + (*ta* → 0) (A. 6.4.104 *ciṇo luk*[96])
(6) *a* + *bha* (*ñ* → 0) *j* + *i* (A. 6.4.33 *bhañjeś ca ciṇi*[97])
(7) *a* + *bhaj* + *i*
(8) *a* + *bh* (*a* → *ā*) *j* + *i* (A. 7.2.116 *ata upadhāyāḥ*[98])
abhāji

The problematic stage in the above derivation is the stage (6) when the deletion of *ñ* by A. 6.4.33 takes place. This *sūtra* belongs to the *asiddhavat* section. To derive the correct form *abhāji*, with the vowel *ā*, we need to apply the rule A. 7.2.116 prescribing the *vṛddhi* substitution of the penultimate *a* in a stem when the same is followed by a suffix marked with *Ṇ* or *Ñ*. The suffix *CiṆ* is such a suffix but, as the deletion of *ñ* belongs to the *asiddhavat* section, it should be treated as if suspended. As a result of this suspension, the vowel *a* of the stem *bhañj* would not be penultimate; for A. 7.2.116 the stem would still contain the consonant *ñ* which constitutes its penultimate sound. As such, the stem would not be able to undergo the *vṛddhi* substitution. However, the *sūtra* A. 7.2.116 does

---

[92] A. 3.1.43 *cli luṅi* || ("[The suffix] *Cli* [comes after a verbal root] before the *l*-substitutes of *lUṄ* (aorist).")

[93] A. 3.4.78 *tiptasjhisipthasthamibvasmastātāmjhathāsāthāmdhvamiḍvahimahiṅ* || ("[The substitute suffixes] *tiP* etc. [come in place of the *l*-members introduced after a verbal root].")

[94] A. 3.1.66 *ciṇ bhāvakarmaṇoḥ* || ("[The substitute aorist suffix] *CiṆ* [comes in place of *Cli* after a verbal stem before *lUṄ* substitute *ta*] when denoting the action itself or the object.")

[95] A. 6.4.71 *luṅlaṅlṛṅkṣv aḍudāttaḥ* || ("[The initial augment] *aṬ udātta*-accented comes [at the beginning of a verbal *aṅga* stem] before [the *l*-substitutes of] aorist (*lUṄ*), imperfect (*lAṄ*) and conditional (*lṚṄ*).")

[96] A. 6.4.104 *ciṇo luk* || ("[The suffix introduced] after [the aorist suffix] *CiṆ* is deleted.")

[97] A. 6.4.33 *bhañjeś ca ciṇi* || ("[The penultimate sound *n*] of [the verbal root] *bhañjO* ('to break', DhP VII:16) [is not optionally deleted] before [the aorist suffix] *CiṆ*.")

[98] A. 7.2.116 *ata upadhāyāḥ* || ("[The vowel *ā*] comes in place of the penultimate vowel *a* [before suffixes marked with *Ñ* or *Ṇ*].")

not belong to the domain prescribed by A. 6.4.22, it lies outside it, which makes *asiddhavattva* inapplicable in this case. For the suspension principle to operate, the conflict between two rules has to arise between rules belonging to the same domain.

If the expression *ā bhāt* determines the domain, the question remains as to the significance, and purpose of *atra*. What is the purpose in using an additional expression? It is used to show that one rule can be suspended with respect to another only if they have the same conditions for operation. The word *papuṣas* ('of the one that has drunk', gen. sg.) can serve as an example:

(1) *pa* + *pā* + *KvasU* + *Śas* (A. 3.2.107 *kvasuś ca*,[99] A. 4.1.2 *svaujasamauṭśas-ṭābhyāmbhisṅebhyāmbhyasṅasibhyāmbhyasṅasosāmṅyossup*[100])
pa + *pā* + *vas* + *as*
(2) *pa* + *pā* + (*v* → *u*) *as* + *as* (A. 6.4.131 *vasoḥ saṃprasāraṇam*[101])
(3) *pa* + *pā* + (*u* + *a* → *u*) *s* + *as* (A. 6.1.108 *saṃprasāraṇāc ca*[102])
(4) *pa* + *p* (*ā* → 0) + *us* + *as* (A. 6.4.64 *āto lopa iṭi ca*[103])
pap + *us* + *as*
(5) *papu* (*s* → *ṣ*) + *as* (A. 8.3.59 *ādeśapratyayayoḥ*[104])
papuṣas

In this case, the stages that are of interest to us are (4) and (2). The deletion of the final *ā* (4) takes place only when the stem is followed by a suffix beginning with a vowel marked with *K*. The suffix *KvasU* is marked with *K* and it does begin with a vowel when it goes through *samprasāraṇa* (2). On the other hand, the *samprasāraṇa* in *KvasU* depends on the following case ending. Therefore, the conditions for both operations are different and, furthermore, the *samprasāraṇa* is not treated as suspended with respect to the *ā*-deletion. In other words, the

---

[99] A. 3.2.107 *kvasuś ca* || ("[In Vedic literature the *kṛt* suffix] *KvasU* also [comes in place of the *l*-substitutes of *lIṬ* introduced after a verbal root to denote general past tense].")

[100] A. 4.1.2 *svaujasamauṭśasṭābhyāmbhisṅebhyāmbhyasṅasibhyāmbhyasṅasisāmṅyossup* || ("[The suffixes] *sU* etc. [are introduced after expressions ending in feminine suffixes or other nominal stems].")

[101] A. 6.4.131 *vasoḥ saṃprasāraṇam* || ("The vocalization of the semivowel of [the suffix] *vasU* (=*KvasU*) [occurring as an *aṅga* final of a *bha* stem] takes place.")

[102] A. 6.1.108 *samprasāraṇāc ca* || ("[A single substitute vowel homogenous to the first of two vowels] also comes in place of [both] the vocalised semivowel (*saṃprasārana*, *iK*) [and the vowel following it in close proximity].")

[103] A. 6.4.64 *āto lopa iṭi ca* || ("[The final] *ā* [of the *aṅga* stem] is deleted before [the infix] *iṬ* and [the *ārdhadhātuka* suffixes beginning with a vowel and marked with *K* or *Ṅ*].")

[104] A. 8.3.59 *ādeśapratyayayoḥ* || ("[The retroflex *ṣ* comes in place of a non-*pada* final sound *s*] of a substitute or a suffix [occurring after vowels other than *a*, and semivowel *r*, velar stops, even when there is intervention by the infix *nuM*, *ḥ* or sibilants].")

samprasāraṇa in *KvasU* allows for the deletion of *ā*, otherwise the correct result would not be possible.

As we can see from this brief description, there are significant differences between the *Ābhīya* and *Tripādī* section not only as far as their contents are concernced, but also, most importantly, regarding the conditions behind the application of the suspension principle.

4.3 *Tripādī* versus *Sapādasaptādhyāyī*

4.3.1 Technical terms (*saṃjñā*) and rules of interpretation (*paribhāṣā*): *yathoddeśapakṣa* and *kāryakālapakṣa*

As mentioned briefly in Chapter 1, there are rules in the *Aṣṭādhyāyī* being employed in the grammatical process only alongside operational rules (*vidhi*), namely *saṃjñā* (technical terms) and *paribhāṣā* (rules of interpretation). Given the *asiddhatva* principle governing the *Tripādī*, the question arises whether they are allowed to operate within that section. This question is vital because certain technical terms appear in the *Tripādī sūtra*s and their proper understanding, according to definitions provided by Pāṇini, is essential. The first example that comes to mind is the term *pada* because, as mentioned earlier, the entire section operates on grammatical elements defined as *pada*s. Were we not allowed to employ the definition of a *pada*, it would be impossible to interpret the *Tripādī sūtra*s correctly. We would be forced to operate under the assumption that it does not possess any special meaning and employ its dictionary definition, which in many aspects differs from the way Pāṇini defines it. MW defines *pada* as 'a step, position, verse' amongst others and none of these are compatible with Pāṇini's system. It would have consequences for forming correct derivatives and the forms such as *rājabhis* (instr. pl. from the stem *rājan* 'a king'), where *rājan* has to be treated as a *pada* before the suffix *bhis* in order for the deletion of the final *n* to take place, would not be possible.

Similarly, the rules of interpretation (*paribhāṣā*) are valid regardless of the *asiddhatva* principle. Those rules can refer either to whole *sūtra*s or only their particular elements. Proper constructions, however, would appear impossible if we did not accept the *paribhāṣā*s. The standard example analysed by all the commentators discussing this issue is the metalinguistic usage of certain case endings, namely genitive, locative and ablative. Their functions differ from the usual, hence the need for Pāṇini to define them. The technical meaning of genitive in the *Aṣṭādhyāyī* is 'instead of, in place of'.[105] It is used in *sūtra*s prescribing substitution and shows an element to be replaced. Ablative and locative

[105] A. 1.1.49 *ṣaṣṭhī sthāneyogā* || ("The genitive is used to indicate the expression after which it is introduced is the substituend.")

distinguish an element that is subject to operations, the one that stands 'immediately after'[106] (ablative) or 'immediately before'[107] (locative) those elements that are expressed by these two case endings. This interpretation of case endings is indispensable also within the *Tripādī*.

Sanskrit grammatical tradition distinguishes two views regarding technical terms and rules of interpretation: the *yathoddeśapakṣa* (lit. 'according to the place') and *kāryakālapakṣa* (lit. 'at the time of an operation'). These are presented as the *paribhāṣā*s 2 and 3 respectively in Nāgeśa's *Paribhāṣenduśekhara*: *yathoddeśaṃ saṃjñāparibhāṣam* and *kāryakālaṃ saṃjñāparibhāṣam*. The former means that *saṃjñā* and *paribhāṣā* rules are to be understood in their own place in the *Aṣṭādhyāyī*; the latter, on the other hand, indicates that they are to be read together with operational rules forming a single expression (*ekavākyatā*).[108] The text defines *yathoddeśa* as: *uddeśam anatikramya yathoddeśam* | *uddeśa upadeśadeśaḥ* | ("According to the place (*yathoddeśa*) means 'not going beyond the [proper] place (*uddeśa*)'. And [the word] *uddeśa* means the place where [a technical term or a rule of interpretation] is taught.");[109] whereas *kāryakāla* as: *kāryakālam ity asya ca kāryeṇa kālyate svasaṃnidhiṃ prāpyata ity arthaḥ* | ("The time of an operation (*kāryakāla*), on the other hand, means 'attracted by an operation'.").[110] According to Joshi, who views them as two ways of interpreting Pāṇinian system calling them analytical (*yathoddeśa*) and synthetic (*kāryakāla*) respectively, the terms *saṃjñā* and *paribhāṣā* should not be taken only in their technical sense; these two views should be considered from the perspective of a student. The former (*yathoddeśapakṣa*) aims to demonstrate how the system works, to present a general notion without the practical aspect of rules. It is useful for those who do not look for any immediate utility from acquired knowledge and should be seen as the mere study of the system. The second method (*kāryakālapakṣa*), on the other hand, serves only the application of rules. These methods represent two approaches to the reading of Pāṇini's treatise: according to the arrangement of rules and according to the grammatical process. Joshi quotes Patañjali, who claims that *kāryakālapakṣa* means the actual change of rule order. The *Kāśikā* follows the first method of interpreting Pāṇinian system; the *Siddhāntakaumudī*, on the other hand, focuses on the *kāryakāla* view, as it stresses the importance of rule application. The former method analyses the sys-

[106] A. 1.1.67 *tasmād ity uttarasya* || ("A form stated in the ablative case denotes an element, the unit following which [is subject to the grammatical operation introduced by the rule].")

[107] A. 1.1.66 *tasminn iti nirdiṣṭe pūrvasya* || ("A form stated in the locative case denotes an element, the unit preceding which is subject to the grammatical operation introduced by that statement.")

[108] DVIVEDI 1978:178.

[109] PŚ vol. I:1, vol. II:6.

[110] PŚ vol. I:4, vol. II:14.

tem, the latter shows how the system works. For Joshi they are not actually opposite views but rather two aspects that complement each other.[111]

Dvivedi states that these *paribhāṣās* are formed to ease formational difficulties. The *yathoddeśa* view is a natural *paribhāṣā*, whereas *kāryakāla* requires shifting *saṃjñās* and *paribhāṣās* into the domain of an operational rule. In the case of the *Tripādī* section, the latter has the purpose of a constraint on A. 8.2.1 not to let certain irregularities be created, which is why it is employed in the *asiddhatva* section only in certain cases.[112] Theoretically, the position of technical terms and the rules of interpretation is static but in practice they are often used in various places in the *Aṣṭādhyāyī* to explain operational rules.

Patañjali, in his *Mahābhāṣya*, favours *kāryakālapakṣa* and employs both *saṃjñā* and *paribhāṣā* rules to interpret the *Tripādī* rules regardless of the *asiddhatva* principle.[113]

4.3.2 *Paribhāṣā* A. 1.4.2

There is, however, one *paribhāṣā* whose interpretation was open to question, namely A. 1.4.2 *vipratiṣedhe paraṃ kāryam*, which establishes that in the case of conflict (*vipratiṣedha*) of two (or more) rules we employ the one which is placed later in the *Aṣṭādhyāyī*. This metarule is obviously contradictory to the *asiddhatva* principle according to which later *sūtras* are suspended with respect to prior ones and, consequently, cannot take precedence. It is impossible to apply both these principles at the same time but determining which principle prevails seems impossible. Traditionally, this particular rule of interpretation applies to the entire *Aṣṭādhyāyī*, as do other *paribhāṣās*. According to modern researchers,[114] however, and in fact as indicated by Pāṇini himself, its application is limited only to a set of rules in the first and second chapters. We can think of A. 1.4.2 as a local rule of interpretation rather than a global one based on the rule that precedes it. A. 1.4.1 *ā kaḍārād ekā saṃjñā* states: "Up to the rule A. 2.2.38 [one grammatical element] gets one definition". The *paribhāṣā* A. 1.4.2 therefore serves as a tool to decide between two conflicting technical terms applying to one element; the one introduced later takes precedence.[115] The fact that A. 1.4.2 belongs to the group introduced by the *sūtra* A. 1.4.1, which is a *paribhāṣā* and an

---

[111] JOSHI 1965:53-57.

[112] For examples see DVIVEDI 1978:188&191.

[113] BANERJEE 1984:16-17, see also BUISKOOL 1939:26ff.

[114] See for example CARDONA 1997:189-191.

[115] A good example is the case of a short vowel that is defined in A. 1.4.10 *hrasvaṃ laghu* || ("[That which is] short [is called] *laghu*"). However, A. 1.4.11 *saṃyoge guru* states that "Before a cluster [of consonants a short vowel is called] *guru* – a long one". Obviously, one and the same vowel cannot be short and long at the same time and this is when the *paribhāṣā* A. 1.4.2 applies and a vowel before a consonantal cluster is always long.

adhikāra at the same time, allows us to determine that it does not refer to the entire *Aṣṭādhyāyī* but is only used locally with respect to this particular set of rules. In fact, this interpretation of the *sūtra* A. 1.4.2 solves a lot of problems when it comes to the application of other rules in the *Aṣṭādhyāyī*.

Kiparsky in his article[116] points out that in the *Mahābhāṣya* on A. 1.4.1 the discussion takes place as to the wording of these first two rules, namely A. 1.4.1 and A. 1.4.2. Patañjali discusses whether the expression *ā kaḍārād ekā saṃjñā* (as it is read according to the editions we have nowadays) or *prāk kaḍārāt paraṃ kāryam* should be used. The latter would limit the application of the *para paribhāṣā* solely to the domain of A. 1.4.1-2.2.38, which is exactly what is desired. Kiparsky concludes that these must have been two versions of the *sūtra* (i.e., *ā kaḍārād ekā saṃjñā* and *prāk kaḍārāt paraṃ kāryam*) in Patañjali's time and as the former was chosen, the *paribhāṣā* came to be traditionally applicable in the entire *Aṣṭādhyāyī*. The text in the *Mahābhāṣya* suggests, however, that this viewpoint is incorrect.

4.3.3 *kāryāsiddhatva* and *śāstrāsiddhatva*

Pāṇini's commentators also discussed the issue of the actual subject of suspension, whether it should be a rule (*śāstra*) or an operation itself (*kārya*). The *Kāśikāvṛtti* on A. 8.2.1 *pūrvatrāsiddham* states:

> *ita uttaraṃ cottarottaro yogaḥ pūrvatrapūrvatrāsiddho bhavati = asiddhavad bhavati | siddhakāryaṃ na karoti ||*
> "Therefore, a following rule [here in the section of the *Tripādī*] is considered suspended with respect to what precedes. The operation does not take effect."[117]

Later commentators generally agree that it must be a rule that is *asiddha*. The author of the *Padamañjarī* states that *śāstra* is primary, it comes before an operation (*kārya*) which can be understood only through the rule and is, therefore, secondary. As such, it cannot take precedence over the primary element.

> *kāryasya tu śāstradvārakam aupacārikaṃ, na hi mukhye sambhavati gauṇasya grahaṇaṃ yuktam ||*
> "The operation is secondary, [understood] via the rule, when the primary is possible, it is not proper to understand the secondary."

---

[116] KIPARSKY 1982:114.
[117] KV VI.330.1-2.

In the *Nyāsa* as well as in the *Uddyotana* of Annaṃbhaṭṭa[118] the maxim is quoted: *devadattasya hantari hate na punar devadattasya prādurbhāvo bhavati* || ("When the killer of Devadatta has been killed, it does not bring Devadatta back to life"). These two commentators use it to explain that when an operation takes place and is consequently suspended, an earlier stage of the grammatical process cannot be restored. This is the argument against the *kāryāsiddhatva* viewpoint; a rule has applied and an operation has taken place, but its result has been suspended. The author of the *Nyāsa* gives the example of *amuṣmai* – the dat. sg. of *adas*.

(1) *adas* + *Ṅe*
(2) *ada* (*s* → *a*) + *e* (A. 7.2.102 *tyadādīnām aḥ*[119])
(3) *ad* (*a* + *a* → *a*) + *e* (A. 6.1.97 *ato guṇe*[120])
(4) *a* (*da* → *mu*) + *e* (A. 8.2.80 *adaso 'ser dād u do maḥ*[121])
(5) *amu* + (*e* → *smai*) (A. 7.1.14 *sarvanāmnaḥ smai*[122])
(6) *amu* + (*s* → *ṣ*) *mai* (A. 8.3.59 *ādeśapratyayayoḥ*[123])
amuṣmai

The final sound *s* is replaced by *a* and then two vowels *a* are substituted by *guṇa* (again *a*). Thus, we arrive at the stem *ada* + the dative ending *Ṅe* (3). This ending is to be replaced by *smai* in the case of pronouns by A. 7.1.14 when the preceding stem ends in *a*. Before this happens, however, we should apply A. 8.2.80 which allows for the *da* → *mu* substitution of the stem *ada*. After this substitution has taken place, it would be impossible to apply A. 7.1.14. On the other hand, the *sūtra* A. 8.2.80 is placed within the *Tripādī* section, which makes it suspended with respect to the preceding rule A. 7.1.14. If the rule itself is subject to suspension, the correct result, namely the form *amuṣmai* is achieved. If, on the

---

[118] MPV X.345.8-9.

[119] A. 7.2.102 *tyadādīnām aḥ* || ("[The vowel] *a* comes in place of [the final sound of] the pronominal stems *tyad* ('that') etc.")

[120] A. 6.1.97 *ato guṇe* || ("[A single substitute comprising of the second of two continuous sounds comes in place of a non-*pada* final vowel] *a* and a *guṇa* vowel which follows it.")

[121] A. 8.2.80 *adaso 'ser dād u do maḥ* || ("[The sound] *u* comes in place of [the sound occurring] after [the sound] *d* of [the pronominal stem] *adas* 'that' when it does not end in *s*, and [the sound] *m* comes in place of [the sound] *d*.")

[122] A. 7.1.14 *sarvanāmnaḥ smai* || ("[The element] *smai* comes in place of [the dative singular ending] *Ṅe* [introduced] after pronominal stems [ending in the sound *a*].")

[123] A. 8.3.59 *ādeśapratyayayoḥ* || ("[The retroflex *ṣ* comes in place of the sound *s* which is not at the end of a *pada* occurring after the sounds *i*, *u* or those belonging to the consonantal group *kU*] when it is a substitute or [a part of] a suffix [even if it is separated by the infix *nUM*, the *visarjanīya* or the sounds denoted by *śaR* in close proximity].")

other hand, the operation were to be suspended, the stem *ada* would not end in *a*, even though the *da* → *mu* substitution is considered suspended. It happens because the rule has been applied and it is only the result that is temporarily suspended. Thus, the rule A. 7.1.14 could not apply at all.

The commentators agree, therefore, that suspension must refer to a rule (*śāstra*) and not to an operation (*kārya*). Although the authors of the *Kāśikāvṛtti* disagree and maintain operation suspension, both *Padamañjarī* and *Nyāsa* try to explain that it refers to an operation through the suspension of a rule.

4.3.3.1 *kāryāsiddhatva* and *śāstrāsiddhatva* vs *asiddhavat*

I find that the problem of either a rule or an operation suspension is closely linked to the interpretation of *asiddhatva* and *asiddhavattva*. They are traditionally considered to be synonymous, and both terms (*asiddha* and *asiddhavat*) are understood as 'as if not having taken place'. The former term, used in A. 8.2.1 *pūrvatrāsiddham* is explained, by the *Kāśikā* and later commentaries, as equalling *asiddhavat* with the suffix *vatI* simply omitted.

The question that should be asked is, in my opinion, how the *kāryāsiddhatva* and *śāstrāsiddhatva* views relate to the very term *asiddha*; or *asiddhavat* as the tradition prefers to understand it. As mentioned above, *kāryāsiddhatva* is traditionally explained via the 'killing of the Devadatta's killer' maxim (*devadattasya hantari hate na punar devadattasya prādurbhāvo bhavati*); which means that after the *sūtra* has been applied and the operation has taken place, it is not possible to restore the previous stage of derivation even if the operation is suspended. However, in the final result this operation can be seen, it has taken place and it prevents the undesired rules from applying. Such a situation is most certainly not desired in the *Tripādī* section, particularly if we operate on *sūtra*s from within the section. When two rules are potentially applicable, the later one is suspended so it does not take effect at all, unless, of course, at a later stage of the process conditions for its application are met. The problem is that when an earlier *sūtra* from the *Tripādī* section is chosen to apply over the later one, we do not see an operation of a later *sūtra* only temporarily suspended; we do not see the result later on as we would, should we interpret suspension in terms of *kāryāsiddhatva*. Therefore, it can be safely stated that in the case of *Tripādī* the only acceptable interpretation is *śāstrāsiddhatva*. I would be inclined to think that the suspension of a rule corresponds to the *asiddhatva* principle, but not *asiddhavattva*. The rule has not taken effect, it may not take effect at all so cannot be treated 'as if it has not taken effect' because it simply has not. At the same time, traditional commentators claim that it is only a rule that is subject to suspension and that *asiddhavat* should be interpreted 'as if it has not taken effect'. In my opinion these two claims are mutually exclusive. Obviously, we cannot understand *kāryāsiddhatva* in the *Tripādī* section but I would like to stress that we could make use of it in the *Ābhīya* section.

The suspension of an operation (*kāryāsiddhatva*) can be interpreted traditionally, but another interpretation of this view is also possible. The maxim: *devadattasya hantari hate na punar devadattasya prādurbhāvo bhavati* ("When the killer of Devadatta has been killed, it does not bring Devadatta back to life") does not have to be used. As Cardona points out,[124] an assumption is made that it is the result of an operation that is suspended. Consequently, if we understand the *kāryāsiddhatva* as suspension of an operation, the question of impossibility to restore the preceding stage of the process does not arise. A good example is the form *śādhi* (2nd sg. impv. of the verb *śās* – 'to instruct') where two rules have to apply, both belonging to the section.

(1) *śās* + *si* → *hi* (A. 3.4.87 *ser hy apic ca*[125])
(2) (*śās* → *śā*) + *hi* (A. 6.4.35 *śā hau*[126])
śā + *hi*
(3) *śā* + (*hi* → *dhi*) (A. 6.4.101 *hujhalbhyo her dhiḥ*[127])
śādhi

To derive a proper form we need to replace both the stem *śās* with the form *śā* and the ending *hi* with *dhi*. In this case, the substitution *śās* → *śā* eliminates the context for the *hi* → *dhi* substitution because *dhi* can come in place of *hi* only when the preceding stem ends in the sound denoted by the term *jhaL*, which includes the sound *s*. When the stem has been replaced by the form *śā*, the conditions for the *dhi*-substitution are no longer met. If, however, the ending substitution takes place first, the stem substitution cannot take place because it depends on the following suffix *hi*. This is why A. 6.4.35, prescribing the stem substitution, is treated as suspended with respect to the suffix substitution prescribed by A. 6.4.101. It seems that *kāryāsiddhatva* is perfectly acceptable here; the operation has taken place (*śas* → *śā*) but is temporarily suspended. By restoring the preceding stage of the process we are able to apply the *dhi*-substitution yet at the same time to preserve the replacement of the stem. The *śā*-substitution can be seen in the final result. If the *sūtra* A. 6.4.35 were not treated as if suspended, the result would be as follows:

---

[124] CARDONA 1989:53.

[125] A. 3.4.87 *ser hy apic ca* ll ("[The suffix] *hi* without the marker *P* comes in place of *siP* [substitutes of the *l*-member *lOṬ* introduced after a verbal stem].")

[126] A. 6.4.35 *śā hau* ll ("[The substitute] *śā* [comes in place of the verbal stem *śāsU* (DhP II:66, 'to instruct')] before [the suffix] *hi*.")

[127] A. 6.4.101 *hujhalbhyo her dhiḥ* ll ("[The substitute] *dhi* comes in place of [the suffix] *hi* [introduced after the verbal stem] *hu* ('to sacrifice', DhP III:1) or those [verbal stems] ending in [a sound denoted by] *jhaL* (non-nasal consonants).")

(1) *śās* + *si* → *hi* (A. 3.4.87)
(2) (*śās* → *śā*) + *hi* (A. 6.4.35)
**śā* + *hi*
**śāhi*

Some grammarians, while commenting on A. 6.4.22 *asiddhavad atrā bhāt* do in fact discuss the possibility of applying *kāryāsiddhatva* in the case of the *Ābhīya* section. Kaiyaṭa and the author of the *Padamañjarī*[128] say that an operation is primary in this case and a rule secondary as it expresses the meaning of an operation. However, they reach the conclusion that the *kāryāsiddhatva* (operation suspension) view would not agree with the *vārttika*: *ādeśalakṣaṇa-pratiṣedhārtham utsargalakṣaṇabhāvārthaṃ ca* ("[The *asiddhatva* principle is used] in order to prohibit [an operation] conditioned by a substitute and allow [an operation] conditioned by a substituend"). It would yield the correct results in the case of the first part of the *vārttika* but would not result in correct forms for *utsargalakṣaṇabhāva*. The *Padamañjarī* explains that an operation to be prohibited is connected with an operation that has taken place and is suspended. In other words, the suspension of a rule stops another one from applying. This is where *kāryāsiddhatva* would work. However, in the case of *śādhi*, the *sthānin śās* does not reappear after the application of the *śā*-substitution, therefore the *dhi*-substitution, which is contingent on the existence of the *sthānin śās*, would not take place. This happens only if we understand *kāryāsiddhatva* via the 'killing of the Devadatta's killer' maxim. If we do not, or rather, if we understand *kārya* as Cardona proposes, that is 'an operation' rather than 'a result of an operation', the word *śādhi* could be an example of *kāryāsiddhatva* and it would not go against the *vārttika* either. Interestingly, Bronkhorst claims that Kātyāyana's *vārttika* mentioned above explains the *asiddhavattva* principle rather than *asiddhatva*.[129]

The majority of scholars and Sanskrit traditional grammarians solely accept *śāstrāsiddhatva* (rule suspension) in all the three sections governed by both *asiddhatva* and *asiddhavattva*. However, I find that the solution proposed by Cardona is far more acceptable.

4.3.4 Metarule *pūrvaparanityāntaraṅgāpavādānām uttarottaraṃ balīyaḥ*

[128] KV V.363-364.
[129] BRONKHORST 1980:79.

Sanskrit grammatical tradition accepts the following *paribhāṣā*: *pūrvaparanityāntaraṅgāpavādānām uttarottaraṃ balīyaḥ*[130] as determining the order of rule application in the *Aṣṭādhyāyī* in the case of conflict between two *sūtras*. This rule of interpretation was not formulated by Pāṇini but is a later invention of the Pāṇinīyas. Determining the order of rule application based on the order in which they appear in the treatise (*pūrva - para*) forms the bottom level in this hierarchy of importance. It does happen, as Patañjali suggests, that sometimes it is actually an earlier rule which has to take precedence over the later one; he mentions the *aṅga* domain (i.e., A. 6.4-7.4)[131] in the *Aṣṭādhyāyī* as controlled by this principle. The *paratva* principle, which has been explained above (see **4.3.2**), merely on the basis of the prescription of A. 8.2.1 cannot be considered valid within the *Tripādī* section or wherever the *asiddhatva* principle operates. The *nityatva* principle, establishing the primacy of this rule, in the case of conflict, which remains applicable even after another has applied, is stronger than the preceding two principles. It is similar to the *siddhatva* principle that was proposed by some scholars (see below in **4.4.1**). On the next level, there is the *antaraṅgatva* principle. Operations in the *Aṣṭādhyāyī* can be externally or internally conditioned. If a conditioning element lies outside the stem (e.g., it is a suffix) or just further from the stem, an operation dependent on such an element is externally conditioned (*bahiraṅga*). Those operations whose conditioning element lies within the stem itself, or closer to the stem, are internally conditioned and those take precedence. Finally, there are exceptions (*apavāda*) to general rules, which are the strongest and always prevail. This principle is also valid within the *Tripādī* section as will be shown in Chapter 6.

The *antaraṅga-bahiraṅga* relation is of a very interesting nature. Traditionally, it is used word-internally, which Kiparsky and Joshi find unacceptable. There are also other *paribhāṣā*s concerning the *antaraṅga-bahiraṅga* relation, the most general being *asiddhaṃ bahiraṅgam antaraṅge* ("An externally conditioned operation is suspended with respect to an internally conditioned operation").[132] As Kiparsky has shown, not only was this *paribhāṣā* not universal, which made the Pāṇinīyas formulate some exceptions, but there are cases when an externally conditioned operation feeds another that is internally conditioned.[133] Kiparsky himself does not find this discussed metarule necessary

---

[130] PŚ 38 vol.I:34, vol. II:185-186 *pūrvaparanityāntaraṅgāpavādānām uttarottaraṃ balīyaḥ* || ("Of [these five kinds of rules] a preceding [rule], a subsequent [rule], a *nitya* (i.e., obligatory) [rule], an *antaraṅga* (i.e., internally conditioned) [rule] and an exception – each following [rule] possesses greater force [than any of, or all, the rules which in this *paribhāṣā* are mentioned before it").

[131] SCHARF 2012:328.

[132] PŚ 50, vol. I:41-42, vol. II:221-266.

[133] KIPARSKY 1982:89-90, JOSHI&ROODBERGEN 1987:545.

as he proposes the existence of the *siddhatva* principle governing the entire *Aṣṭādhyāyī* (see below in **4.4.1**).

4.3.5 *sthānivadbhāva*

There is one more device in the *Aṣṭādhyāyī* often mentioned in the context of the *asiddhatva* principle. It is the principle called *sthānivadbhāva* introduced in the *sūtra* A. 1.1.56 *sthānivad ādeśo 'nalvidhau* || ("A substitute has the status of its substituend except in respect of an operation that depends on the original sound"). This device is traditionally considered very similar to *asiddhatva* as it is supposed to have both a positive aspect (i.e., the application of a rule that is conditioned by a substituend) and a negative one (i.e., the prohibition of application of a rule conditioned by a substitute).[134] A detailed analysis of this principle is beyond the scope of the present book;[135] a few issues, however, need to be addressed because Kātyāyana or Patañjali sometimes refer to this principle in the context of *asiddha* rules.

There are numerous examples in the *Aṣṭādhyāyī* where the commentators employ different, albeit similar in their application, devices to explain grammatical forms and the process we go through to achieve them. The *sthānivadbhāva*, *asiddhatva* and *antaraṅga-bahiraṅga* principles are often used in similar contexts and their distinction is still open to question in certain cases. Some of the problematic situations, in which various solutions could be proposed, are exemplified in the positive function of *sthānivadbhāva*. While Joshi recognises and accepts the fact that *sthānivadbhāva* can have the positive effect, Patañjali employs the *antaraṅga-bahiraṅga* principle in such situations. The reason for Joshi's rejection of *antaraṅga-bahiraṅgatva* is that he accepts it only across word boundaries; he does not think that Pāṇini actually intended this principle to apply word-internally. Joshi's analysis of three examples given by Patañjali for the negative function of *sthānivadbhāva*, on the other hand, leads him to their rejection[136] as he prefers to use the *siddhatva* principle to solve problematic cases instead. The traditional understanding of *sthānivadbhāva* would be identical to *asiddhatva*, which is highly unlikely. There would be no point in Pāṇini introducing two different terms to define one principle, as Joshi rightly points out. Patañjali must therefore be wrong, and he gives examples from the *Ābhīya* section to prove that. If the negative function of *sthānivadbhāva* were to be accepted, many examples from the *Ābhīya* section would be superfluous.[137]

---

[134] JOSHI 1981:155.
[135] For some comments see BUISKOOL 1939:28-44.
[136] JOSHI 1981:157-158.
[137] For the details see JOSHI 1981:161.

Sanskrit grammatical tradition does not clearly distinguish between the three mentioned principles, namely *sthānivadbhāva*, *asiddhatva* and *antaraṅga-bahiraṅga*. Their domains of application often overlap and sometimes it seems that their functions are oddly similar, which would definitely be redundant. The lack of clarity and, occasionally, consistency, led the tradition to formulate additional conditions for these principles to apply so that all the examples could be accounted for. After their analysis, Joshi proposes the following: firstly, the *sthānivadbhāva* principle has only the positive function to feed the application of a rule conditioned by a substituend and it does not block feeding a rule conditioned by a substitute; and secondly, *asiddhatva* works as stated by the tradition and in the remaining parts of the treatise are subject to *siddhatva*.[138]

4.4 State of research

The problem of the *asiddhatva* as well as *asiddhavattva* principles has been analysed and discussed by scholars for many years. According to traditional commentators such as Patañjali, both terms are used in the same meaning, which is more than disputable as Pāṇini did not tend to employ various terms to denote one thing; if the terms are only slightly different they are meant to mean something different. Traditionally, *asiddhatva* serves two purposes, which Kātyāyana explains as follows: *asiddhavacanam ādeśalakṣaṇapratiṣedhārtham utsarga-lakṣaṇabhāvārthaṃ ca*[139] ("The term *asiddha* is used in order to forbid an operation conditioned by a substitute (*ādeśa*) and to allow an operation conditioned by a substituend (*utsarga*[140])"). In a way, it reverses the natural order of grammatical process, where the output of a rule becomes the input for another one to apply. In other words, according to the *asiddhatva* principle, the substitute being the result of application of a certain rule cannot serve as an input for another rule. In modern linguistic terms, it does not feed another rule. The tradition also accepts, as was mentioned above, that it is a rule (*śāstra*) that is subject to suspension, not an operation. This is also the view of Bronkhorst, who accepts *śāstrāsiddhatva* in the *Ābhīya* section as well. According to Cardona, however, rule suspension would presuppose the order as in the *Tripādī* section so the later rules would be suspended with respect to the preceding ones. In this section when two rules are in conflict, when they can both apply, they do apply in the end. So the result of the application of both rules is visible. Rule suspension in

---

[138] JOSHI 1981:167.

[139] It is the *vārttika* 1 under the *sūtra* A. 6.1.86.

[140] The term *utsarga* usually means 'a general rule' in opposition to *apavāda* ('an exception'). In this context its meaning is the same as *sthānin* 'that which is to be substituted' in opposition to *ādeśa* – 'a substitute'.

the *Ābhīya* section would presuppose mutual dependence of rules with respect to one another.[141]

Unlike Kiparsky, who allows the simultaneous application of rules in the *Ābhīya* section,[142] Bronkhorst claims that such an approach is not permitted anywhere in the *Aṣṭāḍhyāyī*, even though it could lead to correct results.[143] The *asiddhatva* principle establishes the linear order of rule application, while *asiddhavattva* does not impose any order whatsoever. Imposing *asiddhavattva* on the *Tripādī* section would imply no prescribed order, which goes against Pāṇini's own statement. Bronkhorst finds that the governing *sūtra* A. 8.2.1 is not merely equivalent to a prescription but is itself a prescription.[144] Some scholars (see below) advance an argument that Pāṇini, by establishing certain rules *asiddha*, indicated the others being *siddha*. The problem lies in the correct interpretation, and consequently, translation of thc term *asiddha*. Should we accept Broknhorst's translation of *asiddha* as 'not having taken effect', the counter-principle (*siddha*) would have to mean 'having taken effect' and this is not always the case, nor is it desirable; the rules are potentially applicable and they may or may not take effect.[145] Kiparsky, on the other hand, perceives reciprocal relation between the rules in the *Ābhīya* section as expressed by *atra*.[146] The suffix *vatI* in *asiddhavat* is used for extension, similarly to the expression *sthānivat* and, consequently, it allows for the rules in this section to be applied simultaneously. If we accept that Pāṇini only allowed for a sequential order of application, mutual *asiddhatva* would be impossible. This is the reason, according to Kiparsky, why the *vat* suffix is added, to make simultaneous application possible. He is of the opinion that the *siddhatva* principle, of which he is the proponent, would set the correct order throughout the *Aṣṭādhyāyī*.[147] It seems very unlikely that Pāṇini would imply the existence of a principle which is supposed to serve the rule application order and which would determine the very order of application also within the section that he, purposefully, exempts from this principle. Kiparsky himself states that by establishing such a chapter as *Tripādī* Pāṇini assumes *siddhatva* everywhere else. Everywhere else means outside the *Tripādī*. This is the problem Bronkhorst raises in his review article.[148]

The natural problem that arises with rule suspension both in A. 6.1.86 and the *Tripādī* section, which was also brought about by the commentators of the *Aṣṭādhyāyī*, is that these rules are stated in the treatise so how could they be

---

[141] CARDONA 1989:56.
[142] KIPARSKY 1987:301.
[143] BRONKHORST 1980:71.
[144] BRONKHORST 1980:73-74.
[145] BRONKHORST 1980:77.
[146] KIPARSKY 1982:106. Cp JOSHI&KIPARSKY 1979. But see JOSHI 1978.
[147] KIPARSKY 1982:109-111.
[148] BRONKHORST 1984:311.

suspended or treated as non-existent? Traditional explanation, as already mentioned, states that the term *asiddha* should be understood as *asiddhavat* ('as if suspended'). A comprehensive analysis of Pāṇini's understanding of *asiddha* and *asiddhavat* principles goes beyond the scope of the present work but I would like to point out that there might be a simpler solution to the rule suspension problem. We can operate on two levels: one is the set of rules, which is the *Aṣṭādhyāyī*, and the other the level of the grammatical process. We can treat the former as an abstract collection of rules to which the principles of interpretation are not assigned. On the latter, though, we have to conform to the technical devices Pāṇini used, including the order in which rules are to apply. In such a way, there is no contradiction between the existence of a rule in the treatise and its actual suspension during the process and we do not need to explain *asiddhatva* in the *Tripādī* section via *asiddhavattva*.

In my opinion, the conflicting views of Cardona and Bronkhorst can be reconciled. I agree with Bronkhorst as to the different interpretations and, consequently, different applications of the principles of *asiddhatva* and *asiddhavattva*. On the other hand, I find the *kāryāsiddhatva* (operation suspension) operating in the *Ābhīya* section more plausible than the *śāstrāsiddhatva* (rule suspension). And this is where I think the difference Bronkhorst discussed lies.[149]

Buiskool in his work claimed that apart from the sections where *asiddhatva* is mentioned, a rule is always *siddha* with respect to any other rule.[150] He distinguishes two types of *asiddhatva* in the *Tripādī* section, which he calls the primary and secondary. The former can be found when the rule belonging to the *Tripādī* is suspended with respect to the rule belonging to the *Sapāda-saptādhyāyī* and the latter when both *sūtra*s belong to the *Tripādī* itself.[151]

4.4.1 *siddhatva*

Based on the existence of the sections in the *Aṣṭādhyāyī* governed by *asiddhatva*, some scholars have postulated another principle that is to govern the remaining parts of the treatise called the *siddhatva* principle. They have claimed that merely by mentioning *asiddha* Pāṇini implies the existence of *siddha*, which is supposed to be the most general rule-ordering and conflict-solving principle. Joshi and Kiparsky formulated the *siddhatva* theory and defined it thus:

1) A is *siddha* w.r.t. B = for all x such that $B(A(x)) \neq B, A(x)$, A is applied before B to x.

---

[149] The summary and comparison of different views can also be found in YAGI 1992.

[150] BUISKOOL 1939:65. For the notion of *siddha* see also the section 4.4.1 below.

[151] BUISKOOL 1939:66-67.

2) A is *asiddha* w.r.t. B = for all x such that $B(A(x)) \neq B, A(x)$, A is not applied before B to x.[152]

The expression B(A(x)) means the rules A and B apply to the input x in such an order, whereas B, A(x) – the rules A and B apply to the input x simultaneously. They have claimed that as Pāṇinian grammar is constructed on the basis of *sāmānya* ('general') and *viśeṣa* ('particular'), the most general principles do not have to be stated if they are understood implicitly through the restrictions.[153] They have, therefore, postulated the general principle governing the *Aṣṭādhyāyī* that they formulate thus: all rules are *siddha* with respect to all rules – they can feed and bleed other rules, with environment-changing rule applying first.[154] Joshi and Roodgerben describe it either by the expression *sarvatra siddham* (lit., "[a rule] is *siddha* everywhere") or *anyatra siddham* (lit., "[a rule] is *siddha* somewhere else").[155]

This specific understanding of the term *siddha* has not been generally accepted. Cardona is of the opinion that what is meant by *siddhatva* with respect to a rule is that it is a finished entity, that has been formulated and set forth and that is in force with respect to others. He also finds that the ability of *siddhatva* to allow for feeding other rules is a natural process, while bleeding does not have to take place at all. The rules that are *siddha* can interact when the conditions are met – only that; it does not mean that one rule must bleed the other.[156] Bronkhorst also criticised Kiparsky's definition of *siddha*:

A is *asiddha* w.r.t. B = A is relevant to B, A does not take effect before B.

He agrees with the second part but the first one deviates from the literal meaning of *asiddha* and, consequently, causes problems. The definition that 'all rules are *siddha* w.r.t. all rules' cannot mean that they 'have taken effect'.[157] The rule A is relevant to B when the application of A and B to F in that order is different from applying them simultaneously.[158] The example he gives is *vakti* (A. 8.2.30 and A. 8.4.40). In this case A. 8.2.30 is relevant to A. 8.4.40 but not vice versa. When we apply the rules simultaneously, we achieve the form *vakci*. When A. 8.2.30 applies first, we will arrive at the correct form *vakti*, but when A. 8.4.40 is chosen first, the formation is again *vakci*. The result, therefore, will be the same as in the case of simultaneous application. Bronkhorst concludes that according to Kiparsky's definition, neither *siddhatva* nor *asiddhatva* determine the order of rules.

---

[152] JOSHI&KIPARSKY 1979:225.
[153] JOSHI&KIPARSKY 1979:228.
[154] JOSHI 1981:153, KIPARSKY 1982:87.
[155] KIPARSKY 1987:301.
[156] CARDONA 1989:57-60.
[157] BRONKHORST 1989:310.
[158] KIPARSKY 1987:296.

Both *asiddhatva* and *siddhatva* operate in the case of conflict, which can be of two kinds: two-way and one-way. We can talk about a two-way conflict when rule A prevents the application of B and vice versa. A one-way conflict takes place when the application of A (or B) does not prevent the application of B (or A), but the application of B (or A) prevents the application of A (or B).[159] The former is usually resolved either by the *utsarga-apavāda* principle with the exception of the *ekā saṃjñā* section (see above **4.3.2**) or *asiddhatva* if one rule belongs to the *Tripādī*. According to these scholars, both *asiddhatva* and *siddhatva* are basically designed to solve a one-way conflict. The *siddhatva* principle states that this rule applies which destroys the *nimitta* ('cause') of another rule. On the other hand, *asiddhatva* allows the rule that destroys the cause of another rule to apply later because the previous rule is suspended.

The two-way conflict can theoretically be of two types: when two rules mutually feed each other and bleed each other. While the former is not present in the *Aṣṭādhyāyī*, the latter is very common. Many cases can be resolved by resorting to the *utsarga-apavāda* principle, which does not only refer to single rules (where a special rule blocks a general one) but also operates on sets of rules (where a set of general rules can be blocked by one special rule).[160] In this case, the domain of a special rule is completely included in the domains of different general rules. It is also possible for a special rule to share some of its domain with other general rules (and this is when it blocks them) but also have its own separate domain.[161] Cardona calls it 'limited blocking' but here Kiparsky invokes the extended *siddhatva* principle, that is, when two rules A and B are mutually bleeding, the preference is given to that one which bleeds or feeds rule C. In other words, the *siddhatva* principle in its basic form is equivalent to the *nityatva* principle accepted by the Pāṇinīyas. Joshi and Roodbergen claim, however, that *siddhatva* has a wider scope (extended *siddhatva* principle) and it can be also referred to when the rules are not simultaneously applicable.[162]

As *asiddhatva* and *asiddhavattva* form a constraint on how rules operate, they are considered 'traffic rules'.[163] Their purpose is anti-feeding (*ādeśa-lakṣaṇapratiṣedha*) and anti-bleeding (*utsargalakṣaṇabhāva*). The *siddhatva* principle, on the other hand, has both feeding and bleeding properties. The latter is similar to *nityatva*, where the rule A is *nitya* when it is applicable whether or not B applies, but not vice versa. Traditionally, however, the *nityatva* principle can work only when two rules are applicable simultaneously;[164] the extended *siddhatva* principle can also apply when the rules are not in conflict. It scans the

[159] JOSHI&ROODBERGEN 1987:542.
[160] KIPARSKY 1982:112,115.
[161] SCHARF 2012:319-321.
[162] JOSHI&ROODBERGEN 1987:544 fn 8.
[163] See also YAGI 1992:49.
[164] JOSHI&KIPARSKY 2006:1-4.

whole grammatical process to choose the greatest interaction between rules; it requires 'looking ahead' in the process. Joshi and Kiparsky redefined *siddhatva*:
In B(A(**x**))
a) A is *asiddha* with respect to B if B(A(**x**)) = B,A(**x**) and A(B(**x**)) ≠ B,A(**x**)
b) A is *siddha* w.r.t. B if B(A(**x**)) ≠ B,A(**x**)
c) otherwise the *siddha* and *asiddha* relations are undefined.[165]
According to the *padasaṃskārapakṣa* (the view that every word is formed independently and only afterwards they are syntactically connected), first we line all the morphemes and then apply all augmentation and substitution rules; at the end we apply phonological rules because we combine all the words to form a sentence. However, this constraint seems wrong in the *Aṣṭādhyāyī* as Pāṇini did not give, as a principle, morphological rules the priority;[166] this priority follows from the extended *siddhatva* principle.

As mentioned before (see **4.3.4**), the Sanskrit tradition has five ways of solving conflict:[167] *paravipratiṣedha*, *pūrvavipratiṣedha*, *nityatva*, *antaraṅgatva* and *utsargāpavādatva*. Similarly, *siddhatva* and *asiddhatva* also apply as the principles solving a conflict.[168] The *siddhatva* principle requires a redefinition according to Joshi and Roodbergen – "two rules A and B are in conflict, if the order of their application – whether A first, or B first – at a given stage of the derivation gives rise to different forms, one of which is desired and one of which is not."[169] Conflict is also possible when one rule at a given stage of grammatical process is applicable to different linguistic elements. As Joshi notes: "We therefore extend the *siddha* principle to mean that in the case of two conflicting rules A and C in which C destroys the *nimitta* ('cause') of A or changes the phonetic form to which A was to become applicable, a rule B which feeds rule C also takes priority with regard to A."[170] In the *asiddha* section we can think of the example *bhugna*: *bhuj* + *Kta*, when A. 8.2.30 (*j* → *g*) and A. 8.2.45 (*t* → *n*) could both apply (and we need them both to apply but in a particular, in this case sequential, order). If the latter applies first, the conditions for A. 8.2.30 to apply are destroyed (because it is conditioned by *jhaL* – a non-nasal consonant) and we are only able to derive the form **bhujna*. Joshi and Roodbergen distinguish two

---

165 JOSHI&KIPARSKY 2006:5.
166 JOSHI&KIPARSKY 2006:12.
167 JOSHI&ROODBERGEN 1993:vi-vii.
168 This is a change from the position presented by Kiparsky (1982:112), who stated that when two rules are in conflict, Pāṇini never uses *asiddhatva* to determine their order, he merely states that one can be suspended. The *asiddhatva* principle does not serve to solve conflicts. It is used to counter the application of *siddhatva*.
169 JOSHI&ROODBERGEN 1993:viii.
170 JOSHI&ROODBERGEN 1993:x.

asiddhatva principles: the conflict solving one as in the above case and rule-ordering by A. 8.2.1.[171] They conclude the following:

One-way conflict-solving principles:

- *siddhatva*
- *asiddhatva*

Two-way conflict-solving principles:

- *paravipratiṣedha* (only in A. 1.4.1-2.2.38)
- *antaraṅgatva* (not word-internally)
- *utsargāpavādatva*

The *siddhatva* principle suggested by Joshi, Kiparsky and Roodbergen seems rather controversial. The terminological issues discussed above appear to be serious. It seems that these scholars are trying to adapt the understanding of the term *siddhatva* so that it is compatible with the principle they create. The extended version is no less problematic as it requires looking ahead in the grammatical process. It might not be wrong in principle but it is at least dubious. Whether knowledge of Sanskrit is necessary to read and apply the Pāṇinian system is irrelevant because it does not exclude the possibility that we should be able to derive the correct forms solely on the basis of the system itself, rather than infer the form from our knowledge of what the form should be. As Scharf rightly points out: "Indeed, if the grammar were meant to validate correct speech forms, it would be circular for knowledge of correct speech forms to be required in order to comprehend what the grammar provided."[172]

[171] JOSHI&ROODBERGEN 1993:xi.
[172] SCHARF 2012:329.

5 Translation and analysis of A. 6.1.86 and the *Tripādī*

5.1 A. 6.1.86

A. 6.1.86 *ṣatvatukor asiddhaḥ*
[A single substitute coming in place of preceding and succeeding sounds in close proximity] is suspended with respect to the *ṣ*-substitute and [the insertion of the infix] *tUK*.

VMBh_1: III.65.7-12; VMBh_2: IV.414.11-415.1

[Question:] Why is this said?

1) The statement [that a single substitute is] *asiddha* ('suspended') with respect to the *ṣ*-substitute and [the infix] *tUK* [is made] in order to prohibit [the application of] a rule [conditioned by] a substitute (*ādeśa*) and allow [the application of] a rule [conditioned by] a substituend (*utsarga*).

[Bhāṣya:] [Suspension] with respect to the *ṣ*-substitute and [the infix] *tUK* is mentioned in order to prohibit [the application of] a rule [conditioned by] a substitute (*ādeśa*) and allow [the application of] a rule [conditioned by] a substituend (*utsarga*).[173] So, in order to prohibit [the application of] a rule [conditioned by] a substitute – *ko 'siñcat* or *yo 'siñcat* ('who emitted, poured out?' and '[he] who emitted, poured out' respectively). When the single substitute has been done (by A. 6.1.109), the *ṣ*-substitute [of the sound *s* occurring] after a sound other than the vowel *a* (*iṆ*) would result (by A. 8.3.59). It does not occur due to [its (i.e., the single substitute)] suspension.

{Explanation:
The derivation of *ko 'siñcat* is as follows:

(1) *kim* + *sU* + *asiñcat*
(2) (*kim* → *ka*) + *s* + *asiñcat* (A. 7.2.103 *kimaḥ kaḥ*)
(3) *ka* + (*s* → *rU*) + *asiñcat* (A. 8.2.66 *sasajuṣo ruḥ*)
(4) *ka* + (*r* → *u*) + *asiñcat* (A. 6.1.113 *ato ror aplutād aplute*)
(5) *k* (*a* + *u* → *o*) + *asiñcat* (A. 6.1.87 *ād guṇaḥ*)
(6) *ko 'siñcat* (A. 6.1.109 *eṅaḥ padāntād ati*)
ko 'siñcat

---

173 The term *utsarga* used in the present *vārttika* usually means 'a general rule' in Pāṇini's grammar. Here, however, it is used to denote *sthānin* ('a substituend, an element to be substituted').

As can be seen above, at the last stage (6) the operation of a single substitute prescribed by the rule A. 6.1.109 is performed. It allows for two sounds (in this case the vowels *o* and *a*) to be replaced by one of them, the preceding one. Thus, we arrive at the correct form *ko 'siñcat*. This final form, however, opens the possibility for the application of A. 8.3.59 *ādeśapratyayayoḥ*[174] prescribing the *ṣ*-substitute in place of the sound *s* under the condition that *s* is preceded by a vowel other than *a*; we can see such a situation at the stage (6) where the preceding sound is the vowel *o*. The *ṣ*-substitution does not take place, however, because the present rule makes the single substitution suspended with respect to *ṣ*, which means that the sound *s* is still perceived as preceded by *a* as if the single substitute (of *o* + *a*) did not take place. This makes the *sūtra* A. 8.3.59 impossible to apply. If it were not the case, the stage (6) would be followed by one more, replacing *s* by *ṣ* and we would arrive at the incorrect form **ko 'ṣiñcat*.}

VMBh_1: III.65.12-13; VMBh_2: IV.415.2-3

[Bhāṣya:] Moreover, [suspension is mentioned] in order to allow [the application of] a rule [conditioned by] a substituend – *adhītya* or *pretya* ('having studied' and 'having died' respectively). When the single substitute has been done (by A. 6.1.101), the infix *tUK* [introduced] after a short vowel [of the stem] would not result (by A. 6.1.71). It does occur (i.e., the infix *tUK* is inserted) due to [its (i.e., the single substitute)] suspension. This is the purpose.

{Explanation:
The derivation of the form *adhītya* is as follows:

(1) *adhi* + *iṄ* (DhP II:37) + *Ktvā* (A. 3.4.21 *samānakartṛkayoḥ pūrvakāle*)
(2) *adhi* + *i* + *LyaP* (A. 7.1.37 *samāse 'nañpūrve ktvo lyap*)
(3) *adh* (*i* + *i* → *ī*) + *ya* (A. 6.1.101 *akaḥ savarṇe dīrghaḥ*)
(4) *adhī* + *tUK* + *ya* (A. 6.1.71 *hrasvasya piti kṛti tuk*)
adhī + *t* + *ya*
adhītya

The crucial stage in the above process is the stage (3) when both vowels *i* are replaced by *ī*. The insertion of *tUK* requires the preceding stem to end in a short vowel. After the single substitute has been implemented (by A. 6.1.101), the stem

174 A. 8.3.59 *ādeśapratyayayoḥ* || ("[The sound *ṣ* comes in place of the sound *s*] of a substitute or of a suffix [occurring after vowels other than *a*, semivowel *r* or velar stops, even when there is an intervention by the infix *nUM*, the sound *ḥ* or sibilants in close proximity].")

no longer ends in a short vowel. As this operation (namely $i + i \rightarrow \bar{ı}$) is considered suspended with respect to the insertion of *tUK*, the stem does not end in a long vowel yet and the conditions for A. 6.1.71 (that is for conditioned by the substituend, the original vowel *i*) the rule to apply are fulfilled. Otherwise, we would obtain the incorrect form **adhīya*.}

VMBh_1: III.65.13-20; VMBh_2: IV.415.4-12

[Question:] How then?

2) In that case [an operation prescribed by] a rule [conditioned by] a substituend would not take place due to lack of a substituend.

[Answer:] In that case an operation [prescribed by] a rule [conditioned by] a substituend would not take place. [For example,] *adhītya* or *pretya* ('having studied' and 'having died' respectively).
[Question:] What is the reason?
[Answer:] Due to lack of a substituend. It is said "[if the preceding stem ends in] a short vowel" (A. 6.1.71) and we do not see any short vowel here.
[Answer:] It is certainly achieved here due to using [the term] 'suspended'.

3) If [you say that] it has been achieved due to using [the term] 'suspended', [this is not correct because] when one [element] is said to be suspended, another one does not appear.

[Bhāṣya:] If [you say that] it has been achieved due to using [the term] 'suspended', [this is] not [correct].
[Question:] What is the reason?
[Answer:] Because when one [element] is mentioned as suspended, another one does not appear. [It does not happen that] when one [element] is mentioned as suspended, another one reappears. For when the killer of Devadatta has been killed, Devadatta is not brought back to life.

{Explanation:
According to Kaiyaṭa (VMBh_2: IV.415.20 ff), this is the *kāryāsiddhatva* standpoint meaning that what is subject to suspension here is an operation itself, not a rule. Even if by means of substitution a substituend is removed and its substitute is considered suspended, it does not mean that a substituend appears again.

It seems to be the explanation of what the term *asiddha* actually means rather than how it is applied. The above passage analyses this term as having a meaning similar to 'absence' and apparently it does not really seem convicing. The *Nyāsa*

(KV IV.550.28 ff) explains that if the term *asiddha* were to be interpreted as *abhāva* 'absence', then the form *adhītya* would not be possible. The infix *tUK* could not be added because after the single substitute has been applied (namely *i* + *i* → *ī*), the vowel *i* is removed. So *i* being the condition for the infix *tUK* to be added is no longer there and even if the single substitute is *asiddha*, it does not bring back two vowels *i* in place of *ī*.
According to the commentators, therefore, the term *asiddha* cannot be equal in meaning to *abhāva* because it leads to undesired results. Further in the discussion the author of the *Nyāsa* explains *asiddha* as *kāryāsāmarthya* – 'incapability of affecting an operation'. A substituend (*sthānin*) does not vanish when its replacement is treated as suspended. He also compares it to a son that can be treated like a non-son when he does not perform the duties of a son (*putrakāryakaraṇe 'sāmarthyāt*). Thus, what is normally *siddha* is *asiddha* here, as it does not perform what it is supposed to perform.}

VMBh_1: III.66.1-3; VMBh_2: IV.415.13-15

4) It should be stated, therefore, that [both principles, namely, a substitute] is like a substituend and suspension [apply].

[Bhāṣya:] It should be stated, therefore, that [both principles, namely, a substitute] is like a substituend and suspension [apply]. [In the cases of] *adhītya* and *pretya* [the principle according to which a substitute] is like a substituend [operates]. In the case of *ko 'siñcat* and *yo 'siñcat* there is suspension.

{**Explanation:**
The reference is made here to the rule A. 1.1.56 *sthānivad ādeśo 'nalvidhau* ॥ ("A substitute [for a substituend] is treated like a substituend except with regard to an operation dependent on a sound."). In the case of *adhītya*, the restoration of a previous stage of the grammatical process is required because we need the short vowel *i* for the infix *tUK* to be inserted. The rule prescribing the infix *tUK* is a rule conditioned by a substituend in this case.
In the examples *ko 'siñcat* and *yo 'siñcat*, on the other hand, using the *asiddhatva* principle is sufficient to prohibit the application of the *ṣ*-substitute that is conditioned by a substitute.}

VMBh_1: III.66.4-7; VMBh_2: IV.415.16-19

5) Stating that [a substitute] is like a substituend is superfluous due to the suspension of a rule.

[Bhāṣya:] Stating that [a substitute] is like a substituend is superfluous.

[Question:] What is the reason?
[Answer:] Since it is a rule that is suspended. It is not the suspension of an operation that is accomplished [here].
[Question:] What then?
[Answer:] It is the suspension of a rule that is accomplished. The rule [prescribing] a single substitute is suspended with respect to the rule [prescribing the infix] *tUK*.

{Explanation:
Kaiyaṭa, commenting on this passage, states that the rule prescribing *tUK* should apply first and only afterwards we can apply the rule prescribing a single substitute. It obviously indicates that *asiddhatva* serves to establish the order of rule application. If one rule is suspended with respect to another, it must apply after the one with respect to which it is suspended. In the case of *adhītya* then, the infix *tUK* is added before the rule A. 6.1.101 which allows the *ī*-substitute of both vowels *i*.}

VMBh_1: III.66.8-10; VMBh_2: IV.416.1-3

[Bhāṣya:] It is not suspended with respect to vocalisation (*saṃprasāraṇa*), the locative singular ending *Ṅi* and the 1st singular *ātmanepada* ending *iṬ*. The single substitute should be mentioned as unsuspended with respect to vocalisation (*saṃprasāraṇa*), the locative singular ending *Ṅi* and the 1st singular *ātmanepada* ending *iṬ*. [For example,] *śakahūṣu* and *parivīṣu* (loc. pl. of 'calling Śakas' and 'tied round', respectively). [The examples of] vocalisation [have been discussed]. [The examples of] the locative singular ending *Ṅi*: *vṛkṣe cchatram* or *vṛkṣe chatram* ('a bee-hive on a tree'). [The examples of] the locative singular ending *Ṅi* [have been discussed]. [The examples of] the 1st singular *ātmanepada* ending *iṬ*: *apace cchatram* or *apace chatram* ('I cooked a mushroom').

{Explanation:
The form *śakahūṣu* is formed as follows:

(1) *śaka* + *hveÑ* (DhP I:1057) + *KviP* + *suP* (A. 3.2.76 *kvip ca*, A. 4.1.2 *svaujasamauṭśasṭābhyāmbhisṅebhyāmbhyasṅasibhyāmbhyasṅasosāmṅyossup*)
(2) *śaka* + *hve* + 0 + *su* (A. 6.1.67 *ver apṛktasya*)
(3) *śaka* + *h* (*v* → *u*) *e* + *su* (A. 6.1.15 *vacisvapiyajādīnāṃ kiti*)
(4) *śaka* + *hu* (*e* → *ā*) + *su* (A. 6.1.45 *ād eca upadeśe 'śiti*)
(5) *śaka* + *h* (*u* + *ā* → *u*) + *su* (A. 6.1.108 *saṃprasāraṇāc ca*)
(6) *śaka* + *h* (*u* → *ū*) + *su* (A. 6.4.2 *halaḥ*)
(7) *śakahū* + (*s* → *ṣ*) *u* (A. 8.3.59 *ādeśapratyayayoḥ*)
śakahūṣu

The following *vārttika* proposal to consider a single substitute unsuspended in certain situations makes the above form possible. Firstly, vocalisation in a verbal stem takes place according to the *sūtra* A. 6.1.15 (stage (3)) because the stem is followed by the suffix marked with *K* (i.e., *KviP*) and the verbal root *hveÑ* belongs to the sub-group of roots beginning with *yajA* (DhP I:1051) in the *Dhātupāṭha*. Then the final vowel *e* of the verbal stem is replaced by the vowel *ā* on the basis of A. 6.1.45 (stage (4)). The subsequent substitution (*u* + *ā* → *u*) is not suspended according to the *vārttika* that follows. After the locative plural suffix is added, A. 8.3.59 can apply provided the consonant *s* follows a vowel other than the vowel *a* (or *ā*). Now, if the single substitute of *u* and *ā* were suspended, the stem would still end in the vowel *ā* and as such would not meet the requirements for the *ṣ*-substitute. We would, consequently, arrive at the form **śakahūsu*; the problem which is solved with the help of the proposed *vārttika*.

Let us now see the expression *vṛkṣe chatram* / *vṛkṣe cchatram*. In this case, the problem would be the insertion of *tUK*, which should be optionally added after the *pada* final long vowel on the basis of A. 6.1.76.

(1) *vṛkṣa* + *Ṅi* + *chatram*
(2) *vṛkṣa* + *i* + *chatram*
(3) *vṛkṣ* (*a* + *i* → *e*) + *chatram* (A. 6.1.87 *ād guṇaḥ*)
(4) *vṛkṣe* + *tUK* / 0 + *chatram* (A. 6.1.76 *padāntād vā*)
(5) *vṛkṣe* (*t* → *c*) *chatram* (A. 8.4.40 *stoḥ ścunā ścuḥ*)
vṛkṣe cchatram or *vṛkṣe chatram*

The crucial operation here is stage (3). A. 6.1.87 establishes the *guṇa* substitute resulting in the vowel *e*. Now, the optional insertion of *tUK* (stage (4)) depends on the length of the preceding vowel; according to A. 6.1.76 it must be long. In our example, after the single substitute has applied, we achieve the vowel *e* – which is a long vowel – as a result; in consequence, the infix *tUK* can be inserted only optionally when the operation prescribed by the rule A. 6.1.87 is not suspended. If, however, the *guṇa* substitution were suspended, the rule A. 6.1.76 would not apply because the preceding stem would end in *i*. In such a case, *tUK* would be inserted on the basis of A. 6.1.73 but this operation would be compulsory and the only possible form would be *vṛkṣe cchatram*, which is an undesired outcome. What we need is the the option of the form without *tUK*, which is only possible if single substitution is unsuspended. And this is what is provided by the *vārttika*.

The examples of the 1st singular *ātmanepada* ending *iṬ*: *apace cchatram* or *apace chatram* ('I cooked a mushroom') are exactly the same as the example explained above – *vṛkṣe cchatram* or *vṛkṣe chatram*. If the single *guṇa* substitute were suspended, *tUK* would have to be inserted obligatorily and the form *apace chatram* would not be possible.}

VMBh_1: III.66.11-15; VMBh_2: IV.416.4-8

6) It is not suspended with respect to vocalisation (*saṃprasāraṇa*), the locative singular ending *Ṅi* and the 1st singular *ātmanepada* ending *iṬ* because a single substitute of the final [sound] of [one] *pada* and of the initial [sound] of [the following] *pada* is stated to be *asiddha*.

[Bhāṣya:] A single substitute is not suspended with respect to vocalisation (*saṃprasāraṇa*), the locative singular ending *Ṅi* and the 1st singular *ātmanepada* ending *iṬ*.
[Question:] How?
[Bhāṣya:] Because a single substitute of the final [sound] of [one] *pada* and of the initial [sound] of [the following] *pada* is stated to be *asiddha*. It is said that a single substitute of the final [sound] of [one] *pada* and of the initial [sound] of [the following] *pada* is suspended; this is not, however, a single substitute of the final [sound] of [one] *pada* and of the initial [sound] of [the following] *pada*.
[Objection:] If a single substitute of the final [sound] of [one] *pada* and of the initial [sound] of [the following] *pada* were suspended, then in these examples the *ṣ*-substitute would result: *susasyā oṣadhīs kṛdhi* ("Cut the plants well-grown with corn")[175] and *supippalā oṣadhīs kṛdhi* ("Cut the plants bearing good berries").[176]

{Explanation:
The problem with the above examples is that the single substitute does not apply to the final and initial sounds of two *padas*; it applies to the final sound of a *pada* and the initial sound of a suffix. It means that the single substitution in the case of *oṣadhīs kṛdhi* is not going to be suspended, which will, consequently, allow for the following *ṣ*-substitute. The process is as follows:

(1) *oṣadhi* + *Śas* + *kṛdhi*
(2) *oṣadh* (*i* → *ī*) + *as* + *kṛdhi* (A. 6.3.132 *oṣadheś ca vibhaktāv aprathamāyām*)
(3) *oṣadh* (*ī* + *a* → *ī*) *s* + *kṛdhi* (A. 6.1.102 *prathamayoḥ pūrvasavarṇaḥ*)
oṣadhīs + *kṛdhi*
(4) *oṣadhī* (*s* → *rU*) + *kṛdhi* (A. 8.2.66 *sasajuṣo ruḥ*)
(5) *oṣadhī* (*r* → *ḥ*) + *kṛdhi* (A. 8.3.15 *kharavasānayor visarjanīyaḥ*)

---

175 VS 4.10, ŚB 3.2.1.30.
176 MS 1.2.2 [11.7].

(6) *oṣadhī* (*ḥ* → *s*) + *kṛdhi* (A. 8.3.50 *kaḥkaratkaratikṛdhikṛteṣv anaditeḥ*)
oṣadhīs kṛdhi

At this point, the *sūtra* A. 8.3.59 could apply prescribing the *ṣ*-substitute in place of *s* that occurs after the vowel other than *a*. The form **oṣadhīṣ kṛdhi*, however, is not desired. The *ṣ*-substitute would be possible because according to the above interpretation, the single substitute of the vowels *ī* and *a* (by A. 6.1.102) is not suspended with respect to the *ṣ*-substitute. If it is not suspended, the penultimate vowel of the word *oṣadhīs* is the vowel *ī* and not *a* which makes the rule A. 8.3.59 possible to apply. It does not happen though, because single substitution prescribed by A. 6.1.102 <u>is</u> suspended in this case. And this is how it is explained:}

VMBh_1: III.66.15-20; VMBh_2: IV.416.8-417.5

[Answer:] A single substitute of the final [sound] of [one] *pada* and of the initial [sound] of [the following] *pada* is suspended with respect to the rule prescribing [the infix] *tUK*; a single substitute is suspended only with respect to the *ṣ*-substitute.
[Objection:] If a single substitute were suspended only with respect to the *ṣ*-substitute, then the *ṣ*-substitute would not result in the case of *śakahūṣu* and *parivīṣu* (loc. pl. of 'calling Śakas' and 'tied round', respectively).
[Answer:] Let it be without any special distinction then.
[Question:] How [would the forms] *susasyā oṣadhīs kṛdhi* and *supippalā oṣadhīs kṛdhi* [be explained]?
[Answer:] This is not a mistake. The use of the word *bhrātuṣputra* ('a brother's son, nephew') is an indication [that there is the prohibition of the *ṣ*-substitute] due to its cause being a single substitute (see vt. 4 on A. 8.3.41). Since he includes this very word *bhrātuṣputra* in the *kaskādi* (A. 8.3.48) [group], by that the teacher indicates that there is no *ṣ*-substitute due to its cause being a single substitute.

{Explanation:
Let us analyse the example mentioned by Patañjali, the form *bhrātuṣputra* ('a brother's son, nephew').

(1) *bhrātṛ* + *Ṅas* + *putra*
(2) *bhrātṛ* + *as* + *putra* (A. 6.3.23 *ṛto vidyāyonisambandhebhyaḥ*)
(3) *bhrāt* (*ṛ* + *a* → *u*) + *r* + *s* + *putra* (A. 6.1.111 *ṛta ut*, A. 1.1.51 *ur aṇ raparaḥ*)
bhrāturs + *putra*
(4) *bhrātur* (*s* → 0) + *putra* (A. 8.2.24 *rāt sasya*)
(5) *bhrātu* (*r* → *ḥ*) + *putra* (A. 8.3.15 *kharavasānayor visarjanīyaḥ*)

(6) *bhrātu* (*ḥ* → *ṣ*) + *putra* (A. 8.3.48 *kaskādiṣu ca*)
bhrātuṣputra

This analysed example serves as an exception, the form in which we can observe the *ṣ*-substitute to have taken place. The form *bhrātuṣputra* is a part of the *kaskādi* group mentioned in A. 8.3.48 and this inclusion makes the substitution possible. The most important stage in the above process is (3), where the single substitute *u* is achieved because it allows the rule A. 8.3.41 *idudupadhasya cāpratyayasya*[177] to apply at the final stage. A. 8.3.41 introduces the *ṣ*-substitute of the *visarjanīya* preceded by the vowels *i* or *u* and followed by velar or labial sounds. Should this rule be considered unsuspended and allowed to apply, the correct form would result anyway but the inclusion of the form *bhrātuṣputra* in *kaskādi* would be superfluous. Thus, an indication is made – the *ṣ*-substitute of the sound *s* that occurs after the single substitute does not take place; because, as the above example shows, the single substitute is the cause of the rule prescribing the *ṣ*-substitute.}

VMBh_1: III.66.20-22; VMBh_2: IV.417.5-7

[Objection:] If this were indicated, then the *ṣ*-substitute would not result in *śakahūṣu* and *parivīṣu*.
[Bhāṣya:] This indication concerns what is similar.
[Question:] And what is similar [here]?
[Bhāṣya:] That which concerns velar and labial sounds.
[Objection:] If this were so, [then] when [the verbal root] *veÑ* ('to weave', DhP I:1055) is followed by a non-suffix (i.e., *KviP*), [the form] *uḥ* (= *us*) would result; however [the form] *ut* is required (the sounds *ut* in the past passive participle form *uta* – 'sewn, woven').

{Explanation:
The expression *yady evam* ('if this is so') refers to *vārttika* 6 and non-suspension of single substitution. As will be shown, one of the conditions is that the stem in question was termed *pada*. Let us see the example given in the *Mahābhāṣya*:

(1) *veÑ* + *KviP* + *sUP* (A. 3.2.76 *kvip ca*, A. 4.1.2 *svaujasamauṭśasṭābhyām-bhisṅebhyāmbhyasṅasibhyāmbhyasṅasosāmṅyossup*)
(2) *ve* + 0 + *s* (A. 6.1.67 *ver apṛktasya*)
(3) *v* (*e* → *ā*) + *s* (A. 6.1.45 *ād eca upadeśe 'śiti*)

177 A. 8.3.41 *idudupadhasya cāpratyayasya* || ("[The sound *ṣ* comes] in place of [the *visarjanīya* of] that which is not a suffix and has the vowel *i* or *u* as its penultimate [before the consonantal groups *kU* and *pU* in close proximity].")

(4) (*v* → *u*) *ā* + *s* (A. 6.1.15 *vacisvapiyajādīnāṃ kiti*)
u ā s
(5) (*u* + *ā* → *u*) *s* (A. 6.1.108 *saṃprasāraṇāc ca*)
us

This is the crucial point of the formation process. What we need to derive the correct form is the infix *tUK* applied on the basis of A. 6.1.71 *hrasvasya piti kṛti tuk*,[178] but it requires the stem ending in a short vowel. If the single substitute of the vowels *u* and *ā* (stage (5)) were suspended, the stem would not obviously end in a short vowel but in the vowel *ā*. Thus, the infix *tUK* could not be inserted and we would arrive at the incorrect form **us* (**uḥ* after applying the sandhi rules). If, on the other hand, we apply the *vārttika*, we will achieve the correct form *ut* in such a way:

u + *tUK* (A. 6.1.71) + *s*
u + *t* + *s*
u + *t* (*s* → 0) (A. 8.2.23 *saṃyogāntasya lopaḥ*)
ut

Here, however, a problem arises: single substitution discussed in the *vārttika* refers to the final and initial sounds of a *pada*. The stem before the case ending gets the designation *pada*, which is done by dividing A. 1.4.17 *svādiṣv asarvanāmasthāne* into: *svādiṣu* and *asarvanāmasthāne*. In such a way, even though the nom. sg. suffix is termed *sarvanāmasthāna*, the technical term *pada* can be assigned to this particular stem and as a result the infix *tUK* can be added.}

VMBh_1: III.66.22-23; VMBh_2: IV.417.8-418.1

[Bhāṣya:] When [forms] are not met in use [amongst people or in literature, they should be understood as] derived according to the rules [of grammar]. Alternatively, it is not understood in such a way: [a single substitute takes place] of the end of the preceding *pada* and the beginning of the following *pada*.
[Question:] How then?
[Answer:] [It should be understood that a single substitute takes place] of that which follows the beginning of a *pada* and that which precedes the end of a *pada*.

{Explanation:

---

[178] A. 6.1.71 *hrasvasya piti kṛti tuk* || ("[The infix] *tUK* is inserted [at the end of a verbal stem] before a *kṛt* [suffix] marked with *P* when [the preceding stem ends] in a short vowel.")

Kaiyaṭa (VMBh_2: IV.417.18 ff) explains this passage in the following manner: "The single substitute of the end of the preceding *pada* and the beginning of the following *pada* is suspended." In the case of *ut*, the vowel *ā* is not the initial sound of a *pada* and the vowel *u* is not the final sound of a *pada*; consequently, there can be no suspension and the infix *tUK* can be added. The problem Kaiyaṭa finds is that single substitution is an operation depending on two *pada*s and as such, it is externally conditioned. He believes that it indicates non-suspension of an externally conditioned operation in the case of immediate sequence of vowels. The *Uddyotana* and *Nārāyaṇīya* (MPV IX.77-78) claim that this *sūtra* implies the existence of a *paribhāṣā* according to which an operation based on immediate sequence of vowels should not be treated as externally conditioned (PŚ:51, VPV:74). According to another *paribhāṣā*: *asiddhaṃ bahiraṅgam antaraṅge*, an externally conditioned operation is suspended with respect to an internally conditioned one. However, commentators claim that the indication made in the present *sūtra* is that when an internally conditioned operation depends on vowels which are not separated, an externally conditioned operation is not suspended at all. As an example they analyse the form *akṣadyū* given by Kaiyaṭa:

(1) *akṣa* + *div* + *KviP* (A. 3.2.76 *kvip ca*)
(2) *akṣa* + *di* (*v* → *ūṬH*) + 0 (A. 6.4.19 *cchvoḥ śūḍ anunāsike ca*, A. 6.1.67 *ver apṛktasya*)
akṣa + *di ū*
(3) *akṣa* + *d* (*i* → *y*) *ū* (A. 6.1.77 *iko yaṇ aci*)
akṣadyū

In this example the vocalisation *v* → *ū* depends on the following suffix *KviP* on the basis of A. 6.4.19. It is obviously externally conditioned because it is dependent on the suffix that follows. On the other hand, the *i* → *y* substitution prescribed by A. 6.1.77 is internally conditioned, because it is dependent on *ūṬH*. If the vocalisation were suspended, the *yaṆ*-substitution could not take place.}

5.2 *Tripādī* (A. 8.2.1-8.4.68)

A. 8.2.1 ***pūrvatrāsiddham***
[From this rule up to the end of the chapter, i.e., to A. 8.4.68, a rule] is [considered] suspended with respect to a prior [rule and with respect to a rule of the section preceding this one, i.e., A. 1.1.1-8.1.74].

VMBh_1: III.385.2; VMBh_2: V.354.3-4

[Bhāṣya:] This *adhyāya* without one *pāda* should be considered suspended with respect to the [section of] seven *adhyāya*s and one *pāda* just finished.

{Explanation:
It is important to determine what actually should be considered *asiddha* – is it a rule or is it an operation? Rules are arranged and have a certain order, whereas operations have a combination of purposes and order does not apply to them. Moreover, the order in which operations apply is achieved through the order of rules, therefore this order relation is primary in the case of *sūtra*s. It could also show that, contrary to the rest of the treatise, a general rule takes precedence over an exception. It is thought that according to *śāstrāsiddhatva* (see **4.3.4** for details on *śāstrāsiddhatva* and *kāryāsiddhatva*), when a rule is suspended, we go back to the previous level of derivation, and an operation performed by a rule contained within the *Tripādī* section is not visible. This allows us to perform other operations dependent on the conditions from an earlier level. On the other hand, in the view of *kāryāsiddhatva*, an operation performed on the basis of the rule from the *Tripādī* section cannot be reversed. The principle discussed earlier – *na hi devadattasya hantari hate devadattasya prādurbhāvo bhavati* ("When the killer of Devadatta has been killed, Devadatta is not brought back to life") – is quoted by Annaṃbhaṭṭa (MPV X.345) to illustrate this interpretation.
Additionally, Kaiyaṭa (VMBh_2: V.354.9 ff) discusses the issue whether the present rule itself can be subject to suspension; this cannot happen though as it would lead to the annulment of suspension of all other rules within the *Tripādī*. Similarly, the sentence "All I am saying is false" establishes the falseness of all the other sentences apart from this one. If such a sentence were *considered* false in itself, all the others would not be. If the present rule were considered suspended, the others could not be taken as such. Consequently, the present rule would be superfluous.}

VMBh_1: III.385.2-4; VMBh_2: V.354.4-5

[Objection:] If it is said: "this *adhyāya* without one *pāda* is [considered] suspended with respect to the seven *adhyāya*s and one *pāda*", then those [*sūtra*s that] specify usages of locative, ablative and genitive should also be suspended here [i.e., in the forthcoming section].

{Exaplantion:
This is the beginning of the discussion regarding the manner in which *saṃjñā*s and *paribhāṣā*s function in the *Aṣṭādhyāyī*, and especially within the *Tripādī* section; whether they should be understood in the place where they are stated or to be used at the time of an operation (see **4.3.1** for details on *yathoddeśapakṣa* and *kāryakālapakṣa*). The *paribhāṣā*s in question describe the usage of certain cases, and their proper – technical – interpretation allows for the correct results.}

VMBh_1: III.385.4-7; VMBh_2: V.354.5-355.1

[Question:] What is the problem with this?
[Answer:] Those *paribhāṣā*s, namely A. 1.1.66, A. 1.1.67 and A. 1.1.49 would not operate due to the suspension of these instructions, i.e., A. 8.2.26, A. 8.2.27, A. 8.2.23 [with respect to the mentioned *paribhāṣā*s].

{Explanation:
The rules of interpretation mentioned by Patañjali determine the use of locative, ablative and genitive in Pāṇini's *Aṣṭādhyāyī*. They are: A. 1.1.66 *tasminn iti nirdiṣṭe pūrvasya* || ("A form stated in the locative case denotes an element, the unit preceding which [is subject to the grammatical operation introduced by that statement]"), A. 1.1.67 *tasmād ity uttarasya* || ("A form stated in the ablative case denotes an element, the unit following which [is subject to the grammatical operation introduced by that statement]") and A. 1.1.49 *ṣaṣṭhī sthāneyogā* || ("The sixth [*sUP* triplet] is used to indicate that the expression after which it is introduced is the substituendum"). If the *yathoddeśa* view were to be accepted, we could not correctly interpret the locative, ablative and genitive in A. 8.2.26 *jhalo jhali*, A. 8.2.27 *hrasvād aṅgāt* and A. 8.2.23 *saṃyogāntasya lopaḥ* respectively, which would, consequently, lead to wrong derivatives.}

VMBh_1: III.385.7-10; VMBh_2: V.355.1-4

[Answer:] This is not a problem. Even if these (i.e., A.8.2.26, A. 8.2.27, A.8.2.23) are suspended with respect to those (i.e., *paribhāṣā*s), they are not suspended here.
[Question:] How?
[Answer:] "Technical terms and rules of interpretation [apply only] along with an operation." It should be understood that when there is an operation, [technical terms and rules of interpretation] are used. [The operations are] A. 8.2.26, A. 8.2.27, A. 8.2.23 and those [i.e., A. 1.1.66, A. 1.1.67, A. 1.1.49] are used [there].

{**Explanation:**
Technical terms and rules of interpretation depend on other rules; they achieve their proper meaning only when used with other rules. Therefore the *sūtra* A. 1.1.66 defining the locative is meaningless alone; similarly the rule A. 8.2.26 prescribing the *s*-deletion before the sounds denoted by the abbreviatory term *jhaL* (i.e., non-nasal stops and fricatives). Formulating separate *sūtra*s defining technical terms and rules of interpretation was used for the sake of brevity; repeating them in the relevant rules would make the treatise much more complex. The rule A. 8.2.26 forms one sentence with A. 1.1.66, which allows us to avoid the problem concerning the order of their appearance in the *Aṣṭādhyāyī*. Therefore the issue of suspension of one with respect to another does not arise.}

VMBh_1: III.385.10-12; VMBh_2: V.355.4-7

[Objection:] If it is said: "technical terms and rules of interpretation [apply only] along with an operation", then this *paribhāṣā*, namely A. 1.4.2, should be used here as well.
[Question:] What is the problem with this?
[Answer:] [Because there are forms] *visphorya* ('to be broken forth, flashed'), *avagorya* ('to be menaced'). On the basis of [the rule A. 1.4.2 regarding] conflict [between two *sūtra*s], the lengthening [of a penultimate vowel] should [take precedence] over the *guṇa* [substitute of a penultimate vowel].

{**Explanation:**
Sūtra A. 1.4.2 *vipratiṣedhe paraṃ kāryam*, which is referred to in this passage, was discussed in greater detail in the previous chapter (see **4.3.2**). It is a conflict-solving *paribhāṣā*, which was evoked in the context of two examples given by Patañjali and the application of which would yield the wrong result: *visphorya* and *avagorya*. The applicable rules are: A. 8.2.77 *hali ca* prescribing the long vowel in place of a penultimate vowel denoted by *iK* (i.e., *i*, *u*, *ṛ*, *ḷ*) of the verbal *pada* ending in the sounds *r* or *v* before the suffix beginning with a consonant; and A. 7.3.86 *pugantalaghūpadhasya ca* ॥ ("[A substitute *guṇa* vowel comes in place of] a penultimate [vowel of a presuffixal stem ending in] the infix *pUK* or containing a short [penultimate vowel denoted by *iK* (i.e., *i*, *u*, *ṛ*, *ḷ*) before *sārvadhātuka* and *ārdhadhātuka* suffixes]"). If we accept A. 1.4.2 as valid in these cases, we would have to apply the rule A. 8.2.77 allowing for the substitution of a long vowel in both cases as this *sūtra* is placed after A. 7.3.86 (therefore, it is *para*). This is not desired, however. Therefore Patañjali replies.}

VMBh_1: III.385.13-18; VMBh_2: V.355.7-356.4

[Bhāṣya:] Therefore it reads as follows:

1) In the *pūrvatrāsiddha* [section] the conflict [between two *sūtra*s] does not occur due to absence of the latter [*sūtra*].

[Bhāṣya:] In the *pūrvatrāsiddha* [section] the conflict [between two *sūtra*s] does not occur.
[Question:] For what reason?
[Answer:] Due to absence of the latter [*sūtra*]. The conflict occurs between two mentioned [*sūtra*s, both] having the scope of application, but the latter does not exist with respect to the previous [one] in the *asiddha* [section].
[Objection:] If so, [in these forms] *dogdhā* ('a milkman'), *dogdhum* ('to milk'), the *ḍh*-substitute [of the sound *h*] would result due to the suspension of the *gh*-substitute. [Similarly, in these forms] *kāṣṭhataṭ*, *kūṭataṭ* ('a carpenter') the deletion of the last [sound] in a cluster would result [instead of] the deletion of the first sound in a cluster due to the suspension [of the latter].

{Explanation:
There are two pairs of examples given: *dogdhā*, *dogdhum* and *kāṣṭhataṭ*, *kūṭataṭ*. In the first case two applicable rules are A. 8.2.31 *ho ḍhaḥ* prescribing the *ḍh*-substitute in place of *h* and A. 8.2.32 *dāder dhātor ghaḥ* prescribing the substitute *gh*. According to *asiddhatva*, the posterior *sūtra* cannot apply due to its absence. What we need, however, is the *gh*-substitute rather than *ḍh*. The derivation of *dogdhum* must be as follows:

(1) *duhIR* (DhP I:774) + *tumUN* (A. 3.3.10 *tumunṇvulau kriyāyāṃ kriyārthāyām*)
(2) *d* (*u* → *o*) *h* + *tum* (A. 7.3.86 *pugantalaghūpadhasya ca*)
(3) *do* (*h* → *gh*) + *tum* (A. 8.2.32 *dāder dhātor ghaḥ*)
(4) *dogh* + (*t* → *dh*) *um* (A. 8.2.40 *jhaṣas tathor dho 'dhaḥ*)
(5) *do* (*gh* → *g*) + *dhum* (A. 8.4.53 *jhalāṃ jaś jhaśi*)
dogdhum

In the second example, two applicable *sūtra*s are A. 8.2.23 *saṃyogāntasya lopaḥ* prescribing the deletion of the final sound of a cluster and A. 8.2.29 *skoḥ saṃyogādyor ante ca* prescribing the deletion of the initial sound *s* or *k* of a cluster. Due to suspension of the later rule, the deletion of the final sound would apply, which is not desired as the derivation should be as follows:

(1) *kāṣṭha* + *takṣA*/*takṣŪ* (DhPI:695,685) + *KviP* + *sU* (A. 3.2.76 *kvip ca*, A. 4.1.2 *svaujasamauṭśasṭābhyāmbhisṅebhyāmbhyasṅasibhyāmbhyasṅasosāmṅyossup*)
(2) *kāṣṭha* + *takṣ* + 0 + *sU* (A. 6.1.67 *ver apṛktasya*)

(3) *kāṣṭha* + *takṣ* + 0 (A. 6.1.68 *halṅyābbhyo dīrghāt sutisy apṛktam hal*)
(4) *kāṣṭha* + *ta* (*k* → 0) *ṣ* (A. 8.2.29 *skoḥ saṃyogādyor ante*)
(5) *kāṣṭha* + *ta* (*ṣ* → *ṭ*) (A. 8.4.56 *vāvasāne*)
kāṣṭhataṭ

In both these cases the rule that appears later in the *Aṣṭādhyāyī* must apply in order to derive the correct form. As they both, namely A. 8.2.32 and A. 8.2.29, belong to the *Tripādī* section, it would go against the *asiddhatva* principle. Therefore Patañjali explains that they should be treated as exceptions to general rules.}

VMBh_1: III.385.19-21; VMBh_2: V.356.5-7

2) An exception [applies] by force of the statement itself.

[Answer:] Those two [i.e., A. 8.2.32 and A. 8.2.29] would not have the scope of application; [therefore,] by force of the statement itself they will apply. Therefore, [the statement saying] that "technical terms and rules of interpretation [apply only] along with an operation" is not false.

{**Explanation:**
Kaiyaṭa (VMBh_2: V.356.17 ff) explains that the suspension principle refers to whole domains and not individual rules, which is why a later rule, being an exception to a prior one, can still apply. These pairs of *sūtra*s: A. 8.3.31-A. 8.3.32, and A. 8.2.23 and A. 8.3.29 are part of two larger domains. Suspension does not regard individual rules within a given domain, which allows for a posterior rule, being an exception, to apply in the above contexts.}

VMBh_1: III.386.1-2; VMBh_2: V.356.8-9

3) [The *sūtra*] A. 8.2.1 [should be seen as] a governing rule.

[Bhāṣya:] [The *sūtra*] A. 8.2.1 should be seen as a governing rule.

{**Explanation:**
The discussion starts regarding the character of the present rule. It cannot be treated as a *vidhi* rule, because it is lacking an element to be prescribed. Moreover, treating A. 8.2.1 as a *vidhi* would result in suspension referring to two sections rather than individual *sūtra*s; the entire *Tripādī* would be suspended with respect to the entire preceding section of the treatise. It could not refer to the internal order of rules within the *pūrvatrāsiddha* section. For obvious reasons this rule cannot be considered as introducing either a technical term or a restriction. Accepting this rule as a rule of interpretation would result in over-application. It

cannot be treated as an extension either due to lack of the suffix *vatI*. Thus we are left with an *adhikāra* interpretation which accounts for the rule versus rule suspension and which Patañjali elaborates on.}

VMBh_1: III.386.2-9; VMBh_2: V.356.9-357.3

[Question:] What is the purpose?

4) In order to recognise that every posterior [*sūtra*] is suspended with respect to every prior [one].

[Bhāṣya:] Every posterior rule should be suspended with respect to every prior rule.

5) If [the *sūtra* A. 8.2.1 were] not a governing rule, [rules would be] recognised as suspended with respect to the whole.

[Bhāṣya:] If [the *sūtra* A. 8.2.1] were not a governing rule, the whole should be recognised suspended with respect to the whole.
[Question:] What is the fault with this?

6) In this case, there is a potential involvement of something which is not as desired.[179]

[Answer:] That which is not desired might be involved. [There are the forms] *godhuṅmān* ('a milkman') and *guḍaliṇmān* ('having sugar-lickers'(?) – meaning unclear). Having applied the *gh*-substitute (by A. 8.2.32) and the *ḍh*-substitute (by A. 8.2.31) [respectively], [the sound] *v* [replacing *m* in the *matUP* suffix on the basis of the *sūtra*] A. 8.2.10 might be involved.

{**Explanation:**
The derivation of *godhuṅmat* is as follows:

(1) *goduh + matUP* (A. 5.2.94 *tad asyāsty asminn iti matup*)
(2) *godu (h → gh) + mat* (A. 8.2.32 *dāder dhātor ghaḥ*)
(3) *go (d → dh) ugh + mat* (A. 8.2.37 *ekāco baśo bhaṣ jhaṣantasya sdhvoḥ*)
(4) *godhu (gh → g) + mat* (A. 8.2.39 *jhalāṃ jaśo 'nte*)
(5) *godhu (g → ṅ) + mat* (A. 8.4.45 *yaro 'nunāsike 'nunāsiko vā*)

---

[179] This translation of *prasaṅga* has been adopted after FRESCHI&PONTILLO 2013:70. For more on the interpretation of *prasaṅga* in Sanskrit grammatical literature see FRESCHI&PONTILLO 2013:65 ff.

godhuṅmat / *godhugmat* (as the *sūtra* A. 8.4.45 is optional).

If the present rule were not treated as an *adhikāra*, after the stage (5) we could apply A. 8.2.10 *jhayaḥ* prescribing the substitution of *m* in the suffix *matUP* by *v*. It does not happen, however, because this substitution is conditioned by the final sound of the stem being a non-nasal stop (*jhaY*). The original sound *h* is not included in the *pratyāhāra jhaY* and further substitutions (i.e., *gh*, *dh* and *g*) are posterior with respect to the *v*-substitution, so the condition for it is not met.
On the other hand, considering A. 8.2.1 a *vidhi* would not allow for the suspension of posterior rules with respect to prior ones within the *Tripādī* section, which would lead to the application of the undesired *v*-substitute.}

VMBh_1: III.386.10-21; VMBh_2: V.357.4-358.3

7) Therefore [the *sūtra* A. 8.2.1 is] a governing rule.

[Bhāṣya:] Therefore [the *sūtra* A. 8.2.1] should be viewed as a governing rule.
[Question:] What is the purpose of mentioning *asiddha*?

8) It has [already] been explained in the statement on *asiddha*.

[Question:] What has been explained?
[Answer:] With reference to that, that much has been said [in the *vt.* 1 on A. 6.1.86]: "The term *asiddha* with respect to the *ṣ*-substitution and [the infix] *tUK* is used to allow [the application of] a rule [conditioned by] a substituend (*utsarga*) and prohibit [the application] of a rule [conditioned by] a substitute (*ādeśa*)." In the same way, here also the statement *pūrvatrāsiddham* [is used] to allow [the application of] a rule [conditioned by] a substituend and prohibit [the application] of a rule [conditioned by] a substitute. First, [let us see how it is used to] prohibit [the application of] a rule [conditioned by] a substitute: *rājabhiḥ*, *takṣabhiḥ* (instr. pl. of *rājan* – 'a king', *takṣan* – 'a carpenter' respectively), *rājabhyām*, *takṣabhyām* (instr. du.), *rājasu*, *takṣasu* (loc. pl.). When [the sound] *n* has been deleted [by A. 8.2.7, the endings] *ais* etc. would result by A. 7.1.9 etc. They will not apply due to suspension [of A. 8.2.7 with respect to A. 7.1.9]. And [the examples of application of] a rule [conditioned by] a substituend: *amuṣmai*, *amuṣmāt*, *amuṣya*, *amuṣmin* (dat., abl., gen., loc. sg. m./n. of *adas* – 'that one'). [In this case,] when *da* has been replaced by *mu* [in the pronoun *adas* by A. 8.2.80, the endings] *smai* etc. would not result. They do apply due to suspension [of A. 8.2.80 with respect to the rules prescribing the endings]. [Other examples are:] *suparvāṇau*, *suparvāṇaḥ* (nom./acc. du. and nom. pl. respectively of *suparvan* – 'having beautiful wings'). When [the sound *n*] has been made retroflex [by A. 8.4.2], the lengthening [of the penultimate vowel] by

A. 6.4.7 would not take result. It does result due to suspension [of A. 8.4.2. with respect to A. 6.4.7].

{**Explanation:**
Kaiyaṭa (VMBh_2: V.357.17 ff) asks whether it is a rule or an operation that is suspended; the fact that a rule is a part of the treatise makes it impossible to consider it suspended in his opinion. Kaiyaṭa, being in favour of *śāstrāsiddhatva*, explains that a previously unsuspended element becomes suspended; thus a *sūtra* that was not suspended before becomes suspended. This interpretation would make the present rule an extension. In his opinion, only in such a way can one restore the application of a rule conditioned by a substituend (*utsarga-lakṣaṇa*). If we accept *kāryāsiddhatva*, after the suspension of a rule conditioned by a substitute, such a restoration would not be feasible because of the maxim *na hi devadattasya hantari hate devadattasya prādurbhāvaḥ* ("When the killer of Devadatta has been killed, Devadatta is not brought back to life").}

A. 8.2.2 *nalopaḥ supsvarasaṃjñātugvidhiṣu kṛti*
The deletion of [the final sound] *n* [is suspended] with respect to the rules [regarding] case endings, accent, technical terms and [the infix] *tUK* before primary suffixes (*kṛt*).

VMBh_1: III.386.22-387.3; VMBh_2: V.358.4-8

[Bhāṣya:] It is said that deletion of [the sound] *n* is suspended with respect to the rules regarding case endings. In these cases, *rājabhiḥ* and *takṣabhiḥ* (instr. pl. of the nouns *rājan* 'a king' and *takṣan* 'a carpenter' respectively), when the deletion of [the sound] *n* has taken place (by A. 8.2.7), the ending *ais* by A. 7.1.9 should not be added.
[Objection:] But here [in the forms] *rājabhyām*, *takṣabhyām*, *rājasu*, *takṣasu* (instr./dat./abl. du. and loc. pl. of the nouns *rājan* 'a king' and *takṣan* 'a carpenter'), when the deletion of [the sound] *n* has taken place, the lengthening [of the final vowel by the *sūtra* A. 7.3.102] and the *e*-substitute [of the final vowel by the *sūtra* A. 7.3.103 in plural] would result.
[Answer:] It is not a fault. [The compound] *subvidhi* is a compound ending in all the case endings. [The compound] *subvidhi* [means both] 'a rule of case endings' and 'a rule before case endings'.

{**Explanation:**
The word *vidhi* combines with all the preceding words separately, not together, which allows for the interpretation presented by Patañjali. A rule 'of case endings' means such a rule that refers to case endings themselves, while a rule 'before case endings' means a rule that describes the attachment of a case ending

and the changes in the preceding stem. The compounds in the text of the *sūtra* are genitive compounds with genitive expressing general relationship; it should not be understood in its technical sense 'in place of'. Later commentators such as the authors of the *Kāśikāvṛtti* (KV VI.337) point to two interpretations of the compound in the text of the *sūtra*: *bhāvasādhana* ('prescribed in the sense of a state') and *karmasādhana* ('prescribed in the sense of an object'). The former refers to a completed verbal activity, the latter, however, to an object of a rule. The *bhāvasādhana* refers to a previously non-existent element. In other words, when we adopt this interpretation to the compound *svaravidhi*, it will yield the meaning 'when an operation relative to the accent is to be performed'. The same applies to technical terms and the infix *tUK*. In the case of *subvidhi*, however, we need the *karmasādhana* interpretation, which accounts for the double meaning: when an operation takes place before a case ending or when a substitution of the case ending is to be performed.

The examples given in the *Mahābhāṣya* illustrate this problem. In the form *rājabhiḥ* there is the possibility of applying the rule A. 7.1.9 *ato bhisa ais*,[180] replacing the case ending *bhis* with *ais* after the stem ending in *a*. In both *rājabhiḥ* and *rājabhyām* the *sūtra*s A. 7.3.102 *supi ca*[181] and A. 7.3.103 *bahuvacane jhaly et*[182] can apply allowing for the lengthening of the final vowel *a* before a case ending and its substitution with *e* before a case ending beginning with a sound belonging to the the group termed *jhaL* respectively. The first *sūtra* prescribes the substitute of the suffix itself whereas the other two prescribe changes in the stem preceding the suffix. The suspension of the final *n*-deletion by A. 8.2.7 *nalopaḥ prātipadikāntasya* is possible only if the interpretation of *karmasādhana* is accepted. In all the examples above the case ending already exists, therefore the *bhāvasādhana* interpretation would not allow for the necessary suspension.}

VMBh_1: III.387.4-5; VMBh_2: V.359.1-2

[Question:] And what is the example in the case of rules regarding technical terms?

[Answer:] [There are the forms] *pañca* and *sapta* ('five' and 'seven' respectively). When the deletion of [the sound] *n* has taken place, [the *sūtra*] A.

---

180 A. 7.1.9 *ato bhisa ais* || ("[The substitute element] *ais* comes in place of [the case ending] *bhis* after [a nominal stem ending in the vowel] *a*.")

181 A. 7.3.102 *supi ca* || ("[A long vowel comes in place of the final *a* of the *aṅga* stem] before a case ending [beginning with the consonant denoted by *yaÑ* (semivowels, nasals or *bh*)].")

182 A. 7.3.103 *bahuvacane jhaly eT* || ("The vowel *e* [comes in place of the final vowel *a* of the *aṅga* stem] before [a case ending] beginning with [the sound denoted by] *jhaL* (i.e., non-nasal stops and fricatives) denoting plural.")

1.1.24[183] and the technical term *ṣaṭ* would not result. It does result due to suspension [of the present *sūtra* with respect to A. 1.1.24].

{Explanation:
The derivation of the word *pañca* is as follows:

(1) *pañcan* + *Jas* (A. 4.1.2 *svaujasamauṭśasṭābhyāmbhisṅebhyāmbhyasṅasibhyāmbhyasṅasosāmṅyossup*)
(2) *pañca* (*n* → 0) + *Jas* (A. 8.2.7 *nalopaḥ prātipadikāntasya*)
(3) *pañca* + 0 (A. 7.1.22 *ṣaḍbhyo luk*)

The problem with this derivation is that the application of A. 7.1.22 depends on the stem *pañcan* having the designation *ṣaṭ*, which is possible only if it ends in *n*. If A. 8.2.7 were not suspended, the plural ending *Jas* could not be deleted.}

VMBh_1: III.387.6-10; VMBh_2: V.359.3-8

1) The word *saṃjñā* [used in the *sūtra*] is superfluous due it being the cause of deletion [of *n*].

[Bhāṣya:] The word *saṃjñā* is superfluous.
[Question:] What is the reason?
[Answer:] Due to it being the cause of deletion [of the sound *n*]. If the technical term *ṣaṭ* did not apply, the deletion of *Jas* and *Śas* (nom., acc. pl.) [by A. 7.1.22] would not take place. If the deletion did not take place, the technical term *pada* would not apply [to the stem]. If the technical term *pada* did not apply, the deletion of [the sound] *n* would not take place. This precisely is resolved by applying the correct order.
[Bhāṣya:] Therefore, this is the purpose [of the use of the term *saṃjñā*]: *pañcabhiḥ*, *saptabhiḥ* (instr. pl. of the words *pañcan* 'five' and *saptan* 'seven' respectively). The accent [concerning the forms mentioned above] should be [determined by the *sūtras*] A. 6.1.179[184] and A. 6.1.180.

{Explanation:
It is argued in the above passage that the word *saṃjñā* is superfluous in the wording of the *sūtra*, because correct interpretation – and, consequently, application – of the rule can be achieved by a series of logical steps. Such an approach would

[183] A. 1.1.24 *ṣṇāntā ṣaṭ* || ("[The technical term] *ṣaṭ* denotes [a subclass of numbers] ending in *ṣ* or *ṇ*.")

[184] A. 6.1.179 *ṣaṭtricaturbhyo halādiḥ* || ("[The case ending] beginning with a consonant [bears the *udātta* accent when introduced] after [numbers with the designation] *ṣaṭ*, *tri* ('three') and *catur* ('four').")

not, however, allow for proper accentuation of forms. When the *n*-deletion has been done, the stem not ending in *n* will not obtain the designation *ṣaṭ*, which will prevent the form *saptabhiḥ* from obtaining the *udātta* accent on the penultimate syllable (by A. 6.1.180 *jhaly upottamam*[185]). It would achieve the *udātta* accent on the first syllable on the basis of the *phiṭsūtra* 2.5 *nraḥ saṃkhyāyāḥ* || ("A numeral ending in [the sound] *n* or *r* [bears the *udātta* accent on the first syllable]").

It is noted that even though the final consonant *n* has been deleted, we can still restore the previous state of the word and thus apply the technical term *ṣaṭ* as if the stem still ended in *n*.[186] Kaiyaṭa points out (VMBh_2: V.359.14), however, that this solution would not replace the lack of the term *saṃjñā* in the rule. Proper forms would be achieved in the case of the stem *ṣaṭ*, but not other stems covered by the term *ṣaṭ*. The author of the *Nyāsa* (KV VI.339.29 ff) explains that we need the term *saṃjñā* in the *sūtra* due to acceptance of *kāryakālatva*; as we need the stems in question to be termed *ṣaṭ* for the purpose of other operations, we also need to state the term *saṃjñā* in the present *sūtra*.}

VMBh_1: III.387.11-12; VMBh_2: V.359.9-360.1-2

2) And due to restriction in accent.

[Bhāṣya:] And the word *saṃjñā* is superfluous due to restriction in accent. [By saying:] "with respect to rules [regarding] accent", restriction in accent is made.

{Explanation:

Patañjali does not seem to find this a very engaging problem. Kaiyaṭa (VMBh_2: V.359-360), however, has much more to say about this. He points out that the suspension of deletion has been established only with respect to accent; the suspension of the term *ṣaṭ*, having accent as its purpose, should not be established. He also quotes other, unnamed, grammarians for whom the purpose of suspension is exhibited by examples such as *pañca brāhmaṇyaḥ* ('five brahmin women'), where the feminine suffix *ṬāP* (by A. 4.1.10) is prohibited. If the *n*-deletion did not taken place, the stem *pañcan* could be subject to the application of

[185] A. 6.1.180 *jhaly upottamam* || ("The penultimate [syllable of a polysyllabic *pada* derived from the numbers with the designation *ṣaṭ*, *tri* ('three') and *catur* ('four') bears the *udātta* accent] before [the case ending beginning with the sound denoted by] *jhaL* (i.e., non-nasal stops and fricatives).")

[186] It is the *paribhāṣā* 76 in PŚ *sāṃpratikābhāve bhūtapūrvagatiḥ* || ("When [a word] cannot denote something that actually is, it must denote something which formerly was"), vol. I:81, vol. II:386-387. See also WUJASTYK 1993: vol. I:18-19, vol. II:91-94; he quotes another version of the *paribhāṣā*: *bhūtapūrvagatir iha śāstre saṃbhavati* || ("Here in the discipline [of grammar] the previous state [of an item] may prevail.", *paribhāṣā* 11)

the rule A. 4.1.5 *ṛnebhyo ṅīp*[187] which is, according to Kaiyaṭa, blocked by the term *ṣaṭ*. After the deletion of the final consonant the suffix *ṬāP* could be added because the stem ends in the vowel *a*, but it is negated by A. 4.1.10 *na ṣaṭsvasrādibhyaḥ*.[188] We need the *n*-deletion to be suspended for the stem *pañca* to be termed *ṣaṭ*. As was mentioned before, it can be so termed only when it ends in *n*, so consequently the deletion must be considered suspended.}

VMBh_1: III.387.13-14; VMBh_2: V.360.3-4

[Question:] What are the examples of the rules regarding the infix *tUK*?
[Answer:] [There are the forms] *vṛtrahabhyām*, *vṛtrahabhiḥ* (instr./dat./abl. du. and instr. pl. of the noun *vṛtrahan* 'the killer of Vṛtra'). When the deletion of *n* has taken place, the infix *tUK* by [the *sūtra*] A. 6.1.71 would result. It does not happen due to suspension [of the present rule with respect to A. 6.1.71].

{Explanation:
The derivation of *vṛtrahabhis* is as follows:

(1) *vṛtrahan* + *KvIP* + *bhis* (A. 3.2.87 *brahmabhrūṇavṛtreṣu kvip*, A. 4.1.2 *svaujasamauṭśasṭābhyāmbhisṅebhyāmbhyasṅasibhyāmbhyasṅasosāmṅyossup*)
(2) *vṛtrahan* + 0 + *bhis* (A. 6.1.67 *ver apṛktasya*)
(3) *vṛtraha* (*n* → 0) + *bhis* (A. 8.2.7 *nalopaḥ prātipadikāntasya*)
vṛtrahabhis

After the *n*-deletion has taken place, there is the possibility of inserting the infix *tUK* by A. 6.1.71 *hrasvasya piti kṛti tuk*[189] because the preceding stem ends in *a*. It would lead to the incorrect form **vṛtrahadbhis*. It does not happen, however, due to suspension of the *n*-deletion with respect to the *tUK*-insertion. The stem is still considered as ending in *n* and the conditions for A. 6.1.71 are not met.}

VMBh_1: III.387.15-18; VMBh_2: V.360.5-361.1-2

3) But it has been mentioned with respect to the rules [regarding] the infix *tUK*.

[Question:] What has been mentioned?

---

[187] A. 4.1.5 *ṛnebhyo ṅīp* || ("[The suffix] *ṄīP* is introduced after [a nominal stem ending in either] *ṛ* or *n* [to derive a feminine nominal stem].")

[188] A. 4.1.10 *na ṣaṭsvasrādibhyaḥ* || ("[The suffix generating a feminine nominal stem] is not introduced after [the nominal stems denoted by] *ṣaṭ* and *svasṛ* ('a sister') etc.")

[189] A. 6.1.71 *hrasvasya piti kṛti tuk* || ("[The infix] *tUK* comes [at the end of a verbal stem] before a primary suffix (*kṛt*) marked with *P* when [the stem ends in] a short vowel.")

[Answer:] "[That which is taught in] a rule [the application of] which is occasioned by the condition [of two things], does not become the cause of the destruction of that [combination]." This is the purpose then: "Before the suffix *kṛt* – thus I will say". Therefore here it [i.e., the lack of *tUK*] must not occur: *brahmahacchatra* ('an umbrella that killed a brahmin'), *bhrūṇahacchāyā* ('protection of that who killed the embryo'). In this case, [the *n*-deletion] is not an operation depending on the combination [of two phonetic elements].

{**Explanation:**
Patañjali quotes here the *vt*. 3 on the *sūtra* A. 1.1.39, which became *paribhāṣā* 85 in the *Paribhāṣenduśekhara*.[190] In the examples such as *vṛtrahabhis* there is a combination between the final *n* and the following case ending. The assignment of the term *pada* to the stem preceding the case ending causes the *n*-deletion. This deletion is considered as based on a combination, which is why it cannot be the reason for the insertion of *tUK*, because it destroys said combination. All this implies the superfluity of *tUK* in the *sūtra*.
Not only does the rule depend on a combination, but it is also externally conditioned. As the *n*-deletion has as its cause the combination with the following case ending, it cannot be the cause for the application of the rule prescribing the infix *tUK*. The infix *tUK* has its cause in the non-suffix *KviP* so its introduction is an internally conditioned operation. The *n*-deletion, depending on the case ending following the stem is externally conditioned and as such must be considered suspended. Kaiyaṭa (VMBh_2: V.361) reaches the conclusion that the purpose to include *tUK* in the *sūtra* is restriction, that is, if the primary suffix follows, the *n*-deletion should be suspended with respect to *tUK*.
The insertion of the infix will take place, however, before the consonant *ch* by A. 6.1.73 *che ca*[191] as evidenced by *brahmahacchatram*. The word *chatra* is not a primary suffix and does not cause the *n*-deletion, which in this case depends on the fact that the stem *brahmahan* is termed *pada*, causing the operation to be internally conditioned. In such a case the insertion of *tUK* takes place.}

A. 8.2.3 *na mu ne*
[The substitute, by the *sūtra* A. 8.2.80,] *mu* [for *da* of the pronoun *adas* ('that one')] is not [suspended] before the [instrumental suffix] *nā*.

VMBh_1: III.387.19-21; VMBh_2: V.361.3-5

---

[190] PŚ I.85-89, II.410-422. See also WUJASTYK 1993: vol. I:14-16, vol. II:69-82.

[191] A. 6.1.73 *che ca* || ("[The infix *tUK* comes after a short vowel] also before [the sound] *ch* [in close proximity].")

[Bhāṣya:] Here it is said that "the substitution *mu* [for *da* of the pronoun *adas*] is not suspended with respect to a grammatical operation that takes place before the [instrumental suffix] *nā*"; and, to begin with, the very occurence of the [suffix] *nā* would not result.

{Explanation:
There are two options of what the locative *ne* in the *sūtra* could mean. It can be interpreted either as "when *nā* is to be introduced" or "before *nā*". Commentators explain that the first meaning simply turns into the latter, and the locative denotes scope. Therefore it is proper to say that when *nā* is to be brought about, the *mu*-substitute is not suspended with respect to an operation that is supposed to be performed before *nā*. The example is the form *amunā* whose derivation is as follows:

(1) *adas* + *āṄ*[192] (A. 4.1.2 *svaujasamauṭśasṭābhyāmbhisṅebhyāmbhyasṅasibhyāmbhyasṅasosāmṅyossup*)
(2) *ada* (*s* → *a*) + *āṄ* (A. 7.2.102 *tyadādīnām aḥ*)
(3) *ad* (*a* + *a* → *a*) + *āṄ* (A. 6.1.97 *ato guṇe*)
(4) *a* (*da* → *mu*) + *āṄ* (A. 8.2.80 *adaso 'ser dād u do maḥ*)
(5) *amu* + (*āṄ* → *nā*) (A. 7.3.120 *āṅo nāstriyām*)
amunā

In this case the rule A. 7.3.120 must apply to substitute the ending *āṄ* with *nā*. It can apply only when the preceding stem is termed *ghi* and it can be so termed only when ending in the vowel *i* or *u* by the *sūtra* A. 1.4.7 *śeṣo ghy asakhi*.[193] The stem *ada*, after the rules A. 7.2.102 (stage (2)) and A. 6.1.97 (stage (3)) have applied, does not end in either *i* or *u*. Only after *mu* replaces the element *da* does it qualify for A. 7.3.120. However, as the substitution is prescribed by A. 8.2.80, and consequently considered suspended, the present *sūtra* is formed to negate this suspension. Otherwise, if the *mu*-substitute were suspended, A. 7.3.102 *supi ca*[194] could apply lengthening the final *a* before the instrumental ending.}

VMBh_1: III.387.21-388.15; VMBh_2: V.361.5-362.10

---

[192] Pāṇini uses two terms for the instrumental singular: *āṄ* and *Ṭā*. The basic *sūtra* introducing the case endings A. 4.1.2 prescribes *āṬ* but because the *sūtra* A. 7.3.120 uses *āṄ*, I chose this option for the derivation.

[193] A. 1.4.7 *śeṣo ghy asakhi* ll ("[The technical term] *ghi* denotes remaining [stems ending in the sounds *i* or *u*, not only feminine as well as only feminine stems which are not termed *nadī*] with the exception of *sakhi* ('a friend').")

[194] A. 7.3.102 *supi ca* ll ("[A substitute long vowel comes in place of the final vowel *a* of the *aṅga* stem] before *sUP* [triplets beginning with a sound denoted by *yaÑ* (i.e., semivowels, nasals or *bh*)].")

[Bhāṣya:] Thus, in that case:

1) [The substitute, by the *sūtra* A. 8.2.80,] *mu* [for *da* of the pronoun *adas* ('that one')] is not [suspended] before the *Ṭā*-substitute.

[Bhāṣya:] It should be said that [the substitute, by the *sūtra* A. 8.2.80,] *mu* [for *da* of the pronoun *adas* ('that one')] is not [suspended] before the *Ṭā*-substitute.
[Question:] What is this *Ṭā*-substitute?
[Answer:] The *Ṭā*-substitute is the substitute of [the instrumental suffix] *Ṭā*.
[Objection:] If it is said, in that case, that the *Ṭā*-substitute is the substitute *of* [the instrumental suffix] *Ṭā*, [the operation] is not prohibited when [the *Ṭā*-substitute is] the substitution *before* [the instrumental suffix] *Ṭā*.
[Question:] What is the fault with this?
[Answer:] Here, [in the example of] *amunā*, due to the *mu*-substitute being suspended, the lengthening of [the penultimate vowel] *a* [before the *sārvadhātuka* suffix beginning with semivowels, nasal consonants or *bh* (*yaÑ*) prescribed] by [the *sūtra*s] A. 7.3.101[195] and A. 7.3.102 might be involved.
[Bhāṣya:] That is not a fault. This compound (i.e., *Ṭādeśa*) can end in all case endings. [Therefore] *Ṭādeśa* [can mean] the substitute *of* the [instrumental suffix] *Ṭā* [as well as] the substitute *before* the [instrumental suffix] *Ṭā*. It is established.
[Objection:] The *sūtra*, in that case, splits.
[Bhāṣya:] It should be according to the instruction (i.e., the *sūtra*).
[Objection:] Has it not been said that "the substitute *mu* [for *da* of the pronoun *adas*] is not suspended with respect to a grammatical operation that takes place before the [instrumental suffix] *nā*'; and, to begin with, the very occurence of the [suffix] *nā* would not result"?
[Bhāṣya:] This is not a fault. Here the teacher's intention is indicated by the composition of the *sūtra*s; hinted at, [shown] through a gesture, [expressed] through winking of an eye or [expressed] through the full composition [of the *sūtra*]. Since he teaches the prohibition of suspension when *nā* follows, the teacher makes known precisely the following: replacement by *nā* occurs here.
[Bhāṣya:] Alternatively, there are causes having two objects (i.e., fulfill two purposes). For example: "Mango trees are watered and the ancestors are gratified"; in the same way sentences are seen as having two objects. [One can say:] *śveto dhavati* [which means] "The white one runs" [or] "The dog runs from here"; and *alambusānāṃ yātā* [which means] "He will go [to the country] of Alambusas" [or] "He is able to obtain/reach the waters". Alternatively, this may be viewed as

---

195 A. 7.3.101 *ato dīrgho yañi* || ("A long vowel comes in place of [the final vowel of the verbal stem ending in] *a* before [a *sārvadhātuka* suffix beginning with] a nasal, semivowel or *bh* (*yaÑ*).")

comparable to the statement regarding an elderly virgin. When an old virgin was asked by Indra, "Choose a boon", she chose a boon [by saying], "May my sons eat rice with much milk and curds from a copper vessel".
[Question:] But she has not had a husband so far, how [could she have] the sons or how [could she have] the cows, how [could she have] the wealth?
[Answer:] In the former case, she (i.e., the old virgin) has brought together [as her boon] by means of one utterance all the following: a husband, sons, cows, and grain. In the same way here [in the sūtra], the teacher who states the prohibition of suspension [of the substitute *mu* for *da* of the pronoun *adas*] before [the instrumental suffix] *nā*, he also comprises (i.e., indicates) the occurrence of [the instrumental suffix] *nā*.

{**Explanation:**
These examples, which can be interpreted in two different ways and which serve to explain the ambiguity of locative interpretation, are an illustration of a technique called *tantra*. As Kaiyaṭa explains, by uttering one sentence we achieve two completely different meanings; this distinction is based on phonic division. If we divide given sentences thus: *śveto dhāvati* and *alambusānāṃ yātā*, we will achieve the first pair of meanings, namely, "The white one runs" and "He will go [to the country] of Alambusas" respectively. If, however, we divide the expressions differently: *śvā-ito-dhāvati* and *alam-busānām-yātā*, we will achieve the second pair of meanings, namely, "The dogs run from here" and "He is able to obtain/reach the waters".[196] The device of *tantra* can be compared to the way a lamp works, which illuminates everything around it. The lamp might illuminate the main object but also others in the vicinity. Similarly, one sentence can possess various meanings for various speakers.[197]

Patañjali gives another explanation as well. He refers to the maxim *vṛddhakumārīvākyavaranyāya* which regards requesting a boon. If an unmarried woman asks for milk and ghee, and wealth for her sons, it implies that at the same time she will be granted a husband, because otherwise she would have no sons. Thus by asking for one thing she gets two. This line of thought brings the commentators to two meanings that the rule A. 8.2.3 *na mu ne* is supposed to express:

a) it negates the suspension of the *mu*-substitute when the ending *nā* is to be introduced;

[196] See JOSHI&ROODBERGEN 1986:209.
[197] FRESCHI&PONTILLO 2013:85 ff. Both these examples, namely the watered mango tree and ambiguous sentences, are discussed in detail by Bhartṛhari in his works, both in the *Dīpikā* as well as *Vākyapadīya*. Interestingly, they serve to illustrate the difference between two devices employed by grammarians: *prasaṅga* and *tantra*. For more detail, see the cited article.

b) it negates the suspension of the *mu*-substitute with respect to any operation that might be performed when the ending *nā* follows (i.e., A. 7.1.12[198]).

The use of this rule is a little obscure as it results in a circular argument – the *mu*-substitution is not suspended when *nā* follows but the ending *nā* will follow only when *da* has been replaced by *mu*. The negation of substitute suspension does not really solve the problem. This is the reason why commentators were trying to find the solution to the interpretation of the locative.[199]}

A. 8.2.4 *udāttasvaritayor yaṇaḥ svarito 'nudāttasya*
A *svarita* comes in place of an *anudātta* appearing after a semivowel (*yaṆ*), [which is the substitute of a vowel with] an *udātta* or *svarita* accent.

VMBh_1: III.388.16-19; VMBh_2: V.362.11-363.1

1) The *yaṆ* accent (i.e., the accent achieved by vowel sandhi, when a semivowel appears) is [used] for the sake of a *svarita* of a semivowel [being a substitute of a vowel] with a *svarita* accent (*svaritayaṆ*) when there is the *yaṆ*-substitute.

[Bhāṣya:] It should be said that the accent *yaṆ* (i.e., of a semivowel) is not suspended with respect to the *yaṆ*-substitute.
[Question:] What is the purpose?
[Answer:] For the sake of a *svarita* of a semivowel [being a substitute of a vowel] with a *svarita* accent (i.e., *svaritayaṆ*). A *svaritayaṆ* should have a *svarita* accent [as well]. [As in the expressions:] *khalapvy aṭati* and *khalapvy aśnati* ('a female cleaner wanders' and 'a female cleaner eats' respectively).

{**Explanation:**
The examples given by Patañjali could be understood in two ways. The form *khalapvy* could be a feminine formation *khalapvī* but it would not be an example of *svarita* accent on the final syllable. The derivation of *khalapvy aṭati* is as follows:

---

198 In other words it negates the suspension of the *mu*-substitution with respect to other rules that potentially could apply. In our case it is the rule A. 7.1.12 which would replace the ending *Ṭā* with *ina*, consequently yielding the incorrect result **adena*.

199 For a proposed explanation of this problem see SULICH-COWLEY 2016.

(1) *khala* + *pūÑ*/*pūṄ* (DhP IX:12, I:1015) + *KviP* + *sU* (A. 3.2.178 *anyebhyo 'pi dṛśyate*, A. 4.1.2 *svaujasamauṭśasṭābhyāmbhisṅebhyāmbhyasṅasibhyāmbhyasṅasosāmṅyossup*)
(2) *khala* + *pū* + 0 + *s* (A. 6.1.67 *ver apṛktasya*)
(3) *khala* + *pū* + *ṄīP* + *s* (A. 4.1.6 *ugitaś ca*, A. 6.2.139 *gatikārakopapadāt kṛt*)
(4) *khala* + *p* (*ū* → *v*) *ī* + *s* (A. 6.1.77 *iko yaṇ aci*)
(5) *khala* + *pvī* + 0 (A. 6.1.68 *halṅyābbhyo dīrghāt sutisy apṛktam hal*)
(6) *khalapvī* (A. 6.1.174 *udāttayaṇo halpūrvāt*)
(7) *khalapvī* + *aṭati* (A. 8.1.28 *tiṅ atiṅaḥ*)
(8) *khalapv* (*ī* → *y*) + *aṭati* (A. 6.1.77 *iko yaṇ aci*)
khalapvy àṭati (A. 8.2.4 *udāttasvaritayor yaṇaḥ svarito 'nudāttasya*)

The compound *khalapvī* is an *upapada* compound by A. 2.2.19 *upapadam atiṅ*.[200] The final syllable of this compound bears the *udātta* accent by A. 6.2.139 *gatikārakopapadāt kṛt*. After the *v*-substitute has taken place, the feminine suffix *ṄīP* will be *udātta* accented on the basis of A. 6.1.174 *udāttayaṇo halpūrvāt*. The semivowel *y* coming in place of *ī* of *khalapvī* will be *udāttayaṆ*. Consequently, the following *a* of *aṭati*, which is *anudātta* on the basis of A. 8.1.28 will receive *svarita* on the basis of the present rule.
The example can be understood, however, as *khalapvy* ('a cleaner') ending in the locative ending *Ṅi*, which makes the situation slightly different. The semivowel *v* replacing *ū* on the basis of A. 6.4.83 *oḥ supi*[201] will be *udātta* accented as before. But the ending *Ṅi* bears the *anudātta* accent both on the basis of A. 3.1.4 *anudāttau suppitau*[202] and because A. 6.1.174 is negated by A. 6.1.175 *noṅdhātvoḥ*[203]. It becomes *svarita* accented on the basis of the present rule. When *y* comes in place of *i* of *khalapvì* before the form *aṭati*, the following vowel *a* should become *anudātta* accented by A. 8.1.28. It would be impossible if the *svarita* accent prescribed by the present rule to the locative ending were suspended and, consequently, it could not be marked with the *svarita* accent; which is why suspension does not apply to the accent of *yaṆ*.

[200] A. 2.2.19 *upapadam atiṅ* || ("An *upapada* which does not terminate in a verbal personal ending [necessarily combines with a syntactically connected nominal *pada* to form a *tatpuruṣa* compound].")

[201] A. 6.4.83 *oḥ supi* || ("[The semivowel substitute *v* of *yaṆ*] comes in place of [the final vowel] *u* [of an *aṅga* stem of a polysyllabic verbal stem, not preceded by a consonant cluster] before *sUP* [triplets beginning with a vowel].")

[202] A. 3.1.4 *anudāttau suppitau* || ("Case endings and [suffixes] marked with *P* have vowels *anudātta* accented.")

[203] A. 6.1.175 *noṅdhātvoḥ* || ("[Case endings excluding those termed *sarvanāmasthāna* beginning with a vowel introduced after a nominal stem whose final *udātta* vowel of the feminine suffix] *ūṄ* or of a verbal root [is replaced by a semivowel preceded by a consonant] do not [bear an *udātta* accent].")

Kaiyaṭa (VMBh_2: V.363.15 ff) quotes another explanation as well, attributing it to 'others'. They claim that assigning *svarita* is an internally conditioned operation because it depends on a single *pada* whereas the *yaṆ*-substitute, being dependent on two *padas*, is externally conditioned. An externally conditioned operation is suspended with respect to an internally conditioned one, therefore the *yaṆ*-substitute would be suspended and the *svarita* accent would not result. However, according to the *paribhāṣā* 51 in the *Paribhāṣenduśekhara* reading *nājānantarye bahiṣṭvaprakḷptiḥ* ("It is not counted as external when the rule depends on the immediate sequence of vowels"),[204] suspension of the *bahiraṅga yaṆ*-substitute is negated because *yaṆ* depends on the immediate sequence of two vowels. Thus the *svarita* accent is achieved.}

VMBh_1: III.388.19-23; VMBh_2: V.363.2-6

[Question:] Should it be said then?
[Answer:] It should not be said. He says "of a semivowel [being a substitute of a vowel] with a *svarita* accent"; and the *svarita* accent is suspended. With respect to that, its non-suspension will take place due to dependancy.

2) If non-suspension takes place due to dependency, there is a fault regarding the *svarita* accent after the *udātta* accent.

[Objection:] If non-suspension takes place due to dependency, there is a fault regarding the *svarita* accent after the *udātta* accent [as in the examples:] *dadhy āśā* and *madhv āśā* ('hope for yoghurt' and 'hope for mead' respectively).

{Explanation:
The word *dádhi* bears the *udātta* accent on the first vowel on the basis of the *Phiṭsūtra* 2.3 *nabviṣayasyānisantasya*.[205] By A. 8.4.66 *udāttād anudāttasya svaritaḥ* the vowel *i* becomes *svarita*. The word *āśā* on the basis of the PhS 1.18 *āśāyā adigākhyā ced*[206] gets the *udātta* accent on the final vowel, therefore its first vowel is *anudātta* accented on the basis of A. 6.1.158 *anudāttaṃ padam ekavarjam*.[207] The *yaṆ*-substitute of the vowel *i* would be *svarita* accented, which, due to non-suspension of the accent of *yaṆ*, would consequently lead to the vowel *ā* getting the undesired *svarita* accent.}

---

[204] PŚ I.51-53, II.267-277. See also WUJASTYK 1993: vol. I:74-74, vol. II:243-245.

[205] PhS 2.3 *nabviṣayasyānisantasya* || ("Neuter [nominal stems get the accent *udātta* on the first vowel] when they do not end in *is*.")

[206] PhS 1.18 *āśāyā adigākhyā ced* || ("[The nominal stem] *āśā* ('hope') [gets the accent *udātta* on the final vowel] if it does not denote ('a direction, space').")

[207] A. 6.1.158 *anudāttaṃ padam ekavarjam* || ("A *pada* is *anudātta* accented with the exception of one [syllable which bears an *udātta* or a *svarita* accent].")

VMBh_1: III.388.24-389.6; VMBh_2: V.363.6-364.2

[Bhāṣya:] In such a case then the division of the rule will be done [into]: *udāttayaṇaḥ* – "a *svarita* comes in place of an *anudātta* that follows a semivowel [being a substitute of a vowel] with an *udātta*" [and] then *svaritayaṇaḥ* – "a *svarita* occurs in place of an *anudātta* that follows a semivowel with a *svarita*." Exactly so, "of a semivowel with an *udātta*". Alternatively, the term '*svarita*' will not be used.
[Objection:] [If the term *svarita* is not used], how in this case will a *svarita* in place of an *anudātta* following a semivowel [which is a substitute of a vowel] with a *svarita* be achieved?
[Answer:] Just [by saying] "a semivowel [which is the substitute of a vowel] with an *udātta*".
[Objection:] But is it not that it would not result due to it being separated with a *svarita* accented semivowel?
[Answer:] [It is said that] "with respect to rules regarding accent, a consonant is [regarded] as if non-existent"; therefore there is no separation [in this case]. Alternatively, it is not understood like this: *svaritayaṆ* is a semivowel replacing a *svarita* accented [vowel]; [therefore we have the expression in the *sūtra*] "of a semivowel [which is substituted for] the *svarita* accented [vowel]."
[Question:] How then?
[Answer:] [It should be understood:] *svaritayaṆ* is a semivowel [that comes] before a *svarita* accented [vowel]; [therefore we have the expression in the *sūtra*] "of a semivowel [that comes] before a *svarita* accented [vowel]."

{**Explanation:**
Patañjali proposes two solutions to the problem, the first being the division of the *sūtra* and the second the ommision of the term *svarita* in the text of the rule altogether. A *svarita* accented vowel comes in place of an *anudātta* accented one when it follows a *svarita* originated from the *udāttayaṆ*. In other words, the vowel *i*, being the locative ending in the form *khalapvi*, gets the *svarita* accent. When the stem combines with the verbal form *aṭati*, the vowel *a*, being *anudātta* accented, gets the *svarita* accent by the present rule (*khalapvy àṭati*). And only such a *svarita* can be considered unsuspended. In the example *dadhy āśā svarita* is prescribed by A. 8.4.66 *udāttād anudāttasya svaritaḥ*[208] and comes from *udātta*, therefore the following vowel *ā* will not be *svarita* accented.
The objection is raised regarding the omission of *svarita* in the text of the rule; the term *udātta* would not be sufficient as during the derivation process the *sva-*

[208] A. 8.4.66 *udāttād anudāttasya svaritaḥ* || ("The *svarita* accent comes in place of the *anudātta* accent occurring after the *udātta* accent [in close proximity].")

rita comes in between. The answer to that is contained by the *paribhāṣā*: *svara-vidhau vyañjanam avidyamānavat* ("In an operation concerning accent a consonant is treated as non-existent").[209]
Yet another proposal is made that the term *svarita* should be interpreted as the locative meaning posteriority, not the genitive. Therefore when in every-day usage there is a *svarita* accent, followed by a semivowel, it is proper to say on the basis of a rule that a *svarita* accented vowel comes in place of the following *anudātta* vowel. In the example *dadhy āśā* the vowel *ā* is not *svarita* accented in every-day usage so there is no fault. We get no suspension of such a semivowel substitute which depends on *svarita* accented vowels in every-day usage.}

{A. 8.2.5 *ekādeśa udāttenodāttaḥ*
A single substitute [of an *anudātta*] with an *udātta* becomes *udātta*.} *This *sūtra* was not commented upon by Patañjali.

A. 8.2.6 *svarito vā 'nudātte padādau*
[A single substitute] of an initial [sound] of a *pada*, which is an *anudātta* [and a preceding *udātta* vowel] preferably becomes a *svarita*.

VMBh_1: III.389.7-9; VMBh_2: V.364.3-5

[Bhāṣya:] It is possible not to use the term *svarita* [in the *sūtra*].
[Question:] How come?
[Answer:] It is achieved [by saying that] "an *udātta* is optional when followed by an initial [sound] of a *pada* which is an *anudātta*".
[Question:] How in this case will *svarita* be [obtained] – *gāṅge 'nūpe* ('at the bank of the river Ganges')?

{Explanation:
The derivation of *gāṅge 'nūpe* is as follows:

(1) *gaṅgā* + *aṆ* (A. 4.3.120 *tasyedam*) + *apo 'nugatam* (A. 2.2.18 *kugati-prādayaḥ*)
(2) *g* (*a* → *ā*) *ṅgā* + *a* + *anūpa* + *Ṅi* (A. 7.2.117 *taddhiteṣv acām ādeḥ*, A. 4.1.2 *svaujasamauṭśasṭābhyāmbhisṅebhyāmbhyasṅasibhyāmbhyasṅasosāmṅyossup*)
(3) *gāṅgā* + *a* + *anūp* + (*a* + *i* → *e*) (A. 6.1.87 *ād guṇaḥ*)
(4) *gāṅg* (*ā* → 0) + *a* + *anūpe* (A. 6.4.148 *yasyeti ca*)
(5) *gāṅgá* (A. 3.1.3 *ādyudāttaś ca*) + *Ṅi* (A. 3.1.4 *anudāttau suppitau*) + *anūpe*
(6) *gāṅg* (*a* + *i* → *e*) + *anūpe* (A. 6.1.87 *ād guṇaḥ*)

[209] PŚ 79 I.82-83, II:393-395. See also WUJASTYK 1993: vol I:37, vol II:137.

(7) *gāṅgé* (A. 8.2.5 *ekādeśa udāttenodāttaḥ*) + *anūpé* (A. 6.2.189 *anor apradhānakanīyasī*)
(8) *gāṅge 'nūpe* (A. 6.1.109 *eṅaḥ padāntād ati*)
(*gāṅgé 'nūpe* – A. 8.2.5 or *gāṅgè 'nūpe* – A. 8.2.6)

The stem *gāṅga*, after the *taddhita* suffix has been added, is *udātta* accented on the final syllable by A. 3.1.3 (stage (5)) which prescribes the *udātta* accent to the suffix. The case ending, on the other hand is *anudātta* accented by A. 3.1.4. Consequently, the stem *gāṅge* receives the *udātta* accent on the final syllable by A. 8.2.5. As in the stem *anūpe* the final member of a compound receives the *udātta* accent (stage (7)), the first syllable is *anudātta* accented. Therefore when the stems *gāṅge* and *anūpe* are combined, there are two options – either the single replacement might be marked with an *udātta* (by A. 8.2.5) or with a *svarita* (A. 8.2.6).}

VMBh_1: III.389.9-10; VMBh_2: V.364.5-7

[Answer:] A single substitute of an *udātta* and an *anudātta* will be a *svarita* thanks to proximity [of the two]. This is the purpose then: because of this [i.e., the use of the word *svarita*] 'the exclusion' (i.e., the application of the *sūtra* A. 6.1.158 *anudāttaṃ padam ekavarjam*[210]) must not take place.

{**Explanation:**
Kaiyaṭa (VMBh_2: V.364.18 ff) comments that the *svarita* accent obtained due to extreme proximity of two sounds should be considered unsuspended. If so, the syllable *pe* in the word *anūpe* would get the *anudātta* accent by the rule A. 6.1.158, which allows for only one syllable in a word to be *svarita* or *udātta* accented. However, what we need in the *anūpe* is the final *udātta*, which is impossible if the *svarita* of *ekādeśa e + a* is not suspended. He concludes that this *svarita* is suspended, so there is no fault here.}

VMBh_1: III.389.10-12; VMBh_2: V.364.7-365.1

[Question:] But even if the term *svarita* is used, and because of this *svarita* which is unsuspended, why won't 'the exclusion' (A. 6.1.158) take place [in this case]: *kanyānūpe* ('the girl is at the river bank')?

{**Explanation:**

[210] A. 6.1.158 *anudāttaṃ padam ekavarjam* || ("A *pada* is *anudātta* accented with the exception of one [syllable which bears an *udātta* or a *svarita* accent].")

The word *kanyā̀* is *svarita* accented on the final syllable by the PhS 4.8 *tilya-śikyamatyakārṣmaryadhānyakanyārājanyamanuṣyāṇām antaḥ.*[211] The single substitute of *svarita* accented *ā* and *anudātta* accented *a* of the word *anūpe* takes place and it becomes *svarita* accented due to proximity (*kanyā̀nūpe*). Because this *svarita* is not suspended, when 'the exclusion' (A. 6.1.158) applies, the simultaneity of *udātta* and *svarita* cannot result. This simultaneity is, however, required according to Annaṃbhaṭṭa (MPV X.355). Therefore, it should also be considered suspended, as in the example *gāṅge 'nūpe*.}

VMBh_1: III.389.12-15; VMBh_2: V.365.1-4

[Answer:] Due to it being externally conditioned. [The *paribhāṣā* says:] "an externally conditioned operation (*bahiraṅga*) is suspended with respect to an internally conditioned operation (*antaraṅga*)"; and thus ['the exclusion', the rule A. 6.1.158] will not apply.
[Objection:] However, just as the term *svarita* is used, and because of this *svarita* which is unsuspended, 'the exclusion' (A. 6.1.158) does not apply; in exactly the same way, when the term *svarita* is not used, it does not apply either. Therefore, there is no point in using the term '*svarita*' [in the *sūtra*]. The same is achieved by treating it as an externally conditioned operation.

{**Explanation:**
The application of a *svarita* is an externally conditioned operation due to the *ekādeśa* depending on two separate *pada*s. Therefore, as a *svarita* is externally conditioned, it will be suspended and we can achieve it together with the *udātta* accent in one word.}

VMBh_1: III.389.16-21; VMBh_2: V.365.5-10

1) The accent of a single substitute is internally conditioned.

[Bhāṣya:] The accent of a single substitute, being an internally conditioned operation, should be mentioned as unsuspended.
[Question:] What is the purpose?

2) It is for the sake of [the accent in rules regarding] the substitutes of *ay*, *av*, *āy* and *āv*, the accent of a single substitute and [the suffix] *śatṛ*, [accent of a

[211] PhS 4.8 *tilyaśikyamatyakārṣmaryadhānyakanyārājanyamanuṣyāṇām antaḥ* || ("The final [syllable] of *tilya* ('suitable for sesamum'), *śikya* ('a loop'), *matya* ('a roler'), *kārṣmarya* ('the arborea tree'), *dhānya* ('grain'), *kanyā* ('a girl'), *rājanya* ('kingly') and *manuṣya* ('a man') [bears the *svarita* accent].")

***pada* where all] except for one [syllables are] *anudātta* accented and [the accent of a *pada* where] all [syllables are] *anudātta* accented.**

[Bhāṣya:] [The examples for] *ay*: *vṛkṣa idam, plakṣa idam* ('it is on a tree', 'it is on a fig-tree' respectively). There is a single substitute of an *udātta* and an *anudātta*. That single substitute will be *udātta* [accented] by A. 8.2.5. Its [i.e., *udātta* prescribed by A. 8.2.5] non-suspension should be mentioned. The *ay*-substitute should be *udātta* accented due to proximity with an *udātta*.

{Explanation:
The alternative to an *udātta* in this example is a *svarita*. The derivation of the expression *vṛkṣa idam* is as follows:

(1) *vṛkṣá* + *Ṅi* (A. 3.1.4 *anudāttau suppitau*)
vṛkṣá + *i*
(2) *vṛkṣ* (*á* + *i* → *é*) (A. 6.1.87 *ād guṇaḥ*, A. 8.2.5 *ekādeśa udāttenodāttaḥ*)
vṛkṣe + *idam*
(3) *vṛkṣ* (*é* → *áy*) + *idám* (A. 6.1.78 *eco 'yavāyāvaḥ*)
(4) *vṛkṣa* (*y* → 0) + *idám* (A. 8.3.19 *lopaḥ śākalyasya*)
vṛkṣá idam

The stem *vṛkṣa* is *udātta* accented by PhS 1.1 *phiṣo 'nta udāttaḥ*.[212] The following locative ending is *anudātta* accented by A. 3.1.4 and *ekādeśa* of the vowels *a* and *i* bears the *udātta* accent by A. 8.2.5. As the stem *idam* is also *udātta* accented on the final syllable by the same PhS 1.1, its initial *i* is an *anudātta*. The *ay*-substitute must also bear the *udātta* accent and similarly the single substitute *e*, from which follows that the accent of this single substitute must be unsuspended.}

VMBh_1: III.389.21-23; VMBh_2: V.365.10-366.3

[Bhāṣya:] There are no [examples for] the *av*-substitute. [The example for] *āy*: *kumāryā idam* ('it is for a girl'). [There is] a single substitute of an *udātta* and an *anudātta*, and this single substitute will become *udātta* [accented] by [the *sūtra*] A. 8.2.5. Its [i.e., *udātta* prescribed by A. 8.2.5] non-suspension should be mentioned. The *āy*-substitute should be *udātta* accented due to proximity with an *udātta*.

{Explanation:

---

212 PhS 1.1 *phiṣo 'nta udāttaḥ* || ("A nominal stem bears the *udātta* accent on the final.")

The word *kumārī* is formed from the nominal stem *kumāra* (bearing an *udātta* on the final by PhS 1.1) with the feminine suffix *ṄīP* (A. 4.1.20 *vayasi prathame*[213]) and the deletion of the final *a* by A. 6.4.148 *yasyeti ca.*[214] The feminine form is *udātta* accented on the final vowel by A. 6.1.161 *anudāttasya ca yatrodāttalopaḥ.*[215]

(1) *kumārī́* + *Ṅe*
(2) *kumārī́* + *āṬ* + *e* (A. 7.3.112 *āṇ nadyāḥ*)
(3) *kumār* (*ī* → *y*) + *ā́* + *e* (A. 6.1.77 *iko yaṇ aci*, A. 6.1.174 *udāttayaṇo halpūrvāt*)
(4) *kumāry* + (*ā́* + *e* → *ā́i*) (A. 6.1.90 *āṭaś ca*)
(5) *kumāryā́i* + *idám* (A. 8.2.5 *ekādeśa udāttenodāttaḥ*)
kumāry (*ā́i* → *ā́y*) + *idám* (A. 6.1.78 *eco 'yavāyāvaḥ*)
kumāryā́ (*y* → 0) + *idám* (A. 8.3.19 *lopaḥ śākalyasya*)
kumāryā́ idam

The infix *āṬ*, due to being marked with *Ṭ*, is inserted at the beginning of the following element.[216] It should be marked with an *anudātta* because the following case ending *e* bears an *anudātta* by A. 3.1.4 *anudāttau suppitau*, and the infix *āṬ* becomes the part of this case ending. It is marked with an *udātta*, however, by the *sūtra* A. 6.1.174 (stage (3)) before it is added to the case ending *e*. Only afterwards does the single *vṛddhi* substitute apply, which is marked with an *udātta* by A. 8.2.5. And this *udātta* should be considered unsuspended.}

VMBh_1: III.389.23-24; VMBh_2: V.366.3-4

[Bhāṣya:] This is not the purpose. When the single substitute has been done, there will be an *udātta* by [the *sūtra*] A. 6.1.174.

{Explanation:
First, the single substitute is composed of the *anudātta* accented infix *āṬ* and the case ending *Ṅe*, and then an *udātta* is prescribed to the entire ending by A. 6.1.174.}

---

[213] A. 4.1.20 *vayasi prathame* || ("[The suffix *ṄīP* comes after a nominal stem] denoting the first part of life [to derive feminine].")

[214] A. 6.4.148 *yasyeti ca* || ("[The final vowels] *i* or *a* [of a *bha* stem are deleted] before the vowel *ī* as well as [*taddhita* suffixes beginning with a vowel or the consonant *y*].")

[215] A. 6.1.161 *anudāttasya ca yatrodāttalopaḥ* || ("[The *udātta* accent] comes in place of the *anudātta* syllable when the preceding *udātta* syllable has been deleted.")

[216] A. 1.1.46 *ādyantau ṭakitau* || ("[An infix] marked with *Ṭ* constitutes the initial [of the unit to which it is added, and one] marked with *K* constitutes the final.")

VMBh_1: III.389.24-390.11; VMBh_2: V.366.4-367.3

[Question:] This is to be considered here: should the single substitute be done or the *udātta* accent, what should be done here?
[Answer:] The *udātta* accent [should apply] due to its posteriority. A single substitute is obligatory (*nitya*); if the *udātta* accent applied, it (i.e., a single substitute) would result; and if it did not apply, it would result as well.
[Objection:] But a single substitute is not obligatory. If the *udātta* accent came in place of a different accent, it (i.e., a single substitute) would result [and] if it did not come in place of a different accent, [the *paribhāṣā* stating that] "a rule is not obligatory when it applies to a different accent"[217] [would apply].
[Answer:] A single substitute is therefore an internally conditioned operation.
[Question:] What kind of internal condition is there?
[Answer:] A single substitute is [an operation] which depends on two sounds and the *udātta* accent [depends] on a stem being termed *pada*.
[Question:] In such a way then, this should be considered here: should the infix *āṬ* apply or the *udātta* accent, what should be done here?
[Answer:] The infix *āṬ* [should apply] due to its posteriority. The *udātta* accent is obligatory. If the infix *āṬ* applied, [the *udātta* accent] would result and if it did not apply, [the *udātta* accent] would result as well.
[Objection:] The infix *āṬ* is also obligatory. If the *udātta* accent applied, [the infix *āṬ*] would result and even if it did not apply, [the infix *āṬ*] would result as well.
[Answer:] The infix *āṬ* is not obligatory. If the *udātta* accent came in place of a different accent, it (i.e., the infix *āṬ*) would result and if it did not come in place of a different accent, [the *paribhāṣā* stating that] "a rule is not obligatory when it applies to a different accent" [would apply].
[Objection:] [Then,] the *udātta* accent is not obligatory either. When the infix *āṬ* to a different one has applied, [the *udātta* accent] would result and even if it has not been applied to a different one, it would result; "a rule which would apply to a different form is not obligatory."[218]
[Answer:] As neither [rule] is obligatory, the infix *āṬ* [applies] due to its posteriority. When the infix *āṬ* has applied, a single substitute [becomes] an internally conditioned [operation].

{**Explanation:**

[217] PŚ 49 *svarabhinnasya ca prāpnuvan vidhir anityo bhavati* ॥ ("When [the word form] in reference to which a rule teaches something, [after the taking effect of another rule simultaneously] would be different [from what it was before that other rule had taken effect] in consequence of some difference in accentuation, then the former rule is *anitya*."), vol. I:40-41, vol. II:219-220.
[218] Vyāḍi's *paribhāṣā* 71 (WUJASTYK 1993: vol I:72, vol II:236).

The issue discussed in the above passage refers to the order of rule application, whether the priority should be given to the *udātta* accent or to a single *vṛddhi* substitute of *ā* and *e*. Firstly, the argument is raised that a single substitute is an obligatory operation as it would take place regardless of the assignment of accent. However, according to the *paribhāṣā* 49, *vṛddhi* will not be obligatory because it would bring about a different accent. The ending *e* is *anudātta* accented by A. 3.1.4. After the *vṛddhi* substitution takes place, the ending *ai* would be assigned an *udātta* by A. 6.1.174 as it appears after the *yaṆ*-substitute following a consonant. Two different accents make the rule A. 6.1.90 prescribing the *vṛddhi* substitution *anitya*. On the other hand, the ending *e* could bear the *udātta* accent by A. 6.1.174, which would be an *anitya* rule as well. The reason for this is that the accent remains the same after the substitution and it is only the form that changes (from *e* to *ai*), and in such a case the rule will not be obligatory.
Another solution is proposed, that *ekādeśa* is internally conditioned because it depends on two sounds, whereas the assignment of an *udātta* depends on the stem being a *pada*. In other words, an *udātta* depends on the case ending to which the accent is prescribed. However, the problem arises whether the infix *āṬ* should be applied before the accent as they could be both considered *nitya* operations. Patañjali says that the insertion of *āṬ* is *anitya* again on the basis of the same *paribhāṣā* 49; and Kaiyaṭa (VMBh_2: V.367.15 ff) explains that if the *yaṆ*-substitute were applied before *āṬ*, the preceding stem would not end in a vowel any more. It would make it impossible to apply the infix as the rule A. 7.3.112 *āṇ nadyāḥ*[219] specifies that *āṬ* can be added after *nadī* stems. After the *yaṆ*-substitute it would not meet these conditions. Kaiyaṭa states, however, that the expression *nadyāḥ* should be understood as "that which is prescribed after *nadī*", which would allow for the insertion of *āṬ*. Moreover, the *udātta* accent is also *anitya* because it applies to two different forms as was stated earlier. The conclusion is that as both the accentual rule and the insertion of *āṬ* are *anitya*, the infix is inserted first due to posteriority. And the single *vṛddhi* substitute is considered an internally conditioned operation.}

VMBh_1: III.390.11-15; VMBh_2: V.367.3-8

[Bhāsya:] [The example for:] *āv* – *vṛkṣāv idam* ('these are two trees'). [There is] a single substitute of an *udātta* and an *anudātta*, which is *udātta* accented by A. 8.2.5. Its (i.e., A. 8.2.5) non-suspension should be mentioned. The *āv*-substitute should be *udātta* accented due to proximity with an *udātta*.
[The example for:] the accent of a single substitute – *gāṅge 'nūpe* ('at the Ganges bank'). [There is] a single substitute of an *udātta* and an *anudātta*. This is [on the

---

[219] A. 7.3.112 *aṇ nadyāḥ* || ("[The initial infix] *āṬ* is inserted at the head of [*sUP* triplets marked with *Ṅ* introduced] after [nominal stems termed] *nadī*.")

basis of the *sūtra*] A. 8.2.5. Its (i.e., A. 8.2.5) non-suspension should be mentioned; the accent should be assigned on the basis of [the *sūtra*] A. 8.2.6.

{**Explanation:**
The example *gāṅge 'anūpe* has been discussed above. In the case of the stem *gāṅge* we arrive at the stage where the single substitute replaces the final vowel *a* of *gāṅga* and the following vowel *i* of locative. The former is an *udātta* whereas the case ending bears an *anudātta*, and the resulting *e* would receive an *udātta* by A. 8.2.5. However, later we combine the word *gāṅge* with the stem *anūpe*. The single *e* substitute replaces *e* of *gāṅge* and the following *a* by A. 6.1.109.[220] A. 8.2.5 is suspended with respect to A. 6.1.109, which means that the vowel *e* would be marked with a *svarita* due to close proximity with what is replaced. Thus, when in combination with the stem *anūpe*, it would be marked with a *svarita* again as we would have the final vowel *e svarita* accented and the initial vowel *a anudātta* accented; an *udātta* would not be possible. If the rule A. 8.2.5 were considered unsuspended, however, we would get the *udātta* accent prescribed to *e* and the *svarita* accent by the present rule as an alternative.}

VMBh_1: III.390.15-20; VMBh_2: V.367.9-14

[Bhāṣya:] [The example for:] the accent of [the suffix] *ŚatṚ* – *tudatī, nudatī* (both meaning 'a pushing female'). [There is] a single substitute of an *udātta* and an *anudātta*, which is *udātta* accented by A. 8.2.5. Its (i.e., A. 8.2.5) non-suspension should be mentioned and the accent should apply based on [the *sūtra*] A. 6.1.173.

[Answer:] This is not the purpose. The teacher's usage indicates that the accent of a single substitute is not suspended with respect to the accent of [the suffix] *ŚatṚ* because he ordains the prohibition [in the *sūtra* A. 6.1.173] by [saying] "without the infix *nUM*".

[Question:] How has the indication been made?

[Answer:] Because there is no word ending in [the suffix] *ŚatṚ* with the infix *nUM* being *udātta* accented on the final syllable without a single substitute of an *udātta* and an *anudātta*.

{**Explanation:**
The derivation of the form *tudatī* is as follows:

[220] A. 6.1.109 *eṅaḥ padāntād ati* ǁ ("[A single substitute vowel homogenous to the first of the two vowels denoted by] *eṄ* (i.e., *e*, *o*) comes in place of [both] the *pada* final *eṄ* and the following vowel *a* [of the following *pada* in close proximity].")

(1) *tud* + *Śa* + *ŚatṚ* + *ṄīP* + *sU* (A. 3.1.77 *tudādibhyaḥ śa*, A. 3.2.124 *laṭaḥ śatṛśānacāv aprathamāsamānādhikaraṇe*, A. 4.1.6 *ugitaś ca*, A. 4.1.2 *svaujasamauṭśasṭābhyāmbhisṅebhyāmbhyasṅasibhyāmbhyasṅasosāmṅyossup*)
(2) *tud* + *á* + *at* + *ī* + *s* (A. 3.1.3 *ādyudāttaś ca*, A. 6.1.186 *tāsyanudātteṅṅidadupadeśāl lasārvadhātukam anudāttam ahnviṅoḥ*)
(3) *tud* + *á* + *at* + *ī* + 0 (A. 6.1.68 *halṅyābbhyo dīrghāt sutisy apṛktam hal*)
(4) *tud* + (*á* + *a* → *á*) *t* + *ī* (A. 6.1.97 *ato guṇe*, A. 8.2.5 *ekādeśa udāttenodāttaḥ*)
(5) *tud* + *át* + *ī´* (A. 6.1.173 *śatur anumo nady ajādī*)
tudatī´

The suffix *ŚatṚ* is *anudātta* accented by A. 6.1.186 whereas the infix *Śa* is *udātta* accented by A. 3.1.3. Their *ekādeśa* will be an *udātta* by A. 8.2.5. It is said that this *sūtra* has to be considered unsuspended for the sake of A. 6.1.173 prescribing an *udātta* to the feminine suffix *ṄīP*. The negation *anumaḥ* in the *sūtra* A. 6.1.173 is an indicator that the accent of a single substitute is not suspended in the case of forms ending in the suffix *ŚatṚ*. Commentators say that it is impossible to find the form ending in *ŚatṚ* with the infix *nUM* inserted that is *udātta* accented on the final syllable.}

VMBh_1: III.390.20-391.1; VMBh_2: V.368.1-9

[Objection:] But there are the following [forms such as]: *yāntī* and *vāntī* ('going one', 'vomiting one' – feminine).
[Answer:] Even if an *anudātta* has applied, there is no word ending in [the suffix] *ŚatṚ* with the infix *nUM* being *udātta* accented on the final syllable without a single substitute of an *udātta* and an *anudātta*.
[Question:] This is what should be considered here: should the single substitute be done or the *anudātta* accent, what should be done here [first]?
[Answer:] The *anudātta* accent [should apply] due to its posteriority. A single substitute is obligatory. If the *anudātta* accent applied, [a single substitute] would result, and even if it did not apply, [a single substitute] would result.
[Answer:] But a single substitute is not obligatory. If the *anudātta* accent came in place of a different accent, it (i.e., a single substitute) would result and if it did not come in place of a different accent, [the *paribhāṣā* stating that] "a rule is not obligatory when it applies to a different accent"[221] [would apply].
[Answer:] A single substitute is therefore an internally conditioned operation.

---

[221] PŚ 49 *svarabhinnasya ca prāpnuvan vidhir anityo bhavati* ॥ ("When [the word form] in reference to which a rule teaches something, [after the taking effect of another rule simultaneously] would be different [from what it was before that other rule had taken effect] in consequence of some difference in accentuation, then the former rule is *anitya*."), vol. I:40-41, vol. II:219-220.

[Question:] What kind of internal condition is there?
[Answer:] A single substitution is [an operation] which depends on two sounds and the *anudātta* accent [depends] on a stem being termed *pada*.
[Answer:] The *anudātta* accent is also an internally conditioned [operation].
[Question:] How?
[Answer:] It has been said that the word *pada* [has been used] to indicate the size (A. 4.3.140, vt. 4). As both [operations are] internally conditioned, the *anudātta* accent [will apply] due to its posteriority; when the *anudātta* accent has applied, there is no final *udātta* accent without a single substitute of an *udātta* and an *anudātta*. The accent of [the suffix] *ŚatṚ* [has been discussed].

{**Explanation:**
In the presented counter-examples *yāntī* and *vāntī* the suffix *ŚatṚ* cannot bear the *anudātta* accent by A. 6.1.186 as it does not meet the requirements specified in that *sutra*; therefore it must be *udātta* accented. Similarly, the verbal root *yā́*, which is *udātta* accented by A. 6.1.162 *dhātoḥ*[222]: the single substitute of the sounds *ā́* and *á* of the verbal root and the suffix *ŚatṚ* respectively, both *udātta* accented, will bear the *udātta* accent. The remaining part of the word – the ending – will be *anudātta* accented on the basis of A. 6.1.158 *anudāttaṃ padam ekavarjam*. The problem arising here is that according to this very rule, when the suffix *ŚatṚ* is *udātta* accented, the verbal root should not bear an *udātta*, it should be *anudātta*. Annaṃbhaṭṭa (MPV X.357) points to the fact that a verbal root cannot be termed *pada*, which excludes it from the scope of A. 6.1.158. These forms are thus an example of constructions ending in the suffix *ŚatṚ* and having the infix *nUM* inserted, which cannot be *antodātta* accented.
The above discussion also regards the operation primacy: should the substitution take precedence or the assignment of the *anudātta* accent? They are both considered internally conditioned. Patañjali refers to the *vt.* 4 *padagrahaṇaṃ parimāṇārtham* on the rule A. 4.3.140 which states that the term *pada* is used for the sake of determining the limit; it denotes one word and cannot refer to words in an utterance. Therefore, as both operations are considered internally conditioned, the application of an *anudātta* takes place due to its later position in the *Aṣṭādhyāyī*.}

VMBh_1: III.391.1-3; VMBh_2: V.368.10-12

[Bhāṣya:] [The example for:] *ekānudātta* (all syllables but one are marked with an *anudātta*) – *tudanti* and *likhanti* ('they push', 'they scratch' respectively). [There is] a single substitute of an *udātta* and an *anudātta*, which is *udātta* accented by A. 8.2.5. Its (i.e., A. 8.2.5) non-suspension should be mentioned;

---

[222] A. 6.1.162 *dhātoḥ* || ("[The final syllable] of the verbal root [bears the *udātta* accent].")

thanks to this non-suspension, 'the exclusion' results (i.e., the *sūtra* A. 6.1.158 applies).

{**Explanation:**
The derivation of the example *tudanti* is as follows:

(1) *tudA* (DhP VI:1) + *Śa* + *jhi* (A. 3.1.77 *tudādibhyaḥ śa*, A. 3.4.78 *tiptasjhisipthasthamibvasmastātāṃjhathāsāthāmdhvamiḍvahimahiṅ*)
(2) *tud* + *Śa* + (*jh* → *ant*) *i* (A. 7.1.3 *jho 'ntaḥ*)
(3) *tud* + *Śá* (A. 3.1.3 *ādyudāttaś ca*) + *anti* (A. 6.1.186 *tāsyanudātteṅṅidadupadeśāl lasārvadhātukam anudāttam ahnviṅoḥ*)
tud + *á* + *anti*
(4) *tud* + (*á* + *a* → *á*) *nti* (A. 6.1.97 *ato guṇe*, A. 8.2.5 *ekādeśa udāttenodāttaḥ*)
tud + *ánti*
tudánti (A. 6.1.158 *anudāttaṃ padam ekavarjam*)

The accent of a single substitute is *udātta* and so is the accent of the verbal root by the *sūtra* A. 6.1.162 *dhātoḥ*. Should the rule A. 8.2.5 prescribing the *ekādeśa* accent be suspended, we would have to apply A. 6.1.162 and the verbal root would have to bear the *udātta* accent. What we need, however, is the verbal stem to be *anudātta* accented and this can be achieved only by unsuspending the accent of a single substitute. Thus the rule A. 6.1.158 prescribing the *anudātta* accent to all the syllables but one in a *pada* can apply.
The objection is raised in Kaiyaṭa's commentary (VMBh_2: V.368.19 ff) that A. 6.1.158 would determine the accent even if an *udātta* were suspended, because a *svarita* would replace the *anudātta* and *udātta* due to close proximity with what is being replaced. As a *svarita* is unsuspended, the desired result is obtained. Kaiyaṭa, however, points to the nature of the process itself; it can be viewed as substitution (an *udātta* replaces a *svarita*), in which the suspension of *udātta* allows for the substituend *svarita* to resurface and for the application of A. 6.1.158. On the other hand, an *udātta* can be considered an exception to a *svarita*, which causes certain difficulties. The *udātta* accent is prescribed for *ekādeśa*; in the case of its suspension, there is no *svarita* and consequently the *sūtra* A. 6.1.158 cannot apply. Therefore, Kaiyaṭa concludes, one has to accept the non-suspension of the rule A. 8.2.5 for the sake of *ekānudātta* examples.}

VMBh_1: III.391.3-6; VMBh_2: V.368.13-369.2

[Bhāṣya:] [The example for:] *anudātta* accent for all [vowels] – *brāhmaṇās tudanti, brāhmaṇā likhanti* ('the Brahmins push' and 'the Brahmins scratch' respectively). [There is] a single substitute of an *udātta* and an *anudātta*, which is

udātta accented by A. 8.2.5. Its (i.e., A. 8.2.5) non-suspension should be mentioned.
[Question:] What is the purpose?
[Answer:] There should be an *anudātta* based on [the *sūtra*] A. 8.1.28.

{Explanation:
The examples given by Patañjali focus on accent in verbal *pada*s: *tudanti* and *likhanti*, which should be *anudātta* accented in their entirety as they follow non-verbal *pada*s. Such a situation is covered by the *sūtra* A. 8.1.28 *tiṅ atiṅaḥ*[223]. The form *tudanti* was analysed above; the final stages of its derivation are the following:

tud + á + anti
tud + (á + a → á) nti (A. 6.1.97 *ato guṇe*, A. 8.2.5 *ekādeśa udāttenodāttaḥ*)
tudánti (A. 6.1.158 *anudāttaṃ padam ekavarjam*)

The single substitute *á* can bear the *udātta* accent as the rule A. 8.2.5 is accepted as unsuspended; it could also bear the *svarita* accent (*à*). In combination with *brāhmaṇas* the verbal form *tudanti* will all be *anudātta* accented. Kaiyaṭa evokes the same argument as in the preceding examples stating that we can interpret the *udātta* accent as a substitute for *svarita* or as its exception. In the first case there is no point in prescribing the *udātta* as unsuspended because an *anudātta*, prescribed by A. 8.1.28, would replace a *svarita* and the desired result would follow. In the second case, however, when an *udātta* is an exception to a *svarita*, an *udātta* should be stated unsuspended.}

VMBh_1: III.391.7-9; VMBh_2: V.369.3-5

[Question:] Is it said that [the accent of a single substitute that is] an internally conditioned [operation]?
[Answer:] Only that [operation] which is externally conditioned is suspended; just like here – *prapacatīti* ('he begins to cook'), *somam utpacatīti* ('he begins to prepare soma').
[Question:] Should it be said then?
[Answer:] It should not be said. There is a prohibition of [the infix] *nUM* indicated in every case; the accent of a single substitute, which is an internally conditioned [operation], is not suspended.

{Explanation:

223 A. 8.1.28 *tiṅ atiṅaḥ* || ("After a non-verbal [*pada*], a verbal *pada* [is marked with an *anudātta* accent].")

Commentators explain that only the accent of a single substitute that is internally conditioned can be unsuspended. Patañjali gives two examples where this non-suspension does not take place. In the example *prapacati* + *iti* the particle *íti* is *udātta* accented on the initial on the basis of PhS 4.12 *nipātā ādyudāttāḥ*.[224] By A. 8.1.28 *tiṅ atiṅaḥ* the stem *prapacati* is *anudātta* accented. When these two words are combined, single substitution gives us the *udātta* accented (by A. 8.2.5) *ī́*. If this rule were considered unsuspended, we could apply the *sūtra* A. 8.1.71 *tiṅi codāttavati*,[225] which would make *ī* an *anudātta*. However, this does not happen because this single substitution is externally conditioned as depending on two words. Consequently, the accent assigned to such a single substitute is also externally conditioned; as such, it cannot be considered unsuspended and in the case *prapacatī́ti* the vowel *ī́* stays *udātta* accented.
Patañjali concludes the above discussion by saying that it is not necessary to require the single substitution to be internally conditioned anyway, because this can be inferred from the prohibition regarding the infix *nUM*. This prohibition can be extended to such situations where single substitution is externally conditioned. What we find here is an inference that depends on the general domain and this is how the indication is made – through the prohibition in the case of the infix *nUM* we achieve the prohibition of the non-suspension of A. 8.2.5 in the cases of externally conditioned single substitution.}

VMBh_1: III.391.10-12; VMBh_2: V.369.6-8

3) The deletion of a final [sound] of a cluster (A. 8.2.23) [should not be suspended] with respect to the *u*-substitute of *rU* (A. 6.1.114) [for the sake of the expression] *harivo medinaṃ tvā*.

[Bhāṣya:] The deletion of a final [sound] of a cluster should be mentioned unsuspended with respect to the *u*-substitute of *rU* (A. 6.1.114).
[Question:] What is the purpose?
[Answer:] [For the sake of the expression:] *harivo medinaṃ tvā* ("Oh Lord of horses, [we make] you [our] ally").[226] If the deletion of a final [sound] of a cluster were suspended, the *u*-substitute before [the sounds denoted by] *haŚ* (i.e., voiced consonants) would not result.

{**Explanation:**
The derivation of *harivo medinam* is as follows:

[224] PhS 4.12 *nipātā ādyudāttāḥ* || ("The particles are *udātta* accented on the initial [syllable].")
[225] A. 8.1.71 *tiṅi codāttavati* || ("[A *gati* co-ocurring] with a verbal *pada* containing the *udātta* accent [becomes *anudātta* accented].")
[226] ṚgVKh 4.3.1. The version of the text is *harivo vedinan tvā*.

(1) *hari + matUP + sU* (A. 5.2.94 *tad asyāsty asminn iti matup*, A. 4.1.2 *svaujas-amauṭśasṭābhyāmbhisṅebhyāmbhyasṅasibhyāmbhyasṅasosāmṅyossup*)
(2) *hari + ma + nUM + t + s* (A. 7.1.70 *ugidacāṃ sarvanāmasthāne 'dhātoḥ*)
(3) *hari +* (*m* → *v*) *ant + s* (A. 8.2.15 *chandasīraḥ*)
(4) *hari + vant +* (*s* → 0) (A. 6.1.68 *halṅyābbhyo dīrghāt sutisy apṛktam hal*)
(5) *harivan +* (*t* → 0) (A. 8.2.23 *saṃyogāntasya lopaḥ*)
(6) *hariva* (*n* → *rU*) (A. 8.3.1 *matuvaso ru sambuddhau chandasi*)
harivar + medinam
(7) *hariva* (*r* → *u*) *+ medinam* (A. 6.1.114 *haśi ca*)
(8) *hariv* (*a + u* → *o*) *medinam* (A. 6.1.87 *ād guṇaḥ*)
harivo medinam

The *u*-substitute (stage (7)) requires the consonant *r* to be followed by one of the sounds denoted by *haŚ*, which includes *m* but does not include *t*. If A. 8.2.23 (stage (5)) were suspended with respect to A. 6.1.114, the given substitution would never take place because the consonant *t* would still be considered present and the conditions for the substitution would not be met.}

VMBh_1: III.391.13-15; VMBh_2: V.369.9-11

4) And the prolation [of a vowel] (A. 8.2.84) [should not be suspended with respect to the *u*-substitute of *rU* (A. 6.1.114)].

[Bhāṣya:] And the prolation [of a vowel] should be mentioned unsuspended with respect to the *u*-substitute [of *rU*]. In this case – *susrotā3 atra nv asi* ("You are indeed Susrotas here"[227]) – if the prolation of a vowel (A. 8.2.84) were suspended, the *u*-substitute on the basis of [the *sūtra*] A. 6.1.113 would result. And [the *sūtra*] A. 6.1.113 should not be mentioned.

{**Explanation:**
The prolation in the form *susrotā3* results from the application of A. 8.2.84 *dūrād dhūte ca*. The final *s* of the stem *susrotas* is replaced by *rU* by A. 8.2.66 *sasajuṣo ruḥ* after the deletion of the vocative ending *sU* has taken place by A. 6.1.68 *halṅyābbhyo dīrghāt sutisy apṛktam hal*. If A. 8.2.84 were suspended, another *sūtra*, namely, A. 6.1.113 *ato ror aplutād aplute*[228] would force the *u*-substitute of the final sound, as the prolation would not be seen, and the *u*-substitute cannot apply after the prolated vowel. It would lead to an incorrect

---

[227] Rau does not identify the appearance of this passage.

[228] A. 6.1.113 *ato ror aplutād aplute* ǁ ("[The vowel *u*] comes in place of *rU* (A. 8.2.66) when it is preceded and followed by a non-prolated vowel *a* [in close proximity].")

result **susroto atra*. On the other hand, after the *rU*-substitute has taken place, the consonant *r* is fur-ther replaced by *y* (A. 8.3.17 *bhobhagoaghoapūrvasya yo 'śi*), which is sub-sequently deleted by A. 8.3.19 *lopaḥ śākalyasya* yielding the correct result.}

VMBh_1: III.391.15-19; VMBh_2: V.369.11-370.1-3

[Bhāṣya:] This is not the purpose. The maxim is done:

5) The deletion of [the suffix] *sIC* (A. 8.2.28) [should not be suspended] with respect to a single substitute (A. 6.1.101).

[Bhāṣya:] The deletion of [the suffix] *sIC* should be mentioned as unsuspended with respect to a single substitute. [For example:] *alāvīt* and *apāvīt* ('he cut, divided' and 'he cleaned' respectively, 3rd sg. aor.). If the deletion of [the suffix] *sIC* were suspended, the lengthening of [two] homogenous vowels would not result.

{Explanation:
The derivation of the form *alāvīt* is as follows:

(1) *lūÑ* (DhP IX:13) + *lUṄ*
(2) *lū* + *Cli* + *tiP* (A. 3.1.43 *cli luṅi*, A. 3.4.78 *tiptasjhisipthasthamibvasmas-tātāmjhathāsāthāmdhvamiḍvahimahiṅ*)
(3) *lū* + *Cli* + *t* (*i* → 0) (A. 3.4.100 *itaś ca*)
(4) *lū* + *sIC* + *t* (A. 3.1.44 *cleḥ sic*)
(5) *aṬ* + *lū* + *sIC* + *t* (A. 6.4.71 *luṅlaṅlṛṅkṣv aḍudāttaḥ*)
(6) *a* + *l* (*ū* → *au*) + *s* + *t* (A. 7.2.1 *sici vṛddhiḥ parasmaipadeṣu*)
(7) *a* + *lau* + *iṬ* + *s* + *t* (A 7.2.35 *ārdhadhātukasyeḍ valādeḥ*)
(8) *a* + *lau* + *iṬ* + *s* + *īṬ* + *t* (A. 7.3.96 *astisico 'pṛkte*)
(9) *a* + *lau* + *i* + (*s* → 0) + *ī* + *t* (A. 8.2.28 *iṭa īṭi*)
(10) *a* + *lau* + (*i* + *ī* → *ī*) + *t* (A. 6.1.101 *akaḥ savarṇe dīrghaḥ*)
(11) *a* + *l* (*au* → *āv*) + *ī* + *t* (A. 6.1.77 *iko yaṇ aci*)
alavīt

The derivation shows that single substitution performed by A. 6.1.101 (stage (10)) could not take place if the suffix *sIC* deletion were suspended simply because the two vowels would still be separated by the consonant *s*. There is, however, an objection raised.}

VMBh_1: III.391.19-22; VMBh_2: V.370.3-7

[Question:] But is it the deletion of [the suffix] *sIC* containing [the infix] *iṬ* at the beginning?
[Answer:] It is not possible like that, because in these cases – *mā hi lāvīt* and *mā hi pāvīt* ('he must not cut' and 'he must not clean' respectively) – if there were not the infix *iṬ*, the *anudātta* accented infix *īṬ* might be involved. If there is, however, the infix *iṬ*, this is said: "Because of the use of the marker *C* [in the suffix *sIC*] the infix *īṬ* bears the *udātta* accent."[229] Therefore [a single substitute of *i* and *ī*] will have the *udātta* accent by A. 8.2.5 and the rule will not be suspended.

{**Explanation:**
The question is asked whether the suffix *sIC* is deleted together with the infix *iṬ* that precedes it. As the infix is marked with *Ṭ*, it is attached at the beginning of the following element, namely the suffix *sIC*, and as it would be considered a part of said suffix, it would be deleted as well by A. 8.2.28. In the example *mā hi lāvīt* the prefix *aṬ* is not added to the verbal stem by A. 6.4.74 *na māṅyoge*[230]. The augment *aṬ* is *udātta* accented according to A. 6.4.71 but as it is not added in this case; the verbal root will bear an *udātta* on the final syllable by A. 6.1.162 *dhātoḥ*. The rest of the stem will be *anudātta* accented on the basis of A. 6.1.158 *anudāttaṃ padam ekavarjam*. Consequently, the infix *īṬ* will be *anudātta* accented as well. This is not desired, however, as it should be *udātta* accented on the basis of the *vt*. 2 on A. 3.1.44. The infix *iṬ* inserted before the suffix *sIC* cannot be deleted together with this suffix, which allows for the *ekādeśa udātta* accent by A. 8.2.5 when combining an *udātta* of *īṬ* and an *anudātta* of *iṬ* after the *sIC* deletion has taken place.}

VMBh_1: III.391.23-392.2; VMBh_2: V.370.8-11

6) The deletion of an initial [sound] of a cluster (A. 8.2.29) [should not be suspended] with respect to the deletion of a final [sound] of a cluster (A. 8.2.23).

[Bhāṣya:] The deletion of an initial [sound] of a cluster should be mentioned unsuspended with respect to the deletion of a final [sound] of a cluster. [For example:] *kāṣṭhataṭ* and *kūṭataṭ* ('a carpenter'). If the deletion of an initial

[229] See A. 3.1.44 *vt*. 2. The accent is prescribed by the *sūtra* A. 6.1.163 *citaḥ* || ("[The final syllable of a nominal stem] marked with *C* [or ending in the suffix with the marker *C* bears the *udātta* accent].")

[230] A. 6.4.74 *na māṅyoge* || ("[The initial augments *aṬ* and *āṬ*] are not [inserted at the beginning of the verbal *aṅga* stem before the *l*-substitutes of *lUṄ*, *lAṄ* and *lṚṄ*] when co-ocurring with the prohibitive particle *māṄ*.")

[sound] of a cluster (A. 8.2.29) were suspended, the deletion of a final [sound] of a cluster would result.
[Answer:] This is not a fault. It has been said: "An exception [applies] by force of the statement itself" (A. 8.2.1 *vt* 2).

{**Explanation:**
The above problem has already been discussed under the *vārttika* 2 on A. 8.2.1. The derivation of the stem *kāṣṭhataṭ* should be as follows:

(1) *kāṣṭha* + *takṣA*/*takṣŪ* (DhPI:695,685) + *KviP* + *sU* (A. 3.2.76 *kvip ca*, A. 4.1.2 *svaujasamauṭśasṭābhyāmbhisṅebhyāmbhyasṅasibhyāmbhyasṅasosāmṅyos-sup*)
(2) *kāṣṭha* + *takṣ* + 0 + *sU* (A. 6.1.67 *ver apṛktasya*)
(3) *kāṣṭha* + *takṣ* + 0 (A. 6.1.68 *halṅyābbhyo dīrghāt sutisy apṛktam hal*)
(4) *kāṣṭha* + *ta* (*k* → 0) *ṣ* (A. 8.2.29 *skoḥ saṃyogādyor ante ca*)
(5) *kāṣṭha* + *ta* (*ṣ* → *ṭ*) (A. 8.4.56 *vāvasāne*)
kāṣṭhataṭ

In this case the rule that appears later in the *Aṣṭādhyāyī*, that is A. 8.2.29 prescribing the deletion of the initial sound of the consonant cluster, must apply in order to derive the correct form. It should apply instead of A. 8.2.23 prescribing the deletion of a cluster initial. As A. 8.2.29 is a posterior rule, it should theoretically be considered suspended, but it being an exception to A. 8.2.23 blocks this suspension.}

VMBh_1: III.392.3-5; VMBh_2: V.370.12-371.2

7) The substitute of the *niṣṭhā* suffix (A. 1.1.26) [should not be suspended] with respect to operations regarding the *ṣ*-substitute, accent, suffixes and [the infix] *iṬ*.

[Bhāṣya:] The substitute of the *niṣṭhā* suffix should be mentioned unsuspended with respect to operations regarding the *ṣ*-substitute, accent, suffixes and [the infix] *iṬ*. [For example:] *vṛkṇaḥ* or *vṛkṇavān* ('broken, cut' and 'one who has cut' respectively). If the *niṣṭhā*-substitute were suspended, the *ṣ*-substitute would result (A. 8.2.36).

{**Explanation:**
The derivation of the form *vṛkṇa* is as follows:

(1) *OvraścŪ* (DhP VI:11) + *Kta* (A. 1.1.26 *ktaktavatū niṣṭhā*, A. 3.2.102 *niṣṭhā*)

(2) *v* (*r* → *ṛ*) *aśc* + *ta* (A. 6.1.16 *grahijyāvayivyadhivaṣṭivicativṛścatipṛcchatibhṛjjatīnāṃ ṅiti ca*)
(3) *v* (*ṛ* + *a* → *ṛ*) *śc* + *ta* (A. 6.1.108 *samprasāraṇāc ca*)
(4) *vṛśc* + (*t* → *n*) *a* (A. 8.2.45 *oditaś ca*)
(5) *vṛ* (*ś* → 0) *c* + *na* (A. 8.2.29 *skoḥ saṃyogādyor ante ca*)
(6) *vṛ* (*c* → *k*) + *na* (A. 8.2.30 *coḥ kuḥ*)
(7) *vṛk* + (*n* → *ṇ*) *a* (A. 8.4.2 *aṭkupvāṅnumvyāvāye 'pi*)
vṛkṇa

The rule A. 8.2.45 introducing the *t* → *n* substitution is not suspended with respect to A. 8.2.36 *vraścabhraśjasṛjamṛjayajarājabhrājacchaśāṃ ṣaḥ*[231] prescribing the *ṣ*-substitute. However, it must be suspended with respect to A. 8.2.30 (stage (6)), which prescribes the substitution *c* → *k*, because this operation takes place only before a non-nasal consonant (*jhaL*). If A. 8.2.45 were not suspended with respect to A. 8.2.30, the following suffix would begin with a nasal consonant, which would mean that A. 8.2.30 would have no scope of application and the form *vṛkṇa* would not be possible.}

VMBh_1: III.392.5-6; VMBh_2: V.371.2-4

[Bhāṣya:] [The example for a rule regarding] accent: *kṣībaḥ* ('drunk, intoxicated'). If the *niṣṭhā*-substitute were suspended, the accent based on [the *sūtra*] A. 6.1.205 *niṣṭhā ca dvyaj anāt*[232] would not result.

{**Explanation:**
The derivation of *kṣība* is as follows:

(1) *kṣībṚ* (DhP I:407) + *Kta* (A. 1.1.26 *ktaktavatū niṣṭhā*, A. 3.2.102 *niṣṭhā*)
(2) *kṣīb* + *iṬ* + *ta* (A. 7.2.35 *ārdhadhātukasyeḍ valādeḥ*)
kṣīb + (*i* + *t* → 0) + *a*
kṣība

---

[231] A. 8.2.36 *vraścabhraśjasṛjamṛjayajarājabhrājacchaśāṃ ṣaḥ* || ("[The final sound] of [the verbal roots] *OvraścŪ* ('to cut', DhP VI: 11), *bhrasjA* ('to roast', DhP VI:4), *sṛjA* ('to create', DhP VI:121), *mṛjŪ* ('to cleanse', DhP II:57), *yajA* ('to sacrifice', DhP I:1051), *rājĀ* ('to shine, rule', DhP I:874), *bhrājĀ* ('to shine, sparkle', DhP I:194) and [those which end in the sounds] *ch* and *ś* [is replaced by] *ṣ* [when the sound to be replaced occurs at the end of a *pada* or before the sound denoted by *jhaL* (i.e., consonants except nasals)].")

[232] A. 6.1.205 *niṣṭhā ca dvyaj anāt* || ("[The initial syllable] of a dissyllabic [stem ending in the suffixes termed] *niṣṭhā*, excluding those having *ā* [in the first syllable, when denoting a name, bears an *udātta* accent].")

This form is irregularly formed by the *sūtra* A. 8.2.55 *anupasargāt phullakṣība-kṛśollāghāḥ*; the deletion of the suffix *iṬ* and the sound *t* is achieved via *nipātana*. If this deletion were suspended, the form *kṣī́ba* could not be *udātta* accented on the first syllable by A. 6.1.205, because the word would still have three syllables instead of two.}

VMBh_1: III.392.6-7; VMBh_2: V.371.4-5

[Bhāṣya:] [The example for a rule regarding] a suffix: *kṣībika* ('one who crosses drunk / with a drunk'). If the *niṣṭhā*-substitute were suspended, [the *taddhita* suffix] *ṭhaN* on the basis of [the *sūtra*] A. 4.4.7 would not apply.

{**Explanation:**
The form *kṣībika* is derived from *kṣība* with the suffix *ṭhaN* added by A. 4.4.7 *naudvyacaṣ ṭhan*.[233] It has to be added to the stem containing only two syllables, therefore A. 8.2.55 allowing for the deletion of the infix *iṬ* and the sound *t* of the *niṣṭhā* suffix *Kta* has to be considered unsuspended.

(1) *kṣība* + *ṭhaN*
(2) *kṣība* + *ika* (A. 7.3.50 *ṭhasyekaḥ*)
(3) *kṣīb* (*a* → 0) + *ika* (A. 6.4.148 *yasyeti ca*)
kṣībika}

VMBh_1: III.392.7-8; VMBh_2: V.371.5-6

[Bhāṣya:] [The example for] a rule [regarding the infix] *iṬ*. If the *niṣṭhā*-substitute were suspended, the infix *iṬ* would result on the basis of the expression *valādi* (A. 7.2.35).

{**Explanation:**
The example is still the same – the word *kṣība* – where the consonant *t* is deleted by A. 8.2.55. According to Kaiyaṭa, A. 8.2.55 can also be perceived as prescribing the deletion of *t* of the suffix *Kta*. Afterwards, the infix *iṬ* could be inserted if the *Tripādī* rule were suspended; this insertion of the infix requires that the consonant other than *y* follow the stem. With A. 8.2.55 suspended, the consonant *t* would still be there.}

VMBh_1: III.392.8-11; VMBh_2: V.371.6-9

---

[233] A. 4.4.7 *naudvyacaṣ ṭhan* ‖ ("[The *taddhita* suffix] *ṭhaN* comes after [the nominal stem] *nau* ('a boat') and those containing two syllables [to denote 'crosses with it'].")

[Objection:] Is it not, however, that which is not suspended with respect to the rule regarding a suffix, that is not suspended with respect to a rule [regarding the infix] *iṬ* [either].
[Answer:] This is the purpose then: [the past participle of the verbal root] *OlasjĪ* ('to be ashamed, blush', DhP VI:10) *lagna*. The *niṣṭhā*-substitute should be mentioned unsuspended because the prohibition of the infix *iṬ* on the basis of [the *sūtra*] A. 7.2.8 should apply. The rule A. 7.2.14 should not apply.

{**Explanation:**
The situation in the case of *lagna* is the same as with the word *vṛkṇa* explained above. The *sūtra* A. 8.2.45 prescribing the *t* → *n* substitution in the suffix *Kta* to derive past passive participle must not be suspended with respect to the rule A. 7.2.8 *neḍ vaśi kṛti*[234] which prohibits the infix *iṬ*. However, the prohibition of insertion of the infix *iṬ* could still apply, even if the *n*-substitute were suspended, by A. 7.2.14 *śvīdito niṣṭhāyām*[235] as it requires the verbal root being marked with *Ī*. Patañjali disagrees with the application of A. 7.2.14 in this case; he prefers A. 7.2.8 with A. 8.2.45 considered unsuspended.}

VMBh_1: III.392.11-14; VMBh_2: V.371.9-372.2

[Bhāṣya:] This is not the purpose. The maxim is done:

8) The *d*-substitution [of the final sound] of [the suffix] *KvasU* etc. (A. 8.2.72) [should not be suspended with respect to the lengthening before [the non-vocative suffix] *sU* (A. 6.4.14).

[Bhāṣya:] The *d*-substitution [of the final sound] of [the suffix] *KvasU* etc. (A. 8.2.72) should be mentioned unsuspended with respect to the lengthening before [the non-vocative suffix] *sU* (A. 6.4.14 *atvasantasya cādhātoḥ*[236]). [For example:] *ukhāsrat* or *parṇadhvat* ('dropping from a cauldron' and 'causing the leaves to fall' respectively). [The *sūtra*] A. 6.4.14 should not apply.

{**Explanation:**
The derivation of *ukhāsrat* is as follows:

---

234 A. 7.2.8 *neḍ vaśi kṛti* || ("[The initial infix] *iṬ* does not come at the beginning of a *kṛt* [suffix beginning with semivowels and] voiced stops (*vaŚ*) excluding [the consonant] *y*.")

235 A. 7.2.14 *śvīdito niṣṭhāyām* || ("[The initial infix *iṬ* does not come at the beginning of] a *niṣṭhā* [suffix introduced] after [the verbal roots] *ṬUOśvi* ('to swell', DhP I:1059) and those marked with *Ī* [in the first enunciation].")

236 A. 6.4.14 *atvasantasya cādhātoḥ* || ("[Before a non-vocative suffix *sU* a long vowel comes in place of the penultimate vowel of an *aṅga* stem] other than a verbal one, [ending in *atU* or *as*.")

(1) *ukhā-sraṃs* + *KviP* + *sU* (A. 3.2.76 *kvip ca*, A. 4.1.2 *svaujasamauṭśasṭā-bhyāmbhisṅebhyāmbhyasṅasibhyāmbhyasṅasosāmṅyossup*)
(2) *ukhā-sraṃs* + *KviP* + (*s* → 0) (A. 6.1.68 *halṅyābbhyo dīrghāt sutisy apṛktam hal*)
(3) *ukhā-sra* (*ṃ* → 0) *s* + *KviP* (A. 6.4.24 *aniditāṃ hala upadhyāyāḥ kṅiti*)
(4) *ukhā-sra* (*ṃ* → 0) *s* + (*KviP* → 0) (A. 6.1.67 *ver apṛktasya*)
(5) *ukhāsra* (*s* → *d*) + *s* (A. 8.2.72 *vasusraṃsudhvaṃsvanaḍuhāṃ daḥ*)
(6) *ukhāsra* (*d* → *t*) (A. 8.4.56 *vāvasāne*)
ukhāsrat

If the *d*-substitute (stage (5)) were considered suspended, the stem would still end in *as* and, consequently, the lengthening of the penultimate vowel of *ukhāsrat* by A. 6.4.14 could apply. It would yield the incorrect form **ukhāsrāt*. However, Patañjali rightly rejects this *vārttika*. The rule A. 6.4.14 could not apply in this case anyway because the stem *sraṃs* is a verbal root; and as such, it is not in the scope of that rule.}

VMBh_1: III.392.15-19; VMBh_2: V.372.2-6

[Bhāṣya:] This is not the purpose. The maxim is done:

9) The *ī* and *ū* substitutes in [the pronominal stem] *adas* ('that one') [should not be suspended] with respect to the rule regarding a vowel being a part of an external *pada*.

[Bhāṣya:] The *ī* and *ū* substitutes in [the pronominal stem] *adas* ('that one') should be mentioned unsuspended with respect to the rule regarding a vowel being a part of an external *pada*. [For example:] *amī atra* ('those ones [are] here', nom. pl. m.), *amī āsate* ('those ones are sitting', nom. pl. m.), *amū atra* ('those two [are] here', nom./acc. du.), *amū āsate* ('those two are sitting', nom./acc. du.). If the *ī* and *ū* substitutes were suspended, the *ay* and *av* substitutes of the sounds denoted by *eC* (A. 6.1.78 *eco 'yavāyāvaḥ*) would result.

{**Explanation:**
The term *svara* used by Patañjali refers in this case to a vowel, not to accent. And the expression *bahiṣpadalakṣaṇa* means "that which is a part of an external *pada*". In the following example the *ī*-substitute should be considered unsuspended with respect to the vowel *a* of the following stem *atra*. The derivation of the expression *amī atra* is as follows:

(1) *adas* + *Jas* + *atra*
(2) *ada* (*s* → *a*) + *Jas* + *atra* (A. 7.2.102 *tyadādīnām aḥ*)

(3) *ada + a + Śī + atra* (A. 7.1.17 *jasaḥ śī*)
(4) *ad (a + a → a) + ī + atra* (A. 6.1.97 *ato guṇe*)
(5) *ad (a + ī → e) + atra* (A. 6.1.87 *ād guṇaḥ*)
(6) *a (de → mī) + atra* (A. 8.2.81 *eta īd bahuvacane*)
amī atra (A. 1.1.12 *adaso māt*)

If the rule A. 8.2.81 were suspended, it would be possible to apply the *sūtra* A. 6.1.78 *eco 'yavāyāvaḥ*, and consequently *ay* would result in place of the vowel *e*. It would lead to an incorrect derivation **ade atra* → **adayatra*.}

VMBh_1: III.392.19-20; VMBh_2: V.372.6-7

[Question:] Why is [the expression] "that which is a part of an external *pada*" used?
[Answer:] Because another one and only that one is suspended. [For example:] *amuyā* and *amuyoḥ* (instr. sg. f. and gen./loc. du. respectively).

{**Explanation:**
By the expression 'another one' Patañjali means such an element that is not a part of an external *pada* and he exemplifies it with the help of two inflectional forms; there is no combination with another word in such cases. One of them is *amuyā* whose derivation is as follows:

(1) *adas + ṬāP + Ṭā* (A. 4.1.4 *ajādyataṣ ṭāp*)
(2) *ada (s → a) + ā + ā* (A. 7.2.102 *tyadādīnām aḥ*)
(3) *ad (a + a → a) + ā + ā* (A. 6.1.97 *ato guṇe*)
(4) *ad (a + ā → ā) + ā* (A. 6.1.101 *akaḥ savarṇe dīrghaḥ*)
(5) *ad (ā → e) + ā* (A. 7.3.105 *āṅi cāpaḥ*)
(6) *ad (e → ay) + ā* (A. 6.1.78 *eco 'yavāyāvaḥ*)
(7) *a (de → mu) + yā* (A. 8.2.80 *adaso 'ser dād u do maḥ*)
amuyā

In the above example the *e*-substitute by A. 7.3.105 must be performed before the *mu*-substitute by A. 8.2.80 takes place due to the suspension of the latter. Here we do not consider the *Tripādī* rule unsuspended as there is no external *pada* that could have influence on the derivation.}

VMBh_1: III.392.21-393.6; VMBh_2: V.372.8-17

10) And [the *ī* and *ū* substitutes should not be suspended] when they are termed *pragṛhya*.

[Bhāṣya:] And [the *ī* and *ū* substitutes] should be mentioned unsuspended when they are termed *pragṛhya*. [For example:] *amī atra* ('those ones [are] here', nom. pl. m.), *amī āsate* ('those ones are sitting', nom. pl. m.), *amū atra* ('those two [are] here', nom./acc. du.), *amū āsate* ('those two are sitting', nom./acc. du.). If the *ī* and *ū* substitutes were suspended, the term *pragṛhya* by [the *sūtra*] A. 1.1.12 *adaso māt* would not apply.
[Question:] Why are these both said? Shouldn't [the expression] "with respect to the rule regarding the vowel which is a part of an external *pada*" be indicated just by [the expression] "when they are termed *pragṛhya*"?
[Answer:] Firstly, this [expression] was seen by the teacher "with respect to the rule regarding the vowel which is a part of an external *pada*" and it was recited. Then, later, this was seen "when they are termed *pragṛhya*" and was recited as well. And in such a case the teachers (i.e., Pāṇini and Katyāyana), having done the *sūtra*s, did not remove [them].

11) The prolation [of a vowel should not be suspended] with respect to an operation regarding the infix *tUK* before [the sound] *cha*.

[Bhāṣya:] The prolation of a vowel should be mentioned unsuspended with respect to an operation regarding the infix *tUK* before [the sound] *cha*. [For example:] *agnā3i cchattram* or *paṭā3u cchattram* ('an umbrella over fire' and 'an umbrella over a smart one' respectively, the meaning being ambiguous). If the prolation were suspended, the insertion of the infix *tUK* on the basis of [the *sūtra*] A. 6.1.73 would not result.

{**Explanation:**
The derivation of the the expression *agnā3i cchattram* is as follows:

(1) *agni + sU*
(2) *agn (i → e) + s* (A. 7.3.108 *hrasvasya guṇaḥ*)
(3) *agne + (s →* 0) (A. 6.1.69 *eṅhrasvāt sambuddheḥ*)
(4) *agnā3i* (A. 8.2.107 *eco 'pragṛhyasyādurād dhūte pūrvasyārdhasyād-uttarasyedutau*)
(5) *agnā3i + tUK + chattram* (A. 6.1.73 *che ca*)
agnā3i + t + chattram
(6) *agnā3i + (t → ch) chattram* (A. 8.4.40 *stoḥ ścunā ścuḥ*)
agnā3i cchattram

If the prolation prescribed by the *sūtra* A. 8.2.107 were suspended, the stem would still be seen as ending in *e* which is not a short vowel; this would, in turn, make it impossible for A. 6.1.73 prescribing the necessary insertion of *tUK* to apply. Theoretically, with the suspension of A. 8.2.107 the infix *tUK* could still apply but it would be only optional by A. 6.1.76 *padāntād vā*[237] as the preceding *e* is long.}

VMBh_1: III.393.6-7; VMBh_2: V.372.17-18

[Question:] Why is [the expression] "before [the sound] *cha*" said?
[Answer:] Because another one and only that one is suspended. [For example:] *agnicī3t* and *somasū3t* ('oh, the one who arranges the sacrificial fire!!' and 'oh, the one who presses Soma!!' respectively').

{**Explanation:**
The derivation of the form *somasū3t* is as follows:

(1) *soma-su* + *KviP* + *sU* (A. 3.2.90 *some suñaḥ*)
(2) *soma-su* + *tUK* + *KviP* + *s* (A. 6.1.71 *hrasvasya piti kṛti tuk*)
(3) *soma-su* + *t* + 0 + *s* (A. 6.1.67 *ver apṛktasya*)
(4) *soma-su* + *t* + (*s* → 0) (A. 6.1.68 *halṅyābbhyo dīrghāt sutisy apṛktam hal*)
soma-sut
(5) *somasū3t* (A. 8.2.106 *plutāv aica idutau*)

In this case, as the infix *tUK* is inserted within a *pada*, the question regarding the prolation being suspended does not arise; prolation must be applied after the infix has been inserted. Kaiyaṭa adds that the rule A. 8.2.106 is doubly suspended: due to it being in the *Tripādī* section and due to the operation being externally conditioned.}

VMBh_1: III.393.8-10; VMBh_2: V.373.1-3

12) The *ś* and *cU* substitutes (A. 8.4.40) [should not be suspended] with respect to the insertion of [the infix] *dhuṬ* (A. 8.3.29).

[Bhāṣya:] The *ś* and *cU* substitutes (A. 8.4.40) should be mentioned unsuspended with respect to the insertion of [the infix] *dhUṬ* (A. 8.3.29). [For example:] *aṭ ścyotati* and *paṭ ścyotati* ('walking and dripping/sprinkling', the meaning being ambiguous). If the *ś* and *cU* substitution (A. 8.4.40) were suspended, [the insertion of the infix] *dhuṬ* on the basis of [the *sūtra*] A. 8.3.29 would result.

{**Explanation:**

---

[237] A. 6.1.76 *padāntād vā* || ("[The final increment *tUK*] is optionally inserted after [a long vowel occurring] at the end of a *pada* [before the sound *ch* in close proximity].")

The verbal stem *scyutIR* ('to drop, flow', DhP I:41) is specified with the sound *s* in the *Dhātupāṭha*, not *ś*. Due to the following sound *c*, the sound *s* is replaced by *ś* on the basis of A. 8.4.40 *stoḥ ścunā ścuḥ*. If this operation were suspended, the infix *dhuṬ* (to be inserted before *s* and after *ḍ*) by the rule A. 8.3.29 *ḍaḥ si dhuṭ* could apply. In the forms *aṭ* and *paṭ* we add the non-suffix *KviP* and the case ending goes through deletion. The final sound *ṭ* is then replaced by *ḍ* based on A. 8.2.39 *jhalāṃ jaśo 'nte*, which means that the conditions for the application of A. 8.3.29 could be met. However, if the *sūtra* A. 8.4.40 is made unsuspended, the sound *s* is not there any more and *dhuṬ* cannot be inserted.
Kaiyaṭa (VMBh_2: V.373.11 ff) raises the question as to why the verbal root *scyutIR* cannot be already specified with the initial *ś*. It is for the sake of the derivative *madhuk* ('dripping honey'). If the verb were specified with *ś*, we would achieve the incorrect form **madhuṭ*.

(1) *madhu + scyut + KviP + sU*
(2) *madhu + scyut + KviP +* (*s* → 0) (A. 6.1.68 *halṅyābbhyo dīrghāt sutisy apṛktam hal*)
(3) *madhu + scyut* + 0 + *ṆiC* (A. 6.1.67 *ver apṛktasya*)
(4) *madhu + scy* (*ut* → 0) + *ṆiC* (A. 6.4.155 *vt*. 1 *ṇāv iṣṭhāvat prātipadikasya*[238])
(5) *madhu + scy + ṆiC + KviP* (A. 3.2.76 *kvip ca*)
(6) *madhu + scy* + 0 + 0 (A. 6.4.51 *ṇer aniṭi*, A. 6.1.67 *ver apṛktasya*)
(7) *madhu + sc* (*y* → 0) (A. 8.2.23 *saṃyogāntasya lopaḥ*)
(8) *madhu +* (*s* → 0) *c* (A. 8.2.29 *skoḥ saṃyogādyor ante*)
(9) *madhu +* (*c* → *k*) (A. 8.2.30 *coḥ kuḥ*)
(10) *madhu +* (*k* → *g*) (A. 8.2.39 *jhalāṃ jaśo 'nte*)
(11) *madhu +* (*g* → *k*) (A. 8.4.56 *vāvasāne*)
madhuk

Were the verbal root specified with the initial *ś* instead of *s*, after the deletion of the suffixes, at the stage (7), we would obtain the deletion of both the sounds *y* and *c* by A. 8.2.23. The sound *ś* could not be deleted because the rule A. 8.2.29 specifies *s*, not *ś*. Consequently, *ś* would go through the *ṣ*-substitution by A. 8.2.36 *vraścabhraśjasṛjamṛjayajarājabhrājacchaśāṃ ṣaḥ*. Further, *ṣ* would be replaced by *ḍ* (A. 8.2.39 *jhalāṃ jaśo 'nte*) and finally it would be devoiced (A. 8.4.56 *vāvasāne*). Thus we would achieve the incorrect form **madhuṭ*. And for this reason the verbal root *scyutIR* must be mentioned with *s*.}

---

[238] A. 6.4.155 *vt*. 1 *ṇāv iṣṭhāvat prātipadikasya* || ("When a nominal stem is followed by [the suffix] *ṆiC*, it goes through similar operations as when it is followed by *iṣṭha*.") A. 6.4.155 *ṭeḥ* || ("The *Ṭi* part [of an *aṅga* stem termed *bha* is deleted when the suffixes *iṣṭhaN*, *imanIC* and *īyasUN* follow.")

VMBh_1: III.393.11-13; VMBh_2: V.373.4-6

13) The *jaŚ* and *caR* substitutes in a reduplicated form [should not be suspended] with respect to the *e*-substitute (A. 6.4.120) and the infix *tUK*.

[Bhāṣya:] The *jaŚ* and *caR* substitutes in a reduplicated form should be mentioned unsuspended with respect to the *e*-substitute (A. 6.4.120) and the infix *tUK*. [For example:] *babhaṇatuḥ* and *babhaṇuḥ* ('two of them have said' and 'they have said', 3rd du. and pl. perfect respectively). If the substitute in a reduplicated syllable were suspended, the *e*-substitute would result.

{**Explanation:**
The derivation of the form *babhaṇatus* is as follows:

(1) *bhaṇA* (DhP I:474) + *lIṬ*
(2) *bhaṇ* + *tas* (A. 3.4.78 *tiptasjhisipthasthamibvasmastātāmjhathāsāthāmdhvamiḍvahimahiṅ*)
(3) *bhaṇ* + *atus* (A. 3.4.82 *parasmaipadānāṃ ṇalatususthalatusaṇalvamāḥ*)
(4) *bhaṇ* + *bhaṇ* + *atus* (A. 6.1.8 *liṭi dhātor anabhyāsasya*)
(5) *bha* (*ṇ* → 0) + *bhaṇ* + *atus* (A. 7.4.60 *halādiḥ śeṣaḥ*)
(6) (*bh* → *b*) *a* + *bhaṇ* + *atus* (A. 8.4.54 *abhyāse car ca*)
babhaṇatus

The suspension of A. 8.4.54 would open the possibility for A. 6.4.120 *ata ekahalmadhye 'nādeśāder liṭi*[239] to apply because the reduplicated syllable would be considered as not having undergone the substitution. This would lead to an incorrect form **bheṇatus*.}

VMBh_1: III.393.13-14; VMBh_2: V.373.6-7

[Bhāṣya:] [Another example is] *ucicchiṣati* ('he wants to bind', 3rd sg. desid.). If the substitute in a reduplicated syllable were suspended, the infix *tUK* on the basis of [the *sūtra*] A. 6.1.73 would result.

{**Explanation:**
The form *ucicchiṣati* is derived in the following way:

[239] A. 6.4.120 *ata ekahalmadhye 'nādeśāder liṭi* ॥ ("The vowel *e*] comes in place of the vowel *a* between single consonants [in a verbal *aṅga* stem] where the initial was not replaced [in a reduplicated syllable] before [the *l*-substitutes of] *lIṬ* (perfect) [with marker *K* or *Ṅ* and deleted reduplicated syllable].")

(1) *uchI* (DhP I:230) + *saN* + *ŚaP* + *tiP* (A. 3.1.7 *dhātoḥ karmaṇaḥ samāna-kartṛkād icchāyāṃ vā*, A. 3.1.68 *kartari śap*)
(2) *u* + *tUK* + *ch* + *sa* + *a* + *ti* (A. 6.1.73 *che ca*)
(3) *u* + *t* + *ch* + *s* (*a* + *a* → *a*) + *ti* (A. 6.1.97 *ato guṇe*)
(4) *u* + *t* + *ch* + *iṬ* + *sa* + *ti* (A. 7.2.35 *ārdhadhātukasyeḍ valādeḥ*)
(5) *u* + *tchi* + *tchi* + *sa* + *ti* (A. 6.1.2 *ajāder dvitīyasya*)
(6) *u* + (*t* → 0) *chi* + *tchi* + *sa* + *ti* (A. 7.4.61 *vt*. 1 *kharpūrvāḥ khayaḥ*[240])
(7) *u* + *chi* + *tchi* + (*s* → *ṣ*) *a* + *ti* (A. 8.3.59 *ādeśapratyayayoḥ*)
(8) *u* + *chi* + (*t* → *c*) *chi* + *ṣa* + *ti* (A. 8.4.40 *stoḥ ścunā ścuḥ*)
(9) *u* + (*ch* → *c*) *i* + *cchi* + *ṣa* + *ti* (A. 8.4.54 *abhyāse car ca*)
ucicchiṣati

The final stage of the derivation must be considered unsuspended with respect to the insertion of the infix *tUK*. Otherwise, we would still have the stem with the sound *ch* in the reduplicated syllable, which would make it possible to apply the *sūtra* A. 6.1.73 *che ca* and to insert *tUK* after the initial vowel *u*.}

VMBh_1: III.393.15-17; VMBh_2: V.373.8-10

14) [A single substitute] homogenous with what follows [should not be suspended] with respect to reduplication.

[Bhāṣya:] [A single substitute] homogenous with what follows should be mentioned unsuspended with respect to reduplication. [Form example:] *sam̐yyantā* ('the one that holds together'), *sam̐vvatsaraḥ* ('a full year'), *tam̐llokam* ('this world'), *yam̐llokam* ('which world'). If [a single substitute] homogenous with what follows were suspended, the reduplication (A. 8.4.47) would not result.

{**Explanation:**
The derivation of *sam̐yyantā* is as follows:

(1) *sam* + *yantā*
(2) *sa* (*m* → *ṃ*) + *yantā* (A. 8.3.23 *mo 'nusvāraḥ*)
(3) *sa* (*ṃ* → *m̐y*) + *yantā* (A. 8.4.58 *anusvārasya yayi parasavarṇaḥ*)
(4) *sam̐ym̐y* + *yantā* (A. 8.4.47 *anaci ca* with A. 8.4.45 *yaro 'nunāsike 'nunāsiko vā*)
sam̐ym̐yyantā

[240] A. 7.4.61 *vt*. 1 *kharpūrvāḥ khayaḥ* || ("Unvoiced stops preceded by unvoiced consonants [of the reduplicated syllable remain and the preceded consonant is deleted]."); it is the *vārttika* 1 on the rule A. 7.4.61 *śarpūrvāḥ khayaḥ* || ("Unvoiced stops (*khaY*) preceded by sibilants [of the reduplicated syllable remain and the sibilants are deleted].")

As can be seen from the derivation, the correct form would not result if A. 8.4.58 were suspended; we would obtain the reduplication of the *anusvāra* instead which would yield the incorrect stem **saṃṃyantā*.}

VMBh_1: III.393.18-19; VMBh_2: V.374.1-3

15) The *l* (A. 8.2.21), *gh* (A. 8.2.33), *n* (A. 8.2.56), *rU* (A. 8.2.74, A. 8.2.75), *ṣ* (A. 8.3.85), *ṇ* (A. 8.4.11), nasal (A. 8.4.45) and *ch* (A. 8.4.63) substitutes [should not be suspended with respect to reduplication] if the governing term is *pada* (A. 8.1.16).

[Bhāṣya:] The *l* (A. 8.2.21 *aci vibhāṣā*), *gh* (A. 8.2.33 *vā druhamuhaṣṇuhaṣṇihām*), *n* (A. 8.2.56 *nudavidondatrāghrāhrībhyo 'nyatarasyām*), *rU* (A. 8.2.74 *sipi dhāto rur vā*, A. 8.2.75 *daś ca*), *ṣ* (A. 8.3.85 *mātuḥpiturbhyām anyatarasyām*), *ṇ* (A. 8.4.11 *prātipadikāntanumvibhaktiṣu ca*), nasal (A. 8.4.45 *yaro 'nunāsike 'nunāsiko vā*) and *ch* (A. 8.4.63 *śaś cho 'ṭi*) substitutes should be mentioned as unsuspended [with respect to reduplication] if the governing term is *pada* (A. 8.1.16 *padasya*[241]).

{**Explanation:**
The non-suspension of abovementioned operations relies on the governing term *pada*. If the term *pada* governs the *sūtra*s above, reduplication (by the rule A. 8.1.1 *sarvasya dve*[242] applies first, as the *l*-substitution etc. are suspended, leading to incorrect forms. If, on the other hand, the *adhikāra pada* is not read in the rules prescribing these substitutions, reduplication will apply at a later stage, after the substitutions have taken place, due to it being externally conditioned. In such a case, the *vārttika* would be unnecessary.
All the substitutions are optional. If they were suspended with respect to reduplication, they would take place only in the second part of the expression and not in both as desired. I explain some of the examples here, others are analysed under relevant *sūtra*s.}

VMBh_1: III.393.20-22; VMBh_2: V.374.3-5

[Bhāṣya:] The *l*-substitute: *garo garaḥ* or *galo galaḥ* ('every swallowing'). The *l*-substitute [has been considered]. The *gh*-substitute: *drogdhā drogdhā* or *droḍhā droḍhā* ('every ill-wisher'). The *gh*-substitute [has been considered]. The *n*-

---

[241] A. 8.1.16 *padasya* || ("[In the section beginning here and extending up to and inclusive of A. 8.3.54 all operations are introduced] to a *pada*.")

[242] A. 8.1.1 *sarvasya dve* || ("Two [expressions] come in place of the whole [sequence].")

substitute: *nunno nunnaḥ* or *nutto nuttaḥ* ('pushed away, dispatched repeatedly'). The *n*-substitute [has been considered]. The *rU*-substitute: *abhino 'bhinaḥ* or *abhinad abhinat* ('he divided repeatedly'). The *rU*-substitute [has been considered].

{**Explanation:**
The derivation of *abhinaḥ* is as follows:

(1) *bhidIR* (DhP VII:2) + *lAṄ*
(2) *bhid* + *ŚnaM* + *siP* (A. 3.1.78 *rudhādibhyaḥ śnam*, A. 3.4.78 *tiptasjhisipthasthamibvasmastātāmjhathāsāthāmdhvamiḍvahimahiṅ*)
(3) *aṬ* + *bhid* + *ŚnaM* + *siP* (A. 6.4.71 *luṅlaṅlṛṅkṣv aḍudāttaḥ*)
(4) *a* + *bhi* + *na* + *d* + 0 (A. 6.1.68 *halṅyābbhyo dīrghāt sutisy apṛktam hal*)
(5) *a* + *bhi* + *na* + (*d* → *rU* / *d*) (A. 8.2.74 *sipi dhāto rur vā*, A. 8.2.75 *daś ca*)
(6) *abhina* (*r* → *ḥ*) (A. 8.3.15 *kharavasānayor visarjanīyaḥ*) / *abhina* (*d* → *t*) (A. 8.4.56 *vāvasāne*)
abhinaḥ / *abhinat*}

VMBh_1: III.393.22-24; VMBh_2: V.374.5-7

[Bhāṣya:] The *ṣ*-substitute: *mātuḥṣvasā mātuḥṣvasā* or *mātuḥsvasā mātuḥsvasā* ('every aunt'); *pituḥṣvasā pituḥṣvasā* or *pituḥsvasā pituḥsvasā* ('every aunt'). The *ṣ*-substitute [has been considered]. The *ṇ*-substitute: *māṣavāpāṇi māṣavāpāṇi* or *māṣavāpāni māṣavāpāni* ('sowing the beans'). The *ṇ*-substitute [has been considered].

{**Explanation:**
The derivation of this last form is as follows:

(1) *māṣa* + *ḌUvapA* (DhP I:1052) + *aṆ* + *Jas* (A. 3.2.1 *karmaṇy aṇ*, A. 4.1.2 *svaujasamauṭśasṭābhyāmbhisṅebhyāmbhyasṅasibhyāmbhyasṅasosāmṅyossup*)
(2) *māṣa* + *v* (*a* → *ā*) *pa* + *Jas* (A. 7.2.115 *aco ñṇiti*)
(3) *māṣa* + *vāpa* + (*Jas* → *Śi*) (A. 7.1.20 *jaśśasoḥ śi*)
(4) *māṣa-vāpa* + *nUM* + *i* (A. 7.1.58 *idito num dhātoḥ*)
(5) *māṣa-vāp* (*a* → *ā*) + *n* + *i* (A. 6.4.8 *sarvanāmasthāne cāsambuddhau*)
(6) *māṣavāpā* (*n* → *ṇ*) *i* / *māṣavāpāni* (A. 8.4.11 *prātipadikāntanumvibhaktiṣu ca*)
māṣavāpāṇi / *māṣavāpāni*

The rule A. 8.4.11 is optional so in the alternative form the *ṇ*-substitute does not take place.}

VMBh_1: III.393.24-394.4; VMBh_2: V.374.8-375.2

[Bhāṣya:] A nasal substitute: *vāṅnayanaṃ vāṅnayanam* or *vāgnayanaṃ vāgnayanam* ('carrying the speech repeatedly'). A nasal substitute [has been considered]. The *ch*-substitute: *vākchayanaṃ vākchayanam* or *vākśayanaṃ vākśayanam* ('resting in speech').
[Objection:] And there is a fault in both cases: if [reduplication is understood as] 'two come in place of one' as well as 'doubling the existing element'.
[Question:] How?
[Answer:] If [reduplication is understood as] 'two come in place of one', there is no *l*-substitute etc. due to the confusion between the base and the suffix.
[Bhāṣya:] Then, [reduplication is understood as] 'doubling the existing element'; due to its suspension the *l*-substitute etc. would not occur.

A. 8.2.7 *nalopaḥ prātipadikāntasya*
[There is] the deletion of [the sound] *n* [occurring] at the end of a nominal stem [being termed *pada*].

VMBh_1: III.394.5-9; VMBh_2: V.375.3-8

[Question:] What is the purpose of the word *anta*?

1) The word *anta* [is used] with respect to the *n*-deletion because the governing term *pada* is a qualifier.

[Bhāṣya:] The word *anta* is used with respect to the *n*-deletion.
[Question:] What is the reason?
[Answer:] Due to the governing term *pada* being a qualifier. The governing term *pada* is a qualifier.
[Question:] How?
[Answer:] [The genitive] *padasya* [used in the *sūtra*] A. 8.1.16 is not a *sthānaṣaṣṭhī*.
[Question:] What [kind of genitive is it] then?
[Answer:] It is a *viśeṣaṇaṣaṣṭhī* (i.e., 'differentiating one').

{**Explanation:**
Patañjali in his explanation refers to the term *pada* which should be read into this *sūtra* from A. 8.1.16 *padasya*. The meaning required in the present rule is "the deletion of the sound *n* appearing at the end of a *pada*". Had the word *anta* not been used here, the *sūtra* would read *nalopaḥ prātipadikasya* (*padasya*), which would mean that the term *pada* is qualified by *n*. The deletion would result in the case of any *n* being a part of a *pada* and not only that constituting the final sound

of it. Kaiyaṭa (VMBh_2: V.375.19) gives the example of the form *narābhyām* ('for/by/from two people', instr./dat./abl. du.) where the consonant *n* would be subject to deletion as well because it is a part of a *pada* and *prātipadika* at the same time, even though it is not its final sound.

The argument can be raised, however, that the word *anta* is compounded with the word *prātipadika*, which would lead to the deletion of such an *n* that appears at the end of a *prātipadika* being a part of a *pada*. According to the author of the *Padamañjarī* (KV VI.362.20), the relation between the terms *pada* and *prātipadika* has to be that of coreferentiality (*sāmānādhikaraṇya*); in other words, the consonant *n* has to form the final sound of a *pada* that is a *prātipadika*. As can be seen in the *sūtra*, the word *anta* is compounded with *prātipadika*, which could theoretically allow for the interpretation "the final sound *n* of a nominal stem". With the term *pada* continuing and the non-coreferential relation (*vyadhikaraṇa*) between the two, the expression *prātipadikāntasya* would be qualified by the term *padasya* yielding the meaning "the final sound *n* of a nominal stem being a part of a *pada*". With the help of A. 1.1.72 *yena vidhis tadantasya*[243] we would be able to delete the consonant *n* in the form *rājānau* (nom./acc./voc. du. from *rājan* 'a king') because in *rājan* it constitutes the final sound and this stem is a part of a *pada rājānau*. As this is not a desired outcome, we have to accept the *sāmānādhikaraṇya* view instead. In that case, *n* has to be the final of a *pada* that is also a *prātipadika*, meaning that it is neither a verbal stem (*dhātu*) nor a suffix (*pratyaya*).[244] The stem *rājan* cannot be termed *pada* before any strong suffix (*sarvanāmasthāna*) by A. 1.4.17 *svādiṣv asarvanāmasthāne*.[245] As the suffix *au* is a *sarvanāmasthāna* suffix, the preceding consonant *n* is not the final sound of a *pada* but only of a *prātipadika* and as such cannot be subject to deletion prescribed by the present rule.
Even though the word *anta* is compounded with the word *prātipadika*, it should not be read with it. The tradition solves this problem by stating that the genitive ending of *prātipadikasya* was deleted by the *sūtra* A. 7.1.39 *supāṃ sulukpūrvasavarṇātśeyāḍāḍyāyājālaḥ*,[246] similarly to Vedic.}

---

[243] A. 1.1.72 *yena vidhis tadantasya* || ("When an operation is stated by means of a unit X which is a part of a larger unit which it qualifies, that X denotes the element ending in it [as well as itself].")

[244] A. 1.2.45 *arthavad adhātur apratyayaḥ prātipadikam* || ("[The technical term] *prātipadika* denotes a meaningful unit other than a verbal stem or a suffix.")

[245] A. 1.4.17 *svādiṣv asarvanāmasthāne* ("[The technical term *pada*] denotes an item before the class of suffixes *sU* etc. excluding those termed *sarvanāmasthāna*.")

[246] A. 7.1.39 *supāṃ sulukpūrvasavarṇātśeyāḍāḍyāyājālaḥ* || ("[In Vedic literature the substitutes] *sU*, *luK*, a long vowel corresponding to the preceding one, *ā*, *āt*, *Śe*, *Ḍā*, *Ḍyā*, *yāC* and *āL* come in place of case endings [introduced after an *aṅga* stem].")

VMBh_1: III.394.10-14; VMBh_2: V.375.9-376.2

2) [There is] the prohibition of the *n*-deletion with respect to [the word] *ahan* ('a day').

[Bhāṣya:] The prohibition of the *n*-deletion should be mentioned with respect to [the word] *ahan*. [For example:] *ahobhyām*, *ahobhiḥ* (instr./dat./abl. du. and instr. pl. respectively).
[Question:] Should the prohibition be mentioned then?
[Answer:] It should not be mentioned. The *rU*-substitute (A. 8.2.68) will be a blocker here.
[Objection:] The *rU*-substitute is suspended [with respect to the *n*-deletion] and due to its suspension the *n*-deletion would result.
[Answer:] The *rU*-substitute, having no scope of application, will block the *n*-deletion.
[Objection:] The *rU*-substitute has the scope of application.
[Question:] What is its scope of application?
[Answer:] The penultimate sound *a*. The teacher's [own] use indicates that *rU* replaces not that which precedes the final; that is what the use of [the word] *ahan* does.

{**Explanation:**
The above discussion refers to the validity of the second *vārttika*. The examples given by Patañjali are *ahobhyām* and *ahobhiḥ* where the relevant substitution rules are as follows:

(1) *ahan* + *bhyām* (A. 4.1.2 *svaujasamauṭśasṭābhyāmbhisṅebhyāmbhyasṅasibhyāmbhyasṅasosāmṅyossup*)
(2) *aha* (*n* → *rU*) + *bhyām* (A. 8.2.68 *ahan*)
(3) *aha* (*r* → *u*) + *bhyām* (A. 6.1.113 *ato ror aplutād aplute*)
(4) *ah* (*a* + *u* → *o*) + *bhyām* (A. 6.1.87 *ād guṇaḥ*)
ahobhyām

The derivation of *ahobhiḥ* is the same as far as the *sūtra*s applied are concerned. The problem under discussion is connected with the *rU*-substitute prescribed by the *sūtra* A. 8.2.68 (stage (2)). This is a rule placed later in the *Tripādī* and as such it would be suspended with respect to the present *sūtra*, which would result in the deletion of the final *n* of *ahan* in the given forms. Hence this *vārttika* proposal, which is ultimately rejected by Patañjali because the rule A. 8.2.68 would not have the scope of application if it could not apply in cases such as *ahobhyām* or *ahobhiḥ*. The possibility of applying the *rU*-substitute to the penultimate *a* of *ahan* is also rejected. Rule A. 8.2.68 prescribes the *rU*-substitute of the final sound of the stem, which should be the consonant *n*. The existence of *n* as final makes the preceding vowel *a* non-final, which should not be the subject of substitution. Pāṇini gives the form *ahan* in A. 8.2.68 thus indicating that the *n*-deletion did not take place by A. 8.2.7. Kaiyaṭa (VMBh_2: V.375.21 ff) states that even if the *n*-deletion were done, we could still treat the stem as if the deletion did not take place on the basis of a maxim: "An item altered in part does not behave like something else".[247] The stem where the *rU*-substitute is to apply by A. 8.2.68 is *ahan*; if the *n*-deletion were done, the form mentioned in the *sūtra* should be **aha* instead.}

VMBh_1: III.394.15-19; VMBh_2: V.376.3-7

3) If it is due to the use of [the form] *ahan*, it is mentioned for the sake of the vocative.

[Bhāṣya:] If it is due to the use of [the form] *ahan*, it should be in order to [apply it in] the vocative (A. 8.2.8). [For example:] *he 'har* ('Oh, day!'). Therefore, when he teaches the *rU*-substitute, it should be in order to [apply it in] the vocative only then. [For example:] *he dīrghāho 'tra* ('Oh, it is a long day.'). Therefore, when [the teacher says that the words] *rūpa*, *rātri*, *rathaṃtara* are to be counted [as well],[248] that is what the teacher indicates: the *rU*-substitute does not take place of that which precedes the final.
[Question:] How was this indication made?
[Answer:] For there would be no difference between [applying] the *rU*-substitute [by the *sūtra*] A. 8.2.68 or the *r*-substitute [by the *sūtra*] A. 8.2.69 to that [sound] which precedes the final [in the stem *ahan*], when [in combination with the words] *rūpa*, *rātri* and *rathaṃtara*.

{Explanation:
The present *vārttika* states that the use of the form *ahan* in the *sūtra* A. 8.2.68 is for the sake of the vocative where the *n*-deletion is negated by A. 8.2.8. The example given by Patañjali is *dīrghāho 'tra* whose derivation is as follows:

(1) *dīrghāhan* + *sU* (A. 4.1.2 *svaujasamauṭśasṭābhyāmbhisṅebhyāmbhyasṅasibhyāmbhyasṅasosāmṅyossup*)
(2) *dīrghāhan* + 0 (A. 6.1.68 *halṅyābbhyo dīrghāt sutisy apṛktam hal*)
(3) *dīrghāha* (*n* → *rU*) (A. 8.2.68 *ahan*)

---

[247] WUJASTYK 1993: vol. I:8, vol. II:37; PŚ 37, I.33-34, II.179-184. Wujastyk notices that it was the rule commonly accepted by the commentators, even by Katyāyana and Patañjali already. Vyāḍi, however, does not comment on it independently, which is surprising.

[248] See *vt*. 1 under A. 8.2.68.

(4) *dīrghāha* (*r* → *u*) + *atra* (A. 6.1.113 *ato ror aplutād aplute*)
(5) *dīrghāh* (*a* + *u* → *o*) + *atra* (A. 6.1.87 *ād guṇaḥ*)
(6) *dīrghāho* + *'tra* (A. 6.1.109 *eṅaḥ padāntād ati*)
dīrghāho 'tra

In this example, the case ending is deleted by the *sūtra* A. 6.1.68 with the help of *lopa*, which makes the suffix still visible despite its absence as a result of A. 1.1.62 *pratyayalope pratyayalakṣaṇam*.[249] If the suffix is considered visible, we cannot apply the *r*-substitute by A. 8.2.69 because it is conditioned by the lack of the case ending (*asupi*). In the case of the stem *dīrghāhan* the suffix cannot be deleted by A. 7.1.23 *svamor napuṃsakāt*[250] because *dīrghāhan* is a *bahuvrīhi* compound and in given examples it is not neuter but masculine, which means that it does not fall within the scope of A. 7.1.23. Consequently, the *luK* deletion does not take place and A. 1.1.63 *na lumatāṅgasya*[251] does not apply. When A. 1.1.63 does not apply, the *r*-substitute by A. 8.2.69 cannot apply either.

Patañjali mentions the *vārttika* under the *sūtra* A. 8.2.68 that extends the *rU*-substitute to formations where *ahan* precedes the stems *rūpa*, *rātri* and *rathaṃtara*. Mentioning said *vārttika* under A. 8.2.68, and not the following rule, indicates that the consonant *n* in *ahan* is not deleted by the present *sūtra*. It indicates that substitution can affect only the final *n* and not the penultimate *a*. Should the *n*-deletion take place, the substitution would have to take place of the penultimate *a*, which would mean no difference between the *rU* or *r* substitution. The derivation would be: *ah* (*a* → rU/*r*). At this stage it would be impossible to apply the *u*-substitute of *rU* by A. 6.1.113 due to the lack of the preceding *a*, and there would be no way to derive the correct forms *ahorūpa*, *ahorātri* and *ahorathaṃtara*.

In the example *he 'har* the final *n* of the stem *ahan* is not deleted due to the prohibition stated in A. 8.2.8. It is further replaced by *r* on the basis of A. 8.2.69. This is so because the case ending *sU* is deleted with the help of luK prescribed by A. 7.1.23 due to *ahan* being a neuter stem, which means that after the suffix has been deleted it is not visible any more. Consequently, we can apply the rule A. 8.2.69 whose condition is the lack of the case ending following the stem. The scope of application of the *r*-substitute in the vocative indicates that *rU* was pre-

---

[249] A. 1.1.62 *pratyayalope pratyayalakṣaṇam* || ("When a suffix is deleted, operations conditioned by it still operate [as if the suffix was still present].")

[250] A. 7.1.23 *svamor napuṃsakāt* || ("[The case endings] *sU* (nom. sg.) and *am* (acc. sg.) [introduced] after the neuter [*aṅga* stem are deleted by *luK*].")

[251] A. 1.1.63 *na lumatāṅgasya* || ("[When the deletion of a suffix is conditioned] by [the use of technical terms] containing *lu* (i.e., *luK*, *Ślu* or *luP*, [operations conditioned by this suffix] on the *aṅga* stem do not take place.")

scribed for cases other than the vocative and it indicates the lack of the *n*-deletion. The *rU*-substitute prescribed by A. 8.2.68 would have no other scope of application if it did not block the *n*-deletion; all the above makes the *vārttika* unnecessary.}

A. 8.2.8 *na ṅisaṃbuddhyoḥ*
[There is] no [deletion of the sound *n* occurring at the end of a nominal stem being a *pada*] before the locative singular and vocative endings.

VMBh_1: III.394.20-23; VMBh_2: V.377.1-4

1) The prohibition [of the deletion of the sound *n*] before the locative singular and vocative endings does not take place when another *pada* follows.

[Bhāṣya:] The prohibition [of the *n*-deletion] before the locative singular and vocative endings does not take place when another *pada* follows. Here it must not be: *carmaṇi tilā asya – carmatilaḥ* ('he on whose skin there are moles'), *rājan vṛdāraka – rājavṛdāraka* ('oh, the best of kings!').

{Explanation:
The present rule would block the *n*-deletion in the cases of *carmatilaḥ* and *raja-vṛndāraka*; which is why the *vārttika* is proposed. The commentators analyse both examples. The argument is raised that the stem *carman* before the singular locative suffix *Ṅi* can be termed *bha* on the basis of the *sūtra* A. 1.4.18 *yaci bham,*[252] which makes this rule inapplicable due to the *adhikāra pada*. The suffix *Ṅi* is deleted after the stem *carman* when the compound is formed, based on the *sūtra* A. 2.4.71 *supo dhātuprātipadikayoḥ.*[253] Due to the fact that the deletion is caused by *luK*, A. 1.1.62 *pratyayalope pratyayalakṣaṇam* does not apply, and the locative ending cannot be seen. Consequently, the stem cannot be termed *bha* and the deletion could take place if it was not for the present rule. On the other hand, the stem can be termed *pada* even after the deletion of the suffix has taken place because the suffix is still visible; the *sūtra* A. 1.1.62 applies in this case. The negation in the rule A. 1.1.63 *na lumatāṅgasya* refers to an *aṅga* stem, that is a presuffixal stem. Therefore it cannot refer to a *pada*. Thus the desired *n*-deletion could be blocked by the present *sūtra*. Hence the *vārttika*.}

VMBh_1: III.395.1-18; VMBh_2: V.377.5-378.8

---

[252] A. 1.4.18 *yaci bham* || ("[The technical term] *bha* denotes [an element] before [the suffix beginning with] a semivowel *y* or a vowel.")
[253] A. 2.4.71 *supo dhātuprātipadikayoḥ* || ("The case ending of [a *pada* consisting of] a verbal or a nominal root [is deleted by *luK*].")

2) [The prohibiton of the *n*-deletion is] optional in the case of neuter stems.

[Bhāṣya:] It should be mentioned that [the prohibition of the *n*-deletion is] optional in the case of neuter stems. [For example:] *he carma* or *he carman* ('oh skin!'); *he varma* or *he varman* ('oh shelter!').
[Question:] Should it be mentioned that [it refers to the situation] when there is no *pada* following?
[Answer:] It should not be mentioned. It is said: "no [deletion] before the locative singular and vocative endings" and we see neither locative nor vocative here.
[Objection:] [We do see it] by [the rule] A. 1.1.62.
[Answer:] [There is] the prohibition of [the *sūtra*] A. 1.1.62 by the *vt*. 13 under [the *sūtra*] A. 1.1.63. The locative suffix is nowhere deleted by *lopa*; it is always deleted by [one of the suffixes] with *lu* (i.e., A. 7.1.39[254] and A. 2.4.71[255]). Just as it is here: *ārdre carman* ('skin soaked with water') and *lohite carman* ('skin soaked with blood'), in the same way it should be here as well: *carmaṇi tilā asya – carmatilaḥ*. Therefore, it should be counted [as well].
[Objection:] Thus there is no reason in using 'locative'.

3) But the prohibition [of the prohibition of the *n*-deletion] before the locative singular is superflous due to [the application of the term] *bha*.

[Bhāṣya:] The prohibition [of the prohibition of the *n*-deletion] before the locative singular is superfluous.
[Question:] What is the reason?
[Answer:] Due to [the application of the term] *bha*. The term *bha* will apply here (by the *sūtra* A. 1.4.20[256]).
[Objection:] Therefore, if the term *bha* applies here [in the expression] *rathaṃtare sāman* ('hymn to Agni'), the deletion of [the penultimate vowel] *a* would result by [the *sūtra*] A. 6.4.134.[257]
[Answer:] That is not a fault. It has been said that "[words referring to] Vedic metre are perceived as having both designations". As [here]: *sa suṣṭubhā sa ṛkvatā gaṇena* ("He with his well-singing group which has the knowledge of

---

[254] A. 7.1.39 *supāṃ sulukpūrvasavarṇātcheyāḍāḍyāyājālaḥ* || ("[In Vedic literature the substitutes] *sU*, *luK*, a long vowel corresponding to the preceding one, *ā*, *āt*, *Śe*, *Ḍā*, *Ḍyā*, *yāC* and *āL* come in place of case endings [introduced after an *aṅga* stem].")

[255] A. 2.4.71 *supo dhātuprātipadikayoḥ* || ("The case ending of [a *pada* consisting of] a verbal or a nominal root [is deleted by *luK*].")

[256] A. 1.4.20 *ayasmayādīni chandasi* || ("In Vedic literature [the technical term *bha* denotes the class of expressions] *ayasmaya* ('made of metal') etc. [before the suffix].")

[257] A. 6.4.134 *allopo 'naḥ* || ("[The vowel *a* [of the final syllable] *an* [of the presuffixal stem termed *bha*] is deleted.")

verses").[258] The *kU*-substitute [by the *sūtra* A. 8.2.30] applies due to [the stem being] termed *pada* and the *jaŚ*-substitute [by the *sūtra* A. 8.2.39] does not apply due to [the stem being] termed *bha*. In the same way here, the deletion of [the penultimate vowel] *a* will not take place due to [the stem being] termed *pada* and the *n*-deletion will not take place due to [the stem being] termed *bha* as well. Therefore, there is no point in using 'locative'.
[Bhāṣya:] And there is no point in using 'vocative'.
[Question:] How?
[Answer:] It is not the compound of [elements] ending in the vocative – *rājavṛdāraka* ("oh, the best of kings!").
[Question:] Should it be mentioned?
[Answer:] No.
[Question:] How will that which has not been mentioned be achieved?
[Answer:] Here, the same meaning should be [expressed] by the phrase and by the compound; here however the meaning understood by the phrase is by no means the one understood by the compound. The vocative [meaning] is understood in a phrase in parts, and in a compound as a whole.
Therefore only this should be mentioned: "[the prohibition of the *n*-deletion is] optional in case of neuter [stems]".

{**Explanation:**
In Vedic, stems can be assigned two technical terms at the same time, which is exemplified by a stanza from the *Ṛgveda*: *sa suṣṭubhā sa ṛkvatā gaṇena*. The form *ṛkvat* is formed from the stem *ṛc* ('a hymn') with the suffix *matUP* (A. 5.2.94 *tad asyāsty asminn iti matup*[259]). Further, the consonant *m* of *matUP* is replaced by *v* on the basis of A. 8.2.10 *jhayaḥ*. The sound *k* in *ṛkvat* is achieved by the application of A. 8.2.30 *coḥ kuḥ*, which can apply because the stem is termed *pada*. On the other hand, further substitution *k* → *g* prescribed by A. 8.2.39 *jhalāṃ jaśo 'nte* cannot take place due to the stem being termed *bha*. The stem can be so termed on the basis of A. 1.4.20 *ayasmayādīni chandasi*. The same situation occurs with the stem *rathaṃtara* where the deletion of *a* in the syllable *an* could take place by A. 6.4.134 *allopo 'naḥ* due to the stem being termed *bha*. It does not happen, however, because for the purpose of this rule the stem is termed *pada*. The *n*-deletion will not take place either due to the stem being termed *bha*. It is possible because the stem can be found in Vedic literature.

The conclusion is drawn that the first *vārttika* proposing an exception to the prohibition of the *n*-deletion in the case of the locative and vocative constituting the

---

[258] ṚgV 4.50.5.

[259] A. 5.2.94 *tad asyāsty asminn iti matup* ‖ ("[The *taddhita* suffix] *matUP* [comes after a nominal stem ending in] the nominative case to denote 'belongs to this' or 'exists in this'.")

first member of a compound is unnecessary. The compound *rājavṛndāraka* is considered to be ending in the vocative case as a whole. The vocative suffix is not added to the stem *rājan* and then deleted. It rarely happens that the vocative-ending stem combines into a compound; such a situation is impossible here. The *n*-deletion in the case of locative-ending stems, on the other hand, can be explained without the help of an additional *vārttika*.

The only *vārttika* that is accepted is the second one, reading *vā napuṃsakānām*. The discussion takes place regarding the prohibition of the *pratyayalakṣaṇa* in the *sūtra* A. 1.1.63 *na lumatāṅgasya* with respect to neuter stems. The deletion of the suffix *sU* after a neuter stem takes place on the basis of A. 7.1.23 *svamor napuṃsakāt*. As the deletion is performed with the help of *luK*, the prohibition of *pratyayalakṣaṇa* prescribed by A. 1.1.63 would take effect. However, the interpretation of the term *aṅga* in A. 1.1.63 is crucial. If we were to understand it technically as 'a presuffixal stem' and limit the application of this prohibition strictly to the domain of *aṅga*, then the prohibition of *pratyayalakṣaṇa* cannot apply, because the stem in question is a *pada*, not an *aṅga* (due to the governing term *padasya* from the *sūtra* A. 8.1.16). Consequently, the rule A. 1.1.63 would not apply and we could see the vocative suffix (as in the example *he carman*) even though it has been deleted. In such a case, the option in a *vārttika* would be *prāptavibhāṣā*, that is an option of that which has already been established. As the prohibition of the *n*-deletion would be valid in the case of neuter stems due to presence of the vocative suffix, which in turn is the result of the non-application of A. 1.1.63, the *vārttika* would propose an optional deletion of the sound *n*. The conclusion drawn is that the prohibition of *pratyayalakṣaṇa* stated in A. 1.1.63 does not refer to an *aṅga* understood in its technical sense. It refers to any presuffixal stem, be it an *aṅga* or a *pada*, which makes this rule applicable in our case.

It appears that the *pratyayalakṣaṇa* principle can be either applied or ignored. The result for the neuter stems would be the same, the difference being in the type of optional application of the *vārttika*. If the rule A. 1.1.63 applies, there is no *pratyayalakṣaṇa*, and the deleted suffix is not visible. Consequently, the *n*-deletion prescribed by the previous *sūtra* can apply. The *vārttika* proposing the optional *n*-deletion in the case of neuter stems should therefore be treated as the one establishing the lack of *n*-deletion. It would be the *aprāptavibhāṣā*. If, on the other hand, the prohibition A. 1.1.63 is prohibited resulting in the application of *pratyayalakṣaṇa*, the present *sūtra* applies and there is no *n*-deletion. In this case the option in the *vārttika* should be treated as the *prāptavibhāṣā* – optionally allowing for the deletion of *n*.}

A. 8.2.9 *mād upadhāyāś ca mator vo 'yavādibhyaḥ*

[The sound] *v* comes in place of [the sound] *m* of [the suffix] *matUP* [occurring] after [nominal stems ending in the sounds] *m* or *a*, or [after those whose] penultimate [sounds] are *m* or *a*; with the exception of [the words] *yava* ('barley') etc.
A. 8.2.42 *radābhyāṃ niṣṭhāto naḥ pūrvasya ca daḥ*
[The sound] *n* comes in place of [the sound] *t* of the *niṣṭhā* [suffix occurring] after [the sounds] *r* and *d* as well as of the preceding [sound] *d*.

VMBh_1: III.395.19-24; VMBh_2: V.378.9-14

1) The substitute also occurs in the [suffixes] *niṣṭhā* and *matUP* in place of [those sounds that] do not occur at the end (but that directly precede the final sounds).

[Bhāṣya:] It should be mentioned that the substitute also occurs in the [suffixes] *niṣṭhā* and *matUP* in place of [those sounds that] do not occur at the end (but that directly precede the final sounds). [For example:] *bhinnavantau* ('those two who have divided'), *bhinnavantaḥ* ('those – many – who have divided'), *vṛkṣavantau* ('two abounding in trees'), *vṛkṣavantaḥ* ('many abounding in trees').
[Answer:] It should not be mentioned. It will be [achieved] from the statement itself. The purpose is in the *sūtra*.
[Question:] What?
[Answer:] [The forms] *bhinnavān* ('that one who has divided'), *chinnavān* ('that one who has cut'), *vṛkṣavān* ('abounding in trees'), *plakṣavān* ('surrounded by fig trees').

{**Explanation:**
The following derivations could serve as examples:

(1) *bhidIR* (DhP VII:2) + Kta (A. 3.2.102 *niṣṭhā*, A. 1.1.26 *ktaktavatū niṣṭhā*)
bhid + ta
(2) *bhi (d → n) + (t → n) a* (A. 8.2.42 *radābhyāṃ niṣṭhāto naḥ pūrvasya ca daḥ*)
bhinna

(1) *vṛkṣa + matUP* (A. 5.2.94 *tad asyāsty asminn iti matup*)
vṛkṣa + mat
(2) *vṛkṣa + (m → v) at* (A. 8.2.9 *mād upadhāyāś ca mator vo 'yavādibhyaḥ*)
vṛkṣavat

There are two possible interpretations of the terms *niṣṭhā* and *matUP*; they can be treated as qualifiers to the term *pada* from the *sūtra* A. 8.1.16 *padasya*, in which case the rule A. 1.1.72 *yena vidhis tadantasya* would apply. It would mean that the proposed substitutions can take place only in such *pada*s that end in the suffixes *niṣṭhā* and *matUP*. This is why the first *vārttika* is proposed, which allows for the inclusion of other examples where one of the suffixes is not the final. On the other hand, the commentators agree that the genitive *padasya* from the *sūtra* A. 8.1.16 cannot be understood as *sthānaṣaṣṭhī*, that is in its technical meaning. It should be understood as *viśeṣaṇaṣaṣṭhī* – 'a qualifying genitive' – with the meaning of 'of a *pada*'. In this case it would be the term *pada* that is the qualifier to *niṣṭhā* and *matUP*. The substitutions would take place when these suffixes constitute a part of a *pada*. We would not need to apply *tadantavidhi*; all of the above makes the *vārttika* unnecessary.}

VMBh_1: III.396.1-2; VMBh_2: V.378.15-16

2) [There is] prohibition in the case of [the word] *nārmata* ('belonging to one who abounds in men').

[Bhāṣya:] Prohibition should be mentioned in the case of [the word] *nārmata*. [The word] *nārmata* [means 'belonging to one] who abounds in men'.

{**Explanation:**
The derivation of *nārmata* is as follows:

(1) *nṛ* + *matUP* + *aṆ* (A. 5.2.94 *tad asyāsty asminn iti matup*, A. 4.3.120 *tasyedam*)
nṛmat + *a*
(2) *n* (*ṛ* → *ār*) *mata* (A. 7.2.117 *taddhiteṣv acām ādeḥ*, A. 1.1.51 *ur aṇ raparaḥ*)
nārmata

The substitution could take place because the vowel *ā* is the penultimate sound of the stem before the suffix *matUP*. However, this is not desired and hence the *vārttika* is proposed. The *vārttika* is ultimately rejected because both situations can be resolved using Pāṇini's own devices.}

VMBh_1: III.396.3-5; VMBh_2: V.378.17-379.2

3) Or it has been explained.

[Question:] What has been explained?
[Answer:] This has been said with respect to [the suffixes] *niṣṭhā* and *matUP*: "It is not so because the governing term *pada* is a qualifier [here]."[260] In the case of

---

[260] Compare A. 8.1.16-17 *vt*. 5.

[the word] *nārmata* it has also been explained: "Due to the rule being externally conditioned."[261]

{**Explanation:**
The first two *vārttikas* do not need to be formulated. The former can be omitted if proper interpretation of the genitive *padasya* is accepted as was shown above. As for *nārmata* case, the problem with substitution is solved with the help of *antaraṅga* and *bahiraṅga* rules. As can be seen from the derivation above, the substitution prescribed by the rule A. 8.2.9, namely *m* → *v*, is internally conditioned because it depends on the vowel *ā* preceding the suffix *matUP*. This *ā*, however, results from the application of the *taddhita* suffix *aṆ*, which causes *vṛddhi* of the first vowel of the stem, in this case the vowel *ṛ*. This makes the operation externally conditioned due to its dependence on the external suffix *aṆ*. According to the *paribhāṣā*: *asiddhaṃ bahiraṅgam antaraṅge*,[262] the *ār* substitute of *ṛ* is not visible for the *v*-substitute. The conditions for the *v*-substitution are not met and therefore it cannot take place.}

{**A. 8.2.10** ***jhayaḥ***
[The sound *v* comes in place of the sound *m* in the suffix *matUP* occurring] after [nominal stems ending in the sounds denoted by] *jhaY* (i.e., consonants with the exception of nasals, sibilants and semivowels).} *This *sūtra* was not commented upon by Patañjali.

A. 8.2.11 ***saṃjñāyām***
[The sound *v* comes in place of the sound *m* of the suffix *matUP*] when the derivative denotes a name.
A. 8.2.12 ***āsandīvadaṣṭhīvaccakrīvatkakṣīvadrumaṇvaccarmaṇvatī***
[The forms] *āsandīvat* (name of a king), *aṣṭhīvat* ('knee-joints'), *cakrīvat* (name of a king), *kakṣīvat* (name of a sage), *rumaṇvat* (name of a mountain), *carmaṇvatī* (name of a river) [are derived in an irregular way when they denote names].

VMBh_1: III.396.6-12; VMBh_2: V.379.3-9

[Question:] Is this one *sūtra* or two different *sūtras*?
[Question:] What of it?

---

[261] Compare A. 8.3.15 *vt*. 3.
[262] PŚ 50, I.41-51, II.221-266. See also WUJASTYK 1993: vol I:40 & 73-74, vol. II:144-148 & 240-242.

[Answer:] If this is one *sūtra*, [substitution] would not result here – *ahīvatī* and *kapīvatī* would not result. However, if they are two different *sūtra*s, [substitution] would also result here – *ikṣumatī* and *drumatī*.
[Answer:] Let it be as you want. Let it be therefore one *sūtra*.
[Question:] How [are the forms] *ahīvatī* and *kapīvatī* [derived then]?
[Answer:] The teacher's use indicates that there is the *v*-substitute in that kind of [words] as [the *sūtra*s] A. 6.1.220[263] and A. 6.1.221[264] say.

{**Explanation:**
Both of the mentioned *sūtra*s refer to accent. However, they use the form *vat* of the suffix *matUP*, which indicates that the substitution must take place.

(1) *ahi* + *matUP* (A. 4.2.85 *nadyāṃ matup*)
(2) *ah* (*i* → *ī*) + *mat* + (A. 6.3.120 *śarādīnāṃ ca*)
(3) *ahī* + (*m* → *v*) *at* (A. 8.2.11 *saṃjñāyām*)
(4) *ahī* + *vat* + *ṄīP* (A. 4.1.6 *ugitaś ca*)
ahī + *vat* + *ī*
(5) *ahīvatī́* (A. 6.1.220 *anto 'vatyāḥ* – which gives the *udātta* accent on the final syllable)}

VMBh_1: III.396.12-13; VMBh_2: V.379.9-11

[Answer:] Alternatively then, there should be two different *sūtra*s.
[Objection:] Has it not been said that [substitution] would also result here – *ikṣumatī* and *drumatī*?
[Answer:] They will be read into [the *gaṇa*] *yavādi* (A. 8.2.9).

{**Explanation:**
The *gaṇa yavādi* from the *sūtra* A. 8.2.9 is an open group (*ākṛtigaṇa*), which allows us to include the words *ikṣumatī* and *drumatī* in it. This group lists the nominal stems that are excluded from the *v*-substitution. The inclusion of these stems into *yavādi* eliminates the problem appearing when the above *sūtra*s are treated separately.

The commentators Kaiyaṭa (VMBh_2: V.379.19 ff) and Annaṃbhaṭṭa (MPV X.367) point out that if there were one *sūtra* instead of two, the use of the word *saṃjñā* would be superfluous, because it could be easily understood from the use

263 A. 6.1.220 *anto 'vatyāḥ* || ("The final [of the stem] ending in *avatī* [is marked with an *udātta* accent when it denotes a name].")
264 A. 6.1.221 *īvatyāḥ* || ("[The final of the stem] ending in *īvatī* [is marked with an *udātta* accent when it denotes a name].")

of irregular forms in A. 8.2.12. If, on the other hand, there were two *sūtra*s, A. 8.2.11 would prescribe the *v*-substitute in the words enlisted in the following rule. The rule A. 8.2.12 would prescribe irregular substitution of the stems though. Therefore two *sūtra*s are needed.
The substitutions of the stems are as follows: *āsana* → *āsandī*, *asthi* → *aṣṭhī*, *cakra* → *cakrī*, *kakṣya* → *kakṣī*, *lavaṇa* → *rumaṇ*, *carman* → *carman*. In the last case there is no deletion of the final *n*, which would regularly take place according to A. 8.2.7 *nalopaḥ prātipadikāntasya*. Then, the suffix *matUP* is added on the basis of A. 4.2.85 and the feminine suffix *ṄīP* by A. 4.1.6.
In other cases, where the denotation is not the name, the stems enlisted in A. 8.2.12 do not get replaced. Consequently, the forms would be *asthimān*, *āsanavān*, *cakravān*, *kakṣyāvān*, *lavaṇavān* and *carmavatī*.}

{A. 8.2.13 *udanvān udadhau ca*
[The form] *udanvān* [is derived in an irregular way] when it denotes 'the ocean' and a name.
A. 8.2.14 *rājanvān saurājye*
[The form] *rājanvān* [is derived in an irregular way] when it denotes 'good sovereignty'.} *These *sūtra*s were not commented upon by Patañjali.

A. 8.2.15 *chandasīraḥ*
[The sound *v* comes in place of the sound *m* of the suffix *matUP* occurring] after [a nominal stem] ending in *i* or *r* in Vedic literature.

VMBh_1: III.396.14-22; VMBh_2: V.379.12-380.3

[Objection:] It is said *chandasīraḥ,* therefore [in the forms such as] *te viśvakarmāṇaṃ te saptarṣimantam* ("[Let them praise] you Viśvakarman, you attended by seven sages")[265] [the *v*-substitute] would result as well.
[Answer:] That is not a fault. It is not understood in such a way: *chandasi i-raḥ*.
[Question:] How then?
[Answer:] [It is understood as] *chandasi ī-raḥ*.
[Objection:] In such a way, [in the forms such as] *tviṣīmān* ('vehemently excited') and *patīmān* ('accompanied by birds', the meaning is uncertain) [the *v*-substitute] would result as well.
[Answer:] That is not a fault. The use of the sound *ī* serves as an adjective to what has been prescribed [meaning] "that which is prescribed comes after [nominal stems] ending in the sound *ī*".
[Objection:] Thus, [in the forms such as] *sūryaṃ te dyāvāpṛthivīmantam* ("[Let them praise] Sūrya attended by the Dyāus and Pṛthivī")[266] [the *v*-substitute]

265 AVŚ 19.18.7a.

would result as well. And here [in the forms such as] *trivatīr yājyānuvakyā bhavanti* ("Sacrificial verses contain the word 'three'")[267] it would not result.
[Answer:] Then, they should be counted as well: *tri*, *hary*, *adhipaty*, *agni* and *re*. [For example:] *tri – trivatīr yājyānuvakyā bhavanti* ("Sacrificial verses contain the word 'three'"). [The word] *tri* [has been considered]. [The word] *hari – harivo medinaṃ tvā* ("Oh Lord of horses, [we make] you [our] ally").[268] [The word] *hari* [has been considered]. [The word] *adhipati – adhipativatīr juhoti* ("Containing the lord in herself sacrifices").[269] [The word] *adhipati* [has been considered]. [The word] *agni – carur agnivān iva* ("[It is] like an oblation being near the fire")[270]. [The word] *agni* [has been considered]. [The word] *re – ā revān etu no viśa* ("Let the rich one come and protect us").

{**Explanation:**
The examples from Vedic literature quoted in the *Mahābhāṣya* are not easily derivable on the basis of Pāṇinian rules, which is why Patañjali considers the present rule and the *v*-substitute optional; it should take place only when it is necessary. The only problematic form is *revān* thought to be formed from the stem *re*. The *sūtra* prescribes the substitution only in the case of stems ending in sounds *i* (or *ī*) and *r*; the vowel *e* is not included. This is why the commentators discuss two options for its correct derivation. The first option is to achieve the form *re* from the verbal root *ri* (Nāgeśa (VMBh_2: V.379.29 ff) and Nārāyaṇa (MPV X.368), *ri pi gatau* – DhP VI.111-112) or from *rī* (Annaṃbhaṭṭa (MPV X.368), *rī gatireṣaṇayoḥ* – DhP IX.30). Kaiyaṭa does not give the verbal root itself. Then, the primary suffix *viC* is added by A. 3.2.75 *anyebhyo 'pi dṛśyate*[271] which is ultimately dropped by A. 6.1.67 *ver apṛktasya*[272] but the root vowel is raised to *guṇa* by A. 7.3.86 *pugantalaghūpadhasya ca*.[273] We achieve the form *re* to which the suffix *matUP* is added and the *v*-substitute results by the present *sūtra*.
The other option, which conforms with the text of the present *sūtra*, is to derive it from the stem *rayi*. Its derivation is as follows:

(1) *rayi* + *matUP* (A. 5.2.94 *tad asyāsty asminn iti matup*)
(2) *rayi* + *ma* + *nUM* + *t* (A. 7.1.70 *ugidacāṃ sarvanāmasthāne 'dhātoḥ*)

---

266 AVŚ 19.18.5.
267 KS 11.1.
268 ṚgVKh 4.3.1.
269 KS 11.1.
270 ṚgV 7.104.2.
271 A. 3.2.75 *anyebhyo 'pi dṛśyate* || ("[The suffixes *maniN*, *KvaniP* and *vaniP*] are also seen after other [verbal roots (i.e., not ending in *ā*) along with the suffix *viC*].")
272 A. 6.1.67 *ver apṛktasya* || ("The single sound [suffix] *vi* [is always deleted].")
273 A. 7.3.86 *pugantalaghūpadhasya ca* || ("[A *guṇa* vowel] comes in place of the penultimate vowel [of the *aṅga* stem] ending in [the infix] *pUK* or containing a short [penultimate] vowel [denoted by *iK* (i.e., *i*, *u*, *ṛ*, *ḷ*), before *sārvadhātuka* and *ārdhadhātuka* suffixes].")

rayi + mant
(3) *ra (y→ i) + i + mant* (A. 6.1.37 vt. 6 *rayer mato bahulam*[274])
(4) *ra + (i + i → ī) + mant* (A. 6.1.101 *akaḥ savarṇe dīrghaḥ*)
(5) *r (a + ī → e) + mant* (A. 6.1.87 *ād guṇaḥ*)
(6) *re + (m → v) ant* (A.8.2.15 *chandasīraḥ*)
(7) *revan* (A. 8.2.23 *saṃyogāntasya lopaḥ*)
(8) *revan + sU* (A. 4.1.2 *svaujasamauṭśasṭābhyāmbhisṅebhyāmbhyasṅasibhyāmbhyasṅasosāmṅyossup*)
(9) *revan* + 0 (A. 6.1.68 *halṅyābbhyo dīrghāt sutisy apṛktam hal*)
(10) *rev (a → ā) n* (A. 6.4.8 *sarvanāmasthāne cāsambuddhau*)
revān}

VMBh_1: III.396.22-397.2; VMBh_2: V.380.3-5

[Objection:] If, therefore, such enumeration is done, [substitution] would not result here: *sarasvatīvān* ('accompanied by Sarasvatī'), *bhāratīvān* ('accompanied by Bhāratī'),[275] *apūpavān* ('possessing cakes')[276] and *dadhivāṃś caru* ('an oblation prepared with sour milk').
[Answer:] Thus it should be said that [the sound *v* comes in place of the sound *m* of the suffix *matUP* occurring] after [nominal stems] ending in *i* or *r* variously in Vedic literature.

A. 8.2.16 *ano nuṭ*
[The infix] *nUṬ* comes after [nominal stems ending in] *an* [before the suffix *matUP* in Vedic literature].

VMBh_1: III.397.3-7; VMBh_2: V.380.6-10

[Objection:] If it is [the infix] *nUṬ*, it should be added at the end of what precedes.

1) [There should be] prohibition of the rule [prescribing] the *rU*-substitute and [injunction of] the *ṇ*-substitute in the case of [the infix] *nUK* added after [nominal stems ending in] *an*.

---

[274] A. 6.1.37 *vt.* 6 *rayer mato bahulam* || ("[In Vedic literature vocalisation] variously takes place [of the semivowel] of [the stem] *rayi* ('property, wealth') before [the suffix] *matUP*.")
[275] ṚgVKh 1.7.4, AB 2.24.5.
[276] ṚgV 3.52.1, 8.91.2.

[Objection:] If [the infix] *nUK* [is added] after [a nominal stem ending in] *an*, the *ṇ*-substitute should be prescribed. [And in the form] *akṣaṇvṇn* ('having eyes') prohibition [of the *ṇ*-substitute] would result by [the *sūtra*] A. 8.4.37.

{**Explanation:**
The discussion concerns whether the infix prescribed by the present rule should be treated as having the marker *Ṭ* or *K*. Different markers show a different position in which said infix is placed. Were it marked with *Ṭ,* it would be added at the beginning of the following element – in this case at the beginning of the sufix *matUP*. If, on the other hand, it were marked with *K*, the infix would be added at the end of the preceding element, that is, the stem followed by the suffix *matUP*. Both interpretations cause some problems discussed by Patañjali. Let us consider the infix *nUK* first. The example given by the author of the *Mahābhāṣya* is *akṣaṇvān*, where the *ṇ*-substitute would not take place if the infix were marked with *K*. The derivation is as follows:

(1) *akṣi* + *matUP* (A. 5.2.94 *tad asyāsty asminn iti matup*)
(2) *akṣ* (*i* → *anAṄ*) + *mat* (A. 7.1.76 *chandasy api dṛśyate*)
akṣan + *mat*
(3) *akṣa* (*n* → 0) + *nUK* + *mat* (A. 8.2.7 *nalopaḥ prātipadikāntasya*, A. 8.2.16 *ano nuṭ*)
(4) *akṣa* + *n* + (*m* → *v*) *at* (A. 8.2.9 *mād upadhāyāś ca mator vo 'yavādibhyaḥ*)
(5) *akṣa* + (*n* → *ṇ*) + *vat* (A. 8.4.1 *raṣābhyāṃ no ṇaḥ samānapade*)
akṣaṇvat

The *ṇ*-substitute would be prohibited, if the infix in question were *nUK*, by A. 8.4.37 *padāntasya* because *n* would appear at the end of a *pada*. If, on the other hand, we accepted the *nUṬ* interpretation, the infix would be attached to the following suffix *matUP*, which would consequently lead to the *v*-substitute of the sound *n* rather than *m* as it is required. This problem can be easily omitted because the insertion of the infix is suspended with respect to the *v*-substitute. Thus we achieve both the *v*-substitute of *m* and the *ṇ*-substitute of *n* of *nUṬ*.}

VMBh_1: III.397.7-8; VMBh_2: V.380.10-11

[Objection:] And the *rU*-substitute should be prohibited. [For example:] *supathintaraḥ* ('a better road'). The *rU*-substitute would result by [the *sūtra*] A. 8.3.7.
[Answer:] Therefore, let [the infix] be [added] at the beginning of what follows.

{**Explanation:**

Another problematic example is *supathintara*. The infix is added on the basis of the following *sūtra*. If it were treated as marked with *K*, it would be added at the end of the stem *supathi*. This would lead to the application of A. 8.3.7 *naś chavy apraśān* prescribing the *rU*-substitute of the final *n* (resulting from the addition of *nUK*). As the *rU*-substitute is not desired, the conclusion is reached that the infix should be *nUṬ*, and should be added at the beginning of the following element.}

VMBh_1: III.397.9-12; VMBh_2: V.380.12-15

2) When [the infix is added] at the beginning of what follows, [there is] prohibition of the *v*-substitute and [there is] also the separation of a compound.

[Bhāṣya:] It should be mentioned that [there is] prohibition of the *v*-substitute if [the infix is added] at the beginning of what follows. [For example:] *akṣaṇvān* ('possessing eyes'). The *v*-substitute would result by [the *sūtra*] A. 8.2.9. And the separation would result in an undesired place – *akṣaṇvān* ('having eyes').

{**Explanation:**
If the infix *nUṬ* is added to the suffix *matUP*, then *v* will replace *n* (of *nmat*) rather than the sound *m*. Annaṃbhaṭṭa (MPV X.369) explains that if the *v*-substitute is to apply and the insertion of the infix *nUṬ* is suspended, the *v*-substitute will not take place because the stem preceding the suffix *matUP* will not end in *n*. Therefore, the suffix *matUP* should be taken as having the infix *nUṬ* included. He quotes a part of a rule of interpretation discussed by both Nāgeśa and Vyāḍi. There are, however, three options for which *paribhāṣā* it could be. The author of the *Uddyotana* says that it is the *paribhāṣā* 11 in Nāgeśa's *Paribhāṣenduśekhara*: *yadāgamās tadguṇībhūtās tadgrahaṇena gṛhyante* ("That to which an infix is added denotes (because the infix forms a part of it) whatever results from its combination with an infix"[277]) and as far as Nāgeśa is concerned, it cannot be any other rule. We find it, however, in the *Vyāḍīyaparibhāṣāvṛtti* as one of the two possible rules. It can be the rule 14: *tadbhaktas tadgrahaṇena gṛhyate* ("The mention of an item includes that what has been annexed to it") or 56: *tadekadeśabhūtas tadgrahaṇena gṛhyate* ("The mention of an item includes what is a part of that item").[278] According to these *paribhāṣās*, the infix *nUṬ* must be a part of the suffix *matUP*, which of course causes problems discussed above.}

VMBh_1: III.397.12-16; VMBh_2: V.380.15-19

[277] PŚ 11, I.9-11, II.54-65.

[278] WUJASTYK 1993: vol. I:22 & 61, vol. II:103 &203.

[Answer:] Therefore, let [the infix] be [added] at the end of what precedes.
[Objection:] But has it not been said: "[There should be] prohibition of the rule [prescribing] the *rU*-substitute and [the injunction of] the *ṇ*-substitute in the case of [the infix] *nUK* added after [the nominal stem ending in] *an*"?

3) It is achieved by [assigning the term] *bha*.

[Bhāṣya:] The term *bha* should be mentioned.
[Objection:] If, therefore, the term *bha* [applies], the deletion of the sound *a* on account of [the *sūtra*] A. 6.4.134[279] would result.

{**Explanation:**
The term *bha* is assigned in this case by 1.4.20 *ayasmayādīni chandasi*. The problem here is that if the term *bha* applies to the stem, we would be forced to delete *a* based on A. 6.4.134 *allopo 'naḥ*. As the *n*-deletion (A. 8.2.7) is suspended, the stem still finishes in *an*, which forms the condition for A. 6.4.134 to apply. Therefore Kaiyaṭa claims the non-suspension of the *n*-deletion with respect to the *a*-deletion on account of the restriction in the *sūtra* A. 8.2.2. The *n*-deletion specified therein refers only to the operations regarding case endings, accent, technical terms and the infix *tUK*. As the author of the *Nārāyaṇīya* states (MPV X.369), in other cases, this deletion is not suspended. However, it is not possible to state that the infix *nUK* is an exception to the *n*-deletion, which is why we do not get the stem ending in *an* but in *ann*. This is not the right explanation. If it were so, we would get the *ṇ*-substitution of the first *n*, it not being at the end of the *pada*, the prohibition of the *sūtra* A. 8.4.37 *padāntasya* would not apply, and then we would obtain the *ṇ*-substitution of the second *n* by A. 8.4.41 *ṣṭunā ṣṭuḥ* as the first one is obviously not suspended, which would result in the incorrect **akṣaṇṇvān*.}

VMBh_1: III.397.17-19; VMBh_2: V.381.1-3

4) But [the suffix] *matUP* in Vedic literature is used after [nominal stems ending in] *an* in their basic form.

[Bhāṣya:] It should be mentioned that [the suffix] *matUP* in Vedic literature is used after [nominal stems ending in] *an* in their basic form. Here, then, [in the form] *supathintaraḥ* ('a better road') there would be the deletion of the final *an*

---

[279] A. 6.4.134 *allopo 'naḥ* || ("The vowel *a* [of the final syllable] *an* [of the *aṅga* stem termed *bha*] is deleted.")

which, [being an element] *Ṭi*, is deleted before a *taddhita* [suffix] by A. 6.4.144.[280]

{Explanation:
The issue with the form *supathintara* regards the suffix *taraP*, which is a *taddhita* suffix. By the rule A. 6.4.144 *nas taddhite* the *Ṭi*-element, that is a syllable beginning with the last vowel of a stem, is deleted when the stem ends in *n*. The deletion of *in* in *supathin* is not desired though. The solution is proposed in the following *vārttika*, where it is stated that the infix *nUṬ* is added before the suffixes taraP and tamaP which are termed *gha*.[281]}

VMBh_1: III.397.20-398.8; VMBh_2: V.381.4-382.2

5) The term *gha* [is used] as well.

[Bhāṣya:] The term *gha* should be mentioned as well.
[Objection:] In that case, a lot should be mentioned. It should be mentioned that [the infix is] *nUK*. And it should be mentioned that the term *bha* [applies]. It should be mentioned that [the suffix] *matUP* in Vedic literature is used after [a nominal stem ending in] *an* when its form is not altered. And the term *gha* should be mentioned as well.
[Answer:] It should not be done. If it is said that [the infix] should be [accepted as] *nUK*, the difficulty connected with *nUK* is removed due to [assigning the term] *bha*. [If] it is said that the term *bha* [applies], the actual maxim is done, [namely the *sūtra*] A. 1.4.20.[282] And if it is said that [the suffix] *matUP* in Vedic literature is used after [a nominal stem ending in] *an* when its form is not altered and the term *gha* should apply as well. [But] it should not apply. [The words referring to] Vedic metre, however, are seen as being designated with both terms (i.e., *pada* and *bha* at the same time). As [here]: *sa suṣṭubhā sa ṛkvatā gaṇena* ("He with his well-singing group which has the knowledge of verses").[283] The *kU*-substitute [by the *sūtra* A. 8.2.30] takes place on account of the term *pada* and the *jaŚ*-substitute [by the *sūtra* A. 8.2.39] does not take place on account of the term *bha*. In the same way here as well the deletion of [the vowel] *a* and [the element] *Ṭi* will not take place on account of the term *pada* and the prohibition of

[280] A. 6.4.144 *nas taddhite* || ("[There is the deletion of the *Ṭi* element of the *aṅga* stem termed *bha* ending in] *n* before a *taddhita* [suffix].")

[281] A. 1.1.22 *taraptamapau ghaḥ* || ("[The technical term] *gha* denotes [the suffixes] *taraP* and *tamaP*.")

[282] A. 1.4.20 *ayasmayādīni chandasi* || ("In Vedic literature [the technical term *bha* denotes the class of expressions] *ayasmaya* ('made of metal') etc. [before the suffix].")

[283] ṚgV 4.50.5.

the *rU*-substitute and [the prescription of] the *ṇ*-substitute will take place on the account of the term *bha*. [This is what] is achieved; the *sūtra,* therefore, splits.
[Answer:] Let it be as in the *sūtra*.
[Objection:] But has it not been said that "when [the infix is added] at the beginning of what follows, [there is] prohibition of the *v*-substitute and [there is] also the separation of a compound"?
[Answer:] If it is said that [there is] prohibition of the *v*-substitute, the substitutes will take place of that which has [actually] been prescribed, [but] it will not be in such a way. [The substitute] of that which is prescribed would not result then.
[Question:] What is the reason?
[Answer:] Because [the infix] *nUṬ* intervenes. [The infix] *nUṬ* is suspended and due to its suspension [the *v*-substitute of the sound *m*] will result.

{**Explanation:**
The above discussion focuses on the necessity of the proposed *vārttika*s. If we specify the infix as *nUK*, the assignment of the term *bha* to the stem solves the problems regarding the application of the *ṇ* and *rU* substitutions. If the stem is termed *bha*, the prohibition of the *ṇ*-substitution will not take place on account of A. 8.4.37 *padāntasya* because the stem would not be termed *pada*. At the same time the *rU*-substitution will be prohibited for the same reason; the *sūtra* A. 8.3.7 *naś chavy apraśān* will not apply because the stem is not termed *pada*. The *vārttika*s regarding Vedic stems and the term *gha* are also unnecessary. As the stems in Vedic can get both designations at the same time, that is *pada* and *bha*, the problem with the application of *sūtra*s is solved. The designation of a *pada* to the stem blocks the deletion of the vowel *a* prescribed by A. 6.4.134 *allopo 'naḥ* and the deletion of the element *Ṭi* prescribed by A. 6.4.144 *nas taddhite*. The conclusion might be drawn then that the only acceptable and necessary *vārttika* is the one introducing the reference to the term *bha*.

The last argument *nirdiśyamānasyādeśā bhavanti* is a rule of interpretation (PŚ 12[284]); only such an element that was explicitly specified in a rule can be subject to the substitution. In this case, what has been prescribed for the substitution is not the consonant *n* of the infix *nUṬ* but it is the consonant *m* of the suffix *matUP*. Therefore, the substitution may take place only of *m* and not of *n*. The conclusion is that the infix *nUṬ* is added at the beginning of *matUP* and as it is suspended with respect to the *v*-substitute, the sound *v* will replace *m*, not *n*.}

VMBh_1: III.398.8-10; VMBh_2: V.382.3-4

---

[284] PŚ 12, I.11-13, II.67-76.

[Bhāṣya:] In the case of separation, the rule should not follow the creators of *padapāṭha*, it is the rule that should be followed by the creators of *padapāṭha*. The *padapāṭha* should be formed according to the rules.[285]

A. 8.2.17 *nād ghasya*
[The infix *nUṬ* is added] to the element termed *gha* (the suffixes *taraP* and *tamaP*) after [nominal stems ending in the sound] *n* [in Vedic literature].

VMBh_1: III.398.11-13; VMBh_2: V.382.5-7

1) [It should be mentioned that] the vowel *ī* comes in place of [the final sound of the nominal stem] *rathin* ('a charioteer').

[Bhāṣya:] It should be mentioned that the vowel *ī* comes in place of [the final sound of the nominal stem] *rathin* ('charioteer'). [Thus we get the form] *rathītara* ('a superior charioteer').

{**Explanation:**
The derivation of *rathītara* is as follows:

(1) *rathin* + *taraP* (A. 5.3.57 *dvivacanavibhajyopapade tarabīyasunau*)
(2) *rathi* (*n* → 0) + *tara* (A. 8.2.7 *nalopaḥ prātipadikāntasya*)
(3) *rath* (*i* → *ī*) + *tara* (present *vārttika*)
rathītara

In this case the vowel *ī* is an exception to the infix *nUṬ*, which means that the infix is not inserted at all. Otherwise, if it were an exception to the *n*-deletion and were supposed to come in place of the final *n*, we would not be able to derive the correct form, because the *ī*-substitute would be suspended and *ekādeśa* (of the vowels *i* and *ī*) could not take place. The form would stay **rathi ītara*.}

VMBh_1: III.398.14-15; VMBh_2: V.382.8-9

2) [It should be mentioned that] after [the nominal stem] *bhūridāvan* [the infix] *tUṬ* [should be added].

[Bhāṣya:] It should be mentioned that after [the nominal stem] *bhūridāvan* [the infix] *tUṬ* [should be added]. [Thus we get the form] *bhūridāvattaro janaḥ* ('an extremely generous person').

---

[285] By saying that the *padapāṭha* should follow the rules of grammar Patañjali also says that it is man-made, which, in turn, might imply that the *saṃhitāpāṭha* is not the creation of a man.

{**Explanation:**
The derivation of *bhūridāvattara* is as follows:

(1) *bhūri + dā + vaniP + taraP* (A. 3.2.74 *āto maninkvanibvanipaś ca*, A. 5.3.57 *dvivacanavibhajyopapade tarabīyasunau*)
bhūri + dā + van + tara
(2) *bhūri+ dā + va (n* → 0) + *tara* (A. 8.2.7 *nalopaḥ prātipadikāntasya*)
(3) *bhūri+ dā + va + tuṬ + tara* (present *vārttika*)
bhūri + dā + va + t + tara
bhūridāvattara.}

A. 8.2.18 *kṛpo ro laḥ*
[The sound] *l* comes in place of [the sound] *r* of [the verbal root] *kṛpŪ* ('to be able to', DhP I:799).

VMBh_1: III.398.16-17; VMBh_2: V.382.10-12

[Bhāṣya:] Prohibition should be mentioned in the case of [the words] *kṛpaṇa* ('miserable, pitiable') etc. [Thus we get the forms] *kṛpaṇa, kṛpāṇa* ('a sword'), *kṛpīṭa* ('wood, fuel').[286]

{**Explanation:**
All these forms are the *Uṇādi* formations. The word *kṛpaṇa* is formed with the suffix *KyuN* (=*ana*) that is added to the stem *rañj* (US 239, 2.79 *rañjeḥ kyun*[287]). The note under this *Uṇādisūtra* states that the suffix may be also added to form *kṛpaṇa*. The word *kṛpāṇa* on account of the US 250, 2.90 *yudhibudhidṛśibhyaḥ kic ca*[288] is formed with the suffix *ānaC*. As those suffixes are applied variously, according to the *sūtra* A. 3.3.1 *uṇādayo bahulam*,[289] some forms can be created, others cannot. Similarly with the form *kṛpīṭa*, which is formed with the suffix *KīṭaN* (US 627, 4.184 *kṝtṝkṛpibhyaḥ kīṭan*).[290]

---

286 VMBh_2 quotes it as a *vārttika* and adds yet another example: *kṛpā* ('pity, compassion'). Kielhorn does not mark any *vārttika*s for this *sūtra*. *Kāśikā* marks two later ones.

287 US 239, 2.79 *rañjeḥ kyun* || ("[The verbal root] *rañjA* ('to colour, DhP I:1048) takes [the suffix] *KyuN*.")

288 US 250, 2.90 *yudhibudhidṛśibhyaḥ kic ca* || ("[The suffix *ānaC*] is added to [the verbal roots] *yudhA* ('to fight', DhP IV:64), *budhIR* ('to know', DhP I:924) and *dṛśIR* ('to see', DhP I:1037) and is treated as marked with *K*.")

289 A. 3.3.1 *uṇādayo bahulam* || ("[The suffixes] *uṆ* etc. [are introduced] variously [after verbal stems when the action refers to the present time to form the names].")

290 US 627, 4.184 *kṝtṝkṛpibhyaḥ kīṭan* || ("[The suffix] *KīṭaN* comes after [the verbal roots] *kṝ* ('to scatter', DhP VI:116), *tṝ* ('to cross', DhP I:1018) and *kṛpŪ* ('to be able to', DhP I:799).")

The VMBh_2 edition of the *Mahābhāṣya* includes the stem *kṛpā* ('compassion') as one where the *l*-substitute should be prohibited. Kielhorn does not do this. This stem, however, is not derived from the verbal root *kṛpŪ* but from *krapA* (DhP I:808 *krapa kṛpāyāṃ gatau* "[The verbal root] *krap* [is used] to denote 'compassion' and 'movement'"). Vocalisation takes place on account of the *vārttika* (*krapeḥ saṃprasāraṇam* "There is vocalisation in [the verbal stem] *krapA*") being quoted in the *gaṇa bhidādi* (A. 3.3.104[291]). The sound *ṛ* is the result of a grammatical operation, therefore the substitution will not take place. As Annaṃbhaṭṭa points out: "According to this viewpoint, the forms *kṛpaṇa* etc. are uderived nominal stems."[292]
The sound *r* in the *sūtra* is to be understood as a single consonant *r* or a consonantal part in the vowel *ṛ*. Thus, we will achieve the *l*-substitute of the consonant *r* and *ḷ*-substitute of the vowel *ṛ* where necessary.}

VMBh_1: III.398.18-20; VMBh_2: V.383.1-5

[Bhāṣya:] It should be mentioned that [the sound] *l* optionally becomes *r* in the case of [the words] *bāla* ('a boy' or *vāla* 'a tail'), *mūla* ('a root'), *laghu* ('light, short'), *alam* ('enough, sufficient'), *aṅguli* ('a finger').[293] [Thus we get the forms] *aśvavālaḥ* or *aśvavāraḥ* ('a young horse' or 'a tail of a horse'), *mūladevaḥ* or *mūradevaḥ* (a name), *varuṇasya laghusyadaḥ* or *varuṇasya raghusyadaḥ* ('a quick movement of Varuna'), *alaṃ bhaktāya* or *araṃ bhaktāya* ('enough of worship'), *subāhuḥ svaṅguliḥ* or *subāhuḥ svaṅguriḥ* ('[someone] with very strong arms and beautiful fingers').

{Explanation:
Most of the words above can be explained with the help of the *Uṇādi* suffixes. The word *vāla* is understood as something that encloses or covers according to the DhP I:520 (*vala saṃvaraṇe* "The verbal root *val* is used in the sense of covering"). The form *vāla* is constructed with the help of the primary suffix *GHaÑ*.[294] The word *mūla* is formed from the verbal root *mūlA* used in the meaning 'fixing, resting' (DhP I:562 *mūla pratiṣṭhāyām*) with the suffix *Ka*.[295]

---

[291] A. 3.3.104 *ṣidbhidādibhyo 'ṅ* || ("[The *kṛt* suffix] *aṄ* comes after [a verbal stem] marked with *Ṣ* and [the class of stems] *bhidIR* ('to break', DhP VII:2) etc. [to form feminine action nouns].")

[292] MPV X.370.

[293] VMBh_2 considers this a *vārttika*.

[294] A. 3.3.19 *akartari ca kārake saṃjñāyām* || ("[The *kṛt* suffix *GHaÑ* comes after a verbal root] to derive forms denoting *kāraka*s other than the agent when the derivative as a proper name.")

[295] A. 3.1.135 *igupadhajñāprīkiraḥ kaḥ* || ("[The *kṛt* suffix] *Ka* comes after [the verbal roots containing the sound denoted by] *iK* (i.e., *i*, *u*, *ṛ*, *ḷ*) as penultimate or [the roots] *jñā* ('to know', DhP IX:36), *prīÑ* ('to please', DhP IX:2) and *kṝ* ('to scatter', DhP VI:116) [to denote the agent].")

The word *aṅguli* is formed with the *Uṇādi* suffix *uli* (US 445, 4.2[296]) and due to it being mentioned in the *gaṇa kapilakādi*, the consonant *r* is usually replaced by *l*. The stem *laghu* is formed with the help of the *Uṇādi* suffix *Ku* (US 29, 1.29).[297]}

VMBh_1: III.398.21-23; VMBh_2: V.383.6-9

[Bhāṣya:] It should be mentioned that [the substitution] is optional in the case of Vedic names such as *kapilaka* ('reddish') etc.[298] [Thus we get the forms] *kapilakaḥ* or *kapirakaḥ*, *tilvirīkaḥ* or *tilvilīkaḥ* ('fertile', the meaning being uncertain), *romāṇi* or *lomāṇi* ('hair'), *pāṃsuram* or *pāṃsulam* ('dusty, sandy'), *karma* or *kalma* ('a deed'), *śukraḥ* or *śuklaḥ* ('clear, bright').

{**Explanation:**
The word *roman* is formed in an irregular way by adding the *Uṇādi* suffix *maniN*[299] to the verbal root *ru* ('to sound, cry', DhP II:24). In this *Uṇādisūtra* two words are mentioned: *roman* and *loman*. They are apparently not considered to be merely two options of one stem, but two separate stems. The word *pāṃsura* is formed by adding the suffix *ra* to the stem *pāṃsu* to denote 'belonging to this or being in this' (A. 5.2.107 vt. 2[300]). The word *karman* is formed by adding the suffix *maniN* to the verbal root *ḌUkṛÑ* ('to do', DhP VIII:10). The words *śukra* and *śukla* are again treated as two separate stems; they are derived from the verbal root *śucA* ('to shine, flame', DhP I:198) or *ĪśucIR* ('to be clean', DhP IV:56) respectively by adding the suffix *ra*.[301] Additionally, in the word *śukla* the sound *r* is

---

[296] US 445, 4.2 *ṛtanyañjavanyañjyarpimadyatyaṅgikuyukṛśibhyaḥ katnijyatujalijiṣṭujiṣṭajisansyanithinulyasāsānukaḥ* || ("[The suffixes] *KatniC*, *yatuC*, *aliC*, *iṣṭuC*, *iṣṭaJ*, *isaN*, *syaN*, *ithiN*, *uli*, *asa*, *āsa* and *ānuka* come after [the verbal roots] *ṛ* ('to go', DhP I:983), *tanU* ('to spread', DhP VIII:1), *añjŪ* ('to decorate', DhP VII:21), *vanU* ('to beg', DhP VIII:8), *añjŪ* ('to go', DhP VII:21), *arpi* (caus. from *ṛ* 'to go'), *madĪ* ('to be pleased', DhP IV:99), *atA* ('to go', DhP I:38), *aṅgI* ('to go', DhP I:155), *ku* ('to sound', DhP II:33), *yu* ('to mix', DhP II:23) and *kṛśA* ('to become thin', DhP IV:117).")

[297] US 29, 1.29 *laṅghibahyor nalopaś ca* || ("[The suffix *Ku*] comes after [the verbal roots] *laṅghI* ('to leap, dry', DhP I:108, 172, X:220, 254) and *baṁhI* ('to increase', DhP I:664), and the nasal is deleted.")

[298] VMBh_2 considers this a *vārttika*.

[299] US 593, 4.150 *nāmansīmanvyomanromanlomanpāpmandhyāman* || ("[The stems] *nāman* ('a name'), *sīman* ('a boundary'), *vyoman* ('space'), *roman*, *loman* ('hair'), *pāpman* ('sin, evil') and *dhyāman* ('measure, splendour') [are irregularly formed with the help of the suffix *maniN*].")

[300] A. 5.2.107 *vt.* 2 *nagapāṃsupāṇḍubhyaś ca* || ("[The suffix *ra* should be added] also after [the nominal stems] *naga* ('a mountain, snake'), *pāṃsu* ('dust, sand') and *pāṇḍu* ('white').")

[301] US 188, 2.28 *ṛjrendrāgravajraviprakubracubrakṣurakhurabhadrograbherabhelaśukraśuklagauravanrerāmālā* || ("[The nominal stems] *ṛjra* ('a leader'), *indra* (name), *agra* ('first'), *vajra* ('thunder'), *vipra* ('wise'), *kubra* ('a forest'), *cubra* ('a face'), *kṣura* ('a razor'), *khura* ('a hoof'), *bhadra* ('auspicious'), *ugra* ('mighty'), *bhera* ('a drum'), *bhela* ('foolish, timid'), *śukra*

changed into *l*. Kaiyaṭa (VMBh_2: V.383.22 ff) says that it is not correct and Nāgeśa adds that there is a mistake in the *Uṇādisūtras* and treating the words *śukra* and *śukla* as two different words is not a Pāṇinian view.}

A. 8.2.19 *upasargasyāyatau*
[The sound *l*] of an *upasarga* [comes in place of the sound *r*] when [a verb] *ayA* ('to go', DhP I:503) follows.

VMBh_1: III.399.1-6; VMBh_2: V.383.10-384.2

[Question:] Is the word *ayati* a qualifier to the sound *r*? [If so,] the sound *l* comes in place of *r* followed by [the verb] *ayA* if that [*r*] is [a part of] an *upasarga*. Or, is [the word *ayati*] a qualifier to the [word] *upasarga*? [If so,] the sound *l* comes in place of *r* of an *upasarga* followed by [the verb] *ayA*. What is the difference then?

1) If [the word] *ayati* [is a qualifier to] the sound *r*, then [the *upasarga*] *pari* is to be added [as well].

[Answer:] If [the word] *ayati* [is a qualifier to] *r*, then [the *upasarga*] *pari* should be added [as well]. [For example:] *palyayate* ('he goes around').

{Explanation:
If the verb *ayati* is the qualifier to the sound *r*, then it must follow *r* immediately. This is why the *vārttika* is stated; we need the substitution in the form *palyayate* and the sound *r* of the *upasarga pari* is separated from the verbal stem by the vowel *i*. The derivation of *palyayate* is as follows:

(1) *pari* + *ayA* (DhP I:503) + *ŚaP* + *tiP* (A. 3.1.68 *kartari śap*, A. 3.4.78 *tiptasjhisipthasthamibvasmastātāmjhathāsāthāmdhvamiḍvahimahiṅ*)
(2) *pari* + *ay* + *a* + *t* (*i* → *e*) (A. 3.4.79 *ṭita ātmanepadānāṃ ṭer e*)
(3) *par* (*i* → *y*) + *ay* + *a* + *te* (A. 6.1.77 *iko yaṇ aci*)
pary + *ay* + *a* + *te*
(4) *pa* (*r* → *l*) + *y* + *ay* + *a* + *te* (A. 8.2.19 *upasargasyāyatau*)
palyayate.}

VMBh_1: III.399.6-7; VMBh_2: V.384.2-3

('bright'), *śukla* ('white'), *gaura* ('white, yellowish'), *vanra* ('a divider, co-heir'), *irā* ('water, fluid') and *mālā* ('a garland') [are formed with the help of the suffix *ra*].")

[Answer:] That will be done on account of the statement itself. That is the purpose in the rule.

{Explanation:
Kaiyaṭa's (VMBh_2: V.384.18 ff) problem is that the *l*-substitution could not take place because the semivowel *y* intervenes, which can be solved by the *paribhāṣā*: *yena nāvyavadhānaṃ tena vyavahite 'pi vacanaprāmaṇyāt* ("By virtue of the assertion, in spite of the intervention of an item which never fails to intervene"[302]). If, therefore, a sound necessarily intervenes between *r* and the verbal stem *ayati*, the substitution will take place nonetheless. The *upasarga*s *nir* and *dur*, however, having no scope of application in such a case, should be included as well; the sound *r* of these *upasarga*s will be replaced by *l* (e.g., *nilayate* 'he is taking a rest' and *dulayate* 'he is going the wrong way'). The *upasarga nir* is used by Pāṇini in the *sūtra* A. 7.2.46 *niraḥ kuṣaḥ*[303] with the consonant *r*. Annaṃbhaṭṭa (MPV X.391-392) claims that rule should also apply in the case of *dur* in order to derive the forms *nilayate* and *dulayate*; yet at the same time he rejects the substitution in the case of *nirayaṇa* and *durayaṇa*. The *upasarga*s are considered to end in *s*, which is subsequently replaced by *rU* (A. 8.2.66) and as this substitution is suspended with respect to the *l*-substitution, the latter cannot take place.}

VMBh_1: III.399.7-10; VMBh_2: V.384.3-7

[Question:] What [is the purpose]?
[Answer:] [For example:] *plāyate, palāyate*.
[Answer:] Therefore, let [the word *ayati*] be a qualifier to an *upasarga*.

2) If [the word *ayati* is a qualifier to] an *upasarga*, then there is no accomplishment [of the *l*-substitute] in the case of a single substitute.

[Objection:] If [the word *ayati* is a qualifier to] an *upasarga*, then there is no accomplishment [of the *l*-substitute] in the case of a single substitute. [As in the examples:] *plāyate*, *palāyate* ('he goes away/escapes'). When a single substitute has been applied, [the *l*-substitute] would not result due to the absence of separation [with the verb *ayati*].

{Explanation:

---

302 WUJASTYK 1993: vol. I:43, vol. II:154-156.

303 A. 7.2.46 *niraḥ kuṣaḥ* || ("[The initial infix *iṬ* is optionally inserted at the beginning of the *ārdhadhātuka* suffixes beginning with semivowels or consonants excluding *y*] after [the verbal root] *kuṣA* ('to hurt', DhP IX:46) occurring with [the *upasarga*] *nir*.")

The derivation of the example *plāyate* is as follows:

(1) *pra* + *ayA* (DhP I:503) + *ŚaP* + *tiP* (A. 3.1.68 *kartari śap*, A. 3.4.78 *tiptasjhisipthasthamibvasmastātāmjhathāsāthāmdhvamiḍvahimahiṅ*)
(2) *pra* + *ay* + *a* + *t* (*i* → *e*) (A. 3.4.79 *ṭita ātmanepadānāṃ ṭer e*)
(3) *pr* (*a* + *a* → *ā*) *y* + *a* + *te* (A. 6.1.101 *akaḥ savarṇe dīrghaḥ*)
(4) *p* (*r* → *l*) + *āy* + *a* + *te* (A. 8.2.19 *upasargasyāyatau*)
plāyate

The *vyapavarga* issue discussed in the *Mahābhāṣya* refers to the single substitute of the vowels *a* of *pra* and *ayati*. Due to this substitution, the division between the preverb and the verb is no longer to be noticed, which is why the word is treated as a whole and the *l*-substitute cannot result.}

VMBh_1: III.399.10-11; VMBh_2: V.384.7-9

[Bhāṣya:] *Vyapavarga* means being either the final or the initial. Being treated as either the final or the initial does not mean depending on both [at the same time]. Therefore, a single substitute is treated like the substituend with respect to an operation on what precedes it [and] due to the rule treating [a substitute] like the substituend [there is] *vyapavarga*.

{**Explanation:**
In order to draw the distinction between the verb and the preverb we need to refer to the *sthānivadbhāva* principle. The single substitute *ā* of two vowels *a* (the final of *pra* and the initial of *ayati*) should be treated as its constituent parts, as if the substitution has not taken place yet. Only in such a way can we talk about *vyapavarga*.}

VMBh_1: III.399.11-19; VMBh_2: V.384.9-17

[Objection:] But here the rule treating [a substitute] like the substituend is prohibited; [it has been said that] "in the *pūrvatrāsiddha* [section] the *sthānivadbhāva* does not [operate]."[304]
[Answer:] That rule of interpretation has mistakes though [according to the *vārttika*:] "There is a fault in [forbidding the *sthānivadbhāva* in the cases of] the deletion of the initial [sound] of a cluster (A. 8.2.29), the *l*-substitute (A. 8.2.18 etc.) and the *ṇ*-substitute (A. 8.4.1 etc.)" (A. 1.1.58 *vt*. 10).
[Answer:] Alternatively, let [the word *ayati*] be a qualifier to the sound *r*.

---

[304] A. 1.1.58 vt. 3 *pūrvatrāsiddhe ca*.

[Objection:] But has it not been said that "if [the word] *ayati* [is a qualifier to] the sound *r,* then [the preverb] *pari* should be added [as well]. That will be done by the statement itself"? But has it not been said that "that is the purpose in the rule. What [is the purpose]? [For example:] *plāyate, palāyate*"?
[Answer:] Here, therefore, [the substitution] would not result due to the intervening sound *a*.
[Objection:] When the single substitution has been applied there is no separation.
[Answer:] A single substitute is treated like the substituend with respect to an operation on what precedes it and due to the rule treating [a substitute] like the substituend [there is] an intervention then.
[Objection:] The rule treating [a substitute] like the substituend is prohibited here; [as has been said:] "In the *pūrvatrāsiddha* [section] the *sthānivadbhāva* does not [operate]."
[Answer:] That rule of interpretation has mistakes though [according to the *vārttika*:] "There is a fault in [forbidding the *sthānivadbhāva* in the cases of] the deletion of the initial [sound] of a cluster (A. 8.2.29), the *l*-substitute (A. 8.2.18 etc.) and the *ṇ*-substitute (A. 8.4.1 etc.)".

{**Explanation:**
In both interpretations (i.e., when the verb *ayati* is a qualifier to *r* and when it is a qualifier to the preverb) the desired result is achieved. In the latter case is it achieved through the application of the *sthānivadbhāva* principle and in the former because the intervention of one sound is treated as if there was no intervention. If the verb *ayati* is a qualifier to the preverb, *vyapavarga* is necessary and we need to see the single substitute as consisting of two elements. If it is a qualifier to *r*, the *l*-substitute takes place anyway.}

{**A. 8.2.20** ***gro yaṅi***
[The sound *l* comes in place of the sound *r*] of [the verbal stem] *gṝ* ('to swallow', DhP VI:117) before [the intensive suffix] *yaṄ*.} *This *sūtra* was not commented upon by Patañjali.

A. 8.2.21 ***aci vibhāṣā***
[The sound *l*] usually [comes in place of the sound *r* of the verbal root *gṝ* ('to swallow', DhP VI:117)] before [a suffix beginning with] a vowel.

VMBh_1: III.399.20-22; VMBh_2: V.385.1-3

[Bhāṣya:] It should be added that [the substitution takes place also] before [the suffix] *Ṇi*.[305] As it should be here: e.g. *nigāryate*, *nigālyate* ('it is made to swallow').
[Question:] Why is it not achieved?
[Answer:] It is said: "before a vowel" and we do not see [anything] beginning with a vowel here.

{**Explanation:**
The derivation of the form *nigāryate/nigālyate* is as follows:

(1) *ni* + *gṝ* (DhP VI:117) + *ṆiC* + *yaK* + *tiP* (A. 3.1.26 *hetumati ca*, A. 3.1.67 *sārvadhātuke yaK*, A. 3.4.78 *tiptasjhisipthasthamibvasmastātāmjhathāsāthāmdhvamiḍvahimahiṅ*)
(2) *ni* + *gṝ* + *ṆiC* + *yaK* + *t* (*i* → *e*) (A. 3.4.79 *ṭita ātmanepadānāṃ ṭer e*)
(3) *ni* + *g* (*ṝ* → *ār*) + *ṆiC* + *ya* + *te* (A. 7.2.115 *aco ñṇiti*, A. 1.1.51 *ur aṇ raparaḥ*)
(4) *ni* + *gār* + 0 + *ya* + *te* (A. 6.4.51 *ṇer aniṭi*)
(5) *ni* + *gā* (*r* → *l*) + *ya* + *te* (A. 8.2.21 *aci vibhāṣā*)
nigāryate / *nigālyate*

This derivation creates some problems. The *l*-substitution depends on the following suffix beginning with a vowel. As the suffix *ṆiC* is deleted by A. 6.4.51 (stage (4)), the consonant *r* is not followed by a vowel any more. One of the solutions could be to apply the substitution first. However, it would be suspended with respect to the deletion of the suffix *ṆiC* and again we would not reach the required form. Yet another solution is proposed; the reference to the *sthānivadbhāva* by which the substitute is treated as the substituend, which would result in the suffix *ṆiC* being still visible there.}

VMBh_1: III.399.22-23; VMBh_2: V.385.4-5

[Objection:] [We can see it] according to the rule A. 1.1.62.[306]
[Answer:] The rule A. 1.1.62 does not apply when it depends on sounds. It will be [achieved], therefore, by the rule treating [a substitute] like a substituend.

{**Explanation:**
The *sūtra* only contains the expression "before a vowel", which makes it unclear whether it denotes a vowel itself or a suffix beginning with a vowel. Nāgeśa

---

305 The term *Ṇi* refers to the suffix *ṆiC* used to form the 10th class of verbs and the causative forms.
306 A. 1.1.62 *pratyayalope pratyayalakṣaṇam* ǁ ("When a suffix is deleted, operations conditioned by it still operate [as if the suffix was still present].")

(VMBh_2: V.385.25 ff) and Nārāyaṇa (MPV X.373) refer to a *paribhāṣā-vārttika* 2 under A. 7.2.114,[307] which is used by Patañjali in the subsequent *sūtra* as well, *dhātoḥ svarūpagrahaṇe tatpratyaye kāryavijñānam* ("An expression of the term of a verbal root indicates an operation relative to a suffix introduced after it") and to the *vārttika* 29 under the *sūtra* A. 1.1.72 *yena vidhis tadantasya* (*yasmin vidhis tadādāv algrahaṇe* – "When a term denoting a sound is used [in a rule in locative and qualifying something else standing in locative], the rule refers to such [a qualified element] which begins with that [sound and not ending with it]"). On the basis of these two *paribhāṣā*s they claim that the expression "before a vowel" is an attribute to the word 'suffix' and the *l*-substitute is prescribed. Moreover, the *sūtra* A. 1.1.62 could also apply in this case because the suffix *ṆiC* is deleted with the help of the general term *lopa*.}

VMBh_1: III.399.23-400.2; VMBh_2: V.385.5-8

[Objection:] But here the rule treating [a substitute] like a substituend is prohibited; [as has been said:] "In the *pūrvatrāsiddha* [section] the *sthānivadbhāva* does not [operate]."
[Answer:] Then he says further:

1) In the case of the *l*-substitute of [*r̥̄* of the verb] *gr̥̄*, it has been explained [that the substitution takes place] before [an affix] *Ṇi*.

[Question:] What has been explained?
[Answer:] "There is a fault in [forbidding the *sthānivadbhāva* in the cases of] the deletion of the initial [sound] of a cluster (A. 8.2.29), the *l*-substitute (A. 8.2.18 etc.) and the *ṇ*-substitute (A. 8.4.1 etc.)" (A. 1.1.58 *vt*. 10).

{**Explanation:**
There are a number of ways of achieving the correct result then. We could apply the *pratyayalakṣaṇatva* (A. 1.1.62) or the *sthānivadbhāva* (A. 1.1.56). As the authors of the *Kāśikāvr̥tti* (KV VI.382-383) say, it is also possible to apply the *l*-substitute before deleting the suffix *ṆiC* as this substitution is internally conditioned with respect to suffix deletion, which depends on the following element.}

A. 8.2.22 *pareś ca ghāṅkayoḥ*

---

[307] A. 7.2.114 *mr̥jer vr̥ddhiḥ* || ("[The substitute sound denoted by] *vr̥ddhi* comes in place of [the *aṅga* stem final denoted by *iK*] of the [verbal stem] *mr̥jŪ* ('to wash, purify', DhP II:57) [before *vibhakti l*-substitutes of *l*-members].")

[The sound *l* optionally comes in place of the sound *r*] of [the preverb] *pari* before [the verbal root] *gha* (form of the verbal root *hanA* 'to kill', DhP II:2) and [the noun] *aṅka* ('a curve').

VMBh_1: III.400.3-12; VMBh_2: V.385.9-386.2

[Bhāṣya:] It should be mentioned that [the substitution also takes place] in the case of [the word] *yoga* ('a yoke'). As it should be here: *pariyoga*, *paliyoga* ('joining around').

1) [It should be added that] the *l*-substitute (A. 8.2.18 etc.), the *s*-deletion (A. 8.2.24 etc.), the deletion of the initial of a cluster (A. 8.2.29), the *kU*-substitute (A. 8.2.30) and the substitution by a long vowel [of the penultimate vowel] (A. 8.2.77) [also take place] before [the suffixes] *saṄ*.

[Bhāṣya:] Having mentioned "before [the suffixes] *saṄ*",[308] the *l*-substitute (A. 8.2.18 etc.), the *s*-deletion (A. 8.2.24 etc.), the deletion of the initial of a cluster (A. 8.2.29), the *kU*-substitute (A. 8.2.30) and the substitution by a long vowel [of the penultimate vowel] (A. 8.2.77) should be added.
[Question:] What is the purpose?

2) The purpose is [to derive the words] *girau*, *giraḥ* ('two songs' and 'many songs' respectively), *payo dhāvati* ('milk flows'), *dviṣṭarām* ('better two'), *dṛṣatsthānam* ('a rocky place'), *kāṣṭhaśaksthātā* (??), *kruñcā* ('a female snipe, curlew') and *dhurya* ('fit or chief').

[Objection:] [In the words] *girau* and *giraḥ* the *l*-substitute would result [optionally] by [the *sūtra*] A. 8.2.21; it does not occur on account of the expression "before [the suffixes] *saṄ*."
[Answer:] That is not the purpose. It has been said: "When the proper form of the verbal root is mentioned, an operation refers to the suffix introduced after it." (A. 7.2.114 *vt*. 2).

{Explanation:
The forms *girau* and *giraḥ* should additionally be mentioned because the case ending is added after the nominal stem here, not the verbal form. Therefore the rule

---

[308] The abbreviation *saṄ* is used to denote the suffixes prescribed in the *sūtras* from A. 3.1.5 *guptijkidbhyaḥ saN* || ("The suffix *saN* is added after [the verbs] *gupA* ('to hide', DhP X:231), *tijA* ('to sharpen', DhP I:1020) and *kitA* ('to know, perceive', DhP I:1042).") to A. 3.4.78 *tiptasjhisipthasthamibvasmas-tātāmjhathāsāthāmdhvamiḍvahimahiṅ* || ("[The substitute suffixes] *tiP* etc. [come in place of the *l*-members introduced after a verbal root].")

A. 8.2.21 could not apply and the optional *l*-substitute would not take place. The derivation of the form *girau* is as follows:

(1) *gr̥̄* (DhP VI:117) + *KviP* + *au* (A. 3.2.76 *kvip ca*, A. 4.1.2 *svaujasamauṭśasṭābhyāmbhisṅebhyāmbhyasṅasibhyāmbhyasṅasosāmṅyossup*)
(2) *gr̥̄* + 0 + *au* (A. 6.1.67 *ver apr̥ktasya*)
(3) *g* (*r̥̄* → *ir*) + *au* (A. 7.1.100 *r̥̄ta iddhātoḥ*, A. 1.1.51 *ur aṇ raparaḥ*)
girau}

VMBh_1: III.400.12-14; VMBh_2: V.386.3-5

[Bhāṣya:] [Let us consider the example] *payo dhāvati*. Here [by the *sūtra*] A. 8.2.25 the deletion of *s* would result; it does not occur on account of the expression "before [the suffixes] *saṄ*."
[Answer:] That is not the purpose. He will say: "Before [the suffix] *dhi* the sound *s* of [the suffix] *siC* is deleted" (A. 8.2.25 *ślokavārttika* 1).

{**Explanation:**
The derivation of the expression *payo dhāvati* is as follows:

(1) *payas* + *dhāvati*
(2) *paya* (*s* → *rU*) + *dhāvati* (A. 8.2.66 *sasajuṣo ruḥ*)
(3) *paya* (*r* → *u*) + *dhāvati* (A. 6.1.113 *ato ror aplutād aplute*)
paya + *u* + *dhāvati*
(4) *pay* (*a* + *u* → *o*) + *dhāvati* (A. 6.1.87 *ād guṇaḥ*)
payo dhāvati

The *s*-deletion does not take place because it is an externally conditioned operation as depending on two *pada*s. The *rU*-substitution, on the other hand, requiring only one *pada*, is internally conditioned, which is why it prevails over the *s*-deletion. A. 8.2.66 prescribing *rU* should, theoretically, be considered suspended with respect to A. 6.1.113 due to its placement in the *Tripādī* but Pāṇini mentions *rU* in the text of A. 6.1.113 itself thus indicating that this substitution cannot be considered suspended.
Patañjali in his commentary on A. 8.2.25 reaches the conclusion that the sound *s* appearing before *dh* to be deleted can only come from the suffix *sIC*; therefore the *s*-deletion does not apply in the case of *payo dhāvati* anyway as there is no suffix *sIC* added.}

VMBh_1: III.400.14-15; VMBh_2: V.386.6-7

[Bhāṣya:] [Let us consider the example:] *dviṣṭarām*. Here [by the *sūtra*] A. 8.2.27 the deletion of *s* would obtain; it does not occur on account of the expression "before [the suffixes] *saṄ*."
[Answer:] That is not the purpose. Here also [the expression] "of [the suffix] *siC*" will continue.

{**Explanation:**
The derivation of the form *dviṣṭarām* is as follows:

(1) *dvi* + *suC* + *taraP* (A. 5.4.18 *dvitricaturbhyāṃ suc*, A. 5.3.57 *dvivacanavibhajyopapade tarabīyasunau*)
(2) *dvis* + *tara* + *āmU* (A. 5.4.11 *kimettiṅavyayaghād āmvadravyaprakarṣe*)
(3) *dvi* (*s* → *ṣ*) + *tara* + *ām* (A. 8.3.101 *hrasvāt tādau taddhite*)
(4) *dviṣ* + (*t* → *ṭ*) *ara* + *ām* (A. 8.4.41 *ṣṭunā ṣṭuḥ*)
dviṣṭarām

The sound *s* would be deleted by A. 8.2.27 but according to Patañjali, this *s* would have to be a part of the suffix *siC* to be subject to deletion; the expression "of [the suffix] siC" from the *ślokavārttika* 1 under A. 8.2.25 is thought to continue there as well.}

VMBh_1: III.400.16-17; VMBh_2: V.386.8-9

[Bhāṣya:] [Let us consider the example:] *dṛṣatsthānam*. Here [by the *sūtra*] A. 8.2.26 the deletion of *s* would result; it does not occur on account of the expression "before [the suffixes] *saṄ*."
[Answer:] That is not the purpose. Here also [the expression] "of [the suffix] *siC*" will continue.

{**Explanation:**
In the case of *dṛṣatsthāna* two stems join to form the compound – *dṛṣat* and *sthāna*. The initial *s* of the stem *sthāna* could be subject to deletion on the basis of A. 8.2.26 *jhalo jhali*, which prescribes such a deletion when the sound appears before and after a non-nasal consonant. The lack of deletion is explained via *jñāpaka*, which the commentators see in A. 8.4.61 *udaḥ sthāstanbhoḥ pūrvasya*. It prescribes the substitution of the initial *s* in the roots *sthā* and *stambh* by a homogenous consonant following it, that is the consonant *t*, when the root is preceded by the preverb *ud*. It indicates that the *s*-deletion in A. 8.2.26 can still apply to a sound *s* that is a part of the suffix *sIC* as was specified in the *vārttika* under the rule A. 8.2.25.}

VMBh_1: III.400.17-20; VMBh_2: V.386.10-12

[Bhāṣya:] [Let us consider the example:] *kāṣṭhaśaksthātā*. Here, [by the *sūtra*] A. 8.2.29 the deletion of the sound *k* would result; it does not occur on account of the expression "before [the suffixes] *saṄ*."
[Answer:] That is not the purpose. There is really no [such a word as] *kāṣṭhaśak* so how someone could stand on *kāṣṭhaśak*.

{Explanation:
In the example *kāṣṭhaśaksthātā*, the sound *k* could be deleted by A. 8.2.29 because it forms a part of a cluster *ks*. The deletion does not take place because *k* is not included in the suffixes *saṄ*. The problem lies with the form *kāṣṭhaśak* itself, as it seems that the word is meaningless, at least according to Patañjali. The stem could, theoretically be derived with the help of the suffix *KviP* added by A. 3.2.76 *kvip ca*, which is further deleted. Kaiyaṭa (VMBh_2: V.386.20 ff) points out, however, that this is not the case. As in A. 3.2.76 the expression *dṛśyate* ('is seen') continues from the preceding rule, the suffix could be added after some verbal roots and after others it could not. Kaiyaṭa says that the common usage does not allow the suffix *KviP* after roots that end in *k*.}

VMBh_1: III.400.20-22; VMBh_2: V.387.1-3

[Bhāṣya:] [Let us consider the example:] *kruñcā*. Here [by the *sūtra*] A. 8.2.30 the *k*-substitute would result; it does not occur on account of the expression "before [the suffixes] saṄ."
[Answer:] That is not the purpose. It is accomplished through irregularity.
[Question:] What is the irregularity?
[Answer:] It is in [the *sūtra*] A. 3.2.59 *ṛtvijdadhṛksragdiguṣṇihañcuyujikruñcāṃ ca*.[309]

{Explanation:
The verbal root *kruñcA* ('to make crooked', DhP I:205) takes the suffix *KviN* which is subsequently deleted by A. 6.1.67 *ver apṛktasya*. To the form *kruñc* the feminine suffix is added by A. 4.1.4 *ajādyataṣ ṭāp* and the irregularity shows retention of the nasal sound *ñ* against A. 6.4.24 *aniditāṃ hala upadhāyāḥ kṅiti*.[310] This last *sūtra* would allow for the nasal *ñ* to be deleted because the zero suffix

---

[309] A. 3.2.59 *ṛtvijdadhṛṣsrajdiśuṣṇihañcuyujikruñcāṃ ca* ‖ ("[The forms] *ṛtvij* ('a priest'), *dadhṛṣ* ('audacious'), *sraj* ('a garland'), *diś* ('a direction'), *uṣṇih* (the name of a metre) [are formed in an irregular way with the suffix *KviN* which is] also [added after verbal roots] *añcU* ('to worship, go', DhP I:203), *yujIR* ('to join', DhP VII:7) and *kruñcA* ('be crooked', DhP I:201).")

[310] A. 6.4.24 *aniditāṃ hala upadhāyāḥ kṅiti* ‖ ("The penultimate [*n* of an *aṅga* verbal stem] not marked with *I* [ending in] a consonant [is deleted] before [the suffixes] marked with *K* or *Ṅ*.")

KviN is marked with *K*, even though it is always deleted when added after the verbal root.}

VMBh_1: III.400.22-24; VMBh_2: V.387.4-6

[Bhāṣya:] [Let us consider the example:] *dhurya*. Here [by the *sūtra*] A. 8.2.77 the substitution by a long vowel [of the penultimate vowel] would result; it does not occur on account of the expression "before [the suffixes] *saṄ*."
[Answer:] That is not the purpose. There will be the prohibition [of the substitution] by [the *sūtra*] A. 8.2.79.

{Explanation:
The form *dhurya* is formed with the help of the *taddhita* suffix *yaT*:

(1) *dhur* + *yaT* (A. 4.4.77 *dhuro yaḍḍhakau*)
dhurya

The sound *u* could be lengthened by A. 8.2.77, which prescribes such a substitution in a verbal stem before a consonant; this operation is negated by A. 8.2.79, which is an exception to A. 8.2.77 so suspension does not apply in this case. As mentioned before, the order of rules in the *Aṣṭādhyāyī* does not affect the relation between general rules and exceptions.
In conclusion, the *vārttika* is superfluous, because all the above cases can be easily explained with the help of other rules.}

A. 8.2.23 *saṃyogāntasya lopaḥ*
[There is] the deletion of a final [sound of a *pada* ending] in a cluster.

VMBh_1: III.401.1-3; VMBh_2: V.387.7-9

1) There is prohibition in the case of the *yaṆ*-substitute regarding the deletion of a final [sound of a *pada* ending] in a cluster.

[Bhāṣya:] It should be mentioned that there is prohibition in the case of the *yaṆ*-substitute regarding the deletion of a final [sound of a *pada* ending] in a cluster. [For example:] *dadhy atra* ('here's the yoghurt') or *madhv atra* ('here's the mead').

{Explanation:
The derivation of one of the above examples is as follows:

(1) *dadhi* + *atra*

(2) *dadh* (*i* → *y*) + *atra* (A. 6.1.77 *iko yaṇ aci*)
dadhyatra

What seems interesting here is that Patañjali does not appeal to the conflict between internally and externally conditioned operations. This *vārttika* could easily be rejected because the *y*-substitute in *dadhi* depends on the following *pada*, which makes it externally conditioned. On the other hand, deletion prescribed by this rule would be internally conditioned because the place of the operation is a single *pada*. Due to the suspension of the former the question of the *y*-deletion would not arise at all. Patañjali does not suggest that, which seems odd and inconsistent because he refers to *antaraṅga-bahiraṅga* solution in other cases, regardless of whether this principle could be employed within the *Tripādī* section.}

VMBh_1: III.401.4; VMBh_2: V.387.10-11

[Bhāṣya:] It should be mentioned that there is also a prohibition in the case of the *yaṆ*-substitute regarding the deletion of an initial [sound *s* or *k*] of a cluster occurring at the end of a *pada*.[311] [For example:] *kākyartham* or *vāsyartham* ('for the sake of Kāki' and 'for the sake of the carpenter's adze' respectively, the meaning being uncertain).

{**Explanation:**
This statement is rejected by Kaiyaṭa. He says that by the rule treating the substitute like the substituend and on account of the *vt*. 10 under A. 1.1.58: "There is a fault in [forbidding *sthānivadbhāva* in the cases of] the deletion of the initial [sound] of a cluster (A. 8.2.29), the *l*-substitute (A. 8.2.18 etc.) and the *ṇ*-substitute", the deletion can be avoided. According to this *vārttika*, we can treat *y* as *i* it replaced, in which case the question of a cluster does not arise.}

VMBh_1: III.401.5-7; VMBh_2: V.387.12-14

2) Alternatively, [it should be said that it happens] due to the deletion of a non-nasal consonant (*jhaL*).

[Bhāṣya:] An alternative should be mentioned.
[Question:] What is the reason?
[Answer:] Due to the deletion of a non-nasal consonant. It should be mentioned that the deletion of a final [sound of a *pada* ending] in a cluster is the deletion of [any] consonant except for nasals and semivowels.

---

311 See the *sūtra* A. 8.2.29.

{**Explanation:**
There can also be another explanation of the lack of *y*-deletion in the examples listed above. According to Patañjali, the condition *jhalo jhali* ("before and after a non-nasal consonant") from A. 8.2.26 should be read into the present *sūtra* as well. Kaiyaṭa (VMBh_2: V.388.16 ff) explains this operation with the maxim called *siṃhāvalokita* ('the look of a lion'); it refers to a lion's habit of looking backwards when he walks. In other words, we can say that it is the opposite of *anuvṛtti*, which is also often called *apakarṣa*. The problem that the commentators find is that the form *jhalaḥ* in A. 8.2.26 is the ablative not the genitive, which would be necessary to properly interpret the *vārttika*. The interpretation, either genitive or ablative, of *jhalaḥ* depends on the context in which it is used; it seems adaptable. In A. 8.2.29 prescribing the deletion of an initial sound of a cluster, we need the ablative again. As deletion is prescribed when said cluster is followed by a sound denoted by *jhaL*, the deletion of *y* in *kakyartham* does not take place.

The *apakarṣa* device seems far-fetched. Even in the preceding part of the treatise it is often considered a controversial method of explaining the *sūtra*. In the *Tripādī* section, however, it seems almost impossible due to *asiddhatva*; it would be rather difficult to use the elements of the *sūtra* that does not exist in the preceding one.}

VMBh_1: III.401.8-12; VMBh_2: V.387.14-388.4

3) Alternatively, [that is done] on account of [the *yaṆ*-substitute] being an externally conditioned operation.

[Bhāṣya:] Alternatively, the *yaṆ*-substitute is externally conditioned and the deletion is internally conditioned; and an externally conditioned [operation] is suspended with respect to an internally conditioned one.

4) [The sound] *s* [should be] mentioned regarding the deletion of a final [sound of a *pada* ending] in a cluster.

[Bhāṣya:] [The sound] *s* should be mentioned regarding the deletion of a final [sound of a *pada* ending] in a cluster. It should also be said that there is the deletion of [the sound] *s* [occurring] at the end of a cluster. Here it should be [done] as well: *śreyān* ('the best, most splendid'), *bhūyān* ('greater, more') and *jyāyān* ('older').

{**Explanation:**
The derivation of the example *śreyān* is as follows:

(1) *praśasya* + *īyasUN* + *sU* (A. 5.3.57 *dvivacanavibhajyopapade tarabīyasunau*, A. 4.1.2 *svaujasamauṭśasṭābhyāmbhisṅebhyāmbhyasṅasibhyāmbhyasṅasosāmṅyossup*)
(2) *praśasya* → *śra* + *īyas* + *s* (A. 5.3.60 *praśasyasya śraḥ*)
(3) *śr* (*a* + *ī* → *e*) *yas* + *s* (A. 6.1.87 *ād guṇaḥ*)
(4) *śreya* + *nUM* + *s* + *s* (A. 7.1.70 *ugid acāṃ sarvanāmasthāna 'dhātoḥ*)
(5) *śreya* + *n* + *s* + 0 (A. 6.1.68 *halṅyābbhyo dīrghāt sutisy apṛktam hal*)
(6) *śrey* (*a* → *ā*) + *n* + *s* (A. 6.4.10 *sāntamahataḥ saṃyogasya*)
(7) *śreyā* + *n* + 0 (A. 8.2.23 *saṃyogāntasya lopaḥ*)
śreyān}

VMBh_1: III.401.12-19; VMBh_2: V.388.4-11

[Question:] Why is it not accomplished?
[Answer:] The *rU*-substitute would result due to posteriority (A.8.2.66).
[Answer:] The *rU*-substitute is suspended and due to its suspension, the deletion [of the sound *s*] will take place.
[Answer:] It is not accomplished.
[Question:] What is the reason?

5) Because the prescription of the *rU*-substitute would be without the scope of application.

[Answer:] The *rU*-substitute having [otherwise] no scope of application would block the deletion.
[Objection:] The *rU*-substitute has its scope of application.
[Question:] What is its scope of application?
[Answer:] [For example:] *payaḥ* ('milk'), *śiraḥ* ('a head').
[Objection:] But would the *jaŚ*-substitute not result (A. 8.2.39) here?
[Opponent:] Just as this *rU*-substitute blocks the *jaŚ*-substitute (A. 8.2.39), in the same way it should block the deletion.
[Answer:] It does not block it.
[Question:] What is the reason?
[Answer:] Because the [rule which is introduced] when another necessarily applies, this one blocks [the one that necessarily applies], and when the *jaŚ*-substitute necessarily applies, the *rU*-substitute takes place [instead]. In the case of the deletion, however, [the *rU*-substitute has its scope of application] whether [the deletion] applied or not.

{**Explanation:**
The derivation of the form *payaḥ* is as follows:

(1) *payas* + *sU* (A. 4.1.2 *svaujasamauṭśasṭābhyāmbhisṅebhyāmbhyasṅasibhyāmbhyasṅasosāmṅyossup*)
(2) *payas* + 0 (A. 6.1.68 *halṅyābbhyo dīrghāt sutisy apṛktam hal*)
(3) *paya* (*s* → *rU*) (A. 8.2.66 *sasajuṣo ruḥ*)
(4) *paya* (*r* → *ḥ*) (A. 8.3.15 *kharavasānayor visarjanīyaḥ*)
payaḥ

There are two cases mentioned above – *śreyān* and *payas*, and the others similarly. In the former case, the *rU*-substitute does not apply because it is suspended with respect to the present rule. In the latter case two rules could apply – the one prescribing the *rU*-substitute (A. 8.2.66) and the one prescribing the *jaŚ*-substitute (A. 8.2.39 *jhalāṃ jaśo 'nte*), by which the sound *s* could be replaced with *d*. According to *asiddhatva*, *rU* should not apply at all due to its later position in the *Aṣṭādhyāyī*. However, in this case the rule A. 8.2.66 blocks the rule A. 8.2.39, so the question arises why it cannot block the deletion of the final *s* in the case of *śreyān*. The problem is solved with the help of the *paribhāṣā* mentioned in the above passage. The domain of the *rU*-substitute is entirely included in the domain of the *jaŚ*-substitute. In such a case, a rule covering a smaller domain, which is A. 8.2.66, will apply because otherwise, it would not have the scope of application. What regards *śreyān*, on the other hand, *rU* can still be applicable in other cases, so we can resort to the *asiddhatva* principle.}

VMBh_1: III.401.20-23; VMBh_2: V.388.12-15

6) It is achieved due to separation of a rule.

[Bhāṣya:] Alternatively, the separation of a rule will be done. Thus I will say: *saṃyogāntasya lopo 'rāt*; there is the deletion of a final [sound of a *pada*] but not [the one] occurring after *r* in a cluster. Then *sasya*; and there is the deletion of [the sound] *s*, which is at the end of a cluster [in a *pada*].
[Question:] What is the reason for saying that?
[Answer:] In order to [state] the prohibition and block the *rU*-substitute.

{**Explanation:**
Patañjali does not elaborate on the examples with the sound *r* in question. Kaiyaṭa (VMBh_2: V.389.19 ff), however, gives some examples – *ūrk* ('strength, vigour') and *amārṭ* ('he purified'). The word *ūrk* (=*ūrj*) is derived from the verbal root *ūrjA* ('to strengthen, animate', DhP X:16) with the suffix *KviP* subsequently deleted. The form *amārṭ* is derived from the verbal root *mṛjŪ* ('to clean, purify', DhP II:57) with the augment *a*. The process is as follows:

(1) *mṛjŪ* (DhP II:57) + *ŚaP* + *tiP* (A. 3.1.68 *kartari śap*, A. 3.4.78 *tiptasjhisipthasthamibvasmastātāmjhathāsāthāmdhvamiḍvahimahiṅ*)
(2) *mṛj* + 0 + *ti* (A. 2.4.72 *adiprabhṛtibhyaḥ śapaḥ*)
(3) *mṛj* + *t* (*i* → 0) (A. 3.4.100 *itaś ca*)
(4) *m* (*ṛ* → *ār*) *j* + *t* (A. 7.2.114 *mṛjer vṛddhiḥ*)
(5) *aṬ* + *mārj* + *t* (A. 6.4.71 *luṅlaṅlṛṅkṣv aḍudāttaḥ*)
(6) *a* + *mārj* + 0 (A. 6.1.68 *halṅyābbhyo dīrghāt sutisy apṛktam hal*)
(7) *a* + *mār* (*j* → *ṣ*) (A. 8.2.36 *vraścabhraśjasṛjamṛjayajarājabhrājacchaśāṃ ṣaḥ*)
(8) *a* + *mār* (*ṣ* → *ḍ*) (A. 8.2.39 *jhalāṃ jaśo 'nte*)
(9) *a* + *mār* (*ḍ* → *ṭ*) (A. 8.4.56 *vāvasāne*)
amārṭ

Kaiyaṭa further states that the examples *mātuḥ* and *pituḥ* ('of a mother' and 'of a father' respectively) are of the same kind as the example *śreyān* given by Patañjali and serve to show the lack of application of *rU*. Annaṃbhaṭṭa (MPV X.375) shows, however, that in the forms *mātuḥ* and *pituḥ* the question of the *rU*-substitution does not arise at all; they are formed with the help of the *sūtra* A. 6.1.111 which prescribes the substitution of the vowel *ṛ* of the stem *mātṛ* and the following vowel *a* of the genitive case ending *as* by the *u*, which is followed by *r* (according to A. 1.1.51). The sound *s* of the suffix is then deleted by A. 8.2.24 as it is preceded by *r*. Then the final *r* is replaced by the *visarjanīya* (A. 8.3.15).

(1) *mātṛ* + *ṄasI* (A. 4.1.2 *svaujasamauṭśasṭābhyāmbhisṅebhyāmbhyasṅasibhyāmbhyasṅasosāmṅyossup*)
(2) *māt* (*ṛ* + *a* → *u*) + *r* + *s* (A. 6.1.111 *ṛta ut*, A. 1.1.51 *ur aṇ raparaḥ*)
mātur + *s*
(3) *mātur* (*s* → 0) (A. 8.2.24 *rāt sasya*)
(4) *mātu* (*r* → *ḥ*) (A. 8.3.15 *kharavasānayor visarjanīyaḥ*)
mātuḥ

The aforementioned example *śreyān* is quoted as the one proving the interpretation of blocking the application of *rU*. The prohibition mentioned by Patañjali refers to the deletion of the final sound of such a cluster that does not follow *r*. There would be no deletion if the last sound is preceded by *r* unless it is the sound *s* (see A. 8.2.24). The rule separation proposed by the *vārttikakāra* aims to block the *rU*-substitute, as evidenced by the form *śreyān*. The counter-argument is that blocking would refer not to the *rU*-substitute but, to the prohibition *arāt* due to proximity,[312] which is not desired. The commentators (Kaiyaṭa,

[312] Annaṃbhaṭṭa quotes two rules of interpretation: PŚ 61 *anantaryasya vidhir vā bhavati pratiṣedho veti* || ("[The rule] is an injunction or a prohibition only of that which is the nearest")

Annaṃbhaṭṭa and Nārāyaṇa – MVP X.375) find the solution by splitting the sentence. They say that two sentences are as follows: *rāt sasyaiva lopo bhavati* ("The deletion of [the sound] *s* takes place only if [this sound *s* appears] after [the sound] *r*") and *saṃyogāntasya lopaḥ* ("There is deletion of the final [sound] of a cluster'). If both of them were made into one, then due to the restriction proposed in *rāt sasya* the form *śreyān* could not be formed.}

VMBh_1: III.401.23-402.2; VMBh_2: V.389.1-4

[Bhāṣya:] Alternatively, mentioning [the sound] *s* [in the *sūtra* A. 8.2.23] will be drawn back from [the *sūtra*] A. 8.2.24. [The *sūtra*s sould be:] *saṃyogāntasya lopaḥ*; then *sasya* – "And there is the deletion of [the sound] *s* occurring at the end of [a *pada* ending] in a cluster"; then *rāt* – "There is the deletion of [the sound] *s* occurring at the end of [a *pada*] only if [the sound *s* occurs] after [the sound] *r* in a cluster".
Alternatively, here, [in the *sūtra*] A.8.2.24 [the expression] "[There is] the deletion of a final [sound of a *pada* ending] in a cluster" will continue.

{A. 8.2.24 *rāt sasya*
[There is the deletion of the sound] *s* [occurring at the end of a *pada* if that sound *s* occurs] after [the sound] *r* [in a cluster].} *This *sūtra* was not commented upon by Patañjali.

A. 8.2.25 *dhi ca*
And [there is the deletion of the sound *s*] before [the suffix beginning with] *dh*.

VMBh_1: III.402.3-7; VMBh_2: V.389.5-9

a) [There is] the deletion [of the sound *s* being the part] of [the suffix] *sIC* when the sound *s* is before [the suffix beginning with] *dh*.

[Bhāṣya:] The deletion [of the sound *s* being the part] of [the suffix] *sIC* should be mentioned when the sound *s* is before [the suffix beginning with] *dh*.
[Question:] What is the purpose?

b) The purpose is [to be able to derive the form] *cakāddhi* (2nd sg impv. of the verb *cakāsṚ* 'to shine', DhP II:65).

---

and PŚ 60 *madhye 'pavādaḥ pūrvān vidhīn bādhante nottarān* ॥ ("The exceptions being in the middle [of other rules] block those rule that precede them not those that follow"), I.70, II.337-340 and I.69-70, II.336-337 respectively.

[Answer:] In this case [the *s*-deletion] must not take place: *cakāddhi palitaṃ śiraḥ* ('Make the grey head shine!').

{Explanation:
The derivation of the form *cakāddhi* is as follows:

(1) *cakāsṚ* (DhP II:65) + *siP* (A. 3.4.78 *tiptasjhisipthasthamibvasmastātāmjha-thāsāthāmdhvamiḍvahimahiṅ*)
(2) *cakās* + *ŚaP* + *si* (A. 3.1.68 *kartari śap*)
(3) *cakās* + 0 + *si* (A. 2.4.72 *adiprabhṛtibhyaḥ śapaḥ*)
(4) *cakās* + (*si* → *hi*) (A. 3.4.87 *ser hyapic ca*)
(5) *cakās* + (*hi* → *dhi*) (A. 6.4.101 *hujhalbhyo her dhiḥ*)
(6) *cakā* (*s* → *d*) + *dhi* (A. 8.4.53 *jhalāṃ jaś jhaśi*)
cakāddhi}

VMBh_1: III.402.7-16; VMBh_2: V.389.9-390.1

[Objection:] If, therefore, it is said that [there is] the deletion [of the sound *s* being the part] of [the suffix] *sIC*....

c) how then should [the form] *āśādhvam* (2nd pl impf. of the verb *ā√śāsU* 'to wish, desire', DhP II:12) be [created]?

[Answer:] [The *s*-deletion] would not result here – *āśādhvam*.

1) There will be the *jaŚ*-substitute (A. 8.2.39) of [the sound] *s*.

[Answer:] There will be the *jaŚ*-substitute (A. 8.2.39) of the sound *s*.

d) It should be brought about in such a way in every case.

[Objection:] It should be brought about by the *jaŚ*-substitute in every case. In these cases as well – *āyandhvam* and *arandhvam* ('stretch!' – 2nd pl. impv., and 'you were happy' – 2nd pl. aor., respectively) are accomplished by the *jaŚ*-substitute (A. 8.4.65).

e) Because there is no difference in sound.

[Objection:] Because there is no difference in sound.

{Explanation:

The commentators explain that there is no difference in hearing two sounds or one; so it does not matter whether *s* will be deleted or substituted by one of the sounds denoted by *jaŚ* in the end. In pronunciation we will hear no difference.}

VMBh_1: III.402.17-20; VMBh_2: V.390.2-5

f) And in the case of retroflex sounds there is no [need in] using [the term] *lUṄ* [in the *sūtra* A. 8.3.78].

[Bhāṣya:] With respect to that, this is the aim – the term *lUṄ* should not be used in [the *sūtra*] A. 8.3.78. Because these [forms] *acyoḍḍhvam* ('you stirred, moved', 2nd pl. aor., *cyuṄ* DhP I:1004) and *aploḍḍhvam* ('you bathed, moved', 2nd pl. aor., *pluṄ* DhP I:1007) are accomplished by the *jaŚ*-substitute after the *ṣ*-substitute of [the sound *s* of the suffix] *sIC* and the retroflex substitute of [the sound] *dh* have been applied.

{**Explanation:**
As shown above and in the example analysed below, there is no need to mention the term *lUṄ* in A. 8.3.78 *iṇaḥ ṣīdhvaṃluṅliṭāṃ dho 'ṅgāt*. This particular rule is not necessary in the derivational process as the correct result can be achieved in another way.

(1) *cyuṄ* (DhP I:1004) + *lUṄ*
(2) *aṬ* + *cyu* + *dhvam* (A. 6.4.71 *luṅlaṅlṛṅkṣv aḍudāttaḥ*, A. 3.4.78 *tiptasjhisipthasthamibvasmastātāmjhathāsāthāmdhvamiḍvahimahiṅ*)
(3) *a* + *cy* (*u* → *o*) + *dhvam* (A. 7.3.84 *sārvadhātukārdhadhātukayoḥ*)
(4) *a* + *cyo* + *Cli* + *dhvam* (A. 3.1.43 *cli luṅi*)
(5) *a* + *cyo* + *sIC* + *dhvam* (A. 3.1.44 *cleḥ sic*)
a + *cyo* + *s* + *dhvam*
(6) *a* + *cyo* + (*s* → *ṣ*) + *dhvam* (A. 8.3.59 *ādeśapratyayayoḥ*)
(7) *a* + *cyo* + *ṣ* + (*dh* → *ḍh*) *vam* (A. 8.4.41 *ṣṭunā ṣṭuḥ*)
(8) *a* + *cyo* + (*ṣ* → *ḍ*) + *ḍhvam* (A. 8.4.53 *jhalāṃ jaś jhaśi*)
acyoḍḍhvam

The argument is raised that the *ḍ*-substitute of *ṣ* (i.e., *jaŚ*) would take place whether the term *lUṄ* is included in the *sūtra* A. 8.3.78 or not. The original sound *s* of the suffix *siC* will be replaced by *ṣ*, which will lead to the *ḍh*-substitution in the ending *dhvam*. That, in turn, will enforce the *jaŚ*-substitution of the preceding *ṣ*. In such a way, we do not need to specify *lUṄ* in A. 8.3.78.}

VMBh_1: III.402.21-23; VMBh_2: V.390.6-8

2) It is wrong in the case of [the *sūtra*] A. 8.3.79.

[Objection:] There is a fault in the case of [the *sūtra*] A. 8.3.79. This is the form that should be – *alaviḍḍhvam,* this one should not – *alavidhvam*. Therefore, the term *sIC* should be used [in the *sūtra*].

{Explanation:
This argument refers to the *sūtra* A. 8.3.78 in which, according to the previous part of the *ślokavārttika*, the term *lUṄ* is unnecessary. However, if it is not used in that *sūtra*, it will not be automatically read in the following one, i.e., A. 8.3.79 *vibhāṣeṭaḥ*, in which it is indispensable to derive the correct form *alaviḍḍhvam* rather that *alavidhvam*.

(1) *lūÑ* (DhP IX:13) + *lUṄ*
(2) *aṬ* + *lū* + *dhvam* (A. 6.4.71 *luṅlaṅlṛṅkṣv aḍudāttaḥ*, A. 3.4.78 *tiptasjhisipthasthamibvasmastātāmjhathāsāthāmdhvamiḍvahimahiṅ*)
(3) *a* + *lū* + *Cli* + *dhvam* (A. 3.1.43 *cli luṅi*)
(4) *a* + *lū* + *sIC* + *dhvam* (A. 3.1.44 *cleḥ sic*)
a + *lū* + *s* + *dhvam*
(5) *a* + *lū* + *iṬ* + *s* + *dhvam* (A. 7.2.35 *ārdhadhātukasyeḍ valādeḥ*)
(6) *a* + *l* (*ū* → *o*) + *i* + *s* + *dhvam* (A. 7.3.84 *sārvadhātukārdhadhātukayoḥ*)
(7) *a* + *l* (*o* → *av*) + *i* + *s* + *dhvam* (A. 6.1.78 *eco 'yavāyāvaḥ*)
(8) *a* + *lav* + *i* + (*s* → *ṣ*) + *dhvam* (A. 8.3.59 *ādeśapratyayayoḥ*)
(9) *a* + *lav* + *i* + *ṣ* + (*dh* → *ḍh*) *vam* (A. 8.4.41 *ṣṭunā ṣṭuḥ*)
(10) *a* + *lav* + *i* + (*ṣ* → *ḍ*) + *ḍhvam* (A. 8.4.53 *jhalāṃ jaś jhaśi*)
alaviḍḍhvam

If the term *lUṄ* is not included in A. 8.3.79 and we accept that the sound *s* to be deleted by the present rule should be a part of the aorist suffix *siC*, the form *alavidhvam* will result. The consonant *s* would be deleted and would not be replaced by *ṣ* by A. 8.3.59, which would mean that we could not get the retroflex *ḍh* by A. 8.3.79 either. We need to include the term *lUṄ* in that *sūtra* if we want to achieve the form *alaviḍhvam*, which is also correct, with the retroflex *ḍh* and the sound *s* deleted.
The above derivation shows the example given by Patañjali, where *s* is not deleted but made retroflex. However, the same result could be achieved in a different way; we could get the *ḍh*-substitute of *dh* by the rule A. 8.3.79 and then double it by applying A. 8.4.47 *anaci ca* prescribing the gemmination of consonants. The final applied *sūtra* would be A. 8.4.53 by which the substitution of the first *ḍh* with *ḍ* would take place. The result would be the same and the order of rule application would also be preserved.}

VMBh_1: III.402.23-403.3; VMBh_2: V.390.8-12

[Objection:] If, therefore, the term *sIC* is used....

g) [The deletion of the sound *s*] of *ghasḶ* ('to eat', DhP I:747) and *bhasA* ('to chew, shine', DhP III:18) would not result.

[Objection:] [The *s*-deletion] of *ghasḶ* and *bhasA* is not accomplished. Here [the forms *sagdhi* and *babdha* in the expressions] *sagdhiś ca me sapītiś ca me* ("Eating together with me and drinking with me"),[313] *babdhāṃ te harī dhānā* ("You're your [two steed] devour tawny grain")[314] would not result.

{**Explanation:**
The derivations of the forms *sagdhi* and *babdham* are as follows:
A.
(1) *adA* + *KtiN* (A. 3.3.94 *striyāṃ ktin*)
(2) *ad* → *ghas* + *ti* (A. 2.4.39 *bahulaṃ chandasi*)
(3) *gh* (*a* → 0) *s* + *ti* (A. 6.4.100 *ghasibhasor hali ca*)
(4) *gh* (*s* → 0) + *ti* (A. 8.2.26 *jhalo jhali*)
(5) *gh* + (*t* → *dh*) *i* (A. 8.2.40 *jhaṣas tathor dho 'dhaḥ*)
(6) (*gh* → *g*) + *dhi* (A. 8.4.53 *jhalāṃ jaś jhaśi*)
samāna + *gdhi*
(7) *sa* + *gdhi* (A. 6.3.84 *samānasya chandasy amūrdhaprabhṛtyudarkeṣu*)
sagdhi
B.
(1) *bhas* + *lOṬ* → *tas* (A. 3.4.78 *tiptasjhisipthasthamibvasmastātāmjhathās-āthāmdhvamiḍvahimahiṅ*)
(2) *bhas* + (*tas* → *tām*) (A. 3.4.85 *loṭo laṅvat*, A. 3.4.101 *tasthasthamipāṃ tāntantāmaḥ*)
(3) *bhas* + *ŚaP* + *tām* (A. 3.1.68 *kartari śap*)
(4) *bhas* + 0 + *tām* (A. 2.4.75 *juhotyādibhyaḥ śluḥ*)
(5) *bhas* + *bhas* + *tām* (A. 6.1.10 *ślau*)
(6) *bha* (*s* → 0) + *bhas* + *tām* (A. 7.4.60 *halādiḥ śeṣaḥ*)
(7) (*bh* → *b*) *a* + *bhas* + *tām* (A. 8.4.54 *abhyāse car ca*)
(8) *ba* + *bh* (*a* → 0) *s* + *tām* (A. 6.4.100 *ghasibhasor hali ca*)
(9) *ba* + *bh* (*s* → 0) + *tām* (A. 8.2.26 *jhalo jhali*)

---

[313] TS 4.7.4.1.

[314] ṚgVKh 5.7.4q. It is a part of a Vedic quotation cited in the *Nirukta* by Yaska: *babdhāṃ te harī dhānā upa ṛjīṣaṃ jighratām* || ("Let thy steeds devour grain and sniff at the residue'). Yaska derives the form *babdhām* from the root *bhas* by reduplicating the first syllable and removing the penultimate sound. Nir 5.12: part II:80, part III:100.

(10) *ba + bh + (t → dh) ām* (A. 8.2.40 *jhaṣas tathor dho 'dhaḥ*)
(11) *ba + (bh → b) + dhām* (A. 8.4.53 *jhalāṃ jaś jhaśi*)
babdhām

In these cases the sound *s* is not a part of the suffix *sIC*. If we accept the condition of the suffix *sIC* in the present rule, the above forms will not be derivable. The *sūtra* A. 8.2.26, by which *s* is deleted in the examples just given, will read the condition "being a part of *sIC*" as well.}

VMBh_1: III.403.4-8; VMBh_2: V.390.13-391.1

h) Therefore, the term *sIC* should not be used.

[Answer:] And therefore, the term *sIC* should not be used in [the *sūtra*] A. 8.2.25.
[Question:] How [then are we able to derive the form] *cakāddhi* [in *cakāddhi*] *palitaṃ śiraḥ*?
[Answer:] Then the term *sIC* should be used.
[Question:] How [then are we able to derive the forms like *sagdhi* and *babdha* in the expressions] *sagdhiś ca me sapītiś ca me* and *babdhāṃ te harī dhānā*?
[Answer:] To begin with, here, the form *sagdhi* is not [derived] from [the verb] *ghasḶ*.
[Question:] How then?
[Answer:] It is the form of [the verb] *ṣaghA* ('to hurt', DhP V:21). [And the form *babdhām* in the expression] *babdhāṃ te harī dhānā* is not [derived] from [the verb] *bhasA*.
[Question:] How then?
[Answer:] It is the form of [the verb] *bandhA* ('to tie', DhP IX:37).

{**Explanation:**
As the forms *sagdhi* and *babdhām* are problematic, Patañjali proposes to derive them from different roots: *sagh* and *bandh* respectively. In both cases the question of the *s*-deletion does not arise. The following examples give yet another solution to this problem. Patañjali claims that the *s*-deletion in the case of *sagdhi* and *babdhām* can be explained by Vedic anomaly, where sometimes the sounds are deleted and sometimes they are not. It seems that Patañjali does not see the need to specify *s* as being a part of the suffix *sIC* in the present rule. Alternatively, it seems obvious that such a restriction has to be taken into account and all the examples that could go against it, can be explained in other ways.}

VMBh_1: III.403.8-24; VMBh_2: V.391.2-18

3) Alternatively, [there is] the sound deletion in a Vedic word as [in the form] *iṣkartāram adhvare*.

[Bhāṣya:] Alternatively, there will be the sound deletion in a Vedic word as [in the form] *iṣkartāram adhvare*. Just like in *tubhyedam agne* ("This is for you, Agni")[315] when the form [should be] *tubhyam idam agne*; *āmbānāṃ caruḥ* ("the vessel for grain")[316] when the form [should be] *nāmbānāṃ caruḥ*; *āvyādhinī ruganāḥ* ("shooting the Mātṛs")[317] when the form [should be] *āvyādhinī suganāḥ*; *iṣkartāram adhvarasya* ("[to] the one preparing an oblation")[318] when the form [should be] *niṣkartāram*; *śivā udrasya bheṣajīḥ* ("auspicious and healing [form] of Rudra")[319] when the form [should be] *śivā rudrasya bheṣajīḥ*. Therefore, the term *sIC* should be used [in the *sūtra*].
[Answer:] It should not be used. [There is] this [*sūtra*] A. 8.2.24 [where] the sound *s* is used and this *s* will be understood as being a part of [the suffix] *sIC*.
[Question:] How?
[Answer:] It is said that [there is the deletion of the sound] *s* [occurring at the end of a *pada* if that *s* occurs] after [the sound] *r* [in a cluster]; it is [such] a sound *s* which [occurs] after [the sound] *r* and not the other one. Therefore, another one [is that] of [the affix] *sIC*.
[Objection:] But there are [forms such as] *mātuḥ*, *pituḥ*,[320] therefore, the term *sIC* should be used [in the *sūtra*].
[Answer:] It should not be used.
[Question:] Why is it not in [the form] *cakāddhi* [in *cakāddhi*] *palitaṃ śiraḥ*?
[Answer:] What is desired should also be included. So, here should be [the form] *cakādhi*.

***Ślokavārttika*:**
1) [There is] the deletion [of the sound *s* being the part] of [the suffix] *sIC* when the sound *s* is before [the suffix beginning with] *dh* and the purpose is [to be able to derive the form] *cakāddhi* (2nd sg impv. of the verb *cakāsR̥* 'to shine', DhP II:65). How then should [the form] *āśādhvam* (2nd pl impf. of the verb *ā√śāsU* 'to wish, desire', DhP II:12) be [accomplished]? There will be the *jaŚ*-substitute (A.8.2.39) of [the sound] *s*.
2) It should be brought about in such a way in every case, because there is no difference in sound. And in the case of retroflex sounds there would be no [need to]

[315] R̥gV 5.11.5.
[316] TS 1.8.10.1. The form in the TS is *carum*, not *caruḥ*.
[317] MS 2.6.6.
[318] R̥gV. 10.140.5.
[319] TS 4.5.10.1.
[320] Here the sound *s* of the suffix *ṄasI* does not follow *r* directly.

use [the term] *lUṄ* [in the *sūtra* A. 8.3.78]. [The *jaŚ*-substitute cannot be applied in every case as] it is wrong in the case of [the *sūtra*] A. 8.3.79.
3) [The deletion of the sound *s*] of *ghasḶ* and *bhasA* would not result. Therefore, the term *sIC* should not be used. Alternatively, [there is] the sound deletion in a Vedic word as [in the form] *iṣkartāram adhvare*.

{A. 8.2.26 *jhalo jhali*
[There is the deletion of the sound *s* occurring] after [a sound denoted by] *jhaL* (i.e., consonants except nasals) before [a sound denoted by] *jhaL*.
A. 8.2.27 *hrasvād aṅgāt*
[There is the deletion of the sound *s* occurring] after an *aṅga* ending in a short vowel [before a sound denoted by *jhaL* (i.e., consonants except nasals)].
A. 8.2.28 *iṭa īṭi*
[There is the deletion of the sound *s* occurring] after [the initial infix] *iṬ* before [the infix] *īṬ*.
A. 8.2.29 *skoḥ saṃyogādyor ante ca*
[There is the deletion] of the initial [sounds] *s* or *k* [being a part] of a cluster [occurring] at the end [of a *pada*] and [also before a sound denoted by *jhaL* (i.e., consonants except nasals)].
A. 8.2.30 *coḥ kuḥ*
[A sound belonging to the group] *kU* comes in place of [a sound belonging to the group] *cU* [when *cU* occurs at the end of the *pada* or before a sound denoted by *jhaL* (i.e., consonants except nasals)].
A. 8.2.31 *ho ḍhaḥ*
[The sound] *ḍh* comes in place of [the sound] *h* [when it occurs at the end of the *pada* or before a sound denoted by *jhaL* (i.e., consonants except nasals)].}
*These *sūtras* were not commented upon by Patañjali.

A. 8.2.32 *dāder dhātor ghaḥ*
[The sound] *gh* comes in place of [the sound *h*] of a verbal root beginning with [the sound] *d* [when the sound *h* occurs at the end of a *pada* or before a sound denoted by *jhaL* (i.e., consonants except nasals)].

VMBh_1: III.403.25-404.2; VMBh_2: V.392.1-5

[Objection:] Here [in the forms] *dogdhā*, *dogdhum* ('a milker' nom. sg. and 'to milk' inf., respectively), due to suspension of the *gh*-substitute (A. 8.2.32) the *ḍh*-substitute (A. 8.2.31) would result.
[Bhāṣya:] That is not a fault. It has been said that "an exception [applies] by force of the statement itself."[321] Alternatively, thus I will say *hoḍho 'dādeḥ* –

[321] See A. 8.2.1 *vt*. 2.

"[The sound] *ḍh* comes in place of [the sound] *h* [when it occurs at the end of the *pada* or before a sound denoted by *jhaL*] but not of that which begins with [the sound] *d*." Then, *dhātor ghaḥ* – "In a verbal root (i.e., that which begins with *d*) [the substitution with the sound] *gh* [takes place]." [The word] *dāder* continues and negation (*na*) stops.

{**Explanation:**
The derivation of the example *dogdhā* is as follows:

(1) *duhA* (DhP II:4) + *tṛC* + *sU* (A. 3.1.133 *ṇvultṛcau*, A. 4.1.2 *svaujasamauṭśasṭābhyāmbhisṅebhyāmbhyasṅasibhyāmbhyasṅasosāmṅyossup*)
(2) *d* (*u* → *o*) *h* + *tṛ* + *s* (A. 7.3.84 *sārvadhātukārdhadhātukayoḥ*)
(3) *doh* + *t* (*ṛ* → *an*) + *s* (A. 7.1.94 *ṛduśanaspurudaṃśonehasāṃ ca*)
(4) *doh* + *tan* + 0 (A. 6.1.68 *halṅyābbhyo dīrghāt sutisy apṛktam hal*)
(5) *doh* + *t* (*a* → *ā*) *n* (A. 6.4.8 *sarvanāmāsthāne cāsambuddhau*)
(6) *doh* + *tā* (*n* → 0) (A. 8.2.7 *nalopaḥ prātipadikāntasya*)
(7) *do* (*h* → *gh*) + *tā* (A. 8.2.32 *dāder dhātor ghaḥ*)
(8) *dogh* + (*t* → *dh*) *ā* (A. 8.2.40 *jhaṣas tathor dho 'dhaḥ*)
(9) *do* (*gh* → *g*) + *dhā* (A. 8.4.53 *jhalāṃ jaś jhaśi*)
dogdhā

In the examples given by Patañjali the *gh*-substitute could be superseded by the *ḍh*-substitute of the preceding *sūtra* due to suspension of the present one. Two alternative solutions are proposed: either we can take the present rule as an exception which always prevails over the general rule, even in the *Tripādī* section; or we accept different wording of the *sūtras* A. 8.2.31 and A. 8.2.32. The condition *adādi* ("not beginning with [the sound] *d*") would be included in the preceding rule and the condition *dādi* would continue into the present one. Negation would cease. The latter is the solution accepted by Kaiyaṭa (VMBh_2: V.392). He claims that in this case we cannot accept the view when the exception prevails over the general rule. The following *sūtra*, that is A. 8.2.33, prescribes the optional *gh*-substitute in the case of some verbal roots, including the verb *druh* ('to injure', DhP IV:88), which begins with *d*. The optionality would be useless if the exception were to be stronger.}

VMBh_1: III.404.3; VMBh_2: V.392.6

[Objection:] It is said: "of [the verbal roots] beginning with [the sound] *d*". Here, it is not accomplished – *adhok* ('he milked', 3 sg. imperf.).

{**Explanation:**
The derivation of *adhok* is as follows:

(1) *duhA* (DhP II:4) + *lUṄ* → *tiP* (A. 3.4.78 *tiptasjhisipthasthamibvasmastātām-jhathāsāthāmdhvamiḍvahimahiṅ*)
(2) *duh* + *ŚaP* + *ti* (A. 3.1.68 *kartari śap*)
(3) *duh* + 0 + *ti* (A. 2.4.72 *adiprabhṛtibhyaḥ śapaḥ*)
(4) *duh* + *t* (*i* → 0) (A. 3.4.100 *itaś ca*)
(5) *aṬ* + *duh* + *t* (A. 6.4.71 *luṅlaṅlṛṅkṣv aḍudāttaḥ*)
(6) *a* + *d* (*u* → *o*) + *t* (A. 7.3.84 *sārvadhātukārdhadhātukayoḥ*)
(7) *a* + *doh* + 0 (A. 6.1.68 *halṅyābbhyo dīrghāt sutisy apṛktam hal*)
(8) *a* + *do* (*h* → *gh*) (A. 8.2.32 *dāder dhātor ghaḥ*)
(9) *a* + (*d* → *dh*) *ogh* (A. 8.2.37 *ekāco baśo bhaṣ jhaṣantasya sdhvoḥ*)
(10) *a* + *dho* (*gh* → *g*) (A. 8.2.39 *jhalāṃ jaśo 'nte*)
(11) *a* + *dho* (*g* → *k*) (A. 8.4.56 *vāvasāne*)
adhok / *adhog*

The above form begins with the vowel *a* so it could be claimed that the *gh*-substitute of *h* at the stage (8) cannot take place as the stem does not begin with *d*.}

VMBh_1: III.404.3-7; VMBh_2: V.392.6-393.1

[Question:] Where would it be then?
[Answer:] [It would be in the form] *mā sma dhok* ('Do not milk'!).
[Bhāṣya:] That is not a fault. [The form] *dhātoḥ* is the genitive that does not stand in coreferential relationship to [the word] *dādi*. [The expression] *dāder dhātoḥ* [would not mean] "of that which begins with [the sound] *d* and is a verbal root."
[Question:] What [kind of genitive] is it then?
[Answer:] It is the genitive in the meaning 'of a part'. [The expression means] "the initial [sound] *d* which is a part of a verbal root." And, of course, it should be understood that the purpose of the genitive in the meaning 'of a part' is what follows.
[Question:] What is the purpose?
[Answer:] As here, in [the *sūtra*] in A. 8.2.37. [The form] *gardhap* [which is formed by adding] a non-suffix [*KviP*] after [the form] *gardabhaya*.

{**Explanation:**
The interpretation of the genitive in the present *sūtra* as *avayavaṣaṣṭhī* is necessary in the rule A. 8.2.37 *ekāco baśo bhaṣ jhaṣantasya sdhvoḥ*. The example given is *gardhap* whose derivation is as follows:

(1) *gardabha* + *ṆiC* + *KviP* (A. 3.1.26 *hetumati ca*, A. 3.2.76 *kvip ca*)
(2) *gardabh* (*a* → 0) + *ṆiC* + *KviP* (A. 6.4.155 *vt*. 1 *ṇāv iṣṭhāvat prātipadikasya*)

(3) *gardabh* + 0 + KviP (A. 6.4.51 *ṇer aniṭi*)
(4) *gardabh* + 0 (A. 6.1.67 *ver apṛktasya*)
(5) *gar* (*d* → *dh*) *abh* (A. 8.2.37 *ekāco baśo bhaṣ jhaṣantasya sdhvoḥ*)
(6) *gardha* (*bh* → *b*) (A. 8.2.39 *jhalāṃ jaśo 'nte*)
(7) *gardha* (*b* → *p*) (A. 8.4.56 *vāvasāne*)
gardhap / *gardhab*

The problem arises when the *sūtra* A. 8.2.37 at stage (5) is to apply. The term *dhātoḥ* recurring there from the present rule could stand in coreferential relationship with *ekāco jhaṣantasya*, which would mean that the substitution of sounds denoted by *baŚ* with those denoted by *bhaṢ* would take place in a monosyllabic verbal root that ends in a sound denoted by *jhaṢ*. The sound subject to replacement in the above example is *d*, which is a part of a syllable *dabh* but which is not a root. Therefore, we need to reinterpret the rule in the following manner: a sound denoted by *baŚ*, which is contained in a monosyllabic part of the verbal root ending in a sound denoted by *jhaṢ*, is replaced by a sound denoted by *bhaṢ*.}

VMBh_1: III.404.8-9; VMBh_2: V.393.1-2

[Objection:] If it is the genitive in the meaning of a part, [the forms such as] *dogdhā* or *dogdhum* would not result.
[Answer:] By treating secondary as principal, the initial *d* is considered a part of a verbal root.

{Explanation:
When we reject the *samānādhikaraṇa* interpretation of the genitive and accept the *avayava* interpretation, the expression *dhātoḥ* will become a qualifier to the expression *adādi*. The substitution prescribed by the rule will refer to such a *h* which is a part of *d*-initial part of the verbal root. This interpretation will make it possible to derive the form *adhok* which begins with a vowel. In the case of *dogdhā* and *dogdhum* the sound *h* is not a part of any *d*-initial part of the root. It is a part of the whole verbal root that begins with *d*. Here Patañjali evokes *vyapadeśivadbhāva* ("treating secondary as principal"), according to which that part of a verbal root which begins with *d* should be treated as the whole verb. In such a way, we can achieve the correct forms both in the case of *adhok* or *gadhap* and *dogdhā* or *dogdhum*.
We can see, therefore, that the interpretation of this *sūtra* can be twofold; as a rule, genitive is interpreted as 'a part of a whole' but in order to account for all the forms another maxim is used, which allows us to treat 'a part as a whole'}.

VMBh_1: III.404.9-11; VMBh_2: V.393.3-5

1) In [the verbal roots] *hṛÑ* ('to carry', DhP I:947) and *grahA* ('to seize', DhP IX:61), in Vedic literature, [the sound] *bh* [comes in place of the sound] *h*.

[Bhāṣya:] It should be mentioned that in Vedic literature in [the verbal roots] *hṛÑ* and *grahA* [the sound] *bh* [comes in place of the sound] *h*. [As in the forms] *gardabhena saṃbharati* ("He brings together by means of a donkey");[322] *marud asya grabhītā* ("Marut is the one who seizes him");[323] *sāmidhenyo jabhrire* ("They grasped the verses recited while the sacrificial fire is kindled");[324] *udgrābhaṃ ca nigrābhaṃ ca brahma devā avivṛdhan* ("The gods glorified rising Brahman as well as falling one").[325]

{A. 8.2.33 *vā druhamuhaṣṇuhaṣṇihām*
[The sound *h* of the verbal roots] *druhA* ('to seek to hurt', DhP IV:88), *muhA* ('to be bewildered', DhP IV:89), *ṣṇuhA* ('to vomit', DhP IV:90) and *ṣṇihA* ('to be attached to', DhP IV:91) [is] preferably [replaced by the sound *gh* when *h* occurs at the end of a *pada* or before a sound denoted by *jhaL* (i.e., consonants except nasals)].
A. 8.3.34 *naho dhaḥ*
[The sound *h*] of [the verbal root] *ṇahA* ('to tie', DhP IV:57) [is replaced by the sound] *dh* [when *h* occurs at the end of a *pada* or before a sound denoted by *jhaL* (i.e., consonants except nasals)].
A. 8.2.35 *āhas thaḥ*
[The sound *h*] of [the verbal root] *āh* ('to speak', the substitute for *brūÑ*, DhP II:35 A. 3.4.84) [is replaced by the sound] *th* [before a sound denoted by *jhaL* (i.e., consonants except nasals)].
A. 8.2.36 *vraścabhraśjasṛjamṛjayajarājabhrājacchaśāṃ ṣaḥ*
[The final sound] of [the verbal roots] *OvraścU* ('to cut', DhP VI:11), *bhrasjA* ('to roast', DhP VI:4), *sṛjA* ('to create', DhP VI:121), *mṛjŪ* ('to cleanse', DhP II:57), *yajA* ('to sacrifice', DhP I:1051), *rājĀ* ('to shine, rule', DhP I:874), *bhrājĀ* ('to shine, sparkle', DhP I:194) and [those which end in the sounds] *ch* and *ś* [is replaced by the sound] *ṣ* [when the sound to be replaced occurs at the end of a *pada* or before a sound denoted by *jhaL* (i.e., consonants except nasals)].
A. 8.2.37 *ekāco baśo bhaṣ jhaṣantasya sdhvoḥ*
[A sound denoted by] *baŚ* (i.e., *b*, *g*, *ḍ*, *d*) being a part of a monosyllabic [verbal root] ending in [a sound denoted by] *jhaṢ* [is replaced] by [a sound deno-

[322] KS 19.2.
[323] AV 1.17.2. The closest quote to the one given by Patañjali comes from the *Paippalāda* recension and takes the form *parur asya grabhītā*.
[324] ṚgV 10.64.6. The form in this passage is *samitheṣu jabhrire*.
[325] TS 1.1.13.1.

ted by] *bhaṢ* (i.e., *bh*, *gh*, *ḍh*, *dh*) [when it occurs at the end of a *pada* or] before *s* or *dhva*.} *These *sūtra*s were not commented upon by Patañjali.

A. 8.2.38 *dadhas tathoś ca*
[A sound denoted by *baŚ* (i.e., *b*, *g*, *ḍ*, *d*) being a part] of [a verbal root] *dadh* (*DUdhāÑ* 'to bear, support', DhP III:10) [ending in a sound denoted by *jhaL* (i.e., consonants except nasals) is replaced by a sound denoted by *bhaṢ* (i.e., *bh*, *gh*, *ḍh*, *dh*) when it occurs at the end of a *pada* or] before [the sounds] *t*, *th*, [*s* or *dhva*].

VMBh_1: III.404.12-14; VMBh_2: V.393.6-8

[Question:] What is the purpose of the word *ca*?
[Answer:] [The expression] "before *s* or *dhva*" is drawn [into this *sūtra*].
[Objection:] That is not the purpose. That [condition]: "before *s* or *dhva*" is achieved by the previous [*sūtra*].
[Answer:] It is not achieved.
[Question:] What is the reason?
[Answer:] Because it (i.e., the verbal stem *dadh*) does not begin with [a sound denoted by] *baŚ* (i.e., *b*, *g*, *ḍ*, *d*).

{**Explanation:**
It may seem that it does actually. However, one has to remember that the form *dadh* mentioned in the *sūtra* is the reduplicated stem of the verbal root *dhā* and the reduplication proceeds as follows: *dhā* + *dhā*, so in fact, it begins with a sound belonging to the group *bhaṢ*. The *jaŚ*-substitute, which would yield the form *dadh*, should be considered suspended with respect to A. 8.2.37. Moreover, the stem *dhā* does not end in a sound denoted by *jhaṢ*, therefore the substitution in question could not be achieved by the previous rule. Patañjali discussed these issues further on.
The whole derivational process is as follows:

(1) *DUdhāÑ* (DhP III:10) + *lAṬ*
(2) *dhā* + *ŚaP* + *tas* (A. 3.1.68 *kartari śap*, A. 3.4.78 *tiptasjhisipthasthamibvasmastātāmjhathāsāthāmdhvamiḍvahimahiṅ*)
(3) *dhā* + 0 + *tas* (A. 2.4.75 *juhotyādibhyaḥ śluḥ*)
(4) *dhā* + *dhā* + *tas* (A. 6.1.10 *ślau*)
(5) *dh* (*ā* → *a*) + *dhā* + *tas* (A. 7.4.59 *hrasvaḥ*)
(6) *dha* + *dh* (*ā* → 0) + *tas* (A. 6.4.112 *śnābhyastayor ātaḥ*)
(7) (*dh* → *d*) *a* + *dh* + *tas* (A. 8.4.53 *jhalāṃ jaś jhaśi*)
(8) (*d* → *dh*) *a* + *dh* + *tas* (A. 8.2.38 *dadhas tathoś ca*)
(9) *dha* + (*dh* → *t*) + *tas* (A. 8.4.54 *khari ca*)

(10) *dhatta* (*s* → *rU*) (A. 8.2.66 *sasajuṣo ruḥ*)
(11) *dhatta* (*r* → *ḥ*) (A. 8.3.15 *kharavasānayor visarjanīyaḥ*)
dhattaḥ

It may seem that the *jaŚ*-substitute prescribed by A. 8.4.53 at the stage (7) should be considered suspended with respect to the present rule as it is placed later in the *Tripādī* section. However, Pāṇini uses the form *dadh* in the text of the present rule which would suggest that the *jaŚ*-substitute cannot actually be suspended; this form presupposes the application of A. 8.4.53 for the purpose of A. 8.2.38.}

VMBh_1: III.404.14-17; VMBh_2: V.393.8-11

[Objection:] But does it not begin with [a sound denoted by] *baŚ* when the *jaŚ*-substitute (*dh* → *d*) [by the *sūtra* A. 8.4.53] has taken place?
[Answer:] The *jaŚ*-substitute is suspended [with respect to the present rule] and due to its suspension, [the verbal stem] does not begin with [a sound denoted by] *baŚ*.
[Objection:] In such a way, therefore, [there is] in the *siddha* section the *vt*. 13 "The *jaŚ* and *caR* substitutes in a reduplicated form [should not be suspended] with respect to the *e*-substitute (A. 6.4.120[326]) and the infix *tUK*" under the *sūtra* A. 8.2.6.
[Answer:] It will not be done with respect to the *e*-substitute and [the infix] *tUK*. [It should] only [be said:] "The *jaŚ* (A. 8.4.53) and *caR* (A. 8.4.54) substitutes in a reduplicated form are not suspended."

{Explanation:
The *vārttika* 13 under the *sūtra* A. 8.2.6 proposes non-suspension of the *jaŚ* and *caR* substitutes with respect to the *e*-substitute and the infix *tUK*. The rule Patañjali has in mind is A. 6.4.120 *ata ekahalmadhye 'nādeśāder liṭi* which includes the condition *anādeśādi* – 'not having its initial substitute'. It refers to the reduplicated syllable of the verbal stem whose sound should not undergo the substitution; as for example by *jaŚ* (i.e., voiced unaspirated stops) or *caR* (i.e., voiceless unaspirated stops and sibilants). If these substitutions were considered suspended, the condition would not be necessary. Moreover, the inclusion of the stems *phalA* and *bhajA* in the *sūtra* A. 6.4.122 *tṝphalabhajatrapaś ca*[327] would be

[326] A. 6.4.120 *ata ekahalmadhye 'nādeśāder liṭi* || ("The vowel *e*] comes in place of the vowel *a* between single consonants [in a verbal *aṅga* stem] where the initial was not replaced [in a reduplicated syllable] before [the *l*-substitutes of] *lIṬ* (perfect) [with marker *K* or *Ṅ* and deleted reduplicated syllable].")

[327] A. 6.4.122 *tṝphalabhajatrapaś ca* || ("[The vowel *e* comes in place of the vowel *a* of the verbal *aṅga* stem of] *tṝ* ('to cross, traverse', DhP I:1018), *phalA* ('to be fruitful, DhP I:563), *bhajA* ('to serve', DhP I:1047) and *trapŪṢ* ('to be ashamed', DhP I:399) [before the *l*-substitutes of *lIṬ*

superfluous. The same result would be achieved by the preceding *sūtra*, that is, A. 6.4.120.
I find that specifying the non-suspension of the *jaŚ*-substitute in the case of the present rule is unnecessary. Pāṇini uses the form *dadh* in the text of the rule, thus indicating that the *jaŚ*-substitute has taken place and, consequently, must not be considered suspended.}

VMBh_1: III.404.14-24; VMBh_2: V.393.11-19

[Objection:] Then in such a way it would not result either because it does not end in *jhaṢ* (i.e, voiced aspirates stops).
[Answer:] When the deletion has been done (A. 6.4.112 *śnābhyastayor ātaḥ*), it ends in *jhaṢ*.
[Objection:] It does not end in *jhaṢ* because of the rule A. 1.1.56 (on the basis of which the substitute is treated like the substituend), which is why he further reads:

1) Drawing [the expression] "of [the verbal root] *dadh* before *t* and *th*" into the preceding rule is superfluous due to prohibition of *sthānivadbhāva*.

[Bhāṣya:] Drawing [the expression] "of [the verbal root] *dadh* before *t* and *th*" into the preceding rule is superfluous.
[Question:] What is the reason?
[Answer:] Due to prohibition of *sthānivadbhāva*. The rule A. 1.1.56 is prohibited here; [it has been said that] "in the *pūrvatrāsiddha* section the rule A 1.1.56 does not [operate]" (A. 1.1.58 *vt*. 3). And this prohibition is necessarily to be applied.

2) On the other hand, [there is] prohibition in the case of absence of deletion.

[Bhāṣya:] What I mean here, though, is that by force of drawing [from the previous *sūtra*], prohibition should be mentioned in the case of absence of deletion. [For example:] *dadhāti* or *dadhāsi* ('I support' and 'you support' respectively).

{**Explanation:**
The above discussion regards the possibility that the substitution in the verbal root *dhā* would take place based on the previous rule. That would mean, however, the necessity of the stem to end in one of the sounds denoted by *jhaṢ*. The stem *dhā* does not originally end in any of such sounds; it becomes such after the deletion of the final *ā* has taken place by A. 6.4.112. Theoretically, the de-

(perfect) with marker *K* or *Ṅ* as well as before the *lIṬ* substitute *thaL* occurring with the initial infix *iṬ*].")

leted *ā* could be treated as the substituend based on A. 1.1.56 *sthānivad ādeśo 'nalvidhau* and we would not get *dh*, which is included in *jhaṢ*, as final. Consequently, the substitution would not take place at all. As, however, according to A. 1.1.58 *vt*. 3, *sthānivadbhāva* does not operate in the *pūrvatrāsiddha* section, we could still get the stem ending in *dh* after the *ā*-deletion.
There are some cases of the forms of *dhā* which could undergo the substitution by the previous *sūtra*; there are others though that should not undergo such a change, for example *dadhāti* or *dadhāsi*, where the verbal endings begin in *t* and *s* respectively, and thus they fall under the scope of application of the rules A. 8.2.37-38. This is why the *vārttika* is formulated negating deletion of the final *ā*.}

VMBh_1: III.405.1-7; VMBh_2: V.394.1-8

[Bhāṣya:] The expression "and before *t* and *th*" could also be omitted.
[Question:] How come?
[Answer:] It is said "of [the verbal root] ending in [a sound denoted by] *jhaṢ* before [a sound denoted by] *jhaL*" and this [expression] "before *t* and *th*" [is included in the expression] "before [a sound denoted by] *jhaL*"; and it should be [the verbal root] ending in [a sound denoted by] *jhaṢ*, not otherwise.
Moreover, it is not so that "in the *pūrvatrāsiddha* [section] the rule treating the substitute like the substituend does not apply", in the same way the meaning is not [understood] either by the means of drawing, with the help of the particle *ca* or by the use of [the expression] "before [the sounds] *t* and *th*". It depends on close proximity: "of [the verbal root] ending in [a sound denoted by] *jhaṢ* before [a sound denoted by] *jhaL*". Sometimes, close proximity is accomplished by contact, and distance by instruction; and sometimes it is accomplished neither by contact nor by instruction. In the case of deletion, close proximity is accomplished by contact and distance by instruction; in the case of absence of deletion, it is accomplished neither by contact nor by instruction. Wherever this close proximity [comes from], there we will apply [the substitution].

{**Explanation:**
Commentators give two types of close proximity of sounds: *śāstrakṛtānantarya* ('rule-derived') and *śrutikṛtānantarya* ('originally heard'). Patañjali uses the term *saṃnipātakṛtānantarya* for the latter. As stated above, the condition "ending in the sounds denoted by *jhaṢ*" is still valid in the present rule. In the case of the verbal root *dhā* we can achieve the form ending in *dh* only by deleting the final vowel *ā*. This is why Kaiyaṭa (VMBh_2: V.394.17 ff) states that it should be treated as *śrutikṛtānantarya*. Now, Patañjali in the discussion uses the term *śāstrakṛtam anānantaryam*, which would mean 'rule-derived distance'.
According to Kaiyaṭa, this is the correct version and he explains that due to the application of *sthānivadbhāva*, we still have the final *ā* at the end of *dhā*, which

causes separation (*vyavadhāna*) – presumably between the sound *dh* and the following verbal ending. In other words, close proximity between the sound *dh* and the ending is natural, not rule-derived, because *dh* is originally in a verbal stem. On the other hand, distance caused by the existence of the vowel *ā* is not considered original because the sound is first deleted and only later brought about by the rule. According to Kaiyaṭa, the separation is not problematic because the following condition: "of [the verbal root] ending in [a sound denoted by] *jhaṢ* before [a sound denoted by] *jhaL*" continues in the present rule.

In conclusion, the present *sūtra* should read only *dadhas* with the omission of *tathoś ca*. The consonants *t* and *th* are included in the abbreviation *jhaL* (i.e., non-nasal consonants) and the endings beginning with other sounds are not possible after the form of the stem *dadh*. Thus, all the forms will be derived. For the same reason the conjuntion *ca* does not have to be used. Its purpose is to read the expression *sdhvoḥ* into the present rule, which is also unnecessary if we accept the condition *jhali* (both *s* and *dh* are included in this abbreviation). The forms such as *dadhāmi* do not fall under the scope of the application of the present *sūtra* at all. The question of deletion of the final vowel *ā* does not arise; consequently, the present rule cannot apply and we are able to derive the correct forms.}

{A. 8.2.39 *jhalāṃ jaśo 'nte*
[The sounds denoted by] *jaŚ* (i.e., voiced unaspirated stops) come in place of [the sounds denoted by] *jhaL* (i.e., consonants except nasals) when [they occur] at the end [of a *pada*].} *This *sūtra* was not commented upon by Patañjali.

A. 8.2.40 *jhaṣas tathor dho 'dhaḥ*
[The sound] *dh* comes in place of [the sounds] *t* and *th* [occurring] after [the sounds denoted by] *jhaṢ* (i.e., voiced aspirated stops) except for [the verbal root] *ḌUdhāÑ* ('to support, bear', DhP III:10).

VMBh_1: III.405.8-12; VMBh_2: V.394.9-14

[Question:] What is the purpose of [saying] "except for [the verbal root] *ḌUdhāÑ*"?
[Answer:] [The forms] *dhattaḥ* (3rd du. praes. ind. 'they both support') and *dhatthaḥ* (2nd du. praes. ind. 'you both support').
[Objection:] [The expression] "except for [the verbal root] *ḌUdhāÑ*" could be omitted.
[Question:] Why does [the substitution] not [apply in] *dhattaḥ* and *dhatthaḥ*?

[Answer:] The separation of a rule will be done in the case of the *jaŚ*-substitute. There is [the *sūtra*] A. 8.2.38 *dadhas tathoś ca*. Then I will say *jhalāṃ jaśaḥ* – "[The sounds denoted by] *jaŚ* come in place of [the sounds denoted by] *jhaL* of [a verbal stem] *dadh* before *t, th*". Then, *ante* – "And [the sounds denoted by] *jaŚ* come in place of [the sounds denoted by] *jhaL* when [they occur] at the end [of a *pada*]". Therefore, when the *jaŚ*-substitute has been done, it (i.e., the *dh*-substitute) will not be due to it (that is, the verbal stem) not ending in [a sound denoted by] *jhaṢ* (i.e., voiced aspirated stops).

{**Explanation:**
The present rule prescribes the *dh*-substitution of *t* and *th* being part of suffixes following the verbal root ending in a sound denoted by *jhaṢ*. Theoretically, it could apply also in the case of the forms such as *dhattaḥ* and *dhatthas*. The relevant piece of the derivation of *dhattaḥ* is as follows:[328]

(1) *dhā + dhā + tas* (A. 6.1.10 *ślau*)
(2) *dh (ā → a) + dhā + tas* (A. 7.4.59 *hrasvaḥ*)
(3) *dha + dh (ā →* 0) *+ tas* (A. 6.4.112 *śnābhyastayor ātaḥ*)
(4) *(dh → d) a + dh + tas* (A. 8.4.53 *jhalāṃ jaś jhaśi*)
(5) *(d → dh) a + dh + tas* (A. 8.2.38 *dadhas tathoś ca*)
(6) *dha + (dh → t) + tas* (A. 8.4.54 *khari ca*)

After the deletion of the final *ā* has taken place at the stage (3), the stem ends in *dh* which is a part of the abbreviation *jhaṢ*. The present rule would allow the *dh*-substitute of *t* of the verbal ending if the condition excluding the verbal root *dhā* were not stated. At the stage (4), another *sūtra* could apply as well, that is A. 8.3.39 prescribing the *jaŚ*-substitute of the sound *dh* at the end of a *pada*. This *jaŚ*-substitute is, however, suspended with respect to the *d → dh* change applied at the stage (5) so it does not take place. The *sūtra* A. 8.4.53 cannot be suspended for the reasons explained above under A. 8.2.38. As the final *dh* is not subject to substitution, the stem still ends in a *jhaṢ* (i.e., voiced aspirated stops) sound. However, the *sūtra* A. 8.2.40 is placed after the one prescribing the *jaŚ*-substitute and thus *jaŚ* would not be suspended. The stem would, theoretically, undergo the substitution and would not meet the conditions for the present rule to apply, as it would not be *jhaṢanta* any more.
The conclusion of the above discussion is that the condition *adhaḥ* could be dispensed with because we can employ other *sūtra*s to derive the correct forms. Patañjali's proposal is the separation of the previous *sūtra* into two.}

{A. 8.2.41 *ṣaḍhoḥ kaḥ si*

---

[328] For the whole derivation check the *sūtra* A. 8.2.38.

[The sound] *k* comes in place of [the sounds] *ṣ* and *ḍ* before [the sound] *s*.}
*This *sūtra* was not commented upon by Patañjali.

This was the first *āhnika* of the second *pada* of the eighth *adhyāya* in the *Vyākaraṇamahābhāṣya* composed by Patañjali.

A. 8.2.42 *radābhyāṃ niṣṭhāto naḥ pūrvasya ca daḥ*
[The sound] *n* comes in place of [the sound] *t* of the *niṣṭhā* [suffix occurring] after [the sounds] *r* and *d* and it (i.e., *n*) also comes in place of the preceding *d*.

VMBh_1: III.406.1-2; VMBh_2: V.395.1-2

[Question:] What is the purpose of [saying] "after [the sounds] *r* and *d*"?
[Answer:] [The forms] *caritam* ('gone') and *muditam* ('glad, joyful').

{Explanation:
The sounds *r* and *d* must directly precede the suffix *niṣṭhā*, otherwise the substitution does not take place. The examples given are *carita* and *mudita* where the infix *iṬ* is inserted thus preventing the substitution.

(1) *carA* (DhP I:591) + *Kta* (A. 3.2.102 *niṣṭhā*, A. 1.1.26 *ktaktavatū niṣṭhā*)
car + ta
(2) *car + iṬ + ta* (A. 7.2.35 *ārdhadhātukasyeḍ valādeḥ*)
carita}

VMBh_1: III.406.2-5; VMBh_2: V.395.2-5

[Objection:] But would it (e.g., the *n*-substitute) not also result in this case if it is said "after [the sounds] *r* and *d*"? Here as well [the suffix] *niṣṭhā* [comes] after the sound *r* and the sound *d*.
[Answer:] [The suffix] *niṣṭhā* is not qualified by [the expression] "after the sound *r* and the sound *d*."
[Question:] What then?
[Answer:] The sound *t* is qualified. [The sound] *n* comes in place of the sound *t* [occurring] after the sound *r* or the sound *d* if it is [a part] of [the suffix] *niṣṭhā*.

{Explanation:
In the counter-examples given by Patañjali the suffix *niṣṭhā* also follows the sounds *r* and *d* respectively. So the question arises why the substitution could not be performed there as well. The key is the proper interpretation of the qualified-qualifier relation. The sounds *r* and *d* serve as qualifiers here. However, they do

not qualify the suffix *niṣṭhā* as such; they qualify the consonant *t* that is a part of this suffix. Therefore, this *t* must follow the consonants *r* or *d* in order for the substitution to take place. Such an interpretation is possible when we do not consider the expression *niṣṭhātaḥ* as a compound; the word *niṣṭhā* has its genitive deleted. It allows for the meaning "the sound *t* of the suffix *niṣṭhā*." In the case of *racita* and *mudita*, the infix *iṬ* is inserted and, as it is marked with *Ṭ*, it is added at the beginning of the following suffix. In such a way the consonant *t* of the suffix does not follow *r* or *d* any more.
Kaiyaṭa (VMBh_2: V.395.14-15) also explains why it is not the suffix *niṣṭhā* that is qualified but the sound *t*. He says that it is so because of the instruction of the compound *niṣṭhātaḥ* where there is no relation of the word *niṣṭhā* with the qualifier as it is not the primary member of a compound. The sound *t*, however, is the principal member of a compound and we can see its relation with the qualifier.}

VMBh_1: III.406.6-8; VMBh_2: V.395.6-9

[Question:] But what is the purpose [in using] the word *pūrva*?

1) The word *pūrva* in the case of the substitute in [the suffix] *niṣṭhā* is used to prohibit the substitute of [such a sound *d*] that follows.

[Bhāṣya:] The word *pūrva* is used in the case of the substitute in [the suffix] *niṣṭhā* so that there is not the substitute of [such a sound *d*] that follows. [For example:] *bhinnavadbhyām*, *bhinnavadbhiḥ* (instr./dat./abl. du. and instr. pl. of the word *bhinnavat* 'one who has divided' respectively).

{Explanation:
These forms are derived from the verbal root *bhidIR* ('to split, divide', DhP VII:2) with the suffix *KtavatŪ*. We get: *bhid* + *KtavatŪ* + *bhyām/bhis* → *bhid* + *tavat* + *bhyām/bhis*. At this point the *sūtra* A. 8.2.39 applies prescribing the *jaŚ*-substitute of the final *t* of the suffix *KtavatŪ*. The result is *bhid* + *tavad* + *bhyām/bhis*. Now, our present rule applies changing both the initial sound *t* of the suffix into *n* and the preceding sound *d* also into *n*, which yields *bhin* + *navad* + *bhyāṃ/bhis* → *bhinnavadbhyām* / *bhinnavadbhis*. The present *sūtra* allows for the *n*-substitute of the sound *d* preceding *t* but not the following one. Therefore, only the first *d* is changed to *n*. Were we allowed to change any *d* into *n*, the result would be **bhinnavanbhyām/*bhinnavanbhis*.
In the final analysis the *n*-substitute of the consonant *d* that is a part of the suffix *niṣṭhā* is not required. This is the purpose of the word *pūrva* in the *sūtra*. In the above examples we can see that *d* is rule-derived, it is not originally a part of the suffix. The lack of the word *pūrva* would allow both sounds *t* and *d* of the suffix, due to proximity in the text of the rule, to be replaced by *n*. Annaṃbhaṭṭa (MPV

X.380) states that the second consonant *d* in *bhinnavadbhyām* / *bhinnavadbhis*, being the result of the *jaŚ*-substitution (A. 8.2.39), is dependent on the term *pada* assigned to the element in which the operation is to take place and is externally conditioned. On the contrary, the consonant *d* of the verbal root *bhidIR* is independent and only this one should be subject to substitution. On the other hand, the substitution refers to such a *d* that is a part of a *pada* (due to governing term *padasya* from A. 8.1.16) and both sounds *d*, of the verbal root and of the suffix, are part of a *pada*; they would be both *antaraṅga*.
Two *paribhāṣā*s are mentioned by the commentators: *lakṣaṇapratipadoktayoḥ pratipadoktasyaiva grahaṇam* ("Of the derived and the explicitly stated it is only the explicitly stated that is taken [into consideration]")[329] and *anantarasya vidhir vā pratiṣedho vā* ("A prescription or a prohibition applies to the nearest item").[330] According to the former, only the element explicitly stated in the enunciation should be taken into consideration; in our case it would be the verbal root *bhidIR*. As mentioned before, the consonant *d* of the suffix is derived by a rule. Kaiyaṭa (VMBh_2: V.395.20 ff) rejects this *paribhāṣā*, however, saying that it cannot apply in the case of single sounds. The second *paribhāṣā* would allow for the substitution of *d* being a part of *niṣṭhā* because, if the rule read *niṣṭhāto daḥ*, the sound *d* would appear close to the term *niṣṭhā*; on the basis of this proximity the substitution would take place. Both these *paribhāṣā*s are rejected and it is accepted that the word *pūrva* must be used in the *sūtra*. The reason is the interpretation of the ablative as explained below.}

VMBh_1: III.406.9-10; VMBh_2: V.395.10-11

2) But [there is the substitution] of what follows on the basis of the ablative.

[Objection:] [The substitution] of what follows would result on the basis of the ablative [according to the *sūtra*] A. 1.1.67.

{**Explanation:**
A. 1.1.67 *tasmād ity uttarasya*[331] states the purpose of the ablative; by this *paribhāṣā* then, without the word *pūrva*, the *n*-substitute would replace *d* that follows the sounds *r* or *d*. It would not, however, replace such a consonant *d* that precedes the suffix and is a part of the verbal root. That is why the word *pūrva* is necessary.}

---

[329] WUJASTYK 1993: vol. I:5-7, vol. II:20 ff., the *paribhāṣā* 2. PŚ 105, I.104-105, II.486-489.

[330] WUJASTYK 1993: vol. I:20-21, vol. II:98 ff., the *paribhāṣā* 13. PŚ 61, I.70, II.337-340.

[331] A. 1.1.67 *tasmād ity uttarasya* || ("A form stated in the ablative denotes an element that follows [which is subject to grammatical operations].")

VMBh_1: III.406.11-14; VMBh_2: V.396.1-4

3) Prohibition [should be mentioned] when the cause is *vṛddhi*.

[Bhāṣya:] It should be mentioned that there is prohibition when the cause is *vṛddhi*.
[Question:] What is the purpose?

4) The purpose is [the forms] *kārti* ('a descendent of Kṛta'), *kṣaiti* ('a descendant of Kṣita'), *phaulli* ('a descendant of Phulla').

[Answer:] [In the form] *kārti,* when *vṛddhi* has been done, the *n*-substitute would result [by the *sūtra*] A. 8.2.42.

{**Explanation:**
The derivation of *kārti* is as follows:

(1) *kṛta* + *iÑ* (A. 4.1.95 *ata iñ*)
(2) *kṛt* (*a* → 0) + *i* (A. 6.4.148 *yasyeti ca*)
(3) *k* (*ṛ* → *ār*) *t* + *i* (A. 7.2.117 *taddhiteṣv acām ādeḥ*, A. 1.1.51 *ur aṇ raparaḥ*)
kārti}

VMBh_1: III.406.14-21; VMBh_2: V.396.4-12

[Answer:] [In the form] *kṣaiti,* when *vṛddhi* has been applied, the *n*-substitute would result [by the *sūtra*] A. 8.2.46. [In the form] *phaulli*, when *vṛddhi* has been applied, the mentioned *l*-substitute connected with the penultimate [vowel] *u* would not result (as it should by the *sūtra* A. 8.2.55).
[Question:] Therefore, when the prohibition is stated "because *vṛddhi* is the cause", how is this understood: [the expression] *vṛddhinimitta* [would mean that] "it is only *vṛddhi* that is the cause"; [hence the expression] "caused by *vṛddhi*", or [the expression] *vṛddhinimitta* [would mean] "the one that has *vṛddhi* as its cause"; [hence the expression] "because of the one that has *vṛddhi* as its cause"?
[Question:] And what of it?
[Answer:] If it is understood that [the expression] *vṛddhinimitta* [means that] "it is only *vṛddhi* that is the cause"; [hence the expression] "caused by *vṛddhi*", [the word] *kṣaiti* is included [but the word] *kārti* is not included. However, if it is understood as "the one that has *vṛddhi* as its cause"; [hence the expression] "because of the one that has *vṛddhi* as its cause", [then the word] *kārti* is included [but the word] *kṣaiti* is not included. And in both of the cases [the word] *phaulli* is not included.

{**Explanation:**
The expression *vṛddhinimitta* can be understood as a *tatpuruṣa* ('caused by *vṛddhi*') or *bahuvrīhi* ('having *vṛddhi* as its cause') compound. According to the former interpretation, the word *kṣaiti* falls under the scope of prohibition because the diphthong *ai*, which is the *vṛddhi* of *i*, would be the cause of the *n*-substitute. The *sūtra* A. 8.2.46 *kṣiyo dīrghāt* prescribes the *n*-substitute of *t* of the suffix *niṣṭhā* that appears after the forms of the verbal root *kṣi* ('to perish, lose', DhP I:255) with a long vowel. The *vṛddhi* diphthong *ai* forms the condition for this substitution to take place. It is not desired in the form *kṣaiti*, hence the prohibition.
The word *kārti*, however, does not fall under the scope of prohibition. One of the conditions of the present rule is the existence of the sound *r*. According to Pāṇini, the *vṛddhi* grade of the vowel *ṛ* is *ā*, after which only the consonant *r* is added. The vowel *ā* cannot be the cause of the *n*-substitution so the prohibition would not apply in this case.
If, on the other hand, the expression *vṛddhinimitta* is treated as a *bahuvrīhi* compound, the situation is reversed; the word *kārti* falls under the scope of prohibition and *kṣaiti* does not. The consonant *r* that is added after the vowel *ā* by A. 1.1.51 has *vṛddhi* as its cause. If it were not for the *vṛddhi* substitution, there would be no consonantal *r*. It is not the situation with *kṣaiti* though, where a vowel is just upgraded so there is no element that has its cause in *vṛddhi*.
The problem, however, is with the form *phulli*, whose derivation is as follows:

(1) *phal* + *Kta* (A. 3.2.102 *niṣṭhā*, A. 1.1.26 *ktaktavatū niṣṭhā*)
phal + *ta*
(2) *ph* (*a* → *u*) *l* + *ta* (A. 7.4.89 *ti ca*)
(3) *phul* + *la* (A. 8.2.55 *anupasargāt phullakṣībakṛśollāghāḥ*)
(4) *phulla* + iÑ (A. 4.1.95 *ata iñ*)
(5) *phull* (*a* → 0) + *i* (A. 6.4.148 *yasyeti ca*)
(6) *ph* (*u* → *au*) *ll* + *i* (A. 7.2.117 *taddhiteṣv acām ādeḥ*)
phaulli

In the case of *phaulli* there is no *n*-substitute replacing *t* of the suffix *niṣṭhā* but the sound *l* is achieved instead by the *sūtra* A. 8.2.55. However, including this word in a *vārttika* seems pointless, regardless of how the expression *vṛddhinimitta* is understood. In this case the *l*-substitute is not conditioned by *vṛddhi* but by the vowel *u* being the substitute for *a* in the verbal root *phalA*. Such is the explanation when the expression *vṛddhinimitta* is a *tatpuruṣa* compound. If it is treated as a *bahuvrīhi* compound, the prohibition stated in a *vārttika* does not influence it either; the *l*-substitution does not cause *vṛddhi*, whose cause is the *taddhita* suffix *iÑ*, but it is done before the *vṛddhi* substitution.}

VMBh_1: III.406.21-24; VMBh_2: V.396.12-15

[Answer:] Let it be as you want. Let it be then that [the expression] *vṛddhi-nimitta* [means that] "it is only *vṛddhi* that is the cause"; [hence the expression] "caused by *vṛddhi*".
[Objection:] But has it not been said that "[the word] *kṣaiti* is included [but the word] *kārti* is not included"?
[Answer:] [The word] *kārti* is also included.
[Question:] How come?
[Answer:] There is *vṛddhi,* there is *guṇa*; *rephaśiras* being the name for *vṛddhi* and *guṇa* [of the sound *r*] that follows as a result.

{**Explanation:**
The term *rephaśiras* is used for the consonant *r* that appears after *guṇa* and *vṛddhi* substitution of the vowel *ṛ* in writing; it is placed above the following letter, hence the name. The question arises how it is possible to assign the term *vṛddhi* to *ār* if it has a defined form and length (i.e., in this case it means the vowel *ā* which is of two *mātras*). The problem here is with the interpretation of the *sūtra* A. 1.1.51 *ur aṇ raparaḥ*. It should be understood according to Patañjali's explanation on *vt*. 3 under that rule: "The sounds denoted by *aṆ* coming in place of the vowel *ṛ* should be understood as being followed by the consonant *r* as soon as it (i.e., *aṆ*) becomes applicable". It means that the *guṇa* or *vṛddhi* substitutions cannot be separated from the injunction of the sound *r*, as both of the operations take place at the same time, at the same stage of derivation. Kaiyaṭa states that even if *r* were prescribed subsequently, the word *kārti* would still be included in the scope of the prohibition because it (i.e., the sound *r*) is a part of *ār*. In such a way we get the consonant *r* being the condition for the *n*-substitute, which makes the prohibition valid in the case of *kārti*.}

VMBh_1: III.406.24-407.3; VMBh_2: V.397.1-3

[Answer:] Alternatively, let it be again that [the expression means] "the one that has *vṛddhi* as its cause"; [hence the expression] "because of the one that has *vṛddhi* as its cause".
[Objection:] But has it not been said that "[the word] *kārti* is included [but the word] *kṣaiti* is not included"?
[Answer:] [The word] *kṣaiti* is also included.
[Question:] How come?
[Answer:] Because the word *vṛddhi* is used in [the meaning of] the rule [that prescribes] *vṛddhi*.

{**Explanation:**

The term *vṛddhi* that appears in the *vārttika* refers to the rule that prescribes the *vṛddhi* substitution and not to the substitution itself. It is the secondary meaning of the term but, as this is what the prohibition depends on, we resort to the secondary rather than the primary meaning. In such a way, the rule prescribing *vṛddhi* is the cause of *vṛddhi* itself and the consonant *r* after it; we can include both *kārti* and *kṣaiti*.}

VMBh_1: III.407.3-7; VMBh_2: V.397.3-8

[Question:] Should this prohibition be mentioned then?

5) Alternatively, it should [be said that the substitution does not take place] due to the rule being externally conditioned.

[Answer:] Alternatively, it should not be mentioned.
[Question:] What is the reason?
[Answer:] Due to the rule being externally conditioned. [The] *vṛddhi* [operation] is externally conditioned and the *n*-substitute is internally conditioned. An externally conditioned [operation] is suspended with respect to an internally conditioned one. And having done thus, the *l*-substitute is not suspended [and the form] *phaulli* is accomplished.

{**Explanation:**
In the cases of both *kārti* and *kṣaiti* the *vṛddhi* of the initial vowel is caused by the *taddhita* suffix *iÑ*, which makes it an externally conditioned operation. The *n*-substitute would not depend on any external element, thus being internally conditioned. The prohibition does not need to be specified at all then.
In the case of the form *phaulli*, when the *l*-substitution is to be done, *vṛddhi* is suspended due to it being externally conditioned, so we apply the *l*-substitution first and then *vṛddhi*. In such a way, the substitution is not suspended and the form can be correctly derived.}

{**A. 8.2.43 *saṃyogāder āto dhātor yaṇvataḥ***
[The sound *n* comes in place of the sound *t* of the *niṣṭhā* suffix occurring] after the verbal root ending in [the vowel] *ā* and beginning with a cluster and containing [a sound denoted by] *yaṆ* (i.e., semivowels).} *This *sūtra* was not commented upon by Patañjali.

A. 8.2.44 *lvādibhyaḥ*
[The sound *n* comes in place of the sound *t* of the *niṣṭhā* suffix occurring] after [the verbal roots] *lūÑ* ('to cut', DhP IX:13) etc.

VMBh_1: III.407.8-10; VMBh_2: V.397.9-12

1) [The sound *t* in the suffix] *KtiN* similar to [the suffix] *niṣṭhā* is replaced [by the sound *n* when it occurs] after [the verbal roots] *lūÑ* ('to cut', DhP IX:13) etc. or after [verbal roots] ending in the sound *ṝ*.

[Bhāṣya:] It should be mentioned that [the sound *t* in the suffix] *KtiN* similar to [the suffix] *niṣṭhā* is replaced [by the sound *n* when it occurs] after [the verbal roots] *lūÑ* ('to cut', DhP IX:13) etc. or after [verbal roots] ending in the sound *ṝ*. [For example:] *kīrṇiḥ* ('scattering, throwing'), *gīrṇiḥ* ('praise', 'swallowing'); *lūniḥ* ('cutting'), *dhūniḥ* ('shaking').

{**Explanation:**
In this *sūtra* four *vārttika*s are proposed specifying either other verbal roots that fall under the scope of substitution or other suffixes where the substitution also takes place. The example derivations are as follows:
A.
(1) *lūÑ* (DhP IX:13) + Kta (A. 3.2.102 *niṣṭhā*, A. 1.1.26 *ktaktavatū niṣṭhā*)
lū + ta
(2) *lū* + (*t* → *n*) *a* (A. 8.2.44 *lvādibhyaḥ*)
lūna

B.
(1) *kṝÑ* (DhP IX:15) + KtiN (A. 3.3.94 *striyāṃ ktin*)
kṝ + ti
(2) *k* (*ṝ* → *ir*) + *ti* (A. 7.1.100 *ṝta iddhātoḥ*, A. 1.1.51 *ur aṇ raparaḥ*)
(3) *kir* + (*t* → *n*) *i* (A. 8.2.44 *lvādibhyaḥ*)
(4) *k* (*i* → *ī*) *r* + *ni* (A. 8.2.77 *hali ca*)
(5) *kir* + (*n* → *ṇ*) *i* (A. 8.4.1 *raṣabhyām no ṇaḥ samānapade*)
kīrṇi

This *vārttika* forms the rule extension. The expression *ktinniṣṭhāvat* is problematic as it could mean that all the operations that are connected with the suffix *niṣṭhā* refer to the suffix *KtiN* as well. For example, the insertion of the infix *iṬ* (as in *carita* or *mudita*), which sometimes comes before the suffixes *Kta* and *KtavatŪ*, but never before *KtiN*. This extension refers only to the *n*-substitution prescribed by the rule.}

VMBh_1: III.407.11-12; VMBh_2: V.397.13-14

2) [The vowel *u*] of [the verbal roots] *du* ('to go', DhP I:991) and *gu* ('to void solid matter from the body', DhP VI:106) [is replaced by] its long counterpart and [the sound *n* comes in place of the sound *t* of the suffix *niṣṭhā*].

[Bhāṣya:] It should be mentioned that [the vowel *u*] of [the verbal roots] *du* ('to go', DhP I:991) and *gu* ('to void solid matter from the body', DhP VI:106) [is replaced by] its long counterpart and [the sound *n* comes in place of the sound *t* of the suffix *niṣṭhā*]. [For example:] *ādūnaḥ* ('consumed with grief'[332]), *vigūnaḥ* ('devoid of solid matter').

{Explanation:
There are two verbal roots *du* that could be taken into account here: *du* ('to go', DhP I:991) and *ṬUdu* ('to burn, to afflict, DhP V:10). However, only the first is meant here according to the *paribhāṣā*: *niranubandhagrahaṇe na sānubandhakasya* ("When an item is mentioned without a marker, that item with a marker is not meant").[333]}

VMBh_1: III.407.13-15; VMBh_2: V.397.15-17

3) [The sound *n* comes in place of the sound *t* of the suffix *niṣṭhā* when it occurs] after [the verbal root] *pūÑ* when [it means] 'to destroy'.

[Bhāṣya:] It should be mentioned that [the sound *n* comes in place of the sound *t* of the suffix *niṣṭhā* when it occurs] after [the verbal root] *pūÑ* when [it means] 'to destroy'. [For example:] *pūnā yavāḥ* ('destroyed barley').
[Question:] What is the purpose [in using the expression] "when [it means] 'to destroy'"?
[Answer:] [The expression] *pūtaṃ dhānyam* ('cleaned grains').

{Explanation:
In the *dhātupāṭha* we find two verbal roots whose basic meaning is 'to clean': *pūṄ* (DhP I:1015) and *pūÑ* (DhP IX:12). The commentators disagree as to which of these should be understood here. Kaiyaṭa opts for the one marked with *Ṅ* but Nāgeśa claims that reading with the marker *Ñ* is correct.}

VMBh_1: III.407.16-18; VMBh_2: V.398.1-3

---

332 MW gives the meaning 'to be filled with grief' for the stem *ā√du* (MW:137), which goes against Patañjali's commentary.

333 WUJASTYK 1993: vol. I:51, vol. II:173. See also PŚ 81, I.84-85, II.400-404.

4) [The sound *n* comes in place of the sound *t* of the suffix *niṣṭhā* when it occurs] after [the verbal root] *ṣiÑ* ('to bind', DhP V:12) and the object (*karman*) *grāsa* ('a mouthful, a piece') becomes an agent (*kartṛ*).

[Bhāṣya:] It should be mentioned that [the sound *n* comes in place of the sound *t* of the suffix *niṣṭhā* when it occurs] after [the verbal root] *ṣiÑ* ('to bind', DhP V:12) and the object (*karman*) *grāsa* ('a mouthful, a piece') becomes an agent (*kartṛ*). [For example,] *sino grāsaḥ* ('a mouthful rolled up').
[Question:] What is the purpose [in using the expression] "and the object (*karman*) *grāsa* ('a mouthful, a piece') becomes an agent (*kartṛ*)"?
[Answer:] [The expression] *sitā paśena sūkarī* ('the female pig has been caught by the animal').

{**Explanation:**
The word *grāsa* ('a mouthful'), which is normally an object of an action, when it is fit for the action of binding is required to become an agent. Nāgeśa gives an example of such a situation: "When a mouthful is mixed with curd etc., it becomes rounded itself and is fit for swallowing and this is when [what is] an object is used as an agent."}

{**A. 8.2.45** ***oditaś ca***
[The sound *n* comes in place of the sound *t* of the *niṣṭhā* suffix occurring] after [the verbal roots marked with] *O*.} *This *sūtra* was not commented upon by Patañjali.

A. 8.2.46 ***kṣiyo dīrghāt***
[The sound *n* comes in place of the sound *t* of the *niṣṭhā* suffix occurring] after the long [vowel of the verbal root] *kṣi* ('to decay', DhP I:255).

VMBh_1: III.407.19-22; VMBh_2: V.398.4-7

[Question:] What is the purpose [in using the expression] "after the long [vowel]"?
[Answer:] [The expression] *akṣitam asi mā me kṣeṣṭhāḥ* ("You are uninjured, do not harm me").[334]
[Bhāṣya:] [The expression] "after the long [vowel]" could be omitted.
[Question:] Why does [the substitution] not take place [in the expression] *akṣitam asi mā me kṣeṣṭhāḥ*?
[Answer:] The use of the long [vowel] is evident from the instruction itself. If the short vowel were used, only *kṣeḥ* would be said.

---

[334] TS 1.6.5.1.

{**Explanation:**
The suffix *Kta* added to the verbal stem *kṣi* in the form *akṣitam* has the impersonal meaning (*bhāva*). Substitution takes place in the root *kṣi* before the *niṣṭhā* suffixes *Kta* and *KtavatŪ* when the implied meaning is not the one expressed by the suffix *ṆyaT* (i.e., impersonal (*bhāva*) or passive (*karman*)). In other words the substitution takes place only if the meaning is active (A. 6.4.60[335]).
The argument is raised that the condition "after the long vowel" can be omitted, as it is self-evident from the form *kṣiyaḥ* used in the rule. This is the genitive of the form *ksī* which is formed with the help of the *iyaṄ*-substitute by the *sūtra* A. 6.4.77 *aci śnudhātubhruvāṃ yvor iyaṅuvaṅau.*[336] If the form *kṣi* were meant rather than *kṣī*, the form used in the rule would be *kṣeḥ* where the *iyaṄ*-substitute would be blocked by *guṇa* prescribed by the rule A. 7.3.111 *gher ṅiti*[337] due to it being a later *sūtra*.}

VMBh_1: III.407.22-408.10; VMBh_2: V.398.8-399.4

[Bhāṣya:] Here the instruction cannot be made an authoritative statement; just as the case ending is inapplicable here, in the same way the *iyAṄ*-substitute [is not applicable] either.
[Answer:] The case ending is not inapplicable here. In this case, the case ending is achieved on the basis of [the technical term] *prātipadika*.
[Question:] How is the term *prātipadika* [used here]?
[Answer:] [On the basis of the *sūtra*] A. 1.2.45.
[Objection:] But wouldn't the prohibition "not a verbal root" result?
[Answer:] It (the word *kṣiyaḥ*) is not a verbal root, it is an imitation of a verbal root.
[Objection:] If it is an imitation, the *iyAṄ*-substitute would not result.
[Answer:] The imitation is like the base, thus the *iyAṄ*-substitute will take place.
[Objection:] If it is said that the imitation is like the base, the addition of case endings would not result.
[Bhāṣya:] In such a way then "those [operations] referring to the thing itself with relation to those which have extension as their purpose are not stopped." More-

---

[335] A. 6.4.60 *niṣṭhāyām aṇyadarthe* || ("[A long vowel comes in place of the final vowel of the verbal stem *kṣi* ('to decay', DhP I:255)] before [the suffixes termed] *niṣṭhā* when the meaning is not the one of [the suffix] *ṆyaT*.")

[336] A. 6.4.77 *aci śnudhātubhruvāṃ yvor iyaṅuvaṅau* || ("[The elements] *iyAṄ* and *uvAṄ* come in place of [the vowels] *i* and *u* [respectively] before [the suffix beginning with] a vowel [when they are the final sounds of an *aṅga* stem ending in the infix] *Śnu* or of a verbal root or of [the nominal stem] *bhrū* ('a brow').")

[337] A. 7.3.111 *gher ṅiti* || ("[The substitute *guṇa* vowel comes in place of the final vowel denoted by *iK* (i.e., *i*, *u*, *ṛ* and *ḷ*) of the *aṅga* stem termed] *ghi* before [case endings] marked with *Ṅ*.")

over, it does not happen that "those [operations] referring to the thing itself with relation to those which have extension as their purpose are not stopped", in such a way it is not a fault. It is necessary here in every case that the case ending is mentioned for instruction. For example: A. 1.3.17,[338] A. 1.3.18,[339] A. 1.3.19[340]. Moreover, it is not that "the imitation is like the base", in such a way it is not the fault either. That form of a verbal root which is before a vowel is imitated.

{Explanation:
At this point, the discussion concerns whether the *iyAṄ*-substitute of the vowel in the verbal root *kṣi* for the purpose of the rule could take place at all. If the case ending is not applicable after the verbal root, then the *iyAṄ*-substitute is not either because it depends on the following suffix; if the case ending cannot be added, there is no suffix and hence no *iyAṄ*. So the main question is whether the form *kṣi* should be treated as a verbal root or a nominal stem, for the purpose of the wording of the present *sūtra*. Firstly, it is argued in favour of a nominal stem designation based on A. 1.2.45 *arthavad adhātur apratyayaḥ prātipadikam*,[341] which stresses the meaningful character of a *prātipadika*. This *saṃjñā* rule, however, also specifies that a nominal stem is something other than a verbal stem (*adhātu*). The form *kṣi* could be treated as both a nominal or verbal root, with each solution imposing certain morphological behaviour on the root. A suggestion that *kṣi* is not a verbal root but merely its imitation allows for the abandonment of *iyAṄ*-insertion. However, according to a *paribhaṣā*: *prakṛtivad anukaraṇaṃ bhavati*,[342] an imitation is to be treated as a base (i.e., as the thing to be imitated) which causes another problem, namely, it is impossible to apply any case ending to a verbal root. Kaiyaṭa (VMBh_2: V.398-399) explains that due to the difference in meaning, not in the word-form, between the imitation and the thing to be imitated the extension of an operation is stated. By extension, those rules that apply to the basic form will apply to the imitation as well. Therefore, because the assignment of the term *prātipadika* to the basic form is prohibited, the imitation will not obtain this designation either; hence, the case ending cannot be added.

---

[338] A. 1.3.17 *ner viśaḥ* || ("[The *ātmanepada l*-substitutes] come after [the verbal root] *viśA* ('to enter', DhP VI:130) with [the *upasarga*] *ni*.")

[339] A.1.3.18 *parivyavebhyaḥ kriyaḥ* || ("[The *ātmanepada l*-substitutes] come after [the verbal root] *ḌUkrīÑ* ('to buy', DhP IX:1) with [the *upasargas*] *pari*, *vi* and *ava*.")

[340] A. 1.3.19 *viparābhyāṃ jeḥ* || ("[The *ātmanepada l*-substitutes] come after [the verbal root] *ji* ('to win, conquer', DhP I:593, 993) with [the *upasargas*] *vi* and *parā*.")

[341] A. 1.2.45 *arthavad adhātur apratyayaḥ prātipadikam* ("[The technical term] *prātipadika* denotes a meaningful unit other than a verbal stem or a suffix.")

[342] WUJASTYK 1993: vol. I:78-79, vol. II:256-258; PŚ 36, I.33, II.168-171.

Patañjali says that with respect to those rules whose purpose is extension, the ones referring to the thing itself are not stopped. Kaiyaṭa, however, raises an issue: an operation that refers to the thing itself and is consistent with the operation of extension must not be stopped, so why shouldn't the one that is not consistent be stopped? And what is not consistent is the word being a nominal stem as referring to the thing itself. It is blocked by the negation *adhātu*. This negation could be understood either as exclusion (*paryudāsa*), or prohibition of an application (*prasajya*). If it is exclusion, the term *prātipadika* referring to the thing itself is valid due to it being different from the verbal root, because the operation (i.e., the one that contradicts the word being a nominal stem) applied by extension does not exist. If it were prohibition of an application though, the negation only would apply by extension. And the *iyAṄ*-substitution, applying by extension to the imitation of a verbal root, would take place as it is not contradictory. And this substitution takes place only of a long *ī*, which makes the expression *dīrghāt* unnecessary; the substitution cannot apply to the short vowel *i* because it is blocked by *guṇa* (A. 7.3.111 *gher ṅiti*). Patañjali's conclusion is that a case ending is always necessary; regardless of whether it has been prohibited based on terminological grounds (the stem not being nominal) or whether it has been deleted. The *sūtra*s quoted in the commentary serve as examples that the case ending has the purpose of instruction. In case of the form *ner* (A. 1.3.17 *ner viśaḥ*), it would normally be deleted by A. 2.4.82 *avyayād āpsupaḥ*[343] but the form ends in the ablative to show the technical meaning of ablative 'after'.

The last discussed problem refers to the form *jeḥ* in A. 1.3.19 which is specified with the short vowel *i*, rather than the long one *ī*. The question is where the difference comes from between the forms *kṣiyaḥ* and *jeḥ*; in the latter case we could also use the form *jiyaḥ*. The imitator sometimes imitates the general (as in A. 1.3.19 *viparābhyāṃ jeḥ*) and sometimes the particular (as in A. 1.3.18 *parivyavebhyaḥ kriyaḥ*). The form *jeḥ* refers to the general form *ji*, not to any particular one. Whereas in the case of *kṣi* the general form is *kṣi* being treated as a *dhātu* and *adhātu*; the particular form is just a *dhātu*. So when the general is imitated, the operation having the cause in a particular form (in this case it is the *iyAṄ*-substitute, when the suffix beginning with the vowel follows) does not take place in an imitation due to it being inferred in a context, and due to its lack in the general form. When the particular form is imitated, however, the operation caused by it takes place; if the verb *kṣi* were to be taken in a general meaning, the *iyAṄ*-substitute would not take place. Here it does, but it is still the substitution of the short vowel. So, when we deal with an imitation, we will not get the condition

---

[343] A. 2.4.82 *avyayād āpsupaḥ* || ("[The feminine suffixes covered by] *āP* (i.e., *CāP*, *ṬāP*, *ḌāP*) and case endings [are deleted by *luK*] after the indeclinable [nominal stems].")

dīrghāt ("after a long vowel") without using the word *dīrgha* in the *sūtra* because the suffix *iyAṄ* will come only in place of the short *i*.}

{A. 8.2.47 *śyo 'sparśe*
[The sound *n* comes in place of the sound *t* of the *niṣṭhā* suffix occurring] after [the verbal root] *śyaiṄ* ('to congeal, to freeze', DhP I:1012) when it does not [mean] 'a touch'.} *This *sūtra* was not commented upon by Patañjali.

A. 8.2.48 *añco 'napādāne*
[The sound *n* comes in place of the sound *t* of the *niṣṭhā* suffix occurring] after [the verbal root] *añcU* ('to bend', DhP I:203) when it is not [used] with the ablative.

VMBh_1: III.408.11-18; VMBh_2: V.400.1-8

1) When there is the *n*-substitute [taking place] in [the verbal root] *añcU*, prohibition [should be stated] with respect to [the form] *vyakta*.

[Bhāṣya:] When there is the *n*-substitute [taking place] in [the verbal root] *añcU*, prohibition should be mentioned in the case of [the form] *vyakta*. He says that [the form] *vyakta* is false.

2) It has been achieved by understanding [the verbal root as] *añjŪ* ('to manifest, anoint, decorate, move', DhP VII:21).

[Bhāṣya:] It (i.e., the form *vyakta*) is not the form of [the verbal root] *añc*. It is the form of [the verbal root] *añj*. The meaning of *añcati* is indeed understood.
[Question:] What is, however, the meaning of *añcati*?
[Answer:] [The verb] *añcati* is [used] in the [meaning] of 'illuminating'. [For example,] *añcitaṃ gacchati* ("He is walking giving away the light/showing [himself]"). It is understood as 'he shines/shows himself'.
[Objection:] But among the people [the expression] *añcitaṃ gacchati* is not understood as "[he is walking] shining/showing [himself]".
[Question:] How [is it understood] then?
[Answer:] It is understood as 'with [the mind] focused'. [So,] "he is walking having his mind focused on something".

{**Explanation:**
The verbal root *añcU* (DhP I:203) means both 'to honour' and 'to move'. The form *añcita* can be formed only from the verb with the first meaning, as only

then the nasal *ñ* remains intact, according to A. 6.4.30 *nāñceḥ pūjāyām*.[344] Thus, the meaning would be 'honoured'. The form *añcita* does not emphasise walking; it would be superfluous as when one walks the action of walking is obvious. On the other hand, it means walking 'without trouble, easily'.}

VMBh_1: III.408.18-19; VMBh_2: V.400.8-9

[Objection:] Then in such a way [the word] *aṅka* ('a mark') [is derived] from [the verbal root] *añcati* and 'a mark' is what illuminates/shows. It is said *aṅkitā gāvaḥ* ('marked cows') and they shine among other cows (i.e., differ from other cows).

{**Explanation:**
The word *aṅka* is derived from the verbal root *añcU* with the suffix *GHaÑ* (A. 3.3.121 *halaś ca*[345]) added in the sense of an instrument. Then the *kU*-substitution takes place (A. 7.3.52 *cajoḥ ku ghiṇṇyatoḥ*[346]) replacing the final *c* and the preceding palatal nasal *ñ* becomes a velar *ṅ*. The word means something that helps showing, distinguishing something else. We cannot derive *aṅka* from the verbal root *añjŪ* though, because the result would be *aṅga* where the consonant *g* would replace *j*. The word *aṅkita*, in the example given above by Patañjali, is explained as having the suffix *matUP* that despite being subsequently deleted (A. 5.3.65[347]) left the meaning behind; which is why the form means 'possessed with marks'.}

VMBh_1: III.408.20-409.2; VMBh_2: V.400.10-401.6

3) If it is the meaning of [the verb] *añcati*, it is achieved because of [the verb] *añjŪ* having the same meaning.

[Objection:] If it is the meaning of [the verb] *añcati*, [the verb] *añjŪ* has the meaning of [the verb] *añcati* as well.

---

[344] A. 6.4.30 *nāñceḥ pūjāyām* || ("[The sound *n*] of [the verbal root] *añcU* ('to move, honour', DhP I:203) is not [deleted before the suffixes marked with *K* or *Ṅ* and beginning with a consonant] when [the verbal root denotes] 'honour'.")

[345] A. 3.3.121 *halaś ca* || ("[The suffix *GHaÑ*] comes also after [a verbal root ending in] a consonant [to form a masculine noun denoting a name signifying an instrument or place].")

[346] A. 7.3.52 *cajoḥ ku ghiṇṇyatoḥ* || ("[A sound denoted by] *kU* come in place of [the sounds] *c* or *j* [of an *aṅga* stem] before [the suffixes] marked with *GH* or [the suffix] *ṆyaT*.")

[347] A. 5.3.65 *vinmator luk* || ("[The *taddhita* suffixes] *vin* and *matUP* [introduced after nominal stems and before the *taddhita* suffixes beginning with a vowel (i.e., *iṣṭhaN* and *īyasuN*)] are deleted (by *luK*).")

[Question:] How is it [possible] that a different name is [used] in the meaning of another one? How is it [possible] that [the verb] *añjŪ* [is used] in the meaning of [the verb] *añcati*?
[Answer:] Verbal roots have more than one meaning.
[Question:] Does it appear anywhere else as well that [the verb] *añjŪ* [is used] in the meaning of [the verb] *añcati*?
[Answer:] He said that it does. From [the verbal root] *añjŪ* [we get the word] *añjana* [meaning] 'applying the ointment', and *añjana* [has the same meaning as] *prakāśana* [meaning] 'causing to appear, illuminating'. It is said "she applies an ointment on [her] eyes" and whether it is white or black it illuminates (i.e., makes the eyes visible). In the same way from [the verbal root] *añjŪ* [we get the word] *vyañjana* [meaning] 'manifesting', and *vyañjana* [has the same meaning as] *prakāśana* [meaning] 'causing to appear, illuminating'. Like that which is settled in one's own body by the sweet fondness of confounded senses, that [is called] 'affection' (*rāga*), that is 'manifesting' (*vyañjana*). The derivation is clear then: 'Manifestation' (*vyañjana*) is [that] by which [something] is manifested/shown.

{**Explanation:**
Kaiyaṭa (VMBh_2: V.400) notices a problem; even if the verb *añjati* is used in the same meaning as the verb *añcati*, the form *vyakta* would not be accomplished, only the form *vyakna* (with the *n*-substitute prescribed by the present rule). In such a way, when we say *vyakna*, the meaning 'illuminating' is not understood. The only base for the form *vyakta* is the verb *añjati* used in the meaning of 'illuminating', not the verb *añcati*. Consequently, the prohibition of *n* in the case of the form *vyakta* is necessary; if it were not stated, the form achieved would be *vyakna* and because the meaning 'illuminating' would not be understood, the verb *añc* would not have that meaning either.
The last *vārttika* proposes the unity of meanings of the verbal roots *añc* and *añj* and there are indeed some derivatives where the desired meaning 'illuminating, showing' is read, for example the words *añjana* and *vyañjana*. The unity of meanings is possible because verbal roots are polysemic and can have other meanings from those stated in the *Dhātupāṭha*. The difference in understanding *añjana* and *vyañjana* is that the former is considered conventional and the latter derived.}

{**A. 8.2.49 *divo 'vijigīṣāyām***
[The sound *n* comes in place of the sound *t* of the *niṣṭhā* suffix occurring] after [the verbal root] *divU* ('to play, gamble, praise, pleasure, intoxicate, dream, desire, go', DhP IV:1) when it does not mean 'the desire to conquer'.} *This *sūtra* was not commented upon by Patañjali.

A. 8.2.50 *nirvāṇo 'vāte*

[The sound *n* comes in an irregular way in place of the sound *t* of the *niṣṭhā* suffix occurring after the verbal root *vā* ('to blow, to hurt', DhP II:41) to derive the form] *nirvāṇa* ('calmness, extinguished') when it does not mean 'the wind'.

VMBh_1: III.409.3-6; VMBh_2: V.401.7-402.3

1) When the name is not 'the wind'.

[Bhāṣya:] It should be mentioned that [the substitution takes place] when the name is not 'the wind'. Here then it should be: *nirvāṇo 'gnir vātena* ("The fire has been extinguished by the wind"), *nirvāṇaḥ pradīpo vātena* ("The lamp has been extinguished by the wind").

{**Explanation:**
There are two possible interpretations of substitution negation in the case of the past passive participle of the verb *vā*. Patañjali says that as the wind is the agent of an action of extinguishing, the substitution must not take place; it can take place only when the suffix *niṣṭhā* denotes the state. Consequently, in the example *nirvāto vātaḥ* ('the wind has subsided') the *n*-substitute will not apply. However, the example *nirvāṇo 'gnir vātena* ("The fire has been extinguished by the wind") is possible because here the wind is merely an instrument. According to Kaiyaṭa (VMBh_2: V.402.13), there are some commentators who claim that in both cited examples the substitution should be prohibited. For the *Kāśikāvṛtti* (KV VI.417.1 ff) the key is the locus (*adhikāraṇa*) of the action; in the examples given by Patañjali this place of action is in the lamp and the fire respectively, which allows for the substitution.}

{A. 8.2.51 *śuṣaḥ kaḥ*
[The sound] *k* [comes in place of the sound *t* of the *niṣṭhā* suffix occurring] after [the verbal root] *śuṣA* ('to dry', DhP IV:74).
A. 8.2.52 *paco vaḥ*
[The sound] *v* [comes in place of the sound *t* of the *niṣṭhā* suffix occurring] after [the verbal root] *ḌUpacAṢ* ('to cook', DhP I:1045).
A. 8.2.53 *kṣāyo maḥ*
[The sound] *m* [comes in place of the sound *t* of the *niṣṭhā* suffix occurring] after [the verbal root] *kṣai* ('to burn, catch fire', DhP I:961).
A. 8.2.54 *prastyo 'nyatarsyām*
[The sound *m*] optionally [comes in place of the sound *t* of the *niṣṭhā* suffix occurring] after [the verbal root] *prastyai* ('to sound, to be collected', DhP I:959).} *These *sūtras* were not commented upon by Patañjali.

A. 8.2.55 *anupasargāt phullakṣībakṛśollāghāḥ*
[The forms] *phulla* ('blown, split open'), *kṣība* ('intoxicated, drunk'), *kṛśa* ('lean, thin'), *ullāgha* ('recovered from sickness') [are derived in an irregular way if they] do not [occur] after an *upasarga*.

VMBh_1: III.409.7-13; VMBh_2: V.402.4-10

[Objection:] It is said "[if they] do not [occur] after an *upasarga*", therefore this [form] *parikṛśa* is not accomplished.

a) There is [the suffix] *Ka* prescribed after [the verbal root] *kṛśA* ('to make thin', DhP IV:117) because it has [the sound which is denoted by] *iK* (i.e., *i*, *u*, *ṛ* and *ḷ*) as penultimate.

[Bhāṣya:] This [form *kṛśa*] does not end in [the suffix] *niṣṭhā*.
[Question:] What then?
[Answer:] There is [the suffix] *Ka* prescribed after [the verbal root] *kṛś* because it has [the sound which is denoted by] *iK* (i.e., *i*, *u*, *ṛ* and *ḷ*) as penultimate.

b) But in the case of [the form] *parikṛśa* ('very thin, wasted') there is a problem with accent.

[Objection:] It is not possible. Here then, in the case of [the form] *parikṛśa* ('very thin, wasted'), there would be a fault with accent. The accent would result based on [the *sūtra*s] A. 6.2.143[348] and A. 6.2.144.[349]

{**Explanation:**
There are two ways of deriving the stems *phulla*, *kṣība* and *ullāgha*. They can be formed with the help of the *niṣṭhā* suffix *Kta*. In the case of *kṣība* and *ullāgha* the consonant *t* of the suffix is deleted. The derivation of *phulla* is as follows:

(1) *phal* + *Kta* (A. 1.1.26 *ktaktavatū niṣṭhā*, A. 3.2.102 *niṣṭhā*)
phal + *ta*
(2) *ph* (*a* → *u*) *l* + *ta* (A. 7.4.89 *ti ca*)
(3) *phul* + *la* (A. 8.2.55 *anupasargāt phullakṣībakṛśollāghāḥ*)
phulla

---

348 A. 6.2.143 *antaḥ* || ("[From this *sūtra* up to the end of the *pāda*] the final [syllable of the final member of a compound bears the *udātta* accent].")

349 A. 6.2.144 *thāthaghañktājabitrakāṇām* || ("[The final syllable of the last member of a compound ending in the suffixes] *tha*, *atha*, *GHaÑ*, *Kta*, *aC*, *aP*, *itra* and *Ka* [is *udātta* accented when occurring after a *gati* particle, a *kāraka* or a subordinate word (*upapada*)].")

The *l*-substitution is the irregularity here. This form can be derived from a couple of verbal roots; the above derivation shows *phalA* (DhP I:563) or *ÑIphalA* (DhP I:549) as its base with the necessary substitution of the root vowel *a* by *u*. However, the forms *phulla*, *kṣība* and *ullāgha* can be derived from the verbal roots *phullA* ('to open, spread', DhP I:565), *kṣībR̥* ('to get drunk, DhP I:407) and *lāghR̥* ('to be able to', DhP I:114) respectively by adding the suffic *aC* on the basis of A. 3.1.134 *nandigrahipacādibhyo lyuṇinyacaḥ*.[350] These verbal roots are thought to be part of an open *gaṇa pacādi*. They will not be ending in the suffix *niṣṭhā*. The accent asigned to these stems depends on their derivation. If they are formed with the *niṣṭhā* suffix, they will bear the *udātta* accent on the initial syllable by A. 6.1.205 *niṣṭhā ca dvyaj anāt*[351] (*phúlla*, *kṣī́ba* and *úllāgha*). If, on the other hand, we accept the derivation with the suffix *aC*, they are accented on the final by A. 6.2.144 *thāthaghañktājapitrakāṇām* (*phullá*, *kṣībá* and *ullāghá*).

The word *kr̥śa* can also be derived in two different ways. The verbal root *kr̥śA* (DhP IV:117) can end either in the suffix *Ka* or *Kta*. If it ends in *Ka* prescribed by A. 3.1.135 *igupadhajñāprīkiraḥ kaḥ*,[352] the *sūtra* A. 6.2.144 applies and the derived form *parikr̥śá* is *udātta* accented on the final syllable. If, on the other hand, the verb ends in the suffix *Kta* added in the sense of an object, the *sūtra* A. 6.2.49 *gatir anantaraḥ*[353] applies allowing the retention of original accent, so the derivative is *udātta* accented on the initial syllable (*párikr̥śa*). Moreover, the verbal root *kr̥śA* is explained in the DhP as 'making thin' (*tanūkaraṇa*), which makes it transitive. As such, it can have the suffix *Kta* added in the sense of an object and the rule A. 6.2.49 will apply, and this is the solution Patañjali chooses. Even though it is possible to add the suffix *Kta* in the sense of an agent when we treat the verb *kr̥śA* as intransitive (as in the example *kr̥śo devadattaḥ* – 'thin Devadatta'), this would lead to the undesired application of A. 6.2.144.}

VMBh_1: III.409.14-15; VMBh_2: V.402.11-403.1

c) The thought is that there is the deletion of the word prescribed.

[350] A. 3.1.134 *nandigrahipacādibhyo lyuṇinyacaḥ* || ("[The *kr̥t* suffixes] *Lyu*, *Ṇini* and *aC* [respectively] come after [the verbal roots] *ṬUnadI* ('to be glad, rejoice', DhP I:67) etc., *grahA* ('to seize', DhP IX:61) etc. and *ḌUpacAṢ* ('to cook', DhP I:1045) etc. [to denote the agent].")

[351] A. 6.1.205 *niṣṭhā ca dvyaj anāt* || ("[The initial syllable] of a dissyllabic [nominal stem ending in the suffixes] *niṣṭhā* excluding those with [the vowel] *ā* [being proper names, is *udātta* accented].")

[352] A. 3.1.135 *igupadhajñāprīkiraḥ kaḥ* || ("[The suffix] *Ka* [comes] after [verbal roots that] have [the sound denoted by] *iK* (i.e., *i*, *u*, *r̥* and *l̥*) as their penultimate sound and after [the verbal roots *jñā* ('to know', DhP IX:36), *prīÑ* ('to please', DhP IX:2) and *kr̥̄* ('to scatter', DhP VI:116).")

[353] A. 6.2.49 *gatir anantaraḥ* || ("A *gati* particle [being the first member of a compound retains its original accent before the nominal stem ending in the suffix *Kta* added to denote an object] without intervention.")

[Bhāṣya:] In such a case it should be seen as the deletion of a word. [The word] *parikṛśa* [is derived from the expression] *paryagataḥ kārśyena* [which means] 'pervaded by thinness'.

{**Explanation:**
The main problem with the derivative *parikṛśa* is that it cannot be derived on the basis of the present rule because of the restriction *anupasargāt*. Patañjali explains that the *upasarga pari* does not serve the verbal root *kṛś* but the verbal root *gam* (as in the example mentioned above). Consequently, there is no *upasarga* as such before the word *kṛśa* and accent is established neither by the *sūtra* A. 6.2.144 (because the derivative does not end in the suffix *Ka* but *Kta*) nor by A. 6.2.49 (because there is no *gati* particle). The accent *udātta* on the initial syllable is regulated by A. 6.2.2 *tatpuruṣe tulyārthatṛtīyāsaptamyupamānāvyayadvitīyākṛtyāḥ*.[354]}

VMBh_1: III.409.16-24; VMBh_2: V.403.2-9

d) Everything in the world is shining.

1) It should be added that the *l*-substitute [takes place also] in [the verbal root] *phul* preceded by [the *upasarga*] *ut*.

[Objection:] It should be added that the *l*-substitute [takes place also] in [the verbal root] *phul* preceded by [the *upasarga*] *ut*. [For example:] *utphullo 'nṛtaṃ kathayati* ('The insolent one tells a lie').
[Bhāṣya:] It is too little to say "preceded by [the *upasarga*] *ut*". It should be said that [it refers to the forms both] *utphulla* ('insolent') and *saṃphulla* ('fully blossomed'). [The correct forms are] *utphulla* and *saṃphulla*.

ślokavārttika
There is [the suffix] *Ka* prescribed after [the verbal root] *kṛśA* ('to make thin', DhP IV:117) because it has [a sound which is denoted by] *iK* (i.e., *i*, *u*, *ṛ* and *ḷ*) as penultimate. But in the case of [the form] *parikṛśa* ('very thin, wasted'), there is a problem with accent.
The thought is that there is the deletion of the word prescribed. Everything in the world is shining.

---

354 A. 6.2.2 *tatpuruṣe tulyārthatṛtīyāsaptamyupamānāvyayadvitīyākṛtyāḥ* ‖ ("In a *tatpuruṣa* compound [the prior member retains its original accent] if it consists of synonyms of *tulya* ('similar, comparable') or [ends in] the instrumental or the locative, or [serves as] an object of comparison, is an indeclinable or [ends in] the accusative or is a *kṛtya* [suffix].")

A. 8.2.56 *nudavidondatrāghrāhrībhyo 'nyatarasyām*
[The sound *n*] optionally [comes in place of the sound *t* of the *niṣṭhā* suffix occurring] after [the verbal roots] *nudA* ('to set in motion', DhP VI:2, 132), *vidA* ('to consider', DhP VII:13), *undĪ* ('to make wet', DhP VII:20), *traiṄ* ('to protect', DhP I:1014), *ghrā* ('to smell', DhP I:973) and *hrī* ('to be shy', DhP III:3).

VMBh_1: III.410.1-11; VMBh_2: V.403.10-404.7

[Question:] Is this an operational rule or a prohibition?
[Question:] And what of it?
[Objection:] If it is really an operational rule, the word *na* should be used.
[Answer:] It should not be used. The context continues.
[Question:] Where is the context?
[Answer:] [It is in the rule] A. 8.2.42 *radābhyāṃ niṣṭhāto naḥ pūrvasya ca daḥ.*
[Objection:] But it is not possible to continue that which is separated by many exceptions.
[Answer:] Then it is a prohibition and the word *hrī* is superfluous, hence it is not an operational rule.
[Answer:] Let is be as you want. Let it be an operational rule then.
[Objection:] But has it not been said: "The word *na* should be used. It should not be used. The context continues. Where is the context? [It is in the rule] A. 8.2.42 *radābhyāṃ niṣṭhāto naḥ pūrvasya ca daḥ*. But it is not possible to continue that what is separated by many exceptions."?
[Answer:] The connection will continue. Alternatively, a maxim is created that the instruction consists of a double sound *n*. [Thus the expression should be] *nudavidondatrāghrāhrībhyo 'nyatarasyāṃ nna dhyākhyāpṝmūrchimadām*. Alternatively, let it be again a prohibition.
[Opponent:] But has it not been said: "The word *hrī* is superfluous, therefore it is not an operational rule."?
[Answer:] It is not superfluous. This is what the teacher indicates: because the rule includes the word *hrī*, this is an operational rule.

{**Explanation:**
It is not clear whether the present rule should be treated as an operational rule (*vidhi*) or a prohibition (*pratiṣedha*). All the verbal roots listed here apart from *hrī* had the *n*-substitute prescribed by the previous rule, that is the *sūtras* A. 8.2.42 *radābhyāṃ niṣṭhāto naḥ pūrvasya ca daḥ* and A. 8.2.43 *saṃyogāder āto dhātor yaṇvataḥ*. In their case, the substitution by *n* is made optional, which makes it a *prāptavibhāṣā*, an option of a previously established operation. The verbal root *hrī*, however, requires an operational rule because the sound *n* has not

been prescribed for it before. Therefore, the suggestion is made to supplement the rule with *n*. The expression would read *nudavidondatrāghrāhrībhyo 'nyatarasyāṃ nna dhyākhyāpṝmūrchimadām*; two *sūtra*s would be joined. The purpose of the first *n* would be prescribing the substitution and the second *n* would serve as a negation for the following stems. The conclusion to treat the present rule as operational is based on the conviction that something that has not been applied yet cannot be prohibited. As the root *hrī* was not addressed before, an option becomes *aprāpta*.}

{A. 8.2.57 *na dhyākhyāpṝmūrcchimadām*
[The sound *n*] does not [come in place of the sound *t* of the *niṣṭhā* suffix occurring] after [the verbal roots] *dhyai* ('to concentrate, meditate', DhP I:957), *khyā* ('to relate', DhP II:51), *pṝ* ('to fill', DhP III:4, IX:19), *murcchĀ* ('to solidify, confuse', DhP I:227) and *madĪ* ('to be happy', DhP IV:99).}
*This *sūtra* was not commented upon by Patañjali.

A. 8.2.58 *vitto bhogapratyayayoḥ*
[The word] *vitta* [is formed in an irregular way] when [the meaning is] *bhoga* ('possession, enjoyment') or *pratyaya* ('belief, intellect').

VMBh_1: III.410.12-411.2; VMBh_2: V.404.8-405.5

[Bhāṣya:] There are many [verbs] *vid* taught. With respect to that, it is not known the *n*-substitute of which is obligatory, of which it is optional, of which there is negation and to which there is [the augment] *iṬ* [added]. Therefore he reads what follows:

a) In this [verbal root] *vid* for which the *vikaraṇa*s *ŚnaM* and *Śa* [are prescribed] when [the suffix] *ta* follows meaning *tana* (2nd pl. imp., Vedic), these [*vikaraṇa*s] are optional and prohibited [respectively].

[Bhāṣya:] There is an option regarding the *vikaraṇa ŚnaM* and there is a prohibition regarding the *vikaraṇa Śa*.

b) What regards [the verbal root *vidA* after which] the *vikaraṇa ŚyaN* [is prescribed], the rule [introducing] the *n*-substitute is the same as in the case of [the verbal root] *chidIR* ('to cut, divide', DhP VIII:3).

[Bhāṣya:] What regards [the verbal root *vidA*, after which] the *vikaraṇa ŚyaN* [is prescribed], the rule [introducing] the *n*-substitute is the same as in the case of [the verbal root] *chidIR* ('to cut, divide', DhP VIII:3).

c) The *vikaraṇa* is thrown away by *luK* before [a suffix] beginning with [a sound denoted by] *vaL* (i.e., all consonants except the semivowel *y*).

[Bhāṣya:] [The verbal root] *vid* has the *vikaraṇa* deleted by *luK* before [a suffix] beginning with [a sound denoted by] *vaL* (i.e., all consonants except the semivowel *y*).

This is the meaning:
In those two [verbal roots] *vid* for which [the *vikaraṇa*s] *ŚnaM* and *Śa* are taught, the *n*-substitute is optional and prohibited respectively.
But in those, for which [the *vikaraṇa*] *ŚyaN* or the deletion by *luK* [are prescribed], [the behaviour] like with [the verbal root] *chid* and [the augment] *iṬ* is required.

The other one has said:
Of [the verb] *vetti* ('he knows', 2nd class) the passive participle is *vidita* (with the infix *iṬ*), of [the verb] *vidyate* ('he is, exists', 4th class) [the passive participle] *vinna* is required.
Of [the verb] *vinatti* ('he considers', 7th class)[355] [there are two forms of the passive participle] *vinna* and *vitta*, and [the form] *vitta* [is required for the verb] *vindati* ('he gains', 6th class) when [the meaning is] 'gaining, possessing'.

{**Explanation:**
The verbal root *vid* appears in the *Dhātupāṭha* in two forms – *vidA* and *vidḶ* – and with different meanings: 'to understand, to communicate, to live' (DhP X:168), 'to know' (DhP II:55), 'to reflect, consider' (DhP VII:13), 'to be' (DhP IV:62) and *vidḶ* ('to gain', DhP VI:138). As it belongs to different conjugational groups, when the suffix *niṣṭhā* is added, the forms are different. The first part of the *ślokavārttika* mentions two of them, i.e., *vidA* – 'to reflect, consider' of the 7th class, to which the *vikaraṇa ŚnaM* is added and *vidḶ* – 'to gain' of the 6th class, to which the *vikaraṇa Śa* is added. In the former case the *n*-substitute is optional and in the latter it is prohibited. This last case is the purpose of the present rule, which specifies the meaning of the form *vitta*; in any other meaning the passive past participle will be *vinna* by A. 8.2.42 *radābhyāṃ niṣṭhāto naḥ pūrvasya ca daḥ*.

[355] In the *śloka* we find the form *vintteḥ* in the genitive which should be *vinatteḥ*, but Kaiyaṭa explains that the form used is the imitation of a verbal form. The 1st sg. *ātmanepada* of present tense is in this case *vintte* and the stem of this form (*vint*) was used to create the form *vintti* (by adding the syllable *ti* which is often used to denote the root or grammatical operations). Therefore the form in the genitive – *vintteḥ*.

In the case of the verbal root *vidA* of the 4th class to which the *vikaraṇa ŚyaN* is added, the form of the past passive participle is the same as in the case of the verb *chid*, that is, the *n*-substitute applies. Hence, the form is *vinna*. The last analysed verb in the *ślokavārttika* is *vidA* of the 2nd class (meaning 'to know') where the *vikaraṇa* is deleted by A. 2.4.72 *adiprabhṛtibhyaḥ śapaḥ*, and after which the augment *iṬ* is added by A. 7.2.35 *ārdhadhātukasyeḍ valādeḥ* accomplishing the final form *vidita*.}

A. 8.2.59 *bhittaṃ śakalam*
[The word] *bhitta* [is formed in an irregular way] when [the meaning is] *śakala* ('a chop, piece').

VMBh_1: III.411.3-6; VMBh_2: V.405.6-406.2

[Objection:] It is said: "[The word] *bhitta* [is formed in an irregular way] when [the meaning is] *śakala* ('a chop, piece')". With respect to that, [the following expression] would not result: *bhittaṃ bhinnam* ('a broken piece').
[Answer:] That is not a fault. For here in every case [the verbal root] *bhidIR* ('to cut, divide', DhP VII:2) is used in general meaning of 'splitting', the qualifier should certainly be additionally employed with the meaning of difference. Broken (*bhinna*). What [is broken]? A piece (*bhitta*).

{**Explanation:**
According to Kaiyaṭa (VMBh_2: V.406.8-9), the prohibition should be stated altogether because the word also occurs in the meaning of 'a piece'. Therefore, the expression should be *bhittaṃ bhittam* and not *bhittaṃ bhinnam*. However, in the expression *bhittaṃ bhinnam* the latter word expresses the general (*bhinna*), common notion of the action of 'splitting' and the former expresses the particular (*bhitta*); thus, it is possible to use them together. It is also possible to say *bhinnaṃ śakalam* and *bhinno ghaṭaḥ* ('a broken piece' and 'a broken jar' respectively). Therefore, they do not mean the same thing but stand in the 'general-particular' relation.}

VMBh_1: III.411.7-8; VMBh_2: V.406.3-4

[Bhāṣya:] Let us sum up: if [the word] *bhitta* is the expressive one, the use of [the word] *śakala* would be superfluous. And if [the same] has been expressed by [the word] *śakala*, there would be no *bhitta* – this is what we conclude.

{**Explanation:**

The words *bhitta* and *śakala* are considered synonymous, which means that the stem *bhitta* can be used only in the meaning of 'a piece'. Consequently, we can use one or the other, and the expression *bhittaṃ śakalam* is not possible.}

{A. 8.2.60 *ṛṇam ādhamarṇye*
[The word] *ṛṇa* [is formed in an irregular way] when [the meaning is] *ādhamarṇya* ('the state of being a debtor').
A. 8.2.61 *nasattaniṣattānuttapratūrttasūrtagūrtāni chandasi*
[The words] *nasatta* ('not seated'), *niṣatta* ('seated'), *anutta* ('not cast down'), *pratūrtta* ('quick'), *sūrta* ('trodden') and *gūrta* ('approved') [are formed in an irregular way] in Vedic literature.[356]} *These *sūtra*s were not commented upon by Patañjali.

A. 8.2.62 *kvinpratyayasya kuḥ*
[A sound belonging to the group] *kU* (i.e., velar sounds) comes in place of [the final element of a *pada* ending] in a suffix *KvIN*.

VMBh_1: III.411.9-12; VMBh_2: V.406.5-407.1

[Question:] What is the purpose in the word *pratyaya* ('suffix')? Why is it not said *kvinaḥ kuḥ* only?
[Answer:] When only so much is said – *kvinaḥ kuḥ*, the *kU*-substitute of the sound *v* only would result.
[Objection:] But will it not happen when the deletion is done? The *kU*-substitute, having no scope of application, would block the deletion.

{Explanation:
The substituend in the present rule seems problematic: should it be the final sound of a *pada* preceding the suffix *KviN* or the sound *v* of the suffix itself. Normally, the suffix would be deleted by A. 6.1.67 *ver apṛktasya* but the *kU*-substitute might be treated as an exception, and then it would prevail over the deletion. On the other hand, the deletion is an internally conditioned operation (because it depends only on the suffix), whereas the substitution is externally conditioned (because the present *sūtra* belongs to the *Tripādī* section). Yet, the deletion has the scope of application with regard to other suffixes as well, for example *KviP*. The *kU*-substitute, on the other hand, has been prescribed precisely for this particular situation. So if it did not apply here, it could have no scope of application whatsoever.

---

[356] Kobayashi in his article states that there is no such form as *nasatta* in Vedic literature. However, the form *na satta* appears. He quotes Knobl's suggestion that it could be a negative *sūtra* prohibiting the *n*-substitute in the stems mentioned. See KOBAYASHI 2006:6 with fn. 9.

The expression *kvinpratyayasya* should be treated as a *bahuvrīhi* compound and should refer to a verbal root; it would mean a stem that ends in the suffix *KviN*. Hence, the *kU*-substitute should apply to the end of a verbal root to which the suffix *KviN* is added and not in the suffix itself.}

VMBh_1: III.411.12-13; VMBh_2: V.407.1-2

[Answer:] The *kU*-substitute has the scope of application.
[Question:] What is its scope of application?
[Answer:] It does not refer to the final.
[Question:] How [is it possible that] when it is the final, the *kU*-substitute should not replace the final?

{**Explanation:**
An additional rule that should be taken into consideration in this case is A. 8.1.16 *padasya* and the interpretation of the genitive form; it could be understood as the *sthānaṣaṣṭhī* (meaning 'in place of') or the *avayavaṣaṣṭhī* ('being a part of'). According to the former interpretation, the *kU*-substitute will take place of the last sound of a *pada*. According to the latter though, it would take place of any sound being a part of a *pada*. This would lead to the incorrect *k*-substitute of *ś* in *ghṛtaspṛśā* ('by touching clarified butter', instr. sg.). So the conclusion is that the substitution prescribed by the present rule is to refer not of the last sound (which would be *v* of the suffix *KviN*) but the last sound of a *pada*. The example can be the following:

(1) *ghṛta* + *am* + *spṛśA* (DhP VI:128) + *KviN* + *sU* (A. 3.2.58 *spṛśo 'nudake kvin*, A. 4.1.2 *svaujasamauṭśasṭābhyāmbhisṅebhyāmbhyasṅasibhyāmbhyasṅas-osāmṅyossup*)
(2) *ghṛta* + *am* + *spṛś* + 0 + *s* (A. 6.1.67 *ver apṛktasya*, A. 1.2.41 *apṛkta ekāl pratyayaḥ*)
(3) *ghṛta* + 0 + *spṛś* + *s* (A. 2.4.71 *supo dhātuprātipadikayoḥ*)
(4) *ghṛta-spṛś* + (*s* → 0) (A. 6.1.68 *halṅyābbhyo dīrghāt sutisy apṛktam hal*)
(5) *ghṛta-spṛ* (*ś* → *k*) (A. 8.2.62 *kvinpratyayasya kuḥ*)
ghṛtaspṛk}

VMBh_1: III.411.13-16; VMBh_2: V.407.2-6

[Answer:] The teacher's use indicates that the *kU*-substitute does not replace the final because [the expression "there is the substitution] of [the suffix] *KvIN* by [a sound belonging to the group] *kU*" makes the instruction about the *k*-class. Because otherwise, it would indicate only its quality. Therefore, this is the purpose: in those [verbal roots] after which the suffix *KvIN* is prescribed, and also in those ending in another suffix, the *kU*-substitute should take place at the end of a *pada*. [For example,] *mā no asrāk* and *mā no adrāk* ("Do not let us go"[357] and "Do not look at us" respectively).

{**Explanation:**
The wording of the *sūtra* itself shows that the substitution cannot regard the sound *v* of the suffix *KviN*. Pāṇini specifies the *k*-class (*ka-varga*) as a substitute, which means that there is more that one substitute replacing more than one substituend. If the consonant *v* were supposed to be the only substituend, the replacement would only refer to *gh* as they share the same phonetic qualities. This is why it is agreed that the expression *kvinpratyaya* refers to such a verbal root which ends in *KviN* (or other suffixes such as *KviP* etc.), and not the suffix itself and substitution regards the final sound of a *pada* being such a verbal root:

(1) *sṛjA* (DhP VI:121) + *lUṄ* (A. 3.3.175 *māṅi luṅ*)
(2) *sṛj* + tiP (A. 3.4.78 *tiptasjhisipthasthamibvasmastātāṃjhathāsāthāmdhvamiḍvahimahiṅ*)
(3) *aṬ* + *sṛj* + *Cli* + *ti* (A. 6.4.71 *luṅlaṅlṛṅkṣv aḍudāttaḥ*, A. 3.1.43 *cli luṅi*)
(4) *a* + *sṛj* + *sIC* + *ti* (A. 3.1.44 *cleḥ sic*)
(5) *a* + *sṛ* + *aM* + *j* + *ti* (A. 6.1.58 *sṛjidṛśor jhaly am akiti*)
(6) *a* + *s* (*ṛ* → *r*) + *aj* + *ti* (A. 6.1.77 *iko yaṇ aci*)
(7) *a* + *sr* + (*a* → *ā*) *j* + *ti* (A. 7.2.3 *vadavrajahalantasyācaḥ*)
(8) *a* + *sr* + *āj* + 0 (A. 6.1.68 *halṅyābbhyo dīrghāt sutisy apṛktam hal*)
(9) *a* + *sr* + *ā* (*j* → *g*) (A. 8.2.62 *kvinpratyayasya kuḥ*)
(10) *a* + *sr* + *ā* (*g* → *k*) (A. 8.4.56 *vāvasāne*)
asrāk

Kaiyaṭa (VMBh_2: V.407) points out that the consonant *j* could be replaced by *ṣ* based on A. 8.2.36 *vraścabhraśjasṛjamṛjayajarājabhrājacchaśāṃ ṣaḥ*, but as A. 8.2.62 is considered an exception to A. 8.2.36, despite its posteriority, it takes precendence.}

VMBh_1: III.411.17-18; VMBh_2: V.407.7-8

Śloka:
The word *pratyaya* is used when [the expression "the sounds belonging to the group] *kU* come in place of *KvIN*."
The *kU*-substitute is required everywhere (i.e., also when another suffix follows, like *KviP* etc.) at the end of a *pada* of [the verbal root ending in] the suffix *KvIN*.

---

357 AV 11.2.19; the direct quote is *mā no 'bhi srāḥ*.

{A. 8.2.63 *naśor vā*
[A sound belonging to the group *kU* (i.e., the velar consonants)] usually comes in place of [the final sound of the verbal root forming a *pada*] *ṇaśA* ('to perish', DhP IV:85).
A. 8.2.64 *mo no dhātoḥ*
[The sound] *n* comes in place of *m* [being the final sound of] a verbal root [forming a *pada*].
A. 8.2.65 *mvoś ca*
[The sound *n*] also [comes in place of *m* being the final sound of a verbal root forming a *pada*] before [the suffixes] beginning with [the sounds] *m* or *v*.
A. 8.2.66 *sasajuṣo ruḥ*
[The sound] *rU* comes in place of [the final sound] *s* [of a *pada*] and [the final sound *ṣ*] of [the word] *sajuṣ* ('a companion').
A. 8.2.67 *avayāḥ śvetavāḥ puroḍāś ca*
[The words] *avayāḥ* ('those who share ritual oblations'), *śvetavāḥ* ('borne by white horses'), *puroḍāḥ* ('a ritual oblation with rice balls') [are formed in an irregular way with the *rU*-substitute of the final sound].} *These *sūtra*s were not commented upon by Patañjali.

A. 8.2.68 *ahan*
[The sound *rU* comes in place of the final sound of a *pada*] *ahan* ('a day').

VMBh_1: III.411.19-22; VMBh_2: V.408.1-4

1) An addition [should be made] that in the case of the rule prescribing the *rU*-substitute, [substitution also regards the final sound] of [a *pada*] *ahan* ('a day') before [the words] *rūpa* ('a form'), *rātri* ('a night') and *rathaṃtara* ('a better chariot, a type of hymn *sāman*').

[Bhāṣya:] An addition should be made that in the case of the rule prescribing the *rU*-substitute, [substitution also regards the final sound] of [a *pada*] *ahan* ('a day') before [the words] *rūpa* ('a form'), *rātri* ('a night') and *rathaṃtara* ('a better chariot, a type of hymn *sāman*'). [For example:] *ahorūpam* ('a form of a day'), *ahorātraḥ* ('a day and night'), *ahorathaṃtaraṃ sāma* (a type of *sāman* called *ahorathaṃtara*).

{Explanation:
This *vārttika* is an exception to A. 8.2.69 prescribing the *r*-substitute of the final *n* in *ahan* when the case ending does not follow. What we need in this case is the *rU*-substitution to be able to achieve the vowel *o* in examples such as *ahobhis* ('with/by the days', instr. pl.).

(1) *ahan* + *bhis* (A. 4.1.2 *svaujasamauṭśasṭābhyāmbhisṅebhyāmbhyasṅasi-bhyāmbhyasṅasosāmṅyossup*)
(2) *aha* (*n* → *rU*) + *bhis* (A. 8.2.68 *ahan*)
(3) *aha* (*r* → *u*) + *bhis* (A. 6.1.114 *haśi ca*)
(4) *ah* (*a* + *u* → *o*) + *bhis* (A. 6.1.87 *ād guṇaḥ*)
ahobhis

The *rU*-substitute applies not only in suggested compounds but also when *ahan* is uncompounded. The following case ending is deleted by A. 2.4.71 *supo dhātu-prātipadikayoḥ* in the case of a compound or A 7.1.23 *svamor napuṃsakāt* when there is no formation. As both these deletions are done via *luK*, the rule A. 1.1.62 *pratyayalope pratyayalakṣaṇam*, allowing for the retention of an operation conditioned by a suffix despite its absence, does not apply. This is strengthened by the vārttika 5 on A. 1.1.63 *na lumatāṅgasya*,[358] which specifies the *rU*-substitution in particular (*ahno ruvidhau*).
Analysing the form *ahorātra* ('day and night') with the words *ahan* and *rātri* compounded we delete the vowel *i* by the *sūtra* A. 6.4.148 *yasyeti ca* but the form changed in one part is still treated as the original.[359] Then the *samāsānta* suffix is added. According to Nāgeśa (VMBh_2: V.408) and Nārāyaṇa (MPV X.398) following him, it is the suffix *ṬaC* (A. 5.4.91 *rājāhaḥsakhibhyaṣ ṭac*[360]). According to Annaṃbhaṭṭa (MPV X.398), it is the suffix *aC* (A. 5.4.87 *ahaḥ-sarvaikadeśasaṃkhyātapuṇyāc ca rātreḥ*[361]). It seems that the latter is correct because the suffix *ṬaC* is added when the word *ahan* appears at the end of a compound. Therefore we have obtained:

(1) *ahan* + *sU* + *rātri* (A. 4.1.2 *svaujasamauṭśasṭābhyāmbhisṅebhyāmbhyas-ṅasibhyāmbhyasṅasosāmṅyossup*)
(2) *ahan* + 0 + *rātri* (A. 2.4.71 *supo dhātuprātipadikayoḥ*)
(3) *ahan* + *rātr* (*i* → 0) (A. 6.4.148 *yasyeti ca*)
(4) *aha* (*n* → *rU*) + *rātr* (A. 8.2.68 *ahan*)

---

358 A. 1.1.63 *na lumatāṅgasya* || ("[When the deletion of a suffix is conditioned] by [the use of technical terms] containing *lu* (i.e., *luK*, *Ślu* or *luP*, [operations conditioned by this suffix] on the *aṅga* stem do not take place.")

359 PŚ 37 *ekadeśavikṛtam ananyavat* || ("That [element] which has undergone a change in one of its parts is like nothing else [but this very element].")

360 A. 5.4.91 *rājāhaḥsakhibhyaṣ ṭac* || ("[The *taddhita samāsānta* suffix] *ṬaC* is introduced after [the nominal stems] *rājan* ('a king'), *ahan* ('a day') and *sakhi* ('a friend') [occurring at the end of a compound].")

361 A. 5.4.87 *ahansarvaikadeśasaṃkhyātapuṇyāc ca rātreḥ* || ("[The *taddhita samāsānta* suffix *aC*] comes after [the nominal stem] *rātri* ('a night') preceded by *ahan* ('a day'), *sarva* ('whole, all'), [expressions signifying] *ekadeśa* ('a portion'), *saṃkhyāta* ('counted') and *puṇya* ('auspicious') as well as [with numerals and indeclinables in a *tatpuruṣa* compound].")

(5) *ahar* + *rātr* + *aC* (A. 5.4.87 *ahaḥsarvaikadeśasaṃkhyātapuṇyāc ca rātreḥ*)
ahar + *rātra*
(6) *aha* (*r* → *u*) + *rātra* (A. 6.1.114 *haśi ca*)
(7) *ah* (*a* + *u* → *o*) + *rātra* (A. 6.1.87 *ād guṇaḥ*)
ahorātra.}

A. 8.2.69 *ro 'supi*
[The sound] *r* [comes in place of the final sound of a *pada ahan* ('a day')] when not before [case endings] *sUP*.

VMBh_1: III.412.1-4; VMBh_2: V.408.5-8

1) There is the prohibition of the *r*-substitute when not before [case endings] *sUP* in the case of a compound with a subordinate word (*upasarjana*), when [case endings] are not deleted by *luK*.

[Bhāṣya:] It should be mentioned that there is the prohibition of the *r*-substitute when not before [case endings] *sUP* in the case of a compound with a subordinate word (*upasarjana*), when [case endings] are not deleted by *luK*. [For example:] *dīrghāhā nidāghaḥ* ('summer when days are long').

{Explanation:
The derivation of the example *dīrghāhā nidāghaḥ* is as follows:

(1) *dīrghāhan* + *sU* + *nidāghaḥ* (A. 4.1.2 *svaujasamauṭśasṭābhyāmbhisṅebhyāmbhyasṅasibhyāmbhyasṅasosāmṅyossup*)
(2) *dīrghāhan* + 0 + *nidāghaḥ* (A. 6.1.68 *halṅyābbhyo dīrghāt sutisy apṛktam hal*)
(3) *dīrghāha* (*n* → *rU*) + *nidāghaḥ* (A. 8.2.68 *ahan*)
(4) *dīrghāh* (*a* → *ā*) *r* + *nidāghaḥ* (A. 6.4.8 *sarvanāmasthāne cāsambuddhau*)
(5) *dīrghāhā* (*r* → *y*) + *nidāghaḥ* (A. 8.3.17 *bhobhagoaghoapūrvasya yo 'śi*)
(6) *dīrghāhā* (*y* → 0) + *nidāghaḥ* (A. 8.3.22 *hali sarveṣām*)
dīrghāhā nidāghaḥ

There are two possibilities when interpreting the prohibition *asupi*. It can be a *paryudāsa* prohibition (the rule applies when not a *sUP* but anything similar to *sUP* follows) or a *prasajya* prohibition (the rule applies when anything other than *sUP* follows). According to the former, we would obtain the *r*-substitute of *n* in *ahan* in the example mentioned above because the case ending is deleted, but it is still visible on the basis of the *sūtra* A. 1.1.62 *pratyayalope pratyayalakṣaṇam* because the deletion is obtained with the help of general *lopa*. As this is not a desired outcome, we should treat the expression *asupi* as *prasajyapratiṣedha*. What

we need, is the *rU*-substitution, which is further replaced by, subsequently deleted, *y* (due to the connection with a following word). Otherwise, we could obtain the *u*-substitute (A. 6.1.114 *haśi ca*), which is not possible because it requires a non-prolated penultimate vowel. As can be seen from the example, the penultimate vowel in the word *dīrghāhan* was substituted by its longer counterpart (A. 6.4.8), which eliminated the conditions for A. 6.1.114 to apply. This substitution was possible only because *rU* is treated as suspended with respect to A. 6.4.8.
Annaṃbhaṭṭa (MPV X.394) explains the necessity of the expression *aluki* in the *vārttika*. In the case of the single word *ahan* the deletion of the case ending takes place on the basis of A. 7.1.23 *svamor napuṃsakāt* because the word is neuter. However, the word *dīrghāhan* is not neuter but masculine in gender (because it serves as a *bahuvrīhi* compound describing the stem *nidāghaḥ*) and therefore the deletion takes place on the basis of A. 6.1.68 (by the general term *lopa*). It results in A. 1.1.62 (*pratyayalope pratyayalakṣaṇam*) being applicable and consequently, an operation conditioned by a suffix that was deleted takes place as if it was still there. Due to the condition of the present rule requiring no case ending after the word, the prohibition must be stated.}

VMBh_1: III.412.5-7; VMBh_2: V.409.1-3

2) But it (i.e., the prohibition) has been achieved from the prohibition *asUPi* ("before [suffixes] *sUP*").

[Objection:] It has been achieved.
[Question:] How?
[Answer:] From the prohibition *asUPi*. This is the prohibition of possible application of the rule (*prasajyapratiṣedha*); [the substitution] does not [take place] before [suffixes] *sUP*.
[Objection:] Here therefore, it (i.e., the substitution) would not result either: *ahar dadāti* ('a day gives'), *ahar bhuṅkte* ('he enjoys the day').

{**Explanation:**
In the examples *ahar dadāti* ('a day gives'), *ahar bhuṅkte* ('he enjoys the day') the *r*-substitute could not be accomplished by the present *sūtra* because the deleted case ending would still be operative on the basis of A. 1.1.62 *pratyayalope pratyayalakṣaṇam*. It is not the case though, because the deletion of the case ending takes place on the basis of A. 7.1.23 *svamor napuṃsakāt*, which is a *luK* deletion, hence A. 1.1.62 does not apply.}

VMBh_1: III.412.8-9; VMBh_2: V.409.4-5

3) And it has been said "before the *luK*-deletion".

[Question:] What has been said?
[Answer:] "In the case of the rule prescribing the *r*-substitute after [the *pada*] *ahan* ('a day'), when [the suffix] has been deleted by [the technical term] containing [the element] *lu*, rule A. 1.1.62 does not apply."[362]

A. 8.2.70 *amnarūdharavarity ubhayathā chandasi*
[There is the substitution of the final sound of *padas*] *amnas* ('unawares'), *ūdhas* ('an udder') and *avas* ('downwards') in both ways [by *r* or *rU*] in Vedic literature.

VMBh_1: III.412.10-13; VMBh_2: V.409.6-9

1) It should be added that in Vedic literature and common language [there is the substitution in both ways] in [the word] *pracetas* ('clever, wise') before [the word] *rājan* ('a king').

[Bhāṣya:] It should be added that in Vedic and common language [there is the substitution in both ways] in [the word] *pracetas* ('clever, wise') before [the word] *rājan* ('a king'). [For example:] *praceto rājan* or *pracetā rājan* ('a wise king').

{**Explanation:**
The respective derivations are as follows:
A.
(1) *pracetas* + *rājan*
(2) *praceta* (*s* → *rU*) + *rājan*
(3) *praceta* (*r* → *u*) + *rājan* (A. 6.1.114 *haśi ca*)
(4) *pracet* (*a* + *u* → *o*) + *rājan* (A. A. 6.1.87 *ād guṇaḥ*)
praceto rājan

B.
(1) *pracetas* + *rājan*
(2) *praceta* (*s* → *r*) + *rājan*
(3) *praceta* (*r* → 0) + *rājan* (A. 8.3.14 *ro ri*)
(4) *pracet* (*a* → *ā*) + *rājan* (A. 6.3.111 *ḍhralope pūrvasya dīrgho 'ṇaḥ*)
pracetā rājan.

[362] A. 1.1.63 *vārttika* 5.

A. 8.3.14 is not considered suspended with respect to A. 6.3.111 because the latter explicitly mentions the deletion of *r* and is consequently dependent on the application of A. 8.3.14.}

VMBh_1: III.412.14-15; VMBh_2: V.409.10-13

[Bhāṣya:] It should be added that [there is the substitution in both ways] in [the words] *ahar* etc. followed by *pati* ('lord') etc.[363] [For example:] *aharpatiḥ* or *ahaḥpatiḥ* ('lord of the day, the sun'), *aharputraḥ* or *ahaḥputraḥ* ('the son of the day'), *gīrpatiḥ* or *gīḥpatiḥ* ('a learned man').

{**Explanation:**
It should be noted that the above passage already mentions the form *ahar*, after substitution has taken place. Naturally, the question arises why the *vārttika* prescribes the consonant *r* in place of the *r*-substitute. As Kaiyaṭa (VMBh_2: V.409.21) and others say, it is to block the *visarjanīya*, which would otherwise be the only option.
A.
(1) *aharU + pati*
(2) *ahar + pati*
aharpati
B.
(1) *aharU + pati*
(2) *aha (rU → r) + pati* (by this *vārttika*, this *r* is the same as in the rule A. 8.2.69)
(3) *aha (r → ḥ) + pati* (A. 8.3.15 *kharavasānayor visarjanīyaḥ*)[364]
ahaḥpati
In the first example we cannot obtain the *u*-substitute of *r* by A. 6.1.114 *haśi ca* because *p* is not included in the *haŚ* abbreviation; it is not a voiced consonant.}

{**A. 8.2.71 *bhuvaś ca mahāvyāhṛteḥ***
[There is] also [the substitution of the final sound of a *pada*] *bhuvas* ('air') [in both ways (by *r* or *rU*) in Vedic language] when the meaning is the name of the magical formula (*mahāvyāhṛti*).} *This *sūtra* was not commented upon by Patañjali.

A. 8.2.72 *vasusraṃsudhvaṃsvanaḍuhāṃ daḥ*

---

[363] VMBh_2 makes this statement a *vārttika*.

[364] This *visarjanīya* can be further replaced by *ẖ* (*upadhmānīya*) by A. 8.3.37 *kupvoḥ ẖkẖpau ca* before the following sound *p*. It is also pointed out in the VMBh_2 edition.

[The sound] *d* comes in place of [the final sound *s*] of [the *pada*s ending in] *vasU*, *sraṃsU*, *dhvaṃsU* and of [the *pada*] *anaḍuh* ('an ox, bull').

VMBh_1: III.412.16-22; VMBh_2: V.409.14-410.5

[Question:] Why does it not happen in these cases: *papivān* and *tasthivān* (nom. sg. masc. of *papivas* and *tasthivas* respectively)? [The expression] "of *s*" [from the *sūtra* A. 8.2.66] continues [here] and in such a way it would result here as well. When the deletion has been done, [the substitution] will not take place.
[Answer:] The *d*-substitute, having no scope of application, would block the deletion.
[Bhāṣya:] The *d*-substitute has its scope of application.
[Question:] What is its scope of application?
[Answer:] [For example:] *papidbhyām* and *papidbhiḥ* (instr./dat./abl. du. and instr. pl. respectively of the form *papivas*).
[Objection:] Here *rU* could result as well. Just as it (i.e., the *d*-substitute) would block *rU*, in the same way it would block the deletion.
[Answer:] It does not block [the deletion].
[Question:] What is the reason?
[Answer:] Because the [rule which is introduced] when another necessarily applies, blocks [the one that necessarily applies], and when the *rU*-substitute necessarily applies, the *d*-substitute takes place [instead]. In the case of deletion, however, [the *d*-substitute has its scope of application] whether [deletion] applied or not.[365]

{Explanation
The above discussion refers to potentially conflicting rules applicable during the formation of *papivān* and *tasthivān*. To focus on the stages of the derivation that regard the present rule I will start from the level *papivas* and omit the derivation from the verb *pā* ('to drink'):

(1) *papivas* + *sU* (A. 4.1.2 *svaujasamauṭśasṭābhyāmbhisṅebhyāmbhyasṅasibhyāmbhyasṅasosāmṅyossup*)
(2) *papiva* + *nUM* + *s* + *s* (A. 7.1.70 *ugidacāṃ sarvanāmasthāne 'dhātoḥ*)
papiva + *n* + *s* + *s*
(3) *papiv* (*a* → *ā*) *ns* + *s* (A. 6.4.14 *atvasantasya cādhātoḥ*)
(4) *papivāns* + (*s* → 0) (A. 6.1.68 *halṅyābbhyo dīrghāt sutisy apṛktam hal*)
(5) *papivān* + (*s* → 0) (A. 8.2.23 *saṃyogāntasya lopaḥ*)
papivān

[365] See WUJASTYK 1993: vol. I:46-48, vol. II:163-165.

The problem raised in the above discussion is whether the sound *s* continues from the *sūtra* A. 8.2.66 *sasajuṣo ruḥ* or not. If it did not continue, at the stage (2) of derivation, that is, *papivanss* the *sūtra* A. 6.1.68 would apply deleting the final *s*, followed by A. 8.2.23 *saṃyogāntasya lopaḥ* deleting the final of a cluster (also the sound *s*), and finally *d* would replace *n*. As this rule application does not lead us to the correct result, it is accepted that an element of A. 8.2.66 is also read in the present *sūtra*. Commentators point out that deletion is prescribed by an earlier rule, therefore the *d*-substitution might take place anyway. However, because both of the *sūtra*s belong to the *Tripādī* section, substitution is suspended with respect to deletion. Thus, if *s* continues in the present rule, after the deletion has been performed, the conditions for the *d*-substitution are not met as the stem ends in *n*, not *s*. The suggested notion that the *d*-substitution has no scope of application because its scope is fully covered by other rules and other applications, namely the deletion or the *rU*-substitute, is also rejected. The *d*-substitute has to block the *rU*-substitute because otherwise the present rule would be superfluous; it does not, however, block deletion.}

VMBh_1: III.412.22-413.1; VMBh_2: V.410.6-7

[Objection:] If therefore [the expression] "of *s*" [from the *sūtra* A. 8.2.66] continues [here, the forms] *anaḍudbhyām* and *anaḍudbhiḥ* (instr./dat./abl. du. and instr. pl. respectively of the form *anaḍuh* 'an ox') would not result.
[Answer:] [The substitution] will take place in the case of [the word] *anaḍuh* on the basis of the rule itself.

{**Explanation:**
The expression "of *s*" continued in the present rule serves as a qualifier; it cannot, however, serve as a qualifier to all the words and forms mentioned. The commentators refer here to *sambhava* ('possibility') and *vyabhicāra* ('possibility of absence'). In the case of words ending in the suffix *vasU*, it is possible that the form will end in *s* as well as that it will not. Therefore, *s* can be the qualifier to the suffix *vasU*. On the other hand, it cannot be one with respect to the suffixes *sraṃsU* and *dhvaṃsU* because the consonant *s* is always there; it is not possible for it to disappear. It does not qualify the word *anaḍuh* either.}

VMBh_1: III.413.2-10; VMBh_2: V.410.8-15

[Objection:] If so…

1) [There is] prohibition of [substitution of] the sound *n* in the case of the *d*-substitute in [the word] *anaḍuh*.

[Objection:] Prohibition should be mentioned of the sound *n* in case of the *ḍ*-substitute in [the word] *anaḍuh*. [For example,] *anaḍvān* ('an ox', nom. sg.).

2) But it has been accomplished by ordaining [the infix] *nUM* after a nominal stem.

[Answer:] It has been accomplished.
[Question:] How?
[Answer:] From [the infix] *nUM* (A. 7.1.82 *sav anaḍuhaḥ*) by force of ordaining it after a nominal stem; the *ḍ*-substitute will not take place.
[Objection:] If therefore, whatever has been applicable after [the word] *anaḍuh*, that exactly is blocked by force of ordaining [the infix] *nUM* after a nominal stem; the *rU*-substitute would not result either. [For example:] *anaḍvāṃs tatra* ('an ox is there').
[Answer:] This is not a fault. That rule with respect to which the instruction is superfluous, is blocked; but the one of which it is a cause, is not blocked. The injuction prescribing [the infix] *nUM* is superfluous with respect to the *ḍ*-substitute but, on the other hand, it is the cause for the *rU*-substitute.

{Explanation:
The derivation of the form *anaḍvān* is as follows:

(1) *anaḍuh* + *sU* (A. 4.1.2 *svaujasamauṭśasṭābhyāmbhisṅebhyāmbhyasṅasibhyāmbhyasṅasosāmṅyossup*)
(2) *anaḍu* + *āM* + *h* + *s* (A. 7.1.98 *caturanaḍuhor ām udāttaḥ*)
anaḍu + *ā* + *h* + *s*
(3) *anaḍ* (*u* → *v*) + *ā* + *h* + *s* (A. 6.1.77 *iko yaṇ aci*)
(4) *anaḍvā* + *nUM* + *h* + *s* (A. 7.1.82 *sav anaḍuhaḥ*)
(5) *anaḍvān* + *h* + (*s* → 0) (A. 6.1.68 *halṅyābbhyo dīrghāt sutisy apṛktam hal*)
(6) *anaḍvān* + (*h* → 0) (A. 8.2.23 *saṃyogāntasya lopaḥ*)
anaḍvān

If the sound *n* of the infix *nUM* were to be replaced by *ḍ*, it would not have any scope of application. Patañjali explains that prescribing the infix *nUM* is irrelevant with respect to the *ḍ*-substitute. It is not irrelevant, however, with respect to the *rU*-substitute prescribed in A. 8.3.7 *naś chavy apraśān* which renders the given example *anaḍvāṃs tatra*. In this example the final *n* is first replaced by *rU*, then the preeding vowel in nasalised and finally the sound *r*, through *visarjanīya*, is replaced by *s*. That is why the *rU*-substitute takes place in the case of *n* of *nUM* but the *ḍ*-substitute does not.

(1) *anaḍvān* + *tatra*

(2) *anaḍvā* (*n* → *rU*) + *tatra* (A. 8.3.7 *naś chavy apraśān*)
(3) *anaḍvā* + *ṃ* + *r* + *tatra* (A. 8.3.4 *anunāsikāt paro 'nusvāraḥ*)
(4) *anaḍvāṃ* + (*r* → *ḥ*) + *tatra* (A. 8.3.15 *kharavasānayor visarjanīyaḥ*)
(5) *anaḍvāṃ* + (*ḥ* → *s*) + *tatra* (A. 8.3.34 *visarjanīyasya saḥ*)
anaḍvāṃs tatra.}

{A. 8.2.73 *tipy anas teḥ*
[The sound *d* comes in place of the final sound *s* of verbal roots] apart from [the root] *asA* ('to be', DhP II:56) before [the verbal ending] *tiP*.
A. 8.2.74 *sipi dhāto rur vā*
[The sound *d* as well as the sound] *rU* usually [come in place of the final sound *s*] of a verbal root before [the verbal ending] *siP*.
A. 8.2.75 *daś ca*
And [the sound *d* as well as the sound *rU* usually come in place] of [the final sound] *d* [of a verbal root before the verbal ending *siP*].
A. 8.2.76 *rvor upadhyāyā dīrgha ikaḥ*
The long vowel comes in place of a penultimate [vowel denoted] by *iK* (i.e., *i*, *u*, *ṛ*, *ḷ*) [of a verbal root ending] in [the sounds] *r* or *v*.
A. 8.2.77 *hali ca*
And [the long vowel comes in place of a penultimate vowel denoted by *iK* (i.e., *i*, *u*, *ṛ*, *ḷ*) of a verbal root ending in the sounds *r* or *v*] before a consonant.} *These *sūtra*s were not commented upon by Patañjali.

A. 8.2.78 *upadhyāyāṃ ca*
And [the long vowel comes in place of a vowel denoted by *iK* (i.e., *i*, *u*, *ṛ*, *ḷ*) of a verbal root] before the penultimate sounds *r* or *v* [of that root before a consonant].

VMBh_1: III.413.11-14; VMBh_2: V.411.1-5

[Question:] Why is this said? Has [the same result] not been accomplished by [the *sūtra*] A. 8.2.77?
[Answer:] It is not accomplished [by the previous *sūtra*]. [The expression] "of a verbal root" continues there, so the verbal root is qualified by the sounds *r* or *v*. [The expression means] "of the verbal root ending in the sounds *r* or *v*."
[Question:] Why then is the verbal root in the previous rule qualified by the sounds *r* or *v*?
[Answer:] [Because] here it must not be: *agnir vayur iti* ('the fire and the wind').

{Explanation:
According to the previous rule A. 8.2.77 *hali ca*, a long vowel replaces a short one (denoted by *iK*) if it precedes the sounds *r* or *v*, which in turn is the final

sound of a word. The word has to be a verbal root; otherwise, the substitution would also take place in the expression *agnir vayuḥ* because the final consonant is preceded by a sound denoted by *iK* and because a general condition for any operation to take place within the *Tripādī* is that the environment is a *pada*. The word *agnir* is such a *pada*, hence the necessity for the *anuvṛtti dhātoḥ*.}

VMBh_1: III.413.15-16; VMBh_2: V.411.6-7

[Objection:] In such a way, then, when in the previous rule the word 'a verbal root' (*dhātu*) [is used] (A. 8.2.76), in the following one (A. 8.2.77) it ceases to be valid. Thus here it would result as well: *kurkuraḥ* ('a dog'), *murmuraḥ* ('the smell of cow urine').

{**Explanation:**
The above examples refer to the present rule, not to the previous one (A. 8.2.77 *hali ca*). If the word *dhātoḥ* did not continue in the present rule, the substitution with a long vowel would take place in words like *kurkuraḥ* or *murmuraḥ*, which are not verbal roots but would fall under the scope of the governing term *pada*. The first *r* is followed by a consonant and preceded by a vowel denoted by *iK*, namely, *u*. Therefore the first vowel could be substituted by its longer counterpart leading to the forms **kūrkuraḥ* and **mūrmuraḥ*.}

VMBh_1: III.413.16-19; VMBh_2: V.411.7-10

[Answer:] In such a way then the word *dhātu* continues there but it is not qualified by the sounds *r* or *v*.
[Question:] What is [qualified] then?
[Answer:] [The expression] *iK* is qualified [by the sound *r* or *v*]. [The expression means] "of the verbal root containing [a sound denoted by] *iK* which ends in the sounds *r* or *v*."
[Objection:] In such a way here it would result as well: *kururīyati* ('behaves like a dog'), *murmurīyati* ('smells like cow urine').
[Answer:] Therefore, it is the verbal root that is to be qualified and when the verbal root is qualified, it should also be mentioned "before the penultimate."

{**Explanation:**
The above discussion determines qualified-qualifier relations in the present *sūtra*. From the previous rule it is understood that the consonants *r* and *v* should be "at the end" (*anta*), but it is proposed that in the present rule *r* and *v* qualify the expression *ikaḥ*. It would mean that the sounds denoted by *iK* are to end with *r* or *v*. However, Kaiyaṭa (VMBh_2: V.411) explains that when those sound are to qualify *iK* and not the verbal root, the meaning of *anta* is not 'the end' but 'proxi-

mity' (*samīpa*). Therefore a sound denoted by *iK* gets replaced by its longer counterpart that is in proximity to (but preceding) either *r* or *v*. It does not have to be the penultimate vowel of a verbal root. In such a case the problem arises because the substitution would also occur in denominative verbal roots such as *kurkurīya* and *murmurīya*. The first vowel *u* would be lengthened producing **kūrkurīya* and **mūrmurīya*, which leads us to the conclusion that the sounds *r* or *v* must qualify the verbal root.
We find two forms of the word *upadhā* ('penultimate') in the present rule. The one that is explicitly stated *upadhāyām* and the one that continues from the rule A. 8.2.76 *upadhāyāḥ*. The fomer should be used as a qualifier to the sounds *r* and *v*, even though these two expressions (*rvoḥ* and *upadhāyām*) do not agree with each other morphologically. It is interpreted as a change (*vyatyaya*), where the genitive dual is changed into the locative singular for the purpose of the present rule. The substitution will take place in such a verbal root that has either *r* or *v* as penultimate. The second *upadhā* qualifies *iK*, which means that *r* and *v* have to be preceded by a sound denoted by the abbreviation *iK*.}

VMBh_1: III.413.20-22; VMBh_2: V.411.11-412.2

1) [There is] prohibition in the case of reduplication, [the words] *jivri* ('old') and *catur* ('four') with respect to the substitution by a long vowel of the penultimate [vowel].

[Bhāṣya:] Prohibition should be mentioned in the case of reduplication, [the words] *jivri* ('old') and *catur* ('four') with respect to the substitution by a long vowel of the penultimate [vowel]. [For example,] *riryatuḥ* and *riryuḥ* (3rd du. and pl. perfect respectively of the verb *rī* 'to release', DhP IX:30); *saṃvivyatuḥ* and *saṃvivyuḥ* (3rd du. and pl. perfect respectively of the verb *vī* 'to go, approach', DhP II:39), *jivriḥ* ('old'), *caturyitā* and *caturyitum* (1st future and infinitive respectively of the verb *caturya* 'to wish for four').

{**Explanation:**
In all the abovementioned cases, a vowel would be replaced by its longer counterpart if prohibition were not stated. Let us consider the perfect forms of the verbal root *rī* as an example.

(1) *rī* + *lIṬ*
(2) *rī* + tas (A. 3.4.78 *tiptasjhisipthasthamibvasmastātāṃjhathāsāthāmdhvamiḍvahimahiṅ*)
(3) *rī* + *atuṣ* (A. 3.4.82 *parasmaipadānāṃ ṇalatususthalatusaṇalvamāḥ*)
(4) *rī* + *rī* + *atus* (A. 6.1.8 *liṭi dhātor anabhyāsasya*)
(5) *r* (*ī* → *i*) + *rī* + *atus* (A. 7.4.59 *hrasvaḥ*)

(6) *ri + r (ī → y) + atus* (A. 6.1.77 *iko yaṇ aci*)
(7) *ri + ry + atu (s → rU)* (A. 8.2.66 *sasajuṣo ruḥ*)
(8) *ri + ry + atu (r → ḥ)* (A. 8.3.15 *kharavasānayor visarjanīyaḥ*)
riryatuḥ

When the *yaṆ*-substitute has applied at the stage (6), the first syllable could be lengthened because it precedes the sound *r*, which in turn is followed a consonant. This would lead to an undesired result, though, **rīryatuḥ*. However, the *yaṆ*-substitute is an externally conditioned operation as it depends on the suffix *atus* and the lengthening is internally conditioned. Before the *yaṆ*-substitute takes place the conditions for lengthening are not met because *r* is followed by a vowel, not a consonant. Thus, the correct form *riryatuḥ* is derived. The *Kāśikāvṛtti* (KV VI.440.3-4) states that we can apply *sthānivadbhāva* to the *yaṆ*-substitute and the consonant *y* can still be treated as the vowel *i*. This is, again, a dubious solution because *sthānivadbhāva* should not be employed within the *Tripādī* section.
Let us now see the form *caturyitā* (1st future from *caturyitṛ*).

(1) *catur + KyaC + tṛC + sU* (A. 3.1.8 *supa ātmanaḥ kyac*, A. 3.1.133 *ṇvultṛcau*, A. 4.1.2 *svaujasamauṭśasṭābhyāmbhisṅebhyāmbhyasṅasibhyāmbhyasṅasosāmṅyossup*)
(2) *catur + y (a → 0) + tṛ + s* (A. 6.4.48 *ato lopaḥ*)
(3) *catur + y + iṬ + tṛ + s* (A. 7.2.35 *ārdhadhātukasyeḍ valādeḥ*)
(4) *catur + yi + t (ṛ → an) + s* (A. 7.1.94 *ṛduśanaspurudaṃśonehasāṃ ca*)
(5) *catur + yi + tan + (s → 0)* (A. 6.1.68 *halṅyābbhyo dīrghāt sutisy apṛktam hal*)
(6) *catur + yi + t (a → ā) n* (A. 6.4.8 *sarvanāmāsthāne cāsambuddhau*)
(7) *catur + yi + tā (n → 0)* (A. 8.2.7 *nalopaḥ prātipadikāntasya*)
caturyitā

When the vowel *a* has been deleted at the stage (2), the consonant *r* of *catur* becomes the penultimate sound of the verbal root. It allows the long vowel *ū* to replace *u* in *caturya*, which would eventually lead to the form **catūryitā*. However, the deletion, depending on the suffix *tṛC*, is externally conditioned; while the substitution is internally conditioned. The former is considered suspended so we still see the vowel *a* there. If it is still there, we cannot apply the lengthening because the consonant *r* is not penultimate in a verbal stem. Consequently, the lengthening does not take place, the vowel *a* is deleted and the correct form *caturyitā* results.

The word *jivri* is formed by adding the *Uṇādi* suffix *KriN*[366] to the verbal root *jṝṢ* ('to grow old', DhP I:863, IV:22) where *r* is changed into *v*. Therefore we get *ji* (*r* → *v*) + *ri* → *jivri*. The lengthening of the first vowel of the stem is prohibited by the *vārttika*.}

VMBh_1: III.413.21-414.3; VMBh_2: V.412.3-8

2) And [there is] prohibition with respect to the *Uṇādi* [suffixes].

[Bhāṣya:] And prohibition should be mentioned with respect to the *Uṇādi* [suffixes]. [For example,] *kiryoḥ* (gen./loc. du. of the word *kiri* 'a pile, a hog'), *giryoḥ* (gen./loc. du. of the word *giri* 'a mountain').
[Objection:] Similarly, prohibition should not be mentioned in the case of reduplication. It is said "before the consonant" but here we do not see [anything] beginning with a consonant.
[Answer:] It would result when the *yaṆ*-substitute has been done.
[Objection:] [The substitution with a long vowel] will not take place due to it (i.e., the *yaṆ*-substitute) being like the substituend.
[Answer:] The rule treating the substitute like the substituend is prohibited here, this rule does not apply to the rule ordaining the substitution with a long vowel (see A. 1.1.58).[367]
[Bhāṣya:] This is not the prohibition. It has been said that: "With reference to the prohibition [of *sthānivadbhāva*, it should be said that] the vowel substitute in the form of deletion is not treated like the substituend with respect to [the rules prescribing] accent, the substitution with a long vowel and the deletion of [the sound] *y*" (A. 1.1.58 *vt*. 1).

{Explanation:
Patañjali quotes *vt* 1 under A. 1.1.58 which enlists other examples of operations where *sthānivadbhāva* is prohibited. However, the same is achieved from the *vt* 3 under the same rule which states that this principle is not valid within the *purvatrāsiddha* section. While analysing the above examples, we can see that the final *i* is replaced by *y* before the initial vowel of the suffix (by A. 6.1.77 *iko yaṇ aci*). The conditions for the present rule to apply are met, and the vowels of the

---

[366] US 730 (5.49): *jīryateḥ krin raś ca vaḥ* || ("[The suffix] *KriN* comes after [the verbal root] *jṝ* ('to grow old') and [the consonant] *v* comes in place of [the consonant] *r*.")

[367] A. 1.1.58 *na padāntadvirvacanavareyalopasvarasavarṇānusvāradīrghajaścarvidhiṣu* || ("[The substitute of a vowel] is not [treated like the substituend] with respect to the operations concerning: the final [sound] of a *pada*, reduplication, the deletion before [the suffixes] *varaC* and *ya*, the accent [of what precedes], homogeneous [sounds], *anusvāra* [substitution of what precedes], lengthening [of what precedes], the *jaŚ* and *caR* substitutions [of what precedes].")

stems could be lengthened, given the inapplicability of *sthānivadbhāva*. As lengthening is not desired here, the *vārttika* is necessary.}

VMBh_1: III.414.4-7; VMBh_2: V.412.9-12

[Answer:] And prohibition with respect to the word *jivri* should not be mentioned. The nominal stems [formed with] the *Uṇādi* [suffixes] are not derivatives. [In the case of the forms] *caturyitā*, *caturyitum* [the negation] *asupi* (from the *sūtra* A. 8.2.69, "not before the case endings") applies.
[Objection:] If so, [there is] no accomplishment of [the forms] *gīrbhyām* and *gīrbhiḥ* (instr./dat./abl. du. and instr. pl. respectively from the word *gīr* – 'praise, verse, song').
[Answer:] [The forms] *gīrbhyām* and *gīrbhiḥ* are not faulty due to the change of the case ending, [the expression "not before the case endings" should be understood as] "not of the case endings".
[Bhāṣya:] Prohibition should be mentioned with respect to the *Uṇādi* [suffixes]; it has been understood that nominal stems [formed with] the *Uṇādi* [suffixes] are not derivatives (which means that the rule of etymologial changes does not apply to them).

{**Explanation:**
In the first *vārttika* of the present *sūtra*, prescribing the prohibition of lengthening, the expression "not before the case endings" continues from A. 8.2.69. This expression should be changed to mean "of the case endings" (from locative singular in the rule A. 8.2.69 to genitive singular in the present rule), which allows the forms *gīrbhyām* and *gīrbhiḥ* to be created. This prohibition is negated when the consonants *r* or *v*, which follow the vowel denoted by *iK* subject to lengthening, are followed by a consonant being a part of a case ending. If *r* or *v* were followed by a consonant not being a part of a case ending, the prohibition would still be valid.
The above discussion starts in the *Mahābhāṣya* with the example *caturyitā*; the question arises why we do not get a long vowel here as well. Commentators explain that the form *caturyitā* ends in a case ending but it is formed with the suffix *KyaC* which is directly followed by this case ending. The very stem, the basis of the final form (*catur*), is not followed directly by the case ending because the suffix *KyaC* intervenes. This does not allow the substitution to take place.}

{**A. 8.2.79 *na bhakurchurām***
[A long vowel] does not [come in place of a penultimate vowel denoted by *iK* (i.e., *i*, *u*, *ṛ*, *ḷ*)] of *bha* stems [ending in the sounds *r* or *v* and] of [the verbal stems] *kur* (from *ḌUkṛÑ* – 'to do, make', DhP VIII:10) and *chur* (from

***churA* – 'to cut', DhP VI:79) [before suffixes beginning with a consonant].}**
*This *sūtra* was not commented upon by Patañjali.

A. 8.2.80 *adaso 'ser dād u do maḥ*
[The sound] *u* comes in place of [the sound occurring] after [the sound] *d* of [the pronominal stem] *adas* ('that one') not ending in [the sound] *s* and [the sound] *m* comes in place of [the sound] *d*.

VMBh_1: III.414.8-14; VMBh_2: V.412.13-413.2

1) [The substitution takes place] in [the pronominal stem] *adas* which does not end in [the sounds] *o*, *s* or *r*.

[Bhāṣya:] It should be mentioned that [the substitution takes place] in [the pronominal stem] *adas* which does not end in [the sounds] *o*, *s* or *r*.
[Question:] What [does the expression] *an-o-s-reḥ* [mean]?
[Answer:] [It means] "not ending in the sound *o*, the sound *s* or the sound *r*." [For example,] not ending in the sound *o* – *ado 'tra* ('that one here'); not ending in the sound *s* – *adasyati* ('he desires that'); not ending in the sound *r* – *adaḥ* ('that one' nom./acc. sg. n.).[368]
[Question:] Should it be mentioned then?
[Answer:] It should not be mentioned. The maxim is done indeed. The instruction is without the case ending; [it should be read as] *adas o*. The prohibition following the sound *o* refers to what precedes it. Then the sound *s* and then the sound *r* (i.e., *adas o a se r*).

{**Explanation:**
The above explanation shows that the *vārttika* is not actually necessary because everything is contained in the *sūtra* itself. The rule looks like this: *adas o a se r* where the vowel *e* is used only to facilitate pronunciation. The words do not contain any case endings; they are *avibhaktika*. The vowel *a* performs a negative function so the question arises how it can negate the elements preceding and following it. In other words, how is it possible that the sound *a* refers to the sound *o* as well as the sounds *s* and *r*? The answer that Annaṃbhaṭṭa (MPV X.396) gives is that all the sounds should be treated as separate words in the *sūtra*, they are not compounded and do not end in a case ending, which why the negative *a* is connected with all of them. The rule says, then, that the *mu*-substitute takes place only when the stem does not end in either *o*, *s* or *r*.}

---

[368] The consonant *s* is replaced by *rU* on the basis of A. 8.2.66 *sasajuṣo ruḥ* and then the rule A. 8.3.15 *kharavasānayor visarjanīyaḥ* applies. As the latter is considered suspended, the stem serves as an example of the one ending in *r*.

VMBh_1: III.414.14-15; VMBh_2: V.413.3-4

[Bhāṣya:] Alternatively, it is not explained in such a way: "of [the stem] *adas* not ending in the sound *s*."
[Question:] How then?
[Answer:] [The expression] *asi* [means] "the one whose sound *s* has been replaced by the sound *a*" [and consequently,] *aseḥ* ("of [such a pronominal stem *adas* whose] sound *s* [has been replaced by the sound] *a*").

{**Explanation:**
This interpretation makes the expression *asi* a *bahuvrīhi* compound to the word *adasas*. The *a*-substitute of *s* referred to is obtained by the *sūtra* A. 7.1.102 *tyadādīnām aḥ*. Thus we obtain the stem: *adas* → *ada* (*s* → *a*, A. 7.2.102) → *adaa* → *ad* (*a* + *a* → *a*) (A. 6.1.87 *ād guṇaḥ*). And only in such a stem the substitutions prescribed in the present rule can take place.}

VMBh_1: III.414.15-16; VMBh_2: V.413.4-5

[Objection:] If [it is] so, [the form] *amumuyaṅ* ('turning in that direction') is not accomplished, [the form] *adadryaṅ* ('inclining to go to that') would result [instead].

{**Explanation:**
The examples above show only two options of possible substitution – either both consonants *d* undergo the substitution or none of them. The former derivatives is desired but not possible given the interpretation of the *sūtra* presented above. In the given interpretation *s* must be replaced by *a*, which requires the application of A. 7.1.102 *tyadādīnām aḥ*. In the case of the form *adadryañc* ('inclining to go to that') that very rule did not apply. Consequently, the objection states, the *m*- and *u*-substitutes will not take place at all.
Let us analyse the derivative process in detail:

(1) *adas* + *añcU* (DhP I:203) + *KviN* (A. 3.2.59 *ṛtvijdadhṛksragdig-uṣṇigañcuyujikruñcāṃ ca*)
(2) *ad* (*as* → *adri*) + *añc* + *KviN* (A. 6.3.92 *viśvagdevayoś ca ṭer adryañcatau vapratyaye*)
(3) *adadr* (*i* → *y*) + *añc* + *KviN* (A. 6.1.77 *iko yaṇ aci*)
(4) *adadry* + *a* (*ñ* → 0) *c* + KviN (A. 6.4.24 *aniditāṃ hala upadhyāyāḥ kṅiti*)
(5) *adadry* + *ac* + 0 (A. 6.1.67 *ver apṛktasya*)
adadryac

This is the starting point where we have three options available:
A. the present rule applies to both of consonants *d* which would yield the form *amumuyaṅ*:
(1) *adadryac* + *sU* (A. 4.1.2 *svaujasamauṭśasṭābhyāmbhisṅebhyāmbhyasṅasibhyāmbhyasṅasosāmṅyossup*)
(2) *adadrya* + *nUM* + *c* + *s* (A. 7.1.70 *ugidacāṃ sarvanāmasthāne 'dhātoḥ*)
(3) *adadryanc* + (*s* → 0) (A. 6.1.68 *halṅyābbhyo dīrghāt sutisy apṛktam hal*)
(4) *adadryan* (*c* → 0) (A. 8.2.23 *samyogāntasya lopaḥ*)
(5) *adadrya* (*n* →*ṅ*) (A. 8.2.62 *kvinpratyayasya kuḥ*)
(6) *a* (*da* → *mu*) (*dr* → *mu*) *yaṅ* (A. 8.2.80 *adaso 'ser dād u do maḥ*)
amumuyaṅ

B. the present rule applies only to the second consonant *d* which would yield the form *adamuyaṅ*:
(1) *adadryac* + *sU* (A. 4.1.2 *svaujasamauṭśasṭābhyāmbhisṅebhyāmbhyasṅasibhyāmbhyasṅasosāmṅyossup*)
(2) *adadrya* + *nUM* + *c* + *s* (A. 7.1.70 *ugidacāṃ sarvanāmasthāne 'dhātoḥ*)
(3) *adadryanc* + (*s* → 0) (A. 6.1.68 *halṅyābbhyo dīrghāt sutisy apṛktam hal*)
(4) *adadryan* (*c* → 0) (A. 8.2.23 *samyogāntasya lopaḥ*)
(5) *adadrya* (*n* →*ṅ*) (A. 8.2.62 *kvinpratyayasya kuḥ*)
(6) *ada* (*dr* → *mu*) *yaṅ* (A. 8.2.80 *adaso 'ser dād u do maḥ*)
adamuyaṅ

C. the present rule does not apply to any of the sounds which would yield the form *adadryaṅ*:
(1) *adadryac* + *sU* (A. 4.1.2 *svaujasamauṭśasṭābhyāmbhisṅebhyāmbhyasṅasibhyāmbhyasṅasosāmṅyossup*)
(2) *adadrya* + *nUM* + *c* + *s* (A. 7.1.70 *ugidacāṃ sarvanāmasthāne 'dhātoḥ*)
(3) *adadryanc* + (*s* → 0) (A. 6.1.68 *halṅyābbhyo dīrghāt sutisy apṛktam hal*)
(4) *adadryan* (*c* → 0) (A. 8.2.23 *samyogāntasya lopaḥ*)
(5) *adadrya* (*n* →*ṅ*) (A. 8.2.62 *kvinpratyayasya kuḥ*)
adadryaṅ}

VMBh_1: III.414.16-19; VMBh_2: V.413.5-8

[Answer:] [The form] should be *adamuyaṅ*; "when the modification does not refer to the final, the grammatical operation applies to what is in the same position as the final."[369]

[369] See WUJASTYK 1993: vol. I:55, vol. II:183.

> Some want the *mu*-substitute [of *da* and *dr*] in [the words] *adas* and *adri* separately, similarly to the *l*-substitute.
> Some see it of [the last portion] standing in the proximity to the final and some do not see [the substitution when *adri* comes] due to [the expression] *aseḥ*.

{**Explanation:**
The verse presents the opinions of other grammarians (*kecit*, *eke*) which can be divided into three groups based on the interpretation of *aseḥ*. Firstly, there are those who claim that the substitution takes place in the case of both consonants *d*. They understand the expression *asi* as "when it does not end in *s*" and they reject the *paribhāṣā* quoted above by Patañjali, which leads them to the form *amumuyaṅ*. It is paralel to the double *l*-substitute in the form *calīkḷpyate* where the verbal root *kṛpA* ('to be fit for', DhP I:808) is reduplicated before the suffix *yaṄ*, then the augment *rīK* comes in place of the sound *r* of the reduplicated syllable and both consonants *r* get replaced by *l* finally.[370] The second view accepts that an operation applies to what is in the same position as the final, which leads to the form *adamuyaṅ*. In this case the substitution refers only of the second consonant *d*. And this is the view accepted by Patañjali. The supporters of the third view claim that the substitution takes place only when the consonant *s* of *adas* has been replaced by *a* (by A. 7.1.102 *tyadādīnām aḥ*). They understand the expression *aseḥ* as a *bahuvrīhi* compound referring to the word *adasas*. In the case, the rule A. 7.1.102 does not apply to the stem *adadryañc* so they claim that the present *sūtra* and the *mu*-substitution does not take place; it would lead to an incorrect form *adadryaṅ*.}

VMBh_1: III.414.20-24; VMBh_2: V.413.9-13

2) Therefore there is no accomplishment of [the substitution of] the non-*pada* final due to the governing term *pada* (A. 8.1.16).

[Objection:] Therefore, due to the governing term *pada* (A. 8.1.16) [the substitution] would not result of the non-*pada* final. [For example:] *amuyā*, *amuyoḥ* (instr. sg. f. and gen./loc. du. respectively).

3) But it has been achieved due to the prohibition of the sound *s*.

---

370 See A. 8.2.18 *kṛpo ro laḥ* and A. 7.4.90 *rīg ṛdupadhasya ca* || ("[There is the infix] *rīK* after [the reduplication of the *aṅga* stem] which has [the sound] *r* as the penultimate [before the suffix *yaṄ* or its deletion by *luK*].")

[Answer:] But it has been achieved.
[Question:] How?
[Answer:] Due to the prohibition of the sound *s*. When the teacher orders the prohibition "not ending in [the sound] *s*", he then indicates that [the substitution] takes place of that which is not the *pada* final.

{**Explanation:**
Kaiyaṭa (VMBh_2: V.413-414), commenting on this passage, discusses the purpose of the negation *aseḥ*. Based on the restriction in A. 1.4.15 *naḥ kye*,[371] the stem *adas* not ending in *n* will not be termed *pada* (which it should due to the governing term *padasya*) and the substitution will not take place in the cases such as *adasyati* ('he wishes that'). The answer is that, thanks to the prohibition in the present *sūtra*, the substitution will take place in an element that is a *pada* as well as in such which is not a *pada*. The examples are *amuṣyai* and *amūbhyām* (dat. sg. f. and instr./dat./abl. du. respectively) for *pada*s (see A. 1.4.17 *svādiṣv asarvanāmasthāne*[372]) and *amuyā* (instr. sg. f.) for a non *pada* (see A. 1.4.18 *yaci bham*[373]).}

VMBh_1: III.415.1-4; VMBh_2: V.414.1-4

[Question:] Then what is the purpose in using [the expression] "after [the sound] *d*"?

4) The expression "after [the sound] *d*" is used in order to prohibit [the *u*-substitute] of the last [sound].

[Answer:] The expression "after [the sound] *d*" is used in order to prohibit [the *u*-substitute] of the last [sound]. [The *sūtra*] A. 1.1.52 must not apply. [For example:] *amuyā*, *amuyoḥ* (instr. sg. f. and gen./loc. du. respectively).

{**Explanation:**
In the above passage Patañjali explains why the expression *dāt* is used in the *sūtra*. According to A. 1.1.52 *alo 'ntyasya*,[374] it is the last sound of the stem that

---

[371] A. 1.4.15 *naḥ kye* || ("[The technical term *pada* denotes an element] ending in [the sound] *n* before [the suffixes] *Kya* (i.e, *KyaṄ*, *KyaC* and *KyaṢ*).")

[372] A. 1.4.17 *svādiṣv asarvanāmasthāne* || ("[The technical term *pada* denotes an element] before [the suffixes] *sU* etc. excluding [those termed] *sarvanāmasthāna* (i.e., strong case endings).")

[373] A. 1.4.18 *yaci bham* || ("[The technical term] *bha* [denotes an element] before [the suffix beginning with the semivowel] *y* or a vowel.")

[374] A. 1.1.52 *alo 'ntyasya* || ("[The substitute ordered in the genitive comes] in place of the final sound.")

is subject to substitution, which would be an undesired outcome in examples such as *amuyā* and *amuyoḥ*. The derivation of the former is as follows:

(1) *adas* + *ṬāP* + *Ṭā* (A. 4.1.4 *ajādyataṣ ṭāp*, A. 4.1.2 *svaujasamauṭśasṭā-bhyāmbhisṅebhyāmbhyasṅasibhyāmbhyasṅasosāmṅyossup*)
(2) *ada* (*s* → *a*) + *ā* + *ā* (A. 7.2.102 *tyadādīnām aḥ*)
(3) *ad* (*a* + *a* → *a*) + *ā* + *ā* (A. 6.1.97 *ato guṇe*)
(4) *ad* (*a* + *ā* → *ā*) + *ā* (A. 6.1.101 *akaḥ savarṇe dīrghaḥ*)
(5) *ad* (*ā* → *e*) + *ā* (A. 7.3.105 *āṅi cāpaḥ*)
(6) *ad* (*e* → *ay*) + *ā* (A. 6.1.78 *eco 'yavāyāvaḥ*)
(7) *a* (*de* → *mu*) + *yā* (A. 8.2.80 *adaso 'ser dād u do maḥ*)
amuyā

Now, if the expression "after [the sound] *d*" were not used, the *m*-substitution of *y*, which is the last sound of the stem, would take place and in order to avoid that, we need to specify the condition.}

A. 8.2.81 *eta īd bahuvacane*
[The vowel] *ī* comes in place of [the vowel] *e* [occurring after the sound *d* of the pronominal stem *adas* ('that one') not ending in the sound *s* and the sound *m* comes in place of the sound *d*] when the meaning is 'many'.

VMBh_1: III.415.5-10; VMBh_2: V.414.5-10

1) [There is] the *ī*-substitute of the final [element] in plural.

[Bhāṣya:] The *ī*-substitute of the final [element] in plural should be mentioned. If it is said only *bahuvacane* (meaning 'in plural'), [the substitution] would only take place here – *amībhiḥ* and *amīṣu* (instr. and loc. pl. respectively). Here it would not be – *amī atra* ('those ones [are] here') and *amī āsate* ('those ones exist').
[Question:] Should it be mentioned then?
[Answer:] It should not be mentioned. This is not the technical use of [the word] *bahuvacana*.
[Question:] What then?
[Answer:] This is the literal meaning [of a word]. [The term] *bahuvacana* [means] 'expression of many things', [therefore] 'when the meaning is many'.

{**Explanation:**
The term *bahuvacana* can be interpreted in two different ways; it can be used in its technical sense 'plural' or in its literal meaning 'many'. Kaiyaṭa (VMBh_2: V.414.17 ff) quotes the *paribhāṣā*: *kṛtrimākṛtrimayoḥ kṛtrime saṃpratyayaḥ*,

according to which when there is a choice between the artificial meaning (i.e., technical) and non-artificial one (i.e., literal, conventional), the former is preferred.[375] This would mean that the term *bahuvacana* should be understood only as specified by Pāṇini in his *sūtra*s A. 1.4.102-103.[376] Consequently, according to these *paribhāṣā*s, the stem ending in the vowel *e* to be replaced by *ī* must be followed by the plural suffix. This interpretation would account for the forms *amībhis* and *amīṣu*.

(1) *adas* + *bhis* (A. 4.1.2 *svaujasamauṭśasṭābhyāmbhisṅebhyāmbhyasṅasibhyāmbhyasṅasosāmṅyossup*)
(2) *ada* (*s* → *a*) + *bhis* (A. 7.2.102 *tyadādīnām aḥ*)
(3) *ad* (*a* + *a* → *a*) + *bhis* (A. 6.1.97 *ato guṇe*)
(4) *ad* (*a* → *e*) + *bhis* (A. 7.3.103 *bahuvacane jhaly et*)
(5) *a* (*d* → *m*) (*e* → *ī*) + *bhis* (A. 8.2.81 *eta īd bahuvacane*)
amībhis

However, the forms *amī atra* or *amī āsate* would not be possible. We would obtain instead:

(1) *adas* + *Jas* (A. 4.1.2 *svaujasamauṭśasṭābhyāmbhisṅebhyāmbhyasṅasibhyāmbhyasṅasosāmṅyossup*)
(2) *adas* + *Śī* (A. 7.1.17 *jasaḥ śī*)
(3) *ada* (*s* → *a*) + *ī* (A. 7.1.102 *tyadādīnām aḥ*)
(4) *ad* (*a* + *a* → *a*) + *ī* (A. 6.1.97 *ato guṇe*)
(5) *ad* (*a* + *ī* → *e*) (A. 6.1.87 *ād guṇaḥ*)
**ade*

The form **ade* could not undergo further substitution because there is no plural suffix following. That is why the *paribhāṣā* has to be rejected in this case and we should interpret the term *bahuvacana* in its literal meaning.}

A. 8.2.82 *vākyasya ṭeḥ pluta udāttaḥ*
The prolated *udātta* accented vowel comes in place of [the vowel of the] *Ṭi*[377] element of an utterance.

---

[375] See WUJASTYK 1993: vol. I:11, vol. II:49-53.

[376] A. 1.4.102 *tāny ekavacanadvivacanabahuvacanāny ekaśaḥ* ‖ ("Those [three and three triplets of verbal endings] taken one by one [are termed] *ekavacana* 'singular', *dvivacana* 'dual' and *bahuvacana* 'plural' [to denote them respectively].") A. 1.4.103 *supaḥ* ‖ ("[The triplets of the suffixes] *sUP* (i.e., case endings) [taken one by one are termed *ekavacana* 'singular', *dvivacana* 'dual' and *bahuvacana* 'plural' to denote them respectively].")

[377] See A. 1.1.64 *aco 'ntyādi ṭi* ‖ ("[That part] of [an item] which begins with its last vowel is called *Ṭi*.")

VMBh_1: III.415.11-17; VMBh_2: V.414.11-415.3

[Question:] What is the purpose [in using] the governing term *vākya*?

1) The governing term *vākya* has as its purpose the annullment of [the governing term] *pada*.

[Answer:] The governing term *vākya* is used in order to annul [the application of the governing term] *pada*. The governing term *pada* (from A. 8.1.16) ceases.
[Objection:] But [as in this expression]: *kāko vāśyate* ("A crow shrieks") the governing terms do not annul each other. This would certainly be the fault if the governing term *vākya* annulled [the application of] the governing term *pada*. Further on, the application of [the term] *pada* is required, [otherwise] those would not result – [e.g., the *sūtra*] A. 8.3.7.

{**Explanation:**
The basic problem here is that according to the general rule, the governing term stops when another comes in its place; it would be natural to have the term *vākya* blocking the term *pada*. This is not what happens here, though. There are further rules, such as A. 8.3.7 *naś chavy apraśān*, where the term *pada* must be read to derive correct forms. The example given by Kaiyaṭa (VMBh_2: V.415.15) is the form *hanti* ('kills'). If the term *pada* were not valid in A. 8.3.7, the final *n* of the verbal root *han* ('to kill') could be replaced by *rU*. It does not happen because the verbal root cannot be termed *pada* so the substitution cannot take place.}

VMBh_1: III.415.17-20; VMBh_2: V.415.4-7

[Answer:] [The expression] *padanivṛttyartham* is not understood in such a way: "in order to annul [the application of a *sūtra*] of [the governing term] *pada*", *padanivṛttyartham*.
[Question:] How then?
[Answer:] [The expression] *padanivṛttyartham* [means] "in order to annul [the application of a *sūtra*] before a *pada*". The prolated vowel of the *Ṭi* [element] would result of all the *pada*s which are in a *vākya* ('utterance'); and it is required that [the substitution] should be in the last *pada* of an utterance; without that the effort does not result;[378] thus this is the purpose of the governing term *vākya*.

{**Explanation:**

[378] Patañjali uses the term *yatna* here which is to show the use of a particular word in a rule to remove some occurring difficulty.

The element *Ṭi* mentioned in the *sūtra* refers to a *pada*. However, it cannot refer to any *pada* in an utterance, which would be the case were the term *vākya* not used in the rule. Prolation is required in the last *pada* of a *vākya* only; there cannot be any more *pada*s following. So the term *vākya* is not used to annul the governing term *pada*. It is used to restrict the application of a rule to a particular *pada* in an utterance.}

VMBh_1: III.415.21-24; VMBh_2: V.415.8-11

[Question:] What is the purpose [in using] the word *Ṭi*?

2) The word *Ṭi* [is used] for the sake of [a word] ending in a consonant with respect to the restriction [in the *sūtra*] A. 1.1.52.[379]

[Answer:] The word *Ṭi* is used in order to restrict [the application] of [the *sūtra*] A. 1.1.52 so that [the substitution] would also take place of [the last vowel in a word] ending in a consonant. [For example:] *agnicī3t* ('one who has arranged the sacrificial fire'), *somasū3t* ('one who offers soma juice').

{Explanation:
According to the rules A. 1.2.27 *ūkālo 'j hrasvadīrghaplutaḥ*[380] and A. 1.2.28 *acaḥ*,[381] the term *pluta* refers to vowels only. According to A. 1.1.72 *yena vidhis tadantasya*, if an operation in a rule refers to a particular element, it also refers to a larger unit ending in said element. When we combine it with the rule A. 1.1.52 *alo 'ntyasya* and cast away the word *Ṭi* from the present *sūtra*, we would have to accept that prolation refers to only such a vowel which constitutes the final sound of a final *pada* of an utterance. This would exclude words ending in a consonant from the scope of the rule. The word *Ṭi* qualifies the vowel to be replaced with its prolated counterpart, so it is such a vowel that is a part of *Ṭi*. It should not be understood the other way round, that it is *Ṭi* which is a vowel, because words ending in a consonant must be included as well.}

VMBh_1: III.415.24-416.3; VMBh_2: V.415.11-416.3

[Question:] Is this the purpose? How then?

---

379 A. 1.1.52 *alo 'ntyasya* || ("[The substitute ordered in the genitive comes] in place of the final sound.")

380 A. 1.2.27 *ūkālo 'j hrasvadīrghaplutaḥ* || ("[The technical terms] *hrasva* ('short'), *dīrgha* ('long') and *pluta* ('prolated') denote vowels having the duration of *u*, *ū* and *ū3* [respectively].")

381 A. 1.2.28 *acaḥ* || ("[A replacement which is specified by *hrasva*, *dīrgha* and *pluta* comes] in place of a vowel (*aC*).")

3) But there is a potential involvement of substitution of the whole.

[Objection:] But the prolated substitution of the whole [element] *Ṭi* would result.
[Question:] What is the reason?
[Answer:] From the rule A. 1.2.28 [the substitution] will not apply to the final [element] and from the rule A. 1.1.52 [the substitution] will not apply to a vowel, [thus,] the prolated vowel would result as the substitution of a whole.

{**Explanation:**
When the *sūtra* A. 1.1.52 *alo 'ntyasya* is qualified by A. 1.2.28 *acaḥ*, a problem might arise resulting in the substitution of an entire *Ṭi* element with a prolated vowel. If such an interpretation were accepted, the substitution prescribed by the present *sūtra* would indeed regard only this vowel which is a final sound of a word. It follows then that these *paribhāṣā*s cannot both apply as they are mutually exclusive, and it is A. 1.1.52 that should be disregarded in this case.}

VMBh_1: III.416.4-6; VMBh_2: V.416.4-6

4) Alternatively, it has been explained.

[Question:] What has been explained?
[Answer:] Where 'short', 'long', 'prolated' are mentioned, with respect to that they should be seen as applying to a vowel.[382]

A. 8.2.83 *pratyabhivāde 'śūdre*
[The prolated *udātta* accented vowel comes in place of a vowel of the *Ṭi* element of an utterance] in response to a reverential salutation, when it does not refer to a *śūdra*.

VMBh_1: III.416.7-8; VMBh_2: V.416.7-8

[Question:] What is the purpose [in saying] "when it does not refer to a *śūdra*"?
[Answer:] [For example,] *kuśaly asi tuṣajaka* ("You are wealthy, Tushajaka").

{**Explanation:**
When the response is made to a *śūdra*, there is no prolation of the last vowel; the answer is a mere sentence expressing kindness in the form of a blessing or a question about health etc.}

---

[382] It is Patañjali's own comment (*evaṃ tarhi hrasvo dīrghaḥ pluta iti yatra brūyād aca ity etat tatropasthitaṃ draṣṭavyam*) under the *vārttika* 2 on the *sūtra* A. 1.2.28 *acaḥ*.

VMBh_1: III.416.8-11; VMBh_2: V.416.8-12

[Objection:] Too little is said here: "when it does not refer to a *śūdra*".

1) [It should be said:] when [the response] does not refer to a *śūdra*, a woman and when 'discontent' [is expressed].

[Objection:] It should be mentioned that [the substitution takes place] when [the response] does not refer to a *śūdra*, a woman and when 'discontent' [is expressed]. In the case of a *śūdra*, the example has been given. In the case of a woman: *gārgy ahaṃ, bhoḥ āyuṣmatī bhava gārgi* ("I [am] Gārgī. O Gārgī, be long-living!").

{**Explanation:**
Kaiyaṭa (VMBh_2: V.416.16 ff) gives the opinion of other grammarians regarding saluting women and whether the prohibition is necessary at all. Some say that a woman does not salute respectfully but she only touches the feet. Others, however, say that a woman salutes respectfully but does not use one's proper name; both salutation and the response to it are connected with the name and the family name, thus the prohibition in the case of women should not be ordained. However, according to those who would employ a woman's name both at salutation as well as at its response, the prohibition should be stated.}

VMBh_1: III.416.11-15; VMBh_2: V.416.12-417.3

[Bhāṣya:] In the case [of expressing] 'discontent': *sthāly ahaṃ, bhoḥ āyuṣmān edhi sthāli3n* ("I [am] Sthālin. O Sthālin, be long-living!").
[Objection:] I did not [intend] '*sthālin*' as a proper name.
[Question:] How then?
[Answer:] I intended it as in the 'ascetic-maxim' (i.e., I am the one carrying a vessel). This [is what] should be said: *sthāly ahaṃ, bhoḥ āyuṣmān edhi sthālin* (without the substitution).
[Objection:] I did not intend the 'ascetic-maxim'.
[Question:] What then?
[Answer:] I [intended] this to be a proper name. [The response would be:] *asūyakas tvam asi jālma na tvaṃ pratyabhivādam arhasi bhidyasva vṛṣala sthālin* ("You are calumnious, vile! You do not deserve reverential salutation! Perish, you wicked Sthālin!").

{**Explanation:**

The situation described above is as follows: someone greets an older person or a teacher saying *sthāly aham*. The teacher thinks that *sthālin* is the person's proper name and responds accordingly: *āyuṣmān edhi sthālī3n* ("Be long-living, Sthālin"). The substitution with a prolated vowel takes place. Then, however, the person says that *sthālin* is not his proper name; he uses it because he carries a vessel. Commentators refer to the maxim of a stick (*daṇḍanyāya*) according to which an ascetic is recognised by the staff he carries. In such a case the teacher, thinking that the person is telling the truth, salutes him thus: *āyuṣmān edhi sthālīn* (no substitution needed). It takes place only in the case of proper names and family names (*gotra*), not in the case of the so-called etymological names (as the name derived from the thing carried). But then the person says again that he does not mean it that way and it is his proper name. At which point the teacher realises that he is being mocked and gets angry because such a wicked person does not deserve any blessing, or any fair response, only a curse. And this is the response the person gets: *asūyakas tvam asi jālma na tvaṃ pratyabhivādam arhasi bhidyasva vṛṣala sthālin* ("You are calumnious, vile! You do not deserve reverential salutation! Perish, you wicked Sthālin!").}

VMBh_1: III.416.16-22; VMBh_2: V.417.4-10

2) [It should be said that the substitution] is optional in the case of warriors (*rājanya*) and tradesmen (*viś*) [when their names are followed by the word] *bhoḥ*.

[Bhāṣya:] It should be mentioned [that the substitution] is optional in the case of warriors (*rājanya*) and tradesmen (*viś*) [when their names are followed by the word] *bhoḥ*. [For example:] *devadatto 'haṃ bhoḥ*; *āyuṣmān edhi devadatta bho3ḥ* ("Hello, I am Devadatta. Oh, Devadatta, be long-living!") or [*āyuṣmān edhi*] *devadatta bhoḥ* ("Oh, [be long-living] Devadatta!"). [Let us see the example of] a warrior: *indravarmāhaṃ bhoḥ*; *āyuṣmān edhi indravarman* ("Hello, I am Indravarman. Oh, Indravarman, be long-living!") or [*āyuṣmān edhi*] *indravarmā3n* ("Oh, [be long-living] Indravarman!"). [The example of] a warrior [has been given]. [Let us see the example of] a tradesman: *indrapālito 'haṃ bhoḥ*; *āyuṣmān edhīndrapālitā3* ("Hello, I am Indrapālita. Oh, Indrapālita, be long-living!") or [*āyuṣmān edhi*] *indrapālita* ("Oh, [be long-living] Indrapālita!"). [The example of] a tradesman [has been given].

Another one has said: the substitute in the word *bhoḥ* should be mentioned in the case of the response to reverential salutation to every name. [For example,] *devadatto 'haṃ bhoḥ*; *āyuṣmān edhi bho3ḥ* ("I am Devadatta. Oh, be long-living!"). Or *āyuṣmān edhi devadattā3* ("Oh, Devadatta! Be long-living!").

{Explanation:

Annaṃbhaṭṭa (MPV X.401) explains why there is no substitution in the word *bhoḥ* when it is used together with the name or the family name. Substitution should take place mainly in the name (or the family name). When the word *bhoḥ* replaces the name (when it is used alone), it is treated like the substitutend, like the proper name and the substitution may take place. According to the commentators, the prescribed option is both *prāpta* and *aprāpta*; it is a *prāptavibhāṣā* with respect to the name, namely the substitution that was considered obligatory when the proper name is used, is now made optional. In the case of the word *bhoḥ*, however, it must an *aprāptavibhāṣā* because the substitution was not prescribed for this word before. It would not take place at all if the option were not stated.}

VMBh_1: III.416.23-417.5; VMBh_2: V.417.11-418.7

[Question:] Why there is no [substitution] in this case: *devadatta kuśaly asi* ("Oh Devadatta, you are happy?")?
[Answer:] Here something is said and something is replied. [Something] secondary is said and [something] principal is replied. The prolation should regard [a vowel] being a part of the element *Ṭi*, which is a part of what is principal, but here the term *Ṭi* is not a part of what is principal.
[Objection:] In this case then it would not result either: *ādheyo 'gnī3r nādheyā3s* ("The fire is to be kindled! Not to be kindled!").
[Answer:] It is not ascertained whether the fire is to be kindled or not to be kindled.
[Question:] What then?
[Answer:] Here, the action accomplished by the means of fire is determined, [whether] the fire is to be kindled or not to be kindled.
[Objection:] If so, the second use of the word *agni* ('fire') would result. [The *paribhāṣā* stating that] "the things that have been stated are not expressed [again"] will not apply.[383]
[Objection:] If so, the use of the second word *ādheya* would not result either. [The *paribhāṣā* stating that] "the things that have been stated are not expressed [again"] does apply.
[Answer:] This is not a fault. The use of the meanings already expressed is seen as well, namely *apūpau dvāv ānaya* ("Bring two cakes!"), *brāhmaṇau dvāv ānaya* ("Bring two Brahmins!").

{Explanation:

[383] See WUJASTYK 1993: vol. I:54, vol. II:181-182.

There are two versions of the beginning of this discussion. Kielhorn accepts *apradhānam ucyate pradhānaṃ pratyucyate*. The VMBh_2 edition reads *pradhānam ucyata 'pradhānaṃ pratyucyate*. The problem seems to be where, if at all, in the example *devadatta kuśaly asi* the substitution should take place. The term *pratyabhivāda* qualifies the governing term *pada* in the present *sūtra*. Taking all *anuvṛtti* into consideration, prolation should take place in the element *Ṭi* of such a *pada* that is placed at the end of an utterance and expresses the meaning of a response. It seems crucial then to determine what is secondary and what is principal in the above example to understand why the substitution does not take place. The commentators accept *devadatta* as principal, and as such it could be subject to substitution. The expression *kuśaly asi* is secondary because it is the response. That view goes along the second reading, that is *pradhānam ucyata 'pradhānaṃ pratyucyate*. According to the former, the word *devadatta* is heard in the reverential salutation and this is what is replied as well. The expression *kuśaly asi* does not appear before and as such cannot be replied. It seems from the commentaries that in both cases the word *devadatta* is considered the principal one. They differ in establishing which expression should be considered a response. However, the word *devadatta* does not appear at the end of an utterance, which is a necessary condition for the substitution, which is why it does not take place. What appears at the end is secondary.

Such an interpretation leads to problems with the example *ādheyo 'gnī3r nādheyā3s* where the substitution takes place on the basis of A. 8.2.97 *vicāryāmāṇām*. Were we to understand that deliberation refers to fire, we should treat it as principal. Patañjali says that this is not the case. Deliberation does not refer to the object of kindling (or not kindling) but to the action itself that is performed with the help of *agni*. That makes *agni* secondary.

It seems that this expression should be divided as we have the prolated vowel twice, which goes against the rules. It should read thus *ādheyo 'gnī3ḥ – nādheyā3s*. In such a way we achieve two *pada*s, both at the end of an utterance, which can undergo the substitution. It also explains the discussion that follows regarding the repetition of words. It is proposed that the word *agni* appeared in the second part or the word *ādheya* were excluded. This difference depends on whether we accept the *paribhāṣā* as valid or not. The conclusion is that we should follow the usage. Repeating the word *agni* in the above example would not be done. However, the expression such as *apūpau dvāv ānaya* where duality is expressed twice – by the word *dvau* and the case ending in *apūpa* – is perfectly acceptable.}

A. 8.2.84 *dūrād dhūte ca*

[The prolated *udātta* accented vowel comes in place of a vowel of the *Ṭi* element of an utterance] when used for calling out [someone] from a distance.

VMBh_1: III.417.6-14; VMBh_2: V.419.1-10

[Objection:] It is said "when used for calling out [someone] from a distance"; and the word *dūra* ('far') does not have a fixed meaning. It refers either to something far away or to something close. In such a way, indeed, someone has said to someone: "This water vessel is near, bring it". That one has said: "Get up and grab [it]. [It is] far away; I will not be able [to do it]". Another one has said: "Pāṭaliputra is far from Mathura". That one has said: "It is not far. It is near". Thus the word *dūra* ('far') does not have a fixed meaning; due to its unfixed meaning one does not know in which place the prolation should take place.
[Answer:] In such a case then the instruction is formed with the help of [the verb] *hve* ('to call') – that which involves calling is far away.
[Question:] What is it then?
[Answer:] When no particular effort [of articulation] is used other than the natural effort and there is a doubt whether it will be heard or not; in such a case it is understood that [a person is] far away.

{**Explanation:**
The word *dūra* is relative in meaning. For some people something can be far away, for others the same thing will be close. How is it possible to determine where the substitution with a prolated vowel should take place, then? The clue is the verb *hveÑ* ('to call', DhP I:1057). If one needs to use additional effort so that the person standing in a distance could hear what is said, then the substitution takes place. We can also determine that something is far away when it involves tiredness. In other words, when one has to use a lot of effort to convey the message and becomes tired, then it means that the person they were shouting to was far away.}

A. 8.2.85 *haiheprayoge haihayoḥ*
[The prolated *udātta* accented vowel comes in place of the *Ṭi* vowel of the particles] *hai* and *he* when [the words] *hai* and *he* are used [for calling out someone from a distance].

VMBh_1: III.417.15-19; VMBh_2: V.419.11-420.4

[Question:] What is the purpose in using *hai* and *he*?

1) [The particles] *hai* and *he* [in the expression] "when [the words] *hai* and *he* are used", are used for the sake of the substitution with a prolated vowel in [the particles] *hai* and *he*.

[Answer:] [The particles] *hai* and *he* [in the expression] "when [the words] *hai* and *he* are used", are used so that the substitution with a prolated vowel took place in [the particles] *hai* and *he*. [For example:] *devadatta hai3* and *devadatta he3* ('Hello, Devadatta!'). If [the particles] *hai* and *he* were not used [in the *sūtra*], when they are used [in speech, the prolation] would result in something else.

{**Explanation:**
The present *sūtra* has two purposes: introducing the *pluta*-substitution in the words *hai* and *he*, and establishing this substitution irrespective of their position in an utterance. We could not achieve that on the basis of the previous *sūtra* as it required that the words used for calling were either names or family names. The words *hai* and *he* do not convey such a meaning, they are used for drawing attention. If the *sūtra* were formulated *prayoge haihayoḥ*, the previous context would continue (i.e., *dūrād dhūte*) and only the words expressing calling would undergo the substitution. Using the words *hai* and *he* specifies that only these forms are subject to substitution.}

VMBh_1: III.417.19-22; VMBh_2: V.420.5-8

[Question:] What is the purpose in using [the word] *prayoga*?

2) The word *prayoga* [is used] for the sake of meaningless [words] when meaningful [words] are used.

[Answer:] The word *prayoga* is used so that [the substitution] also regarded [the vowel of] meaningless [words] when the meaningful one is used. [For example,] *devadatta hai3* and *devadatta he3* ('Hello, Devadatta!').

{**Explanation:**
The words *hai* and *he* are *nipāta*s (particles) and as such do not convey an independent meaning; they are often considered meaningless. Later grammarians thought that such words as particles cannot posses the notion of *vācakatva* ('expressiveness') but rather *dyotakatva* ('suggestiveness'). They show some properties of the words they are attached to, rather than conveying a sense of their own.[384] That is why the problem arises with respect to the present rule. When the word appears in the vocative (e.g., *devadatta*), the substitution should

[384] The issue of different parts of speech being independent meaning carriers goes beyond the scope of the present work. It was first discussed in Yāska's *Nirukta* and further developed by later grammarians and philosophers of language. Whether *nipātas* were *vācaka* or *dyotaka* was the problem that was heavily debated within all philosophical schools in India.

apply to this very word; not to the word which is merely a particle. The word *prayoga* used in the *sūtra* allows for the substitution also in the case of a particle irrespective of the word in the vocative.}

VMBh_1: III.417.22-24; VMBh_2: V.420.8-11

[Question:] Then what is the purpose in using [the particles] *hai* and *he* twice?

3) [The particles] *hai* and *he* are used twice so that [the substitution took place also when the particles] are not in the final position.

[Answer:] [The particles] *hai* and *he* are used twice so that [the substitution] also took place when [the particles] are not in the final position. [For example,] *hai3 devadatta* and *he3 devadatta* ('Hello, Devadatta!').

{**Explanation:**
If the words *hai* and *he* were not used twice in the rule, the substitution could take place only if those words stood at the end of the sentence due to the governing expression *vākyasya ṭeḥ*. The substitution always takes place in the words *hai* and *he*, even though they do not stand at the end of an utterance. Therefore, the possible examples are: *devadatta hai3 / he3* or *hai3 / he3 devadatta*. The present rule allows for the substitution in the particles *hai* and *he* irrespective of their position in an utterance.}

A. 8.2.86 *guror anṛto 'nantyasyāpy ekaikasya prācām*
According to Eastern [grammarians, a prolated *udātta* accented vowel comes in place of] a *guru* vowel other than *ṛ*, one by one, even when it is not a final [vowel when used in response to reverential salutation excluding a *śūdra* or in response to a call from a distance].

VMBh_1: III.418.1-5; VMBh_2: V.420.12-16

1) In the case of prescribing the prolated vowel in place of a *guru* vowel, the substitution with a prolated vowel in place of a short final one would result due to it being prescribed by another [rule].

[Bhāṣya:] In the case of prescribing the prolated vowel in place of a *guru* vowel, the prolated vowel instead of the final short vowel would result. [For example,] *de3vadatta* ('O, Devadatta!').
[Question:] What is the reason?

[Answer:] Due to it being prescribed by another [rule]. It is by another rule that the prolated vowel instead of the final short vowel is prescribed when used for calling [someone] from the distance (A. 8.2.84).

{**Explanation:**
The problem regards the number of substituted vowels. According to previous rules, substitution would take place in the case of the last vowel of the last *pada* in an utterance. According to the present *sūtra*, we get the substitution of a long vowel in a *pada*. Thus when the final vowel is short and the non-final is long, the substitution would refer to both of them simultaneously, and incorrectly. The prolated vowel can be only one in a word, so in the word *devadatta* the possible forms are: *de3vadatta*, *devadā3tta* or *devadattā3*. It is not possible to have forms such as **de3vadā3ttā3* or **devadā3ttā3*.}

VMBh_1: III.418.6-10; VMBh_2: V.421.1-5

2) Alternatively, the expression *anantyasyāpi* [is used] for the sake of specifying both.

[Objection:] Alternatively, this is a fault.
[Question:] What is the reason?
[Answer:] The expression *anantyasyāpi* will be used in order to specify both. [The substitution will take place] of a non-final heavy vowel and also of a final vowel of [the element] *Ṭi*.
[Objection:] But should it not depend on a heavy vowel, i.e., [the substitution will take place] of a non-final heavy vowel and also of a final heavy vowel?
[Answer:] No, he has said. This [should] depend on both.[385] [The substitution will take place] of a non-final heavy vowel and also of a final vowel of [the element] *Ṭi*.

{**Explanation:**
The word *api* does not allow the option between the final and non-final heavy vowel. It rather means that the vowel undergoing the substitution can also be a part of the element *Ṭi*, so the substitution of the heavy vowel might take place when it is the final vowel, non-final or if it is a part of *Ṭi*.}

VMBh_1: III.418.10-12; VMBh_2: V.421.5-7

[Question:] Then what is the purpose of [using the word] *prāñc* (*prācām*)?

---

[385] The VMBh_2 edition has the version *ṭyapekṣam etat* ("It depends on [the element] *Ṭi*"), which seems to be more reasonable given the following sentence.

3) The word *prāñc* (*prācām*) [is used] for the sake of [establishing] an option.

[Answer:] The word *prāñc* (*prācām*) is used so that there could be an option.

{Explanation:
When Pāṇini mentions other grammarians, it can denote either showing respect or making an operation optional. It is the latter in the present rule. In his comment on the *sūtra* A. 8.2.92 Patañjali says: *sarva eva plutaḥ sāhasam anicchatā vibhāṣā vaktavyaḥ* ("Without desire to violate [the authority] every substitution with a prolated vowel should be mentioned as optional"). It means that not only this one but all the other rules prescribing prolation should be considered optional. Consequently, we can obtain forms without a prolated vowel at all.}

VMBh_1: III.418.13-20; VMBh_2: V.421.8-15

4) But the expression *prāñc* (*prācām*) is superfluous because [the same result (i.e., the option) is achieved] by the expression *ekaikasya* ('one by one').

[Objection:] The expression *prāñc* (*prācām*) is superfluous.
[Question:] What is the reason?
[Answer:] Because [the same result (i.e., the option) is achieved] by the expression *ekaikasya* ('one by one'). The word *ekaikasya* is used so that there was an option.
[Bhāṣya:] There is another purpose for using the word *ekaikasya*.
[Question:] What?
[Answer:] There must not be simultaneous prolation. On the basis of the rule A. 6.1.158[386] the simultaneous [substitution with a prolated *udātta* accented vowel of different vowels] is not possible.
[Objection:] The prolated vowel is suspended [with respect to the rule A. 6.1.158] and due to its suspension restriction would not apply.
[Answer:] This is not a fault. Even if in that case it is suspended, it is not suspended here.
[Question:] How come?
[Answer:] [There is the statement:] "Technical terms and rules of interpretation [are used] at the time of the grammatical operation"; where there is a grammatical operation, there they should be seen as present. [The rule reads:] "According to Eastern [grammarians, a prolated *udātta* accented vowel comes in

386 A. 6.1.158 *anudāttaṃ padam ekavarjam* ॥ ("A *pada* (word) bears an *anudātta* accent with the exception of one [syllable]")

place of] a *guru* vowel other than *ṛ*, one by one (*ekaikasya*), even when it is not a final [vowel when used in response to reverential salutation excluding a *śūdra* or in response to a call from a distance]." [The *sūtra*] A. 6.1.158 is present here.

{**Explanation:**
There are a few rules taken into consideration here; A. 6.1.158 *anudāttaṃ padam ekavarjam* allowing for only one syllable accented with *udātta* or *svarita*; A. 1.2.33 *ekaśruti dūrāt sambuddhau*,[387] according to which a *pada* is monotone (i.e., all the three accents merge) when calling someone from a distance; A. 6.1.198 *āmantritasya ca*[388] prescribing *udātta* accent to the initial syllable of the vocative; and finally, A. 8.1.55 *āma ekāntaram āmantritam anantike*[389] stating that when a *pada* termed *āmantrita* (lit. 'addressing, calling') occurs after *ām* and is not intervened by more than a single *pada*, is not *anudātta* accented in its entirety when a person is not close. As can easily be seen, all the above rules are often mutually exclusive and the whole discussion of the commentators is centred around solving the problem as to which of those rules should take precedence in our case.
The reference is made to two views regarding the application of technical terms and rules of interpretation within the *Tripādī* section discussed earlier (See **4.3.1**), namely the *kāryakāla* view where *paribhāṣā*s and *saṃjñā*s are read along with operational rules; and the *yathoddeśa* view where technical terms and rules of interpretation should be read at the place where they were originally stated. Based on the former, the rule A. 6.1.158 is not suspended with respect to the present rule so it should be taken into account while determining the accent of a *pada* with a prolated vowel. According to the latter, though, it is suspended. Patañjali agrees with the first view, which gives us the syllable with a prolated vowel being *udātta* accented on the basis of the application of the present *sūtra*, and with all the other syllables *anudātta* accented.}

VMBh_1: III.418.20; VMBh_2: V.421.15-16

[Answer:] Here, therefore, the simultaneous occurrence would not result: *devadattā3* ('O, Devadatta!').

{**Explanation:**

[387] A. 1.2.33 *ekaśruti dūrāt sambuddhau* || ("When calling someone from a distance, [the utterance is articulated as] monotone.")

[388] A. 6.1.198 *āmantritasya ca* || ("[The initial syllable] of the vocative also [bears an *udātta* accent].")

[389] A. 8.1.55 *āma ekāntaram āmantritam anantike* || ("The vocative [is not all *anudātta* accented when co-occurring with] *ām*, but separated from it by a single [*pada*] except when following it.")

Kaiyaṭa (VMBh_2: V.421.20 ff) says that an initial *udātta* accent by A. 6.1.198 *āmantritasya ca* should apply because it would not merge with the *udātta* of the prolated vowel. Thus the *sūtra* A. 6.1.158 would apply leaving only one *udātta* accented vowel, that is the initial one, and the rest would all be *anudātta*. On the other hand, A. 8.1.55 *āma ekāntaram āmantritam anantike* should block the monotone of A. 1.2.33 *ekaśruti dūrāt sambuddhau* as well as the *nighāta* ('toning down', *anudātta*). Annaṃbhaṭṭa (MPV X.406) says that it is monotone (*ekaśruti*) that applies in this case. It is required for the accent of a prolated vowel and *ekaśruti* to merge because they both cover the same domain of calling somebody from a distance. And when there is no monotone accent, then this is an example of a word with the initial *udātta* accent and the final prolated vowel.}

VMBh_1: III.418.21-23; VMBh_2: V.421.16-422.3

[Answer:] These two are suspended and unsuspended. The restriction applies to those [*sūtra*s] which are suspended or unsuspended.
[Objection:] But when the prolated vowel is *svarita* accented, then the simultaneous occurrence would result. [There is the *sūtra*] A. 8.2.103.
[Answer:] When there is the *svarita* accent, there is also *udātta*.[390]

{Explanation:
The rule prescribing initial *udātta* of the vocative is not suspended as it belongs to the sixth chapter (A. 6.1.198), while the rule prescribing *udātta* to a prolated vowel is suspended as it belongs to the *Tripādī* section. Consequently, we cannot obtain *anudātta* on remaining vowels based on the *Tripādī sūtra*. When it comes to A. 8.2.103 *svaritam āmreḍite 'sūyāsammatikopakutsaneṣu*, prescribing *svarita* to a prolated vowel, its application might result in two accented vowels; the situation accepted by Annaṃbhaṭṭa, according to whom it is possible to have a *pada* with two prolated vowels, one *udātta* accented on the final and the other *svarita* accented, on the basis of A. 6.1.158. The reason it is possible is that there is a difference between *udātta* and *svarita* accents. In order to stop simultaneous occurance of two prolated vowels with acute and circumlex accents respectively in one word, the expression *ekaikasya* ('one by one') is used in the present rule.}

VMBh_1: III.418.23-24; VMBh_2: V.422.3-4

[Bhāṣya:] In that case, when the prolated vowel is *anudātta*, then simultaneous occurrence would result. [There is the *sūtra*] A. 8.2.100. Therefore, the expression *prāñc* (*prācām*) should be used.

---

[390] A. 1.2.32 *tasyādita udāttam ardhahrasvam* ॥ ("The first part of that (a *svarita* accented vowel) which is half a short vowel is *udātta* accented [and the other half is *anudātta* accented].")

{Explanation:
The expression *ekaikasya* is used for the sake of stopping simultaneous occurrence of prolated vowels marked with *udātta* and *anudātta*. The term *prācām*, on the other hand, is used for making the option of no prolation available.}

{A. 8.2.87 *om abhyādāne*
[The prolated *udātta* accented vowel comes in place of a vowel of the *pada*] *om* at the beginning [of a Vedic hymn].} *This *sūtra* was not commented upon by Patañjali.

A. 8.2.88 *ye yajñakarmaṇi*
[The prolated *udātta* accented vowel comes in place of a vowel of the *pada*] *ye* when [it is] used during a sacrificial action.

VMBh_1: III.419.1-5; VMBh_2: V.422.5-10

1) There is potential overapplication if [the expression reads: "the prolated *udātta* accented vowel comes in place of a vowel of the *pada*] *ye* when [it is] used during a sacrificial action".

[Objection:] There is potential overapplication if [the expression reads: "the prolated *udātta* accented vowel comes in place of a vowel of the *pada*] *ye* when [it is] used during the sacrificial action". Here it would result as well: *ye devāso divy ekādaśa sthā*[391] ("Those deities who are eleven in heaven").

2) But it has been achieved "*ye yajāmahe* ("We who sacrifice")" due to its addition in [the *sūtra*] A. 8.2.91.

[Answer:] It has been achieved.
[Question:] How?
[Answer:] The expression *ye yajāmahe* should be added in [the *sūtra*] A. 8.2.91.

{Explanation:
The present rule allows for the prolated substitution in the word *ye* only when the expression is used during a sacrifice. Consequently, in the first example the substitution will not take place, as it is merely a statement. The expression *ye yajāmahe*, however, could be included in the *sūtra* A. 8.2.91.}

---

[391] Ṛ̣gV 1.139.11.

A. 8.2.89 *praṇavaṣ ṭeḥ*
The *praṇava* (the sacred *om* syllable), [prolated and *udātta* accented] comes in place of [a vowel of] the *Ṭi* [element of the final *pada* of an utterance when the same is used during a sacrificial action].

VMBh_1: III.419.6-8; VMBh_2: V.423.1-4

[Question:] It is said '*praṇava*'; what is really '*praṇava*'?
[Answer:] [The term] '*praṇava*' signifies the letter *o* or the syllable *om* with the duration of three morae, that comes in place of what begins with the final vowel and the consonant and the vowel (i.e., the element *Ṭi*) or having taken the final vowel of the verse, or of half of the verse, of a Vedic hymn.

{**Explanation:**
The term *praṇava* is not a technical term used in grammar; nor is it particularly well known from usage, which is why the question is asked. The substitution with the prolated *praṇava* is prescribed for the element *Ṭi* of the verses in Vedic hymns used for a sacrificial activity. Annaṃbhaṭṭa (MPV X.407) explains that in the world the word *praṇava* is used by specialists in Veda to denote the syllable *om*; this meaning is not intended here either, however. If this term is not used in grammar at all and it is not understood in its wordly usage, what does it mean then? The answer is that it is used according to what has been stated in *śāstrāntara* ('another science') which is understood as phonetical treatises – *prātiśākhya*s etc.}

VMBh_1: III.419.9-12; VMBh_2: V.423.5-8

[Question:] What is the purpose [in using] the word *Ṭi*?

1) The word *Ṭi* [is used] in order to substitute the whole.

[Answer:] When there is the sound *o*, then the substitute of a whole should take place. When there is the syllable *om*, then the substitute of a whole will take place [on the basis of the *sūtra*] A. 1.1.55.[392]

{**Explanation:**
The element *Ṭi* should be read into the present rule from A. 8.2.82. That would lead, however, to the substitution of the vowel that forms a part of *Ṭi*, not the en-

[392] A. 1.1.55 *anekāl śit sarvasya* || ("[A substitute ordered for an element in genitive] comes in place of the whole [element when the substitute consists of] more than one sound (*aL*) or is marked with *Ś*.")

tire unit. The rule A. 1.1.52 *alo 'ntyasya* establishes the substitution of the final element; so, if the word *Ṭi* were not used in the *sūtra* but it continued via *anuvṛtti*, it would be possible to substitute the final consonant in a word. The element *Ṭi* can have two forms: it can be a single vowel or it can be a vowel followed by a final consonant in a word. By force of the so-called *acparibhāṣā* (A. 1.2.28 *acaś ca*) it will be the vowel itself (*aC*) that is going to be quallified by *Ṭi* in this rule. This would lead to the conclusion that the vowel that gets replaced forms a part of an element *Ṭi*, yet it would not allow for the substitution of the whole unit *Ṭi*. To summarize, when the word *Ṭi* is not used in the text of the *sūtra*, on the one hand we can apply the *paribhāṣā* A. 1.1.52 which would result in the substitution of the final sound and, on the other, we can apply A. 1.2.28 resulting in the substitution only of the vowel. The purpose of repeating the word *Ṭi* is to allow for the replacement of the entire *Ṭi*.
Naturally, in the case of *praṇava*, we need only refer to the vowel *o* that is going to be prolated. The problem here is again the vowel *paribhāṣā* which, according to Annaṃbhaṭṭa, would not allow for the substitution in the case of words ending in consonants. Nārāyaṇa (MPV X.408) states that A. 1.2.28 applies when the technical term is prescribed, and not when what is prescribed contains three morae. Consequently, A. 1.2.28 is not applied in this case because it would lead to a lack of substitution in the case of the syllable *om*. This syllable consists of a vowel and a consonant, and the technical term *pluta* cannot refer to such a combination. Thus the rule A. 1.2.28 is not present here.
According to some (*kecit*), mentioning the word *Ṭi* in the present rule is superfluous as it would continue from the *sūtra* A. 8.2.82 anyway. This view is held by those who understand the term *praṇava* as the vowel *o* only. According to Nāgeśa (VMBh_2: V.423) then, the present *sūtra* as a whole would be superfluous if that particular view were accepted.}

A. 8.2.90 *yājyāntaḥ*
[The prolated *udātta* accented vowel comes in place of a vowel of *Ṭi* of] the final [sentence] of *yājyā* (a type of a hymn) [when the same is used during a sacrificial action].

VMBh_1: III.419.13-16; VMBh_2: V.424.1-4

[Question:] What is the purpose of the word *anta*?
[Answer:] [The word] *yājyā* is the name of a Vedic hymn and it is a collection of sentences; the prolated vowel of [the element] *Ṭi* would result in all of those sentences. And it is desired that [the substitution] should take place of the last one. Without this the specific effort is not achieved. That is the purpose [in using] the word *anta*.

{Explanation:
The question about the purpose of the word *anta* arises because the element *Ṭi*, continued from the *sūtra* A. 8.2.82, shows that the substitution refers to the last vowel in an utterance. However, *yājyā* is a collection of sentences or verses. Were the word *anta* not used, each sentence would end with a prolated sound, while the required result is to employ prolation only at the end of the last sentence of a hymn.}

{A. 8.2.91 *brūhipreṣyaśrauṣaḍvauṣaḍāvahānām ādeḥ*
[The prolated *udātta* accented vowel comes in place of] the initial vowel of [the words] *brūhi* ('speak!'), *preṣya* ('call upon to recite!'), *śrauṣaṭ* ('may he hear us'), *vauṣaṭ* ('may he lead us') and *āvaha* ('lead!') [when they are used during a sacrificial action].} *This *sūtra* was not commented upon by Patañjali.

A. 8.2.92 *agnītpreṣaṇe parasya ca*
[The prolated *udātta* accented vowel comes in place of an initial vowel of a *pada*] and the following one [when they used during a sacrificial action] in an order given to a priest to kindle the sacrificial fire.

VMBh_1: III.419.17-19; VMBh_2: V.424.5-7

1) There is potential overapplication [if we say:] "when used [during a sacrificial action] in an order given to a priest to kindle the sacrificial fire".

[Objection:] There is potential overapplication [if we say:] "when used [during the sacrificial action] in an order given to a priest to kindle the sacrificial fire". Here it would result as well: *agnīd agnīn vihara* ("O, priest, divide the fires").[393]

{Explanation:
The word *agnīdh* denotes a type of a subordinate priest who helps an *adhvaryu*. Prolation is employed when the call of an *adhvaryu*, the head of a ceremony, to an *agnīdh* performing the function, is made. The prescription in this rule regards two vowels: the initial and the following one, which gives us examples such as *āśrāvaya*→*ā3śrā3vaya* or *ośrāvaya*→*o3śrā3vaya* (both meaning 'announce!').}

VMBh_1: III.420.1-5; VMBh_2: V.424.8-11

2) But it has been achieved due to the statement: "[the prolated *udātta* accented vowel comes in place of an initial vowel of a *pada*] and the following one in *ośrāvaya* ('make them hear, announce!')".

---

[393] TS 6.3.1.2.

[Answer:] It has been achieved.
[Question:] How?
[Answer:] It should be mentioned that "[the prolated *udātta* accented vowel comes in place of an initial vowel of a *pada*] and the following one in *ośrāvaya*" – *o3śrā3vaya* ('Make them hear, announce!').
[Bhāṣya:] Another one has said: it should be mentioned that "[the prolated *udātta* accented vowel comes in place of an initial vowel of a *pada*] and the following one in *ośrāvaya* and *āśrāvaya*" – *o3śrā3vaya* and *ā3śrā3vaya* ('Make them hear, announce!').
It should be mentioned that in other cases it is variously [applicable]. [For example:] *uddharā3* or *uddhara* ('Raise up!') and *āharā3* or *āhara* ('Fetch!').

{Explanation:
The examples given by Patañjali are the only ones where substitution can take place, which is why the *sūtra* needs reformulating in order to exclude other stems from falling under its scope.
The term *bahulam* ('variously') is proposed in the *sūtra*, which would allow for the substitution not only of the first and the following vowels, but also of the final vowel of an utterance. The commentators read the examples *uddharā3 uddhara* and *āharā3 āhara* together, with the repetition. If this is the case, the substitution takes place of the final vowel of the first *pada*.}

VMBh_1: III.420.6-8; VMBh_2: V.424.11-425.3

[Question:] Should it be mentioned then?
[Answer:] It should not be mentioned. The separation of the rule will be done. [The *sūtra*s will be:] *agnītpreṣaṇe parasya ca vibhāṣā* ("[The prolated *udātta* accented vowel] rarely [comes in place of an initial vowel of a *pada*] and the following one [when they are used during a sacrificial action] in an order given to a priest to kindle the sacrificial fire"). Then: *pṛṣṭāprativacane heḥ* ("[The prolated *udātta* accented vowel comes in place of a final element] of *hi* ('surely, indeed') when it is used in response to a question"). [And finally,] *vibhāṣā* ("It is only 'optional'").
Another one has said: without desire to violate [the authority] every substitution with a prolated vowel should be mentioned as optional.

{Explanation:
The separation of two rules is suggested in this passage; it is proposed that optionality (*vibhāṣā*) from the next rule should be incorporated into the present one. Such a solution would make it a fixed option applying only in particular cases. The word *para* used in the *sūtra* could suggest that the substitution takes

place when two vowels to be replaced are separated, as in the example of *uddhara uddhara* when we have two separate words. The word *para* could be understood as 'the following *pada*'. Treating the rule as a fixed option does not allow for such an interpretation because it restricts the application of a rule to the examples *āśrāvaya* and *ośrāvaya* where there is no separation involved. The substitution would be allowed only in the case of supplementing the rule with the word *bahulam*.
Another view proposes it to be such an option as the rule A. 8.2.86, which prescribed every prolation case as optional. The expression *prācām* used in A. 8.2.86 is thought to continue here as well which allows for the optionality of the *sūtra*.}

{A. 8.2.93 *vibhāṣā pṛṣṭaprativacane heḥ*
[The prolated *udātta* accented vowel] rarely [comes in place of the final sound] of *hi* ('surely, indeed') when it is used in response to a question.
A. 8.2.94 *nigṛhyānuyoge ca*
[The prolated *udātta* accented vowel rarely comes in place of the *Ṭi* vowel of the final *pada* of an utterance] when the question, after having been refuted, [is repeated] with reproach.} *These *sūtra*s were not commented upon by Patañjali.

A. 8.2.95 *āmreḍitaṃ bhartsane*
[The prolated *udātta* accented vowel comes in place of the *Ṭi* vowel of] a reduplicated *pada* (*āmreḍita*) when the meaning is 'threat'.

VMBh_1: III.420.9-12; VMBh_2: V.425.4-7

1) [The substitution with a prolated vowel takes place] in the case of [the word] meaning 'threat' alternately.

[Bhāṣya:] It should be mentioned that [the substitution with a prolated vowel takes place] in the case of [the word] meaning 'threat' alternately. [For example,] *caurā3 caura* or *caura caurā3* ('thief!'), *kuśīlā3 kuśīla* or *kuśīla kuśīlā3* ('evil one!').

{Explanation:
The reduplication is a result of application of the *sūtra* A. 8.1.8 *vākyāder āmantritasyāsūyāsammatikopakutsanabhartsaneṣu*.[394] The *vārttika* proposes that

---

[394] A. 8.1.8 *vākyāder āmantritasyāsūyāsammatikopakutsanabhartsaneṣu* ॥ ("[Two come] in place of a vocative (*āmantrita*) occurring at the beginning of an utterance when the meaning is *asūyā*

the *pluta* substitution took place in either word: the first one or the repeated one, even though, technically, it is the repeated word only that is called *āmreḍita* by A. 8.1.2 *tasya param āmreḍitam* || ("[The technical term] *āmreḍita* denotes the second expression of it [i.e., the doubled sentence]").}

{A. 8.2.96 *aṅgayuktaṃ tiṅākāṅkṣam*
[The prolated *udātta* accented vowel comes in place of the *Ṭi* vowel of] a verbal *pada* (*tiṄ*) which shares an expectancy relationship [with something] and is used with connection to [the word] *aṅga* ('indeed, truly') [when the meaning is 'threat'].
A. 8.2.97 *vicāryamāṇānām*
[The prolated *udātta* accented vowel comes in place of the *Ṭi* vowel of an utterance] meaning a deliberation of choice.
A. 8.2.98 *pūrvaṃ tu bhāṣāyām*
But [the prolated *udātta* accented vowel comes in place of the *Ṭi* vowel of] the first [among utterances meaning a deliberation of choice] in common speech.
A. 8.2.99 *pratiśravaṇe ca*
[The prolated *udātta* accented vowel comes in place of the *Ṭi* vowel of an utterance] meaning 'a response to a promise'.
A. 8.2.100 *anudāttaṃ praśnāntābhipūjitayoḥ*
[The prolated] *anudātta* accented vowel [comes in place of the *Ṭi* vowel of a final *pada* of an utterance] being a question or when the meaning is 'praised'.
A. 8.2.101 *cid iti copamārthe prayujyamāne*
[The prolated *anudātta* accented vowel comes in place of the *Ṭi* vowel of a final *pada* of an utterance] used with [the particle] *cit* in the meaning of 'comparison'.
A. 8.2.102 *uparisvid āsīd iti ca*
And [the prolated *anudātta* accented vowel comes in place of the *Ṭi* vowel of] *uparisvid āsīt* ("He/she was perhaps above").} *These *sūtra*s were not commented upon by Patañjali.

A. 8.2.103 *svaritam āmreḍite 'sūyāsammatikopakutsaneṣu*
[The prolated] *svarita* accented vowel [comes in place of the *Ṭi* vowel of] the preceding *pada* before the reduplicated [*pada* in the vocative] when the meaning is *asūyā* ('envy, jealousy'), *sammati* ('sameness of opinion'), *kopa* ('anger') or *kutsana* ('abuse, reproach').

('envy, jealousy'), *sammati* ('sameness of opinion'), *kopa* ('anger'), *kutsana* ('abuse, reproach') and *bhartsana* ('threat').")

VMBh_1: III.420.13-16; VMBh_2: V.425.8-11

1) An option should be mentioned when [the meanings are] *asūyā* etc.

[Bhāṣya:] An option should be mentioned when [the meanings are] *asūyā* etc. [For example:] *kanye3 kanye* or *kanye kanye* ("O, you wicked girl!"), *śaktike3 śaktike* or *śaktike śaktike* ("O, you really strong one!").

{Explanation:
This *sūtra* refers to A. 8.1.8 *vākyāder āmantritasyāsūyāsammatikopakutsana-bhartsaneṣu*, which allows for reduplication of the stem under given meaning conditions; the conditions that almost overlap in A. 8.2.103 and A. 8.1.8, with the sole exception of *bhartsana* which appears in the rule A. 8.2.95 *āmreḍitaṃ bhartsane* assigning *udātta* to a prolated vowel. The examples in the present rule are *svarita* accented.
Commentators (MPV vol. X:410) point out that the *vārttika* is unnecessary, because optionality of the rule would be achieved on the basis of the statement: "Without desire to violate [the authority] every substitution with a prolated vowel should be mentioned as optional" (see the *sūtra* A. 8.2.92). However, this statement was not used by Kātyāyana, it was not a *vārttika*. Patañjali says: "another one has said", so it is neither Pāṇini, nor Kātyāyana nor, obviously, Patañjali himself.}

{A. 8.2.104 *kṣiyāśīḥpraiṣeṣu tiṅākāṅkṣam*
[The prolated *svarita* accented vowel comes in place of the *Ṭi* vowel of] a verbal *pada* (*tiṄ*) which shares an expectancy relationship [with something] when the meaning is *kṣiyā* ('offence against the customs'), *āśīs* ('benediction') or *praiṣa* ('command').
A. 8.2.105 *anantasyāpi praśnākhyānayoḥ*
[The prolated *svarita* accented vowel comes in place of the *Ṭi* vowel] of a non-final *pada* as well as [of the final one] when the meaning is 'a question' or 'a story, relation'.} *These *sūtra*s were not commented upon by Patañjali.

A. 8.2.106 *plutāv aica idutau*
[In the case of the diphthongs] *ai* or *au* (*aiC*), the prolated vowels come in place of the vowels *i* and *u*.

VMBh_1: III.420.17-20; VMBh_2: V.426.1-4

[Question:] Why is this said?

1) The term *pluta* for the vowels *i* and *u* is used because there is potential involvement of the [undesired] growth of both [parts] of [the diphthongs] *ai* and *au*.

[Answer:] The term *pluta* for the vowels *i* and *u* is used because there is potential involvement of the [undesired] growth of both [parts] of [the diphthongs] *ai* and *au*.

{Explanation:
The term *pluta* in the present *sūtra* is not used in order to prescribe the substitution but to settle its domain. In previous rules the substitution referred to single vowels and, occassionaly, the entire element *Ṭi*. Here, however, the substitution will refer to a part of diphthongs *ai* and *au*, which are composed of the vowels *a* + *i* and *a* + *u* respectively. The *sūtra* specifies that only elements *i* and *u* are subject to prolation.}

VMBh_1: III.420.20-421.5; VMBh_2: V.426.4-11

[Question:] Why is it said: "Because there is potential involvement of the [undesired] growth of both" when words are permanent? And when words are permanent, sounds should be unchangeable and immutable, not [being] altered by decrease and increase.
[Answer:] This is not a fault. [The expression] *ubhayavivṛddhiprasaṅgāt* is not understood in such a way: *ubhayavivṛddhi* [meaning] "growth of both", [further] "due to the growth of both".
[Question:] How then?
[Answer:] [The expression] *ubhayavivṛddhi* [means] "that one in which there is the growth of both", [further] "due to the one in which there is the growth of both". These [diphthongs] *ai* and *au* are sound compounds of the sound *a*, and the sounds *i* and *u* [respectively] of one mora each; when the prolation of those two is mentioned, that one in which there is the growth of both would result. As here – when the womb is growing, the whole body grows perfect. There is the purpose then.

{Explanation:
The discussed problem with interpretation of *vivṛddhi* is an interesting one given grammarians' position on the unchangeable character of sounds. If we were to interpret the compound *ubhayavivṛddhi* as a *tatpuruṣa* and accept that sounds are *nitya*, we would face the contradiction, for elements that are eternal cannot grow. If they are unchangeable, how can they change? Even if they are considered *anitya*, there is no growth whatsoever, because in that case the sounds are destroyed after they have been uttered. The comparison to a womb is explained by

Kaiyaṭa; they are not fixed elements that grow in a womb. When the first image is destroyed, another one appears. In the same way new words and sounds appear.}

VMBh_1: III.421.5-14; VMBh_2: V.426.11-427.9

[Question:] What then?

2) With respect to that, there is potential involvement of something which is undesired.

[Answer:] With respect to that, something which is undesired might be involved. A prolated vowel of the duration of four morae would result.

3) But it has been achieved due to mentioning the lengthening of [the vowels] *u* and *i*.

[Answer:] It has been achieved.
[Question:] How?
[Answer:] It should be mentioned that [the vowels] *u* and *i* are long.
[Question:] Having said that, how is that [which is desired] achieved?
[Answer:] If there is the equal division, the vowel *a* is of one mora, and the vowels *i* and *u* are [also] one mora long.
However, a two and a half mora long [vowel] would result if the vowel *a* [had the duration] of half a mora, and the vowels *i* and *u* a mora and a half [each].
However, a three and a half mora long [vowel] would result if the vowel *a* [had the duration] of one and a half mora, and the vowels *i* and *u* half a mora [each].
And the *sūtra* divides.
[Answer:] Let it be as in the text of the *sūtra*.
[Objection:] But has it not been said that "with respect to that, something which is undesired might be involved"?
[Answer:] Vāḍaba, who knows what is undesired, says that it has been said by Sauryabhagavat. A prolated vowel is, indeed, desired [to have] four morae.

{**Explanation:**
The way Patañjali describes the length of prolated diphthongs here is very curious. He himself accepts that the diphthongs have the duration of two morae, which are evenly distributed. That means that the vowel *a* has the duration of one mora, and the vowels *i* and *u* are also one mora long each. The prolated vowel should be three morae long. If, therefore, we make the vowels *i* and *u* prolated, they will be three morae long. Together with the vowel *a* it will make four morae. However, the length in a diphthong can be distributed in a different way.

The vowel *a* can be of half a mora, and vowels *i* and *u* of one and a half mora. Patañjali says that after the prolation has taken place, the whole would have the duration of two and a half morae. It would mean that the vowels are lengthened from one and a half mora to two, which is the length of a simple long vowel.
The other option is to have the vowel *a* with the duration of one and a half mora and the vowels *i* and *u* with half a mora each. After the application of prolation, the whole diphthong would have the duration of three and a half morae. It would happen because the vowels *i* and *u*, with half a mora each, would be lengthened to two morae, which with the vowel *a* would give three and a half morae.
There is also the view that the prolated vowel, whether single or a diphthong, should be three morae long. It would suggest that we are supposed to prolate *i* and *u* only to such extent that the result will give three morae; irrespective of the distribution of length of individual sounds in a diphthong.}

A. 8.2.107 *eco 'pragṛhyasyādūrād dhūte pūrvasyārdhasyāduttarasyedutau*
[The prolated vowel] *ā3* comes in place of the first half of [the vowels denoted by] *eC* (i.e., *e*, *o*, *ai* and *au*) and [the vowels] *i* and *u* come in place of the second half when [the meaning is the one introduced from A. 8.2.83 on, but] it does not denote 'calling from a distance' [and the vowels denoted by *eC*] are not *pragṛhya*.

VMBh_1: III.421.15-18; VMBh_2: V.427.10-428.2

1) In the case of modification of a prolated vowel of [the vowels denoted by] *eC* (i.e., *e*, *o*, *ai* and *au*), [it should be said that it refers to] the end of a *pada*.

[Bhāṣya:] In the case of modification of a prolated vowel of [the vowels denoted by] *eC* (i.e., *e*, *o*, *ai* and *au*), [it should be said that it refers to] the end of a *pada*. Here, it must not be: *bhadraṃ karoṣi gau3ḥ* ("You are doing well, bull!").

{**Explanation:**
This rule also excludes those vowels denoted by *eC* that are termed *pragṛhya* defined by Pāṇini in A. 1.1.11 *īdūded dvivacanaṃ pragṛhyam.*[395] The *vārttika* proposes that the operation only referred to a diphthong that appears at the end of a *pada*. The substitution in the word *gauḥ* ('a bull') cannot take place for two reasons. Firstly, it cannot be termed *pada* due to prohibition in the *sūtra* A. 1.4.17 *svādiṣv asarvanāmasthāne*. The form *gauḥ* is the nominative singular and as such ends in the suffix *sU*, which is a strong case ending. Moreover, the final sound of the stem is the *visarjanīya*; the word does not end in a vowel denoted

[395] A. 1.1.11 *īdūded dvivacanaṃ pragṛhyam* || ("[The technical term] *pragṛhya* denotes [the final vowels] *ī*, *ū* and *e* of dual endings.")

by *eC*. The diphthong *au* is penultimate in the word *gauḥ*, thus it could not be subject to prolation.}

VMBh_1: III.421.19-422.2; VMBh_2: V.428.3-9

2) And the enumeration of the domain [of this rule should be done].

[Bhāṣya:] And the enumeration of the domain [of this rule] should be done. It should be mentioned that [the rule applies] at the end of a question, [in a sentence with the meaning of] 'praised' (see A. 8.2.100), [in a sentence denoting] something discussed (see A. 8.2.97), in response to reverential salutation (see A. 8.2.83) and at the end of a sacrificial formula (see A. 8.2.90). [Let us see the examples] at the end of a question: *agamā3ḥ pūrvā3n grāmā3n agnibhūtā3i paṭā3u* ("Have you gone to the eastern villages, o Agnibhūta, o smart one!?"). [The examples of the substitution] at the end of a question [have been discussed]. [Let us see the examples] 'praised': *siddho 'si māṇavakāgnibhūtā3i paṭā3u* ("You are skilled, o student Agnibhūta, o smart one!"). [The examples of the substitution in a sentence with the meaning of] 'praised' [have been discussed]. [Let us see the examples of a sentence denoting] something discussed: *hotavyaṃ dīkṣitasya gṛhā3i* ("Should one offer [the oblation] in the house of a consecrated person?").[396] [The examples of the substitution in a sentence denoting] something discussed [have been discussed]. [Let us see the examples of] a response to reverential salutation: *āyuṣmān edhy agnibhūtā3i* ("Be long-living, o Agnibhūta!"). [The examples of the substitution in] a response to reverential salutation [have been discussed]. [Let us see the examples] at the end of a sacrificial formula: *ukṣānnāya vaśānnāya somapṛṣṭāya vedhase/stomair vidhemāgnayā3i* ("May we worship Agni with praise, whose food is oxen, who eats cows, who demands soma and who is wise/brave").[397]

{**Explanation:**
According to the *vārttika*, this rule should be limited to the scope of the rules A. 8.2.100, A. 8.2.97, A. 8.2.83 and A. 8.3.90; it is not a general rule. The prolated vowel *ā3* should be accented according to the prescription of a particular rule, that is *anudātta* or *svarita* at the end of a question (A. 8.2.100) and *udātta* everywhere else. The vowels *i* and *u* are always *udātta* accented due to the continuation of the term *udātta* from the rule A. 8.2.82.}

VMBh_1: III.422.3-5; VMBh_2: V.428.10-12

---

[396] TS 6.1.4.5.
[397] ṚgV 8.43.11.

3) It should be added that in Vedic literature [the substitution is limited] to the vocative singular.

[Bhāṣya:] It should be added that in Vedic literature [the substitution is limited] to the vocative singular. [For example:] *agnā3i patnīvā3ḥ sajūr devena tvaṣṭrā somaṃ piba* ("O Agni, carrying wives, drink soma together with the god Tvaṣṭṛ!").[398]

A. 8.2.108 ***tayor yvāv aci saṃhitāyām***
[The semivowels] ***y*** **and** ***v*** **replace those [*****i*** **and** ***u*** **specified as a substitution for the second half of the sounds denoted by** ***eC*** **respectively] before a vowel in close proximity.**

VMBh_1: III.422.6-12; VMBh_2: V.428.13-429.5

[Question:] Then, it is said that these *y* and *v* [replace] which two?
[Answer:] He said [that they replace the vowels] *i* and *u*.
[Objection:] It should be said then "of [the vowels] *i* and *u*".
[Answer:] It should not be said. The context continues.
[Question:] What is the context?
[Answer:] [The *sūtra*] A. 8.2.107. So the meaning is: that which is indicated in the nominative here, [it is prescribed] with what is indicated in the genitive. [The expression] *aci* is in locative; [the expression] *idutau* will be changed into the genitive from the nominative, [on the basis of the rule] A.1.1.66.
[Question:] Why is this [*sutra*] said? Is it not achieved by [the *sūtra*] A. 6.1.77?
[Answer:] It is not achieved. [The substitution with] a prolated vowel is suspended [with respect to the rule A. 6.1.77] and so are these changes in prolated vowels.
[Answer:] The prolated vowel is not suspended with respect to vocalic *saṃdhi*.

{**Explanation:**
The present rule shares the domain of application with A. 6.1.77 *iko yaṇ aci*. On the one hand, it might be said that the rules prescribing prolation, being placed in the *Tripādī*, are suspended with respect to A. 6.1.77, which makes the present *sūtra* necessary. On the other hand, however, the prolation might not be considered suspended. And if it is not, then all the changes that take place in a prolated vowel would not be suspended either, which would make the present rule superfluous.
Nāgeśa (VMBh_2: V.429.24 ff) explains that the expression "changes in prolated vowels", which refers to the vowels *i* and *u* that undergo the change, does not

---

[398] TS 1.4.27.1.

really mean the change in a prolated vowel. This change refers to the second part of a sound whose first half is the prolated *ā3*. Therefore, he understands the expression *plutavikārau* as "the changes in what is attached to a prolated vowel" (*plutasahitau vikārau*) where the middle word (i.e., *sahitau*) is dropped. The domain of *pluta* applies to the vowels *i* and *u* because even though the term *pluta* is prescribed for the vowel *ā3* only, the domain extends to the rest as they are together, due to their closeness.}

VMBh_1: III.422.12-17; VMBh_2: V.429.6-11

[Question:] How is that known?
[Answer:] For he (i.e., Pāṇini) teaches the basic (i.e., unaltered) form of a prolated vowel on the basis of [the rule] A. 6.1.125.[399]
[Question:] How is the indication given?
[Answer:] For an operation should be applied to that which is the subject of an operation. This is therefore the purpose: to prohibit the substitution with a long vowel (A. 6.1.101 *akaḥ savarṇe dīrghaḥ*) and the *śākala* operations (A. 6.1.127 *iko 'savarṇe śākalyasya hrasvaś ca*).[400] The substitution with a long vowel and *śākala* operations must not take place. [For example:] *agnā3y indram* ("O Agni, to Indra…"), *paṭā3v udakam* ("O, smart one, [here is] water").
[Objection:] Surely this is not the purpose. It is formulated: preceded by a prolated vowel; "the *yaṆ*-substitute [of the vowels *i* and *u* that are] preceded by a prolated vowel is in order to prohibit the substitution with a long vowel and *śākala* operations."[401]
[Answer:] It should not be mentioned. It should necessarily be mentioned that those vowels *i* and *u* which are preceded by a prolated vowel are the changes of a prolated vowel; that is the purpose. [For example,] *bho3y indra* ("O! Indra!"), *bho3y iha* ("O! here!").

{**Explanation:**

[399] A. 6.1.125 *plutapragṛhyā aCi nityam* || ("Prolated vowels and *pragṛhya* vowels compulsorily [retain their original form] before vowels [in close proximity].")

[400] The operation called *śākala* is the one prescribed by Śākalya. He was an ancient grammarian whose name is mentioned in the treatise a few times. He claimed that the vowels *i*, *u*, *ṛ* and *ḷ* remain without phonetical combination or they are shortened when long: e.g., A. 6.1.127 *iko 'savarṇe śākalyasya hrasvaś ca* || ("According to Śākalya [the final vowel denoted by] *iK* (i.e., *i*, *u*, *ṛ*, *ḷ*) [of a *pada* retains its form] before non-homogenous [vowels] and [is replaced by] a [corresponding] short vowel.")

[401] See *vārttikas* 1 and 2 under A. 6.1.77: 1) *yaṇādeśaḥ plutapūrvasya ca* 2) *dīrghaśākalapratiṣedhārtham*.

In the above examples the vowel *i* should be treated as a particle (VMBh_2: V.429.20 ff) and by the *sūtra* A. 1.1.14 *nipāta ekāj anāṅ*[402] gets the designation *pragṛhya* which excludes it from sandhi operations. As such, it would retain its original form, which is why this rule was formed, to allow the application of sandhi. The word *bho* by the *vārttika* 2 under the *sūtra* A. 8.2.83 gets its final vowel replaced by *pluta*. This substitution, however, should refer to the final sound in an utterance. This change in positions is irregular (*vyatyaya*) and is possible in Vedic. According to Nāgeśa, however, based on the rule A. 8.2.86 and the expression *ekaikasya* ('one by one') used therein, the substitution with a prolated vowel can refer to different vowels, not necessarily the final one.}

VMBh_1: III.422.18-423.6; VMBh_2: V.429.12-430.6

[Objection:] If therefore this which should be mentioned is the reason for that, it should not be mentioned.
[Answer:] And this should necessarily be mentioned for the sake of accent. If it were by that [rule (i.e., A. 6.1.77)] then, the accent [on the basis of the *sūtra*] A. 8.2.4 might be involved. If, on the other hand, it were by this [rule], it (i.e., the accent) would not apply due to its suspension.
[Objection:] If therefore this what should be mentioned is the reason for that, it should not be mentioned.
[Question:] But has is not been said that "that should necessarily be mentioned that those vowels *i* and *u* which are preceded by a prolated vowel are the changes of a prolated vowel; that is the purpose; [for example,] *bho3y indra* ("O! Indra!"), *bho3y iha* ("O! here!")"? It belongs to Vedic literature, the rule is seen in Vedic literature.
[Answer:] If so, it does not belong to Vedic literature. [For example,] *bho3y indram sāma gāyati* ("O! He sings a great hymn"). This is an additional use of what is seen in Vedic literature.

***Kārika*:** When he (i.e., Pāṇini) prescribes *y* and *v* instead of *i* and *u*, could this not be achieved here by *yaṆ* (A. 6.1.77)? [Even if] those two are not suspended in the case of vocalic sandhi, the lengthening and *śākala* operations are invalid [here].
But when [a vowel denoted by] *iK* (i.e., *i*, *u*, *ṛ*, *ḷ*) is preceded by a prolated vowel, he prescribes the *yaṆ*-[substitute] as an exception to that. Because of that, the lengthening and *śākala* [operations] do not [apply] to those two; but the purpose is really to block the *yaṆ* accent.

---

[402] A. 1.1.14 *nipāta ekāj anāṅ* ‖ ("[The technical term *pragṛhya* denotes] a particle consisting of a single vowel with the exception of [the particle] *āṄ*.")

{**Explanation:**
The *pluta* substitution along with mentioned changes should be considered unsuspended with respect to the section preceding the *Tripādī* because the term *pluta* is explicitly mentioned in A. 6.1.125 *plutapragṛhyā aci*. The present rule could therefore serve to block the lengthening and operations prescribed by Śākalya, but it has already been established by the *vārttika*s on A. 6.1.77 *iko yaṇ aci*. Thus, the purpose of the present *sūtra* must be different. And it is to block the accent prescribed to the *yaṆ*-substitute by the *sūtra* A. 8.2.4.}

This was the second *āhnika* of the second *pada* of the eighth *adhyāya* in the *Vyākaraṇamahābhāṣya* composed by Patañjali. This is the end of a *pada*.

A. 8.3.1 *matuvaso ru saṃbandhau chandasi*
[The final sound of a *pada* ending] in [the suffixes] *matUP* or *KvasU* [is replaced by] *rU* before a vocative [ending, in close proximity] in Vedic.

VMBh_1: III.424.1-3; VMBh_2: V.431.1-5

1) [The suffixes] *vanIP* and *KvanIP* should [also] be included in the scope of substitution regarding [the final sound of a *pada* ending] in [the suffixes] *matUP* or *KvasU*.

[Bhāṣya:] [The suffixes] *vanIP* and *KvanIP* should [also] be included in the scope of substitution regarding [the final sound of a *pada* ending] in [the suffixes] *matUP* or *KvasU*. [For example,] *yas tvāyantaṃ vasunā prātiritvaḥ* ("You, the morning guest, who came with the wealth!").[403]

{**Explanation:**
The word used in the *vārttika* is *vana* (*matuvasor ādeśe vana upasaṃkhyānam*) but it covers two suffixes: *vanIP* and *KvanIP*. The commentators following Kaiyaṭa agree, however, that such an interpretation is a violation of *paribhāṣā*s according to which a suffix without a marker cannot be treated like a suffix with one, which quite clearly do not apply here.[404]

[403] Ṛg V 1.125.2. See A. 3.2.74 *ātaḥ maninkvanibvanipaś ca* || ("[In Vedic the suffixes *vIC*] and *manIN*, *KvanIP* and *vanIP* [are introduced] after [a verbal root ending in] *ā* [co-occurring with a nominal *pada* and with or without an *upasarga*]"); A. 3.2.75 *anyebhyo 'pi dṛśyate* || ("[The suffixes *manIN*, *KvanIP* and *vanIP* together with *vIC*] are also seen after other [verbal roots].")

[404] The *paribhāṣā*s in question are 81 *niranubandhakagrahaṇe na sānubandhakasya* || ("When a term void of an *anubandha* is employed [in grammar], it does not [denote] that which has an *anubandha* attached to it.") and 82 *tad anubandhakagrahaṇe nātad anubandhakasya* || ("When a term with one or more *anubandha*s is employed [in grammar], it does not [denote] that which

The derivation of the word *prātaritvaḥ* used in the Vedic example by Patañjali is as follows:

(1) *prātar* + *iṆ* (DhP II:36) + *KvanIP* (A. 3.2.75 *anyebhyo 'pi dṛśyate*)
prātar + *i* + *van*
(2) *prātar* + *i* + *tUK* (A. 6.1.71 *hrasvasya piti kṛti tuk*) + *van*
prātar + *i* + *t* + *van*
(3) *prātar* + *i* + *t* + *va* (*n* → *r*) (A. 8.3.1 *matuvaso ru saṃbandhau chandasi*)
(4) *prātar* + *i* + *t* + *va* (*r* → *ḥ*) (A. 8.3.15 *kharavasānayor visarjanīyaḥ*)
prātaritvaḥ}

VMBh_1: III.424.4-6; VMBh_2: V.431.6-9

2) [It should be said that] in the case of [the words] *bhavat*, *bhagavat* ('lord') and *aghavat* ('sinful') [the *rU*-substitute] optionally [takes place before a vocative ending] and [the element] *ava* [is replaced by the sound] *o*.

[Bhāṣya:] In Vedic and in common language in the case of [the words] *bhavat*, *bhagavat* ('lord') and *aghavat* ('sinful') the *rU*-substitute should be mentioned as optional [before a vocative ending] and [the sound] *o* should be mentioned [as replacing the element] *ava*. [The examples of the vocative singular are:] *bhoḥ* or *bhavan*; *bhagoḥ* or *bhagavan*; *aghoḥ* or *aghavan*.

{Explanation:
The derivation of the word *bhoḥ*, and the others similarly, is as follows:

(1) *bhavat* + *sU* (A. 4.1.2 *svaujasamauṭśasṭābhyāmbhisṅebhyāmbhyasṅasibhyāmbhyasṅasosāmṅyossup*)
(2) *bhavat* + (*s* → 0) (A. 6.1.68 *halṅyābbhyo dīrghāt sutisy apṛktam hal*)
(3) *bh* (*ava* → *o*) (*t* → *rU*) (A. 8.3.1 *vt*. 2 *vibhāṣā bhavadbhagavadaghavatām oc cāvasya*)
(4) *bho* (*r* → *ḥ*) (A. 8.3.15 *kharavasānayor visarjanīyaḥ*)
bhoḥ

As the *vārttika* proposes optional substitutions, the other possible form would be *bhavan*.}

VMBh_1: III.424.6-8; VMBh_2: V.431.9-10

---

in addition to those has another *anubandha* attached to it.") PŚ: I.84-85, II.400-404. See also WUJASTYK 1993: vol. I:51, vol. II:173 (*paribhāṣā* no. 42).

[Objection:] It is said: "before a vocative singular [ending]", therefore this one does not result: *bho brāhmaṇāḥ* ("Oh, hello Brahmins"). In the same way, with respect to the case ending, the inclusion of the feminine gender (lit. different gender) would not result: *bho brāhmaṇi* ("Oh, hello Brahmin lady!").

{**Explanation:**
Kaiyaṭa (VMBh_2: V.431) explains this passage by saying that the *rU* and *o*-substitutes prescribed in the *vārttika* would not take place before the plural ending, which means that the form *bhoḥ* could not be derived in the example *bho brāhmaṇāḥ*. A slightly different problem appears in the feminine gender; the final *ī* would be replaced by *rU* in the form *bhavatī*, because the substitution of the final sound should take place on the basis of A. 1.1.52 *alo 'ntyasya*. Then, *ava* would be replaced by *o*. The problem arises with the application of A. 8.2.23 *saṃyogāntasya lopaḥ* because of the suspension of *rU* (introduced in the third sub-chapter); the desired form would then not be achieved in this case either.

The author of the *Uddyotana* (MPV X.415) elaborates on Kaiyaṭa's explanations and says that in the first case we would arrive at the form **bhoraḥ*. The second example – the feminine – would be formed as follows: after the substitutions prescribed by the present *sūtra*, we would arrive at the sequence *bho t r*. At this point, A. 8.2.23 would have to apply allowing the deletion of the final *r*. It cannot take place, however, due to suspension of the *rU*-substitution with respect to A. 8.2.23. The consonant *r* comes in place of the vowel *ī* in the feminine; therefore what we have is *bho t ī*. There is, then, no consonant cluster. On the other hand, even if the *rU*-substitution is not considered suspended and it takes effect, the result of this particular derivation would be **bhot*, which is an incorrect form.}

VMBh_1: III.424.8-10; VMBh_2: V.431.10-432.2

[**Answer:**] This is not a fault. The word *bhos* is an indeclinable, it does not have its origin in [the word] *bhavat*.
[Question:] How is it an indeclinable?
[Answer:] The particles (*nipāta*) are similar in form to [the words ending in] a vowel or a case ending, [this is] the definition of a particle and the definition of an indeclinable is that a particle is an indeclinable.

{**Explanation:**
This is how a form *bhoḥ* could be achieved provided it is an indeclinable. It comes from the word *bhū* with the zero-suffix *viC*. Although this suffix is always deleted, it causes *guṇa* of the root vowel and we get the form *bho*. We need to add the case ending to form an indeclinable so we add the suffix *sU*.

(1) *bhū* + *viC* + *sU* (A. 3.2.75 *anyebhyo 'pi dṛśyate*, A. 4.1.2 *svaujasamauṭśasṭā-bhyāmbhisṅebhyāmbhyasṅasibhyāmbhyasṅasosāmṅyossup*)
(2) *bho* + 0 + *s* (A. 6.1.67 *ver apṛktasya*)
(3) *bho* + (*s* → *rU*) (A. 8.3.1 *matuvaso ru saṃbandhau chandasi*)
(4) *bho* + (*r* → *y*) (A. 8.3.17 *bhobhagoaghoapūrvasya yo 'śi*)
(5) *bho* + (*y* → 0) (A. 8.3.19 *lopaḥ śākalyasya*)
bho

This solution to the problem allows forms such as *bho brāhmaṇāḥ* to be derived, which indicates that the *vārttika* is superfluous. We do not need to formulate a separate rule for the word *bhavat* if the same result can be achieved by correctly applying Pāṇini's *sūtras*.}

{A. 8.3.2 *atrānunāsikaḥ pūrvasya tu vā*
But here (i.e., in this section up to A. 8.3.12) [the sound] preceding [the sound to be replaced by *rU*] is usually replaced by a nasalized vowel [in close proximity].
A. 8.3.3 *āto 'ṭi nityam*
[The vowel] *ā* [preceding *rU* is] necessarily [replaced by a nasalized vowel] before [the sounds denoted by] *aṬ* (i.e., vowels and *h*, *y*, *v*, *r*) [in close proximity].
A. 8.3.4 *ananunāsikāt paro 'nusvāraḥ*
The *anusvāra* [is inserted] after that which is other than a nasalized vowel [preceding *rU* in close proximity].} *These *sūtra*s were not commented upon by Patañjali.

A. 8.3.5 *samaḥ suṭi*
[The *rU*-substitute comes in place of the final sound] of [the *upasarga*] *sam* before [the infix] *suṬ* [in close proximity].
A. 8.3.6 *pumaḥ kyayy ampare*
[The *rU*-substitute comes in place of the final sound] of [the nominal stem] *pum* ('a man') before [the sounds denoted by] *khaY* (i.e., voiceless stops) which are followed by [the sound denoted by] *aM* (i.e., vowels, *h*, semivowels and nasals) [in close proximity].
A. 8.3.12 *kān āmreḍite*
[The *rU*-substitute comes in place of the final sound] of [the pronominal stem] *kān* (acc. pl. of *kim* 'what') before its reduplicated form [in close proximity].

VMBh_1: III.424.11-15; VMBh_2: V.432.3-6

1) The *s*-substitute [should be mentioned] in the case of [the *upasarga*] *sam* and [the words] *pum* ('a man') and *kān*.

[Bhāṣya:] The *s*-substitute should be mentioned in the case of [the *upasarga*] *sam* and [the words] *pum* ('a man') and *kān*. [For example:] *saṁsskartā* ('one who prepares, cooks'), *puṁskāmā* ('a woman desirous of a man'), *kāṁskān* ('whom', acc. pl. of the pronoun *kim*).

{**Explanation:**
The examples in this *sūtra* can have different forms and Patañjali gives only some of them. It is a result of application of different rules within the *Tripādī* section. I present the derivational process below; the first example is the word *saṁsskartā* ('one who prepares, cooks'), an example for A. 8.3.5.

(1) *sam* + *ḌUkṛÑ* (DhP VIII:10)
(2) *sam* + *suṬ* + *kṛ* (A. 6.1.137 *samparyupebhyaḥ karotau bhūṣaṇe*)
(3) *sa* (*m* → *rU*) + *s* + *kṛ* (A. 8.3.5 *samaḥ suṭi*)
(4) *sa* + *ṃ* + *r* + *s* + *kṛ* (A. 8.3.4 *ananunāsikāt paro 'nusvāraḥ*)
(5) *saṃ* (*r* → *ḥ*) + *s* + *kṛ* (A. 8.3.15 *kharavasānayor visarjanīyaḥ*)
(6) *saṃ* (*ḥ* → *s*) + *s* + *kṛ* (A. 8.3.34 *visarjanīyasya saḥ*)
saṃsskṛ

To that form the suffix *tṛC* is added by A. 3.1.133 *ṇvultṛcau* to create the form *saṃsskartā*. The derivation presented above is based on the application of A. 8.3.4 *ananunāsikāt paro 'nusvāraḥ* introducing the *anusvāra* after the vowel of *sam* before the *rU*-substitute. There is, however, another option, given by Patañjali, where A. 8.3.2 *atrānunāsikaḥ pūrvasya tu vā* applies and instead of the *anusvāra* we get the *anunāsika*. In such a case, the form will be *saṁsskṛ* and *saṁsskartā* respectively.
According to Kaiyaṭa (VMBh_2: V.432-433), there are even more options. Firstly, he analyses the forms with the *anunāsika* that is introduced by A. 8.3.2. The consonant *m* of the *upasarga sam* is first replaced with *rU* by A. 8.3.5 and then further substitutions follow: *r* → *ḥ* → *s* by A. 8.3.15 and A. 8.3.34 respectively. The vowel *a* being a part of the *upasarga sam* can be nasalised even though nasalisation is prescribed by an earlier *sūtra*. However, in A. 8.3.2 the substitution *rU* continues from A. 8.3.1 as it does in the following ones, including the rule A. 8.3.5. It, therefore, indicates that the *rU*-substitute takes place in this particular context and we can apply the rule that precedes A. 8.3.5 in the *Tripādī*. What we achieve as a result is the form *saṁsskartā* with two sounds *s*. We can, however, apply yet another *sūtra* – A. 8.4.47 *anaci ca*, which would allow for a form that contains three consonants *s* – *saṁssskartā*. By the appli-

cation of A. 8.4.65 *jharo jhari savarṇe* we delete *s* appearing before another *s* and our final form would be containing two consonants *s* – *saṁsskartā*.

When it comes to the *anusvāra*, which can be used instead of the *anunāsika*, it can apply on the basis of A. 8.3.4. Commentators point out that the *anusvāra* is not included in the *pratyāhāra sūtras*; Pāṇini excludes from them such sounds as *visarjanīya*, *upadhmānīya*, *jīhvamūlīya* or *anusvāra*. Therefore, according to Kaiyaṭa, the *anusvāra* can be treated either as a consonant or as a vowel, contrary to the *anunāsika*, which is always a nasalised vowel. If the *anusvāra* is treated as a consonant, then the rule A. 8.4.65 can apply to delete one *s*. It leaves us with the form *saṃskartā*. When deletion does not take place, the form *saṃsskartā* is achieved. If, however, the *anusvāra* is treated as a vowel, the rule A. 8.4.47 can apply yielding a form with three consonants *s* – *saṃssskartā*.

Another example, for A. 8.3.6, is *puṁskāmā* ('a woman desirous of a man') is formed as follows:

(1) *pum* + *kāmā*
(2) *pu* (*m* → *rU*) + *kāmā* (A. 8.3.6 *pumaḥ kyayy ampare*)
(3) *pu* + *ṃ* + *r* + *kāmā* (A. 8.3.4 *ananunāsikāt paro 'nusvāraḥ*)
(4) *puṃ* (*r* → *ḥ*) + *kāmā* (A. 8.3.15 *kharavasānayor visarjanīyaḥ*)
(5) *puṃ* (*ḥ* → *s*) + *kāmā* (A. 8.3.34 *visarjanīyasya saḥ*)
puṃskāmā

In this case we achieve a similar situation as with the word *saṃsskartā*. Here the *anunāsika* (by the rule A. 8.3.2) instead of the *anusvāra* is also possible and then we get the form *puṁskāmā* as quoted by Patañjali.

The form *kān* is the accusative plural of the pronoun *kim*; the stem of which is replaced by the form *ka* by A. 7.2.103 *kimaḥ kaḥ*[405] before the plural case ending.

(1) *kān kān*
(2) *kā* (*n* → *rU*) *kān* (A. 8.3.12 *kān āmreḍite*)
(3) *kā* (*r* → *ḥ*) *kān* (A. 8.3.15 *kharavasānayor visarjanīyaḥ*)
(4) *kā* (*ḥ* → *s*) *kān* (A. 8.3.34 *visarjanīyasya saḥ*)
kāskān

In this case as well there is the possibility of applying the rules A. 8.3.2 or A. 8.3.4 which gives us two additional forms: *kāṁskān* and *kāṃskān* respectively.

---

[405] A. 7.2.103 *kimaḥ kaḥ* || ("[The substitute] *ka* comes in place of [the whole *aṅga* pronominal stem] *kim* ('who, what, which') [before the case endings].")

The commentators point out that in the form *saṁsskartā* or *saṃsskartā*, regardless of the number of *s*, there is also the possibility of reduplication of the consonant *k*. It would yield not six different forms but twelve. This reduplication is possible on the basis of *vārttika* 2 *śaraḥ khayaḥ* on the *sūtra* A. 8.4.47. Annaṃbhaṭṭa (MPV X.417) explains that the forms *śaraḥ* and *khayaḥ* can be interpreted as the ablative and genitive or the genitive and ablative (in this order). For the purpose of the present rule, we need the first interpretation when the form *śaraḥ* is the ablative and, consequently, the whole *vārttika* can be understood as follows: "A sound denoted by *khaY* occurring after a sound denoted by *śaR* is optionally replaced by two." Therefore, we get the following forms: *saṃskartā*, *saṃsskartā*, *saṃssskartā*, *saṃskkartā*, *saṃsskkartā*, *saṃssskkartā* (with *anusvāra*) and *saṁskartā*, *saṁsskartā*, *saṁssskartā*, *saṁskkartā*, *saṁsskkartā*, *saṁssskkartā* (with *anunāsika*). Further Annaṃbhaṭṭa states that the consonant *t* could also be subject to reduplication by the rule A. 8.4.46, which would yield twenty-four forms altogether: *saṃskartā*, *saṃsskartā*, *saṃssskartā*, *saṃskkartā*, *saṃsskkartā*, *saṃssskkartā*, *saṃskarttā*, *saṃsskarttā*, *saṃssskarttā*, *saṃskkarttā*, *saṃsskkarttā*, *saṃssskkarttā* (with *anusvāra*) and *saṁskartā*, *saṁsskartā*, *saṁssskartā*, *saṁskkartā*, *saṁsskkartā*, *saṁssskkartā*, *saṁskarttā*, *saṁsskarttā*, *saṁssskarttā*, *saṁskkarttā*, *saṁsskkarttā*, *saṁssskkarttā* (with *anunāsika*).}

VMBh_1: III.424.16-425.2; VMBh_2: V.432.7-433.5

2) In the case of the *rU*-substitute though, there is potential involvement of something undesired.

[Objection:] If the *rU*-substitute applied though, something undesired might be involved. Here then [in the example] *saṁsskartā* [the *visarjanīya* by the *sūtra*] A. 8.3.36 might be involved. [In the example] *puṁskāmā* the *ṣ*-substitute [by the *sūtra*] A. 8.3.41 might be involved. [In the example] *kāṁskān* the *ẖk*-substitute [by the *sūtra*] A. 8.3.37 might be involved.
[Question:] Should it be mentioned then?
[Answer:] It should not be mentioned. The maxim is done exactly so: a double sound *s* is ordained in [the expression:] *samaḥ suṭi*. There is the sound *s* in [the *upasarga*] *sam* before [the infix] *suṬ*. That context will continue further on.

{**Explanation:**
The maxim given in the *Mahābhāṣya* states that the *sūtra* A. 8.3.5 should be formulated in this way: *samaḥ ssuṭi*; such wording would form a solution to the problem raised earlier. If the *rU*-substitute is prescribed in place of the sound *m* of the *upasarga sam*, there is the possibility of applying the rule A. 8.3.36 *vā śari*.

This rule allows for the optional substitution of the *visarjanīya* with the *visarjanīja* before a sound denoted by *śaR* (i.e., sibilants), which would apply to *s* in the form *saṃsskartā*. According to the derivation presented above, the *visarjanīya*, which comes as a replacement of *r*, is further replaced by *s* by A. 8.3.34, which gives us the correct form. If A. 8.3.36 were allowed to apply, it would give us an optional undesired form *saṃḥskartā* (and all the other derivatives). The commentators explain that A. 8.3.36 is a *vyavasthitavibhāṣā* ('a fixed option'), so the *visarjanīya* must necessarily be replaced by *s*, thus yielding the correct result.
A similar situation is observed with two other examples given by Patañjali, namely *puṃskāmā* and *kāṃskān*. In the case of the former, the rule A. 8.3.37 *kupvoḥ ẖkẖpau ca* could apply before A. 8.3.41 *idudupadhasya cāpratyayasya* prescribing the *ṣ*-substitute in place of the *visarjanīya* as well. It does not happen, however, because the rule *samaḥ suṭi* should be treated as an *adhikāra sūtra* whose context will continue in the following rules, namely A. 8.3.6 and A. 8.3.12 as commented in the *Mahābhāṣya*. The rule A. 8.3.5, as I mentioned above, is read with double *s* – *samaḥ ssuṭi*. Annaṃbhaṭṭa (MPV vol. X: 417) states that the vowel *a* of *samaḥ* is marked with the *svarita* accent. When it is said that the context continues in the following *sūtra*s, what is meant is that the consonant *s* only continues, even though theoretically the whole expression *samaḥ s* should be carried over. He also mentions that according to common understanding of *adhikāra sūtra*s, even without *svarita* in A. 8.3.5, the consonant *s* alone would be carried over to the other two rules.

The explanation given above is the solution to the problem of possible application of A. 8.3.36, A. 8.3.37 and A. 8.3.41 to the examples in this rule. If the *s*-substitute is prescribed in all three *sūtra*s discussed here, then it is made obligatory and further rules, which are optional, cannot apply. In such a way, the problem of undesired forms is solved.}

VMBh_1: III.425.3; VMBh_2: V.433.6

[Objection:] If this continues, it would result in [the *sūtra*] A. 8.3.7 as well.

{**Explanation:**
Kielhorn's edition does not give any examples here, contrary to the VMBh_2 which gives *bhavām̐s tatra* ("The lord is there"). Kaiyaṭa and other commentators (VMBh_2: V.433, MPV X.417) give the example *bhavāṃs tarati* ("The lord crosses"). The use of *anunāsika* and *anusvāra* is arbitrary as they are both possible in these cases on the basis of A. 8.3.2 *atrānunāsikaḥ pūrvasya tu vā* and A. 8.3.4 *ananunāsikāt paro 'nusvāraḥ*; an identical situation to the one discussed previously.

(1) *bhavān + tatra*
(2) *bhavā (n → rU) + tatra* (A. 8.3.7 *naś chavy apraśān*)
(3) *bhavā (r → ḥ) + tatra* (A. 8.3.15 *kharavasānayor visarjanīyaḥ*)
(4) *bhavā (ḥ → s) + tatra* (A. 8.3.34 *visarjanīyasya saḥ*)
(5) *bhavā + ṃ + s + tatra* (A. 8.3.4 *ananunāsikāt paro 'nusvāraḥ*)
bhavāṃs tatra

Kaiyaṭa claims that in this particular instance the difference between prescribing *s* or *r* as a substitute is non-existent. According to the solution presented above, we should read the sound *s* into the rule A. 8.3.7 and thus get immediately the desired result. However, even the *rU*-substitute would yield the same result through the application of the *sūtra*s A. 8.3.15 – replacing *r* with the *visarjanīya* – and then followed by A. 8.3.34 – replacing the *visarjanīya* with *s*.
Kaiyaṭa also gives the counterexample from the rule A. 8.3.9, the expression *mahām̐ indraḥ* ('great Indra') where prescribing the *rU*-substitute or the *s*-substitute does make a difference.

(1) *mahān + indraḥ*
(2) *mahā (n → rU) + indraḥ* (A. 8.3.9 *dīrghād aṭi samānapāde*)
(3) *mahā (r → y) + indraḥ* (A. 8.3.17 *bhobhagoaghoapūrvasya yo 'śi*)
(4) *mahā (y → 0) + indraḥ* (A. 8.3.19 *lopaḥ śākalyasya*)
(5) *mahā + m̐ + indraḥ* (A. 8.3.2 *atrānunāsikaḥ pūrvasya tu vā*)
mahām̐ indraḥ

This derivation is different. After the final *n* has been replaced by *r* on the basis of A. 8.3.9, it is further replaced by *y* by A. 8.3.17 and not by the *visarjanīya*. The consonant *y* is subject to deletion by A. 8.3.19 which, after applying A. 8.3.2 and making the final vowel of the word *mahā* nasalised, allows us to achieve the correct form *mahām̐ indraḥ*. What would happen, however, if the substitution prescribed by the rule A. 8.3.9 were the *s*-substitution? Kaiyaṭa says that there is a difference in this case and it would not yield the desired result. Should the *s*-substitute be prescribed, there would be the lack of *r*, which would result in the impossibility of applying both the rules ordaining *anunāsika* and the *y*-substitute, being conditioned by *rU*. Consequently, the desired result would not be achieved.}

VMBh_1: III.425.3-8; VMBh_2: V.433.7-434.1

[Answer:] The relation [between the qualifier and the qualified] will continue. In [the *upasarga*] *sam* before [the infix] *suṬ*; in [the nominal stem] *pum* ('a man') before [the sounds denoted by] *khaY* (i.e., voiceless stops) which are followed by

[the sounds denoted by] *aM* (i.e., vowels, *h*, semivowels, nasals) there is the sound *s*. There is *rU* in place of [the final] *n* [of a *pada*] before [the sounds denoted by] *chaV* (i.e., palatal, retroflex and dental voiceless stops) [followed by the sounds denoted by *aM* (i.e., vowels, *h*, semivowels, nasals)] except [the word] *praśān* ('painless') [but] in [the nominal stem] *pum* ('a man') before [the sounds denoted by] *khaY* (i.e., voiceless stops) which are followed by [the sounds denoted by] *aM* (i.e., vowels, *h*, semivowels, nasals) there is the sound *s*. There is *rU* in Ṛgvedic hymns in place of [the final *n* of a *pada* before the sounds denoted by *chaV* (i.e., palatal, retroflex and dental voiceless stops) followed by the sounds denoted by *aM* (i.e., vowels, *h*, semivowels, nasals)] (A. 8.3.8); in place of [the final *n* of a *pada* occurring] after a long vowel before [the sounds denoted by] *aṬ* (i.e., vowels, *h*, semivowels except *l*) within the same verse (A. 8.3.9); in place of [the final *n* of a nominal *pada*] *nṝn* (acc. pl. of *nṛ* 'a man') before [the sound] *p* (A. 8.3.10) and in place of [the final *n* of a nominal *pada*] *svatavān* (nom. sg. of *svatavas* 'powerful') before [the expression] *pāyu* ('a protector') (A. 8.3.11) [but] in [the nominal stem] *pum* ('a man') before [the sounds denoted by] *khaY* (i.e., voiceless stops) which are followed by [the sounds denoted by] *aM* (i.e., vowels, *h*, semivowels, nasals) there is the sound *s*. There is the sound *s* in place of [the final sound] of [the pronominal stem] *kān* before its reduplication. In [the *sūtra*] A. 8.3.12 [the sound *s*] finishes [to apply].
Some would rather want deletion in [the *upasarga*] *sam*. [Hence, the forms:] *saṃskartā*, *sam̐skartā*.

{**Explanation:**
This last sentence is understood to be a *vārttika* but is not given as such by Kielhorn. I have discussed the results of applying this statement above. By the deletion of *m* of the *upasarga sam* we can get the forms containing only one sound *s* as the substitution prescribed in the rule refers to *m*.}

{**A. 8.3.7** ***naś chavy apraśān***
[The *rU*-substitute comes in place of the final] *n* [of a *pada*] before [the sounds denoted by] *chaV* (i.e., palatal, retroflex and dental voiceless stops) [followed by the sounds denoted by *aM* (i.e., vowels, *h*, semivowels, nasals)] except [the word] *praśān* ('painless') [in close proximity].
A. 8.3.8 ***ubhayatharkṣu***
In Ṛgvedic hymns both (i.e., the sound *n* or its substitute by *rU*) [occur before the sounds denoted by *chaV* (i.e., palatal, retroflex and dental voiceless stops) followed by the sounds denoted by *aM* (i.e., vowels, *h*, semivowels, nasals) in close proximity].
A. 8.3.9 ***dīrghād aṭi samānapāde***

[The *rU*-substitute comes in place of the final *n* of a *pada* occurring] after a long vowel before [the sounds denoted by] *aṬ* (i.e., vowels, *h*, semivowels except *l*) within the same verse [of a hymn in close proximity].
A. 8.3.10 *nṝn pe*
[The *rU*-substitute comes in place of the final *n* of a nominal *pada*] *nṝn* (acc. pl. of *nṛ* 'a man') before *p* [of a hymn in close proximity].
A. 8.3.11 *svatavān pāyau*
[The *rU*-substitute comes in place of the final *n* of a nominal *pada*] *svatavān* (nom. sg. of *svatavas* 'powerful') before [the expression] *pāyu* ('a protector') [in close proximity].} *These *sūtra*s were not commented upon by Patañjali.

A. 8.3.13 *ḍho ḍhe lopaḥ*
[There is] deletion of [the sound] *ḍh* before [the following sound] *ḍh* [in close proximity].

VMBh_1: III.425.9-12; VMBh_2: V.434.2-5

1) The expression "not at the end of a *pada*" [should be used] with respect to deletion of [the sound] *ḍh*.

[Bhāṣya:] The expression "not at the end of a *pada*" should be used with respect to deletion of [the sound] *ḍh*. Here it must not take place: *śvaliḍ ḍhaukate* ("A licking one approaches"), *guḍaliḍ ḍhaukate* ("A sugar-licking one approaches").
[Question:] Should it be mentioned then?
[Answer:] It should not be mentioned. The *jaŚ*-substitute (A. 8.2.39) will be the blocker here.

{**Explanation:**
It is not clear whether this deletion should take place "at the end of a *pada*" as well as "not at the end of a *pada*." According to Patañjali, the sound *ḍh* that appears at the end of a *pada* should be excluded from the domain of the present rule, as evidenced by examples such as *śvaliḍ ḍhaukate*, whose derivation is as follows:

(1) *śvalih* + *ḍhaukate*
(2) *śvali* (*h* → *ḍh*) + *ḍhaukate* (A. 8.2.31 *ho ḍhaḥ*)
(3) *śvali* (*ḍh* → *ḍ*) + *ḍhaukate* (A. 8.2.39 *jhalāṃ jaśo 'nte*)
śvaliḍ ḍhaukate

After the *ḍ*-substitution has taken place, there is no *ḍh* – substituend – any more. The *jaŚ*-substitution that takes place on the basis of A. 8.2.39 depends on one *pada*, contrary to deletion requiring two *pada*s. What is more, if suspension is taken into account, it would be the *ḍh*-deletion suspended with respect to the *jaŚ*-substitution, not the other way round. That is why A. 8.2.39 has to apply.

The situation is different when *ḍh* does not terminate a *pada*, as in the past participle of the verb *lihA* ('to lick', DhP II:6) – *līḍha* ('licked'):

(1) *lih* + *Kta* (A. 3.2.102 *niṣṭhā*, A. 1.1.26 *ktaktavatū niṣṭhā*)
(2) *li* (*h* → *ḍh*) + *ta* (A. 8.2.31 *ho ḍhaḥ*)
(3) *liḍh* + (*t* → *dh*) *a* (A. 8.2.40 *jhaṣas tathor dho 'dhaḥ*)
(4) *liḍh* + (*dh* → *ḍh*) *a* (A. 8.4.41 *ṣṭunā ṣṭuḥ*)
(5) *li* (*ḍh* → 0) + *ḍha* (A. 8.3.13 *ḍho ḍhe lopaḥ*)
(6) *l* (*i* → *ī*) + *ḍha* (A. 6.3.111 *ḍhralope pūrvasya dīrgho 'ṇaḥ*)
līḍha

Here the deletion takes place not at the end of a *pada* but within a *pada*. The fact that both rules A. 8.3.13 and A. 6.3.111 apply after A. 8.4.41 has already applied, which seems to be in clear violation of *asiddhatva*, is explained by the explicit mention of the *ḍh*-deletion in the wording of A. 6.3.111. The lengthening prescribed therein is directly dependent on the said deletion. This problematic order of rules is explained by the following *vārttika*s and *bhāṣya*.}

VMBh_1: III.425.13-17; VMBh_2: V.434.6-10

2) If there is the *jaŚ*-substitute, further on there is potential involvement of an exception due to absence of [the sound] *ḍh*.

[Objection:] If there is the *jaŚ*-substitute, further on an exception should be recognised due to absence of the sound *ḍh*, due to its suspension.
[Question:] To what?
[Answer:] To the *jaŚ*-substitute (A. 8.2.39).

3) Therefore it should be treated as unsuspended.

[Answer:] Therefore the non-suspension should be mentioned.
[Question:] Of what?
[Answer:] Of the *ṣṭU*-substitute (A. 8.4.41).

{**Explanation:**
As Kaiyaṭa explains (VMBh_2: V.434), whenever in the subsequent *sūtra*s the deletion before *ḍh* is required, it would not take place due to absence of *ḍh* resulting from A. 8.4.41, as that operation would be suspended. Hence, the need to resort to the notion of exception. When we consider the example *līḍha*, however,

A. 8.4.41 cannot be considered suspended with respect to the present one because otherwise the rule A. 8.3.13 would have no scope of application.}

VMBh_1: III.425.18-19; VMBh_2: V.434.11-435.1

4) Alternatively, [the suffixes] *saṄ* [should be] used.

[Bhāṣya:] Alternatively, [the suffixes] *saṄ* should be used. It should be mentioned "when there is [the sound] *ḍh* before [the suffixes] *saṄ*."

{**Explanation:**
The abbreviation *saṄ* refers to the suffixes introduced in the *sūtra*s A. 3.1.5 to A. 3.4.78. The first rule introduces the suffix *saN* (A. 3.1.5 *guptijkidbhyaḥ san*) and the second one the personal ending added to the verbal stem (A. 3.4.78 *tiptasjhisipthasthamibvasmastātāmjhathāsāthāmdhvamiḍvahimahiṅ*). According to the solution proposed in the *vārttika*, the deletion could result only if the sound *ḍh* appears in a word ending in one of the suffixes belonging to the *pratyāhāra saṄ*. Annaṃbhaṭṭa (MPV X.418) explains the lack of deletion in the case of *ḍhaukate* quoted by Patañjali with the help of this *vārttika*.}

VMBh_1: III.425.20-24; VMBh_2: V.435.2-5

[Question:] Should it be mentioned then?
[Answer:] It should not be mentioned. Here it depends on close proximity [between two sounds] "the sound *ḍh* [appearing] before [another sound] *ḍh*." Sometimes close proximity is accomplished by contact, and distance by instruction; and sometimes it is accomplished neither by contact nor by instruction. In the case of the *ṣṭU*-substitute (A. 8.4.41), close proximity is accomplished by contact, and distance by instruction; in the case of the *jaŚ*-substitute (A. 8.2.39), it is neither accomplished by contact nor by instruction. Wherever this close proxymity [comes from], there we will apply [the deletion].

{**Explanation:**
According to grammarians, there are two types of close proximity between sounds: *śāstrakṛtānantarya* ('rule-derived') and *śrutikṛtānantarya* ('originally heard'). Patañjali uses the term *saṃnipātakṛtānantarya* for the latter. The close proximity in the example *līḍha* is achieved via the rule, i.e. A. 8.4.41. The example *śvaliḍ ḍhaukate* is a more complex one. The substitution of *h* in the word *śvaliḍ* with *ḍh* is rule-derived. The sound *ḍh* in the verb *ḍhaukate* is not derived by any rule and as such is treated as *śrutikṛtānantarya* (*saṃnipātakṛtānantarya*). However, when the *jaŚ*-substitute has applied in the form *śvaliḍh ḍhaukate* → *śvaliḍ ḍhaukate*, there is no close proximity at all. What is required

in the present rule is close proximity that is rule-derived only; thus, there is no question of applying the present deletion in the example of *śvaliḍ ḍhaukate*. Moreover, the sound *ḍh* that is resulting from the application of a rule (as in the example of *līḍha*, where *ḍh* is the result of A. 8.4.41) should be treated as unsuspended with respect to deletion prescribed by the present *sūtra*.
Kaiyaṭa (VMBh_2: V.435) also explains that deletion has to necessarily block *asiddhatva*, as it takes place in the case of *līḍha*. However, in the case of *śvaliḍ ḍhaukate* we face double suspension. On the one hand, the *sūtra* prescribing the deletion of *ḍh* is placed further in the *Aṣṭādhyāyī* than the *jaŚ*-substitution, which makes it suspended. On the other, deletion is an externally conditioned operation and as such suspended with respect to the *jaŚ*-substitution. Therefore, the deletion cannot block the *asiddhatva* principle, even though it does so in the case of the past passive participle *līḍha*.}

{A. 8.3.14 *ro ri*
[There is] deletion of [the sound] *r* before [the following sound] *r* [in close proximity].} *This *sūtra* was not commented upon by Patañjali.

A. 8.3.15 *kharavasānayor visarjanīyaḥ*
The *visarjanīya* (*ḥ*) [comes in place of the final *r* of a *pada*] before [a sound denoted by] *khaR* (i.e., voiceless consonants) or at the end [of a speech, in close proximity].

VMBh_1: III.426.1-4; VMBh_2: V.435.6-9

1) [It should be mentioned that] the *visarjanīya* does not take place before the last member of a compound.

[Bhāṣya:] It should be mentioned that the *visarjanīya* does not take place before the last member of a compound. Here it must not be: *nārkuṭaḥ* ('being in a person's house'), *nārpatya* ('an offspring of a king').

{Explanation:
The *vārttika* introduces the constraint on the substitution; it cannot take place in compounds, most specifically, in the initial member of a compound. However, there are cases contradicting the above statement such as *dāsyāḥputraḥ*, discussed by Kaiyaṭa (VMBh_2: V.435.15 ff), in which the *visarjanīya* replaces the consonant *r*. This happens because in this case the following *pada*, namely *putraḥ*, is not the cause for *r* to appear. In the example *dāsyāḥputraḥ* the genitive ending *Ṅas* of the first member of the compound is first changed to *ar* by A.

8.2.66 and is further replaced by the *visarjanīya* by the present rule. The ending is not subject to deletion on the basis of A. 6.3.22 *putre 'nyatarasyām*.[406]
Nāgeśa elaborates on this by interpreting the locative as the locative absolute according to A. 2.3.37 *yasya ca bhāvena bhāvalakṣaṇam*.[407] According to such an interpretation, the meaning of *uttarapade* in the *vārttika* would not be "before a following member of a compound" but "when there is another member of a compound". Nārāyaṇa (MPV X.421) adds that the existence of the following member of a compound is what characterises the existence of *r*, which makes it the cause of *r*. In the examples given by Patañjali, namely *nārkuta* and *nārpatya*, the following member of a compound is not the cause of the consonant *r* that could be replaced by the *visarjanīya*; its cause is the *taddhita* formation and the *vṛddhi* degree to which the first vowel of the derivative is raised. This is the reason why in those two cases the *visarjanīya* does not replace *r*.
The derivation of the word *nārkuta* is as follows:

(1) *nṛkuṭī* + *Ṅi* + *aṆ* (A. 4.3.53 *tatra bhavaḥ*)
(2) *nṛkuṭī* (*Ṅi* → 0) + *a* (A. 2.4.71 *supo dhātuprātipadikayoḥ*)
(3) *n* (*ṛ* → *ār*) *kuṭī* + *a* (A. 7.2.117 *taddhiteṣv acām ādeḥ*, A. 1.1.51 *ur aṇ raparaḥ*)
(4) *nārkuṭ* (*ī* → 0) + *a* (A. 6.4.148 *yasyeti ca*)
nārkuṭa

The *vṛddhi* in the case of *ṛ* is the vowel *ā* automatically followed by the consonant *r* (by the rule A. 1.1.51 as shown). This *r* could be subject to the *visarjanīya* substitution prescribed by the present rule but this is not the case. Its origin does not lie in the *pada* that follows.}

VMBh_1: III.426.5-7; VMBh_2: V.436.1-3

2) Alternatively, it [should] not [be mentioned] because the operation is externally conditioned.

[Bhāṣya:] Alternatively, it should not be mentioned.
[Question:] Why?
[Answer:] Because the operation is externally conditioned. [The appearance of] the sound *r* [in the above examples *nārkuṭa* and *nārpatya*] is externally condi-

---

[406] A. 6.3.22 *putre 'nyatarasyām* || ("Before [the final member of a compound] *putra* ('a son'), [the deletion *luK* does not come in place of the genitive ending introduced after the first member of a compound] optionally [to denote an insult].")

[407] A. 2.3.37 *yasya ca bhāvena bhāvalakṣaṇam* || ("[The locative ending is introduced after a nominal stem] denoting an action which serves to characterise another action.")

tioned and the *visarjanīya* is internally conditioned. [An operation] conditioned externally is suspended with respect to [the one] internally conditioned.

{**Explanation:**
The *visarjanīya* cannot replace such an *r* that results from an externally conditioned operation. In the examples of *nārkuṭa* and *nārpatya* the consonant *r*, resulting from the addition of a *taddhita* suffix, is *bahiraṅga* and, consequently, suspended. It cannot be replaced by the *visarjanīya*, which is internally conditioned for it is supposed to replace *r* occurring at the end of a *pada*. This end of a *pada* being the condition of substitution makes it an *antaraṅga* operation.}

VMBh_1: III.426.7-9; VMBh_2: V.436.3-5

[Bhāṣya:] This is not a proper removal of difficulty. [The terms] *antaraṅga* and *bahiraṅga* are two opposing views. If there is an internally conditioned [operation, there is] an externally conditioned [one]; if there is an externally conditioned [operation, there is] an internally conditioned [one]. But there is no simultaneous appearance of *antaraṅga* and *bahiraṅga* in this case.

{**Explanation:**
The terms *antaraṅga* and *bahiraṅga* do not exist one without the other. Here, however, they do not appear simultaneously. The author of the *Pradīpa* says that by bearing in mind an *antaraṅga* operation we immediately assume the existence of a *bahiraṅga* operation. Nārāyaṇa emphasises that this is a mental process; it does not have to be a real operation. In the same way the opposite situation is explained. This simultaneity of internally and externally conditioned operations is rejected by Patañjali with respect to the current domain; the reason for this being an *adhikāra* A. 8.2.1, which makes the *visarjanīya* substitution suspended. Consequently, there is no *antaraṅga* operation. This means that the appearance of the consonant *r* cannot be *bahiraṅga* with respect to the *visarjanīya*. There is no room for the *paribhāṣā* prescribing the suspension of a *bahiraṅga* operation with respect to an *antaraṅga* one to apply. As a result, we achieve the *visarjanīya* after all.
Annaṃbhaṭṭa (MPV X.419) adds that *paribhāṣā* 50, even though not stated explicitly in the *Aṣṭādhyāyī*, belongs to the *Sapādasaptādhyāyī* section whereas the *visarjanīya* substitution belongs to the *asiddhatva* section. As a result of this latter condition, its status as an internally conditioned operation does not arise in one's mind and consequently the prescription of *r* is not externally conditioned either. The principle of suspension does not operate in this case, which leads to *r* being unsuspended and the possibility of the *visarjanīya* application.}

VMBh_1: III.426.9-13; VMBh_2: V.436.5-437.3

[Question:] Why?
[Answer:] Due to suspension (A. 8.2.1).
[Objection:] And when an externally conditioned [operation] has not resulted, an internally conditioned [operation] would not result, because with respect to that an externally conditioned [operation] is the very cause of an internally conditioned [one].
[Bhāṣya:] An externally conditioned [operation] is not the cause of an internally conditioned [one].
[Question:] Why?
[Answer:] Due to [its] suspension.
[Question:] How [do we get] the suspension if the *paribhāṣā* A. 8.2.1 is not valid?

{**Explanation:**
The problem arises as to how the rule prescribing the consonant *r* can be suspended if by the rule A. 8.2.1 it is the *visarjanīya* substitute that is suspended, because the previous *paribhāṣā* (i.e., PŚ 50) does not operate. Kaiyaṭa responds that it is suspended because A. 8.2.1 is not applicable; and it is not applicable because if an internally conditioned operation is suspended (in this case the *visarjanīya* substitution), the *r*-substitution does not get the status of an externally conditioned operation.}

VMBh_1: III.426.13-19; VMBh_2: V.437.4-439.4

[Answer:] [By the *paribhāṣā* stating that an operation] conditioned externally is suspended with respect to [the one] internally conditioned.
[Question:] How?
[Answer:] Technical terms and rules of intepretation [apply] at the time of an operation. In [the rule] A. 8.3.15 [the *paribhāṣā* stating that] an externally conditioned [operation] is suspended with respect to internally conditioned is placed. Thus this rule of interpretation is not suspended.
[Question:] So, how [will it be] then when both rules of interpretation – *pūrvatrāsiddham* and *asiddhaṃ bahiraṅgam antaraṅge* – have the scope of application and appear together? Having annulled *pūrvatrāsiddham*, the situation will be determined by *asiddhaṃ bahiraṅgam antaraṅge*; but having annulled *asiddhaṃ bahiraṅgam antaraṅge*, the situation will be determined by *pūrvatrāsiddham*?
[Question:] And so what?
[Answer:] Therefore, this is not a proper removal of difficulty: “Alternatively, it [should] not [be said] due to an operation being externally conditioned”.

{Explanation:
The commentators discuss this issue giving examples for the rules where the *pūrvatrāsiddha* prevails or the *bahiraṅga paribhāṣā*. I omit this discussion here as it sums up to the statement that the rule of intepretation we chose depends on the result we wish to achieve. In this case we cannot have the *visarjanīya* in *nārpatya* etc. and thus we should accept the *bahiraṅga paribhāṣā*. Patañjali, however, rejects the second *vārttika* and accepts the first one instead.}

A. 8.3.16 *roḥ supi*
[The *visarjanīya* comes in place of the sound *r*] of the *rU*-substitute before the locative plural ending (*suP*) [in cloxe proximity].

VMBh_1: III.426.20-22; VMBh_2: V.439.5-7

[Question:] What is the purpose of saying that is it not achieved by A. 8.3.15?
[Answer:] This begins the meaning of restriction. [The substitution refers] to that [sound *r* which results from] the *rU*-substitute [appearing] before the locative plural [ending], not any other [sound *r*] before the locative plural [ending].
[Question:] Where must it not be?
[Answer:] [For example here:] *gīrṣu*, *dhūrṣu* (loc. pl. of *gīr* ('a song') and *dhūr* ('a burden') respectively).

{Explanation:
The question arises as to why this rule is considered restrictive rather than an injunction. Kaiyaṭa (VMBh_2: V.440.10 ff) gives the example of the form *payobhyām* (instr./dat./abl. du. of *payas* – 'milk') where the consonant *s* is first replaced by *rU* by A. 8.2.66 and then *rU* is replaced with *u* by A. 6.1.114 *haśi ca*. The vowels *a* and *u* are further substituted by a *guṇa* vowel *o* (by A. 6.1.87 *ād guṇaḥ*). The present *sūtra* forms a restriction on the application of A. 6.1.114; it prescribes the *visarjanīya* in place of *r* rather than the vowel *u*.
The term *suP* must refer to the locative plural ending and not all the nominal endings (*sUP*) which is indicated by the *anuvṛtti* of the word *khaR* form the previous *sūtra*. This shows that the ending must begin with the sound belonging to the abbreviation *khaR* and in this case the sound *s*. By mentioning a particular case ending Pāṇini makes the present rule a restrictive one, not an injunction.

In the examples *gīrṣu* and *dhūrṣu*, the consonant *r* is not the result of the *rU*-substitution. This derivation is as follows:

(1) *gr̥̄* + *KviP* + *suP* (A. 3.2.76 *kvip ca*, A. 4.1.2 *svaujasamauṭśasṭābhyāmbhisṅebhyāmbhyasṅasibhyāmbhyasṅasosāmṅyossup*)
(2) *gir* + 0 + *su* (A. 7.1.100 *r̥̄ta iddhātoḥ*, A. 1.1.51 *ur aṇ raparaḥ*)

gir + su
(3) *g* (*i* → *ī*) *r* + *su* (A. 8.2.76 *rvor upadhāyā dīrgha ikaḥ*)
(4) *gīr* + (*s* → *ṣ*) (A. 8.3.59 *ādeśapratyayayoḥ*)
gīrṣu}

A. 8.3.17 *bhobhagoaghoapūrvasya yo 'śi*
[The sound] *y* comes in place of [the sound *r* of the *rU*-substitute] preceded by [the words] *bho* (an interjection), *bhago* ('illustrious') and *agho* ('a sinner') or [the vowel] *a* before [a sound denoted by] *aŚ* (i.e., voiced sounds) [in close proximity].

VMBh_1: III.427.1-2; VMBh_2: V.440.1-2

1) The word *aŚ* is superfluous because there is [no *rU*-substitute] anywhere else.

{**Explanation:**
The *y*-substitute that comes in place of *r* originating from the *rU*-substitution is always deleted afterwards. One of the examples could be the expression *bho atra* ("Hey, here!"). The derivation is as follows:

(1) *bhos + atra*
(2) *bho* (*s* → *rU*) + *atra* (A. 8.2.66 *sasajuṣo ruḥ*)
(3) *bho* (*r* → *y*) + *atra* (A. 8.3.17 *bhobhagoaghoapūrvasya yo 'śi*)
(4) *bho* (*y* → 0) + *atra* (A. 8.3.20 *oto gārgyasya*)
bho atra

In this example, the initial sound of the word *atra* is covered by the abbreviation *aŚ* (which includes all voiced sounds). Despite using reference to a grammarian Gārgya, the *sūtra* A. 8.3.20 does not describe an optional operation; it is obligatory. The reference to another grammarian is merely an indication of respect (*pūjā*). If, on the other hand, we take an example in which the following word begins with a consonant (as in the example *bhago dadāti* – "An illustrious one gives"), the consonant *y* is deleted by A. 8.3.22 *hali sarveṣām* prescribing this deletion before a consonant. Either way, then, it is an obligatory deletion.

According to Kaiyaṭa (VMBh_2: V.440.14-15), the *vārttika* refers to the rule A. 8.3.15 which prescribes the *visarjanīya* in place of *r*. It does not come in place of *rU* though, which makes the present rule and the *y*-substitution inapplicable in the environment described in the *sūtra* A. 8.3.15. Hence, the argument that the expression *aśi* is superfluous in this rule.}

VMBh_1: III.427.3-8; VMBh_2: V.440.3-9

[Bhāṣya:] The word *aŚ* is superfluous.
[Question:] What is the reason [for that]?
[Answer:] Because [the rule] does not [apply] anywhere else. Because there is no *rU* anywhere else other than before *aŚ*.
[Answer:] But indeed there is: *chandaḥsu* (loc. pl. of *chandas* – 'a hymn'), *payaḥsu* (loc. pl. of *payas* – 'milk').
[Question:] Why is there again an example given [of the word] followed by the sounds *su* only and not this *vṛkṣas tatra* ("There is a tree"), *plakṣas tatra* ("There is a fig-tree")?
[Answer:] There is a difference. When the *visarjanīya* has applied, [the *y*-substitute] will not apply. Here, therefore, when *visarjanīya* has applied, [the *y*-substitute] would not apply either: *chandaḥsu* (loc. pl. of *chandas* – 'a hymn'), *payaḥsu* (loc. pl. of *payas* – 'milk'). It would result on the basis of *sthānivadbhāva*.
[Objection:] But would it not result here as well on the basis of *sthānivadbhāva*: *vṛkṣas tatra*, *plakṣas tatra*?
[Answer:] [The principle of] *sthānivadbhāva* does not [apply] to rules dependent on original sounds.

{**Explanation:**
The above discussion regarding the potential *y*-substitution in *chandaḥsu*, *payaḥsu* and *vṛkṣas tatra*, *plakṣas tatra* evokes the principle of *sthānivadbhāva* formulated by Pāṇini in A. 1.1.56 *sthānivad ādeśo 'nalvidhau*. Theoretically, we could apply the *sūtra* A. 1.1.56 in the cases of *chandaḥsu* and *payaḥsu* because the *visarjanīya* replaces *rU* which does not have to be treated as a single sound (A. 8.3.16 *roḥ supi*). Therefore, *ḥ* could still be treated as *rU* and be further replaced by *y* according to the present rule as the substituend is *rU* and not single *r*. However, in the examples *vṛkṣas tatra* and *plakṣas tatra* the case ending *s* is first replaced by *rU* (A. 8.2.66 *sasajuṣo rUḥ*), then the consonant *r* by *ḥ* (A. 8.3.15 *kharavasānayor visarjanīyaḥ*) and finally *ḥ* by *s* (A. 8.3.34 *visarjanīyasya saḥ*). As can be seen, there is the *rU*-substitution as well. The difference lies in the *sūtra* prescribing the *visarjanīya* which is in this case A. 8.3.15. The subject of substitution in the rule A. 8.3.15 is the individual sound *r* without its specification coming from *rU*. Therefore, the single *r* is replaced by *ḥ* and as such cannot be subject to application of *sthānivadbhāva*. What Kaiyaṭa (VMBh_2: V.441) points out, however, is that in the cases of *chandaḥsu* and *payaḥsu* there is also a single sound that gets replaced, because in the term *rU* the vowel *U* is merely a marker and it is only the single *r* that becomes *ḥ*. The situtation is the same then as with the examples *vṛkṣas tatra* and *plakṣas tatra*. He states that what is heard

while pronouncing the word should be taken into consideration and not that which is understood in a rule.}

VMBh_1: III.427.8-12; VMBh_2: V.440.9-441.5

[Objection:] Then this should be the rule dependent on sounds so is it possible not to use the word *aŚ*?
[Answer:] [It is] really possible. Therefore, it will be the rule dependent on sounds.
[Question:] How come?
[Answer:] There is [the rule] A. 8.3.14. Then I will say that [there is] the *visarjanīya* in place of [the sound] *r* before [a sound denoted by] *khaR* or at the end of a speech (A. 8.3.15). Then [I will say that there is] a *visarjanīya* in place of [the sound] *r* of the *rU*-substitute before the ending *suP* (A. 8.3.16).
[Answer:] In that case the word *aŚ* should be used for the purpose of the following [*sūtra*s] i.e., A. 8.3.22, and it should mean the following: ["Deletion comes in place of the sound *y*] before a consonant [included within the sounds denoted by] *aŚ*". Here it must not be: there is a non-suffix after [the verb] *vṛkṣavayati* [therefore we have the form:] *vṛkṣavkaroti* ('one that calls the tree-cutter').

{**Explanation:**
The derivation of the expression *vṛkṣavkaroti* is quite complex and it is as follows:

(1) *OvraścŪ* (DhP II:11) + KviP (A. 3.2.76 *kvip ca*)
(2) *v* (*r* → *ṛ*) *a* + *śc* + *KviP* (A. 6.1.16 *grahijyāvayivyadhivaṣṭivicativṛścati-pṛcchatibhṛjjatīnāṃ ṅiti ca*)
(3) *v* (*ṛ* + *a* → *ṛ*) + *śc* + *KviP* (A. 6.1.108 *samprasāraṇāc ca*)
(4) *vṛ* + *śc* + 0 (A. 6.1.67 *ver apṛktasya*)
(5) *vṛ* (*ś* → 0) + *c* (A. 8.2.29 *skoḥ saṃyogādyor ante ca*)
(6) *vṛ* (*c* → *ṣ*) (A. 8.2.36 *vraścabhraśjasṛjamṛjayajarājabhrājacchaśāṃ ṣaḥ*)
(7) *vṛ* (*ṣ* → *ḍ*) (A. 8.2.39 *jhalāṃ jaśo 'nte*)
(8) *vṛ* (*ḍ* → *ṭ*) (A. 8.4.56 *vāvasāne*)
vṛṭ

Further:
(1) *vṛkṣavṛṭ* + *ṆiC* + *viC* + *karoti* (A. 3.1.26 *hetumati ca*, A. 3.2.75 *anyebhyo 'pi dṛśyate*)
(2) *vṛkṣav* (*ṛṭ* → 0) + *ṆiC* + *viC* + *karoti* (A. 6.4.155 *vt.* 1 *ṇāv iṣṭhāvat prātipadikasya*)
(3) *vṛkṣav* + 0 + 0 + *karoti* (A. 6.4.51 *ṇer aniṭi*, A. 6.1.67 *ver apṛktasya*)

vṛkṣavkaroti

By a non-suffix Patañjali understands a suffix that is always deleted, which refers to the suffixes containing *vi*. In this particular case there could be the suffixes *viC* or *KviP*. KviP, as we can see, is added at the beginning of this derivation. It cannot, however, be added in the second part where we join *vṛkṣavṛṭ* with *karoti*. Kaiyaṭa explains that were there the suffix *KviP*, the vocalisation of *v* in the form *vṛścati* would take place on the basis of the *paribhāṣā*: *ekadeśavikṛtam ananyavat* ("An item altered in part does not behave like something else").[408] An alternative would be deletion of this sound by A. 6.1.66 *lopo vyor vali*.[409] Moreover, deletion of the suffix *ṆiC* could not be treated as if it had not taken place on the basis of *sthānivadbhāva* due to the prohibition stated in the second *vārttika* under A. 1.1.58.[410] This would lead to the undesired deletion of *v*. Before the suffix *viC*, on the other hand, *sthānivadbhāva* with respect to the suffix *ṆiC* applies and there is no deletion. And even if we accept that *sthānivadbhāva* does not operate in the *pūrvatrāsiddha* section and the *v*-deletion could take place on the basis of the rule A. 8.3.22 *hali sarveṣām*, it is blocked by the condition *aŚi*. This is what the whole above discussion leads to; to explaining the use of the abbreviation *aŚ* in the present rule. Its purpose is not the present rule but the following *sūtra*, namely A. 8.3.22 *hali sarveṣām*. The *pratyāhāra aŚ* qualifies the abbreviation *haL* in A. 8.3.22. In other words, the deletion can take place only before such consonants (*haL*) which are further qualified by *aŚ* (voiced consonants) and the consonant *k* in the word *karoti* is not voiced, which makes the *v*-deletion impossible.}

{A. 8.3.18 *vyor laghuprayatnataraḥ śākaṭāyanasya*
According to Śākaṭāyana, a glide sound (lit. more slightly pronounced) [*y* or *v* comes] in place of [the sounds] *y* and *v* (of the *sūtra*s A. 6.1.78 *eco 'yavāyāvaḥ* and A. 8.3.17 *bhobhagoaghoapūrvasya yo 'śi*) [occurring at the end of a *pada* before a sound denoted by *aŚ* (i.e., voiced sounds) in close proximity].
A. 8.3.19 *lopaḥ śākalyasya*
According to Śākalya, there is deletion [of the sounds *y* and *v* (of the *sūtra*s A. 6.1.78 *eco 'yavāyāvaḥ* and A. 8.3.17 *bhobhagoaghoapūrvasya yo 'śi*) occurring at the end of a *pada* before a sound denoted by *aŚ* (i.e., voiced sounds) in close proximity].} *These *sūtra*s were not commented upon by Patañjali.

---

[408] WUJASTYK 1993: vol. I:8, vol. II:37; PŚ 37; vol I:33-34, vol. II:179-184.

[409] A. 6.1.66 *lopo vyor vali* || ("[The sounds] *v* and *y* are deleted before [a sound denoted by] *vaL*.")

[410] *kvilugupadhātvacaṅparanirhrāsakutveṣūpasaṃkhyānam* || ("[In the prohibition of the *sthānivadbhāva*] should also be counted [the operation before the suffix] *KviP*, the *luK*-deletion, [the operation conditioned by] the penultimate position, the shortening before [the aorist suffix] *CaṄ* and [the operation connected with] the *kU*-substitute.")

A. 8.3.20 ***oto gārgyasya***
According to Gārgya, [there is deletion of the sound *y* occurring at the end of a *pada*] after the sound *o* [before a sound denoted by *aŚ* (i.e., voiced sounds) in close proximity].

VMBh_1: III.427.13-16; VMBh_2: V.442.1-4

[Question:] Why is this said? Has [deletion] not been achieved by [the *sūtra*] A. 8.3.19?

1) The statement regarding deletion [of the sound *y*] after the sound *o* is to make [the operation] obligatory (while it is optional by the preceding rule).

[Bhāṣya:] The statement regarding deletion [of the sound *y*] after the sound *o* is made.[411] This is the beginning of the obligatory meaning.

{**Explanation:**
Kaiyaṭa (VMBh_2: V.442) explains that this deletion must be obligatory. He justifies this by refering to Gārgya's texts in which he always deletes *y* appearing after *o*. He says that Pāṇini also requires such a usage, so the only possibility is *bho atra*; **bhoy atra* is unacceptable (see the example under A. 8.3.17).}

A. 8.3.21 ***uñi ca pade***
[There is deletion of the sounds *y* and *v* (of the *sūtra*s A. 6.1.78 *eco 'yavāyāvaḥ* and A. 8.3.17 *bhobhagoaghoapūrvasya yo 'śi*)] also before the *pada uÑ* [in close proximity].

VMBh_1: III.427.17-21; VMBh_2: V.442.5-10

[Question:] What is the purpose [in using the term] *pada*?
[Answer:] [Because we have the example:] *tantre utam* → *tantray utam* → *tantra utam* ('woven on a loom').
[Objection:] [The term] *pada* does not have to be said.
[Question:] Why does [the rule] not apply in *tantre utam* → *tantray utam* → *tantra utam* ('woven on a loom')?
[Answer:] When there are both – something directly stated and something said through the rule [of grammar] – only [that one should prevail, which] is stated directly. In that case the term *pada* should be used for the sake of what follows, [e.g., the *sūtra*] A. 8.3.32; before a non-*pada* [the operation prescribed by A.

[411] VMBh_2 adds here *nityārtham* ("in order to make it obligatory").

8.3.32] must not take place: *daṇḍinā*, *śakaṭinā* (instr. sg. from the stems *daṇḍin* 'carrying a stick, ascetic' and *śakaṭin* 'an owner of a cart' respectively).

{**Explanation:**
The reason why this rule cannot apply in the example *tantre utam* from which we derive *tantra utam* is that the term *pade* qualifying *uÑ* does not refer to any *pada* that follows the consonant *y* and begins with the vowel *u*; it refers to the particle *u* only. The letter *Ñ* is merely a marker here. This means that this rule can apply in the example *sa u ekāgniḥ* ("He is keeping one fire only") whose derivation is as follows:

(1) *sas + u ekāgniḥ*
(2) *sa* (*s* → *rU*) + *u ekāgniḥ* (A. 8.2.66 *sasajuṣo ruḥ*)
(3) *sa* (*r* → *y*) + *u ekāgniḥ* (A. 8.3.17 *bhobhagoaghoapūrvasya yo 'śi*)
(4) *sa* (*y* → 0) + *u ekāgniḥ* (A. 8.3.21 *uñi ca pade*)
sa u ekāgniḥ

The form *utam* is the passive past participle of the verb *ve* ('to weave'), which in the *Dhātupāṭha* appears with the marker *Ñ* (*veÑ*, DhP: I: 1055). During the formation of the passive past participle the consonant *v* goes through *saṃprasāraṇa*[412] and as a result we achieve *uta*. This vowel *u*, being the result of vocalisation, is not marked with *Ñ* any more and consequently the consonant *y* preceding it cannot be subject to deletion prescribed by this rule. The deletion does take place, but through the application of A. 8.3.19 *lopaḥ śākalyasya*. Patañjali refers to the *paribhāṣā* 105[413] stating that a term used should be taken to denote only that which has been originally stated. In this case we have the word *uÑ* used in the text of the *sūtra* and only such a form should be taken into consideration, the form that originally has the marker *Ñ* attached to it; and not the form *u* (of *uta*) derived from the verb *ve* which is originally marked with *Ñ*.

Patañjali concludes that the term *pada* is used for the sake of the following *sūtra*s, in particular A. 8.3.32 *ṅamo hrasvād aci ṅamuṇ nityam*, which prescribes an obligatory insertion of the infix denoted by the abbreviation *ṅaMUṬ* (i.e., *ṅuṬ*, *ṇuṬ* and *nuṬ*) before a vowel when this vowel appears after a *pada* ending in a sound denoted by *ṅaM*, further used after a short vowel. The word subject to this insertion must be followed by another *pada*. It is not the case with the form *daṇḍinā*. The final sound of the word *daṇḍin* is a dental nasal stop preceded by a

412 A. 6.1.15 *vacisvapiyajādīnāṃ kiti* || ("[Vocalisation replaces the semivowels] of [the verbal stems] *vacI* ('to speak', DhP II: 54), *svapI* ('to sleep', DhP II: 59) and *yajA* etc. ('to sacrifice', DhP I: 1051-59) before [the suffixes] marked with *K*.")

413 PŚ 105 *lakṣaṇapratipadoktayoḥ pratipadoktasyaiva grahaṇam*, I.104-105, II.486-489. WUJASTYK 1993: vol. I:5-7, vol. II:20-31.

short vowel and the following instrumental singular ending is a vowel, but this instrumental suffix cannot be treated as a *pada*. The condition *aci* used in A. 8.3.32 requires the vowel following a *pada* to which it is going to be attached to be also a part of a *pada*. This *pada* condition comes, according to Patañjali, from the present *sūtra*. Therefore, the form *daṇḍinā* does not get the infix and the form **daṇḍinnā* is not possible.}

{A. 8.3.22 *hali sarveṣam*
According to all [grammarians, there is deletion of the *pada* final sound *y* (of the *sūtra* A. 8.3.17 *bhobhagoaghoapūrvasya yo 'śi*)] before a consonant [in close proximity].
A. 8.3.23 *mo 'nusvāraḥ*
The *anusvāra* comes in place of [the *pada* final sound] *m* [before a consonant in close proximity].
A. 8.3.24 *naś cāpadāntasya jhali*
[The *anusvāra*] also comes in place of a non-*pada* final *n* [and the sound *m*] before [a sound denoted by] *jhaL* (i.e., non nasal stops and fricatives) [in close proximity].
A. 8.3.25 *mo rāji samaḥ kvau*
[The sound] *m* comes in places of [a *pada* final *m*] of [the *upasarga*] *sam* before [the verbal stem] *rājṚ* ('to rule', DhP I:874) ending in [the suffix] *KviP* [in close proximity].} *These *sūtra*s were not commented upon by Patañjali.

A. 8.3.26 *he mapare vā*
[The sound *m*] usually [comes in place of a *pada* final *m*] before [the sound] *h* followed by [the sound] *m* [in close proximity].

VMBh_1: III.428.1-4; VMBh_2: V.443.1-4

1) When [the sound *h*] is followed by [the sounds] *y*, *v* or *l*, [the preceding sound *m* is] optionally [replaced by the sounds] *y*, *v* or *l* [respectively].

[Bhāṣya:] It should be mentioned that when the sound *h* is followed by *y*, *v* or *l*, [the preceding sound *m* is] optionally [replaced by the sounds] *y*, *v* or *l* [respectively]. [For example,] *kiy hyas* or *kiṃ hyas* ("What [was] yesterday?"), *kiv hvalayati* or *kiṃ hvalayati* ("What makes it shake?"), *kil hlādayati* or *kiṃ hlādayati* ("What makes it shout [for joy]?").

{A. 8.3.27 *napare naḥ*
[The sound] *n* [usually comes in place of a *pada* final *m*] before [the sound *h*] followed by [the sound] *n* [in close proximity].
A. 8.3.28 *ṅṇoḥ kukṭuk śari*

[The infixes] *kUK* and *ṭUK* [usually come at the end of a *pada* ending in the sounds] *ṅ* and *ṇ* [respectively] before [a sound denoted by] *śaR* (i.e., sibilants) [in close proximity].} *The first *sūtra* was not commented upon by Patañjali, the second one is discussed later on.

A. 8.3.29 *ḍaḥ si dhuṭ*
[The infix] *dhUṬ* [usually comes at the beginning of a *pada*] before [the sound] *s* after [a *pada* ending in the sound] *ḍ* [in close proximity].
A. 8.3.30 *naś ca*
[The infix *dhUṬ* usually comes at the beginning of a *pada* before the sound *s*] also after [a *pada* ending in the sound] *n* [in close proximity].
A. 8.3.31 *śi tuk*
[The infix] *tUK* [usually comes at the end of a *pada* ending in the sound *n*] before [the sound] *ś* [in close proximity].
A. 8.3.28 *ṅṇoḥ kukṭuk śari*
[The infixes] *kUK* and *ṭUK* [usually come at the end of a *pada* ending in the sounds] *ṅ* and *ṇ* [respectively] before [a sound denoted by] *śaR* (i.e., sibilants) [in close proximity].
A. 8.3.32 *ṅamo hrasvād aci ṅamuṇ nityam*
[The infixes denoted by] *ṅaMUṬ* (i.e., *ṅUṬ*, *ṇUṬ*, *nUṬ*) necessarily [come at the beginning of a *pada*] before a vowel after [a *pada* ending in a sound denoted by] *ṅaM* (i.e., the sounds *ṅ*, *ṇ*, *n*) [occuring] after a short vowel [in close proximity].

VMBh_1: III.428.5-11; VMBh_2: V.443.5-9

[Bhāṣya:] Here, in [the *sūtra*s] beginning with A. 8.3.29 some [think that] they [i.e., the infixes] are inserted at the end of what precedes and some [think that] that they are inserted at the beginning of what follows.
[Question:] What is the difference here?

{**Explanation:**
The above *sūtra*s are commented on together as they refer to one operation – the insertion of an infix. The infixes are of different kinds though; they can be inserted at the beginning of the following *pada* or at the end of a *pada* that precedes. Pāṇini marked them with markers *Ṭ* and *K* respectively. The infixes marked with *Ṭ* come at the beginning of the element they are attached to, and those marked with *K* come at the end; on the basis of the *sūtra* A. 1.1.46 *ādyantau ṭakitau*.}

VMBh_1: III.428.12-15; VMBh_2: V.443.10-14

1) [There should be] prohibition of *ṣṭU*- and *ṇ*-substitutes in [the *sūtras*] A. 8.3.29 etc.

[Bhāṣya:] Prohibition of *ṣṭU*- and *ṇ*-substitutes in [the *sūtras*] A. 8.3.29 etc. should be mentioned. Firstly, [the example of] the *ṣṭU*-substitute: *śvaliṭ tsāye* ("Licking up like a dog in the evening"), *madhuliṭ tsāye* ("A bee in the evening"). The *ṣṭU*-substitute would result by A. 8.4.41. If, on the other hand, [the infix is added] at the beginning of what follows, the prohibition by A. 8.4.42 will be achieved.

{**Explanation:**
Let us consider the example *śvaliṭ tsāye* (of the rule A. 8.3.29) where the infix *dhUṬ* is added at the beginning of the *pada sāye*. The consonant *dh* is replaced by *t* before the sibilant *s* of *sāye* on the basis of A. 8.4.55 *khari ca*. The question might arise as to why the infix is not marked with *K* instead of *Ṭ*, which would allow it to continue in the following rule A. 8.3.31. If that were the case, the infix would have to be added to the *pada śvaliṭ* leading to the undesired application of A. 8.4.41 *ṣṭunā ṣṭuḥ* and the retroflex substitute of *s* in *sāye*. If the infix *dhUṬ* were added at the end of *śvaliṭ*, it would become *ṭ* (by the application of A. 8.4.41 and A. 8.4.55) and A. 8.4.41 could still apply. If, on the other hand, it is added to *sāye*, the retroflex substitution is blocked by A. 8.4.42 *na padāntāṭ ṭor anām*, which negates the substitution when *s* appears after the *pada*-final retroflex and the infix *dhUṬ*, though added to *sāye*, can still be treated as such. The situation is the same if we decide not to add *dhUṬ* at all, as it is optional, and we achieve the form *śvaliṭ sāye* where the dental *s* is not replaced by its retroflex counterpart.}

VMBh_1: III.428.15-17; VMBh_2: V.443.14-16

[Bhāṣya:] [The example of] the *ṇ*-substitute: *kurvann āste* ("A doer sits"), *kṛṣann āste* ("A ploughman sits"). The *ṇ*-substitute would result by A. 8.4.1. If, on the other hand, [the infix is added] at the beginning of what follows and not at the end of what precedes, the prohibition by A. 8.4.37 will be achieved.

{**Explanation:**
This is an example of A. 8.3.32. In the expression *kurvann āste* and the like, the infix *ṅaM* (in this case the consonant *n*) should be added at the end of the *pada kurvan* as it is marked with *K*. However, the insertion of the infix at the end of a preceding *pada* would allow A. 8.4.2 *aṭkupvāṅnumvyavāye 'pi* to apply, which prescribes the *ṇ*-substitute in place of *n* when the same follows *r* or *ṣ* even if *n* is separated from *r* or *ṣ* by *aṬ* (i.e., vowels, *h*, semivowels), velar or labial consonants, the particle *āṄ* or infix *nUM*; this is not a desired outcome. If, on the other

hand, *ṅaM* were introduced to the *pada āste*, then the prohibition of the substitution would apply by the rule A. 8.4.37 *padāntasya* which does not allow for the consonant *ṇ* at the end of a *pada*. This, of course, poses a problem as the infix is marked with *K* and should be added at the end of what precedes.}

VMBh_1: III.428.18-429.1; VMBh_2: V.443.16-444.4

[Objection:] In that case, let it be [added] at the beginning of what follows.

2) If the infix [is added] at the beginning of what follows, there [should be] injunction of the *ch*-substitute (A. 8.4.63 *śaś cho 'ṭi*) and prohibition of the *ṣ*-substitute (A. 8.3.59 *ādeśapratyayayoḥ*).

[Bhāṣya:] If the infix [is added] at the beginning of what follows, the *ch*-substitute should be enjoined and the *ṣ*-substitute should be forbidden. [The example of] the *ch*-substitute to be enjoined: *kurvañ cchete* ("A doer lies"), *kṛṣañ cchete* ("A ploughman lies"). If A. 8.4.63 [applies], thus it [should apply] after the *pada*-final [when it] ends in [a sound denoted by] *jhaY* (i.e., non-nasal stops).

{**Explanation:**
In the examples *kurvañ cchete* and *kṛṣañ cchete* the sibilant *ś* needs to be replaced by *ch* on the basis of the *sūtra* A. 8.4.63 *śaś cho 'ṭi*. The substitution occurs when *ś* appears before vowels or the consonants *y*, *r*, *v*, and after a *pada* ending in a non-nasal consonant. Obviously, the word *kurvan* ends in a nasal consonant and therefore the substitution would not be possible. If the infix *tUK*, prescribed by A. 8.3.31, is inserted though, the word *kurvan* will not end in a nasal consonant any more.

(1) *kurvan* + *śete*
(2) *kurvan* + *tUK* + *śete* (A. 8.3.31 *śi tuk*)
(3) *kurvan* + (*t* → *c*) + *śete* (A. 8.4.40 *stoḥ ścunā ścuḥ*)
(4) *kurva* (*n* → *ñ*) + *c* + *śete* (A. 8.4.40 *stoḥ ścunā ścuḥ*)
(5) *kurvañ* + *c* + (*ś* → *ch*) *ete* (A. 8.4.63 *śaś cho 'ṭi*)
kurvañ cchete

The rule A. 8.4.40 will allow us to replace the consonant *t* with *c* before *ś* and subsequently the nasal *n* with *ñ* before *c*. It would seem that in this case it is better to insert the infix at the end of what precedes to be able to apply A. 8.4.63 and the *ch*-substitute.}

VMBh_1: III.429.1-5; VMBh_2: V.444.4-7

[Question:] Why, however, should it be that [it applies] after the *pada*-final [when it] ends in [a sound denoted by] *jhaY* (i.e., non-nasal stops)?
[Answer:] [Because] here it must not be: *purā krūrasya visṛpo virapśin* ("Before the cruel foe slips away, oh glorious one").[414] [The example of] the *ṣ*-substitute to be forbidden: *pratyaṅk siñca* ("Sprinkle to the west!"), *udaṅk siñca* ("Sprinkle to the north!"). The *ṣ*-substitute would result by A. 8.3.59. If, on the other hand, [the infix is added] at the end of what precedes, the prohibition is achieved by A. 8.3.111.

{**Explanation:**
In the examples quoted above there is the possibility to apply the *ṣ*-substitute on the basis of A. 8.3.59 *ādeśapratyayayoḥ* if the infix *kUK* is added at the beginning of what follows, which would result in the incorrect form **pratyaṅ kṣiñca*. When the infix is added to the preceding *pada*, the substitution can be blocked by A. 8.3.111 *sātpadādyoḥ* which denies the *ṣ*-substitute if *s* appears at the beginning of a *pada* and follows the vowels *i*, *u* or velar consonants. After the addition of *kUK* to the *pratyaṅ*, giving *pratyaṅk*, the word *siñca* begins with the sibilant *s* following a velar consonant and as such could be spared the *ṣ*-substitute.}

VMBh_1: III.429.5-10; VMBh_2: V.444.7-12

[Answer:] Let it be then according to the text of the *sūtra*, in some instances at the end of what precedes and in others at the beginning of what follows.
[Objection:] But now, it should be said that [the infix is added] at the end of what precedes according to the command in order to [achieve] the *ch*-substitute of [the sound *t* of] *tUK* inserted before [the sound *ś* on the basis of the *sūtra* A. 8.3.31]. Therefore in these case – *kurvañ cchete* ("A doer lies"), *kṛṣañ cchete* ("A ploughman lies") – the *ṇ*-substitute would result by [the *sūtra*] A. 8.4.1.
[Bhāṣya:] There is no fault here. In [the *sūtra*] A. 8.4.40 the separation of a rule will be done. First, [we have]: "the sound *ṇ* is not [the substitute for the sound *n*] in [the words] *kṣubhnāti* ('he shakes, trembles') etc." (see A. 8.4.39). Then [we have]: *stoḥ ścunā* – the sound *ṇ* does not come in place of the sound *n* when there is the contact of [the sound] *s* and the dental consonants (*tU*) with [the sound] *ś* and the palatal consonants (*cU*). Then [we have]: *ścuḥ* – there is [the substitution of the sound] *ś* and the palatal consonants (*cU*) when there is the contact of [the sound] *s* and the dental consonants (*tU*) with [the sound] *ś* and the palatal consonants (*cU*, see A. 8.4.40).

{**Explanation:**

[414] TS 1.1.9.3. Here, in the word *virapśin* the consonant *ś* is not replaced by *ch* because it is not at the end of a *pada*, even though it appears after a sound denoted by *jhaY*.

Patañjali proposes a split interpretation of the *sūtra* A. 8.4.40 *stoḥ ścunā ścuḥ* in order to block the *ṇ*-substitute in the cases *kurvañ cchete* and *kṛṣañ cchete*. The preceding rule, i.e., A. 8.4.39 *kṣubhnādiṣu ca* negates the *ṇ*-substitute in the stems *kṣubhnā* etc. so that the forms such as *kṣubhnāti* do not get the retroflex *ṇ*. When the rule A. 8.4.40 is split, the first part, i.e., *stoḥ ścunā*, will be joined with the *sūtra* A. 8.4.39 and thus negation will also apply in the situation where *s* and the dental consonants are in contact with *ś* and the palatal consonants.
Let us examine the example *kurvañ cchete* then. As we can see from the derivation presented above, at the very beginning we have the stage *kurvan* + *t* + *śete*. According to A. 8.4.1, the final *n* of *kurvan* could be subject to the *ṇ*-replacement. If we accept the split interpretation of A. 8.4.40 though, it will not be possible. The consonant *t* appears before *ś* and when we read *stoḥ ścunā* together with *kṣubhnādiṣu ca*, we get the prohibition of the *ṇ*-substitution in such a situation. Instead, we will get the *c*-substitute of the dental *t* – thanks to the split interpretation of the rule A. 8.4.40, by the second part of it, i.e., *ścuḥ* – and then the consonant *ś* gets replaced by *ch* by A. 8.4.63.}

A. 8.3.32 *ṅamo hrasvād aci ṅamuṇ nityam*
[The infixes denoted by] *ṅaMUṬ* (i.e., *ṅUṬ*, *ṇUṬ*, *nUṬ*) necessarily [come at the beginning of a *pada*] before a vowel after [a *pada* ending in a sound denoted by] *ṅaM* (i.e., the sounds *ṅ*, *ṇ*, *n*) [occuring] after a short vowel [in close proximity].

VMBh_1: III.429.11-16; VMBh_2: V.444.13-445.4

1) In the case of [the infixes] *ṅaMUṬ* the beginning of a *pada* should be mentioned.

[Bhāṣya:] In the case of [the infixes] *ṅaMUṬ* the beginning of a *pada* should be mentioned. Here it must not be: *daṇḍinā*, *śakaṭinā* (instr. sg. of 'carrying a stick' and 'an owner of a cart' respectively).
[Question:] Should it be mentioned then?
[Answer:] It should not be mentioned. [The expression] "after a *pada*" from [the *sūtra* A. 8.1.17] continues.[415] In the same way [the forms] *paramadaṇḍinā*, *paramacchattriṇā* (instr. sg. of the words 'the best carrier of a stick' and 'the best owner of a cart' respectively) would result.
[Bhāṣya:] This is not a fault. It has been said: "When the second member of a compound is to get the designation of a *pada* with the exception of the rule [applying to] the beginning of a *pada*, when [a suffix] has been deleted by [an

---

[415] A. 8.1.17 *padāt* || ("[All the operations are introduced] after a *pada*.")

element] containing *lu* (i.e., *luK*, *luP* or *Ślu*), [the rule] A. 1.1.62 does not apply."[416] In the same way it should also be said "after a *pada*" (A. 8.1.17).

{Explanation:
The compound *paramadaṇḍin* is formed from *paramaḥ* and *daṇḍin*. During the process of forming a compound the ending of the word *paramaḥ* (i.e., *sU*) is deleted on the basis of the rule A. 2.4.71 *supo dhātuprātipadikayoḥ*. A. 1.1.62 *pratyayalope pratyayalakṣaṇam* allows the suffix that has been deleted to be treated as if it was still there, but the *vārttika* quoted by Patañjali prohibits it when the second member of a compound is to get the designation of a *pada*. The present rule requires the element to be termed *pada* for the insertion of the infix to take place; as *daṇḍin* cannot be so designated due to prohibition of the quoted *vārttika*, the conditions for the infix insertion are not met.}

VMBh_1: III.429.16-19; VMBh_2: V.445.4-7

[Opponent:] If this is the context, in the same way it should be before [the *sūtra*] A. 8.1.69.[417] Thus [the infixes] *ṅaMUṬ* are applied only after [a *pada* ending in the sounds denoted by] *ṅaM*.
[Question:] How [is that]?
[Answer:] [The *sūtra*] A. 8.1.16 continues and [the form] *ṅamaḥ* is not in the ablative.
[Question:] What [is the form] then?
[Answer:] It is the genitive of connection (*sambandhaṣaṣṭhī*). [The infixes] *ṅaMUṬ* are [added] to a following [*pada*] before a vowel after [the sounds denoted by] *ṅaM* (i.e., nasals *ṅ*, *ṇ*, *n*) [occurring] at the end of a *pada* after a short vowel.

{Explanation:
The form *ṅamaḥ* could be interpreted both as the ablative or genitive. However, as the term *pada* continues in this *sūtra* from A. 8.1.16 *padasya* where it is used in the genitive, *ṅamaḥ* is read as the genitive as well; it becomes the qualifier to *pada*. This is the view in the *Mahābhāṣya*.

The commentators (KV VI.512) view it differently though. They claim that the expression *ṅamaḥ* is not the genitive but it is the ablative and the word *padasya*

---

[416] A. 1.1.63 *vt*. 6 *uttarapadatve cāpadādividhau*.

[417] See A. 8.1.69 *kutsane ca supy agotrādau* || ("[A verbal *pada* occurring with or without a *gati* becomes *anudātta* accented] before a *sUP* [suffix] except for [a group of words] *gotra* etc. to mean 'reproach, abuse'].") This rule is quoted because the *anuvṛtti* of the term *padāt* from the *sūtra* A. 8.1.17 ceases there. The term *pada* in the present rule is not continued from A. 8.1.17 as is explained further on.

is transformed into *padāt* being qualified by *ṅaM*. The word *hrasvāt* is used as a qualifier to *ṅamaḥ*. Further, they make use of the *tadantavidhi* rule interpreting the present *sūtra* as *hrasvāt paro yo ṅam tadantād padāt* – "after a *pada* which ends in *ṅaM* (i.e. nasals *ṅ*, *ṇ*, *n*) occurring after a short vowel."}

VMBh_1: III.429.19-24; VMBh_2: V.445.7-446.3

[Objection:] If [the infixes] *ṅaMUṬ* are added only after [the sounds denoted by] *ṅaM* (i.e., nasals *ṅ*, *ṇ*, *n*), [in the examples] *kurvann āste* ("A doer is sitting down") and *kṛṣann āste* ("A ploughman is sitting down"), the *ṇ*-substitute would result by [the *sūtra*] A. 8.4.1.
[Answer:] There will be prohibition – "not at the end of a *pada*" – A. 8.4.37.
[Objection:] It is said "at the end of a *pada*" but this is not the end of a *pada*.
[Answer:] That which is a part of the end of a *pada* will be understood from the expression "the end of a *pada*".
[Objection:] It is not achieved in this way either.
[Question:] What is the reason?
[Answer:] It has been said: "Alternatively, due to the governing term (*adhikāra*) *pada* being a qualifier."[418] Thus [the expression] *pade* continues then.
[Question:] Where is the context?
[Answer:] [The context is the *sūtra*] A. 8.3.21.

{**Explanation:**
The word *pada* is not to be qualified here but it is a qualifier itself. In other words, we should understand that *ṅamaḥ* should refer to a sound denoted by *ṅaM* (i.e., nasals *ṅ*, *ṇ*, *n*) being a part of a *pada* and not a *pada* ending in a sound denoted by *ṅaM*. As Kaiyaṭa (VMBh_2: V.446) points out, the *tadantavidhi*[419] rule will not apply here. This is not the ideal solution, however, because it would allow the insertion of the infix in the example *daṇḍinā*, which is why another solution is proposed. The *vārttika* is considered superfluous by Patañjali because the term *pada*, refering to the following element beginning with a vowel, is continued from the rule A. 8.3.21 *uñi ca pade*. It solves the problem with *daṇḍinā* and *śakaṭinā* as the following element (i.e., the instrumental ending *āṄ*) does not get the designation of a *pada* so the conditions for the present rule are not met.}

A. 8.3.33 *maya uño vo vā*

---

[418] Patañjali states in the *sūtra* A. 8.1.16 *padasya vt.* 5 that the genititive should not be understood as that denoting 'in place of' (*sthānaṣaṣṭhī*) but it should denote 'qualifying' (*viśeṣaṇaṣaṣṭhī*).

[419] A. 1.1.72 *yena vidhis tadantasya* || ("When an operation is stated by means of a unit X which is a part of a larger unit which it qualifies, that X denotes the element ending in it [as well as itself].")

[The sound] *v* usually comes in place of [the particle] *uÑ* [appearing] after [a sound denoted by] *maY* (i.e., all stops except the nasal *ñ*) [in close proximity].

VMBh_1: III.430.1-3; VMBh_2: V.446.4-6

[Question:] Why is it said: "[the sound] *v* usually comes in place of [the particle] *uÑ* [appearing] after [a sound denoted by] *maY* (i.e., all stops except the nasal *ñ*)"? Is it not achieved by [the *sūtra*] A. 6.1.77?
[Answer:] It is not achieved [by the *sūtra* A. 6.1.77]. Having done *pragṛhya*, the original form [of the word] would result.

{**Explanation:**
The particle *uÑ* gets the designation *pragṛhya* by A. 1.1.14 *nipāta ekāj anāṅ*. Theoretically, this particle could be replaced by a corresponding semivowel based on A. 6.1.77 *iko yaṇ aci*; the reason why it cannot happen here, however, is the term *pragṛhya* assigned to *uÑ*. A. 6.1.77 will be blocked by A. 6.1.125 *plutapragṛhyā 'ci nityam*. The examples such as *sam u astu vediḥ* ("May the sacrificial altar be propitious") have an optional version – *sam v astu vediḥ*.}

VMBh_1: III.430.3-6; VMBh_2: V.446.6-9

[Objection:] What if, on the other hand, with respect to that it would be said: "[The sounds denoted by] *yaṆ* come in place of [the sounds denoted by] *iK* before vowels, and [the sound] *v* optionally comes in place of [the particle] *uÑ* [appearing] after [a sound denoted by] *maY* (i.e., all stops except the nasal *ñ*)"?
[Answer:] It is not possible in such a way because there would be a fault here: *kim v āvapanaṃ mahat* ("Is the sowing big?"[420]). The *anusvāra* would result before a consonant by A. 8.3.23. When there is the *v*-substitute, it (i.e., the *anusvāra*) will not [apply] due to its (i.e., the *v*-substitute) suspension.

{**Explanation:**
The undesired outcome of potential application of A. 6.1.77 is that it opens the option to apply A. 8.3.23 *mo 'nusvāraḥ* prescribing the *anusvāra* in place of *m* appearing before a consonant. If, on the other hand, the *v*-substitute applies on the basis of the present *sūtra* rather than A. 6.1.77, the rule A. 8.3.23 cannot apply due to suspension of the *v*-substitute. Consequently, there is no consonant *v* at all; we still have the vowel *u* and the conditions for A. 8.3.23 to apply are not met. In such a situation we accept the *pragṛhya* designation for the particle *uÑ*.

[420] VS 29.9.45.

The situation is different when the particle *uÑ* is followed by the word *iti* like in the example *kim u iti*. There are four forms possible, as Kaiyaṭa (VMBh_2: V.446) points out: *kiṃ v iti*, *kim v iti*, *kim u iti* and *kim ūm̐ iti*. According to A. 1.1.17 *uñaḥ*,[421] the particle *uÑ* is termed *pragṛhya* only optionally before *iti* and so is the case with *ūm̐* which replaces it.[422] That accounts for the last two forms where the *v*-substitution has not taken place. If, however, the *pragṛhya* interpretation is not accepted, then we can achieve the *v*-substitution on the basis of A. 6.1.77 and get the form *kim v iti*. Consequently, the preceding consonant *m* can also be subject to the *anusvāra* substitution and we get *kiṃ v iti*. The application of A. 6.1.77 in the case of *uÑ* is accepted only if the same is not termed *pragṛhya*.
According to commentators, the vowel *u* could also be replaced by *ūm̐* on the basis of the rule A. 1.1.18 leading to the form *kim vm̐ iti*. Therefore, possible forms of the expression *kim u iti* include one without substitution, with the *ūm̐*-substitute, and consequently the *vm̐*-substitute, one with the *v*-substitute and further also with *anusvāra* in place of *m* before the *v*-substitute.}

A. 8.3.34 *visarjanīyasya saḥ*
[The sound] *s* comes in place of the *visarjanīya* [before a sound denoted by *khaR* (i.e., voiceless consonants) in close proximity].

VMBh_1: III.430.7-8; VMBh_2: V.447.1-2

[Question:] Why will it not be here: *vṛkṣaḥ*, *plakṣaḥ* (nom. sg. of 'a tree' and 'a fig-tree' respectively)?
[Answer:] [The term] *saṃhitāyām* ('in close proximity') [continues from A. 8.2.108].

{Explanation:
Kaiyaṭa (VMBh_2: V.447.11 ff) explains that the term *saṃhitā* means the order of sounds not separated by time; it requires two sounds and in the quoted examples there is no sound following the final *visarjanīya*. Hence, no *saṃhitā*. This time the separation condition is necessary not to allow for sandhi in examples such as *dadhi atra* ("Yoghurt is here") where the rule A. 6.1.77 would apply yielding the undesired form **dadhyatra*. The interval of time results when the consonant *r* appearing at the end of the word *dadhi* is replaced by *y* (A. 8.3.17

[421] A. 1.1.17 *uñaḥ* || ("[According to Śākalya, the particle] *uÑ* [is termed *pragṛhya* before a non-Vedic *iti*].")
[422] A. 1.1.18 *ūm̐* || ("[According to Śākalya, the technical term *pragṛhya* denotes the particle] *ūm̐* [which replaces *uÑ*].")

bhobhagoaghoapūrvasya yo 'śi) and further deleted (A. 8.3.19 *lopaḥ śākalyasya*), which is why the expression is not subject to further sandhi.}

VMBh_1: III.430.8-11; VMBh_2: V.447.2-5

[Answer:] Thus, it (i.e., the substitution) would result here as well.
[Question:] What is the reason?
[Answer:] It is said that [the term] *saṃhitā* means the closest proximity (A. 1.4.109 *paraḥ saṃnikarṣaḥ saṃhitā*); just as this closest proximity is with that which follows, in the same way it is with what precedes as well.
[Objection:] In that case then the technical term *avasāna*,[423] having no scope of application, will block the technical term *saṃhitā*.

{**Explanation:**
This passage refers to the section in the *Aṣṭādhyāyī* headed by the *adhikāra* A. 1.4.1 *ākaḍārād ekā saṃjñā*,[424] in which every following rule supersedes the former in the case of conflict between the two (**See 4.3.2**). The technical terms *saṃhitā* and *avasāna* are introduced in two consecutive *sūtra*s A. 1.4.109 and A. 1.4.110 respectively, from which follows that the latter should block the former as it would not have the scope of application otherwise. The objection is raised, however, that there is no blocking here due to the difference of the element to be designated: *saṃhitā* refers to the closest proximity and the *avasāna* to a pause. Nonetheless, the blocked-blocking relation applies here because both these terms share their domain; which is always one sound and the meaning of operations (i.e., designating) is the same, therefore one term is able to block the other.}

VMBh_1: III.430.11-12; VMBh_2: V.447.5-7

[Bhāṣya:] Alternatively, preferential treatment will be recognized with respect to the term *saṃhitā*. That one which means the closest proximity is more correct.
[Question:] Which is more correct?
[Answer:] The one [which includes both] preceding and following ones.

{**Explanation:**
Kaiyaṭa (VMBh_2: V.447) states that as the term *saṃhitā* is understood as close proximity, the word *para* ('the following') gets preferential treatment. It is of special importance and such proximity that has its domain in both the preceeding and the following element gets the designation of *saṃhitā*. Nāgeśa adds that the

---

[423] A. 1.4.110 *virāmo 'vasānam* || ("[The term] *avasāna* means pause.")
[424] A. 1.4.1 *ākaḍārād ekā saṃjñā* || ("[In this section] up to A. 2.2.38 one technical term [applies to one element].")

meaning of *prakarṣagati*, the term used by Patañjali for 'preferential treatment or special consideration', is the close proximity of the preceeding element that is subject to an operation with a following one. In other words, the following element is essential; we cannot do without it in interpreting the present *sūtra*.}

VMBh_1: III.430.12-19; VMBh_2: V.447.8-448.6

[Objection:] If then the technical term *avasāna*, having no scope of application, blocks the technical term *saṃhitā* and also preferential treatment is recognized with respect to the term *saṃhitā*, there is a fault in both cases. From this point further on [the rules] are required [to apply] before a pause (*avasāna*), those operations referring to close proximity (*saṃhitā*) are not achieved; [thus] A. 8.4.57.
[Answer:] In such a way the teacher's use indicates that the *s*-substitute does not replace every *visarjanīya*, as he says in [the *sūtra*] A. 8.3.15. Otherwise he would just say: "[The sound] *s* comes before the sounds [denoted by] *khaR* and in a pause." And this is [made] short, [the sound] *s* comes in place of the *visarjanīya* – this should not be said. It is necessary in [the *sūtra*] A. 8.3.35, the term *visarjanīya* should be [used] there in order to prescribe the base (i.e., the *sthānin*).

{**Explanation:**
The reference is made to the rule A. 8.4.57 *aṇo 'pragṛhyasyānunāsikaḥ* which prescribes the optional *anunāsika* vowel in place of the vowels *a*, *i* or *u* when the vowel is not termed *pragṛhya*, and which also has to appear in a pause understood from the context of the preceeding A. 8.4.56 *vāvasāne*. The example of the rule A. 8.4.57 is as follows:

(1) *madhu* + *sU* (A. 4.1.2 *svaujasamauṭśasṭābhyāmbhisṅebhyāmbhyasṅasibhyāmbhyasṅasosāmṅyossup*)
(2) *madhu* + 0 (A. 7.1.23 *svamor napuṃsakāt*)
(3) *madhu* / *madhum̐* (A. 8.4.57 *aṇo 'pragṛhyasyānunāsikaḥ* – optionally)

However, the term *saṃhitā* is necessary for understanding the following rules properly. For example, if it were not supplied in A. 8.4.60 *tor li*, the rule could not apply in the examples such as *agnicit lunāti* > *agnicil lunāti* ("The one arranging the sacrificial fire cuts"). This is why Kaiyaṭa (VMBh_2: V.448) says the *anunāsika* substitution in A. 8.4.57 depends both on *saṃhitā* and *avasāna*. He further states that if the blocked-blocking relation were accepted in this situation, there would be no connection with the *saṃhitā* in a rule conditioned by the *avasāna*; and what we need in later *sūtra*s is the *anuvṛtti* of *saṃhitā*. So, no fault is found here. Despite the fact that the continuance of *saṃhitā* has been broken by another *adhikāra* (i.e., *avasāna*), the term can still apply in later rules thanks to the device called *maṇḍūkapluti* ('frog's leap') as Annaṃbhaṭṭa explains. According to Kaiyaṭa, both terms (*saṃhitā* and *avasāna*) can occur simultaneously due to various domains of their respective operations.}

VMBh_1: III.430.19-21; VMBh_2: V.448.6-449.1

[Objection:] Then in this case this will also be drawn back in order to [place] it near [the sound] *r*; [so the rule A. 8.3.15 would read:] "[The sound] *s* comes [in place of *rU*] before [a sound denoted by] *khaR* and in a pause"; in the same way also [in the *sūtra*] A. 8.3.37. In such a manner *rU* should be used in [the *sūtra*] A. 8.3.17 [because it is] separated from the first with the following ones.

{**Explanation:**
The necessity of the present rule is discussed further and it is suggested that A. 8.3.15 were amended; it could read *kharavasānayoḥ saḥ* instead of *kharavasānayor visarjanīyaḥ*. Kaiyaṭa (VMBh_2: V.448-449) states that in such a case the order of rules would have to be the following: A. 8.3.14 (prescribing the deletion of *r* before another *r*), A. 8.3.15 (including the *s*-substitute rather than the *visarjanīya*), A. 8.3.16 (prescribing the *visarjanīya* in place of *rU* before the locative plural ending) and finally A. 8.3.35 (prescribing the *visarjanīya* in place of another *visarjanīya* before voiceless stops (*khaR*) followed by sibilants (śaR)), followed by A. 8.3.36 (prescribing an optional *visarjanīya* in place of another *visarjanīya* before sibilants (śaR)) and A. 8.3.37 (prescribing the *jīhvamūlīya* and *upadhmānīya* before velar and labial stops). A problem arises, however, if A. 8.3.16 is immediately followed by A. 8.3.35. A. 8.3.17 prescribes the sound *y* in place of *r* being a part of *rU*; it is done via *anuvṛtti* from A. 8.3.16. By placing A. 8.3.35 before A. 8.3.17 in the *Tripādī* section, the continuance of *rU* is stopped and *y* would replace *r* but not *rU*, which would lead to the undesired *y*-substitute in the cases such as *svar atra* ("Here is the sun"). Kaiyaṭa states that in such a case, due to breaking the continuance of *rU*, it would have to be stated once again. Annaṃbhaṭṭa adds that *rU* could continue thanks to, again, *maṇḍūkapluti* ('frog's leap') in A. 8.3.17 and its repetition would not be necessary.}

VMBh_1: III.430.21-431.1; VMBh_2: V.449.1-6

[Answer:] In this case then one use of [the term] *visarjanīya* is false. Therefore, when it has been achieved by the shorter maxim, when [the teacher] makes a specific effort, the teacher indicates that the *s*-substitute does not come in place of every *visarjanīya*.
[Question:] In this way then an indication is indefinite. So much [only] is indicated – the *s*-substitute does not come in place of every *visarjanīya*. With

respect to that, why will it (i.e., the substitution) be here: *vṛkṣas tatra*, *plakṣas tatra* and not here: *vṛkṣaḥ*, *plakṣaḥ*?

{Explanation:
Kaiyaṭa (VMBh_2: V.449) explains that according to the wording of a rule, there are three substitutions used: the *visarjanīya* is used twice (both in A. 8.3.15 and in the present *sūtra*) and the consonant *s* (in the present rule) is used once. If we accept a different wording, we will achieve only two – *s* and *rU*. The consonant *s* comes as a necessary consequence of the *visarjanīya*, which is why one use of the *visarjanīya* term is superfluous. It is explained, however, with the use of the term *yatna* – specific effort; the term used to describe an addition to the rule in order to remove the difficulty in its application. This is precisely what happens here. By using the word *visarjanīya* in the present *sūtra* and not stating the *s*-substitution directly in A. 8.3.15 Pāṇini makes it clear that the consonant *s* cannot come in a pause, it has to come before the sounds denoted by the abbreviatory term *khaR*.}

VMBh_1: III.431.2-6; VMBh_2: V.449.7-450.2

[Answer:] Therefore, in the same way the teacher's use indicates that there is no *s*-substitute of this *visarjanīya*, that which he says [in] A. 8.3.35. Alternatively, [the expression] "before a consonant" continues.
[Question:] Where is the context?
[Answer:] In A. 8.3.22.
[Objection:] If that continues, [the *sūtra* A. 8.3.33 will read] "[The sound] *v* usually comes in place of [the particle] *uÑ* [appearing] after [a sound denoted by] *maY* and also before a consonant". The *v*-substitute would result also before a consonant, [such as here:] *śam u naḥ, śam u yor astu* ("Let the happiness be for us" and "Let the happiness and wealfare be [for us]" respectively).[425]
[Answer:] Therefore, in the same way here in [the *sūtra*] A. 8.3.34 [the expression]: "before [the sounds denoted by] *khaR*" will continue (from A. 8.3.15). Alternatively, the connection [between the qualifier and the qualified] will continue.

{Explanation:
The word ordering that Pāṇini chose in his *sūtra*s is necessary for the sake of the rules that follow. In A. 8.3.35, the substitute is necessarily the *visarjanīya* so that in the examples such as *puruṣaḥ tsarukaḥ* ('a sword-hilt maker') the final *visarjanīya* of *puruṣaḥ* were not replaced with *s*. Specifying the *s*-substitute only before *khaR* sounds eliminates the possibility of the consonant *s* appearing in a

[425] KS 2.1.

pause. It also allows the *visarjanīya* as a substitute in the example *puruṣaḥ tsarukaḥ* where *t* (i.e., a sound denoted by *khaR*) is followed by a sibilant (śaR).

The objection is raised in the *Pradīpa* (VMBh_2: V.450) that A. 8.3.35 *śarpare visarjanīyaḥ* (comp. *puruṣaḥ tsarukaḥ*) was formed to prohibit the application of *ẖk* and *ẖp* in the examples such as *vāsaḥ kṣaumam adbhiḥ* ("The linen cloth is devoured by waters"). Kaiyaṭa, however, refutes this argument by saying that if it were the only purpose of A. 8.3.35, then it would suffice to change the wording of A. 8.3.37 (the one prescribing *ẖk* and *ẖp*) by formulating the additional condition – *aśari* ("[when a sound denoted by *khaR*] is not followed by [a sound denoted by] *śaR*").}

{A. 8.3.35 *śarpare visarjanīyaḥ*
The *visarjanīya* [comes in place of the *visaranīya* before a sound denoted by *khaR* (i.e., voiceless consonants)] followed by [a sound denoted by] *śaR* (i.e., sibilants) [in close proximity]} *This *sūtra* was not commented upon by Patañjali.

A. 8.3.36 *vā śari*
[The *visarjanīya*] usually [comes in place of the *visaranīya*] before [a sound denoted by] *śaR* (i.e., sibilants) [in close proximity].

VMBh_1: III.431.7-9; VMBh_2: V.450.3-6

1) Optionally, there is deletion [of the *visarjanīya*] in the case of [a sound denoted by] *śaR* (i.e., sibilants) being followed [by a sound denoted by] *khaR* (i.e., voiceless consonants).

[Bhāṣya:] Deletion [of the *visarjanīya*] should optionally be mentioned in the case of [a sound denoted by] *śaR* (i.e., sibilants) being followed [by a sound denoted by] *khaR* (i.e., voiceless consonants). [For example,] *vṛkṣā sthātāraḥ* or *vṛkṣāḥ sthātāraḥ* ("Trees are immovable", nom. pl.).

{Explanation:
The *visarjanīya* substituend continues from the rule A. 8.3.34. As the rule is optional, these are the possible forms: *vṛkṣāḥ sthātarāḥ* (by the present *sūtra*) and *vṛkṣās sthātarāḥ* (by A. 8.3.34). Kātyāyana's *vārttika* presents one more option, which is deletion of the final *visarjanīya* yielding the form *vṛkṣā sthātarāḥ*.}

A. 8.3.37 *kupvoḥ ẖkẖpau ca*
[The *visarjanīya*] as well as *ẖk* and *ẖp* [usually come in place of the *visarjanīya*] before [the consonantal groups] *kU* and *pU* [in close proximity].

VMBh_1: III.431.10-12; VMBh_2: V.450.7-9

1) [It should be said that] the *visarjanīya*, the *jihvamūlīya* (ẖk) and the *upadhmānīya* (ẖp) come in place of [the sound] *s* before [the consonantal groups] *kU* and *pU*.

[Bhāṣya:] The *visarjanīya*, the *jihvamūlīya* (ẖk) and the *upadhmānīya* (ẖp) should be mentioned as replacing [the sound] *s* before [the consonantal groups] *kU* and *pU*.

{**Explanation:**
In the examples *brāhmaṇaḥ pacati* ("A Brahmin is cooking") and *brāhmaṇaḥ karoti* ("A Brahmin is doing [something]") there are options according to the *vārttika*: the *jihvamūlīya* and the *visarjanīya* in the latter, and the *upadhmānīya* and the *visarjanīya* in the former. However, in the example *vāsaḥ kṣaumam adbhiḥ* ("The linen cloth is devoured by waters"), where the consonant *k* of the word *kṣaumam* is followed by *ṣ* belonging to the abbreviation *śaR*, it is only the *visarjanīya* that is possible (on the basis of A. 8.3.35). This rule prescribes the allophones of the *visarjanīya*, which would otherwise be replaced by *s* by A. 8.3.34. The *visarjanīya*, being the substituend, is a result of A. 8.3.15 (so it comes from *rU*). This substitution, however, would not result if velar or labial consonants were followed by sibilants, which means that the present rule blocks the application of A. 8.3.34 under the conditions of velar or labial consonants following, but it does not block the *visarjanīya* prescribed by the rule A. 8.3.35 on the basis of *asiddhatva*.}

VMBh_1: III.431.13-15; VMBh_2: V.451.1-3

2) But what regards the substitute for the *visarjanīya*, there is a potential involment of the allophones ẖk and ẖp [before the sounds belonging to the groups] *kU* or *pU* only when they are followed by [a sound denoted by] *śaR* (i.e., sibilants) (A. 8.3.35).

[Objection:] But what regards the substitute for the *visarjanīya* there would be *ẖk* and *ẖp* [in place of the *visarjanīya*] before [the consonantal groups] *kU* and *pU* only when they are followed by [a sound denoted by] *śaR* (A. 8.3.35). [For example,] *adbhiḥ psātam* ('eaten by waters') and *vāsaḥ kṣaumam* ('the linen cloth').
[Answer:] It will not happen due to the statement.

{**Explanation:**

The problem raised here is that if the *jīhvamūlīya* and the *upadhmānīya* are ordained in place of the *visarjanīya*, substitution would result only when the velar or labial consonants are followed by sibilants due to the *anuvṛtti* from the previous rule. If a sibilant does not follow, the present rule would have to be considered suspended and the only possible substitution would be the consonant *s* of the *sūtra* A. 8.3.34. Moreover, the substitution *s* could not be treated as the *visarjanīya* (i.e., like the substituend) on the basis of A. 1.1.56 *sthānivad ādeśo 'nalvidhau* for the purpose of the present rule because the allophones *ẖk* and *ẖp* are not listed in the *pratyāhāra sūtras* while only sounds that appear in the *upadeśa* can be subject to *sthānivadbhāva*. Patañjali states that the very *sūtra* A. 8.3.35 *śarpare visarjanīyaḥ* shows that the present rule cannot apply to such velar and labial consonants that are followed by a sibilant. If A. 8.3.37 were to be treated as an exception, the rule A. 8.3.35 would be superfluous.}

VMBh_1: III.431.15-16; VMBh_2: V.451.4-6

[Bhāṣya:] There is the purpose in the *sūtra*.
[Question:] What [is the purpose]?
[Answer:] [The expression] *puruṣaḥ tsarukaḥ* ('a sword-hilt maker').
[Question:] Should it be mentioned then?
[Answer:] It should not be mentioned. Because in [the *sūtra*] A. 8.3.34 the term *visarjanīya* is used, it continues in the following [*sūtras*] and with respect to that when [a sound denoted by] *śaR* follows, [the *sūtra*] A. 8.3.35 is suspended.
[Answer:] It is not suspended.

{Explanation:
Kaiyaṭa (VMBh_2: V.451.8 ff) explains that when we consider the rule A. 8.3.34 *visarjanīyasya saḥ* and the *visarjanīya* that is continued in the following rules via *anuvṛtti*, we have to determine what type of the *visarjanīya* we have in mind. He notes that the *visarjanīya* being the substituend for the consonant *s* can be twofold – it can come either from the application of A. 8.3.15 (namely *ḥ* that appears before the *khaR* sounds or in a pause) or from the application of A. 8.3.35 (*ḥ* appears before the *khaR* sounds when they are followed by the *śaR* sounds). However, A. 8.3.35 is placed after A. 8.3.34 and because of *asiddhatva* it cannot be taken into consideration. Hence, Kaiyaṭa's conclusion that the *visarjanīya* to be replaced in the rule A. 8.3.34 can only be the one prescribed in A. 8.3.15. And the substituend to be continued in the *sūtras* A. 8.3.35 and A. 8.3.36 is *s* only in order to achieve the *visarjanīya*.

The objection is raised in Kaiyaṭa's commentary that the rule A. 8.3.35 will not be suspended because suspension refers to the context of application, not individual rules themselves; and the context in question is the same in both cases.

For Kaiyaṭa, however, the division of operations signifies the division of contexts; the *s*-substitute is ordained by one rule and the *visarjanīya* by another. According to Nāgeśa (VMBh_2: V.451), on the other hand, the context is indeed the same because in all the cases it is always the *visarjanīya* that is the substituend. However, even though there is no difference in *sthānin*s, there is the difference in prescribed operations, and in reality it is a rule that is suspended with respect to another rule.}

VMBh_1: III.431.18-432.2; VMBh_2: V.451.7-452.6

[Question:] How come?
[Answer:] The term *adhikāra* ('governing rule') is threefold. One [says that it (i.e., the *adhikāra*)] is situated in one place [that] enlightens the whole instruction just as a well-kindled lamp illuminates the whole house. Another one [says that] it is like a piece of wood that is dragged bound with a rope or iron. Yet another [says that] an *adhikāra* has as its purpose its absence in every rule; [but] it is present in every rule.
According to that very view – the *adhikāra* has as its purpose its absence in every rule – then whichever *visarjanīya* [is replaced by] *s*, here the term *visarjanīya* is used, and this very term continues in the following [rules], something else is produced. With respect to that, [the *sūtra*] A. 8.3.35 is not suspended. And having done that, there would be *ẖk* and *ẖp* [in place of the consonant *s*] before [the consonantal groups] *kU* and *pU* only when they are followed by [a sound denoted by] *śaR* (i.e., sibilants): *adbhiḥ psātam* ('eaten by waters') and *vāsaḥ kṣaumam* ('the linen cloth').

{**Explanation:**
Kaiyaṭa (VMBh_2: V.452.12 ff) analyses the first view. As enlightening the whole instruction is a feature of a *paribhāṣā*, it indicates that there is no difference between an *adhikāra* and a *paribhāṣā* due to the common purpose of serving another rule. The second view is explained with the help of the particle *ca* that draws the elements from previous rules. He passes on to explain the last view to point out that an *adhikāra* is marked with *svarita*. In other types of *sūtra*s other words are inferred corresponding to that which has the *svarita* attached to it. Alternatively, Kaiyaṭa says, we infer that whose purpose is to be employed in other rules. We recognise the difference in meaning even if there is no difference in the word form. In Kaiyaṭa's conclusion A. 8.3.34 *visarjanīya saḥ* cannot be a *paribhāṣā*. Furthermore, the substituend does not continue in the following *sūtra*s. In the present rule the conjunction *ca* does not serve the purpose of drawing the substituend into it but it allows the substitute to continue, which is in this case also the *visarjanīya*. The word *visarjanīya* in A. 8.3.37 shows a connection with another word due to being marked with *svarita*. The rule A. 8.3.35

should not be treated as suspended and it should be the source of the *visarjanīya* (due to its non-suspension and proximity), rather than A. 8.3.15 which is further back. It would thus apply also in the present rule.}

VMBh_1: III.432.3-7; VMBh_2: V.452.7-453.2

[Bhāṣya:] Therefore the separation of the rule will be done. [First we have the *sūtra*] A. 8.3.35 *śarpare visarjanīyaḥ* – "The *visarjanīya* [comes in place of the *visarjanīya* when followed by sounds denoted by *khaR* (i.e., voiceless con-sonants)] being followed by [sounds denoted by] *śaR* (i.e., sibilants)." [Then, there is the *sūtra*] A. 8.3.36 *vā śari* – "[The *visarjanīya*] usually [comes in place of the *visarjanīya*] before [sounds denoted by] *śaR* (i.e., sibilants)." Then, *kupvoḥ*. And there is the *visarjanīya* in place of the *visarjanīya* before [the sounds belonging to the groups] *kU* and *pU* being followed by [the sounds denoted by] *śaR* (i.e., sibilants).
[Question:] Why is this [said]?
[Answer:] [The *sūtra*] A. 8.3.37 will be said – "*ẖk* and *ẖp* [usually come in place of the *visarjanīya*] before [the consonantal groups] *kU* and *pU*". [This is said] in order to block it. Then [the allophones] "*ẖk* and *ẖp*" come only "before [the sounds belonging to the groups] *kU* and *pU*." [The expression] "followed by [the sounds denoted by] *śaR*" is not continued. Alternatively, "the *visarjanīya* [comes in place of the *visarjanīya* followed by sounds denoted by *khaR* (i.e., voiceless consonants)] being followed by [sounds denoted by] *śaR* (i.e., sibilants)"; this [*visarjanīya* comes in place of the *visarjanīya*] as well as *ẖk* and *ẖp* before [the consonantal groups] *kU* and *pU*" – [this] will continue here.

{**Explanation:**
The division of the *sūtra* serves the purpose of blocking the *ẖk* and *ẖp* substitutes that are generally applicable; to allow the *visarjanīya* be the only substitute before velar and labial consonants followed by sibilants. Prescribing *ẖk* and *ẖp* separately as the substitutes for the *visarjanīya* before velar and labial consonants only, not followed by sibilants, leads to desired results. Annaṃbhaṭṭa (MPV X.432) states though that even if all expressions: *śari, khari* and *kupvoḥ* together continue in the following rule, the prescribed substitute will be the *visarjanīya*. Therefore, through the power of *anuvṛtti* itself and even without the division of the rule, thanks to the meaning of the statement, there is no need to divide the *sūtra*.}

A. 8.3.38 ***so 'padādau***
[The sound] *s* [comes in place of the *visarjanīya* before the consonantal groups *kU* and *pU*] which do not occur at the beginning of a *pada* [in close proximity].

VMBh_1: III.432.8-10; VMBh_2: V.453.3-5

1) [The sound] *s* [comes in place of the *visarjanīya* before the consonantal groups *kU* and *pU*] which do not occur at the beginning of a *pada* which is non-indeclinable.

[Bhāṣya:] It should be mentioned that [the sound] *s* [comes in place of the *visarjanīya* before the consonantal groups *kU* and *pU*] which do not occur at the beginning of a *pada* which is non-indeclinable. Here it must not be: *prātaḥkalpam* ('early dawn'), *punaḥkalpam* ('as if again').

{Explanation:
This rule is an exception to the preceding one, and the example for its application can be the expression *payaspāśam* ('unimportant milk'). Katre in his translation of the *Aṣṭādhyāyī* points out that the only possible units here are the following suffixes: *pāśaP* (A. 5.3.47[426]), *kalpaP* (A. 5.3.67[427]), *ka* (A. 5.3.70[428]) and *kāmyaC* (A. 3.1.9[429]). The derivation of *payaspāśam* is as follows:

(1) *payas + pāśaP*
(2) *paya (s → rU) + pāśa* (A. 8.2.66 *sasajuṣo ruḥ*)
(3) *paya (r → ḥ) + pāśa* (A. 8.3.15 *kharavasānayor visarjanīyaḥ*)
(4) *paya (ḥ → s) + pāśa* (A. 8.3.38 *so 'padādau*)
payaspāśa

The first *vārttika* proposes a restriction – the substitution would take place only in such words that are non-indeclinable. Therefore, in the examples given by Patañjali: *prātaḥkalpam* and *punaḥkalpam* the *visarjanīya* remains.}

VMBh_1: III.432.11-23; VMBh_2: V.453.6-454.7

---

426 A. 5.3.47 *yāpye pāśap* ‖ ("[The *taddhita* suffix] *pāśaP* comes [after a nominal stem pleonastically] to denote something unimportant.")

427 A. 5.3.67 *īṣadasamāptau kalpabeśyadeśīyaraḥ* ‖ ("[The *taddhita* suffixes] *kalpaP*, *deśya* and *deśīyaR* come [after a nominal stem] to denote 'not quite fully'.")

428 A. 5.3.70 *prāg ivāt kaḥ* ‖ ("In the section beginning here up to A. 5.3.96 [the *taddhita* suffix] *ka* comes [after a nominal stem to denote the meaning listed in this section].")

429 A. 3.1.9 *kāmyac ca* ‖ ("[The suffix] *kāmyaC* also [optionally comes after a nominal stem ending in case ending when it is the object of a verbal stem expressing desire and which the agent desires for himself].")

2) Before [the verb] *kamU* ('to have a desire for', DhP I:470) [the sound *s* comes in place of the *visarjanīya* being the substitute] of *rU*; in order to restrict.

[Bhāṣya:] It should be mentioned that before [the verb] *kāmya* ('to have a desire for') [the sound *s* comes in place of the *visarjanīya* being the substitute] of *rU*.
[Question:] What is the purpose?
[Answer:] In order to restrict. Before [the verb] *kamU* [the sound *s* comes in place of such a *visarjanīya* that came in place] of *rU* only, not of anything else. [For example,] *payas kāmyati* ("He wants milk").
[Question:] Where should it not be?
[Answer:] [Here:] *gīḥ kāmyati* ("He wants the chant"), *pūḥ kāmyati* ("He wants a town").[430]
[Bhāṣya:] It should be mentioned that there is the *s*-substitute in place of an *upadhmānīya*.
[Question:] What is the purpose?
[Answer:] The [verbal root] *ubjA* ('to make straight', DhP VI:20) is read as having an *upadhmānīya* as penultimate. When the *s*-substitute has been performed and there is the *jaŚ*-substitute (A. 7.3.52 *cajoḥ ku ghiṇṇyatoḥ*,[431] A. 8.4.53 *jhalāṃ jaś jhaśi*), the forms should be *abhyudga*, *samudga*.
[Objection:] If an *upadhmānīya* is read as penultimate, [then in the form] *ubjijiṣati* ('He wants to make straight', 3rd sg. desid.) the double *upadhmānīya* would result. If, on the other hand, there is the sound *d* as penultimate, the prohibition A. 6.1.3 *na ndrāḥ saṃyogādayaḥ* would be achieved.[432]
[Question:] If the sound *d* is read as penultimate, what is the formation of words: *ubjitā* (2nd fut.) and *ubjitum* (inf.)?
[Answer:] In the *asiddha* [section the verbal root] *ubjA* [gets the designation] *bha*. There is [the *sūtra*] A. 8.4.40 *stoḥ ścunā ścuḥ*. Then I will say *bha udbjeḥ*. [The verbal root] *ubjA* is [termed] *bha* when in contact with [the sound] *ś* and [the sounds belonging to the group] *cU*.
[Question:] Should it be mentioned then?
[Answer:] It should not be mentioned. It is achieved due to irregularity.
[Question:] What is the irregularity?

---

[430] In these cases the *visarjanīya* does not have *rU* as its cause but simple *r*.

[431] A. 7.3.52 *cajoḥ ku ghiṇṇyatoḥ* || ("[The sound belonging to the group] *kU* comes in place of [the sounds] *c* and *j* before [the suffixes] with a marker *GH* and [the suffix] *ṆyaT*.")

[432] A. 6.1.3 *na ndrāḥ saṃyogādayaḥ* || ("[The sounds] *n*, *d* and *r*, occurring at the beginning of a consonant cluster [and forming a part of the second syllable of a polysyllabic verbal root beginning with a vowel,] are not [reduplicated].")

[Answer:] It is the [*sūtra*] A. 7.3.61.[433] Here in these examples it would result as well: *abhyudga*, *samudga*. There is the irregularity with respect to the scope of the lack of the *kU*-substitute. Alternatively, that is not the form of [the verbal root] *ubjA*.
[Question:] What is it [the form] of then?
[Answer:] After [the verbal root] *gamḶ* ('to go', DhP I:1031) [preceded by] two *upasargas* (*abhi-ut* and *sam-ut* respectively) [the suffix] *Ḍa* is prescribed. [The form] *abhyudga* [should be understood as] *abhyudgata* and *samudga* as *samudgata*.

{**Explanation:**
The verbal root *ubjA* is considered to have the *upadhmānīya* as its penultimate sound. The *upadhmānīya* is followed by *p* (which does not make it penultimate) but because it cannot appear without *p*, it is considered to be penultimate after all. The consonant *p* is used only for the sake of pronunciation, not for hearing. The consonant *b* appearing in a verbal root is the result of the *jaŚ*-substitute.
The derivation of the form *abhyudga* will be as follows:

(1) *abhyuẖpj* + *GHaÑ* (A. 3.3.121 *halaś ca*)
(2) *abhyuẖp* (*j* → *g*) + *a* (A. 7.3.52 *cajoḥ ku ghitṇyatoḥ*)
(3) *abhyu* (*ẖp* → *b*) + *a* (A. 8.4.53 *jhalāṃ jaś jhaśi*)
**abhyubga*

This is not the desired result. I have marked the *upadhmānīya* here to show its substitution by *b*. Commentators state that it should further be replaced with the consonant *s* and then *d*, to achieve the correct form.

(4) *abhyu* (*b* → *s*) + *a* (by the statement under the present rule)
(5) *abhyu* (*s* → *d*) + *a* (A. 8.4.53 *jhalāṃ jaś jhaśi*)
abhyudga

Annaṃbhaṭṭa (MPV X.433) states that the consonant *s* comes in place of the *visarjanīya* or *upadhmānīya* only when they are followed by *kU* or *pU*, not everywhere. In the form *ubjitā* (fut.) then there is no *k*-substitution and consequently, there will not be the *s*-substitution. He also explains that this is an example where the *upadhmānīya* is heard, not the consonant *b*. The *upadhmānīya* is not found in the *pratyāhāra sūtras*; but because it is a labial sound, due to the *jaŚ*-substitute it is replaced with *b* in writitng.

---

433 A. 7.3.61 *bhujanyubjau pāṇyupatāpayoḥ* || ("[The words] *bhuja* and *nyubja* [are formed in an irregular way without velar substitute of the consonant *j* before the suffix *GHaÑ* (A. 7.3.52)] to denote 'a hand' and 'heat, pain' respectively.")

Patañjali says that in order to achieve *b* we can term the verb *bha* in the *asiddhatva* section; and the verb should be read as *udj*, not *ubj*. The commentators refer to the rule A. 7.3.61 *bhujanyubjau pāṇyupatāpayo* that blocks the *kU*-substitution of *j*. If, however, we accept the verbal root *udj*, we have to apply the rules A. 8.4.40 and A. 8.4.53 to achieve the correct forms *abhyudga* and *samudga*.
Another problem raised in the *Mahābhāṣya* is the potential reduplication of the consonant *b* in the form *ubjijiṣati* ('he wants to make straight', 3rd sg. des.). If we accept the verbal root as *udj*, the problem does not arise because the rule A. 6.1.3 *na ndrāḥ saṃyogādayaḥ* blocks it. If the verb were termed *bha* in the *asiddhatva* section, we could not apply the rules responsible for the reduplication, as the consonant *b* would be suspended, and even if we could apply the reduplication, it would refer to the *upadhmanīya*. This view is rejected as it is enough to refer to the irregularity mentioned above with the *sūtra* A. 7.3.61.
The last option considered is that the forms *abhyudga* and *samudga* do not come from the verb *ubj*/*udj* but from the verb *gam* ('to go'); two *upasarga*s – *abhi* + *ut* and *sam* + *ut* – are added and the verb is followed by the suffix *Ḍa*. Kaiyaṭa explains that the order of the derivation should be the following: there is no reduplication of *d* as it is blocked. In the relevant forms we need to apply the reduplication first and then the consonant *b* via *jaŚ* or via *nipātana*. For example, in the form *nyubja* there must be *b* as the *kU*-substitution is blocked. The problem appears with the accent of the derivatives though. When the suffix *GHaÑ* is added, the accent is *adyudātta*,[434] when *Ḍa* – *antodātta*. Kaiyaṭa is of the opinion that the accent is always *antodātta*, on the element *ga* in *abhyudgá* etc., conditioned by the accent of the suffix.[435]}

A. 8.3.39 *iṇaḥ ṣaḥ*
[The sound] *ṣ* [comes in place of the *visarjanīya* which occurs] after [a sound denoted by] *iṆ* (i.e., all vowels except *a*, semivowels, *h*) [and before the consonantal groups *kU* and *pU* which do not occur at the beginning of a *pada* in close proximity].

VMBh_1: III.432.24-433.28; VMBh_2: V.454.8-456.15

[Question:] Having stated the *s*-substitute, is the *ṣ*-substitute, due to the absence of specification, mentioned [to replace] the sound *s* following [a sound denoted

434 A. 6.1.197 *ñnity ādir nityam* || ("Before [the suffix] marked with *Ñ* or *N* the initial [syllable] necessarily [bears the *udātta* accent].")

435 A. 6.2.144 *thāthaghañktājabitrakāṇām* || ("[The final syllable of the last member of the compound in the suffixes] *tha*, *atha*, *GhaÑ*, *Kta*, *aC*, *aP*, *itra* and *Ka* [bears the *udātta* accent when occurring after a *gati*, *kāraka* or *upapada*].")

by] *iṆ* (i.e., all vowels except *a*, semivowels, *h*) or is it prescribed only instead of the *visarjanīya* following [a sound denoted by] *iṆ*?
[Question:] And what of it?
[Answer:] If, due to the absence of specification, having stated the *s*-substitute, the *ṣ*-substitute were mentioned [to replace] the sound *s* following [a sound denoted by] *iṆ*, [then] in this case – *niṣkṛta* ('removed') and *niṣpīta* ('dried up') – the *ṣ*-substitute would not result due to suspension of the *s*-substitute.[436] But if the *ṣ*-substitute is prescribed only of the *visarjanīya* following [a sound denoted by] *iṆ*, does the *s*-substitute continue or not?
[Question:] And what of it?
[Answer:] If it continued, the *s*-substitute would result as well. But if it does not continue, in A. 8.3.40 the sound *s* should be used. When it is done, does the *ṣ*-substitute continue or not?
[Question:] And what of it?
[Answer:] If it continued, the *ṣ*-substitute would result as well. But if it does not continue, in A. 8.3.41 the sound *ṣ* should be used. When it is done, does the *s*-substitute continue or not?
[Question:] And what of it?
[Answer:] If it continued, the *s*-substitute would result as well. But if it does not continue, in A. 8.3.42 the sound *s* should be used. When it is done, does the *ṣ*-substitute continue as well or not?
[Question:] And what of it?
[Answer:] If it continued, the *ṣ*-substitute would result as well. But if it does not continue, in these [*sūtra*s] A. 8.3.43, A. 8.3.44 and A. 8.3.45 the sound *ṣ* should be used. When it is done, does the *s*-substitute continue or not?
[Question:] And what of it?
[Answer:] If it continued, the *s*-substitute would result as well. But if it does not continue, in A. 8.3.46 the sound *s* should be used.
[Bhāṣya:] Let it be as you want.
[Answer:] In that case let it be that due to absence of specification, having stated the *s*-substitute, the *ṣ*-substitute is mentioned [to replace] the sound *s* following [a sound denoted by] *iṆ*.
[Objection:] But has it not been said that in this case – *niṣkṛta* ('removed') and *niṣpīta* ('dried up') – the *ṣ*-substitute would not result due to the suspension of the *s*-substitute?
[Answer:] This is not a fault. The teacher's use indicates that the rule is not suspended with respect to [another] rule.
[Question:] How then?
[Bhāṣya:] [One] section is suspended with respect to [another] section; in this very [*sūtra*] A. 8.4.14 [the teacher] uses the expression *asamāse 'pi* ("even if this

[436] See A. 8.3.41 *idudupadhasya cāpratyayasya*.

is not the compound"). Alternatively, on the other hand, let it be that the *ṣ*-substitute is prescribed of the a *visarjanīya* following [a sound denoted by] *iṆ*.
[Objection:] But has it not been said: "does the *s*-substitute continue or not?; and so what? If it continued, the *s*-substitute would result as well."?
[Bhāṣya:] This is not a fault. The connection [between the qualifer and the qualified] will continue. [The *sūtra*s] A. 8.3.38, A. 8.3.39 and A. 8.3.40 [state that there is] the sound *s* [as the substitution but] when following [a sound denoted by] *iṆ*, [there is] the sound *ṣ*. [The *sūtra*] A. 8.3.41 [prescribes] the sound *ṣ*, [but] A. 8.3.40 – the sound *s*. [The *sūtra*] A. 8.3.42 [prescribes] the sound *s*, [but] A. 8.3.41 – the sound *ṣ*. [The *sūtra*s] A. 8.3.43, A. 8.3.44 and A. 8.3.45 [prescribe] the sound *ṣ*, [but] A. 8.3.42 – the sound *s*. [And in the *sūtra*] A. 8.4.46 the sound *s* continues and the use of the sound *ṣ* is stopped.

{**Explanation:**
There are two basic problems regarding this rule: whether the substituend is the *visarjanīya* or the consonant *s*, and whether in the subsequent *sūtra*s we get the *s* or the *ṣ*-substitute. Let us analyse the issue of the substituend first. The sound *s* could be subject to substitution because it could continue from the previous rule A. 8.3.38 *so 'padādau*. However, we find a difficulty in deriving the forms such as *niṣkṛtam* and *niṣpītam* as the final sound of the preverb appears before a *pada*. It is the consonant *r* of *nir* that is further replaced by the *visarjanīya* and finally with *ṣ*. It could, theoretically, go through the *s*-substitution as well. The problem is, however, that we cannot achieve the *s*-substitute on the basis of the *sūtra* A. 8.3.38, it would have to be A. 8.3.41 *idudupadhasya cāpratyayasya*. It is impossible because A. 8.3.41 is suspended, for it is posterior in the *Tripādī*. The conclusion is therefore that it must be the *visarjanīya* that serves as the substituend in the present rule.
The next problem refers to the substitutes; in the following rules we sometimes need the sound *s* and sometimes *ṣ* as a replacement. The previous rule introduced the *s*-substitute which could continue later on, but that would mean that in some cases we would need to supplement *ṣ*. Similarly, if it were only the *ṣ*-substitute that continues from the present rule, some later rules would lack *s*. Patañjali refers to A. 8.4.14 *upasargād asamāse 'pi ṇopadeśasya*,[437] in which the word *api* ('also') indicates that the *ṇ*-substitute applies regardless of the elements being in a compound. The restriction allowing for the *ṇ*-substitute only in compounds stated in A. 8.4.3 *pūrvapadāt saṃjñāyām agaḥ* does not apply. The expression

[437] A. 8.4.14 *upasargād asamāse 'pi ṇopadeśasya* || ("[The retroflex *ṇ* comes in place of the dental *n* of the verbal root] containing [the sound] *ṇ* in the original enunciation (*upadeśa*) [used] after the *upasarga* [containing the sounds *r* or *ṣ* even when there is the separation by the sounds denoted by *aṬ*, the sounds belonging to the group *kU* or *pU*, the particle *āṄ* or the infix *nUM* in close proximity] also when not in a compound.")

asamāse 'pi is used to indicate that it should be applied as stated. Consequently, in the case of the present rule, even if there is a division of substituends and substitutes, because the *visarjanīya* is the substituend of the sound *s*, and the sound *s* is the substituend of *ṣ*, and because they fall under the scope of the *adhikāra* of labial and velar sounds following (A. 8.3.37), they have the same cause and therefore the same context of application. Pāṇini shows, yet again, that it is not a rule that is suspended with respect to another rule, but it is the context.
In conclusion it is decided that the continuation of *s* or *ṣ* as substitutes in the following *sūtra*s depends on the context; on what is required. They both carry the *svarita* accent so they can both continue. In the present rule the sound *s* is not possible; the sound *ṣ* blocks it and the lack of the conjunction *ca* does not allow *s* to continue.}

{A. 8.3.40 *namaspurasor gatyoḥ*
[The sound *s* comes] in place of [the *visarjanīya* of the words] *namas* ('obeisance') and *puras* ('in front') when [they are termed] *gati*[438] [before the consonantal groups *kU* and *pU* in close proximity].} *This *sūtra* was not commented upon by Patañjali.

A. 8.3.41 *idudupadhasya cāpratyayasya*
[The sound *ṣ* comes] in place of [the *visarjanīya* of] that which is not a suffix and has the vowel *i* or *u* as its penultimate [before the consonantal groups *kU* and *pU* in close proximity].

VMBh_1: III.434.1-4; VMBh_2: V.456.16-457.2

1) If [the sound *ṣ* comes] in place of [the *visarjanīya* being a part of] that which is not a suffix and has the sound *i* or *u* as its penultimate, [there should be] prohibition in the case of [the words] *pum* ('a male') and *muhur* ('suddenly, in a moment').

[Objection:] If [the sound *ṣ* comes] in place of [the *visarjanīya* being a part of] that which is not a suffix and has the vowel *i* or *u* as its penultimate, prohibition should be mentioned in the case of [the words] *pum* ('male') and *muhur* ('suddenly, in a moment'). [For example,] *puṃskāmā* ('a woman desirous of a lover or a husband'), *muhuḥkāma* ('loving or desiring again and again').

---

[438] These words are termed *gati* by the *sūtras* A. 1.4.73 and A. 1.4.67 respectively. A. 1.4.73 *sākṣātprabhṛtīni ca* || ("[The term *gati* denotes the class of particles] beginning with *sākṣāt* ('before the eyes') and also [rarely when occurring with the verbal root *ḌUkṛÑ* – 'to do', DhP VIII:10].") A. 1.4.67 *puro 'vyayam* || ("[The term *gati* denoted the particle] *puras* ('in front') when it is indeclinable.")

{Explanation:
In order for the present rule to apply the *visarjanīya* cannot be a part of a suffix. The problem arises with the words stated in a *vārttika* as they are both derived with the help of the *Uṇādi* suffixes by *pāter ḍumsun* (US 620; 4.177)[439] and *muheḥ kic ca* (US 280; 2.120)[440] respectively. The word *muhus* is derived with the suffix *usI* and is treated as the one having the marker *K*. The consonant *s* of the word *puṃs* is a part of a suffix so it should not be subject to substitution stated in this rule anyway; prohibition would be superfluous then. Kaiyaṭa (VMBh_2: V.457) explains, however, that these two words are not derived (*avyutpanna*) and this is why the prohibition is stated. On the other hand, the word *pum* has also been mentioned in *vt*. 1 *saṃpuṃkānāṃ satvam* on the *sūtra* A. 8.3.5 as having the consonant *m* replced by *s* before which the *anusvāra* comes; which would also make the present *vārttika* futile.
An argument is raised in Kaiyaṭa's *Pradīpa* that this prohibition might not suffice because *ṣ* can replace both the *visarjanīya* and *s*. According to Annaṃbhaṭṭa (MPV X.436), however, the lack of specification with respect to the substituend makes the prohibition valid in any case; so in the case of it being the consonant *s*, substitution will not take place either. Whether the *ṣ*-substitute applies to the consonant *s* or *s* is prescribed, the consonant *ṣ* can come only in place of the *visarjanīya* replacing *rU* or another *visarjanīya*; therefore, prescribing *s* in the abovementioned examples is pointless.}

VMBh_1: III.434.5-13; VMBh_2: V.457.3-458.1

[Bhāṣya:] The *ṣ*-substitute should be mentioned in [the words] having [the vowels *i* and *u* in the grade] *vṛddhi*. [For example,] *dauṣkulyam* ('born in a low family'), *naiṣpuruṣyam* ('coming not from a male').

2) [The *ṣ*-substitute should be mentioned] in [the words] having the vowels [*i* or *u*] prolated and also before [the *taddhita* suffix] beginning with [the consonant] *t*.

[Bhāṣya:] The *ṣ*-substitute should be mentioned in [the words] having the vowels [*i* or *u*] prolated and also before [the *taddhita* suffix] beginning with [the consonant] *t*, and before [the consonantal groups] *kU* and *pU*. [For example,] *sarpī3ṣṭara* ('more genuine clarified butter'), *bahī3ṣṭara* ('more outside'), *nī3ṣkula* ('without family'), *dū3ṣpuruṣa* ('a bad person').

---

439 US 620 (4.177) *pāter ḍumsun* || ("[The suffix] *ḌumsUN* comes after [the verbal root] *pā* ('to protect', DhP II:47).")

440 US 280 (2.120) *muheḥ kic ca* || ("[The suffix *usI*] comes after [the verbal root] *muhA* ('to faint, lose consciousness', DhP IV:89) and it is treated as if it was marked with *K*.")

3) Alternatively, it is due to the rule being externally conditioned.

[Bhāṣya:] An alternative should be mentioned.
[Question:] Why?
[Answer:] Due to the rule being externally conditioned. The rule [introducing] *vṛddhi* is externally conditioned.
[Question:] Why will it not be in this case: *pituḥ karoti* ("He does for the father"), *mātuḥ karoti* ("He does for the mother")?
[Answer:] The *ṣ*-substitute might be involved in place of the *visarjanīya* that is not a part of a suffix (A. 8.3.41). It is said "in place of the *visarjanīya* that is not a part of a suffix"; but this *visarjanīya* is a part of a suffix.
[Bhāṣya:] In this case the *visarjanīya* which is a part of a suffix is deleted by A. 8.2.24.

{**Explanation:**
Let us examine the derivation of the word *mātuḥ*:

(1) *mātṛ* + *ṄasI* (A. 4.1.2 *svaujasamauṭśasṭābhyāmbhisṅebhyāmbhyasṅasibhyāmbhyasṅasosāmṅyossup*)
(2) *māt* (*ṛ* + *a* → *u*) + *r* + *s* (A. 6.1.111 *ṛta ut*, A. 1.1.51 *ur aṇ raparaḥ*)
mātur + *s*
(3) *mātur* (*s* → 0) (A. 8.2.24 *rāt sasya*)
(4) *mātu* (*r* → *ḥ*) (A. 8.3.15 *kharavasānayor visarjanīyaḥ*)
mātuḥ

The final *visarjanīya* does not have its source in a suffix as the suffix is deleted at the previous stage, because it appears after *r*; such an outcome would qualify for the present rule to apply. It does not happen, though, and the answer is provided by the next *vārttika*.}

VMBh_1: III.434.13-16; VMBh_2: V.458.2-5

[Answer:] In such a way then…

4) The use of [the word] *bhrātuṣputra* ('a brother's son') is an indication that there is prohibition of the *ṣ*-substitute due to its cause being *ekādeśa*.

[Bhāṣya:] In this very word *bhrātuṣputra*, which is read in [the *gaṇa*] *kaskādi* (A. 8.3.48), what the teacher indicates is that there is no *ṣ*-substitute due to its cause being *ekādeśa*.

{**Explanation:**
In the above example of *matuḥ karoti* and *pituḥ karoti* we find *ekādeśa*; the vowel *u* comes in place of two other vowels: *ṛ* and *a*. In the word *bhrātuṣputra* we observe the same operation. The indication is that the *visarjanīya* which is prescribed after the *ekādeśa* rule is not changed into *ṣ*. The inclusion of the word *bhrātuṣputra* in the *gaṇa kaskādi* shows that there would be no point in doing so if the *ṣ*-substitute were regular. The form *bhrātuṣputra* is an exception.}

{**A. 8.3.42 *tiraso 'nyatarasyām***
[The sound *s*] optionally [comes] in place of [the *visarjanīya* of the word] *tiras* ('across') [before the consonantal groups *kU* and *pU* in close proximity].} *This *sūtra* was not commented upon by Patañjali.

A. 8.3.43 *dvistriścatur iti kṛtvo 'rthe*
[The sound *ṣ* optionally comes] in place of [the *visarjanīya* of the words] *dvis* ('two'), *tris* ('three') and *catur* ('four') with the signification of [the suffix] *kṛtvasUC* (A. 5.4.17[441]) [before the consonantal groups *kU* and *pU* in close proximity].

VMBh_1: III.434.17-435.9; VMBh_2: V.458.6-459.8

[Question:] What are [the words] *dvis*, *tris* and *catur* used for?
[Answer:] [Because] in this case it must not be: *pañcakṛtvaḥ karoti* ("He does [it] five times").
[Question:] What is the purpose of [the expression] "the signification of [the suffix] *kṛtvasUC*"?
[Answer:] [Because] in this case it must not be: *catuṣkapālaḥ* ('being in four jars'), *catuṣkaṇṭakaḥ* ('consisting of four thorns').
[Suggestion:] It is not that. Let it be that by this [rule the substiution] is optional and by the previous one (A. 8.3.41) the operation will be obligatory. When it has been necessarily ordained by the previous [*sūtra*], it becomes optional [here]. And just like this one serves as a blocker here: *catuḥ karoti*, *catuṣ karoti*; in the same way in [the form] *catuṣkapāla* it should also be a blocker. In this case the *ṣ*-substitute would not result by the previous [rule].
[Question:] What is the reason?
[Answer:] It is said "in place of the *visarjanīya* that is not a part of a suffix" but this *visarjanīya* is a part of a suffix. This *visarjanīya* which is a part of a suffix is deleted by A. 8.2.24. Therefore, [the expression] "the signification of [the suffix] *kṛtvasUC*" should be used.

---

[441] A. 5.4.17 *saṃkhyāyāḥ kriyābhyāvṛttigaṇane kṛtvasuc* || ("[The suffix] *kṛtvasUC* comes after numbers to denote the counting of the repetition of an action.")

[Suggestion:] The stems *dvis*, *tris* and *catur* could be omitted.
[Question:] Why does [the *ṣ*-substitution] not take place in: *pañcakṛtvaḥ karoti*?
[Answer:] [Because the expression] "of the one having the vowels *i* or *u* as penultimate" (A. 8.3.41) continues.
[Answer:] It is not possible in this way. When [the words] *dvis*, *tris* and *catur* are not used, the *visarjanīya* would be qualified by the expression "the meaning of [the suffix] *kṛtvasUC*".
[Question:] What is the problem with that?
[Answer:] It should be in this case as well: *dviṣ karoti*, *dviḥ karoti* ("He does it twice"). [But] it should not be in this case: *catuṣ karoti*, *catuḥ karoti* ("He does it four times"). When, on the other hand, [the words] *dvis*, *tris* and *catur* are used, [the words] *dvis*, *tris* and *catur* would be qualified by the expression "the meaning of [the suffix] *kṛtvasUC*". [The meaning would be: "The *ṣ*-substitute comes in place of] such a *visarjanīya* which comes in [the words] *dvis*, *tris* and *catur* in the meaning of [the suffix] *kṛtvasUC*".
[Bhāṣya:] But this is not the purpose. [The expression] "of a *pada*" continues [here and] this we will qualify with the expression "the meaning of [the suffix] *kṛtvasUC*". [The meaning would be: "The *ṣ*-substitute comes in place of] such a *visarjanīya* which is a part of a *pada* in the meaning of [the suffix] *kṛtvasUC*".

{**Explanation:**
The example derivation is as follows:

(1) *dvis* + *sUC* (A. 5.4.18 *dvitricaturbhyāṃ suc*) + *karoti*
(2) *dvi* (*s* → *rU*) + *s* + *karoti* (A. 8.2.66 *sasajuṣo ruḥ*)
(3) *dvir* + (*s* → 0) + *karoti* (A. 8.2.24 *rāt sasya*)
(4) *dvi* (*r* → *ḥ*) + *karoti* (A. 8.3.15 *kharavasānayor visarjanīyaḥ*)
(5) *dviḥ karoti* / *dvi* (*ḥ* → *ṣ*) *karoti* (A. 8.3.43 *dvitricatur iti kṛtvo 'rthe*)
dviḥ karoti / *dviṣ karoti*

In the example *catuṣkapāla* the *ṣ*-substitute is not optional. Firstly, the word *catur* does not have the meaning of the suffix *kṛtvasUC* here. Moreover, as Kaiyaṭa explains (VMBh_2: V.458), the *ṣ*-substitute was prescribed necessarily by the previous *sūtra* A. 8.3.41 because the word *catur* is considered underived due to being formed with the *Uṇādi* suffix US 739 (5.58) *cater uran*.[442] The commentators further add that the word *catur* is used in the sense of the suffix *kṛtvasUC* by the association with the words *dvis* and *tris*, from which they conclude that in the example *catuṣkapāla* the optional *ṣ*-substitute (instead of the obligatory one) is impossible, which makes the expression *kṛtvo 'rthe* superfluous.

[442] US 739 (5.58) *cater uran* || ("[The suffix] *urAN* comes after [the verbal root] *catE* ('to ask, beg', DhP I:918).")

According to Patañjali, the present rule serves to complete the meaning, and makes a previously obligatory operation optional. Another problem with the word *catur* concerns its derivation. It is pointed out that when the suffix *sUC* is added on the basis of the rule A. 5.4.18 in the meaning of *kṛtvasUC*, the consonant *s* of the suffix is changed into *r*. Further, the final *r* of *catur* is deleted by A. 8.3.14 *ro ri*, which would yield the same form – *catur* – but the final *r* would come from the suffix. This would mean that the word cannot be subject to the obligatory substitution of A. 8.3.41. This view is rejected based on the suspension of the *r*-deletion with respect to the *s*-deletion prescribed by the *sūtra* A. 8.2.24. Moreover, the vowel *u* preceding the consonant *r* would have to be lengthened by A. 6.3.111 *ḍhralope pūrvasya dīrgho 'ṇaḥ*.
Patañjali reaches the conclusion that the words *dvis*, *tris* and *catur* are not necessary in the *sūtra*. He claims that the expression *kṛtvo 'rthe* would not qualify the *visarjanīya* but *pada* and via *tadantavidhi* the meaning would be: "the *visarjanīya* of a *pada* which is used with the meaning of *kṛtvasUC* is optionally replaced with *ṣ*".
This optional rule is an *ubhayatravibhāṣā*. It makes *ṣ* optional for the stem *catur* as opposed to the obligatory one in A. 8.3.41 (*prāptavibhāṣā*); and it prescribes the optional substitution for the stems *dvis* and *tris*, which has not been done yet because the consonant *s* in these examples comes from the suffix (*aprāptavibhāṣā*). Therefore, they would not qualify for the substitution prescribed by A. 8.3.41.}

VMBh_1: III.435.10-19; VMBh_2: V.459.9-460.6

***kārikas*:**

1) Why is he stating the *ṣ*-substitute when there is the meaning of [the suffix] *kṛtvasUC*? So that in [the example] *catuṣkapāla* the *ṣ*-substitute were not optional but were achieved [necessarily] by the previous [*sūtra* A. 8.3.41].
2) But when it is achieved [by the previous *sūtra*], he is prescribing the *ṣ*-substitute in [the word] *catur* in the meaning of [the suffix] *kṛtvasUC*. When the [suffix] added in the meaning of [the suffix] *kṛtvasUC* (i.e., *sUC*) is deleted (by A. 8.2.24), the *visarjanīya* comes in place of the sound *r* (which will then be replaced by *ṣ* obligatorily by A. 8.3.41).
3) If that is the case, what is the purpose in using [the words] *dvis*, *tris* and *catur* here? There is no other [stem] which would have the vowel *i* or *u* as penultimate [and] in the meaning of [the suffix] *kṛtvasUC*.
4) If [these words] were not used, then [the expression] "in the meaning of [the suffix] *kṛtvasUC*" would qualify the *visarjanīya* (meaning: the *visarjanīya* of the suffix having the meaning of *kṛtvasUC* is replaced by

ṣ). And this would not be achieved in the case of [the word] *catur* as the *visarjanīya* comes in place of the sound *r* (i.e., is not a part of a suffix).

5) Therefore, it is proper to use [the words *dvis*, *tris* and *catur* and the expression "in the meaning of the suffix *kṛtvasUC*"] is the qualifier of [the word] *catur*. It can also be the qualifier of the domain of a *pada* [interpreted via] the *tadantavidhi*.

{A. 8.3.44 *isusoḥ sāmarthye*
[The sound *ṣ* optionally comes] in place of [the *visarjanīya* of a *pada* ending in] *is* and *us* [before the consonantal groups *kU* and *pU* in close proximity] when the two *pada*s are syntactically and semantically related.} *This *sūtra* was not commented upon by Patañjali.

A. 8.3.45 *nityaṃ samāse 'nuttarapadasthasya*
[The sound *ṣ*] necessarily [comes in place of the *visarjanīya* of a *pada* ending in *is* and *us*] and not being the final element of a compound [before the consonantal groups *kU* and *pU* in close proximity].

VMBh_1: III.435.20-22; VMBh_2: V.460.7-9

[Question:] What is the purpose [in saying] "not being the final element [of a compound]"?
[Answer:] [See the example:] *paramasarpiḥkuṇḍikā* ('the jar of the best ghee').
[Question:] But now, why does the optional *ṣ*-substitute not result by the previous [*sūtra*] A. 8.3.44, when by this one it is left out?

{Explanation:
The relation (*sāmarthya*) can be of two kinds: *ekārthībhāva* and *vyapekṣā*. A compound can only be an example for *ekārthībhāvasāmarthya*, the union of meanings. The present *sūtra* specifies this way of understanding the term *sāmarthya* by using the word *samāse*, but the previous one does not specify it at all; which raises the question regarding potentially optional application of the *ṣ*-substitution in the word *paramasarpiḥkuṇḍikā*. The answer is provided by the following *ślokavārttika*.}

VMBh_1: III.435.23-436.2; VMBh_2: V.460.10-461.4

1) When a rule is to be known as referring to two words of different meaning, in this (i.e., *vyapekṣāsāmarthya*) the *ṣ*-substitute should be used, that is proper, but as far as I am concerned it is not [the case] here.

[Bhāṣya:] The previous rule refers to *vyapekṣāsāmarthya* (the relationship in a sentence between two *padas*) but it is not *vyapekṣāsāmarthya* in this case.
[Opponent:] On the other hand, why does it depend on *vyapekṣāsāmarthya* and it is not *ekārthībhāva* like in other cases?

2) If there were the compositeness in the sense of unity of meanings (*aikārthya sāmarthya*), the *ṣ*-substitute, as far as I am concerned, could not be involved in a sentence.

[Bhāṣya:] If there were the compositeness in the sense of unity of meanings (*aikārthya sāmarthya*), the *ṣ*-substitute should not be in the sentence: *sarpiṣ karoti*, *sarpiḥ karoti* ("He/she makes clarified butter").

{**Explanation:**
This *vārttika* refers to the previous rule. Patañjali explains that if the previous *sūtra* were an example of *ekārthībhāvasāmarthya*, the optional *ṣ*-substitution in the sentence *sarpiṣ karoti/sarpiḥ karoti* could not result. Kaiyaṭa (VMBh_2: V.461) considers the possibility of two simultaneous interpretations; two kinds of *sāmarthya* understood in A. 8.3.44, especially given that the general term *sāmarthya* is used without any specification. According to Kaiyaṭa, the present rule specifies the meaning of *sāmarthya* in A. 8.3.44 by using the term *samāse*; it shows that the only correct interpretation here is *ekārthībhāva*, by which it is also implied that the previous rule refers to *vyapekṣā*.}

VMBh_1: III.436.3-7; VMBh_2: V.461.5-9

Therefore they think that here (A. 8.3.44) the compositeness in the sense of mutual relationship (*vyapekṣā sāmarthya*) is a good [intepretation].
3) But if it ends in [the suffix] *kṛt*, then as far as I am concerned it should not result in the subsequent one only.

[Bhāṣya:] If it ends in [the suffix] *kṛt*, the *ṣ*-substitute of the subsequent one would not result.
[Question:] What is the reason?
[Answer:] When the suffix is used, it is used to denote that after which [it was employed], beginning with that [to which the suffix was added and ends with the suffix itself].
[Question:] It would not result in the sentence either then, would it? – *paramasarpiṣ karoti*, *paramasarpiḥ karoti* ("He/she makes the best clarified butter").

{**Explanation:**

Patañjali refers to the rule of interpretation (PŚ 23) *pratyayagrahaṇe yasmāt sa vihitas tadādes tadantasya grahaṇam*[443] stating that a mentioned suffix refers to the whole form after which said suffix was added. The previous rule mentions words ending in *is* or *us*, and the example *paramasarpis* meets the required condition for the *ṣ*-substitution. The word *sarpis* is derived with the *Uṇādi* suffix *isI* (US 268; 2.108),[444] so it could, theoretically, apply to the given example. If, however, it does not apply in *paramasarpiḥkuṇḍikā*, then it should not apply in a sentence either. The answer to that is the following.}

VMBh_1: III.436.8-10; VMBh_2: V.461.10-12

And as far as I am concerned, there is an optional [substitution] in a sentence; prohibition would not be suitable.

[Answer:] As the teacher orders the prohibition [by saying] "of not being the final element [of a compound]", he indicates that there is an optional [substitution] in a sentence.

{**Explanation:**
An indication is made by the expression *anuttarapadasthasya* that the *paribhāṣā* 23 does not apply to these examples, but yet the *ṣ*-substitute will apply in a sentence such as *paramasarpiṣ karoti*. The *ṣ*-substitution does not take place in *paramasarpiḥkuṇḍikā* even by A. 8.3.44 because the compound does not end in the suffix *is*. It is the word *sarpis* only that ends in this suffix, and PŚ 23 is not applied. If we were to apply this *paribhāṣā*, the use of the expression "of not being the final element [of a compound]" would be superfluous.

According to other grammarians quoted by Kaiyaṭa (VMBh_2: V.462.16 ff), another way of solving this difficulty is the division of the *sūtra*. The first part would prescribe the obligatory *ṣ*-substitute in a compound (*nityaṃ samāse*); and the second would block it in the final member of a compound *(anuttarapadasthasya)*. They say that in this case, the two-fold interpretation of *sāmarthya* in the *sūtra* A. 8.3.44 does not create problems.}

VMBh_1: III.436.11-12; VMBh_2: V.462.1-2

---

443 PŚ 23 "An affix denotes [a word-form] which begins with that to which [the suffix] has been added and ends with [the suffix] itself."; I.21-22, II.117-124.

444 US 268 (2.108) *arciśucihusrpichādichardibhya isi* ‖ ("[The suffix] *isI* comes after [the verbal roots] *arcA* ('to worship', DhP I:219), *śucA* ('to grieve', DhP I:198), *hu* ('sacrifice', DhP III:1), *srpḶ* ('to crawl', DhP I:1032), *chadA* ('to cover', DhP X:290) and *chardA* ('to vomit', DhP X:51).")

4) But if the ṣ-substitute is understood as obligatory, then this is optional.

[Objection:] But [this is] an underived nominal stem; so when the obligatory ṣ-substitute has been achieved, this [*sūtra* A. 8.3.44] begins the optional [substitution].

{Explanation:
If the stem *sarpis* is considered as underived, as the stems formed with the *Uṇādi* suffixes are, then even with an additional word (*parama*) it will undergo the obligatory ṣ-substitution by A. 8.3.41 because the *visarjanīya* does not have its source in a suffix. It may further be subject to the optional ṣ-substitution in a sentence by A. 8.3.44 as the *paribhāṣā* 23 is not applicable.}

VMBh_1: III.436.13-14; VMBh_2: V.462.3-4

And as far as I am concerned it is achieved in a compound.

...the ṣ-substitution.
[Question:] Why is this said then?

{Explanation:
The question is raised as to the purpose of the use of the word *nityam* in the present rule. As Kaiyaṭa explains (VMBh_2: V.462-463), if we accept the *vyapekṣā* interpretation of *sāmarthya* in the previous *sūtra*, the ṣ-substitution in a compound in A. 8.3.41 automatically becomes obligatory. The following statement answers the doubt – the ṣ-substitution is blocked in the second member of a compound. It would seem then that the word *nityam* should not be used. Kaiyaṭa refers to two views – *vyutpattipakṣa* and *avyutpattipakṣa* (the stems are considered derivable and underivable respectively). If we accept the latter, the forms such as *sarpiṣā* (instr. sg. of *sarpis*) would not be achieved. The ṣ-substitution would not be possible because the consonant *s* would not be a part of a suffix and consequently, A. 8.3.59 *ādeśapratyayayoḥ* (which prescribes ṣ in place of such an *s* that is a part of a suffix or a substitute) could not apply. In the case of stems ending in *is* and *us*, for the sake of the ṣ-substitution, we have to accept the former then. The conclusion is that the term *nitya* is not necessary in the *sūtra* as the sole expression *anuttarapadasthasya* will serve as prohibition.}

VMBh_1: III.436.15-24; VMBh_2: V.462.5-14

But this particular effort has the meaning of a prohibition.

[Bhasya:] I will state the prohibition: "of not being the final element [of a compound]."

***ślokavārttikas*:**
1) When a rule is to be known as referring to two words of different meaning, in this (i.e., *vyapekṣāsāmarthya*) the *ṣ*-substitute should be used, that is proper but as far as I am concerned it is not [the case] here.
2) If there were the compositeness in the sense of unity of meanings (*aikārthya sāmarthya*), the *ṣ*-substitute, as far as I am concerned, could not be involved in a sentence. Therefore they think that here (A. 8.3.44) the compositeness in the sense of mutual relationship (*vyapekṣā sāmarthya*) is a good [intepretation].
3) But if it ends in [the suffix] *kṛt*, then as far as I am concerned it should not result in the subsequent one only. And as far as I am concerned, there is an optional [substitution] in a sentence; prohibition would not be suitable.
4) But if the *ṣ*-substitute is understood as obligatory, then this is optional. And as far as I am concerned it is achieved in a compound. But this particular effort has the meaning of a prohibition.

{A. 8.3.46 *ataḥ kṛkamikaṃsakumbhapātrakuśākarṇīṣv anavyayasya*
[The sound *s* necessarily comes in place of the *visarjanīya* which comes] after the final vowel *a* [of the element not being the final member of a compound and] non-indeclinable before [the verbal stems] *ḌUkṛÑ* ('to make', DhP VIII:10), *kamU* ('to love', DhP I:470) and [the nominal stems] *kaṃsa* ('a goblet'), *kumbha* ('a jar'), *pātra* ('a vessel'), *kuśā* ('a rope, a cord'), *karṇī* ('a rudder') [in close proximity].
A. 8.3.47 *adhaḥ śirasī pade*
[The sound *s* necessarily comes in place of the *visarjanīya* of the words] *adhas* ('below') and *śiras* ('a head') [not being the final member of a compound] before [the stem] *pada* ('a place') [in close proximity].
A. 8.3.48 *kaskādiṣu ca*
[The sound *ṣ*] and [the sound *s* come in place of the *visarjanīya* of the *padas*] *kaska* ('which of them?') etc. [before the consonantal groups *kU* and *pU* in close proximity].
A. 8.3.49 *chandasi vāprāmreḍitayoḥ*
In Vedic [the sound *s*] usually [comes in place of the *visarjanīya* of a *pada* before the consonantal groups *kU* and *pU* in close proximity] except for [the sound *p*] of [the particle] *pra* or reduplicated element (*āmreḍita*).
A. 8.3.50 *kaḥkaratkaratikṛdhikṛteṣv anaditeḥ*
[In Vedic the sound *s* comes in place of the *visarjanīya* of a *pada*] before [the *padas*] *kaḥ* (*kar* – subj. 2nd/3rd sg.), *karat* (ibid.), *karati* (ind. 3rd sg.), *kṛdhi* (impv. 2nd sg.) and *kṛta* (past pass. part.) [in close proximity].
A. 8.3.51 *pañcamyāḥ parāv adhyarthe*

[In Vedic the sound *s* comes in place of the *visarjanīya* of a *pada*] ending in the ablative (*pañcamī*) before [the particle] *pari* used in the meaning of *adhi* [in close proximity].
A. 8.3.52 *pātau ca bahulam*
[In Vedic the sound *s* comes in place of the *visarjanīya* of a *pada* ending in the ablative] variously before [the verb] *pātu* ('may he protect') [in close proximity].
A. 8.3.53 *ṣaṣṭhyāḥ patiputrapṛṣṭhapārapadapayaspoṣeṣu*
[In Vedic the sound *s* comes in place of the *visarjanīya* of a *pada*] ending in the genitive (*ṣaṣṭhī*) before [the nominal stems] *pati* ('lord'), *putra* ('a son'), *pṛṣṭha* ('back'), *pāra* ('beyond, across'), *pada* ('a place'), *payas* ('milk') and *poṣa* ('prosperity') [in close proximity].
A. 8.3.54 *iḍāyā vā*
[In Vedic the sound *s*] usually [comes in place of of the *visarjanīya*] of *iḍā* ('an oblation') [ending in the genitive (*ṣaṣṭhī*) before the nominal stems *pati* ('lord'), *putra* ('a son'), *pṛṣṭha* ('back'), *pāra* ('beyond, across'), *pada* ('a place'), *payas* ('milk') and *poṣa* ('prosperity') in close proximity].} *These *sūtra*s were not commented upon by Patañjali.

A. 8.3.55 *apadāntasya mūrdhanyaḥ*
The retroflex (*mūrdhanya*) sound comes in place of [a sound] which is not at the end of a *pada* [in close proximity].

VMBh_1: III.436.25-437.6; VMBh_2: V.463.1-9

[Question:] But what is the purpose in using [the term] *mūrdhanya*? Should it not be only said: *apadāntasya ṣaḥ*?
[Answer:] With respect to that this is the meaning: the sound *ṣ* should not be used [because] the context continues.
[Question:] Where is the context?
[Answer:] [In the *sūtra*] A. 8.3.39.
[Bhāṣya:] It is not possible in such a way. It is necessary to use the term *mūrdhanya* for the sake of the present [context] and the following [ones]. For the sake of the present [context] then – in A. 8.3.78 the term *mūrdhanya* should not be used. And for the sake of the following [rules] – in the case of A. 8.4.1 the sound *ṇ* should not be used. With respect to that this is the meaning: the prohibition "not at the end of a *pada*" (see A. 8.4.37) should not be mentioned. The term *mūrdhanya* connected to [the expression] "not at the end of a *pada*" continues.

{Explanation:

The use of the more general term *mūrdhanya* ('retroflex') instead of *ṣaḥ* is being questioned. This is a governing rule whose scope extends up to the end of this *pāda*. The general term allows for the *ḍh*-substitute in the *sūtra* A. 8.3.78 and again the *ṣ*-substitute in A. 8.3.80. Otherwise, a reformulation of these rules would have to be undertaken; they would have to include the expressions *ḍhaḥ* and *ṣaḥ* respectively to allow the correct results.
The expression *apadāntasya* is necessary to indicate that the governing term *pada* from A. 8.1.16 ceases to continue; therefore, the following rules will also apply when the word is not termed *pada*. Patañjali states that A. 8.4.37 *padāntasya* prohibiting the *ṇ*-substitute when *n* appears at the end of a *pada*, is superfluous for the context of the present prohibition will continue there as well.}

This was the first *āhnika* of the third *pada* of the eighth *adhyāya* in the *Vyākaraṇamahābhāṣya* composed by Patañjali.

A. 8.3.56 *saheḥ sāḍaḥ saḥ*
[The retroflex (*mūrdhanya*) *ṣ* comes] in place of [the sound] *s* of *sāḍ* being the form of [the verbal root] *ṣahA* ('to endure', DhP I:905) [in close proximity].

VMBh_1: III.438.1-19; VMBh_2: V.464.1-465.9

[Question:] What is the purpose in using *s*? Should it not be only said: "The retroflex comes in *sāḍ* being the form of [the verbal root] *sah*"?
[Answer:] If this is said: "The retroflex comes in *sāḍ* being the form of [the verbal root] *sah*", [the substitution] might undesiredly be involved in the case what is at the end.[445]
[Objection:] But is it not that there is no point in prescribing the retroflex for the last sound? If that is done, it will [apply to] the sound *s*.
[Question:] How will it then [refer] to the sound *s*, when the meaning of a non-final has begun? Should it not, on the other hand, [refer] to the sound *ā*?
[Answer:] It will [refer] to the sound *s* [on the basis of the *sūtra*] A. 1.1.50.[446] When the effect of the closest [equivalent] is produced with respect to the base, it [i.e., the substitution of *s*] would be achieved. But when the effect of the closest [equivalent] is produced with respect to the substitute, it [i.e., the substitution] might udesiredly be involved with respect to the sound *ā*. That is why the sound *s* should be used [in the *sūtra*]. And the sound *s* is used for the sake of the fol-

[445] A. 1.1.52 *alo 'ntyasya* || ("[The substitute ordered in the genitive comes] in place of the final sound.")
[446] A. 1.1.50 *sthāne 'ntaratamaḥ* || ("[A substitute which is to replace a substituend must be] the closest in place of articulation.")

lowing [*sūtras*]. As in [the *sūtra*] A. 8.3.59 [the substitute] should refer to the sound *s*. Here it must not be: *citam stutam* ('praised a lot').
[Question:] But then, what is the purpose in using [the verbal root] *ṣahA*? Should it not be only said: "[The retroflex] comes in place of [the sound] *s* of *sāḍ*"? The form *sāḍ* comes only from [the verbal root] *sah*, not from anything else.
[Objection:] If so....

1) When there is the ṣ-substitute in *sāḍ*, [there should be] prohibition with respect to similar words (i.e., words of the same form).

[Objection:] When there is the *ṣ*-substitute in *sāḍ*, prohibition with respect to similar words should be mentioned. [For example:] *sāḍo daṇḍaḥ* ('a pointed stick') or *sāḍo vṛścikaḥ* ('a scorpion with a sting').
[Answer:] It is achieved due to the use of the meaningful [unit]. [It should be] the use of the word *sāḍ* which has the meaning, and this one is not meaningful.

2) If it were achieved due to the use of a meaningful [item],[447] prohibition [should be mentioned] in the case of deletion of the *taddhita* [suffix] due to meaningfulness.

[Objection:] If it were achieved due to the use of a meaningful [item], prohibition should be mentioned in the case of deletion of the *taddhita* [suffix] due to meaningfulness. [For example:] *sāḍaḥ* [is the one] 'with a sting'; the offspring of Sāḍa is Sāḍi[448] – here [the substitution] would result.
[Answer:] It should not be mentioned. This is not the word *sāḍ*, due to suspension of the single replacement (*ekādeśa*) with respect to the *ṣ*-substitute and [the operation regarding the infix] *tUK* (see A. 6.1.86). In such a way [these forms:] *sāḍāḥ* [is the one] 'with a sting', the offspring of Sāḍa is Sāḍi would result. That is why [the word] *sahi* (i.e., *saheḥ*) should be used.

{Explanation:
The discussion under this *sūtra* concentrates on what is to be replaced – is it the consonant *s* or perhaps the vowel *ā*, and why. The term *mūrdhanya* used in A. 8.3.55 does not give a clear answer, which is why the form *saḥ* is used in the rule. If it were not used, there would be the possibility to replace the vowel *ā* with the consonant *ṣ* as the former is considered retroflex by Sanskrit gram-

447 PŚ 14 *arthavadgrahaṇe nānarthakasya* || ("When a meaningful item is mentioned, that item should not be mentioned without meaning.")
448 See A. 4.1.95 *ata iñ* || ("[The *taddhita* suffix] *iÑ* comes after [the nominal stem ending in the vowel] *a* [to denote the meaning of a descendant].")

marians. The expression *apadāntasya*, continued from the previous rule, allows for that, undesired, substitution. Moreover, based on A. 1.1.50 *sthāne 'ntaratamaḥ* the closest substitute to *s* is the retroflex *ṣ*, which can also be said to continue from A. 8.3.39. According to Patañjali, the use of *saḥ* in the rule is necessary also for the sake of the following *sūtra*s such as A. 8.3.59 where the *ṣ*-substitution is required, so that there were no *ṭ*-substitutions in the forms *citam* or *stutam*.

The specification *saheḥ* cannot be dispensed with either, because it allows for the exclusion from the domain of the *ṣ*-substitution such forms as Sāḍi ('the offspring of Sāḍa'). As in the forms *sāḍaḥ* and, consequently, Sāḍi there is no meaning covered by the verb *sah*, the substitution does not take place.
The example derivation can be as follows:

(1) *jalaṃ sahate*
(2) *jala + sah + Ṇvi* (A. 3.2.63 *chandasi sahaḥ*)
(3) *jala + sah +* 0 (A. 6.1.67 *ver apṛktasya*)
(4) *jal* (*a* → *ā*) (A. 6.3.137 *anyeṣām api dṛśyate*) + *s* (*a* → *ā*) *h* (A. 7.2.116 *ata upadhāyāḥ*)
(5) *jalā-sāh* + *sU* (A. 4.1.2 *svaujasamauṭśasṭābhyāmbhisṅebhyāmbhyasṅasibhyāmbhyasṅasosāmṅyossup*)
(6) *jalā-sāh* + 0 (A. 6.1.68 *halṅyābbhyo dīrghāt sutisy apṛktam hal*)
(7) *jalā-sā* (*h* → *ḍh*) (A. 8.2.31 *ho ḍhaḥ*)
(8) *jalā-sā* (*ḍh* → *ḍ*) (A. 8.2.39 *jhalāṃ jaśo 'nte*)
(9) *jalā-* (*s* → *ṣ*) *āḍ* (A. 8.3.56 *saheḥ sāḍaḥ saḥ*)
jalāṣāḍ - that which endures water.}

A. 8.3.57 *iṇkoḥ*
[The retroflex *ṣ* comes in place of the sound *s* which is not at the end of a *pada*] occurring after the sounds *i*, *u* or [those belonging to the consonantal group] *kU* [in close proximity].
A. 8.3.58 *numvisarjanīyaśarvyāvaye 'pi*
[The retroflex *ṣ* comes in place of the sound *s* which is not at the end of a *pada* occurring after the sounds *i*, *u* or those belonging to the consonantal group *kU*] even if it[449] is separated by [the infix] *nUM*, the *visarjanīya* or [a sound denoted by] *śaR* (i.e., sibilants) [in close proximity].

VMBh_1: III.438.20-439.5; VMBh_2: V.465.10-466.4

[449] 'It' refers to the consonant *s* being separated from the sounds *i*, *u* or those denoted by *kU*.

1) Prohibition [of the substitution should be mentioned] in the case of [the verbal root] *ṇisI* ('to touch closely, to kiss', DhP II:15) when there is separation by [the infix] *nUM*, the *visarjanīya* or [a sound denoted by] *śaR* (i.e., sibilants).

[Bhāṣya:] Prohibition [of the substitution] should be mentioned in the case of [the verbal root] *ṇisI* ('to touch closely, to kiss', DhP II:15) when there is separation by [the infix] *nUM*, the *visarjanīya* or [a sound denoted by] *śaR* (i.e., sibilants). [For example,] *niṃsse* or *niṃssva* ('you kiss' and 'kiss!' – praes. ind. and impv, 2nd sg., respectively).
[Question:] Should it be mentioned then?
[Answer:] It should not be mentioned. [It is said:] "when there is separation only by [the infix] *nUM*, when there is separation only by the *visaranīya* and where there is separation only by [a sound denoted by] *śaR* (i.e., sibilants)".
[Question:] Should it be mentioned?
[Answer:] No.
[Question:] How is the unsaid understood?
[Answer:] The completion of an idea in a sentence is understood separately.[450] As here: the terms *guṇa* and *vṛddhi* are [applied] one by one.
[Objection:] But is it not an example for the completion of an idea in a sentence [to be understood] collectively?[451] As here: *gargāḥ śataṃ daṇḍyantām* ("The Gargas should be punished with a hundred"). The kings are desirous of gold and [they] do not punish [them] separately (but all of them, the punishment is collective).

{**Explanation:**
The *sūtra*s A. 8.3.57 and A. 8.3.58 are discussed together because the former serves as the governing rule. It is supplied in the following rules so that the substitution took place only after the vowels denoted by *iṆ*, that is, all vowels except *a* and *ā*. As the expression *iṇkoḥ* is interpreted as the ablative, the rule A. 8.3.58 has to be stated. Otherwise, the *ṣ*-substitution could only apply to such an *s* that appears after a vowel denoted by *iṆ* directly.
The *vārttika* introduces prohibition in the case of the forms of the verb *ṇisI* ('to kiss'). In the examples given by Patañjali we can see that the consonant *s* that could undergo the substitution is separated from the vowel *i* with both the infix *nUM* and the sibilant *s*. The question arises whether this prohibiton is necessary

---

450 PŚ 107 *pratyekaṃ vākyaparisamāptiḥ* || ("What is stated [in grammar of several things] must be understood [to have been stated] of each of them separately."), I.105, II.491-492. WUJASTYK 1993: vol. I:33, vol. II:129.

451 PŚ 108 *kvacit samudāye 'pi* || ("Sometimes [it is] also [understood to have been stated of all of them collectively."), I.105-106, II.492-493. WUJASTYK 1993: vol. I:33-34, vol. II:130-131.

because there are two ways of interpreting the *sūtra* A. 8.3.58. It can be interpreted along the lines of the *paribhāṣā* 107 saying that "a sentence is complete with respect to each single one of its constituents"; or the *paribhāṣā* 108, which states that "a sentence is also complete with respect to the aggregate". The analysed problem focuses on the term *vyavāya*, whether it should be read with *nUM*, *visarjanīya* and *śaR* separately or collectively. If we were to read it collectively, we would run into difficulty with the examples: *niṃsse* and *niṃssva*. The *ṣ*-substitute could also take place in these cases; but it does not. The answer Patañjali gives is that we should read *vyavāya* separately with every single word; thanks to which we achieve the meaning – the *ṣ*-substitute relaces the consonant *s* following a vowel denoted by *iṆ* even if there is separation either by the infix *nUM*, *visarjanīya* or a sibilant.
These are the examples of the rule A. 8.3.58:

A. When *nUM* intervenes:
(1) *sarpis* + *Jas* (A. 4.1.2 *svaujasamauṭśasṭābhyāmbhisṅebhyāmbhyasṅasibhyāmbhyasṅasosāmṅyossup*)
(2) *sarpis* + *Śi* (A. 7.1.20 *jaśśasoḥ śi*)
(3) *sarpi* + *nUM* + *s* + *i* (A. 7.1.72 *napuṃsakasya jhalacaḥ*)
(4) *sarpi* + (*n* → *ṃ*) + *s* + *i* (A. 8.3.24 *naś cāpadāntasya jhali*)
(5) *sarp* (*i* → *ī*) + *ṃ* + *s* + *i* (A. 6.4.10 *sāntamahataḥ saṃyogasya*)
(6) *sarpīṃ* + (*s* → *ṣ*) + *i* (A. 8.3.58 *numvisarjanīyaśarvyāvaye 'pi*)
sarpīṃṣi

B. When the *visarjanīya* intervenes:
(1) *sarpis* + *suP* (A. 4.1.2 *svaujasamauṭśasṭābhyāmbhisṅebhyāmbhyasṅasibhyāmbhyasṅasosāmṅyossup*)
(2) *sarpi* (*s* → *rU*) + *su* (A. 8.2.66 *sasajuṣo ruḥ*)
(3) *sarpi* (*r* → *ḥ*) + *su* (A. 8.3.15 *kharavasānyor visarjanīyaḥ*)
(4) *sarpi* (*r* → *ḥ*) + *su* (A. 8.3.36 *vā śari*)
(5) *sarpiḥ* + (*s* → *ṣ*) + *u* (A. 8.3.58 *numvisarjanīyaśarvyāvaye 'pi*)
sarpiḥṣu

C. When a sound denoted by *śaR* intervenes:
(1) *sarpis* + *suP* (A. 4.1.2 *svaujasamauṭśasṭābhyāmbhisṅebhyāmbhyasṅasibhyāmbhyasṅasosāmṅyossup*)
(2) *sarpis* + (*s* → *ṣ*) + *u* (A. 8.3.58 *numvisarjanīyaśarvyāvaye 'pi*)
sarpis + *ṣu*
(3) *sarpi* (*s* → *ṣ*) (A. 8.4.41 *ṣṭunā ṣṭuḥ*) + *ṣu*
sarpiṣṣu}

VMBh_1: III.439.6-9; VMBh_2: V.466.5-8

[Answer:] In such a way then....

2) It is achieved by division of the rule.

[Answer:] Division of the rule will be done. [Firstly, we have:] *numvyavāye* "When there is separation by [the infix] *nUM*." Then, *visarjanīyavyavāye* "when there is separation by the *visarjanīya*." Then, *śarvyavāye* "when there is separation by [a sound denoted by] *śaR* (i.e., sibilants)."
[Question:] Should this division of the rule be done then?
[Answer:] It should not be done. The word 'separation' (*vyavāya*) is joined with every single one (i.e., *nUM*, *visarjanīya* and *śaR*).

A. 8.3.59 *ādeśapratyayayoḥ*
[The retroflex *ṣ* comes in place of the sound *s* which is not at the end of a *pada* occurring after the sounds *i*, *u* or those belonging to the consonantal group *kU*] when it is a substitute or [a part of] a suffix [even if it is separated by the infix *nUM*, the *visarjanīya* or a sound denoted by *śaR* (i.e., sibilants) in close proximity].

VMBh_1: III.439.10-16; VMBh_2: V.466.9-15

1) There is prohibition in the case of [the *Uṇādi* suffix] *saraK* with respect to the *ṣ*-substitute [of the sound *s*] being a substitute or [a part of] a suffix.

[Bhāṣya:] Prohibition should be mentioned in the case of [the *Uṇādi* suffix] *saraK* with respect to the *ṣ*-substitute [of the sound *s*] being a substitute or [a part of] a suffix. [For example,] *kṛsaraḥ* ('a dish of sesamum and grain') and *dhūsaraḥ* ('grey, dust-coloured').
[Opponent:] Too little is said [here] "in case of [the *Uṇādi* suffix] *saraK*". It should be said: "in the case of [the *Uṇādi* suffix] *saraK* etc." because in this case it should be: *varsam* and *tarsam* ('a year' and 'an ocean', respectively).
[Question:] Should it be mentioned then?
[Answer:] It should not be mentioned. [The words ending in the suffixes] *uṆ* etc. are not derived nominal stems.[452] Alternatively, in the case of the *ṣ*-substitute it is possible to understand [the following]: "The words ending in [the suffixes] *uṆ*

[452] PŚ 22 *uṇādayo 'vyutpannāni prātipadikāni* || ("Those words which end in [the suffixes] *uṆ* etc. are underived [and do not undergo or cause such operations as would depend on their etymological formation, or they do not admit of a division into a base and a suffix]."), I.20-21, II.115-117.

etc. are not derived nominal stems". In this case it should not be then: *sarpiṣaḥ*, *yajuṣaḥ* (gen./abl. sg. of 'clarified butter' and 'a sacrifice' respectively).

{**Explanation:**
The first *vārttika* proposes prohibition of the *ṣ*-substitution in the case of the suffix *saraK*; an *Uṇādi* suffix which is, in fact, not *saraK* but merely *sara*, introduced in US 353 (3.70).[453] However, it is treated as a suffix with the marker *K* in the case of certain verbs, such as *ḌUkṛÑ* ('to do', see US 356; 3.73[454]). The proposal is made to extend the prohibition onto other suffixes as well, such as the suffix *sa* prescribed after the verbal roots *vṝ* ('to select', DhP IX:16) or *tṝ* ('to cross', DhP I:1018, see US 345; 3.62[455]). This proposal leads to a discussion whether the *Uṇādi* suffixes can be treated as falling into the scope of the present *sūtra*, because it is generally accepted that the stems derived with the help of such suffixes are treated as underived. According to Kaiyaṭa, the cause of an operation does not lie in the derivation with the help of an *Uṇādi* suffix. This implication is made by Pāṇini himself in the rule A. 8.3.46, where he mentions the form *kaṃsa* ('a drinking vessel'), already derived. This noun is formed with the *Uṇādi* suffix *sa* (US 345; 3.62) added to the verb *kamU* ('to desire', DhP I: 470).
The problem, however, arises with the words *sarpiṣā* ('with clarified butter') and *vṛkṣa* ('a tree'). How do we get the *ṣ*-substitute here? The word *vṛkṣa* is formed with the *Uṇādi* suffix *saN* (which is treated as having the marker *K*; see US 349; 3.66.);[456] the word *sarpis* is derived with the suffix *isI* (US 268; 2.108).[457] When these words are treated as underived, the consonant *s* cannot be treated as a part of the suffix, because formally there is no suffix, and the substitution cannot take place. Similarly, we see this in the examples given by Patañjali. Therefore, they should be treated as derived stems and the solution is proposed in the following *vārttika*.}

---

[453] US 353 (3.70) *aśeḥ saraḥ* || ("[The suffix] *sara* comes after [the verbal root] *aśŪ* ('to pervade', DhP V:180).")

[454] US 356 (3.73) *kṛdhūmadibhyaḥ kit* || ("[The suffix *sara*] comes after [the verbal roots] *ḌUkṛÑ* ('to do', DhP VIII:10), *dhūÑ* ('to shake', DhP V:9) and *madĪ* ('be pleased', DhP IV:99) and it is treated as if marked with *K*.")

[455] US 345 (3.62) *vṝtṝvadihanikamikaṣibhyaḥ saḥ* || ("[The suffix] *sa* comes after [the verbal roots] *vṝÑ* ('to select', DhP IX:16), *tṝ* ('to cross', DhP I:1018), *vadA* ('to speak', DhP I:1058), *hanA* ('to kill', DhP II:2), *kamU* ('to wish, desire', DhP I:470) and *kaṣA* ('to injure', DhP I:716).")

[456] US 349 (3.66) *snuvraścikṛtyṛṣibhyaḥ kit* || ("[The suffix *sa*] comes after [the verbal roots] *ṣnu* ('to flow', DhP II:29), *OvraścŪ* ('to cut, wound', DhP VI:11), *kṛtĪ* ('to cut', DhP VI:141) and *ṛṣĪ* ('to go', DhP VI:7) and it is treated as if marked with *K*.")

[457] US 268; 2.108 *arciśucihusṛpichādichardibhya isi* || ("[The suffix] *isI* comes after [the verbal roots] *arcA* ('to worship', DhP I:219), *śucA* ('to grieve', DhP I:198), *hu* ('sacrifice', DhP III:1), *sṛpḶ* ('to crawl', DhP I:1032), *chadA* ('to cover', DhP X:290) and *chardA* ('to vomit', DhP X:51).")

VMBh_1: III.439.17-21; VMBh_2: V.466.15-467.5

[Bhāṣya:] In such a way then....

2) It is achieved on the basis of the term 'variously' (*bahulam*).

[Bhāṣya:] The term 'suffix' is [applied] variously.
[Question:] But is this the genitive showing a part (*avayavaṣaṣṭhī*) – the sound *s* which is [a part] of a substitute, the sound *s* which is [a part] of a suffix? Or, [is it the genitive of] syntactic coordination (*samānādhikaraṇa*) – the sound *s* which is a substitute, the sound *s* which is a suffix?
[Question:] What is the difference here?

{**Explanation:**
The answer to the problem is the variability of application of the term 'suffix'. Kaiyaṭa (VMBh_2: V.467.13 ff) explains that in the case of the words *kṛsara* ('a dish of sesamum and grain') etc., when the *ṣ*-substitution is to take place, the term 'suffix' does not apply. The term *bahulam*, to which the reference is made, regards the *sūtra* A. 3.3.1 *uṇādayo bahulam* ("[The *kṛt* suffixes] beginning with *uṆ* [come after verbal roots when the action refers to the present time] variously [to form names]").

The genitive *ādeśapratyayayoḥ* could be interpreted either as *avayavaṣaṣṭhī* or *samānādhikaraṇaṣaṣṭhī*. If the former view is accepted, the substitution will refer to such a consonant *s* which is a part of a substitute or a part of a suffix. According to the latter view, we have the consonant *s* which is a substitute or a suffix. Kaiyaṭa explains that in the first view the grammatical change of the form of *s* continued from previous rules should not be done; but then, there is no logical connection between the expression "of the substitute and of the suffix" and the operation (i.e., the *ṣ*-substitution), because they would both qualify *s*. In the *samānādhikaraṇa* view, however, the consonant *s* would have to change its number to dual. Were we to accept either of the views, we run into problems that are explained in the following *vārttika*s.}

VMBh_1: III.439.22-24; VMBh_2: V.467.6-8

3) If [the expression] "of a substitute or of a suffix" is the genitive showing a part, there is prohibition in the case of reduplication (*dvirvacana*).

[Answer:] If [the expression] "of a substitute or of a suffix" is the genitive showing a part, prohibition should be mentioned in the case of reduplication (*dvirvacana*). [For example,] *bisaṃ bisam* ('a shoot'), *musalaṃ musalam* ('a club').

{**Explanation:**
In view of *avayavaṣaṣṭhī*, the forms such as *bisaṃ bisam* and *musalaṃ musalam* could be subject to the undesired *ṣ*-substitution because the consonant *s* is a part of a substitute. The rule A. 8.1.4 prescribes the reduplication in place of a single word; therefore we treat the whole operation as a substitution.[458]}

VMBh_1: III.440.1-2; VMBh_2: V.467.9-10

4) And [the *ṣ*-substitute] would not result [if the words] were syntactically coordinated either.

[Answer:] And the *ṣ*-substitute would not result [if the words] were syntactically coordinated either. [For example,] *eṣaḥ* ('this one'), *akarṣīt* ('he/she/it did' 3rd sg. aor.).

{**Explanation:**
The examples given must be a mistake. In both these cases the consonant *s* is not a part of a substitute but it is a substitute itself. The form *eṣaḥ* is derived from the stem *etad* where the consonant *t* is replaced by *s* on the basis of A. 7.2.106 *tadoḥ saḥ sāvanantyayoḥ*.[459] In the form *akarṣīt* the consonant *s* can be interpreted both as a suffix or a substitute because it comes in place of the suffix *Cli* by the rule A. 3.1.44 *cleḥ sic*, and via *sthānivadbhāva* it can be considered a suffix. So, both these examples could be an argument for the *samānādhikaraṇaṣaṣṭhī* interpretation, not against it.}

VMBh_1: III.440.3-5; VMBh_2: V.467.11-468.1

[Answer:] Let it be [the genitive expressing] syntactic coordination then.
[Objection:] If it were [the genitive expressing] syntactic coordination, in these cases [the substitution] would not result: *siṣeca* (3rd sg. perf. 'to pour out, emit'), *suṣvāpa* (3rd sg. perf. 'to sleep').
[Answer:] It is not possible to establish the reduplication 'in place of' when the reduplication is of a verbal root. Because it would also result in this case:

---

458 See A. 8.1.1 and A. 8.1.4. A. 8.1.1 *sarvasya dve* || ("[Up to A. 8.1.15] two [expressions] come in place of a whole."); A. 8.1.4 *nityavīpsayoḥ* || ("[Two expression come in place of a whole] to denote 'over and over again, continually' or 'pervasion of a thing by property and action.")

459 A. 7.2.106 *tadoḥ saḥ sāvanantyayoḥ* || ("[The consonant] *s* comes in place of a non-final *t* or *d* [of the pronominal stem *tyad* ('that') etc.] before *sU*.")

sarīsṛpyate (3rd sg. intens. 'to creep'). That is why, with reference to that, [the term] *dvirvacana* [means] doubling, using the element twice.

{**Explanation:**
The derivation of *siṣeca* is as follows:

(1) *ṣicA* (DhP VI:140) + *tiP* (A. 3.4.78 *tiptasjhisipthasthamibvasmastātāmjhathāsāthāmdhvamiḍvahimahiṅ*)
(2) (*ṣ* → *s*) *ic* + *ti* (A. 6.1.64 *dhātvādeḥ ṣaḥ saḥ*)
(3) *sic* + *ṆaL* (A. 3.4.82 *parasmaipadānāṃ ṇalatususthalatusaṇalvamāḥ*)
(4) *sic* + *sic* + *a* (A. 6.1.8 *liṭi dhātor anabhyāsasya*)
(5) *si* + *sic* + *a* (A. 7.4.60 *halādiḥ śeṣaḥ*)
(6) *si* + *s* (*i* → *e*) *c* + *a* (A. 7.3.86 *pugantalaghūpadhasya ca*)
si + *sec* + *a*
si + (*s* → *ṣ*) *ec* + *a* (A. 8.3.59 *ādeśapratyayayoḥ*)
siṣeca

The verbal root is presented with the consonant *ṣ* in grammar, not with *s*; what goes through the final *ṣ*-substitution is a substitute and not the original sound of the verb.
Patañjali presents two views regarding the understanding of the term *dvirvacana*. It can be understood as two elements replacing one (*sthāne dvirvacana*) so the result is proper substitution, or as doubling the existing element, which means there is no substitution whatsoever. In the examples *siṣeca* and *suṣvāpa* accepting the *samānādhikaraṇaṣaṣṭhī* interpretation of the rule, and *sthāne dvirvacana*, would make it impossible to derive the correct forms, the *ṣ*-substitution would not result. As will be shown later, *sāmānādhikaraṇya* does not create such a problem, because before we double the verbal root we go through *ṣ* → *s* substitution on the root itself. And in this case we have the consonant *s* that is a substitution itself and not its part.
The problem arises with the form *sarīsṛpyate* (3rd sg. intens.); if we accept the *sthāne dvirvacana* interpretation, the *ṣ*-substitute will apply because *s* will be a part of the substitute. That is, of course, if we accept the *avayavaṣaṣṭhī* interpretation along with it. The argument is raised in the *Pradīpa* (VMBh_2: V.468.17-21) that there is no danger of the *ṣ*-substitution if the *samānādhikaraṇa* view is accepted. Additionally, accepting *dviḥprayoga dvirvacana* view of reduplication solves the problems both with *sarīsṛpyate* as well as with *siṣeca*. The *s* in *siṣeca* appears as a result of the substitution in A. 6.1.64 (so it is a substitution, not a part of it), therefore, accepting the *samānādhikaraṇa* view we get the *ṣ* in place of it.}

VMBh_1: III.440.5-6; VMBh_2: V.468.1-2

[Objection:] In these cases then: *kariṣyati* (3rd sg. fut. 'to do'), *hariṣyati* (3rd sg. fut. 'to bear, carry'), [according to the meaning of the *sūtra*] "the sound *s* which is a suffix", the *ṣ*-substitute would not result.

{Explanation:
In these cases the full suffix is *sya*, not only *s*. As *s* is only a part of a suffix, accepting the *samānādhikaraṇa* view would not allow for the necessary *ṣ*-substitution in these cases.}

VMBh_1: III.440.7-11; VMBh_2: V.468.3-7

[Answer:] Let it be then "the sound *s* which is a substitute, the sound *s* which is a part of a suffix".
[Objection:] In this case then: *akārṣīt* (3rd sg. aor. 'to do') [according to the meaning of the *sūtra*] "the sound *s* which is a part of a suffix", the *ṣ*-substitute would not result.
[Answer:] Let it not be in this way [in this case], it will be in this way: "the sound *s* which is a substitute."
[Objection:] In these cases: *joṣiṣat* (3rd sg. subj. of *juṣ* 'to be pleased'), *mandiṣat* (3rd sg. subj. of *mand* 'to be glad, delighted'), [according to the meaning of the *sūtra*] "the sound *s* which is a part of a suffix", the *ṣ*-substitute would not result. Additionally, when [the addition of the infix] *aṬ* has been done, the sound *s* is a part of a suffix. In this case then: *indro mā vakṣat sa devān yakṣat* ("May Indra not speak, he should sacrifice to gods"[460]).

{Explanation:
The derivation of the form *joṣiṣat* is as follows:

(1) *juṣ* + *lEṬ*
(2) *juṣ* + *sIP* + *tiP* (A. 3.1.34 *sib bahulaṃ leṭi*)
(3) *juṣ* + *iṬ* + *s* + *ti* (A. 7.2.35 *ārdhadhātukasyeḍ valādeḥ*)
(4) *j* (*u* → *o*) *ṣ* + *i* + *s* + *ti* (A. 7.3.84 *sārvadhātukārdhadhātukayoḥ*)
(5) *joṣ* + *i* + *s* + *t* (*i* → 0) (A. 3.4.97 *itaś ca lopaḥ parasmaipadeṣu*)
(6) *joṣis* + *aṬ* + *t* (A. 3.4.94 *leṭo aḍāḍau*)
joṣis + *a* + *t*
(7) *joṣi* (*s* → *ṣ*) + *a* + *t* (A. 8.3.59 *ādeśapratyayayoḥ*)
joṣiṣat

---

[460] ṚgV 3.4.3.

The question might arise whether *s* to be replaced here is a suffix or if it is a part of the suffix. Originally, it is a suffix (*sIP*) but, as Kaiyaṭa explains, it is further augmented with the infix *iṬ*, which makes it a part of the suffix in the end. The suffix should be understood together with its augment.

In the examples *yakṣat* and *vakṣat* (3rd sg. subj. of *vac* – 'to speak' and *yaj* – 'to sacrifice' respectively) the augmentation does not take place. The suffix is merely the consonant *s*. Therefore, the *avayavaṣaṣṭhī* view makes the *ṣ*-substitution impossible. We are able to derive the correct forms with the help of *samānādhikaraṇa* view.}

VMBh_1: III.440.12-13; VMBh_2: V.468.8-9

5) But a compound is not produced of [the words in] different cases.

[Objection:] But [the expression] *ādeśapratyayayoḥ* is not formed as a compound of [the words ending in] different cases.

{Explanation:
A *dvandva* compound cannot be made of two words (in the genitive in this case) that denote two different things at the same time. The genitive *ādeśasya* with respect to the *ṣ*-substitution would be considered the *sthānaṣaṣṭhī* (meaning 'in place of'); and the genitive *pratyayasya* with respect to the consonant *s* would be considered the *avayavaṣaṣṭhī* (meaning 'being a part of'). The solution is presented by the following *vārttika*.}

VMBh_1: III.440.14-24; VMBh_2: V.468.10-469.6

6) It is achieved by division of the rule.

[Answer:] Division of the rule will be done. [First,] *ādeśasya*; "There is [the sound] *ṣ* in place of a substitute." Then, *pratyayasya*; "There is [the sound] *ṣ* in place of the sound *s* of a suffix."
[Question:] Should division of the rule be done then?
[Answer:] It should not be done.
[Question:] How come?
[Answer:] Let it be really the genitive showing a part.
[Objection:] But has it not been said that if [the expression] "of a substitute or of a suffix" is the genitive showing a part, prohibition should be said in the case of reduplication (*dvirvacana*)?
[Answer:] This is not a fault. [The term] *dvirvacana* [means] putting the element twice.

[Objection:] It is also said that the *ṣ*-substitute would not result [if the words] were syntactically coordinated either; it will be by treating [a secondary thing] as the principal one (lit. the one getting the designation).
[Answer:] Alternatively, let it be [the genitive showing] the syntactic coordination.
[Question:] How [will we have the forms] *kariṣyati*, *hariṣyati*?
[Answer:] The teacher's usage indicates that there is the *ṣ*-substitute in that kind [of words] just as he prescribes prohibition [of the substitution] in [the word] *sāt* in A. 8.3.111.
[Proposition:] Alternatively, let it be "the sound *s* which is a substitute, the sound *s* which is [a part] of a suffix".
[Question:] How [will we have the forms] *indro mā vakṣat sa devān yakṣat*?
[Answer:] It will be by treating [a secondary thing] as the principal one (lit. the one getting the designation).
[Question:] Should this maxim about treating [a secondary thing] as the principal one (lit. the one getting the designation) be mentioned then?
[Answer:] It should not be mentioned.

{Explanation:
The above discussion focuses on the *paribhāṣā* 30 in the *Paribhāṣenduśekhara*: *vyapadeśivad ekasmin* ("[An operation which affects] something on account of some special designation which attaches to the latter, [affects] likewise that which stands alone.") This rule of interpretation states that when the suffix is '*s*', the consonant *s* can be considered as a part of the suffix, not only the suffix itself. Kaiyaṭa (VMBh_2: V.469.15 ff) explains that this principle depends on the meaningfulness of the element *s*. In the case of suffixes *sIP* and *sIC*, forming the Vedic subjunctive and aorist respectively, the consonant *s* is meaningful, therefore *vyapadeśivadbhāva* may apply. The problem appears with the form *eṣa* where *s*, being the substitute for *t* of *etad*, does not bear any meaning of its own. Annaṃbhaṭṭa (MPV X.446-447) adds that it is meaningless due to a lack of different forms. However, the *s*-substitute prescribed in the word *eṣa* is prescribed for many words, therefore, we get different forms. This leads Annaṃbhaṭṭa to the conclusion that *vyapadeśabhāva* can be applied in this case as well.
Thus, the principle can apply in a situation when the element is considered a part while constituting a whole. The consonant *s* of the abovementioned suffix *sIP*, for example, can be treated as a part of the suffix even though the suffix consists of the single sound *s*. It is further implied by Pāṇini himself in the rule A. 8.3.111 *sāt padādyoḥ*, which prohibits the *ṣ*-substitution of *s* of *sāt*. Obviously, the consonant *s* is a part of the suffix in this case. By formulating A. 8.3.111 in such a way Pāṇini indicates how the genitive should be understood in the present rule. It shows that the substitution will normally take place if the consonant *s* is a part of the suffix. Otherwise, there would be no point in formulating the prohibition.}

VMBh_1: III.440.25-441.5; VMBh_2: V.469.7-14

7) Alternatively, it has been mentioned.

[Question:] What has been mentioned?
[Answer:] With reference to that, there is the statement about treating [a secondary thing] as the principal one in order to get reduplication (*dve*) of a single vowel (*aC*) of the first [syllbale][461] and with respect to the *ṣ*-substitute in order to correctly comprehend the substitution; it is achieved not from the statement [itself but] through the knowledge of the world.[462]
[Objection:] But a compound of [the words in] different cases is not produced.
[Answer:] The teacher's use indicates that this compound consists of [words in] two different cases just like he uses [the term] *ghasḶ* in A. 8.3.60.
[Question:] How is an indication made?
[Answer:] If [the substitution refers to] the sound *s* which is a part of a substitute, in the same way it should be that the term *ghasI* is superfluous.[463] But the teacher sees [the meaning of the *sūtra* like this]: the *ṣ*-substitute takes place of such a sound *s* that is a substitution; then he uses the term *ghasḶ*.

{**Explanation:**
The conclusion of the above discussion is that the compound *ādeśapratyayayoḥ* should be understood in two different ways. There are four views regarding this *sūtra*:
1) *ādeśāvayavo yaḥ sakāraḥ pratyayāvayavo yaḥ sakāraḥ* – the sound *s* that is a part of the substitution and the sound *s* that is a part of a suffix undergo the *ṣ*-substitution.
2) *ādeśo yaḥ sakāraḥ pratyayo yaḥ sakāraḥ* – the sound *s* that is the substitution and the sound *s* that is the suffix undergo the *ṣ*-substitution.
3) *pratyayo yaḥ sakāraḥ ādeśāvayavo yaḥ sakāraḥ* – the sound *s* that is the suffix and the sound *s* that is a part of the substitution undergo the *ṣ*-substitution.

---

461 A. 6.1.1 *ekāco dve prathamasya* || ("Two [syllables] come in place of the first [syllable of the verbal stem] consisting of a single [syllable].")

462 See A. 1.1.21 *vt*. 1-5.

463 See A. 2.4.37-40: A. 2.4.37 *luṅsanor ghasḷ* || ("[The substitute] *ghasḶ* comes in place of [the whole verbal stem *adA* ('to eat', DhP II:1)] before [*ārdhadhātuka* substitutes of] *lUṄ* and [the desiderative marker] *saN*."); A. 2.4.38 *ghañapoś ca* || ("[The substitute *ghasḶ* comes in place of the whole verbal stem *adA* ('to eat', DhP II:1)] also before [*ārdhadhātuka* suffixes] *GHaÑ* and *aP*."); A. 2.4.39 *bahulaṃ chandasi* || ("In Vedic [the substitute *ghasḶ* comes in place of the whole verbal stem *adA* ('to eat', DhP II:1)] variously."); A. 2.4.40 *liṭy anyatarasyām* || ("[The substitute *ghasḶ*] optionally [comes in place of the whole verbal stem *adA* ('to eat', DhP II:1)] before [*ārdhadhātuka* substitutes of] *lIṬ* (perfect tense).")

4) *ādeśo yaḥ sakāraḥ pratyayāvayavo yaḥ sakāraḥ* – the sound *s* that is the substitution and the sound *s* that is a part of a suffix undergo the *ṣ*-substitution.

The commentators conclude in favour of the last view. If we accepted the third view, there would be no necessity in stating the prohibition in the rule A. 8.3.111; the sound *s* is a part of the element *sāt* so the substitution would not take place anyway. Furthermore, the inclusion of the verbal root *ghasḶ* in the following *sūtra* would be superfluous. The form *ghas* is the substitute of the verbal root *adA* ('to eat', DhP II:1), which makes *s* a part of the substitute. The *ṣ*-substitution would take place in the verb *ghas* by the present rule. Both those rules A. 8.3.60 and A. 8.3.111 serve as an indication that there is the possibility of understanding a *dvandva* compound as consistuting of two genitives with different meanings.}

{A. 8.3.60 *śāsivasighasīnāṃ ca*
[The retroflex *ṣ* comes in place of the sound *s* which is not at the end of a *pada* occurring after the sounds *i*, *u* or those belonging to the consonantal group *kU*] of [the verbal roots] *śāsI* ('to instruct, rule', DhP II:66), *vasI* ('to dwell', DhP I:1054) and *ghasI* ('to eat', DhP I:747) [in close proximity].}
*This *sūtra* was not commented upon by Patañjali.

A. 8.3.61 *stautiṇyor eva ṣaṇyabhyāsāt*
[The retroflex *ṣ* comes in place of the sound *s* which is not at the end of a *pada* occurring after the sounds *i*, *u* or those belonging to the consonantal group *kU*] of the reduplicated [syllable of a root] before [the desiderative suffix] *ṣaṆ* of [the verbal roots] *ṣṭuÑ* ('to praise', DhP II:34) and those ending in [the causative marker] *ṆiC* only [in close proximity].

VMBh_1: III.441.6-11; VMBh_2: V.470.1-6

[Question:] What is the purpose in using [the expression] "of [the verbal roots] *ṣṭuÑ* ('to praise') and those ending in [the causative suffix] *ṆiC*"?
[Answer:] It must not be in [verbal roots] other than *ṣṭuÑ* ('to praise') and those ending in [the causative suffix] *ṆiC*. [For example,] *sisikṣati* ('he wishes to sprinkle').
[Question:] Then what is the purpose [in using] the particle *eva* ('only')?
[Answer:] In order to restrict. [The substitution takes place of the sound *s*] of [the verbal roots] *ṣṭuÑ* ('to praise') and those ending in [the causative suffix] *ṆiC* only, not of others.
[Answer:] This is not the purpose. When it is achieved (i.e., the *ṣ*-substitute by A. 8.3.59), the prescription that starts will have the restriction as its purpose without the use of the particle *eva*.

[Answer:] [The rule] has as its purpose the accurate determination of what is then desired. Thus, it should be understood as "of [the verbal roots] *ṣṭuÑ* ('to praise') and those ending in [the causative suffix] *ṆiC* only before [the desiderative marker] *saN*." It must not be understood in such a way: "of [the verbal roots] *ṣṭuÑ* ('to praise') and those ending in [the causative suffix] *ṆiC* before [the desiderative marker] *saN* only." In this case it would not be: *tuṣṭāva* (3rd sg. perf. from *stu*).

{**Explanation:**
The present rule is formulated for restrictive purposes. The first example given by Patañjali is the form *sisikṣati* ('he wishes to sprinkle'). Its derivation is as follows:

(1) *ṣicA* (DhP VI:140) + *saN* + *ŚaP* + *tiP* (A. 3.1.7 *dhātoḥ karmaṇaḥ samānakartṛkād icchāyāṃ vā*, A. 3.1.68 *kartari śap*, A. 3.4.78 *tiptasjhisipthasthamibvasmastātāmjhathāsāthāmdhvamiḍvahimahiṅ*)
(2) (*ṣ* → *s*) *ic* + *sa* + *a* + *ti* (A. 6.1.64 *dhātvādeḥ ṣaḥ saḥ*)
sic + *sa* + *a* + *ti*
(3) *sic* + *sic* + *sa* + *a* + *ti* (A. 6.1.9 *sanyaṅoḥ*)
(4) *si* + *sic* + *sa* + *a* + *ti* (A. 7.4.60 *halādiḥ śeṣaḥ*)
(5) *si* + *sic* + *s* (*a* + *a* → *a*) + *ti* (A. 6.1.97 *ato guṇe*)
(6) *si* + *si* (*c* → *k*) + *sa* + *ti* (A. 8.2.30 *coḥ kuḥ*)
(7) *si* + *sik* + (*s* → *ṣ*) *a* + *ti* (A. 8.3.59 *ādeśapratyayayoḥ*)
sisikṣati

The verbal root is *ṣicA* (DhP VI:140) specified in the *Dhātupāṭha* with *ṣ*, which is further replaced by *s*. This *s*, being a substitute, could be subject to the *ṣ*-substitution by the rule A. 8.3.59. It does not happen because of the restriction in the present rule. This restriction is further enhanced by the particle *eva*, which Patañjali considers indispensable. The substitution only applies in the case of the verb *stu* and verbs ending in the suffix *ṆiC*, and only when the suffix *saN* follows. If the particle *eva* had not been used, we could understand the rule in two different ways: either the substitution would take place when *stu* or a causative verb alone is followed by *saN*, or when *saN* alone follows *stu* or a causative verb. Accepting the first view allows for the substitution in the form *sisikṣati*, while the second view blocks the substitution in the form *tuṣṭāva*. Its derivation is as follows:

(1) *ṣṭuÑ* (DhP II:34) + *tiP* (A. 3.4.78 *tiptasjhisipthasthamibvasmastātāmjhathāsāthāmdhvamiḍvahimahiṅ*)
(2) (*ṣ* → *s*) *tu* + *ti* (A. 6.1.64 *dhātvādeḥ ṣaḥ saḥ*)
(3) *stu* + *ṆaL* (A. 3.4.82 *parasmaipadānāṃ ṇalatususthalatusaṇalvamāḥ*)

(4) *stu* + *stu* + *a* (A. 6.1.8 *liṭi dhātor anabhyāsasya*)
(5) *tu* + *stu* + *a* (A. 7.4.60 *halādiḥ śeṣaḥ*)
(6) *tu* + *st* (*u* → *au*) + *a* (A. 7.2.115 *aco ñṇiti*)
(7) *tu* + *st* (*au* → *āv*) + *a* (A. 6.1.78 *eco 'yavāyāvaḥ*)
(8) *tu* + (*s* → *ṣ*) *tāv* + *a* (A. 8.3.61 *stautiṇyor eva ṣaṇyabhyāsāt*)
(9) *tu* + *ṣ* (*t* → *ṭ*) *āv* + *a* (A. 8.4.41 *ṣṭunā ṣṭuḥ*)
tuṣṭāva

In this case the verb *stu* is not followed by the suffix *saN* and therefore, if the particle *eva* had not been used in the rule, the substitution would not be possible.}

VMBh_1: III.441.11; VMBh_2: V.470.7

[Question:] Then what is the purpose [in using the expression] "before [the desiderative suffix] *saN*"?
[Answer:] [So that is does not apply in the form] *seṣīvyate* ('he sews intensely', 3rd sg. intens. of the verb *siv* ('to sew').

{**Explanation:**
The restriction regarding the desiderative suffix *saN* does not allow it to apply anywhere else. If the expression "before *saN*" had not been used, the restriction would apply to any suffix, and the forms such as *seṣīvyate* could not be derived correctly as the verbal root is not followed by *saN*. The lack of this expression would allow for the *ṣ*-substitution also in a reduplicated syllable and we would achieve the incorrect form **ṣeṣīvyate*. The derivation is as follows:

(1) *ṣivU* (DhP IV:2) + *yaṄ* + *ŚaP* + *tiP* (A. 3.1.22 *dhātor ekāco halādeḥ kriyāsamabhihāre yaṅ*, A. 3.1.68 *kartari śap*, A. 3.4.78 *tiptasjhisipthastham-ibvasmastātāmjhathāsāthāmdhvamiḍvahimahiṅ*)
(2) (*ṣ* → *s*) *iv* + *ya* + *a* + *ti* (A. 6.1.64 *dhātvādeḥ ṣaḥ saḥ*)
(3) *siv* + *ya* + *a* + *t* (*i* → *e*) (A. 3.4.79 *ṭita ātmanepadānāṃ ṭer e*)
(4) *siv* + *siv* + *ya* + *a* + *te* (A. 6.1.9 *sanyaṅoḥ*)
(5) *si* + *siv* + *ya* + *a* + *te* (A. 7.4.60 *halādiḥ śeṣaḥ*)
(6) *si* + *siv* + *y* (*a* + *a* → *a*) + *te* (A. 6.1.97 *ato guṇe*)
(7) *s* (*i* → *e*) + *siv* + *ya* + *te* (A. 7.4.82 *guṇo yaṅlukoḥ*)
(8) *se* + *s* (*i* → *ī*) *v* + *ya* + *te* (A. 8.2.77 *hali ca*)
(9) *se* + (*s* → *ṣ*) *īv* + *ya* + *te* (A. 8.3.59 *ādeśapratyayayoḥ*)
seṣīvyate}

VMBh_1: III.441.12; VMBh_2: V.470.7-8

[Question:] What is the necessity in making [the sounds *s* and *N*] cerebral [in *saN*]?
[Answer:] [If the sound *s* and *N*] are not cerebral, there must not be the restriction. [For example,] *suṣupsati* ('he wants to sleep', 3rd sg. desid. from *svap*).

{Explanation:
Patañjali explains that this rule will not apply when the general desiderative suffix *saN* is meant; it applies only when the suffix is changed to *ṣaṆ*. The example is *suṣupsati*:

(1) *ÑIṣvapA* (DhP II:59) + *saN* + *ŚaP* + *tiP* (A. 3.1.7 *dhātoḥ karmaṇaḥ samānakartṛkād icchāyāṃ vā*)
(2) (*ṣ* → *s*) *vap* + *sa* + *a* + *ti* (A. 6.1.64 *dhātvādeḥ ṣaḥ saḥ*)
(3) *s* (*v* → *u*) *ap* + *sa* + *a* + *ti* (A. 6.1.15 *vacisvapiyajādīnāṃ kiti*)
(4) *s* (*u* + *a* → *u*) *p* + *sa* + *a* + *ti* (A. 6.1.108 *saṃprasāraṇāc ca*)
(5) *sup* + *sup* + *sa* + *a* + *ti* (A. 6.1.9 *sanyaṅoḥ*)
(6) *su* + *sup* + *sa* + *a* + *ti* (A. 7.4.60 *halādiḥ śeṣaḥ*)
(7) *su* + *sup* + *s* (*a* + *a* → *a*) + *ti* (A. 6.1.97 *ato guṇe*)
(8) *su* + (*s* → *ṣ*) *up* + *sa* + *ti* (A. 8.3.59 *ādeśapratyayayoḥ*)
suṣupsati

The *saṃprasāraṇa* in the verbal stem *svap* takes place because the suffix *saN* is treated as if it had the marker *K* on the basis of the *sūtra* A. 1.2.8 *rudavidamuṣagrahisvapipracchaḥ sañ ca*.[464] Otherwise, vocalisation could not take place.}

VMBh_1: III.441.12-13; VMBh_2: V.470.8-9

[Question:] What is the necessity in presenting the suffix together with the *anubandha* [*N*]?
[Answer:] If there is only the word *ṣa*, there must not be a restriction. [For example,] *suṣupiṣa indram/indriyam* ("Power has slept")[465], *suṣupiṣa iha* ("You have slept here", *suṣupiṣa* is the 3rd sg. perf.).

{Explanation:
The derivation of the expression *suṣupiṣa indram/indriyam* is as follows:

---

[464] A. 1.2.8 *rudavidamuṣagrahisvapipracchaḥ sañ ca* || ("[The suffix *Ktvā*] and [the suffix] *saN* introduced after [the verbal roots] *rudA* ('to cry', DhP II:58), *vidA* ('to know', DhP II:51), *muṣA* ('to steal', DhP IX:58), *grahI* ('to grasp', DhP IX:61), *ÑIṣvapA* ('to sleep', DhP II:59) and *prachA* ('to ask', DhP VI:120) [function like suffixes marked with *K*].")

[465] According to Kielhorn's footnote, there should be *indriyam* instead of *indram*. See TS 6.1.4.7.

(1) *ÑIṣvapA* + *thās*
(2) (*ṣ* → *s*) *vap* +*thās* (A. 6.1.64 *dhātvādeḥ saḥ ṣaḥ*)
(3) *svap* + (*thās* → *se*) (A. 3.4.80 *thāsaḥ se*)
(4) *s* (*v* → *u*) *ap* + *se* (A. 6.1.15 *vacisvapiyajādīnāṃ kiti*)
(5) *s* (*u* + *a* → *u*) *p* + *se* (A. 6.1.108 *saṃprasāraṇāc ca*)
(6) *sup* + *sup* + *se* (A. 6.1.9 *sanyaṅoḥ*)
(7) *su* + *sup* + *se* (A. 7.4.60 *halādiḥ śeṣaḥ*)
(8) *su* + *sup* + *iṬ* + *se* (A. 7.2.35 *ārdhadhātukasyeḍ valādeḥ*)
(9) *susupis* (*e* + *ay*) + *indram* (A. 6.1.78 *eco 'yavāyāvaḥ*)
(10) *susupisa* (*y* → 0) + *indram* (A. 8.3.19 *lopaḥ śākalyasya*)
(11) *su* (*s* → *ṣ*) *upi* (*s* → *ṣ*) *a* + *indram* (A. 8.3.59 *ādeśapratyayayoḥ*)
suṣupiṣa indram

The ending *se* is treated as being marked with *KiT* by A. 1.2.5 *asaṃyogāl liṭ kit*,[466] which allows for vocalisation of A. 6.1.15 to take place in the root. Had the marker *N* not been used but the general suffix *ṣa* been understood, the general *sūtra* A. 8.3.59 would have been restricted by the present rule. Thus, the *ṣ*-substitute of the consonant *s* after the reduplication would not have taken place, because the verb is not the casuative.}

VMBh_1: III.441.14-15; VMBh_2: V.470.10-11

[Question:] What is he purpose [in saying] "after reduplication"?
[Answer:] The restriction should refer to the occurrence [of the sound *s*] in reduplication and the restriction must not refer to the occurrence [of the sound *s*] in an *upasarga*. [For example,] *abhiṣiṣikṣati* ('he wishes to sprinkle, consecrate', 3rd sg. desid. from *abhiṣic*).

{Explanation:
The argument raised here is that this restriction cannot apply to the verb form preceded by a preverb as in the example *abhiṣiṣikṣati* where the *ṣ*-substitution takes place, to the contrary of the verbal form *sisikṣati* (its derivation is shown above). However, this is not so because the *ṣ*-substitute prescribed for verbs with *upasarga*s is placed after the present rule, in A. 8.3.65, and as such it will be considered suspended. Kaiyaṭa (VMBh_2: V.470) explains that in this case, even though both rules refer to the same domain, one rule will be suspended with respect to another. It was mentioned before that in such cases it is the domain that is suspended with respect to another; the view that is not maintained here.}

---

466 A. 1.2.5 *asaṃyogāl liṭ kit* || ("[Substitutes ending of] *lIṬ* (perfect tense) function like those marked with *K* [when introduced after a vebal stem] not ending in a consonant cluster.")

VMBh_1: III.441.15-18; VMBh_2: V.470.11-471.1

[Answer:] This is not [like this]. The *ṣ*-substitute after an *upasarga* is suspended [with respect to the present rule]; due to its suspension there will be no restriction. This is the purpose then. The restriction should refer to that occurrence [of the sound *s*] which follows that reduplication which [takes place] before [the desiderative suffix] *saN*, and the restriction must not refer to that occurrence [of the sound *s*] which follows that reduplication which [takes place] before [the intensive suffix] *yaṄ*. [The desiderative] *soṣupiṣate* [is formed by adding the desiderative suffix] *saN* to [the intensive form] *soṣupyati*.

{Explanation:
The solution proposed here is that the term *abhyāsa* is qualified by *saN*, meaning that reduplication must be caused by the desiderative suffix *saN* and not, for example, by the intensive suffix *yaṄ*. In the form *soṣupiṣate* then, when *saN* is added but to a form ending in *yaṄ*, which primarily caused reduplication, this restriction will not apply.

(1) *ÑIṣvapA* + *yaṄ* + *ŚaP* + *tiP* (A. 3.1.22 *dhātor ekāco halādeḥ kriyāsamabhihāre yaṅ*)
(2) (*ṣ* → *s*) *vap* + *ya* + *a* + *ti* (A. 6.1.64 *dhātvādeḥ ṣaḥ saḥ*)
(3) *svap* + *ya* + *a* + *t* (*i* → *e*) (A. 3.4.79 *ṭita ātmanepadānāṃ ṭer e*)
(4) *s* (*v* → *u*) *ap* + *ya* + *a* + *te* (A. 6.1.19 *svapisyamivyeñāṃ yaṅi*)
(5) *s* (*u* + *a* → *u*) *p* + *ya* + *a* + *te* (A. 6.1.108 *saṃprasāraṇāc ca*)
(6) *sup* + *sup* + *ya* + *a* + *te* (A. 6.1.9 *sanyaṅoḥ*)
(7) *sup* + *sup* + *y* (*a* + *a* → *a*) + *te* (A. 6.1.97 *ato guṇe*)
(8) *su* + *sup* + *ya* + *te* (A. 7.4.60 *halādiḥ śeṣaḥ*)
(9) *s* (*u* → *o*) + *sup* + *ya* + *te* (A. 7.4.82 *guṇo yaṅlukoḥ*)
(10) *so* + (*s* → *ṣ*) *up* + *ya* + *te* (A. 8.3.59 *ādeśapratyayayoḥ*)
soṣupyate

(1) *soṣupya* + *saN* + *te*
(2) *soṣup* (*ya* → 0) + *sa* + *te* (A. 6.4.49 *yasya halaḥ*)
(3) *soṣup* + *iṬ* + *sa* + *te* (A. 7.2.35 *ārdhadhātukasyeḍ valādeḥ*)
(4) *soṣupi* (*s* → *ṣ*) *ate* (A. 8.3.59 *ādeśapratyayayoḥ*)
soṣupiṣate

Kaiyaṭa also points out that one could resort to the conflict between *antaraṅga* and *bahiraṅga* operation; the *ṣ*-substitution is internally conditioned and the restriction is externally conditioned, and as such the latter will be suspended. We can also treat the *ṣ*-substitute depending on the suffix *saN* as externally conditioned, which would yield the same result. The restriction will not apply when the verbal stem is followed by the suffix *saN* in its original form, or when the verbal stem is followed by *ṣaṆ* either.}

VMBh_1: III.441.18-21; VMBh_2: V.471.1-5

[Answer:] Alternatively, the restriction should refer to that occurrence [of the sound *s*] in reduplication and the restriction must not refer to that occurrence [of the sound *s*] in a verbal root. [For example:] *adhīṣiṣati* ('he wants to study', 3rd sg. desid. from *adhī*).
[Objection:] But it is said "before [the desiderative suffix] *saN*." It is not possible to understand [the expression] *ṣaṆi* as the locative [in the sense] of 'what follows', because reduplication is mentioned [to occur] in [the verbs] ending in [the suffixes] *saN* and *yaṆ* (A. 6.1.9 *sanyaṅoḥ*).
[Answer:] Therefore this is the locative [in the sense] of being [meaning] "when there is [the suffix] *ṣaṆ*." It results when it is the locative [in the sense] of being.

{**Explanation:**
The derivation of *adhīṣiṣati* is as follows:

(1) *adhi* + *iṄ* (DhP II:37) + *saN* + *ŚaP* + *tiP* (A. 3.1.7 *dhātoḥ karmaṇaḥ samānakartṛkād icchāyāṃ vā*)
(2) *adh* (*i* + *i* → *ī*) + *sa* + *a* + *ti* (A. 6.1.101 *akaḥ savarṇe dīrghaḥ*)
(3) *adhī* + *sa* + *sa* + *a* + *ti* (A. 6.1.2 *ajāder dvitīyasya*)
(4) *adhī* + *sa* + *s* (*a* + *a* → *a*) + *ti* (A. 6.1.97 *ato guṇe*)
(5) *adhī* + *s* (*a* → *i*) + *sa* + *ti* (A. 7.4.79 *sany ataḥ*)
adhī + *si* + *sa* + *ti*
(6) *adhī* + *si* + (*s* → *ṣ*) *a* + *ti* (A. 8.3.59 *ādeśapratyayayoḥ*)
(7) *adhī* + (*s* → *ṣ*) *i* + *ṣa* + *ti* (A. 8.3.59 *ādeśapratyayayoḥ*)
adhīṣiṣati

The basic meaning of the verb *i* is 'to move, to go' (*iṆ*, DhP II:36) but here it means 'to understand, to study' (*iṄ*, DhP II:37), and this is the reason why it is not changed to the form *gam*. The restriction is made by A. 2.4.47 *sani ca*.[467]
In the above example the consonant *s* of the suffix is changed into *ṣ* first by force of the vowel *i* of the *abhyāsa*; following which the vowel *i* of the root causes the *ṣ*-substitution in the reduplicated syllable. The restriction does not apply in this case because it is the suffix *saN* that is reduplicated.
Patañjali explains that the expression *ṣaṆi* cannot be understood as *parasaptamī*, because reduplication takes place of the root that ends in the suffixes *saN* and

[467] A. 2.4.47 *sani ca* || ("Also before [the desiderative suffix] *saN* [the substitute *gam* comes in place of the verbal stem *iṆ* when it does not signify 'understanding'].")

yaṄ (A. 6.1.9), so it is treated as a whole. The expression is to be understood as "when there is the suffix *saN*." Nāgeśa (VMBh_2: V.461) adds that the meaning of the *sūtra* will be the following: "If the *ṣ*-substitute takes place of a part of a whole ending in the suffix *saN*, when there is *saN*, then it takes place only in the verbs *stu* and those ending in the suffix *ṆiC*." If in the domain of the suffix *saN* the *parasaptamī* interpretation were accepted, we would not get the suffix *iṬ* in the form *adhīṣiṣati* because the whole stem has the form of the suffix *saN*, therefore that is no prior-posterior relation there. Had the expression *abhyāsāt* not been used, the sound *s* of the reduplicated syllable could not be changed into *ṣ* in the above example.}

{A. 8.3.62 *saḥ svidisvadisahīnāṃ ca*
[The sound] *s* comes in place of [the sound *s* occurring after the sounds *i*, *u* or those belonging to the consonantal group *kU* of the reduplicated syllable before the desiderative suffix *ṣaṆ* added] after [the verbal roots] *ÑIṣvidĀ* ('to sweat', DhP I:780, also *ṣvidA* DhP IV:79), *ṣvadA* ('to taste well', DhP I:18, X:263) and *ṣahA* ('to endure', DhP I:905) [ending in the causative suffix *ṆiC* in close proximity].
A. 8.3.63 *prāk sitād aḍvyavāye 'pi*
[The retroflex *ṣ* comes in place of the sound *s* which is not at the end of a *pada*] even with intervention of [the infix] *aṬ* [in the section] before A. 8.3.70 [in close proximity].} *These *sūtra*s were not commented upon by Patañjali.

A. 8.3.64 *sthādiṣv abhyāsena cābhyāsasya*
[The retroflex *ṣ* comes in place of the sound *s* which is not at the end of a *pada*] of [the verbal roots] *ṣṭhā* ('to stand', DhP I:975) etc. [even with intervention] of a reduplicated [syllable] as well as [it comes in place of the sound *s*] of a reduplicated [syllable in the section before A. 8.3.70 in close proximity].

VMBh_1: III.441.22-442.3; VMBh_2: V.472.1-5

[Question:] Why is this said?

1) The word *abhyāsa* with respect to [the verbal roots] *ṣṭhā* etc. is used in order to restrict.

[Answer:] This is the beginning of the restrictive meaning. [The substitution] should take place [of the sound *s*] of [the verbal roots] *ṣṭhā* etc. only. In this case it must not be: *abhisusūṣati* ('he wishes to press out [the juice]', 3rd sg. desid.).

{Explanation:

This rule has the purpose of both a *vidhi* and a *niyama*. It prescribes the *ṣ*-substitute in the verbal stems *ṣṭhā* etc. when reduplication intervenes, and restricts it to the consonant *s* appearing in the reduplicated syllable of those stems. The rule will apply to those verbal stems that are specified in the *sūtra*s from A. 8.3.65 to A. 8.3.70. In the case of *abhisisūṣati* the substitution of *s* in the reduplicated syllable could take place by A. 8.3.65 had it not been for the present restriction. The *ṣ*-substitute in the stem is blocked by A. 8.3.61. The derivation is as follows:

(1) *abhi* + *ṣūṄ* (DhP IV:24) + *saN* + *ŚaP* + *tiP* (A. 3.1.7 *dhātoḥ karmaṇaḥ samānakartṛkād icchāyāṃ vā*, A. 3.1.68 *kartari śap*, A. 3.4.78 *tiptasjhisipthasthamibvasmastātāmjhathāsāthāmdhvamiḍvahimahiṅ*)
(2) *abhi* + (*ṣ* → *s*) *ū* + *sa* + *a* + *ti* (A. 44 *dhātvādeḥ ṣaḥ saḥ*)
(3) *abhi* + *sū* + *sū* + *sa* + *a* + *ti* (A. 6.1.9 *sanyaṅoḥ*)
(4) *abhi* + *s* (*ū* → *u*) + *sū* + *sa* + *a* + *ti* (A. 7.4.59 *hrasvaḥ*)
(5) *abhi* + *su* + *sū* + *s* (*a* + *a* → *a*) + *ti* (A. 6.1.97 *ato guṇe*)
(6) *abhi* + *su* + *sū* + (*s* → *ṣ*) *a* + *ti* (A. 8.3.59 *ādeśapratyayayoḥ*)
abhisusūṣati}

VMBh_1: III.442.4-6; VMBh_2: V.472.6-9

[Question:] Then why is "when [with intervention] of a reduplicated [syllable]" said?

2) [It is said] in order to also [include those verbal roots that] are not [listed with the sound] *ṣ* in the teaching (i.e., in the *Dhātupāṭha*) when there is intervention of that [i.e., reduplication].

[Answer:] When there is intervention of that, [namely] when there is intervention of a reduplicated [syllable, the substitution] should also refer to [those verbal roots that] are not [listed with the sound] *ṣ* in the teaching. [For example,] *abhiṣiṣeṇayiṣati* ('he wishes to march with the army', 3rd sg. desid.).

{**Explanation:**
The substitution prescribed in this *sūtra* also applies in the case of such verbal roots that are not listed in the *Dhātupāṭha* with the consonant *ṣ*. The form given as an example is *abhiṣiṣeṇayati* ('he wishes to march with the army'). The verb *senaya* comes from the noun *senā* ('army') which in turn is derived via the *Uṇādi* suffix *na* (US 293; 3.10[468]) from the verbal root *ṣiÑ* ('to bind'). This verbal root

---

[468] US 293 (3.10) *kr̥̄vr̥jr̥̄sidrupanyanisvapibhyo nit* || ("[The suffix *na*] comes after [the verbal roots] *kr̥̄* ('to scatter', DhP VI:116), *vr̥Ñ* ('to choose', DhP V:8, IX:16), *jr̥̄* ('to become old', DhP

is stated in the *Dhātupāṭha* with *ṣ* which is then replaced by *s* (see A. 6.1.64). Thus the verb *senaya* is not originally presented with the retroflex *ṣ*.

(1) *abhi + senā + ṆiC + saN + ŚaP + tiP* (A. 3.1.25 *satyāpapāśarūpavīṇatūla-ślokasenālomatvacavarmavarṇacūrṇacurādibhyo ṇic*, A. 3.1.7 *dhātoḥ karmaṇaḥ samānakartṛkād icchāyāṃ vā*, A. 3.1.68 *kartari śap*, A. 3.4.78 *tiptasjhisip-thasthamibvasmastātāmjhathāsāthāmdhvamiḍvahimahiṅ*)
(2) *abhi + senā + i + iṬ + sa + a + ti* (A. 7.2.35 *ārdhadhātukasyeḍ valādeḥ*)
(3) *abhi + sen (ā → 0) + i + i + sa + a + ti* (A. 6.4.64 *āto lopa iṭi ca*)
(4) *abhi + sen + sen + i + i + sa + a + ti* (A. 6.1.9 *sanyaṅoḥ*)
(5) *abhi + se (n → 0) + sen + i + i + sa + a + ti* (A. 7.4.60 *halādiḥ śeṣaḥ*)
(6) *abhi + s (e → i) + sen + i + i + sa + a + ti* (A. 7.4.59 *hrasvaḥ*)
(7) *abhi + si + sen + i + i + s (a + a → a) + ti* (A. 6.1.97 *ato guṇe*)
(8) *abhi + si + sen + (i → e) + i + sa + ti* (A. 7.3.84 *sārvadhātukārdhādhātukayoḥ*)
(9) *abhi + si + sen + (e → ay) + i + sa + ti* (A. 6.1.78 *eco 'yavāyāvaḥ*)
(10) *abhi + si + sen + ay + i + (s → ṣ) a + ti* (A. 8.3.59 *ādeśapratyayayoḥ*)
(11) *abhi + (s → ṣ) i + (s → ṣ) en + ay + i + ṣa + ti* (A. 8.3.64 *sthādiṣv abhyāsena cābhyāsasya*)
(12) *abhi + ṣi + ṣe (n → ṇ) + ay + i + ṣa + ti* (A. 8.4.1 *raṣābhyāṃ no ṇaḥ samānapade*)
abhiṣiṣeṇayiṣati}

VMBh_1: III.442.7-8; VMBh_2: V.472.10-12

3) It is in order to [allow the substitution in the case of reduplicated verbal roots] ending in the vowel *a*, and in order to prohibit it before [the desiderative suffix] *ṣaṆ*.

[Bhāṣya:] It is in order to [allow the substitution in the case of reduplicated verbal roots ending in] the vowel *a*, e.g., *abhitaṣṭhau* ('he has stepped upon', 3rd sg. perf. from *abhiṣṭhā*). It is in order to prohibit it before the desiderative suffix] *ṣaṆ* (A. 8.3.61), e.g., *abhiṣiṣikṣati* ('he wishes to sprinkle, consecrate', 3rd sg. desid. from *abhiṣic*).

{**Explanation:**
In the example *abhitaṣṭhau* the consonant *s* could not be replaced by *ṣ* based on A. 8.3.59 because it is preceded by *a*. This rule makes the substitution possible. The derivation is as follows:

IX:24, X:272), *ṣiÑ* ('to bind', DhP V:2), *panA* ('to praise', DhP I:467), *anA* ('to breathe', DhP II:61) and *ÑIṣvapA* ('to sleep', DhP II:59) and it is treated as if marked with N.")

(1) *abhi* + *ṣṭhā* + *tiP*
(2) *abhi* + *ṣṭhā* + *ṆaL* (A. 3.4.82 *parasmaipadānāṃ ṇalatususthalatusaṇalvamāḥ*)
(3) *abhi* + (*ṣ* → *s*) *ṭhā* + *a* (A. 6.1.64 *dhātvādeḥ ṣaḥ saḥ*)
(4) *abhi* + *sthā* + (*a* → *au*) (A. 7.1.34 *āta au ṇalaḥ*)
(5) *abhi* + *sthā* + *sthā* + *au* (A. 6.1.8 *liṭi dhātor anabhyāsasya*)
(6) *abhi* + *sth* (*ā* → *a*) + *sthā* + *au* (A. 7.4.59 *hrasvaḥ*)
(7) *abhi* + (*s* → 0) *tha* + *sthā* + *au* (A. 7.4.61 *śarpūrvāḥ khayaḥ*)
(8) *abhi* + *tha* + *sth* (*ā* + *au* → *au*) (A. 6.1.88 *vṛddhir eci*)
(9) *abhi* + *tha* + (*s* → *ṣ*) *thau* (A. 8.3.64 *sthādiṣv abhyāsena cābhyāsasya*)
(10) *abhi* + *tha* + *ṣ* (*t* → *ṭ*) *hau* (A. 8.4.41 *ṣṭunā ṣṭuḥ*)
(11) *abhi* + (*th* → *t*) *a* + *ṣṭhau* (A. 8.4.54 *abhyāse car ca*)
abhitaṣṭhau

The example *abhiṣiṣikṣati* was presented under the rule A. 8.3.61.}

A. 8.3.65 *upasargāt sunotisuvatisyatistautistobhatisthāsenayasedhasicasañjasvañjām*

[The retroflex *ṣ* comes in place of the sound *s* which is not at the end of a *pada*] of [the verbal roots] *ṣuÑ* ('to press out, extract', DhP III:1), *ṣū* ('to impel', DhP VI:115), *ṣo* ('to terminate', DhP IV:39), *ṣṭuÑ* ('to praise', DhP II:34), *ṣṭubhU* ('to chant, utter', DhP I:421), *ṣṭhā* ('to stand', DhP I:975), *senaya* ('to march with an army'), *ṣidhA* ('to go, move', DhP I:48), *ṣicA* ('to pour out', DhP VI:140), *ṣañjA* ('to attach', DhP I:1036) and *ṣvañjA* ('to embrace, clasp', DhP I:1025) after an *upasarga* [containing the sounds *i*, *u* even with the intervention of the infix *aṬ* in close proximity].

VMBh_1: III.442.9-21; VMBh_2: V.473.1-474.4

1) With respect to the *ṣ*-substitute [in a verbal root] after an *upasarga*, [the *upasarga*] *nis* should be listed because it does not end in either *i* or *u*.

[Bhāṣya:] With respect to the *ṣ*-substitute [in a verbal root] after an *upasarga*, [the *upasarga*] *nis* should be listed. [For example,] *niḥṣuṇoti* ('he presses', 3rd sg. praes. indic.), *niḥṣiñcati* ('he pours away', 3rd sg. indic.).
[Question:] Why is it not obtained [by the text of the *sūtra*]?
[Answer:] Due to its not ending in either *i* or *u*. The *ṣ*-substitute is said [to occur] after an *upasarga* ending in [the vowels] *i* or *u* and [the *upasarga*] *nis* does not end in either *i* or *u*.

2) Alternatively, due to the ṣ-substitute depending on a single sound, an *upasarga* and a verbal root are its [i.e., of *iṆ*] attributes.

[Bhāṣya:] An alternative should be mentioned.
[Question:] Why?
[Answer:] Due to the ṣ-substitute depending on a single sound. The ṣ-substitute [is the operation] depending on a single sound. An *upasarga* and a verbal root are its attributes. It is not understood in such a way: "after an *upasarga* ending in [the vowels] *i* or *u*."
[Question:] How then?
[Answer:] Of [the vowels] *i* or *u* followed by the sound *s*, if these [vowels] *i* or *u* are a part of an *upasarga*; if this sound *s* is a part of [the verbal roots] *sunoti* etc. Therefore, it is just achieved when there is intervention of [a sound denoted by] *śaR* (i.e., sibilants, see A. 8.3.58.).
[Objection:] If it is so, the connection between a verbal root and an *upasarga* has not been established.
[Question:] What is the problem with that?
[Answer:] Here it would result as well: *visecako grāmaḥ* [means that] from this village clouds have gone away (lit., it is the village with the clouds disappeared).
[Answer:] But the connection between a verbal root and an *upasarga* has been established.
[Question:] How?
[Answer:] We will characterise an *upasarga* by [the verbal roots] *sunoti* etc.: [the vowels] *i* or *u* which are [a part] of an *upasarga* which is before [the verbal roots] *sunoti* etc.

{**Explanation:**
Kaiyaṭa explains (VMBh_2: V.473-474) that we can see two kinds of sound dependancy here; the sounds denoted by *iṆ* which are to qualify a preverb and the sound *s* of a verbal root. The sounds *iṆ* constitute the cause of the substitution while *s* is the substituend. They cannot be a qualifier to the consonant *s* of a *dhātu*. The objection is raised that if there is no established connection between an *upasarga* and a verbal root, the ṣ-substitution would be extended to the examples such as *visecako grāmaḥ*. Patañjali's answer to this is a preverb will be qualified by the verbal roots listed; so the sounds denoted by *iṆ* have to be a part of such an *upasarga* that is followed by a verbal root for the ṣ-substitution to take place.
However, if *s* is not qualified by the verbs *sunoti* etc., the ṣ-substitution will take place in other verbs as well. Thus, the substitute of *s* following *iṆ* which is a part of an *upasarga* to the verbs *sunoti* etc. will take place. When the consonant *s* is a part of a preverb, it will not undergo the substitution on the basis of this rule

because the *adhikāra apadāntasya* still governs here (see A. 8.3.55), and the preverbs such as *nis* and *dus* have *s* as their final.
How is it possible that the expression *iṆ* is qualified by the term *upasarga* if the latter is presented in the ablative while the former in the genitive (*iṇaḥ* and *upasargāt* respectively)? Kaiyaṭa says that there is no fault here when the *ṣ*-substitution is recognised as referring to an *s* following a sound denoted by *iṆ* residing in an *upasarga* that precedes the verbs *sunoti* etc.}

VMBh_1: III.442.23-443.2; VMBh_2: V.474.5-8

3) With respect to the ṣ-substitute in [the verbal roots] *sunoti* etc. the addition [should be made] of [those stems] ending in [the causative suffix] *ṆiC*, due to superfluity.

[Bhāṣya:] With respect to the *ṣ*-substitute in [the verbal roots] *sunoti* etc. the addition should be made of [those stems] ending in [the causative suffix] *ṆiC*. [For example,] *abhiṣāvayati* ('he makes to press out', 3rd sg. caus.).
[Question:] Why?
[Answer:] Due to superfluity. Having said that [the expression] *sunotyādi* is excessive, the *ṣ*-substitute would not result in [the verbal roots] *sunoti* etc. after an *upasarga*.

{**Explanation:**
The problem with causative verbs is similar to the example *visecako grāmaḥ*. Here the *ṣ*-substitute does not take place because a preverb is added not to the verbal root *sic* but to the form *secaka*. Thus, it is implied that in the form *abhiṣāvayati* the *upasarga* will be added to the causative form *sāvaya* and not directly to the verbal root *ṣic*, which would exclude the form from undergoing the substitution. Therefore, as the *vārttika* proposes, a specification should be made for those verbs that end in the causative suffix *ṆiC*. We find the superfluity here due to the additional meaning when the attributive meaning of the suffix is concerned. The suffix *ṆiC* bears the meaning of a causal agent (A. 3.1.26 *hetumati ca* || "[The suffix *ṆiC*] also comes [after a verbal stem] to denote a causal agent"). Nārāyaṇa (MPV X.449) elaborates on this and says that when a preverb joins a verbal stem, it qualifies the meaning of that stem; in the case of stems ending in the suffix *ṆiC* due to the qualifying meaning of the suffix ('causing'), the *ṣ*-substitution should not take place after preverbs added to stems.}

VMBh_1: III.443.3-4; VMBh_2: V.474.9-11

4) Alternatively, because the part is identical.

[Bhāṣya:] An alternative should be mentioned.
[Question:] Why?
[Answer:] Because the part is identical. The part here is the same.

{Explanation:
The solution to the problem raised in the previous *vārttika* is the following: an *upasarga* is added to a part of a unit and not to the entire element ending in the suffix *ṆiC*. In other words, it is added to a verbal stem, to which the causative suffix is attached afterwards, which gives the possibility to apply the *ṣ*-substitute. An *upasarga* qualifies the meanings of the verbs *sunoti* etc., not those ending in the suffix *ṆiC*.}

VMBh_1: III.443.5-6; VMBh_2: V.474.12-14

5) But [there should be] prohibition in the case of a denominative root.

[Bhāṣya:] But prohibition should be mentioned in the case of a denominative root. [For example,] *abhisāvakīyati* or *parisāvakīyati* ('he wants the young of an animal').

{Explanation:
The example *abhisāvakīyati* is different from the preceding ones. The preverb *abhi* is added to the form *sāvakīya* that is derived from the noun *sāvaka*, which in turn is derived from the verb *su*. There is, though, no direct connection between the *upasarga* and the verbal root. The derivation is as follows.

(1) *ṣu* + *ṆvuL* (A. 3.1.133 *ṇvultṛcau*)
(2) (*ṣ* → *s*) *u* + *ṆvuL* (A. 6.1.64 *dhātvādeḥ ṣaḥ saḥ*)
(3) *su* + (*vu* → *aka*) (A. 7.1.1 *yuvor anākau*)
(4) *s* (*u* → *au*) + *aka* (A. 7.2.115 *aco ñṇiti*)
(6) *s* (*au* → *āv*) + *aka* (A. 6.1.78 *eco 'yavāyāvaḥ*)
sāvaka
(7) *sāvaka* + *KyaC* + *ŚaP* + *tiP* (A. 3.1.8 *supa ātmanaḥ kyac*, A. 3.1.68 *kartari śap*, A. 3.4.78 *tiptasjhisipthasthamibvasmastātāmjhathāsāthāmdhvamiḍvahi-mahiṅ*)
(8) *sāvak* (*a* → *ī*) + *ya* + *a* + *ti* (A. 7.4.33 *kyaci ca*)
(9) *sāvakī* + *y* (*a* + *a* → *a*) + *ti* (A. 6.1.97 *ato guṇe*)
sāvakīyati
abhi + *sāvakīyati* → *abhisāvakīyati*}

VMBh_1: III.443.7-12; VMBh_2: V.474.15-475.2

6) Alternatively, because it is not an *upasarga*.

[Bhāṣya:] An alternative should be mentioned.
[Question:] What is the reason?
[Answer:] Because it is not an *upasarga*. The terms *gati* and *upasarga* are [used] with respect to that which has become connected with an action (i.e., the verb) and in this case there is no connection with an action with respect to [the verb] *sunoti*.
[Question:] With what then?
[Answer:] [It is] with respect to [the verb] *sāvakīyati*.
[Objection:] In this case then it would not result either: *abhiṣāvayati* ('he moistens', 3rd sg. caus. from *abhiṣu*). In this case there is no connection with an action with respect to [the verb] *sunoti* either.
[Question:] With what then?
[Answer:] [It is] with respect to [the verb] *sāvayati*.
[Bhāṣya:] There is a connection with an action with respect to [the verb] *sunoti* here.
[Question:] How?
[Answer:] That is not intended in such a way: *sunu abhi*.
[Question:] How then?
[Answer:] That is intended towards the action characterized by the *upasarga*: *abhiṣuṇu*.

{**Explanation:**
Kaiyaṭa explains that we can say that the preverb *abhi* is not the preverb to the verb *sunoti* in its final form because the meaning 'desire' is in the suffix *KyaC*. If we were to accept that the *upasarga* comes first, the form **abhiṣāvakīya* could be derived (with the *ṣ*-substitution); we would add the *upasarga* first and then the suffixes *ṆvuL* and *KyaC* would follow.
In the case of *abhiṣuṇoti* the action is qualified by the *upasarga* and it is not known in common usage to put the preverb separately. Nāgeśa (VMBh_2: V.474) adds that *upasarga*s are qualifiers to the base of verbal roots, not to the forms already ending in other suffixes such as the causative suffix *ṆiC*. Kaiyaṭa also states that, if preverbs qualified the meaning of the *ṆiC* suffix, there would be no *ṣ*-substitution. If, however, they qualify the action of the verbal root, there is no obstacle any more.}

{**A. 8.3.66 *sadir aprateḥ***
[The retroflex *ṣ* comes in place of the sound *s* which is not at the end of a *pada*] of [the verbal root] *ṣadĀ* ('to sit down', DhP VI:133) [after an *upasarga* ending in the sounds *i* or *u* even with intervention of the infix *aṬ* in

close proximity] with the exception of [the *upasarga*] *prati*.} *This *sūtra* was not commented upon by Patañjali.

A. 8.3.67 *stambheḥ*

[The retroflex *ṣ* comes in place of the sound *s* which is not at the end of a *pada*] of [the verbal root] *stanbhU* ('to support', DhP IX:7) [after an *upasarga* ending in the sounds *i* or *u* even with intervention of the infix *aṬ* in close proximity].

VMBh_1: III.443.13-18; VMBh_2: V.475.3-9

[Question:] Does [the expression] "with the exception of [the *upasarga*] *prati*" continue or is it finished?
[Answer:] He says it is finished.
[Question:] How is that known?
[Answer:] Through the force of dividing the rule. Otherwise, one should just say: "[The retroflex *ṣ* comes in place of the sound *s* which is not at the end of a *pada*] of [the verbal roots] *ṣadĀ* ('to sit down') and *stanbhU* ('to support) [after an *upasarga* ending in the sounds *i* or *u* even with intervention of the infix *aṬ* in close proximity] with the exception of [the *upasarga*] *prati*."
[Answer:] There is another purpose in dividing the rule.
[Question:] What?
[Answer:] He will say [the *sūtra*] A. 8.3.68; it should take place only in [the verbal root] *stanbhU*, it must not be in [the verbal root] *ṣadĀ*.
[Bhāṣya:] This is not the purpose. Even if [the verbal roots] were in one rule, [the *ṣ*-substitute] would take place in this one to which [the meanings] 'depending, resting upon' (*ālambana*) and 'proximity' (*āvidūrya*) apply.
[Question:] And to which do [the meanings] 'depending, resting upon' (*ālambana*) and 'proximity' (*āvidūrya*) apply?
[Answer:] To [the verbal root] *stanbhU*.

{**Explanation:**
This rule is not commented upon by either of the commentators of Patañjali. The only problem appears to be whether the condition *aprateḥ* ("not after the *upasarga prati*") continues from the previous rule. It is decided that this is not so due to formulating two separate rules. The example for this *sūtra* can be *abhiṣṭabhnāti* ('he rests', 3rd sg. indic.).

(1) *abhi* + *stanbh* + *Śnā* + *tiP* (A. 3.1.82 *stanbhustunbhuskanbhuskunbhuskuñbhyaḥ śnuś ca*)
(2) *abhi* + *sta* (*n* → 0) *bh* + *nā* + *ti* (A. 6.4.24 *aniditāṃ hala upadhāyāḥ kṅiti*)
(3) *abhi* + (*s* → *ṣ*) *tabh* + *nā* + *ti* (A. 8.3.67 *stambheḥ*)

(4) *abhi* + *ṣ* (*t* → *ṭ*) *abh* + *nā* + *ti* (A. 8.4.41 *ṣṭunā ṣṭuḥ*) *abhiṣṭabhnāti*}

{A. 8.3.68 *avāc cālambanāvidūryayoḥ*
[The retroflex *ṣ* comes in place of the sound *s* which is not at the end of a *pada*] of [the verbal root *stanbhU* ('to support', DhP IX:7)] after [the *upasarga*] *ava* when [the meanings are 'depending, resting upon' (*ālambana*) and 'proximity' (*āvidūrya*) in close proximity].
A. 8.3.69 *veś ca svano bhojane*
[The retroflex *ṣ* comes in place of the sound *s* which is not at the end of a *pada*] of [the verbal root] *svanA* ('to sound', DhP I:879)] after [the *upasargas ava*] and *vi* when [the meaning] is 'eating' (*bhojana*) [even with intervention of a reduplicated syllable or the infix *aṬ* in close proximity].
A. 8.3.70 *parinivibhyaḥ sevasitasayasivusahasuṭstusvañjām*
[The retroflex *ṣ* comes in place of the sound *s* which is not at the end of a *pada*] of [the verbal formations] *ṣevṚ* ('to serve', DhP I:530), *sita* ('bound'), *saya* ('binding'), *ṣivU* ('to sew', DhP IV:2), *ṣahA* ('to endure', DhP I:905), *ṣṭuÑ* ('to praise', DhP II: 34), *ṣvañjA* ('to embrace', DhP I:1025) and [the infix] *suṬ* after [the *upasargas*] *pari*, *ni* and *vi* [even with intervention of the infix *aṬ* in close proximity].
A. 8.3.71 *sivādānāṃ vāḍvyavāye 'pi*
[The retroflex *ṣ*] usually [comes in place of the sound *s* which is not at the end of a *pada*] of [the verbal roots] *ṣivU* ('to sew', DhP IV:2) etc. [after the *upasargas pari*, *ni* and *vi*] even with intervention of the infix *aṬ* [in close proximity].} *These *sūtras* were not commented upon by Patañjali.

A. 8.3.72 *anuviparyabhinibhyaḥ syandater aprāniṣu*
[The retroflex *ṣ* usually comes in place of the sound *s* which is not at the end of a *pada*] of [the verbal root] *syandŪ* ('to flow, to rush', DhP I:798) after [the *upasargas*] *anu*, *vi*, *pari*, *abhi* and *ni* when it does not refer to a living creature (*prāṇin*) [in close proximity].

VMBh_1: III.443.19-23; VMBh_2: V.475.10-15

[Question:] But how should it be in the case when it is a living and not living creature [at the same time]? [Should it be] *anuṣyandete matsyodake* or *anusyandete matsyodake* ('the fish and water, both, flow')?
[Answer:] If [this meaning] 'not a living creature' is established by the prescription, [then] there should be the *ṣ*-substitute when we establish: "There is not a living creature here". But [if this meaning] 'a living creature' is prohibited' [then] there should be prohibition [of the substitution] when we establish: "There is a living creature here".

[Question:] What is then the real nature of the meaning here?
[Answer:] The gods are able to know that.

{**Explanation:**
The word *devāḥ* used in the final sentence of Patañjali's commentary refers to scholars and not to divine beings. The prohibition *apraniṣu* can be interpreted in two different ways. It can be treated as *paryudāsa* negation, meaning that the *ṣ*-substitution applies in contexts other than living creatures. Or it can be treated as *prasajya* negation, meaning that it does not apply in the case of words expressing living creatures. The former interpretation has been accepted by Kaiyaṭa and later commentators, as the latter would exclude the form *anuṣyandete matsyodake*. The optional *ṣ*-substitute would not be possible and the only correct form would be *anusyandete matsyodake*. The *paryudāsa* interpretation allows us to use the *sūtra* A. 2.4.6 *jātir aprāṇinām* || ("[A *dvandva* compound is treated as though it denoted a single thing] when the constituent members denote the names of species of inanimate beings"). Therefore, if only one member of a compound denotes a non-living creature, the substitution can apply in a verbal form that goes with it; as in the example shown where *matsya* denotes a living creature but *udaka* does not.}

{**A. 8.3.73 *veḥ skander aniṣṭhāyām***
[The retroflex *ṣ* usually comes in place of the sound *s* which is not at the end of a *pada*] of [the verbal root] *skandIR* ('to leap', DhP I:1028) after [the *upasarga*] *vi* when it is not before [the suffixes termed] *niṣṭhā* [in close proximity].} *This *sūtra* was not commented upon by Patañjali.

A. 8.3.74 *pareś ca*
[The retroflex *ṣ* usually comes in place of the sound *s* which is not at the end of a *pada* of the verbal root *skandIR* ('to leap', DhP I:1028)] also after [the *upasarga*] *pari* [in close proximity].

VMBh_1: III.444.1-4; VMBh_2: V.476.1-4

[Question: Does [the expression] "not before [the suffixes termed] *niṣṭhā*" continue or is it discontinued?
[Answer:] He says it is discontinued.
[Question:] How is that known?
[Answer:] Through the force of dividing the rule. Otherwise though, it would only be said: "Of [the verbal root] *skandIR* also after [the *upasargas*] *vi* and *pari*, not before [the suffixes termed] *niṣṭhā*."

{**Explanation:**

This *sūtra* was not commented upon by Patañjali's commentators either. The only problem that appears is the use of the suffix termed *niṣṭhā*; its use is discontinued here. Therefore, we would get both forms *pariṣkaṇṇa* and *pariskanna*, as the substitution is optional. The basic suffix added here is *Kta* (=*ta*), which is later replaced with *na* by A. 8.2.42 *radābhyāṃ niṣṭhāto naḥ pūrvasya ca daḥ* and by the same rule the final *d* is also substituted with *n*. We achieve the form *pariskann* + *na*. The final *n* of the stem is then deleted by A. 8.2.23 *saṃyogāntasya lopaḥ* and we achieve the form *pariskanna*. First, we can optionally replace *s* with *ṣ* and then the *ṇ*-substitution follows twice by A. 8.4.1 *raṣābhyāṃ no ṇaḥ samānapade* and A. 8.4.41 *ṣṭunā ṣṭuḥ*. This is how we obtain the second form *pariṣkaṇṇa*.}

{A. 8.3.75 *pariskandaḥ prācyabharateṣu*
[The word] *pariskanda* ('a servant running by the side of a carriage') [is formed in an irregular way, without the *ṣ*-substitute] among the Eastern Bharatas.
A. 8.3.76 *sphuratisphulatyor nirnivibhyaḥ*
[The retroflex *ṣ* usually comes in place of the sound *s* which is not at the end of a *pada*] of [the verbal roots] *sphurA* ('to tremble, quiver', DhP VI:95) and *sphulA* ('to tremble, throb', DhP VI:96) after [the *upasargas*] *nir*, *ni* and *vi* [in close proximity].
A. 8.3.77 *veḥ skabhnāter nityam*
[The retroflex *ṣ*] necessarily [comes in place of the sound *s* which is not at the end of a *pada*] of [the verbal root] *skanbhU* ('to support', DhP IX:7) after [the *upasarga*] *vi* [in close proximity].} *These *sūtra*s were not commented upon by Patañjali.

A. 8.3.78 *iṇaḥ ṣīdhvaṃluṅliṭāṃ dho 'ṅgāt*
[The retroflex sound *ḍh*] comes in place of [the sound] *dh* of [the *l*-substitute of *lIṄ* (potentialis)] *ṣīdhvam* and of [the *l*-substitutes of] *lUṄ* (aorist) and *lIṬ* (perfect) after the *aṅga* stem ending in [sound denoted by] *iṆ* (i.e., *i* and *u*) [in close proximity].
A. 8.3.79 *vibhāṣeṭaḥ*
[The retroflex sound *ḍh*] rarely [comes in place of the sound *dh* of the *l*-substitute of *lIṄ* (potentialis) *ṣīdhvam* and of the *l*-substitutes of *lUṄ* (aorist) and *lIṬ* (perfect)] preceded by [the infix] *iṬ* [after the *aṅga* stem ending in a sound denoted by *iṆ* (i.e., *i* and *u*) in close proximity].

VMBh_1: III.444.5-12; VMBh_2: V.476.5-12

[Question:] What is the purpose in using [the expression] "ending in [a sound denoted by] *iṆ* (i.e., *i* and *u*)"?

1) [The expression] "ending in [a sound denoted by] *iṆ* (i.e., *i* and *u*)" is used in the context of the *ḍh*-substitute in order to stop [the substitution] after [a sound belonging to] the *kU*-group.

[Bhāṣya:] [The expression] "ending in [a sound denoted by] *iṆ*" is used so that there would not be the *ḍh*-substitute after [a sound belonging to] the *kU*-group.[469] [For example,] *pakṣīdhvam*, *yakṣīdhvam* (2nd pl. prec. from *pac* 'to cook' and *yaj* 'to sacrifice').
[Question:] However, is this expression "ending in [a sound denoted by] *iṆ*" a qualifier to the suffix, [meaning "that] sound *dh* which is of [the *l*-substitute of *lIṄ*] *ṣīdhvam* and of [the *l*-substitutes] of *lUṄ* and *lIṬ* following [a sound denoted by] *iṆ*"; or is it a qualifier to the sound *dh*, [meaning that the substitution takes place] "of this sound *dh* which follows [a sound denoted by] *iṆ* if this sound *dh* is of [the *l*-substitute of *lIṄ*] *ṣīdhvam* and of [the *l*-substitutes] of *lUṄ* and *lIṬ*"?

{**Explanation:**
The expression *iṇaḥ* has to be repeated in the present *sūtra*; otherwise, it would continue together with *koḥ* from A. 8.3.57 *iṇkoḥ*. The separation of these two expressions would not be possible. What we need here, however, is the continuation of *iṇaḥ* only. This specification is made so that the *ḍh*-substitute did not apply in the forms such as *pakṣīdhvam* and *yakṣīdhvam*.

(1) *pac* + *lIṄ*
(2) *pac* + *ŚaP* + *dhvam* (A. 3.1.68 *kartari śap*, A. 3.4.78 *tiptasjhisipthasthamibvasmastātāmjhathāsāthāmdhvamiḍvahimahiṅ*)
(3) *pac* + *sīyUṬ* + *dhvam* (A. 3.4.102 *liṅaḥ sīyuṭ*)
pac + *sīy* + *dhvam*
(4) *pac* + *sī* (*y* → 0) + *dhvam* (A. 6.1.66 *lopo vyor vali*)
(5) *pa* (*c* → *k*) + *sī* + *dhvam* (A. 8.2.30 *coḥ kuḥ*)
(6) *pak* + (*s* → *ṣ*) *ī* + *dhvam* (A. 8.3.59 *ādeśapratyayayoḥ*)
pakṣīdhvam

In the above example the consonant *dh* appears not only after the vowel *ī* but also after the consonant *k*; therefore the substitution cannot take place.}

VMBh_1: III.444.13-16; VMBh_2: V.476.13-16

[Question:] What is the difference in this case?

---

[469] See A. 8.3.57.

2) With respect to that, when the suffix follows, [there would be no] *ḍh*-substitute after [the infix] *iṬ* before [the *l*-substitutes of] *lIṬ* due to it (i.e., the infix *iṬ*) [being added] at the beginning of what follows.

[Answer:] With respect to that, when the suffix follows, the *ḍh*-substitute would not result after [the infix] *iṬ* [in such examples as] *luluviḍhve*, *luluvidhve* (2nd pl. perf. from *lū* – 'to cut, divide').
[Question:] What is the reason?
[Answer:] Due to [it being added] at the beginning of what follows. [The infix] *iṬ* [is added] at the beginning of what follows.
[Answer:] It will be from the statement. There is a purpose in the statement.
[Question:] What?
[Answer:] [The forms] *alaviḍhvam*, *alavidhvam* (2nd pl. aor. from *lū* – 'to cut, divide').
[Proposition:] Let it be then that [the expression "ending in a sound denoted by *iṆ*" is] a qualifier to the sound *dh*.

{**Explanation:**
As Nārāyaṇa explains, there are two views regarding a qualifier and a qualificand. According to the first view, firstly *ṣīdhvam* etc. are qualified by the infix *iṬ* and then they qualify the sound *dh*. According to the second view, the sound *dh* is qualified by both the infix *iṬ* and *ṣīdhvam* etc.
The problem raised in this *vārttika* is that in the case of *ṣīdhvam* the infix *iṬ* is a part of this form, as it is added at its beginning. The optional *ḍh*-substitution would not be able to take place. Patañjali mentions that we could obtain the *ḍh*-substitution based on the expression *lIṄ* (potential mood) continued from the rule A. 8.3.78, which makes the substitution optional. Annaṃbhaṭṭa further adds (MPV X.450) that in the case of *lIṬ* we can accept that the ending *dhvam* follows the infix *iṬ*, because it is separated from the infix by the aorist suffix *sIC*.
Out of the two given examples – *luluviḍhve* / *luluvidhve* and *alaviḍhvam* / *alavidhvam* – in the latter (the form of *lUṄ*, aorist) the infix *iṬ* is separated from the ending by the suffix *sIC* which is deleted in the process. It is not the case in the former example where the infix is placed directly before the ending (the form of *lIṬ*, perfect), which means it can be treated a part of the ending to which it is attached. The derivations are as follows:

A.
(1) *lūÑ* (DhP IX:13) + *lIṬ*
(2) *lū* + *dhvam* (A. 3.4.78 *tiptasjhisipthasthamibvasmastātāmjhathāsāthāmdhvamiḍvahimahiṅ*)
(3) *lū* + *lū* + *dhvam* (A. 6.1.8 *liṭi dhātor anabhyāsasya*)
(4) *lū* + *lū* + *dhv* (*am* → *e*) (A. 3.4.79 *ṭita ātmanepadānāṃ ṭer e*)

(5) *l* (*ū* → *u*) + *lū* + *dhve* (A. 7.4.59 *hrasvaḥ*)
(6) *lu* + *l* (*ū* → *uvAṄ*) + *dhve* (A. 6.4.77 *aci śnudhātubhruvāṃ yvor iyaṅuvaṅau*)
(7) *lu* + *luv* + *iṬ* + *dhve* (A. 7.2.35 *ārdhahātukasyeḍ valādeḥ*)
(8) *lu* + *luv* + *i* + (*dh* → *ḍh*) *ve* (A. 8.3.79 *vibhāṣeṭaḥ*)
luluviḍhve / *luluvidhve*
B.
(1) *lū* + *lUṄ*
(2) *lū* + *dhvam* (A. 3.4.78 *tiptasjhisipthasthamibvasmastātāmjhathāsāthām-dhvamiḍvahimahiṅ*)
(3) *lū* + *Cli* + *dhvam* (A. 3.1.43 *cli luṅi*)
(4) *lū* + *sIC* + *dhvam* (A. 3.1.44 *cleḥ sic*)
(5) *aṬ* + *lū* + *s* + *dhvam* (A. 6.4.71 *luṅlaṅlṛṅkṣv aḍudāttaḥ*)
(6) *a* + *lū* + *iṬ* + *s* + *dhvam* (A. 7.2.35 *ārdhahātukasyeḍ valādeḥ*)
(7) *a* + *l* (*ū* → *o*) + *i* + *s* + *dhvam* (A. 7.3.84 *sārvadhātukārdhadhātukayoḥ*)
(8) *a* + *l* (*o* → *av*) + *i* + *s* + *dhvam* (A. 6.1.78 *eco 'yavāyāvaḥ*)
(9) *a* + *lav* + *i* + (*s* → 0) + *dhvam* (A. 8.2.25 *dhi ca*)
(10) *a* + *lav* + *i* + (*dh* → *ḍh*) *vam* (A. 8.3.79 *vibhāṣeṭaḥ*)
alaviḍhvam / *alavidhvam*}

VMBh_1: III.444.17-20; VMBh_2: V.477.1-4

3) When the sound *dh* follows, there is the lack of option [of the substitution] after [the infix] *iṬ* due to it not being [placed] immediately before [the sound *dh*], because there is [the suffix] *ṣīdhvam*.

[Objection:] When the sound *dh* follows, an option [of the substitution] after [the infix] *iṬ* would not result due to it not being [placed] immediately before [the sound *dh*], because there is [the suffix] *ṣīdhvam*. [For example,] *laviṣīḍhvam*, *laviṣīdhvam* (2nd pl. prec. from *lū* – 'to cut, divide').
[Answer:] It will be from the statement. There is a purpose in the statement.
[Question:] What?
[Answer:] [The forms] *luluviḍhve*, *luluvidhve* (2nd pl. perf. from *lū* – 'to cut, divide').

{**Explanation:**
This *vārttika* explains that when the verbal root is followed by the ending *ṣīdhvam* preceded by the infix *iṬ*, the *ḍh*-substitute cannot be optionally applied because the element *ṣī* stands between *dh* of the ending and the infix. The example is the form *laviṣīdhvam* where the infix *iṬ* comes after the verbal root *lū* and before the suffix *sīyUṬ* followed by the ending *dhvam*. The optional substitution is valid in the case of the *lIṬ* and *lUṄ* forms presented under the previous *vārttika*.}

VMBh_1: III.444.21-445.3; VMBh_2: V.477.5-9

4) And there might be potential involvement of the *ḍh*-substitute only in the case of [the suffix] beginning with *ṣī*, because the term *iṆ* is not a qualifier.

[Objection:] The *ḍh*-substitute might be involved only in the case of [the suffix] beginning with *ṣī*, because the term *iṆ* is not a qualifier. [For example,] *pakṣīdhvam*, *yakṣīdhvam*.
[Answer:] This is not a fault. I will say: "after an *aṅga* stem."
[Objection:] And there is a fault with the expression "after an *aṅga* stem." In this case it would not result: *upadidīyidhve*, *upadidīyiḍhve* (2nd pl. perf. from *upadī* – 'to fly'); because here there is no [infix] *iṬ* following such [a sound denoted by] *iṆ* which is at the end of an *aṅga* stem. And that [sound denoted by] *iṆ*, after which there is [the infix] *iṬ* following, is not at the end of an *aṅga* stem.

{**Explanation:**
If *dh* is qualified by the expression *iṇaḥ* and not the suffix, then in the case of the ending *ṣīdhvam* the consonant *dh* cannot be considered as following a sound denoted by *iṆ*. In *ṣīdhvam* the element *ṣī* separates *dh* from a sound denoted by *iṆ*, and the vowel *ī* directly preceding *dh* is a part of the element *ṣī*, not the verb. Therefore, the meaning of the above passage should be this: "the *ḍh*-substitute takes place of the sound *dh* that is a part of *ṣīdhvam* and following an *aṅga* stem ending in a sound denoted by *iṆ*." Thus, in the example *cyoṣīḍhvam* (2nd pl. prec. from *cyu* 'to shake, stir') the substitution takes place, but in *pakṣīdhvam* is does not because an *aṅga* stem in the latter case does not end in *iṆ*. In the case of *upadidīyidhve* the infix *yUṬ* is added to the ending *dhve* (preceded by the infix *iṬ*) so it separates the stem ending in *ī* from *dh*. The derivation of the form *upadidīyidhve* is as follows:

(1) *upa* + *dīṄ* (DhP IV:26) + *lIṬ*
(2) *upa* + *dī* + *dhvam* (A. 3.4.78 *tiptasjhisipthasthamibvasmastātāmjhathās-āthāmdhvamiḍvahimahiṅ*)
(3) *upa* + *dī* + *dī* + *dhvam* (A. 6.1.8 *liṭi dhātor anabhyāsasya*)
(4) *upa* + *dī* + *dī* + *dhv* (*am* → *e*) (A. 3.4.79 *ṭita ātmanepadānāṃ ṭer e*)
(5) *upa* + *d* (*ī* → *i*) + *dī* + *dhve* (A. 7.4.59 *hrasvaḥ*)
(6) *upa* + *di* + *dī* + *iṬ* + *dhve* (A. 7.2.35 *ārdhahātukasyeḍ valādeḥ*)
(7) *upa* + *di* + *dī* + *yuṬ* + *i* + *dhve* (A. 6.4.63 *dīṅo yuḍ aci kṅiti ca*)
upadidīyidhve}

VMBh_1: III.445.4-14; VMBh_2: V.478.1-13

[Answer:] Let it be as you want. Let it be then the qualifier to the suffix.
[Objection:] But has it not been said: "With respect to that, when the suffix follows, the *ḍh*-substitute would not result after [the infix] *iṬ* due to [it being added] at the beginning of what follows [in such examples as] *luluviḍhve*, *luluvidhve* (2nd pl. perf. from *lū* – 'to cut, divide')"?
[Answer:] It will be from the statement.
[Objection:] But has it not been said: "There is a purpose in the statement. What? [The forms] *alaviḍhvam*, *alavidhvam* (2nd pl. aor. from *lū* – 'to cut, divide')"?
[Answer:] This [term] *lIṄ*, which is used in this rule (i.e., A. 8.3.78), has no scope of application and due to its lack of applicability, [the substitution] will be based on the statement.
[Answer:] Alternatively, let it be the qualifier to the sound *dh*.
[Objection:] But has it not been said: "When the sound *dh* follows, an option [of the substitution] after [the infix] *iṬ* would not result due to it not being [placed] immediately before [the sound *dh*], because there is [the suffix] *ṣīdhvam*; [for example,] *laviṣīḍhvam*, *laviṣīdhvam* (2nd pl. prec. from *lū* – 'to cut, divide')"?
[Answer:] It will be from the statement.
[Objection:] But has it not been said: "There is a purpose in the statement. What? [The forms] *luluviḍhve*, *luluvidhve* (2nd pl. perf. from *lū* – 'to cut, divide')"?
[Answer:] The [term] *ṣīdhvam*, which is used in this rule (i.e., A. 8.3.78), has no scope of application and due to its lack of applicability [the substitution] will be based on the statement.
[Objection:] And it is also said: "The *ḍh*-substitute would result only in case of [the suffix] beginning with *ṣī* because the term *iṆ* is not a qualifier."
[Answer:] I will say: "after an *aṅga* stem."
[Objection:] But has it not been said: "And there is a fault with the expression "after *an aṅga* stem""?
[Answer:] The [term] '*aṅga* stem', which is used in the first rule (i.e., A. 8.3.78), is discontinued in the latter (i.e., A. 8.3.79). Alternatively, the term *iṆ* in the first rule is the qualifier to the suffix and in the latter it is the qualifier to the sound *dh*.

{**Explanation:**
The conclusion Patañjali reaches is that the technical term *aṅga*, which applies in A. 8.3.78, is discontinued in A. 8.3.79, thus allowing for the optional *ḍh*-substitution in the form *upadidīyidhve* and achieving the alternative correct form *upadidīyiḍhve*.
Another solution is that in the first rule the expression *iṇaḥ* qualifies the suffix and in the second one, the consonant *dh*. According to the *paribhāṣā*: *yena nāvyavadhānaṃ tena vyavahite 'pi vacanaprāmaṇyāt* ("By virtue of the assertion, in spite of the intervention of an item which never fails to

intervene."[470]), even when the forms end in *ṣīdhvam*, there is a substitution. Therefore, whenever the verbal root ending in a sound denoted by *iṆ* is followed by *dh* directly, or is separated with the infix *iṬ*, the *ḍh*-substitution takes place and the option is valid.}

{A. 8.3.80 *samāse 'ṅguleḥ saṅgaḥ*
[The retroflex *ṣ* comes in place of the sound *s* which is not at the end of a *pada*] of [the nominal stem] *saṅga* ('attachment') after [the nominal stem] *aṅguli* ('a finger') in a compound [in close proximity].
A. 8.3.81 *bhīroḥ sthānam*
[The retroflex *ṣ* comes in place of the sound *s* which is not at the end of a *pada*] of [the nominal stem] *sthāna* ('a place') after [the nominal stem] *bhīru* ('fearful, cowardly') [in a compound in close proximity].} *These *sūtra*s were not commented upon by Patañjali.

A. 8.3.82 *agneḥ stutstomasomāḥ*
[The retroflex *ṣ* comes in place of the sound *s* which is not at the end of a *pada*] of [the nominal stems] *stut* ('praising, celebrating'), *stoma* ('praise') and *soma* ('soma juice') after [the nominal stem] *agni* ('fire, name of a god') [in a compound in close proximity].

VMBh_1: III.445.15-17; VMBh_2: V.478.14-16

1) [The retroflex *ṣ* should come in place of the sound *s*] of [the nominal stem] *soma* [when it appears] after [the nominal stem] *agni* with the long vowel (i.e., after *agnī*).

[Bhāṣya:] It should be mentioned that [the retroflex *ṣ* comes in place of the sound *s*] of [the nominal stem] *soma* [when it appears] after [the nominal stem] *agni* with the long vowel (i.e., after *agnī*). [For example,] *agnīṣomau* ('Agni and Soma', nom./acc. du.).

{Explanation:
The commentators point out that this is an example of a *devatādvandva* compound where the constituents denote divinities. In the case of *agnīṣomau* the rule A. 6.3.27 *īd agneḥ somavaruṇayoḥ* applies allowing for the replacement of the final vowel *i* with its longer counterpart.[471] Moreover, in this kind of compound

---

[470] WUJASTYK 1993: vol. I: 43, vol. II: 154-156.

[471] A. 6.3.27 *īd agneḥ somavaruṇayoḥ* || ("[The substitute vowel] *ī* comes in place of [the final sound of] *agni* ('Agni') before [the posterior member of a compound] *soma* ('Soma') or *varuṇa* ('Varuṇa') [in a *devatādvandva* compound].")

both members retain their original accent on the basis of the *sūtra* A. 6.2.141 *devatādvandve ca* || ("In a *dvandva* compound composed of names of divinities also [both first and final members retain their original accents simultaneously].")}

VMBh_1: III.445.18-23; VMBh_2: V.478.17-479.5

2) Because otherwise, there is potential involvement of something undesired.

[Bhāṣya:] Because otherwise, something undesired might be involved. [For example, the *ṣ*-substitute in] *agnisomau māṇavakau* ('Two religious students named Agni and Soma', nom./acc. du.).
[Question:] Should it be mentioned then?
[Answer:] It should not be mentioned. When there are both the principal and the secondary, there is an understanding with reference to the principal one. Just like: the cow is to be tied up and the ram is to be sacrificed to Agni and Soma – the ox is not tied up.
[Question:] How then, in the case of [the word] ox, are the *vṛddhi* and *ā* substitutes [possible]: *gaus tiṣṭhati* ("A cow is standing") and *gām ānaya* ("Bring a cow!")[472]?
[Answer:] In such a way it depends on a meaning.
[Objection:] But what depends on the word (the word-form), that depends only on the word. And when there is the *ā*-substitute and *vṛddhi*, it depends on the word.

{**Explanation:**
Patañjali refers to the *paribhāṣā*: *gauṇamukhyayor mukhye sampratopattiḥ* ("Of the secondary and the primary, the primary is meant");[473] when the word to which the operation applies has two senses, the primary meaning should be taken into account. As Kaiyaṭa points out (VMBh_2: V.479), this is a maxim accepted in the world that should be used in the science of grammar as well. He refers to the *sūtra* A. 1.1.68 *svaṃ rūpaṃ śabdasyāśabdasaṃjñā*,[474] according to which an operation applies to the form mentioned in the *sūtra* and not to its synonyms; with the exclusion of technical terms which are used to designate elements other

---

[472] See A. 7.1.90 *goto ṇit* || ("[The strong *sUP* suffixes introduced] after [the *aṅga* stem] *go* ('a cow, bull') [are treated as] having a marker *Ṇ*."). This particular marker causes *vṛddhi* lengthening of the stem vowel. A. 6.1.93 *auto 'mśasoḥ* || ("[The single substitute] *ā* comes in place of [both the stem final sound] *o* [and the following initial vowel of the suffix] *am* and *Śas* [in close proximity].")

[473] WUJASTYK 1993: vol. I:7-9, vol. II:32-41; PŚ 15, I.14-17, II.81-85.

[474] A. 1.1.68 *svaṃ rūpaṃ śabdasyāśabdasaṃjñā* || ("An expression denotes itself unless it is the name of a linguistic technical term.")

than themselves. The word *rūpa* in A. 1.1.68 Pāṇini also covers the meaning of an element, and this meaning should be primary, not secondary. In the case of religious students (*māṇavaka*) named Agni and Soma, their names constitute the secondary meanings of the words *agni* and *soma*, therefore the *ṣ*-substitution in a *dvandva* compound does not take place.

There are two examples given in which the *vṛddhi* and *ā* substitutions respectively take place – *gaus tiṣṭhati* and *gām ānaya*. These operations are performed on a nominal stem, a notion which does not have a meaning outside the grammatical treatise. In common usage there are only finite words that bear the meaning; we do not perceive words are divided into the base and suffix when we speak. It is only inferred and by this supposition a nominal stem is considered meaningful in grammar. Kaiyaṭa explains (VMBh_2: V.479) that in the given examples, when the case endings are added, the operations must only depend on the word form due to lack of the wordly meaning of words and the primary-secondary relation. On the other hand, a word never appears in another meaning by leaving its basic one. The meaning, however, can be created when it is the cause of the application of a rule on a word; this is when we find the secondary meaning. It means that the *vṛddhi* and *ā* substitutions in the above examples take place when the nominal stem is used in its basic meaning.}

{A. 8.3.83 *jyotir āyusaḥ stomaḥ*
[The retroflex *ṣ* comes in place of the sound *s* which is not at the end of a *pada*] of [the nominal stem] *stoma* ('praise') after [the nominal stems] *jyotis* ('a light') or *āyus* ('duration of life') [in a compound in close proximity].
A. 8.3.84 *mātṛpitṛbhyāṃ svasuḥ*
[The retroflex *ṣ* comes in place of the sound *s* which is not at the end of a *pada*] of [the nominal stem] *svasṛ* ('a sister') after [the nominal stems] *mātṛ* ('a mother') or *pitṛ* ('a father') [in a compound in close proximity].} *These *sūtra*s were not commented upon by Patañjali.

A. 8.3.85 *mātuḥpiturbhyām anyatarasyām*
[The retroflex *ṣ*] optionally [comes in place of the sound *s* which is not at the end of a *pada*] of [the nominal stem *svasṛ* ('a sister')] after [the nominal stems] *mātur* ('mother's') or *pitur* ('father's') [in a compound, in close proximity].

VMBh_1: III.446.1-6; VMBh_2: V.480.1-6

[Bhāṣya:] It should be mentioned: "also after those two ending in [the sound] *s*." Just as in this case it should be: *mātuḥṣvasā* or *mātuḥsvasā* ('mother's sister'), *pituḥṣvasā* or *pituḥsvasā* ('father's sister') as well.

1) [In the case of] *mātur* and *pitur*, the expression "ending in [the sound] *s*" is useless because what has been modified in one place (i.e., in one of its parts) is not something else.

[Bhāṣya:] [In the case of] *mātur* and *pitur* the expression "ending in [the sound] *s*" is useless.
[Question:] What is the reason?
[Answer:] Because what has been modified in one place (i.e., in one of its parts) is not something else. [Based on a rule that] "what has been modified in one place (i.e., in one of its parts) is not like something else", [the substitution] will take place also in that ending in [the sound] *s*.

{Explanation:
Both forms *mātuḥ* and *pituḥ* are taken here as ending in the consonant *r*. The genitive forms are derived as follows:

(1) *mātṛ* + *ṄasI* (A. 4.1.2 *svaujasamauṭśasṭābhyāmbhisṅebhyāmbhyasṅasibhyāmbhyasṅasosāmṅyossup*)
(2) *māt* (*ṛ* + *a* → *u*) + *s* (A. 6.1.111 *ṛta ut*)
(3) *mātu* + *r* + *s* (A. 1.1.51 *ur aṇ raparaḥ*)
(4) *mātur* (*s* → 0) (A. 8.2.24 *rāt sasya*)
(5) *mātu* (*r* → *ḥ*) (A. 8.3.15 *kharavasānayor visarjanīyaḥ*)
mātuḥ

If we accepted that both forms end in the *visarjanīya*, we could optionally replace it with the *visarjanīya* by A. 8.3.36 *vā śari*, but another option would be the consonant *s*. In such a case the *ṣ*-substitute before the word *svasṛ* would be impossible. The proposal that the substitution should take place when they end in *s* as well is rejected. According to Patañjali, this specification is not necessary because we can resort to the *paribhāṣā*: *ekadeśavikṛtam ananyavat*.[475] Thus, even when the genitive forms of *mātṛ* and *pitṛ* end in the *visarjanīya* or the consonant *s*, they are still treated as ending in *r* for the purpose of this *sūtra*.}

{A. 8.3.86 *abhinisaḥ stanaḥ śabdasaṃjñāyām*
[The retroflex *ṣ* optionally comes in place of the sound *s* which is not at the end of a *pada*] of [the verbal root] *stanA* ('to resound', DhP I:489)] after [the *upasarga*s] *abhi* and *nis* [in close proximity] when the technical term is denoted.} *This *sūtra* was not commented upon by Patañjali.

[475] WUJASTYK 1993: vol. I:8, vol. II:37; PŚ 37, I.33-34, II.179-184.

A. 8.3.87 *upasargaprādurbhyām astir yac paraḥ*
[The retroflex *ṣ* optionally comes in place of the sound *s* which is not at the end of a *pada*] of [the verbal root] *asA* ('to be', DhP II:56) after the *upasarga* [ending in the sounds *i* or u,] or [the word] *prādur* ('visible') before [the sound] *y* or a vowel [in close proximity].

VMBh_1: III.446.7-9; VMBh_2: V.480.7-481.1

[Question:] What is the purpose [in using] the term *asti*?
[Answer:] It must not be in this case: *anusṛtam*, *visṛtam* ('followed' and 'dispersed' respectively).
[Answer:] This is not the purpose. The terms *gati* and *upasarga* are used with respect to that which has become connected with an action (i.e., the verb) and there is no connection with an action with respect to this sound *s*.

{**Explanation:**
The question regards the need to specify the verbal root *as* in the *sūtra* when even if the vowel *a* of the stem is deleted, the preverb will still qualify the consonant *s* of this verbal root. This specification is needed because we do not want the substitution in the forms *anusṛtam* or *visṛtam* where the single *s* does not carry the denotation of an action, whereas in the case of *s* of the verb *as* this notion is still there. In these counter-examples, the *upasarga*s refer to the whole verbal root *sṛ*, the vowel *ṛ* is not deleted in any form. However, as there is no notion of an action connected with the consonant *s* in *sṛ*, the counter-example seems to be chosen wrongly.
The example of the derivation where the vowel *a* of *as* is deleted may be as follows:

(1) *anu* + *asA* (DhP II:56) + *jhi* (A. 3.4.78 *tiptasjhisipthasthamibvasmastātām-jhathāsāthāmdhvamiḍvahimahiṅ*)
(2) *anu* + *as* + (*jh* → *ant*) *i* (A. 7.1.3 *jho 'ntaḥ*)
(3) *anu* + (*a* → 0) *s* + *anti* (A. 6.4.111 *śnāsor allopaḥ*)
(4) *anu* + (*s* → *ṣ*) + *anti* (A. 8.3.87 *upasargaprādurbhyām astir yacparaḥ*)
anuṣanti

This example is discussed below by Patañjali.}

VMBh_1: III.446.10-13; VMBh_2: V.481.1-4

[Objection:] In this case, then, it would not result either: *abhiṣanti* ('they surpass' 3rd pl. indic. praes.), *viṣanti* ('they surpass' 3rd pl. indic. praes.) because [the verb] *as* does not have the meaning of an action.

[Question:] But who has said that "[the verb] *as* does not have the meaning of an action"? [The verb] *as* has the meaning of an action. And it does have the meaning of an action for the following reason: *vyatyanuṣate* ('they exceed each other') – by the [*sūtra*] A. 1.3.14 there is an *ātmanepada* ending.
[Question:] And what is *karmavyatihāra*?[476]
[Answer:] [It means] 'reciprocity of an action'.

{Explanation:
The objection made is that the verb *as* does not denote an action. The verbal root can have two meanings: *kriyā* ('an action') and *bhāva* ('a root sense'). An action can be located in its object (*karmasthakriyaka*) or the root sense can have the object as its locus (*karmasthabhāvaka*). Kaiyaṭa explains that the term *kriyā* refers to an action that is qualified by movement on the basis of the above distinction. However, when reference is made to the elements connected with the action, there is no contradiction. The meaning of the verbal root is taken into account, being different from the substantive whether it is in the form of movement or not.}

VMBh_1: III.446.13-18; VMBh_2: V.481.5-10

[Bhāṣya:] It must not be after the word *prādur* though; because the word *prādur* has a limited scope, it is used only with [the verbal roots] *ḌUkṛÑ* ('to do', DhP VIII:10), *bhū* ('to be, exist', DhP I:1) and *asA* ('to be', DhP II: 56).
[Objection:] It must not be in [the verb] *syati* after an *upasarga*.
[Answer:] The *ṣ*-substitute [of the sound *s*] of [the verb] *syati* (*asU* – 'to throw', DhP IV:100) after an *upasarga* is required. And for the following reason it is required, in the same way he says [the *sūtra*] A. 8.3.65.
[Objection:] It must not be of [the sound *s* of the verb] *syati* after the word *prādur* though, because *prādur* has a limited scope, it is used only with [the verbal roots] *ḌUkṛÑ* ('to do', DhP VIII:10), *bhū* ('to be, exist', DhP I:1) and *asA* ('to be', DhP II:56).
[Answer:] This is the purpose then, in this case it must not be: to [the verb] *anusūti* the non-suffix [is added forming] *anusū* and the offspring of Anusū is *ānuseya*.

{Explanation:
The derivation of *ānuseya* is as follows. First the suffix *KviP* is added to the verbal root *anusū* by A. 3.2.61 *satsūdviṣadruhaduhayujavidabhidachidajinī-*

[476] The reference is made to A. 1.3.14 and the expression *karmavyatihāra* used therein.

rājām upasarge 'pi kvip[477] and is further deleted by A. 6.1.67 *ver apṛktasya.* We achieve the nominal form *anusū* to which the suffix *ḍhaÑ* is added in the meaning of 'his offspring'.

(1) *anusū* + *ḍhaÑ* (A. 4.1.135 *catuṣpādbhyo ḍhañ*)
(2) *anusū* + (*ḍh* → *ey*) *a* (A. 7.1.2 *āyaneyīnīyiyaḥ phaḍhakhachaghāṃ pratyayādīnām*)
(3) *anus* (*ū* → 0) + *eya* (A. 6.4.147 *ḍhe lopo 'kadrvāḥ*)
(4) (*a* → *ā*) *nus* + *eya* (A. 7.2.115 *aco ñṇiti*)
ānuseya

If the verb *as* were not specified in the rule, the *ṣ*-substitution would also take place in the form *ānuseya*, which is undesirable.}

A. 8.3.88 *suvinirdurbhyaḥ supisūtisamāḥ*
[The retroflex *ṣ* comes in place of the sound *s* which is not at the end of a *pada*] of [the verbal root] *supI* (*ÑIṣvapA* 'to sleep', DhP II:59) and [the nominal stems] *sūti* ('pressing out') and *sama* ('equal') [after the *upasargas*] *su*, *vi*, *nir* and *dur* [in close proximity].

VMBh_1: III.446.19-22; VMBh_2: V.481.11-14

[Question:] Why is the form *supI* used of the [verbal root] *ÑIṣvapA*?

1) There is the *ṣ*-substitute [of the sound *s*] of [the form] *supI*, but it must not be in [the form] *svapI*.

[Answer:] The *ṣ*-substitute [of the sound *s*] is mentioned in [the form] *supI*, but it must not be in [the form] *svapI*. [For example,] *susvapnaḥ* ('a good dream'), *visvapnaj* ('sleepy').

{Explanation:
The verb *svap* was specified in the *sūtra* in the form *supI* and not *svapI* to show that the substitution takes place only in such forms where vocalisation has taken place, which is why the given examples are exempt from it. Let us analyse the

---

[477] A. 3.2.61 *satsūdviṣadruhaduhayujavidabhidacchidajinīrājām upasarge 'pi kvip* ॥ ("[The *kṛt* suffix] *KviP* comes after [the verbal stems] *sadḶ* ('to sit down', DhP I: 907), *ṣūṄ* ('to produce', DhP II: 21), *dviṣA* ('to hate', DhP II: 3), *druhA* ('to hurt', DhP IV: 88), *duhA* ('to milk', DhP II: 4), *yujA* ('to join', DhP IV: 68), *vidA* ('to know', DhP II: 55), *bhidIR* ('to break', DhP VII: 2), *chidIR* ('to split', DhP VII: 3), *ji* ('to win, conquer', DhP I: 593), *ṇīÑ* ('to lead', DhP I: 950) and *rājṚ* ('to shine', DhP I: 874) also with an *upasarga* [and with nominal *padas*].")

form *visvapnaj*; it is formed with the *kṛt* suffix *najIṄ*.[478] The word *visvapnaj* might mean 'the one who usually sleeps' or, as Kaiyaṭa (VMBh_2: V.481) puts it, 'the one who sleeps very well'. According to the commentators, the problem arises because the *tācchīlika* suffix[479] should be added to the crude stem, not the one preceded by an *upasarga*. The answer to this is that in some other instances we have verbs preceded by *upasarga*s that take this kind of suffixes, for example the verb *āgam* ('to come');[480] it is therefore acceptable in this case as well.}

VMBh_1: III.447.1-2; VMBh_2: V.481.15-16

Why do not we get [the ṣ-substitute in the reduplicated syllable of] form *visuṣvāpa* ('he slept' 3rd sg. perf.)?

[Question:] Why do not we get [the *ṣ*-substitute in the reduplicated syllable of] the form *visuṣvāpa* ('he slept' 3rd sg. perf.)?

{Explanation:
The question was raised whether it would be possible to have the form **viṣuṣvāpa* with the *ṣ*-substitute in the reduplicated syllable. When the vocalisation has been applied (by A. 6.1.17 *liṭy abhyāsasyobhayeṣām*[481]) and the deletion of *p* in the reduplicated *svap* has not been done yet (by A. 7.4.60 *halādiḥ śeṣaḥ*), the *ṣ*-substitution could take place, because the operation depending on the preverb of the verbal root is internally conditioned. We need the form *sup* for the substitution to take place. However, according to Kaiyaṭa (VMBh_2: V.482), even if the *p*-deletion is done, we still can refer to the *paribhāṣā*: *ekadeśavikṛtam ananyavat* ("An item altered in part does not behave like something else").[482]}

---

[478] A. 3.2.172 *svapitṛṣor najiṅ* ‖ ("[The suffix] *najiṄ* comes after [the verbal stems] *ÑIṣvapA* ('to sleep', DhP II:59) and *ÑItṛṣA* ('to be thirsty', DhP IV:118) [to denote the agent's habitual disposition, duty or excellence].")

[479] A. 3.2.134 *ākves tacchīlataddharmatadsādhukāriṣu* ‖ ("Up to and including the *sūtra* A. 3.2.177 [the *kṛt* suffixes introduced after verbal stems] are meant to denote that the agent performs the action as a part of his habitual disposition, as his duty or efficiently.")

[480] A. 3.2.154 *laṣapatapadasthābhūvṛṣahanakamagamaśṝbhya ukañ* ‖ ("[The *kṛt* suffix] *ukaÑ* comes after [the verbal roots] *laṣA* ('to desire', DhP I:937), *patḶ* ('to fall, fly', DhP I:898), *padA* ('to walk', DhP IV:60), *ṣṭhā* ('to stand', DhP I:975), *bhū* ('to be, exist', DhP I:1), *vṛṣU* ('to rain', DhP I:738), *hanA* ('to kill', DhP II: 2), *kamU* ('to love', DhP I:470), *gamḶ* ('to go', DhP I: 1031), *śṝ* ('to destroy', DhP IX:18) [to denote the agent's habitual disposition, duty or excellence].")

[481] 6.1.17 *liṭy abhyāsasyobhayeṣām* ‖ ("Before [the *l*-substitutes of] *lIṬ* (perfect) [the vocalisation of semivowels] of a reduplicated [syllable] of both classes of verbal roots – A. 6.1.15-16 – takes place].")

[482] WUJASTYK 1993: vol. I:8, vol. II:37; PŚ 37, I.33-34, II.179-184.

VMBh_1: III.447.3-9; VMBh_2: V.482.1-7

There is no *supI* due to [the application of the *sūtra*] A. 7.4.60.

[Answer:] When [the *sūtra*] A. 7.4.60 *halādiḥ śeṣaḥ* has been applied, there is no *supI*.
[Objection:] This is what should be considered in this case: whether vocalisation should be done after the application of [the rule] A. 7.4.60. [The *sūtra*] A. 7.4.60 [could apply first] due to its posteriority.

Vocalisation is required to be applied first.

[Answer:] It is required that vocalisation (A. 6.1.17) be prior to [the deletion of the consonant in the reduplicated syllable by] A. 7.4.60. And for the following reason it is required, in the same way he has said: vocalisation of a reduplicated [syllable], through the conflict, [takes places] before [the *sūtra*] A. 7.4.60.[483] In the same way it will not be due to the restriction in [the *sūtra*] A. 8.3.64.

{**Explanation:**
Patañjali replies that vocalisation should apply prior to the deletion of the consonant *p*. Annaṃbhaṭṭa explains (MPV X.455) that if the deletion took place in the form *sup* and not *svap*, only in this case we could apply the *paribhāṣā*: *ekadeśavikṛtam ananyavat*. As the reduplicated syllable is *svap*, other operations take place only afterwards. Kaiyaṭa (VMBh_2: 482) gives the example of the form *vivyādha* ('he pierced', 3rd sg. perf. from *vyadh* – 'to pierce') where the vocalisation also has to take place first. In this case, at the stage of reduplication *vyadh-vyadh*, both consonants *y* and *dh* of the reduplicated syllable would be deleted by A. 7.4.60. What would undergo the vocalisation is the semivowel *v*. In the end, we would achieve the form **uvyādha* which is incorrect, and which shows that *saṃprasāraṇa* precedes the deletion of all the consonants apart from the first one in a reduplicated syllable of the verbal stem. Similarly, in the example *visuṣvāpa*, if the deletion were to apply first, it would apply to both *p* and *v*.
Another argument used is the restriction stated in the rule A. 8.3.64 quoted by Patañjali, which limits the *ṣ*-substitution to those verbs that belong to the *sthādi* group, so in others the substitution does not take place. It would not, therefore, take place in the reduplicated syllable of the verb *svap* in *visuṣvāpa*.}

VMBh_1: III.447.10-12; VMBh_2: V.482.8-10

[483] See A. 6.1.17 *vt*. 1 *abhyāsasaṃprasāraṇaṃ halādiśeṣād vipratiṣedhena* ||

2) The restriction with respect to [the verbal roots] *sthā* etc. [does not apply], as in this case *supI* is later than [the scope of the *sūtra*] A. 8.3.70 (A. 8.3.63 *prāk sitāt…*).

[Bhāṣya:] [The word] *supI* follows this restriction [which is established] from [the rule] A. 8.3.63 to [the rule] A. 8.3.70. In the same way then, [through the *paribhāṣā*: *arthavadgrahane nānarthakasya* stating that:] "when a meaningful unit is used, it does not [denote the same unit] devoid of meaning,"[484] in the same way there will not be [the substitution] of it [i.e., the sound *s* here].

{**Explanation:**
The verbal root *svap* cannot fall into the scope of restriction formed in the *sūtra* A. 8.3.64 because it extends only up to A. 8.3.70. As the present rule follows the said restriction, it cannot be subject to it. Moreover, as Patañjali points out, a meaningful element cannot denote the one that is meaningless. When reduplication is done, the whole reduplicated syllable bears the meaning, not a part of it. Therefore, the form *su*, after the deletion of *p* would be meaningless. The meaning as such is not reduplicated, it is revealed in the reduplication process itself.
The derivation of the form *visuṣvāpa* is as follows then:

(1) *vi* + *ÑIṣvapA* + *tiP* (A. 3.4.78 *tiptasjhisipthasthamibvasmastātāmjhathāsāthāmdhvamiḍvahimahiṅ*)
(2) *vi* + (*ṣ* → *s*) *vap* + *ti* (A. 6.1.64 *dhātvādeḥ ṣaḥ saḥ*)
(3) *vi* + *svap* + (*tiP* → *ṆaL*) (A. 3.4.82 *ṇalatususthalatusaṇalvamāḥ*)
(4) *vi* + *svap* + *svap* + *a* (A. 6.1.8 *liṭi dhātor anabhyāsasya*)
(5) *vi* + *s* (*v* → *u*) *ap* + *svap* + *a* (A. 6.1.17 *liṭy abhyāsasyobhayeṣām*)
(6) *vi* + *s* (*u* + *a* → *u*) *p* + *svap* + *a* (A. 6.1.108 *saṃprasāraṇāc ca*)
(7) *vi* + *su* (*p* → 0) + *svap* + *a* (A. 7.4.60 *halādiḥ śeṣaḥ*)
(8) *vi* + *su* + *sv* (*a* → *ā*) *p* + *a* (A. 7.2.116 *ata upadhāyāḥ*)
(9) *vi* + *su* + (*s* → *ṣ*) *vāp* + *a* (A. 8.3.59 *ādeśapratyayayoḥ*)
visuṣvāpa}

VMBh_1: III.447.13-16; VMBh_2: V.482.11-483.1

If this is meaningless, [how do we get the form] *viṣuṣupuḥ* ('they slept' 3rd pl. perf. from *visvap*)?

[Objection:] If this is used [with respect] to the meaningful [unit], [the substitution] would not be obtained in *viṣuṣupuḥ*.

484 WUJASTYK 1993: vol. I:1-2, vol II:3-10; PŚ 14, vol. I:14, vol. II:81-85.

[Answer:] This is not a fault.
[Question:] How come?

The form *supI* is doubled.

[Answer:] There is reduplication of the form *supI*.

{**Explanation:**
The problem appears to be with the form *viṣuṣupuḥ*, where the *ṣ*-substitution has taken place in the reduplicated syllable. It is possible because we apply the *saṃprasāraṇa* first and then reduplication. If we consider reduplication as substitution of two elements instead of one (*sthāne dvirvacana*), then on the basis of *sthānivadbhāva* we get *sup* as the substituend. The whole form *sup* is there and the *ṣ*-substitution can apply to both sounds *s*. If we treat reduplication as 'putting the element twice' (*dviḥprayoga*), then *sthānivadbhāva* cannot apply due to lack of the substitute, but the *ṣ*-substitution depends on whole form *sup*. In the case of *visuṣvāpa*, however, reduplication comes first and vocalisation takes place only in the reduplicated syllable; not in the verbal root.
The derivation of the form *viṣuṣupuḥ* is as follows then:

(1) *vi* + *ÑIṣvapA* + *tiP*
(2) *vi* + (*ṣ* → *s*) *vap* + *ti* (A. 6.1.64 *dhātvādeḥ ṣaḥ saḥ*)
(3) *vi* + *svap* + (*tiP* → *us*) (A. 3.4.82 *parasmaipadānāṃ ṇalatususthalatusaṇalvamāḥ*)
(4) *vi* + *s* (*v* → *u*) *ap* + *us* (A. 6.1.17 *liṭy abhyāsasyobhayeṣām*)
(5) *vi* + *s* (*u* + *a* → *u*) *p* + *us* (A. 6.1.108 *saṃprasāraṇāc ca*)
(6) *vi* + *sup* + *sup* + *us* (A. 6.1.8 *liṭi dhātor anabhyāsasya*)
(7) *vi* + *su* (*p* → 0) + *sup* + *us* (A. 7.4.60 *halādiḥ śeṣaḥ*)
(8) *vi* + (*s* → *ṣ*) *u* + (*s* → *ṣ*) *up* + *us* (A. 8.3.59 *ādeśapratyayayoḥ*)
(9) *vi* + *ṣu* + *ṣup* + *u* (*s* → *rU*) (A. 8.2.66 *sasajuṣo ruḥ*)
(10) *vi* + *ṣu* + *ṣup* + *u* (*r* → *ḥ*) (A. 8.3.15 *kharavasānayor visarjanīyaḥ*)
viṣuṣupuḥ

According to the commentators, some apply the double *ṣ*-substitute in the form *viṣuṣupuḥ* before reduplication. It is possible because this substitution is not considered suspended with respect to reduplication.[485]}

VMBh_1: III.447.17-20; VMBh_2: V.483.2-5

***ślokavārttika*:**

---

[485] See *vt*. 13 on A. 8.2.4.

1) There is the *ṣ*-substitute [of the sound *s*] of [the form] *supI* [but] it must not be in [the form] *svapI*. Why do not we get [the *ṣ*-substitute in the reduplicated syllable of] form *visuṣvāpa* ('he slept' 3rd sg. perf.)? There is no *supI* due to [the application of the *sūtra*] A. 7.4.60. Vocalisation is required to be applied first.
2) The restriction with respect to [the verbal roots] *sthā* etc. [does not apply], as in this case *supI* is later than [the scope of the *sūtra*] A. 8.3.70 (A. 8.3.63 *prāk sitāt*...). If this is meaningless, [how do we get the form] *viṣuṣupuḥ* ('they slept' 3rd pl. perf. from *visvap*)? The form *supI* is doubled.

{A. 8.3.89 *ninadībhyāṃ snāteḥ kauśale*
[The retroflex *ṣ* comes in place of the sound *s* which is not at the end of a *pada*] of [the verbal root] *snā* ('to take a bath', DhP I:868) [after the *upasarga*] *ni* and [the nominal stem] *nadī* ('a river') when the meaning is 'skillfulness' (*kauśala*) [in close proximity].
A. 8.3.90 *sūtraṃ pratiṣṇāta*
[The word] *pratiṣṇāta* [is formed with the *ṣ*-substitute] when it means 'a rule'.} *These *sūtra*s were not commented upon by Patañjali.

A. 8.3.91 *kapiṣṭhalo gotre*
[The word] *kapiṣṭhala* [is formed with the *ṣ*-substitute] when it means 'a lineage'.

VMBh_1: III.447.21-448.2; VMBh_2: V.483.6-484.3

1) [It should be said that the word] *kapiṣṭhala* [is used] in the basic meaning of *gotra*.

[Bhāṣya:] It should be mentioned [that the word] *kapiṣṭhala* [is formed] in the basic meaning of *gotra*. When [the term] *gotra* is said, it (i.e., the *ṣ*-substitute) should take place in this case: *kāpiṣṭhali* ('the son of Kapiṣṭhala'). In these cases, it should not take place: *kapiṣṭhala* and *kāpiṣṭhalāyana*.
[Question:] Should it be mentioned then?
[Answer:] It should not be mentioned. [The word] *kapiṣṭhala* is not understood in this way: "it is formed in an irregular way to denote 'a lineage'."
[Question:] How then?
[Answer:] There is the irregular *ṣ*-substitute in this word *kapiṣṭhala*, which [is used] in the meaning 'a lineage' whether there or elsewhere.

{Explanation:

The term *gotra* should be understood here in a technical sense, according to the *sūtra* A. 4.1.162 *apatyaṃ pautraprabhṛti gotram.*[486] Annaṃbhaṭṭa, Nārāyaṇa (MPV X.456-457) and Nāgeśa (VMBh_2: V.483) add that when the word can be taken in its technical or non-technical sense, Pāṇini means the technical one.[487] Therefore, when the *taddhita* suffix is added in the meaning of *gotra*, the *ṣ*-substitution of *s* in *sthala* introduced after *kapi* takes place. The term *gotra* should not be understood as the most original base (*kapiṣṭhala*) or the *yuvan* descendant (*kāpiṣṭhalāyana*). However, if the technical meaning were really meant, the only possible form with the *ṣ*-substitution would be *kāpiṣṭhali* ('the son of Kapiṣṭhala'), and *kapiṣṭhala* or *kāpiṣṭhalāyana* ('the *yuvan* descendant of Kapiṣṭhala') could not be formed. The *vārttika* is ultimately rejected. The *ṣ*-substitute applies to the derivatives of the word *kapiṣṭhala* when the term *gotra* is used in its non-technical sense. This *sūtra* establishes the substitution when the general sense of 'a lineage, clan' is meant and at the same time it excludes the *ṣ*-substitute in *kapisthala* when the intended meaning is 'a place' (a place where monkeys live).}

{A. 8.3.92 *praṣṭho 'gragāmini*
[The word] *praṣṭha* [is formed with the *ṣ*-substitute] when it means 'the one taking the lead'.
A. 8.3.93 *vṛkṣāsanayor viṣṭaraḥ*
[The word] *viṣṭara* [is formed with the *ṣ*-substitute] when it means 'a tree' or 'a seat'.
A. 8.3.94 *chandonāmni ca*
And also [the word *viṣṭara* is formed with the *ṣ*-substitute] when it means 'the name of a metre'.
A. 8.3.95 *gaviyudhibhyāṃ sthiraḥ*
[The retroflex *ṣ* comes in place of the sound *s* which is not at the end of a *pada*] of [the nominal stem] *sthira* ('firm, solid') [after the nominal *pada*s] *gavi* ('a cow') and *yudhi* ('a battle') [in a compound in close proximity].
A. 8.3.96 *vikuśamiparibhyaḥ sthalam*
[The retroflex *ṣ* comes in place of the sound *s* which is not at the end of a *pada*] of [the nominal stem] *sthala* ('a place') [after the *upasarga*s] *vi*, *ku*, *pari* and [the nominal stem] *śami* (the name of a tree) [in a compound in close proximity].} *These *sūtra*s were not commented upon by Patañjali.

[486] A. 4.1.162 *apatyaṃ pautraprabhṛti gotram* || ("[The technical term] *gotra* denotes a descendant beginning with a grandson.")

[487] *kṛtrimākṛtrimayoḥ kṛtrime saṃpratyayaḥ* || ("Of the technical and the non-technical, the technical is meant."), WUJASTYK 1993: vol. I:11, vol. II:49-53.

A. 8.3.97 *ambāmbagobhūmisavyāpadvitrikuśekuśaṅkvaṅgumañjipuñjiparame-barhirdivyagnibhyaḥ sthaḥ*
[The retroflex *ṣ* comes in place of the sound *s* which is not at the end of a *pada*] of [the nominal stem] *stha* ('remaining in') [after the nominal stems] *ambā* ('a mother'), *āmba*, *go* ('a cow, bull'), *bhūmi* ('earth'), *savya* ('left'), *apa* ('away'), *dvi* ('two'), *tri* ('three'), *kuśe* ('on a kuśa grass'), *ku* ('bad'), *śaṅku* ('a peg'), *aṅgu* ('a finger'), *mañji* ('a cluster of blossoms'), *puñji* ('a heap, mass'), *parame* ('in the highest'), *barhis* ('kuśa grass'), *divi* ('in heaven') and *agni* ('a fire') [in a compound in close proximity].

VMBh_1: III.448.3-9; VMBh_2: V.484.4-11

[Question:] [The word] *stha*, is it the form of the verbal root [*sthā*] or is it the word form [*stha*]?
[Question:] What of it?
[Objection:] If this is the form of the verbal root, [the substitution] would result in this case: *gosthāna*. But [if this is] the word form [*stha*], in these cases: *savyeṣṭhāḥ* ('warriors standing on the left side [of a chariot]'), *parameṣṭhī* ('a superior woman'), *savyeṣṭhā* ('a warrior standing on the left side [of a chariot]') it would not result.
[Answer:] Let it be as you want. Let it be the form of the verbal root then.
[Question:] How [is the form] *gosthāna* ('a station for cattle') [possible]?
[Answer:] [This word] is read in [the *gaṇa*] *savanādi* [in the *sūtra* A. 8.3.110]. Alternatively, let it be the word form [*stha*].
[Question:] How [are the forms] *savyeṣṭhāḥ*, *parameṣṭhī* and *savyeṣṭhā* possible?
[Answer:] It should be mentioned [that the substitution takes place in] *stha* in [the form of] *sthā*, *sthin* and *sthṛ*.[488]

{**Explanation:**
The form *stha* in the *sūtra* could also, theoretically, refer to a similar verbal root. That would, however, lead to the undesired substitution in the forms such as *gosthāna* or *bhūmisthāna*, where the stem *sthāna* is the derivative of the verbal root. Those forms are considered to be included in the *gaṇa savanādi* in A. 8.3.110, which automatically prevents the *ṣ*-substitution. On the other hand, the forms *savyeṣṭhāḥ*, *parameṣṭhī*, *savyeṣṭhā* do not end in the form *stha*, which prompts a *vārttika* suggesting an amendment and the inclusion of various readings of *stha*, such as *sthā*, *sthin* and *sthṛ* into the rule.

---

[488] The VMBh_2 edition marks this last statement as a *vārttika*.

In all the above examples the locative ending of the first member of a compound is not deleted by the rule A. 6.3.9 *haladantāt saptamyāḥ saṃjñāyām* || ("[Before the final member of a compound] the locative ending [is not deleted when introduced] after [the first member] ending in a consonant or [the vowel] *a* to denote a name"). In the case of *savyeṣṭhā* the locative is considered by commentators to be retained by A. 6.3.14 *tatpuruṣe kṛti bahulam* || ("In a *tatpuruṣa* compound before [a final member ending in a suffix] *kṛt* [the locative ending introduced after the first member is not] variously [deleted]").}

A. 8.3.98 *suṣāmādiṣu ca*
[The retroflex *ṣ* comes in place of the sound *s* which is not at the end of a *pada*] also of [the nominal stems] *suṣāman* ('a beautiful song') etc. [in close proximity].

VMBh_1: III.448.10-11; VMBh_2: V.485.1-2

[Bhāṣya:] The retroflex [*ṣ*-substitute] in the case of [the nominal stems] *suṣāman* ('a beautiful song') etc. should be seen as not having been established.

{Explanation:
This *sūtra* was not commented by Kaiyaṭa or his later commentators. Only Nāgeśa (VMBh_2: V.485) briefly explains this short comment made by Patañjali. The purpose of this rule is to include those stems that should undergo the *ṣ*-substitution but are excluded from it on the basis of other rules, for example A. 8.3.111.}

{A. 8.3.99 *eti saṃjñāyām agāt*
[The retroflex *ṣ* comes in place of the sound *s* which is not at the end of a *pada*] before the vowel *e* [and after the sounds *i*, *u* or those belonging to the consonantal group *kU*] with the exception of [the sound] *g*, to denote the name [in close proximity].
A. 8.3.100 *nakṣatrād vā*
[The retroflex *ṣ*] usually [comes in place of the sound *s* which is not at the end of a *pada* before the vowel *e*] after [the nominal stems denoting] 'lunar houses' [ending in the sounds *i*, *u* or those belonging to the consonantal group kU with the exception of the sound *g*, to denote the name in close proximity].} *These *sūtra*s were not commented upon by Patañjali.

A. 8.3.101 *hrasvāt tādau taddhite*
[The retroflex *ṣ* comes in place of the sound *s* which is not at the end of a *pada*] after a short vowel [*i* or *u*] before a *taddhita* [suffix] beginning with [the sound] *t* [in close proximity].

VMBh_1: III.448.12-14; VMBh_2: V.485.3-5

1) Prohibition [should be mentioned] after a short vowel before [the suffix] beginning with [the sound] *t* in the case of [the suffixes] *tiṄ* (i.e., the verbal endings).

[Bhāṣya:] Prohibition should be mentioned after a short vowel before [the suffix] beginning with [the sound] *t* in the case of [the suffixes] *tiṄ* (i.e., verbal endings). [For example,] *bhindyustarām*, *chindyustarām* ('they would split better' and 'they would cut better' respectively).

{Explanation:
This rule was not commented by either of the commentators. An example for this rule can be the form *sarpiṣṭara* ('more genuine clarified butter').[489] The final *s* of *sarpis* is first replaced by *ṣ* which, consequently, causes the *ṭ*-substitution by A. 8.4.41 *ṣṭunā ṣṭuḥ*. Thus, we arrive at the form *sarpiṣṭara*.
The *vārttika* proposes prohibition of the substitution when the *taddhita* suffix follows the finite verbal form such as *chindyustarām*. Its derivation is as follows:

(1) *chid* + *ŚnaM* + *jhi* (A. 3.1.78 *rudhādibhyaḥ śnam*, A. 3.4.78 *tiptasjhisipthasthamibvasmastātāmjhathāsāthāmdhvamiḍvahimahiṅ*)
(2) *chid* + *ŚnaM* + *yāsuṬ* + *jhi* (A. 3.4.103 *yāsuṭ parasmaipadeṣv udātto ṅic ca*)
(3) *chi* + *na* + *d* + *yās* + *jhi* (A. 1.1.47 *mid aco 'ntyāt paraḥ*)
(4) *chin* (*a* → 0) *d* + *yās* + *jhi* (A. 6.4.148 *yasyeti ca*)
(5) *chind* + *yās* + (*jhi* → *Jus*) (A. 3.4.108 *jher jus*)
(6) *chind* + *yā* (*s* → 0) + *us* (A. 7.2.79 *liṅaḥ salopo 'nantyasya*)
(7) *chind* + *y* (*ā* + *u* → *u*) *s* (A. 6.1.96 *usy apadāntāt*)
(8) *chindyus* + *taraP* (A. 5.3.56 *tiṅaś ca*)
(9) *chindyus* + *tara* + *āmU* (A. 5.4.11 *kimettiṅavyayaghād āmv adravyaprakarṣe*)
(10) *chindyustar* (*a* → 0) + *ām* (A. 6.4.148 *yasyeti ca*)
chindyustarām}

{A. 8.3.102 *nisas tapatav anāsevane*
[The retroflex *ṣ* comes in place of the sound *s* which is not at the end of a *pada*] of [the *upasarga*] *nis* [occurring] after [the verbal root] *tapA* ('to heat',

---

489 The *taddhita* suffix *taraP* is added by A. 5.3.57 *dvivacanavibhajyopapade tarabīyasunau* || ("[The *taddhita* suffixes] *taraP* and *īyasuN* [come after nominal stems and verbal stems ending in *tiṄ*] to express a comparison between two things or that from which something is distinguished.")

DhP I:1034) when it does not mean 'do something repeatedly' [in close proximity].
A. 8.3.103 *yuṣmattattatakṣuḥsv antaḥpādam*
[The retroflex *ṣ* comes in place of the sound *s*] occurring in the middle of the verse [and after the vowels *i* or *u*] of [the pronominal stems] *yuṣmad* ('you') [beginning with the sound *t*], *tad* ('that') and *tatakṣuḥ* (3rd pl. perf. from *takṣ* – 'to cut') [in close proximity].
A. 8.3.104 *yajuṣy ekeṣam*
According to some, [the retroflex *ṣ* comes in place of the sound *s* occurring in the middle of the verse and after the vowels *i* or *u* of the pronominal stems *yuṣmad* ('you') beginning with the sound *t*, *tad* ('that') and *tatakṣuḥ* (3rd pl. perf. from *takṣ* – 'to cut') in Yajurveda [in close proximity].} *These *sūtra*s were not commented upon by Patañjali.

A. 8.3.105 *stutastomayoś chandasi*
In Vedic, [according to some, the retroflex *ṣ* comes in place of the sound *s* occurring after the vowels *i* or *u*] of [the nominal stems] *stuta* ('praised, glorified') and *stoma* ('praise, a hymn') [in close proximity].

VMBh_1: III.448.15-18; VMBh_2: V.485.6-9

1) The use of this *sūtra* is pointless because [the same] is achieved by [the *sūtra*] A. 8.3.106.

[Bhāṣya:] The use of this *sūtra* is pointless.
[Question:] Why?
[Answer:] Because [the same] is achieved by [the *sūtra*] A. 8.3.106. It is achieved just by [the *sūtra*] A. 8.3.106.

{Explanation:
According to Kaiyaṭa (VMBh_2: V.485), the words *stuta* and *stoma* are not necessary in the present rule. The *ṣ*-substitute in them can be obtained by applying the following *sūtra* because it can be applicable both in compounds as well as in expressions. The term *pūrvapada* can be understood as referring to the prior member of a compound or the preceding *pada* in an expression. He concludes that the rule should read *chandasi* only, the condition that should follow to the subsequent rule.}

{A. 8.3.106 *pūrvapadāt*
[In Vedic, according to some, the retroflex *ṣ* comes in place of the sound *s* occurring] after a preceding *pada* [ending in the vowels *i* or *u* in close proximity].

A. 8.3.107 *suñaḥ*
[In Vedic the retroflex *ṣ* comes in place of the sound *s*] of [the particle] *suÑ* [occurring after a preceding *pada* ending in the vowels *i* or *u* in close proximity].} *These *sūtra*s were not commented upon by Patañjali.

A. 8.3.108 *sanoter anaḥ*
[In Vedic the retroflex *ṣ* comes in place of the sound *s*] of [the verbal root] *ṣanU* ('to obtain as a gift', DhP VIII:2) without [the sound] *n* [occurring after a preceding *pada* ending in the vowels *i* or *u* in close proximity].

VMBh_1: III.449.1-13; VMBh_2: V.485.10-486.4

1) [It should be said:] "also of [the verbal root] *san* without [the sound] *n*."

[Objection:] Why? The use [of this *sūtra*] is really pointless.
[Question:] Why?
[Answer:] Because [the same] is achieved by [the *sūtra*] A. 8.3.106 (see also *vt.* 1 under the *sūtra* A. 8.3.105).
[Answer:] Thus, it should be mentioned for the sake of restriction; [the substitution] should take place [of the sound *s*] in [the verbal root] *san* without the sound *n*. In this case it must not be: *gosanim* ('winning/gaining the cattle', acc. sg. from *gosani*).

2) If this *sūtra* [is formed] for the sake of restriction, [the same] is achieved by being placed in [the *gaṇa*] *sevanādi* (in A. 8.3.110).

[Objection:] If this *sūtra* [is formed] for the sake of restriction, it will be read in [the *gaṇa*] *sevanādi* (in A. 8.3.110).

3) But [it should be said] for the sake of [the desiderative suffix] *saN*.

[Answer:] But it should be mentioned for the sake of [the desiderative suffix] *saN*; e.g., *sisaniṣati* ('he wants to gain', 3rd sg. desid.).
[Answer:] But this is not the purpose. [The operation] will not take place because of restriction in [the *sūtra*] A. 8.3.61.
[Proposition:] It should be mentioned for the sake of [the causative suffix] *ṆiC* then; e.g., *sisānayiṣati* ('he wants to give', 3rd sg. desid. of caus.).
[Question:] How, on the other hand, is it possible to understand it as finishing in [the causative suffix] *ṆiC* when there is prohibition with respect to what finishes in [the causative suffix] *ṆiC*?
[Answer:] Because of compositeness. Having said that the purpose is not in stating prohibition with respect to what finishes in [the causative suffix] *ṆiC*, that

which ends in [the causative suffix] *ṆiC* is understood. Alternatively, this [form] does not end in [the causative suffix] *ṆiC*. [The form] *sisanīḥ* ('wanting to gain') [is created when] a non-suffix (i.e., *KvIP*) comes after the desiderative form.

{**Explanation:**
The substitution takes place when the verbal root *san* appears without the consonant *n* as in the example *goṣāḥ* ('acquiring cattle'). Its derivation is as follows:

(1) *go* + *ṣanU* (DhP VIII:2) + *vIṬ* + *sU* (A. 3.2.67 *janasanakhanakramagamo viṭ*, A. 4.1.2 *svaujasamauṭśasṭābhyāmbhisṅebhyāmbhyasṅasibhyāmbhyasṅasosāmṅyossup*)
(2) *go* + (*ṣ* → *s*) *an* + *vIṬ* + *s* (A. 6.1.64 *dhātvādeḥ ṣaḥ saḥ*)
(3) *go* + *sa* (*n* → *ā*) + *vIṬ* + *s* (A. 6.4.41 *viḍvanor anunāsikasyāt*)
(4) *go* + *sa* + *ā* + 0 + *s* (A. 6.1.67 *ver apṛktasya*)
(5) *go* + *s* (*a* + *ā* → *ā*) + *s* (A. 6.1.101 *akaḥ savarṇe dīrghaḥ*)
(6) *go* + *sā* + (*s* → *rU*) (A. 8.2.66 *sasajuṣo ruḥ*)
(7) *go* + *sā* + (*r* → *ḥ*) (A. 8.3.15 *kharavasānayor visarjanīyaḥ*)
(8) *go* + (*s* → *ṣ*) + *ā* + *ḥ* (A. 8.3.108 *sanoter anaḥ*)
goṣāḥ

The substitution does not take place in the form *gosanim*, though, because the consonant *n* is present there. It is argued, however, that this form could be included in the *sevanādi* group so the restriction would be superfluous, which leads us to another argument that the restriction could be stated for the sake of the causative suffix *ṆiC* and the form *sisānayiṣati*. The present *sūtra* does not specify the causative forms, which makes this counter-example dubious. Patañjali offers the form *sisanīḥ* where the substitution does not take place and which is formed from the desiderative base of the verb *san*. Moreover, Kaiyaṭa adds (VMBh_2: V.485) that in the case of *sisānayiṣati*, the *ṣ*-substitution should take place in the verbal root because there is no similar restriction as the one formulated in A. 8.3.61. Thus the form should be *siṣāṇayiṣati* with the retroflex *ṇ* caused by the preceding *ṣ* by A. 8.4.1.
The derivation of *sisanīḥ* from the base *sisanisa* is as follows:

(1) *sisanisa* + *KviP* + *sU* (A. 3.2.76 *kvip ca*, A. 4.1.2 *svaujasamauṭśasṭābhyāmbhisṅebhyāmbhyasṅasibhyāmbhyasṅasosāmṅyossup*)
(2) *sisanisa* + 0 + *sU* (A. 6.1.67 *ver apṛktasya*)
(3) *sisanis* (*a* → 0) + *s* (A. 6.4.48 *ato lopaḥ*)
(4) *sisanis* + (*s* → 0) (A. 6.1.68 *halṅyābbhyo dīrghāt sutisy apṛktam hal*)
(5) *sisani* (*s* → *rU*) (A. 8.2.66 *sasajuṣo ruḥ*)
(6) *sisan* (*i* → *ī*) *r* (A. 8.2.76 *rvor upadhāyā dīrgha ikaḥ*)
(7) *sisanī* (*r* → *ḥ*) (A. 8.3.15 *kharavasānayor visarjanīyaḥ*)

sisanīḥ}

{**A. 8.3.109** ***saheḥ pṛtanartābhyāṃ ca***
[In Vedic the retroflex *ṣ* comes in place of the sound *s*] of [the verbal root] *ṣahA* ('to endure', DhP I:905) [occurring after a preceding *pada*] *pṛtanā* ('a hostile army' or *ṛta* ('universal order') [in close proximity].} *This *sūtra* was not commented upon by Patañjali.

A. 8.3.110 ***na raparasṛpisṛjispṛśispṛhisavanādīnām***
[The retroflex *ṣ*] does not come in place of [the sound *s*] preceded by [the sound] *r* or of [the verbal roots] *sṛpḶ* ('to crawl', DhP I:1032), *sṛjA* ('to emit, let go', DhP VI:121), *spṛśA* ('to touch', DhP VI:128), *spṛhA* ('to envy', DhP X:325) and [the nominal stems] *savana* ('extraction') etc. [even preceded by the vowels *i* or *u* in close proximity].

VMBh_1: III.449.14-20; VMBh_2: V.486.5-11

[Question:] Why is the word *aśvasani* ('gaining horses') read in [the *gaṇa*] *savanādi*?
[Answer:] For the sake of blocking the *ṣ*-substitute obtained by [the *sūtra*] A. 8.3.106.
[Answer:] This is not the purpose. [The expression] "after [that] ending in [the vowels] *i* or *u*" (A. 8.3.76) continues there and this [rule] refers to those not ending in [the vowels] *i* or *u*. This is most certainly the meaning of the prohibition that [the *ṣ*-substitute] would result.
[Objection:] In the same way then, when he reads the word *aśvasani* in [the *gaṇa*] *savanādi*, the teacher indicates that the *ṣ*-substitute also takes place [of the sound *s* appearing] after that which does not end in [the vowels] *i* or *u*.
[Question:] What is the purpose of this indication?
[Answer:] [The expression] *jalāṣāhaṃ māṣa* ('bean subduing water'). Alternatively, it is the beginning of the meaning that modification done in one place [does not mean anything else],[490] thus: *aśvaṣā* ('the one that can endure horse-riding', A. 8.3.108).

{**Explanation:**
This *sūtra* blocks the *ṣ*-substitution under certain circumstances. The form *aśvasani* seems problematic because the consonant *s* is preceded here by the vowel *a*, and as such would not normally undergo the substitution. According to Patañjali, *aśvasani* serves as an indication that the sound *s* does not have to be preceded by *iṆ* to undergo substitution. The present rule also negates the

---

[490] WUJASTYK 1993: vol. I:8, vol. II:37; PŚ 37, I.33-34, II.179-184.

operation when *s* is preceded by *iṆ* but is followed by the consonant *r*. The example can be the form *visrabdha* ('confident, fearless') whose derivation is as follows:

(1) *vi* + *sranbhU* (DhP I:420) + *Kta* (A. 3.2.102 *niṣṭhā*, A. 1.1.26 *ktaktavatū niṣṭhā*)
(2) *vi* + *sra* (*n* → 0) *bh* + *ta* (A. 6.4.24 *aniditāṃ hala upadhyāyāḥ kṅiti*)
(3) *vi* + *srabh* + (*t* → *dh*) *a* (A. 8.2.40 *jhaṣas tathor dho 'dhaḥ*)
(4) *vi* + *sra* (*bh* → *b*) + *dha* (A. 8.4.53 *jhalāṃ jaś jhaśi*)
visrabdha}

{A. 8.3.111 *sāt padādyoḥ*
[The retroflex *ṣ* does not come in place of the sound *s*] of [the adverbial suffix] *sāt* (A. 5.4.64) or a *pada* initial [after the word ending in the sound *i* or *u* or belonging to the *kU* group in close proximity].} *This *sūtra* was not commented upon by Patañjali.

A. 8.3.112 *sico yaṅi*
[The retroflex *ṣ* does not come in place of the sound *s*] of [the verbal root] *ṣicA* ('to sprinkle', DhP VI:140) [after the sounds *i* or *u*] before [the intensive suffix] *yaṄ* [in close proximity].

VMBh_1: III.450.1-8; VMBh_2: V.486.12-487.2

[Question:] Should there be prohibition of this [*ṣ*-substitute] achieved by [the *sūtra*] A. 8.3.65 or not?
[Answer:] It should not be.
[Question:] What is the reason? The *ṣ*-substitute [prescribed] by A. 8.3.65 enters in the scope of prohibition, just like it blocks prohibition in the rule A. 8.3.111, in the same way it blocks this [rule] A. 8.3.112 as well.
[Answer:] It does not block it.
[Question:] What is the reason?
[Answer:] When [a rule is formulated] when [another rule] necessarily applies, it blocks [this rule] and when the prohibition with reference to the term *padādi* [in the rule A. 8.3.111] applies, the *ṣ*-substitute by A. 8.3.65 is composed; whereas this [rule] A. 8.3.112 sometimes applies and sometimes it does not. Alternatively, the exception (*apavāda*) which [appears] earlier [in the treatise] blocks operational rules which [appear] later; in the same way the *ṣ*-substitute of A. 8.3.65 will block the prohibition rule A. 8.3.111 but it will not block [the rule] A. 8.3.112. Therefore, there should be [the form] *abhisesicyate* ('he consecrates intensely', 3rd sg. intens. from *abhiṣic*).

{Explanation:
It is being discussed why the rule A. 8.3.65 *upasargāt sunotisuvatisyatistauti-stobhatisthāsenayasedhasicasañjasvañjām* could not block this prohibition in the same way as it blocks the prohibition in A. 8.3.111 *sāt padādyoḥ*. It happens when rule Y necessarily applies and rule X blocks it, when its domain is within the domain of Y. In such a situation, rule Y is forbidden from applying. In the case of A. 8.3.111, which prohibits the *ṣ*-substitute when *s* appears at the beginning of a *pada*, the domain of A. 8.3.65 is included within the domain of A. 8.3.111. Therefore, the substitution takes place against that prohibition. It is not the case with A. 8.3.112. The domains of A. 8.3.65 and A. 8.3.112 overlap, but there are some instances that are not covered by the *ṣ*-substitute of A. 8.3.65. The present negation has a wider scope than A. 8.3.111, which is why it cannot be blocked. Kaiyaṭa additionally stresses (VMBh_2: V.487) that the order in which these discussed rules appear is irrelevant due to domain versus domain suspension rather than individual *sūtras*.}

{A. 8.3.113 *sedhater gatau*
[The retroflex *ṣ* does not come in place of the sound *s*] of [the verbal root] *ṣidhA* ('to move' DhP I:48) when the meaning is 'movement' [after the sounds *i* or *u* in close proximity].
A. 8.3.114 *pratistabdhanistabdhau ca*
Also [the words] *pratistabdha* ('pressed, leaned against') and *nistabdha* ('stopped, fixed') [are formed in an irregular way without the *ṣ*-substitute].}
*These *sūtra*s were not commented upon by Patañjali.

A. 8.3.115 *soḍhaḥ*
[The retroflex *ṣ* does not come in place of the sound *s*] of [the form] *soḍh-* (of the verbal root *ṣahA* 'to endure', DhP I:905) [after the sounds *i* or *u* or those belonging to the *kU* group in close proximity].

VMBh_1: III.450.9-11; VMBh_2: V.487.3-5

[Question:] Why is [the verbal root] *ṣahA* used in the form *soḍha* [here]?
[Answer:] Where such a form is used of this [verbal root, i.e., of *sahI*], then there should be [prohibition of the *ṣ*-substitute]. In this case it must not apply: *pariṣahate* ('he sustains', 3rd sg. indic. from *pariṣah*).

{Explanation:
The rules until the end of a *pāda* were not commented by either of the commentators. Patañjali explains why the form used in the text of the rule is *soḍha* instead of the pure verbal root. It shows that the substitution will be

prohibited only in the case of such a form, for example *parisoḍha* ('sustained'). Its derivation is as follows:

(1) *pari* + *ṣahA* (DhP I:905) + *Kta* (A. 3.2.102 *niṣṭhā*, A. 1.1.26 *ktaktavatū niṣṭhā*)
(2) *pari* + (*ṣ* → *s*) *ah* + *ta* (A. 6.1.64 *dhātvādeḥ ṣaḥ saḥ*)
(3) *pari* + *sa* (*h* → *ḍh*) + *ta* (A. 8.2.31 *ho ḍhaḥ*)
(4) *pari* + *saḍh* + (*t* → *dh*) *a* (A. 8.2.40 *jhaṣas tathor dho 'dhaḥ*)
(5) *pari* + *saḍh* + (*dh* → *ḍh*) *a* (A. 8.4.41 *ṣṭunā ṣṭuḥ*)
(6) *pari* + *sa* (*ḍh* → 0) + *ḍha* (A. 8.3.13 *ḍho ḍhe lopaḥ*)
(7) *pari* + *s* (*a* → *o*) + *ḍha* (A. 6.3.112 *sahivahor od avarṇasya*)
parisoḍha

The rule A. 6.3.112 has to apply at the end even though it is placed before the *Tripādī* rules. The *ḍh*-deletion is not considered suspended with respect to the *o*-substitution because it is specified as the condition of the operation by Pāṇini.
It is not the case in other forms of the verbal root *sah* where the *ṣ*-substitution takes place on the basis of the *sūtra* A. 8.3.70.}

A. 8.3.116 *stambhusivusahāṃ caṅi*
[The retroflex *ṣ* does not come in place of the sound *s*] of [the verbal roots] *stanbhU* ('to support', DhP IX:7), *ṣivU* ('to sew', DhP IV:2) and *ṣahA* ('to endure', DhP I:905) [after the sounds *i* or *u* or those belonging to the *kU* group] before [the aorist substitute suffix] *CaṄ* [in close proximity].

VMBh_1: III.450.12-16; VMBh_2: V.487.6-10

1) [It should be said that there is no *ṣ*-substitute] in [the verbal roots] *stanbhU* ('to support', DhP IX:7), *ṣivU* ('to sew', DhP IV:2) and *ṣahA* ('to endure', DhP I:905) before [the suffix] *CaṄ* and after an *upasarga*.

[Bhāṣya:] It should be mentioned [that there is no *ṣ*-substitute] in [the verbal roots] *stanbhU* ('to support', DhP IX:7), *ṣivU* ('to sew', DhP IV:2) and *ṣahA* ('to endure', DhP I:905) before [the suffix] *CaṄ* and after an *upasarga*.
[Question:] What is the purpose?
[Answer:] When the application [of the substitution] takes place after an *upasarga*, there should be prohibition of that application. When the application [of the substitution] takes place after reduplication, there must not be prohibition of that application. [For example,] *paryasīṣahat* ('he made endure', 3rd sg. caus. aor. from *pariṣah*).

{Explanation:

This *sūtra* refers to reduplicated aorist forms. The *ṣ*-substitution in the case of the verb *stanbhU* is prescribed by A. 8.3.67 *stambheḥ* and in the case of other verbs by A. 8.3.70 *parinivibhyaḥ sevasitasayasivusahasuṭstusvañjām*. However, the *vārttika* proposes that the prohibition applied only when the *ṣ*-substitution is caused by the preverb and not by the reduplication. Therefore we will have the form *paryatastambhat* but *paryasīṣivat*. Their respective derivations are as follows:

A.

(1) *pari + stanbh + ṆiC + Cli + tiP* (A. 3.1.26 *hetumati ca*, A. 3.1.43 *cli luṅi*, A. 3.4.78 *tiptasjhisipthasthamibvasmastātāmjhathāsāthāmdhvamiḍvahimahiṅ*)
(2) *pari + stanbh + ṆiC + Cli + t (i* → 0) (A. 3.4.100 *itaś ca*)
(3) *pari + stanbh + ṆiC + CaṄ + t* (A. 3.1.48 *ṇiśridrusrubhyaḥ kartari caṅ*)
(4) *pari + aṬ + stanbh + ṆiC + a + t* (A. 6.4.71 *luṅlaṅlṛṅkṣv aḍudāttaḥ*)
(5) *pari + a + stanbh +* 0 *+ a + t* (A. 6.4.51 *ṇer aniṭi*)
(6) *pari + a + stanbh + stanbh + a + t* (A. 6.1.11 *caṅi*)
(7) *pari + a + ta + stanbh + a + t* (A. 7.4.61 *śarpūrvāḥ khayaḥ*, A. 7.4.60 *halādiḥ śeṣaḥ*)
(8) *par (i → y) + a + ta + stanbh + a + t* (A. 6.1.77 *iko yaṇ aci*)
(9) *pary + a + ta + sta (n → ṃ) bh + a + t* (A. 8.3.24 *naś cāpadāntasya jhali*)
(10) *pary + a + ta + sta (ṃ → m) bh + a + t* (A. 8.4.58 *anusvārasya yayi parasavarṇaḥ*)
paryatastambhat

B.

(1) *pari + ṣiv + ṆiC + Cli + tiP* (A. 3.1.26 *hetumati ca*, A. 3.1.43 *cli luṅi*, A. 3.4.78 *tiptasjhisipthasthamibvasmastātāmjhathāsāthāmdhvamiḍvahimahiṅ*)
(2) *pari + ṣiv + ṆiC + Cli + t (i* → 0) (A. 3.4.100 *itaś ca*)
(3) *pari + (ṣ → s) iv + Cli + t* (A. 6.1.64 *dhātvādeḥ ṣaḥ saḥ*)
(4) *pari + siv + ṆiC + CaṄ + t* (A. 3.1.48 *ṇiśridrusrubhyaḥ kartari caṅ*)
(5) *pari + aṬ + siv + ṆiC + a + t* (A. 6.4.71 *luṅlaṅlṛṅkṣv aḍudāttaḥ*)
(6) *pari + a + siv +* 0 *+ a + t* (A. 6.4.51 *ṇer aniṭi*)
(7) *pari + a + siv + siv + a + t* (A. 6.1.11 *caṅi*)
(8) *pari + a + si + siv + a + t* (A. 7.4.60 *halādiḥ śeṣaḥ*)
(9) *pari + a + s (i → ī) + siv + a + t* (A. 7.4.94 *dīrgho laghoḥ*)
(10) *par (i → y) + a + sī + siv + a + t* (A. 6.1.77 *iko yaṇ aci*)
(11) *pary + a + sī + (s → ṣ) iv + a + t* (A. 8.3.59 *ādeśapratyayayoḥ*)
paryasīṣivat

The form *paryasīṣahat* is derived in the same way as *paryasīṣivat*.}

A. 8.3.117 *sunoteḥ syasanoḥ*

[The retroflex *ṣ* does not come in place of the sound *s*] of [the verbal root] *ṣuÑ* ('to press out, extract', DhP V:1) [after the sounds *i* or *u* or those belonging to the *kU* group] before [the future suffix] *sya* and [the desiderative suffix] *saN* [in close proximity].

VMBh_1: III.450.17-21; VMBh_2: V.487.11-15

[Question:] What is the example in the case of [the desiderative suffix] *saN*?
[Answer:] It is *susūṣati* ('he wants to extract', 3rd sg. desid.).
[Bhāṣya:] This is not the purpose. It [i.e., the *ṣ*-substitute] will not take place due to the restriction in [the *sūtra*] A. 8.3.61.
[Objection:] Then this [is the purpose]: *abhisusūṣati* ('he wants to extract', 3rd sg. desid.).
[Bhāṣya:] This is not the purpose either. It [i.e., the *ṣ*-substitute] will not take place due to the restriction in [the *sūtra*] A. 8.3.64. This is the purpose then: to [the verb] *abhisusūṣati* the non-suffix [is added forming] *abhisusūḥ* ('desirous of extracting Soma juice').

{Explanation:
The purpose of this *sūtra* is the form *abhisusūḥ* ('desirous of extracting Soma juice') formed with the suffix *KviP* added to the desiderative base *abhisusūṣa*. The derivation is as follows:

(1) *abhi* + *ṣuÑ* (DhP V:1) + *saN* + *ŚaP* (A. 3.1.7 *dhātoḥ karmaṇaḥ samāna-kartṛkād icchāyāṃ vā*, A. 3.1.68 *kartari śap*)
(2) *abhi* + (*ṣ* → *s*) *u* + *sa* + *a* (A. 6.1.64 *dhātvādeḥ ṣaḥ saḥ*)
(3) *abhi* + *su* + *su* + *sa* + *a* (A. 6.1.9 *sanyaṅoḥ*)
(4) *abhi* + *su* + *s* (*u* → *ū*) + *sa* + *a* (A. 6.4.16 *ajhanagamāṃ sani*)
(5) *abhi* + *su* + *sū* + *s* (*a* + *a* → *a*) (A. 6.1.97 *ato guṇe*)
(6) *abhi* + *su* + *sū* + (*s* → *ṣ*) *a* (A. 8.3.59 *ādeśapratyayayoḥ*)
(7) *abhisusūṣa* + *KviP* (A. 3.2.61 *satsūdviṣadruhaduhayujavidabhidachidajinī-rājām upasarge 'pi kvip*)
(8) *abhisusūṣa* + 0 (A. 6.1.67 *ver apṛktasya*)
(9) *abhisusūṣ* (*a* → 0) (A. 6.4.48 *ato lopaḥ*)

Now, at this stage we go back to A. 8.3.59 which allowed the *ṣ*-substitution. It is considered suspended, so the rule A. 8.2.66 will apply to the original consonant *s*.

(10) *abhisusū* (*s* → *rU*) (A. 8.2.66 *sasajuṣo ruḥ*)
(11) *abhisusū* (*r* → *ḥ*) (A. 8.3.15 *kharavasānayor visarjanīyaḥ*)
abhisusūḥ}

A. 8.3.118 *sadeḥ parasya liṭi*
[The retroflex *ṣ* does not come in place of the sound *s*] of [the verbal root] *ṣadḶ* ('to sit', DhP I:907, VI:133) [after the sounds *i* or *u* or those belonging to the *kU* group occurring] after [the sound *s*], before [the *l*-substitutes of] *lIṬ* (perfect tense) [in close proximity].

VMBh_1: III.451.1-3; VMBh_2: V.487.16-18

1) When there is prohibition [of the *ṣ*-substitute of the sound *s*] in [the verbal root] *ṣadḶ* before [the *l*-substitutes of] *lIṬ* (perfect tense), [the same should be] added regarding [the verbal root] *svañjA* ('to embrace, clasp', DhP I:1025).

[Bhāṣya:] When there is prohibition [of the *ṣ*-substitute of the sound *s*] in [the verbal root] *ṣadḶ* before [the *l*-substitutes of] *lIṬ* (perfect tense), [the verbal root] *svañjA* ('to embrace, clasp', DhP I:1025) should be added: *pariṣasvaje* ('he has embraced' 3rd sg. perf.).

{**Explanation:**
The prohibition stated in this *sūtra* refers to the consonant *s* of the verbal root, not of the reduplicated syllable. The *ṣ*-substitute of the reduplicated syllable is obtained by A. 8.3.66 *sadir aprateḥ* in the case of the verb *ṣadḶ*.}

{A. 8.3.119 *nivyabhibhyo 'ḍvyavāye vā chandasi*
In Vedic [the retroflex *ṣ* does not] usually [come in place of the sound *s* occurring] after [the *upasarga*s] *ni*, *vi* or *abhi*, even when [the infix] *aṬ* intervenes [in close proximity].} *This *sūtra* was not commented upon by Patañjali.

This was the second *āhnika* of the third *pada* of the eighth *adhyāya* in the *Vyākaraṇamahābhāṣya* composed by Patañjali. This is the end of a *pada*.

A. 8.4.1 *raṣābhyāṃ no ṇaḥ samānapade*
[The retroflex sound] *ṇ* comes in place of [the sound] *n* [occurring] after [the sounds] *r* or *ṣ* within the same word [in close proximity].

VMBh_1: III.452.1-6; VMBh_2: V.488.1-7

1) In the case of the *ṇ*-substitute [of the sound *n*, occurring] after [the sounds] *r* or *ṣ*, the vowel *ṛ* [should be] used [as well].

[Bhāṣya:] In the case of the *ṇ*-substitute [of the sound *n*, occurring] after [the sounds] *r* or *ṣ*, the vowel *ṛ* should be used [as well]. It should be mentioned that [the sound] *ṇ* comes in place of [the sound] *n* [occurring] after [the sounds] *r* or *ṣ* within the same word as well as after the sound *ṛ*. In these cases it should take place as well: *mātṝṇām*, *pitṝṇām* ('of mothers', 'of fathers' respectively, gen. pl. from *mātṛ* and *pitṛ*).
[Question:] Should it be mentioned then?
[Answer:] It should not be mentioned. This *ṇ*-substitute will take place which is dependant on this *r* being in the vowel *ṛ*.
[Bhāṣya:] It is not achieved.
[Question:] What is the reason?
[Answer:] Because parts of sounds are not understood as the [whole] sound.

{**Explanation:**
The first *vārttika* proposes the inclusion of the vowel *ṛ* as the cause for the substitution. Such a specification seems dubious as *ṛ* contains the consonantal part *r* in itself and as such could fall into the scope of the present rule. The above discussion presents two views: according to the first one, the consonantal *r* in the vowel *ṛ* allows for the substitution, and according to the second, a part of a sound cannot be treated as a whole sound, which results in blocking the substitution. Kaiyaṭa explains (VMBh_2: V.488.11 ff) that according to some grammarians, the *r* part in the vowel *ṛ* has a duration of half a mora, so in the forms such as *āstīrṇa* ('spread out') etc. the *ṇ*-substitute following *r* takes place due to the absence of a separate sound *r* and dependence on another sound. In the example *āstīrṇa* the consonant *r* should be read together with the preceding vowel *ī*, which is the substitution of the final sound of the verbal root. In the same way, it takes place in the forms *mātṝṇām*, *pitṝṇām*. Yet according to others, the consonant *r* in the vowel *ṛ* has a duration of only a quarter of a mora, and even then the substitution in the form *āstīrṇa* will take place. Kaiyaṭa proposes another solution as well; he says that in the expression *raṣābhyām* the shape of *r* is established. Thus, the *ṇ*-substitute will take place after such a sound *r* which is a part of the vowel *ṛ*.
As for the second view, according to which a part of a sound cannot be treated as a whole sound, the example is given – *narasiṃha* – where the nature of a man and of a lion are understood together, not separately. Similarly, when we say 'the meat is not to be sold', it does not mean that we cannot sell the cow instead. Annaṃbhaṭṭa (MPV X.460) adds another example – *agne indraḥ* – where the vowel *e* is treated as combined of the vowels *a* and *i*. It does not mean, however, that we can apply the rule prescribing the lengthening of two homogenous sounds (in this case two vowels *i*; one of *agne* and another of *indre*). A similar situation is with the sounds *ṛ* and *r*.
The derivation of the form *āstīrṇa* is as follows:

(1) *ā* + *stṝÑ* (DhP IX:14) + *Kta* (A. 3.2.102 *niṣṭhā*, A. 1.1.26 *ktaktavatū niṣṭhā*)
(2) *ā* + *st* (*ṝ* → *i*) + *ta* (A. 7.1.100 *ṝta iddhātoḥ*)
(3) *ā* + *sti* + *r* + *ta* (A. 1.1.51 *ur aṇ raparaḥ*)
(4) *ā* + *stir* + (*t* → *n*) *a* (A. 8.2.42 *radābhyāṃ niṣṭhāto naḥ pūrasya tu daḥ*)
(5) *ā* + *st* (*i* → *ī*) *r* + *na* (A. 8.2.76 *rvor upadhāyā dīrgha ikaḥ*)
(6) *ā* + *stīr* + (*n* → *ṇ*) *a* (A. 8.4.1 *raṣābhyāṃ no ṇaḥ samānapade*)
āstīrṇa}

VMBh_1: III.452.7-8; VMBh_2: V.488.8-489.1

2) And as far as a part of a whole is concerned, it has been said [that the sound *ṛ* should be used] with respect to [the infix] *nUṬ* etc.

[Question:] What has been said?
[Answer:] If it is not included, the sound *ṛ* should be used in the case of the rules regarding [the infix] *nUṬ*, the *l*-substitute and cerebralisation. Therefore, [the parts of sounds] are understood [from the whole sound].

{**Explanation:**
Patañjali refers to the *vārttika* 11 under the *Śivasūtra*s 3 and 4: *agrahaṇaṃ cen nuḍvidhilādeśavināmeṣv ṛkāragrahaṇam*. As Kaiyaṭa explains (VMBh_2: V.469), when a rule refers to the whole element, it cannot apply in the case of a part of this element. He quotes the example *agna indraḥ*, derived from *agne indraḥ*, once again and states that the rule lengthening the final vowel *i* does not apply, even though *i* is thought to be present in the vowel *e*. The rule substituting the final *e* with *ay* applies instead (A. 6.1.78 *eco 'yavāyāvaḥ*) after which the consonant *y* is deleted (A. 8.3.19 *lopaḥ śākalyasya*). In Kaiyaṭa's commentary we find a question regarding the form *mātṝṇām*; whether we apply a rule prescribing an operation or the one negating it, it always refers to a part of an element, not to a whole. Annaṃbhaṭṭa elaborates on this (MPV X.460); when we form the genitive plural of *mātṛ*, we apply A. 6.4.3 *nāmi*.[491] In this case the operation depends on the vowel *ṛ* and not on the consonantal part *r* that it contains. Similarly, when A. 8.2.86 *guror anṛto 'nantyasyāpy ekaikasya prācām* is to apply, negation depends on a vowel and not on the combination of a vowel and a consonant. According to Annaṃbhaṭṭa, further diphtongs are considered undivided, which is not the case with the sounds *ṛ* and *r*; these are considered separate sounds by grammarians. Thus the consonant *r* being a part of the vowel *ṛ* cannot be the cause of the application of this rule.}

---

[491] A. 6.4.3 *nāmi* ‖ ("[A long vowel comes in place of the final vowel of the *aṅga* stem] before [the genitive plural ending] *nām*.")

VMBh_1: III.452.9-10; VMBh_2: V.489.1-2

[Answer:] It is not achieved in such a way either.
[Question:] What is the reason?
[Answer:] Due to it being separated. It would not result due to separation by that part which follows the sound *r*. In the same way it will take place by [the *sūtra*] A. 8.4.2.

{**Explanation:**
The separation mentioned in this passage refers to the vowel *a* intervening between *r* and *n*, which prevents the substitution from taking place. As mentioned before, the vowel *ṛ* is a combination of the consonantal part *r* and two vowel parts *a* preceding and following it. The problem found here is that the consonantal part of *r* does not directly precede the consonant *n* which would make the rule impossible to apply. Therefore, the reference to the following *sūtra*, which allows the substitution despite the intervention of another sound, is proposed.}

VMBh_1: III.452.10-20; VMBh_2: V.489.3-490.5

[Answer:] It is not achieved.
[Question:] What is the reason?
[Answer:] Those parts of sounds, which are understood through a whole sound, those sounds are also divided. And here that part (*bhakti*) which follows the sound *r*, that is nowhere to be seen as divided.
[Bhāṣya:] In such a way then division of the rule will be accomplished. [First,] *raṣābhyāṃ no ṇaḥ samānapade*. Then, *vyāvaye*. And also when there is the intervention, there is the *ṇ*-substitute of *n* [occurring] after [the sounds] *r* or *ṣ*. [And] then, *aṭkupvāṅnum* ("By [the sounds denoted by] *aṬ*, [a sound belonging to the group] *kU* or *pU*, [the particle] *āṄ* or [the infix] *nUM*").
[Question:] What is the purpose of it here?
[Answer:] [It is used] for the sake of restriction. [He says]: when there is the intervention only by those sounds belonging to the *Śivasūtra*s, not the others.[492] Alternatively, the teacher's use indicates that there is the *ṇ*-substitute after the sound *r*, because he mentions the word *nṛnamana* ('bending men', proper name) in [the *gaṇa*] *kṣubhnādi* (A. 8.4.39).
[Bhāṣya:] This is not the indication. It should be done for the sake of *vṛddhi* – *nārnamani* ('the offspring of Nṛnamana').
[Objection:] But just as he mentions the word *tṛpnoti* ('he is satisfied') there (in the *gaṇa* in A. 8.4.39), he also mentions the word *nṛnamana* [there].

---

[492] See the discussion under the *vārttika* 11 on the *Śivasūtra*s 3-4. VMBh_1 I.25-26.

[Objection:] But has it not been said that it should be done for the sake of *vṛddhi*? [The] *vṛddhi* [substitute] is externally conditioned; the *ṇ*-substitute is internally conditioned. An externally conditioned [operation] is suspended with respect to an internally conditioned one.
[Bhāṣya:] Alternatively, the division of the rule will be done later on (A. 8.4.26): *ṛto no ṇaḥ* ("[The sound] *ṇ* comes in place of [the sound] *n* after the sound *ṛ*"). Then: *chandasyavagrahāt* ("In Vedic after a contraction (*avagraha*)"); *ṛtaḥ* ("[The substitute takes place] only after the sound *ṛ*").

{**Explanation:**
Patañjali concludes that there is no intervention of another sound in the vowel *ṛ* as the vocalic part is only a quarter of a mora long. He further adds that the intervention may refer only to such sounds that are mentioned by Pāṇini himself in the *Śivasūtra*s, which means those explicitly stated as well as those which are implicit, that is, their long and prolated counterparts. This, obviously, cannot refer to the vocalic part *a* in *ṛ*. Moreover, the inclusion of such words as *nṛnamana* and *tṛpnoti* in the *sūtra* A. 8.4.39, which negates the *ṇ*-substitute, indicates that the operation usually takes place in words containing the vowel *ṛ*. Otherwise, we can accept the division of a rule at a later stage, in the *sūtra* A. 8.4.26, which would render the *vārttika* unnecessary.}

A. 8.4.2 *aṭkupvāṅnumvyavāye 'pi*
[The retroflex sound *ṇ* comes in place of the sound *n* occurring after the sounds *r* or *ṣ* within the same word] even when there is separation by [a sound denoted by] *aṬ* (i.e., all vowels, *h*, semivowels except *l*), [a sound belonging to the group] *kU* or *pU*, [the particle] *āṄ* or [the infix] *nUM* [in close proximity].

VMBh_1: III.452.21-23; VMBh_2: V.490.6-8

1) Prohibition [should be mentioned] in the case of the *ṇ*-substitute when [a sound denoted by] *aṬ* (i.e., all vowels, *h*, semivowels except *l*) intervenes, when something else [also] intervenes.

[Bhāṣya:] Prohibition should be mentioned in the case of the *ṇ*-substitute when [a sound denoted by] *aṬ* intervenes, when something else [also] intervenes. [For example,] *ādarśena* ('by looking, through a mirror', instr. sg.), *ākṣadarśena* ('by a judge', instr. sg.).

{**Explanation:**

This *vārttika* seems superfluous because by the nature of the ablative *raṣābhyām*, on the basis of A. 1.1.67,[493] the *ṇ*-substitution would take place only when the consonant *n* appears directly after the sounds *r* or *ṣ*, and also when the elements mentioned in the *sūtra* intervene. However, any other intervening sound is excluded, therefore the prohibition is not necessary. The consonant *ś* following *r* in the examples given is not included in any of the conditions mentioned in the rule. Thus, the substitution will not take place.}

VMBh_1: III.453.1-4; VMBh_2: V.490.9-491.1

2) Alternatively, due to the separation by something else.

[Bhāṣya:] An alternative should be mentioned.
[Question:] What is the reason?
[Answer:] Due to the separation by something else. There is the separation by something else in this case.
[Objection:] Even if there is the separation by something else, there is also the separation by [a sound denoted by] *aṬ*. With respect to that, when there is the separation by [a sound denoted by] *aṬ*, [the substitution] would result.
[Answer:] It is only when there is the separation by [a sound denoted by] *aṬ*.

{**Explanation:**
On the basis of the previous *sūtra* the substitution would take place when the consonant *n* appears after *r* or *ṣ* directly due to *paribhāṣā* A. 1.1.67. The present rule established the intervention by other sounds, making the substitution possible in these cases. Enlisting particular conditions excludes other sounds from intervening and consequently from being subject to the application of the rule.
Annambhaṭṭa (MPV X.462) explains that the *paribhāṣā* should apply in full and the present rule is not a restrictive *sūtra* but it establishes the *ṇ*-substitution in such cases that are not covered by A. 8.4.1. It is, therefore, to be treated as a *vidhi* rule.}

VMBh_1: III.453.4-17; VMBh_2: V.491.1-16

[Question:] Should it be mentioned?
[Answer:] No.
[Question:] How will something unexpressed be understood?
[Answer:] By force of the expression "by [a sound denoted by] *aṬ*."

---

[493] A. 1.1.67 *tasmād ity uttarasya* || ("A form stated in the ablative denotes an element, the unit following which [is subject to the grammatical operation introduced by the rule].")

[Objection:] But where there is the separation by [a sound denoted by] *aṬ* and by something else, there should be [the *ṇ*-substitute and] the expression "by [a sound denoted by] *aṬ*" should be superfluous. He should say only this: "[the sound] *ṇ* comes in place of [the sound] *n* where there is the separation [by something]."
[Answer:] The purpose of the expression "by [a sound denoted by] *aṬ*" is different.
[Question:] What?
[Answer:] [The substitution] must not take place where there is the separation by undefined [elements]. [For example,] *kṛtsna*, *mṛtsnā* ('whole, entire' and 'good soil' respectively).
[Objection:] If the purpose should be of that kind, he should say "[there is] no [substitute] when there is the separation by [a sound denoted by] *śaR* (i.e., sibilants)."

3) When there is a combination of that, there is no accomplishment of the *ṇ*-substitute like elsewhere.

[Bhāṣya:] When there is a combination of that, [namely,] when there is a combination of the separation [i.e., of the elements that intervene], there in no accomplishment of the *ṇ*-substitute. [For example,] *arkeṇa*, *argheṇa* ('by the sun' and 'by worth, price' respectively, instr. sg.). Just like elsewhere, when there is a combination of the separation [i.e., of the elements that intervene], the operation does not take place either.
[Question:] Where is elsewhere?
[Answer:] [In the *sūtra*] A. 8.3.58; e.g., *niṃsse*, *niṃssva* ('kiss!', 2nd sg. impv.).
[Question:] Why, however, does the operation not take place when there is a combination of the separation [i.e., of the elements that intervene] elsewhere?
[Answer:] The completion of an idea [to be expressed] in an utterance is seen separately.[494] Just like the terms *guṇa* and *vṛddhi* are [applied] separately.
[Objection:] But this is the example for the completion of the idea [to be expressed] in an utterance when there is a combination.[495] Just like [here:] *gargāḥ śataṃ daṇḍyantām* ("Let the Gargas be punished with a hundred"). Kings desire gold and they are not individually punished.
[Objection:] If it is so, when one [element] intervenes, [the substitute] would not result; e.g., *kiriṇā*, *giriṇā* ('through, by a mountain', instr. sg.).

---

[494] PŚ 107 *pratyekaṃ vākyaparisamāptiḥ* || ("What is stated [in grammar of several things] must be understood [to have been stated] of each of them separately."), I.105, II.491-492. WUJASTYK 1993: vol. I:33, vol. II:129.

[495] PŚ 108 *kvacit samudāye 'pi* || ("Sometimes [it is] also [understood to have been stated of all of them collectively."), I.105-106, II.492-493. WUJASTYK 1993: vol. I:33-34, vol. II:130-131.

[Answer:] The completion of the idea [to be expressed] in an utterance is seen in both cases. Just like: it should not be eaten with Gargas (*gargaiḥ saha na bhoktavyam*), one by one, it is not eaten together with them gathered.

{**Explanation:**
The above discussion focuses on the interpretation of the nature of separation, whether the rule should apply when there is only one intervening element, or when there is more than one. The conclusion is that the *ṇ*-substitution takes place regardless of the number of elements intervening between the sounds *r* or *ṣ* and the sound *n*. It could be only one, two or all of those mentioned in the *sūtra*.}

VMBh_1: III.453.18-21; VMBh_2: V.491.17-492.3

4) When [a sound belonging to the group] *kU* intervenes, prohibition [should be stated] with respect to the substitute of [the verbal root] *hanA* ('to kill', DhP II:2).

[Bhāṣya:] When [a sound belonging to the group] *kU* intervenes, prohibition should be mentioned with respect to the substitute of [the verbal root] *hanA* ('to kill', DhP II:2).
[Question:] What is the purpose?

5) The purpose is [the forms] *vṛtraghna* ('the killer of Vṛtra'), *srughna* (name of a place) and *prāghāṇi* ('let me kill', 1st sg. impv. from *prāhan*).

[Answer:] In [the *sūtra*] A. 8.4.22, the expression "[of the sound *n*] preceded by the sound *a*" should not be included.

{**Explanation:**
The *ṇ*-substitute in the example *vṛtraghna* could take place on the basis of A. 8.4.11 allowing for this substitution when *n* appears as the final element of a nominal stem. The basic form *han* undergoes the *gh* substitution by A. 7.3.54 *ho hanter ñṇitneṣu*,[496] which would make the sound *n* of *ghna* in *vṛtraghna* subject to the *ṇ*-substitution. These two *vārttika*s prevent that.
The answer Patañjali gives under the *vārttika* 5 refers to the form *prāghāṇi* and to the condition stated in the rule A. 8.4.22. The derivation of the form is as follows:

[496] A. 7.3.54 *ho hanter ñṇitneṣu* || ("[A substitute velar stop] comes in place of the sound *h* of [the verbal root] *hanA* ('to kill', DhP II:2) before [the suffix] marked with *Ñ* or *Ṇ*, or the sound *n* [when the penultimate vowel is deleted by A. 6.4.98.")

(1) *pra + hanA* (DhP II:2) + *lUṄ*
(2) *pra + han + Cli + tha* (A. 3.1.43 *cli luṅi*, A. 3.4.78 *tiptasjhisipthasthamibvasmastātāmjhathāsāthāmdhvamiḍvahimahiṅ*)
(3) *pra + han + Cli + (tha → ta)* (A. 3.4.101 *tasthasthamipāṃ tāntantāmaḥ*)
(4) *pra + han + CiṆ + ta* (A. 3.1.66 *ciṇ bhāvakarmaṇoḥ*)
(5) *pra + aṬ + han + CiṆ + ta* (A. 6.4.71 *luṅlaṅlṛṅkṣv aḍudāttaḥ*)
(6) *pra + a + (h → gh) an + i + ta* (A. 7.3.54 *ho hanter ñṇitneṣu*)
(7) *pr (a + a → ā) + ghan + i + ta* (A. 6.1.101 *akaḥ savarṇe dīrghaḥ*)
(8) *prā + gh (a → ā) n + i + ta* (A. 7.2.116 *ata upadhāyāḥ*)
(9) *prā + ghān + i + (ta →*0) (A. 6.4.104 *ciṇo luk*)
prāghāni

As can be seen from the derivation, the consonant *n* is not preceded by the vowel *a*, but by *ā* instead, which excludes this form from the scope of the *ṇ*-substitution. What Patañjali means is that the condition *atpūrvasya* in the *sūtra* A. 8.4.22 is not necessary; he accepts this *vārttika* instead.}

VMBh_1: III.453.22-23; VMBh_2: V.492.4-6

6) When [the infix] *nUM* intervenes, prohibition [should be mentioned] with respect to the *ṇ*-substitute when there is no *anusvāra*.

[Bhāṣya:] When [the infix] *nUM* intervenes, prohibition should be mentioned with respect to the *ṇ*-substitute when there is no *anusvāra*. [For example,] *prenvanam*, *prenvanīyam* ('sending forth' and 'to be sent forth' respectively).

{Explanation:
The *sūtra* prescribes the *ṇ*-substitute even if the infix *nUM* intervenes but according to the present *vārttika*, it takes place only when the consonant *n* of the infix is changed into the *anusvāra*. This is not the case with the examples given. The derivation of *prenvanam* is as follows:

(1) *pra + ivI* (DhP I:618) + *LyuṬ* (A. 3.3.115 *lyuṭ ca*)
(2) *pra + iv + (yu → ana)* (A. 7.1.1 *yuvor anākau*)
(3) *pra + i + nUM + v + ana* (A. 7.1.58 *idito num dhātoḥ*)
pr (a + i → e) nv + ana (A. 6.1.87 *ād guṇaḥ*)
prenvana

The *ṇ*-substitute could apply on the basis of A. 8.4.32 *ijādeḥ sanumaḥ* as the verbal root begins with a sound other than *a* and has the infix *nUM* inserted. This *vārttika* prevents the substitution because *n* of the infix is not turned into the *anusvāra*.}

VMBh_1: III.453.24-25; VMBh_2: V.492.7-8

7) And the *ṇ*-substitute [should be mentioned] in the case of the infix *ana*.

[Objection:] And the *ṇ*-substitute [should be mentioned] in the case of the infix *ana*. [For example,] *tṛmpaṇīya* ('to be satisfied').

{**Explanation:**
Patañjali's commentators do not comment on this *vārttika* but the *Kāśikāvṛtti* does. It states that there is no infix *nUM* inserted in this case but the *anusvāra* is originally in the verbal root (*tṛmphA*, DhP VI:25). Therefore, as the next *vārttika* states, the *anusvāra* is the cause for the substitution; we do not need to make a separate condition for the infix *ana*.}

VMBh_1: III.454.1-7; VMBh_2: V.492.9-16

8) But this is achieved through the *anusvāra*.

[Bhāṣya:] It should be mentioned that [the sound] *ṇ* comes in place of [the sound] *n* when the *anusvāra* intervenes.
[Question:] Should the word *anusvāra* be used then?
[Answer:] It should not be used. The maxim is formulated; it is recommended that an *anusvāra* became homogenous with the [following] sound *n*.
[Objection:] In this case then [the substitute] would result as well – *prenvanam*, *prenvanīyam* ('sending forth' and 'to be sent forth' respectively).
[Answer:] The word *nUM* is a qualifier to the *anusvāra*; [it is] the *anusvāra* that [comes from the infix] *nUM*.
[Objection:] In this case then [the substitute] would not result – *tṛmpaṇa* ('the act of satisfying'), *tṛmpaṇīya* ('to be satisfied').
[Answer:] In such a way then the instruction is produced by the lack of specification of the *ayogavāha* sounds. In that case when the *anusvāra* has been accomplished, [a sound denoted by] *aṬ* intervenes; only then [the substitute] is achieved.
[Objection:] If this is so, the meaning is not [achieved] by the word *nUM*.
[Answer:] When the *anusvāra* has been accomplished, [a sound denoted by] *aṬ* intervenes; only then [the substitute] is achieved.

{**Explanation:**
The above discussion refers to the infix *nUM* mentioned in the text of the *sūtra*. As for the rule to apply we need the *anusvāra* rather than the infix itself, it is the *anusvāra* that should be stated in the *sūtra*. Kaiyaṭa specifies (VMBh_2: V.491)

that Patañjali's actual solution is the inclusion of two consonants *n* in the *sūtra*. It should read *nnum* where the first *n* would refer to the *anusvāra* that is replaced by a sound homogenous with the following sound in a word. Moreover, such an *n* coming from the infix *nUM* is subject to the *ṇ*-substitution that is replaced by the *anusvāra*.
Patañjali refers to the sounds termed *ayogavāha*. These are the *visarjanīya*, *anusvāra*, *upadhmānīya* and *jīhvāmūlīya*, and they are not specified in the *Śivasūtras*. Yet still, there are cases, like in the present *sūtra*, when they need to be subject to an operation. Patañjali specifies this in the *vārttika* 6 on the *Śivasūtra* 5: *ayogavāhānām aṭsu ṇatvam*, referring to the present rule.}

A. 8.4.3 *pūrvapadāt saṃjñāyām agaḥ*
[The retroflex sound *ṇ* comes in place of the sound *n* occurring] after the first member of a compound [containing the sounds *r* or *ṣ* even when there is the separation by a sound denoted by *aṬ* (i.e., all vowels, *h*, semivowels except *l*), a sound belonging to the group *kU* or *pU*, the particle *āṄ* or the infix *nUM*] except for [the sound] *g* [in close proximity] to denote a name.

VMBh_1: III.454.8-16; VMBh_2: V.493.1-9

1) [If it is said] "after the first member of a compound to denote a name", the expression "the second member of a compound" [should be used as well].

[Bhāṣya:] [If it is said] "after the first member of a compound to denote a name", the expression "the second member of a compound" should be used [as well].
[Question:] What is the purpose?

2) In order not to prohibit [the substitute of the sound *n*] being in the first constituent of a *taddhita* [formation].

[Bhāṣya:] There must not be prohitition [of the substitute of the sound *n*] being in the first constituent of a *taddhita* [formation]. [For example,] *khārapāyaṇa* ('a descendant of Kharapa'),[497] *karaṇapriya* ('he to whom doing is dear').
[Question:] Should it be mentioned then.
[Answer:] It should not be mentioned. These words, [that is,] first member and the second member of a compound, are relative terms. When there is the first member of a compound, there is the last one and when there is the last member of a compound, there is the first one. Therefore, due to this relation, it should be

497 See A. 4.1.99 *naḍādibhyaḥ phak* || ("[The *taddhita* suffix] *phaK* comes after [the nominal stems] *naḍa* etc. [to denote the meaning 'his descendant'].")

understood thus: "There is restriction [of the *ṇ*-substitute of the sound *n*] being in that with respect to which there is the prior member [of a compound]."
[Question:] Which is that [applied] to?
[Answer:] To the last member of a compound.

{**Explanation:**
The proposition is made to include the expression *uttarapada* in the *sūtra*. The argument is that otherwise the *ṇ*-substitute would not be able to apply in the *taddhita* formations. Kaiyaṭa explains (VMBh_2: V.493) that the term *pūrvapada* is a qualifier to the sounds *r* and *ṣ*, which means that *ṇ* replaces such an *n* that appears after *r* or *ṣ* contained in the preceding member of a compound. Thus, the ablative *pūrvapadāt* should be interpreted as the locative.
The *vārttika* is, however, rejected. The term *pūrvapada* indicates that there is the *uttarapada* as well. What would be needed for the application of this *sūtra* is the cause in the first member of a compound and the result in the second one. The restriction prescribed in this rule does not have to refer to the *taddhita* formations at all. The *ṇ*-substitute in such derivatives is achieved by the general rule A. 8.4.1. We cannot talk of *pūrva* and *uttara pada*s in a *taddhita* derivative either. The word *khārapāyaṇa* is formed with the suffix *phaK* from the stem *kharapa*. The suffix, whose form is *ayana*, is not a *pada*. Therefore, we can say that the cause of application lies in the previous constituent of a *taddhita* formation, namely in *kharapa*; but not in the preceding *pada*. Consequently, the restriction in the present rule cannot refer to such derivatives.}

VMBh_1: III.454.17-455.9; VMBh_2: V.493.10-494.11

3) When restriction with respect to the name is stated due to prohibition [of substitution] in the case of [the sound] *g*, there is prohibition of restriction.

[Bhāṣya:] When restriction with respect to the name is stated due to prohibition [of substitution] in the case of [the sound] *g*, this prohibition of restriction is understood – not [when it contains the sound] *g*.
[Question:] What is the problem there?

4) In that case, there is potential involvement of the obligatory *ṇ*-substitute.

[Answer:] In that case, on the basis of the previous [*sūtra* A. 8.4.1.] the *ṇ*-substitute would result whether [the word] denotes a name or not.

5) It has been achieved through the division of the rule.

[Bhāṣya:] The division of the rule will be made. [Firstly,] *pūrvapadāt saṃjñāyām* ("after the first member of a compound to denote a name"). Then, *agaḥ* ("not [when it contains the sound] *g*"). Whenever there is the application of the *ṇ*-substitute [of the sound *n*] which occurs after the first member of a compound ending in [the sound] *g*, all of this is prohibited.

6) Alternatively, there is the lack of prohibition like in the case of the terms of pronouns.

[Bhāṣya:] Alternatively, the meaning is thanks to prohibition.
[Question:] Why do we not have the *ṇ*-substitute [here]?
[Answer:] [Just] as in the case of the terms of pronouns. And it has been said in the case of the terms of pronouns: "In the case of the terms of pronouns there is the lack of the *ṇ*-substitute due to irregularity."[498]
[Objection:] If, on the other hand, irregularity is done in [the *sūtra*] A. 1.1.27,[499] what is irregularity now?
[Answer:] In this case there is irregularity as well.
[Question:] What?
[Answer:] [It is the *sūtra*] A. 4.3.73.[500]
[Bhāsya:] Alternatively again, here the *ṇ*-substitute would not result through the previous [*sūtra* A. 8.4.1].
[Question:] Why?
[Answer:] It is said – "within the same word" – and this is not the same word. The same word is when a compound has been done. The same word is what is integral and this is not the integral same word.
[Question:] Should it be mentioned?
[Answer:] No.
[Question:] How will that which is not mentioned be understood?
[Answer:] On the basis of [using] the word 'the same' (*samāna*), because if [the substitution] should take place [whether the cause of the operation and the element to be substituted are] in the same [word] or not, the word 'the same' would be useless.

{**Explanation:**
The above discussion refers to the interpretation of the *sūtra* as either a *niyama* or a *vidhi* rule. The previous rule prescribed the *ṇ*-substitute under the condition that both the cause for the substitution and the element to be substituted appear in

---

498 See A. 1.1.27 *vt*. 1 *sarvanāmasaṃjñāyāṃ nipātanāṃ ṇatvābhāvaḥ*.
499 A. 1.1.27 *sarvādīni sarvanāmāni* || ("[The words] *sarva* ('whole') etc. [are termed] pronouns.")
500 A. 4.3.73 *aṇ ṛgayanādibhyaḥ* || ("[The *taddhita* suffix] *aṆ* comes after [nominal stems] *ṛgayana* etc. [to denote a commentary or 'found therein'].")

the same *pada*. In the case of compounds, however, we do not find one *pada* as the term *pūrvapada* and *uttarapada* show. Therefore, the *ṇ*-substitute would not apply if the present rule were to be considered restrictive, which is why this *sūtra* is a *vidhi* rule. The question is raised as to how it is possible to achieve the *ṇ*-substitute in the *taddhita* formation *khārapāyaṇa*. It does not have *pūrva* and *uttara padas* because the suffix cannot be termed *pada*. Moreover, the cause for the substitution appears in the word *khara* from which *khārapāyaṇa* is derived. Therefore, we cannot speak of the cause for the substitution and the element to be substituted appearing in the same *pada* either. replies that the *ṇ*-substitution applies in this case because the consonant *r*, being the cause of the operation, is used in an irregular way and also the consonant *n* is irregularly considered to be within the same *pada*.
The issue has been raised regarding two restrictions in the present rule: *saṃjñāyām* and *agaḥ*. The third *vārttika* states that the negation *agaḥ* could negate the restriction 'to denote a name', which would result in the obligatory *ṇ*-substitution in some cases. This is not the case, however, as it negates only the substitution itself and not the restriction. This meaning can be achieved by splitting the *sūtra*.}

{A. 8.4.4 *vanaṃ puragāmiśrakāsidhrakāśārikākoṭarāgrebhyaḥ*
[The retroflex sound *ṇ* comes in place of the sound *n* occurring in the last member of a compound] *vana* ('a forest') after [the words] *puragā*, *miśrakā*, *sidhrakā*, *śarikā*, *koṭara* (names of trees) or *agre* ('in front of') [in close proximity to denote a name].
A. 8.4.5 *pranirantaḥśarekṣuplakṣāmrakārṣyakhadirapīyūkṣābhyo 'asaṃjñā-yām api*
[The retroflex sound *ṇ* comes in place of the sound *n* occurring in the last member of a compound *vana* ('a forest')] after [the words] *pra*, *nir*, *antar* ('inside'), *śara* ('reed'), *ikṣu* ('sugar cane'), *plakṣa* ('a waved-leaf fig tree'), *amra* ('a mango tree'), *kārṣya*, *khadira*, *pīyūkṣā* [in close proximity to denote a name] or otherwise as well.} *These *sūtra*s were not commented upon by Patañjali.

A. 8.4.6 *vibhāṣauṣadhivanaspatibhyaḥ*
[The retroflex sound *ṇ*] rarely [comes in place of the sound *n* occurring in the last member of a compound *vana* ('a forest')] after [the names of] plants or forest trees [containing the sounds *r* or *ṣ* even when there is the separation by a sound denoted by *aṬ* (i.e., all vowels, *h*, semivowels except *l*), a sound belonging to the group *kU* or *pU*, the particle *āṄ* or the infix *nUM* in close proximity].

VMBh_1: III.455.10-12; VMBh_2: V.494.12-14

[Bhāṣya:] It should be mentioned [that the substitution takes place only when the word *vana* appears] after two- or three-syllable [stems]. It must not be in this case: *devadāruvana* ('a forest of deodars').
[Bhāsya:] Prohibition should be mentioned [when the word *vana* comes] after [the stems] *irikā* etc. [For example,] *irikāvana*, *timiravana* ('a forest of irikas' and 'a forest of timiras' respectively).

{Explanation:
Patañjali's comments assume the form of *vārttika*s in this rule, yet Kielhorn does not mark them so. Nāgeśa points out (VMBh_2: V.494) that by the term *akṣara* the combination of a vowel with a consonant is meant, implying that a single vowel cannot be so termed. Thus, the second *vārttika* gives the examples of two-syllable stems that are to precede the stem *vana* that have to be excluded from the scope of this *sūtra*.}

A. 8.4.7 *ahno 'dantāt*
[The retroflex sound *ṇ* comes in place of the sound *n* occurring in the last member of a compound] *ahna* ('a day') after [the prior member of a compound] ending in the vowel *a* [containing the sounds *r* or *ṣ* even when there is the separation by a sound denoted by *aṬ* (i.e., all vowels, *h*, semivowels except *l*), a sound belonging to the group *kU* or *pU*, the particle *āṄ* or the infix *nUM* in close proximity].

VMBh_1: III.455.13-16; VMBh_2: V.494.15-495.1

[Bhāṣya:] It should be mentioned [that the *ṇ*-substitution takes place in the last member of a compound] ending in the vowel *a* after [the prior member of a compound] ending in the vowel *a*. It must not be in this case: *dīrghāhnī śarad* ('autumn that has long days').
[Question:] Should it be mentioned then?
[Answer:] It should not be mentioned. This is not the genitive [ending] after the word *ahan*.
[Question:] What then?
[Answer:] There is the nominative [ending] after the word *ahan* as there is the instruction in the previous *sūtra*s. Alternatively, it will be read in [the *gaṇa*] *yuvādi* [in the *sūtra* A. 8.4.11].

{Explanation:
Kaiyaṭa explains (VMBh_2: V.495) that according to previous teachers, the substituend is not specified in the genitive case. By the *sūtra* A. 5.4.88 *ahno ahna*

etebhyaḥ[501] the form *ahan* is replaced with *ahna*. The nominative case is to be interpreted as the genitive here. Moreover, in some other *sūtra*s we also find the nominative case with such a purpose, as for example in A. 8.4.4, where the word *vana* is not specified with genitive. Another proposed solution is that the word *ahan* is read in the *gaṇa yuvādi* in the rule A. 5.1.130 *hāyanāntayuvādibhyo 'ṇ*.[502] According to the *vārttika* 3 on A. 8.4.11, which establishes the optional *ṇ*-substitution, the option does not apply to the stems included in *yuvādi*.}

A. 8.4.8 *vāhanam āhitāt*

[The retroflex sound *ṇ* comes in place of the sound *n* occurring in the last member of a compound] *vāhana* ('a vehicle') after [the prior member of a compound meaning] 'a thing placed' [containing the sounds *r* or *ṣ* even when there is the separation by a sound denoted by *aṬ* (i.e., all vowels, *h*, semivowels except *l*), a sound belonging to the group *kU* or *pU*, the particle *āṄ* or the infix *nUM* in close proximity].

VMBh_1: III.455.17-21; VMBh_2: V.495.2-6

[Bhāsya:] It should be mentioned after [the prior member of a compound meaning] 'a thing placed' and 'a thing that is nearby, approached'. It should be here as well: *ikṣuvāhaṇa*, *śaravāhaṇa* ('a cart to carry sugarcane' and 'a cart to carry reed' respectively).

[Bhāṣya:] Another one has said: "It should be mentioned [that the substitution takes place in the stem] *vāhana* [occurring] after 'that which is to be carried'."[503] Because when the vehicle of Gargas is pierced, then there must not be [the substitution]: *gargavāhana*.

{Explanation:

Patañjali's comments on the present rule can be summed up by saying that the *sūtra* might apply only in such cases when the stem *vāhana* is preceded by a stem denoting something to be carried or placed on a vehicle. It cannot refer to the situation where the ownership of the vehicle is meant. Therefore, if the word *gargavāhana* means 'a vehicle of Gargas', the *ṇ*-substitute will not apply. If, on

---

501 A. 5.4.88 *ahno ahna etebhyaḥ* ‖ ("[The morpheme] *ahna* comes in place of [the whole nominal stem] *ahan* ('a day') [as the last member of a compound] after these [i.e., *sarva* ('whole'), expressions meaning 'a portion' (*ekadeśa*), 'enumerated' (*saṃkhyāta*) and 'auspicious' (*puṇya*) as well as numbers and indeclinables].")

502 A. 5.1.130 *hāyanāntayuvādibhyo 'ṇ* ‖ ("[The *taddhita* suffix] *aṆ* comes after [the nominal stems] ending in *hāyana* ('year') as well as *yuvan* ('youth') etc. [ending in the genitive to denote its essential condition or state, its function or duty.")

503 VMBh_2 marks this statement as a *vārttika*.

the other hand, the word means 'a vehicle for carrying Gargas', we can achieve the substitution.}

{A. 8.4.9 *pānaṃ deśe*
[The retroflex sound *ṇ* comes in place of the sound *n* occurring in the last member of a compound] *pāna* ('a drink') [after the prior member of a compound containing the sounds *r* or *ṣ* even when there is the separation by a sound denoted by *aṬ* (i.e., all vowels, *h*, semivowels except *l*), a sound belonging to the group *kU* or *pU*, the particle *āṄ* or the infix *nUM* in close proximity] to denote a place.} *This *sūtra* was not commented upon by Patañjali.

A. 8.4.10 *vā bhāvakaraṇayoḥ*
[The retroflex sound *ṇ*] usually [comes in place of the sound *n* occurring in the last member of a compound *pāna* ('a drink') after the prior member of a compound containing the sounds *r* or *ṣ* even when there is the separation by a sound denoted by *aṬ* (i.e., all vowels, *h*, semivowels except *l*), a sound belonging to the group *kU* or *pU*, the particle *āṄ* or the infix *nUM* in close proximity] when denoting 'an activity' (*bhāva*) or 'an instrument' (*karaṇa*).

VMBh_1: III.456.1-4; VMBh_2: V.495.7-10

1) In the context of an option, the enumeration of [the nominal stems] *girinadī* ('a mountain river') etc. [should be done].

[Bhāṣya:] In the context of an option, the enumeration of [the nominal stems] *girinadī* ('a mountain river') etc. should be done. [For example,] *giriṇadī* or *girinadī*; *cakraṇitambā* or *cakranitambā* ('a woman with round buttocks').

A. 8.4.11 *prātipadikāntanumvibhaktiṣu*
[The retroflex sound *ṇ* usually comes in place of the sound *n* occurring] at the end of a nominal stem, [being a part of the infix] *nUM* or nominal endings [after the prior member of a compound containing the sounds *r* or *ṣ* even when there is the separation by a sound denoted by *aṬ* (i.e., all vowels, *h*, semivowels except *l*), a sound belonging to the group *kU* or *pU*, the particle *āṄ* or the infix *nUM* in close proximity].

VMBh_1: III.456.5-12; VMBh_2: V.495.11-496.4

1) The expression "at the end of a compound" [should be used] with respect to the *ṇ*-substitute [of the sound *n* occurring] at the end of a nominal stem in order to prohibit [the substitution when *n* appear] not at the end of a compound.

[Bhāṣya:] The expression "at the end of a compound" should be used with respect to the *ṇ*-substitute [of the sound *n* occurring] at the end of a nominal stem.
[Question:] What is the purpose?
[Answer:] In order to prohibit [the substitution when *n* appears] not at the end of a compound. [The substitution] must not take place at the end of what is not a compound. [For example,] *gargabhaginī*, *dakṣabhaginī* ('a sister of Gargas' and 'a sister of Dakṣas' respectively).
[Question:] Alternatively, will it take place in *gargabhagiṇī*?
[Answer:] There is [the *ṇ*-substitute] when the expression is "*gargabhaga* [meaning] the prosperity of Gargas" and "the prosperity of Gargas is hers" (*gargabhagiṇī*). But when the expression is "*gargabhaginī* [meaning] the sister of Gargas", then [the substitution] should not take place. Then it must not be.
[Objection:] If the expression "at the end of a compound" is formulated, in these cases – *māṣavāpiṇī* and *vrīhivāpiṇī* ('a woman sowing beans' and 'a woman sowing rice' respectively) – [the substitution] would not result.

{**Explanation:**
The expression *prātipadikānta* is a qualifier to *n*; the *ṇ*-substitution refers to such a sound *n* that appears at the end of a nominal stem. Moreover, as the *vārttika* proposes, this stem has to be the final member of a compound. If it is not, the substitution does not apply. The example given is *gargabhaginī* meaning 'a sister of Gargas'. The substitution does not take place because the compound is formed of *garga* and *bhaginī*, where the latter does not end in *n*. However, when the meaning is different; when the word means 'she who possesses the prosperity of Gargas', the *ṇ*-substitution will take place. In this case the compound is *gargabhagin* to which the feminine suffix *ṄīP* is added by A. 4.1.5 *ṛnnebhyo ṅīp*.[504] Kaiyaṭa (VMBh_2: V.496) also adds that the *ṇ*-substitute in this case applies on the basis of A. 8.4.1 due to the condition *samānapade*; according to him, both the cause of the substitution (the consonant *r*) and the consonant *n* appear in the same word.
A similar problem appears with words such as *māṣavāpiṇī* and *vrīhivāpiṇī*. According to the *pūrvapakṣa*, these are compounds ending in the vowel *ī* so the *sūtra* could not apply. However, the feminine suffix *ṄīP* is added after the compound has been formed and thus, we find that the stem ends in *n*, which allows the *ṇ*-substitution to take place. The reason for this solution is explained under the second *vārttika*.}

504 4.1.5 *ṛnnebhyo ṅīp* || ("[The suffix] *ṄīP* comes after [nominal stems ending in the sounds] *ṛ* or *n* [to derive a feminine nominal stem].")

VMBh_1: III.456.13-17; VMBh_2: V.496.5-10

2) It has been mentioned that it is also so when the used [element] is characterized by gender.

[Question:] What has been mentioned?
[Answer:] The compound is said [to be formed] of *gati* (preverbs or adverbial prefixes), *kāraka*s (participants in an action) or *upapada*s (subordinate elements) with the stems ending in the *kṛt* suffix before the addition of *sUP* [endings or feminine suffixes].[505]

3) In that case prohibiton [should be mentioned] with respect to [the nominal stems] *yuvan* ('young') etc.

[Bhāṣya:] In that case prohibiton should be mentioned with respect to [the nominal stems] *yuvan* ('young') etc. [For example,] *āryayūnā* ('a noble young person'), *kṣatriyayūnā* ('a young warrior'), *prapakvāni* ('inflamed', nom./acc. pl. n.), *paripakvāni* ('fully riped', nom./acc. pl. n.), *dīrghāhnī śarad* ('long-day-autumn').

{A. 8.4.12 *ekājuttarapade ṇaḥ*
[The retroflex sound] *ṇ* [comes in place of the sound *n* occurring at the end of a nominal stem, being a part of the infix *nUM* or nominal endings after the prior member of a compound containing the sounds *r* or *ṣ* even when there is the separation by a sound denoted by *aṬ* (i.e., all vowels, *h*, semivowels except *l*), a sound belonging to the group *kU* or *pU*, the particle *āṄ* or the infix *nUM*] when the last member of a compound is monosyllabic [in close proximity].} *This *sūtra* was not commented upon by Patañjali.

A. 8.4.13 *kumati ca*
[The retroflex sound *ṇ* comes in place of the sound *n* occurring at the end of a nominal stem, being a part of the infix *nUM* or nominal endings after the prior member of a compound containing the sounds *r* or *ṣ* even when there is the separation by a sound denoted by *aṬ* (i.e. all vowels, *h*, semivowels except *l*), a sound belonging to the group *kU* or *pU*, the particle *āṄ* or the infix *nUM* when the last member of a compound] contains a sound belonging to the group] *kU* [in close proximity].

VMBh_1: III.456.18-457.2; VMBh_2: V.496.11-497.2

---

[505] See A. 4.1.48 *vt*. 4 and PŚ 75, I.79-81, II.380-385.

[Question:] But in this case how should it be: *māṣakumbhavāpeṇa* ('by sowing jars of beans'), *vrīhikumbhavāpeṇa* ('by sowing jars of rice')? Should the *ṇ*-substitute be obligatory or optional?[506]

[Answer:] To begin with, the *ṇ*-substitute should be obligatory when the expression is "*kumbhavāpa* [meaning] sowing a jar" and "sowing a jar of beans" (*māṣakumbhavāpa*). When, however, the expression is "*māṣakumbha* [meaning] a jar of beans" and "sowing a jar of beans", then [the substitution] should be optional.

{Explanation:

The *ṇ*-substitution in the forms *māṣakumbhavāpeṇa* and *vrīhikumbhavāpeṇa* depends on the interpretation of a compound. The substitution can take place when the following *pada* of a compound contains a velar sound (*kU*). This is the purpose of the suffix *matUP* used in the *sūtra*. If the suffix were not used, the following *pada* would have to begin with a sound belonging to the velar group. The examples in question can be analysed in two ways. We can combine the word *kumbha* with *vāpa* first – 'sowing of jars' – and then we compound it with *māṣa*, achieving *māsākumbhavāpa* – 'sowing jars of beans'. Otherwise, we can combine *māṣa* and *kumbha* first – 'jars of beans' – and then we add *vāpa*, achieving 'sowing jars of beans'. As Kaiyaṭa explains (VMBh_2: V.496), the *ṇ*-substitution should not apply because the words *māṣa* and *vāpa* are separated by a *pada*, which would trigger the prohibition stated in A. 8.4.38 *padavyavāye 'pi*. The *nimitta* (sounds *r* or *ṣ*) and *nimittin* (sound *n*) are separated by a *pada kumbha*. On the other hand, some say that in the case of the second analysis, that is *māṣakumbha* + *vāpa*, the word *kumbha* is not given the designation of a *pada*. The reference is made to the *vārttika* 6 on the *sūtra* A. 1.1.63 *na lumatāṅgasya*. The *vārttika* reads: *uttarapadatve cāpadādividhau* || ("And also with respect to the final member of a compound in the case of a rule not refering to the beginning of a *pada*."). When compounds are formed, the case ending is deleted by the suffix *luK* on the basis of the *sūtra* A. 2.4.71 *supo dhātuprātipadikayoḥ*. In our example, the case ending after *māṣakumbha* before compounding with *vāpa* is deleted, and its deletion by *luK* does not affect the following operations. Thus, the word *kumbha* cannot be termed *pada* because it does not end in a suffix. Furthermore, the restriction of A. 8.4.38 cannot apply in this case, as the stems *māṣa* and *vāpa* are not separated by a *pada*. The conclusion is that the *ṇ*-substitution can take place. If, however, we accept the analysis *māṣa* + *kumbhavāpa*, the restriction of the *vārttika* 6 on A. 1.1.63 does not apply, because the word *kumbha* is not the final member of a compound. Which means that the prohibition of the *sūtra* A. 8.4.38 applies and the *ṇ*-substitution does not take place.

[506] Compare: A. 8.4.11.

Patañjali specifies that in the former case, the *ṇ*-substitution would be optional by A. 8.4.11, in the latter though it is obligatory by the present rule. It has to be mentioned that the *sūtra* A. 8.4.38 is placed later in the *Aṣṭādhyāyī* and as such is considered suspended with respect to both A. 8.4.11 and A. 8.4.13.}

A. 8.4.14 *upasargād asamāse 'pi ṇopadeśasya*
[The retroflex sound *ṇ* comes in place of the sound *n* of the verbal root] containing [the sound] *ṇ* in the original enunciation (*upadeśa*) [used] after an *upasarga* [containing the sounds *r* or *ṣ* even when there is the separation by a sound denoted by *aṬ* (i.e., all vowels, *h*, semivowels except *l*), a sound belonging to the group *kU* or *pU*, the particle *āṄ* or the infix *nUM* in close proximity] also when not in a compound.

VMBh_1: III.457.3-14; VMBh_2: V.497.3-498.4

[Question:] What is the purpose in [using] the expression "when not in a compound"?
[Answer:] [The expression] "when in a compound" continues; [the substitution] should take place also when there is no compound. [For example,] *praṇamati* ('he bows'), *pariṇamati* ('he changes').
[Question:] Where was the term 'compound' used then?
[Answer:] In [the *sūtra*] A. 8.4.3.
[Question:] But how is it possible to understand the term 'compound' from this [rule]?
[Answer:] On the basis of the expression "after the prior member of a compound" (A. 8.4.3 *pūrvapadāt*). Only in a compound there are prior and last members.
[Question:] But what is the purpose in [using] the word 'even, also'?
[Answer:] [The substitution] should take place also in a compound. [For example,] *praṇāmaka*, *pariṇāmaka* ('a person who bends down').
[Objection:] If then it is required both in a compound and not in a compound, the meaning is not [achieved] through the expression "also when not in a compound". [The expression] "after the prior member of a compound" is not continued.
[Answer:] I will say [that there is] the *ṇ*-substitute after an *upasarga* without special specification.
[Objection:] It would not result in a compound due to the restriction.
[Answer:] The *ṇ*-substitute after an *upasarga* is suspended [with respect to the operation in the *sūtra* A. 8.4.3] and due to its suspension, there will be no restriction.

[Answer:] In this way then when it is not suspended, when the teacher uses the expression "also when not in a compound", he indicates that one rule is not suspended with respect to another.
[Question:] How then?
[Answer:] One subject is suspended with respect to another.
[Question:] What is the purpose in such an indication?
[Answer:] Whatever has been said, in these cases – *niṣkṛta* and *niṣpīta* ('removed, expelled' and 'drunk out' respectively) – the *ṣ*-substitute would not result due to suspension of the *s*-substitute; there is no problem [in this] (see A. 8.3.39).

{**Explanation:**
The problem discussed here concerns the purpose of using the term *asamāse* in the text of the rule. It is explained that the expression *pūrvapadāt* from the *sūtra* A. 8.4.3 is understood as well, which means that without the word *asamāse* the substitution would take place in compounds only. The rule A. 8.4.3 refers to compounds as we cannot have *pūrvapada* anywhere else. The purpose of the *sūtra* is to allow the substitution in both compounds and non-compounds. The rule A. 8.4.3 could pose restriction on the application of the *ṇ*-substitution in compounds. This argument is refuted, however, because A. 8.4.14 is *asiddha*; the restriction cannot apply. As Kaiyaṭa reminds (VMBh_2: V.497) us, there are two views regarding A. 8.4.3: it might be considered a *niyama sūtra* or a *vidhi sūtra*. According to the former view, the *ṇ*-substitute achieved by A. 8.4.1 is restricted to the situation when the cause of the operation (the sounds *r* or *ṣ*) and the caused (the sound *n*) appear in the same *pada* of a compound. Similarly with the condition *asamāse*, the *ṇ*-substitution takes place. However, the suspension of one domain with respect to another is implied, and here, in the case of both A. 8.4.3 and A. 8.4.14 there is one domain, therefore there is no suspension of a single rule. According to the second view, when the rule A. 8.4.3 is interpreted as a *vidhi sūtra*, the implication regarding the domain suspension as opposed to the rule suspension is not created. Annaṃbhaṭṭa explains (MPV X.467) that the conditions established in A. 8.4.3 do not appear in the present rule, therefore the issue of suspension does not arise and, consequently, the implication of the domain suspension with respect to another domain cannot be made.
Even so, Patañjali accepts the interpretation "it is the domain that is suspended with respect to another domain, not the rule with respect to another rule", due to the meaningfulness that single rules lack.
Yet another solution is proposed with reference to the *ṣ*-substitute in the forms such as *niṣkṛta* and *niṣpīta*. The *ṣ*-substitute could apply by A. 8.3.39 *iṇkoḥ* or A. 8.3.41 *idudupadhasya cāpratyayasya*, the question being whether it shoud replace *s* or the *visarjanīya*. The order would be *ḥ* → *s* → *ṣ*. However, due to suspension of the *s*-substitute, the *ṣ*-substitute would not take place. The difficulty arises because the *s*-substitute is suspended with respect to the *ṣ*-substitute. Even

though the *ṣ*-substitute is prescribed by A. 8.3.34, it does not refer to the examples given. The *s*-substitute in these cases could be prescribed by the rules following A. 8.3.39 or A. 8.3.41, and as such would be suspended. To remove this difficulty, the expression *asamāse 'pi*, indicating that we find the domain suspension rather than the rule suspension here, is used. When we reject this indication in A. 8.3.41, the *ṣ*-substitute will not replace *s*, but the *visarjanīya* only. Thus, Annaṃbhaṭṭa concludes that the implication of the domain suspension is used repeatedly in other places and it is not in the case of *niṣkṛta* and *niṣpīta*.}

VMBh_1: III.457.15-21; VMBh_2: V.498.5-11

1) There is no instruction because an *upasarga* is not [connected with] the original enunciation that is [the sound] *ṇ*.

[Bhāsya:] [The term] *anirdeśa* [means] "the instruction that has not been communicated". The terms *gati* and *upasarga* apply to that which is connected with an action and there is no connection with an action with respect to [the verbal roots] containing [the sound] *ṇ* in the original enunciation. In such a way then he has said: "[The retroflex sound *ṇ* comes in place of the sound *n* of the verbal root] containing [the sound] *ṇ* in the original enunciation (*upadeśa*) [used] after the *upasarga*s [containing the sounds *r* or *ṣ* even when there is the separation by a sound denoted by *aṬ* (i.e., all vowels, *h*, semivowels except *l*), a sound belonging to the group *kU* or *pU*, the particle *āṄ* or the infix *nUM* in close proximity] also when not in a compound" and the *upasarga* is not [connected with] the original enunciation that is [the sound] *ṇ*; it will be on the basis of the *sūtra*.

2) If it is [so] by force of the statement itself, prohibition [should be mentioned] in the case of deletion of a *pada*.

[Objection:] If it is [so] by force of the statement itself, prohibition should be mentioned in the case of deletion of a *pada*. [For example,] *pranāyako grāmaḥ* is a village from which the leaders went away.

{Explanation:
The expression *pranāyaka* in this case is derived from the sentence *pragatā nāyakā asmād grāmāt*, where the *upasarga pra* is not connected with the verbal root *ṇīÑ* (DhP I:950), stated in the *Dhātupāṭha* with *ṇ*. It is connected with the verbal root *gamḶ* (DhP I:1031) which is obviously not specified there with *ṇ*. The *pada gatā* is deleted, and this is how we achieve the form *pranāyakā*, which blocks the application of the *ṇ*-substitution.}

VMBh_1: III.457.22-458.2; VMBh_2: V.498.12-17

3) But it has been achieved through the statement that [the sound *ṇ* comes in place of the sound *n*] being in that to which an *upasarga* refers.

[Bhāṣya:] It has been achieved.
[Question:] How?
[Answer:] It should be said that [the sound] *ṇ* [comes in place of the sound *n*] being in that to which an *upasarga* refers.
[Answer:] It is achieved; the *sūtra* is divided then.
[Proposition:] Let it be according to the text of the *sūtra* then.
[Objection:] But has it not been said that: "There is no instruction because an *upasarga* is not [connected with] the original enunciation that is [the sound] *ṇ*'?
[Answer:] This is not a fault. [The expression] *ṇopadeśa* is not understood in this way: "the original enunciation that is [the sound] *ṇ*", [hence,] "of the original enunciation being [the sound] *ṇ*".
[Question:] How then?
[Answer:] [It should be understood as: "the term] *ṇopadeśa* [refers to] that which original enunciation contains [the sound] *ṇ*", [therefore] "of that which original enunciation contains [the sound] *ṇ*".

{**Explanation:**
In the above passage we find the rejection of the *karmadhāraya* interpretation of the compound *ṇopadeśa*; it is concluded that it should be *bahuvrīhi* meaning "of that [verbal root] whose original enunciation contains [the sound] *ṇ*". Thus, the *upasarga* must precede the verbal root that is specified in the *Dhātupāṭha* with *ṇ*. This sound is further replaced by *n* on the basis of the *sūtra* A. 6.1.65 *ṇo naḥ* ("[The substitute dental] *n* comes in place of [the retroflex] *ṇ* [occurring as initial of the verbal stem when first introduced in the *Dhātupāṭha*]"). And this consonant *n* is subject to the substitution prescribed by the present rule.}

A. 8.4.15 *hinumīnā*
[The retroflex sound *ṇ* comes in place of the sound *n* of the verbal roots] *hi* ('to urge on, incite', DhP V:11) and *mīÑ* ('to destroy', DhP IX:4) [used after an *upasarga* containing the sounds *r* or *ṣ* even when there is the separation by a sound denoted by *aṬ* (i.e., all vowels, *h*, semivowels except *l*), a sound belonging to the group *kU* or *pU*, the particle *āṄ* or the infix *nUM* in close proximity].

VMBh_1: III.458.3-10; VMBh_2: V.499.1-8

1) It should be added that in the case of [using] the words *hinu* and *mīnā* [the substitution refers] to the modified form [as well].

[Bhāṣya:] The addition should be made that in the case of the words *hinu* and *mīnā* [the substitution refers] to the modified form [as well]. [For example,] *prahiṇoti* and *pramīṇīte* ('he incites' and 'he destroys' respectively).
[Answer:] It will be from the statement. There is a purpose in the rule.
[Question:] What [purpose]?
[Answer:] [The forms] *prahiṇutaḥ* and *pramīṇāti* ('they both incite' and 'he incites' respectively).

2) It has been achieved due to [the substitute] being like the substituend in the case of vowels.

[Bhāṣya:] It has been achieved.
[Question:] How?
[Answer:] Due to [the substitute] being like the substituend in the case of vowels. There will be the *ṇ*-substitute in this case on the basis of the principle [that the substitute is treated] like the substituend.
[Objection:] Here the rule [that the substitute is treated] like the substituend is forbidden; *sthānivadbhāva* does not [apply] in the *pūrvatrāsiddha* section.
[Answer:] There are really faults with respect to that rule of interpretation; "its fault is with respect to the deletion of the initial [sound] of a cluster (A. 8.2.29), the *l*-substitute (A. 8.2.18 ff.) and the *ṇ*-substitute (A. 8.4.1 ff.) .

{**Explanation:**
The first *vārttika* proposes an addition which would allow for the inclusion of the changed forms in the domain of substitution. As can be seen from the text of the *sūtra*, the verbal roots were specified with their respective *vikaraṇas* *Śnu* and *Śnā*, according to the class they belong to. The desired derivatives are achieved with the help of the *paribhāṣā*: *ekadeśavikṛtam ananyavat* ("An item altered in part does not behave like something else").[507] Therefore, despite the particular specification in the *sūtra*, even the forms where some changes took place do undergo the *ṇ*-substitution. The derivation of *pramīṇītaḥ* ('the two destroy') is as follows:

(1) *pra* + *mīÑ* (DhP IX:4) + *Śnā* + *tas* (A. 3.1.81 *kryādibhyaḥ śnā*, A. 3.4.78 *tiptasjhisipthasthamibvasmastātāmjhathāsāthāmdhvamiḍvahimahiṅ*)
(2) *pra* + *mī* + *n* (*ā* → *ī*) + *tas* (A. 6.4.113 *ī haly aghoḥ*)
(3) *pra* + *mī* + (*n* → *ṇ*) *ī* + *tas* (A. 8.4.15 *hinumīnā*)
(4) *pra* + *mī* + *ṇī* + *ta* (*s* → *rU*) (A. 8.2.66 *sasajuṣo ruḥ*)
(5) *pra* + *mī* + *ṇī* + *ta* (*r* → *ḥ*) (A. 8.3.15 *kharavasānayor visarjanīyaḥ*)

---

507 WUJASTYK 1993: vol. I:8, vol. II:37; PŚ 37, vol. I:33-34, vol. II:179-184.

pramīṇītaḥ

The second *vārttika* proposes that the same can be achieved through the principle of *sthānivadbhāva*.[508] Thus, in the above example the vowel *ī*, being the replacement for *ā*, would still be considered *ā* for the sake of the *ṇ*-substitution. The argument is raised, however, that this principle does not work in the *pūrvatrāsiddha* section, as was specified in the *vārttika* 3 on A. 1.1.58 *na padāntadvirvacanavareyalopasvarasavarṇānusvāradīrghajaścarvidhiṣu*, which reads *pūrvatrāsiddhe ca* ("[The sustitute of a vowel is not treated like the substituend] also in the *pūrvatrāsiddha* [section]"). As is pointed out by Patañjali, however, this *vārttika* is refuted by yet another one, *vārttika* 10 *tasya doṣaḥ saṃyogādilopalatvaṇatveṣu* on the same *sūtra*. The conclusion is that we do not need to specify other conditions for the substitution when the form of the word changes, because the *sūtra* covers them all either with the help of *sthānivadbhāva* or the *paribhāṣā* 37.}

A. 8.4.16 *āni loṭ*

[The retroflex sound *ṇ* comes in place of the sound *n* of] the first person singular imperative (*āni*) [introduced after a verbal stem used after an *upasarga* containing the sounds *r* or *ṣ* even when there is the separation by a sound denoted by *aṬ* (i.e., all vowels, *h*, semivowels except *l*), a sound belonging to the group *kU* or *pU*, the particle *āṄ* or the infix *nUM* in close proximity].

VMBh_1: III.458.11-15; VMBh_2: V.499.9-13

[Question:] Why is [the expression] *lOṬ* used?
[Answer:] [Because the substitution will not take place in these cases: *prahimāni kulāni* ('the country with severe winters') and *pravapāni māṃsāni* ('meat containing thick membrane').

1) The expression *āni loṭ* is superfluous due to the use of a meaningful [unit].

[Bhāṣya:] The expression *āni loṭ* is superfluous.
[Question:] What is the reason?
[Answer:] Due to the use of a meaningful [unit]. The use of the meaningful word *āni* [makes] the other one (i.e., *lOṬ*) meaningless.

{Explanation:

---

[508] A. 1.1.57 *acaḥ parasmin pūrvavidhau* || ("A vowel [substitute conditioned] by the following [element is treated like the original vowel] with respect to an operation on what precedes it.")

The form *āni* refers to the form *ni* with the augment *āṬ* prescribed by the *sūtra* A. 3.4.92 *āḍ uttamasya pic ca.*[509] The ending *ni*, on the other hand, is the replacement for *miP* by A. 3.4.89 *mer niḥ.*[510] What is disputable, is whether it is necessary to use both expressions *āni* and *lOṬ*. One argument is that *lOṬ* is not superfluous because it allows us to avoid the confusion with the plural neuter ending *āni*, as in *pravapāni* etc. On the other hand, the *paribhāṣā*: *arthavadgrahaṇe nānarthakasya* ("When a meaningful item is mentioned, that item should not be mentioned without meaning")[511] shows that when the item *āni* is used, it is used with a certain meaning, and this meaning is the first person singular of the imperative. The inclusion of the term *lOṬ* in the text of the *sūtra* is thus not necessary to obtain the desired meaning.}

VMBh_1: III.458.16-22; VMBh_2: V.499.14-20

2) [The substitution in a verbal root] not preceded by an *upasarga* is optional.

[Bhāṣya:] Alternatively, the terms *gati* and *upasarga* apply to that which is connected with an action and there is no connection with an action with respect to the word *āni*. In this case then it would not result either: *prayāṇi* and *pariyāṇi* ('let me go' and 'let me go around' respectively).
[Objection:] But in this case the connection with an action is not with respect to the word *āni* either.
[Answer:] There is the connection with an action with respect to the word *āni*.
[Question:] How?
[Answer:] [The expression] *yatkriyāyuktāḥ* is not understood in such a way – "an action of which" (*yatkriyā*) [therefore] "those connected with an action of which, to that the terms *gati* and *upasarga* apply".
[Question:] How then?
[Answer:] [The expression] *yatkriyā* [is to be understood as] "which action", [therefore,] "those connected with which action, to that the terms *gati* and *upasarga* apply".

{Explanation:
The terms *gati* and *upasarga* can apply only to such elements that are connected with a verbal root. As Kaiyaṭa explains (VMBh_2: V.499.21 ff), an action is

509 A. 3.4.92 *āḍ uttamasya pic ca* ‖ ("[The initial augment] *āṬ* comes at the beginning of [the *l*-substitutes of] the first person [of *l*-member *lOṬ* (imperative)] and it functions as if it was marked with *P*.")

510 A. 3.4.89 *mer niḥ* ‖ ("[The substitute suffix] *ni* comes in place of [the whole of *l*-substitute of *lOṬ* (imperative)] *miP* [introduced after the verbal stem].")

511 WUJASTYK 1993: vol. I:1-2, vol II:3-10; PŚ 14, I.14, II.81-85.

viewed in context of its usage and not alone. Therefore, the connection with an action should be understood with respect to the whole element ending in *āni*. According to Kaiyaṭa, the *sūtra* should be understood in the following manner: "The sound *ṇ* comes in place of the sound *n* that appears in *āni* following the whole – verbal root preceded by an *upasarga*". It would mean that the expression *lOṬ* is superfluous in the text of the rule.}

A. 8.4.17 *ner gadanadapatapadaghumāsyatihantiyātivātidrātipsātivapativahati-śāmyaticinotidegdhiṣu ca*
[The retroflex sound *ṇ* comes in place of the sound *n*] of [the *upasarga*] *ni* [used] before [the verbal roots] *gadA* ('to speak', DhP I:53), *nadA* ('to roar', DhP I:55), *patḶ* ('to fly, fall down', DhP I:898), *padA* ('to fall, go', DhP IV:60), [those designated by the term] *ghu*, *māṄ* ('to measure', DhP IV:34), *ṣo* ('to destroy, kill', DhP IV:39), *hanA* ('to kill', DhP II:2), *yā* ('to go', DhP II:40), *vā* ('to blow', DhP II:41), *drā* ('to run', DhP II:45), *psā* ('to eat', DhP II:46), *ṬUvapA* ('to sow', DhP I:1052), *vahA* ('to carry', DhP I:1053), *śamU* ('to become tired, to stop', DhP IV:92), *ciÑ* ('to heap', DhP V:5) and *dihA* ('to anoint', DhP II:5) [after the *upasarga* containing the sounds *r* or *ṣ* even when there is the separation by a sound denoted by *aṬ* (i.e., all vowels, *h*, semivowels except *l*), a sound belonging to the group *kU* or *pU*, the particle *āṄ* or the infix *nUM* in close proximity].

VMBh_1: III.459.1-10; VMBh_2: V.500.1-9

1) It should be added that [the substitution takes place] in [the *upasarga*] *ni* [used] before [the verbal roots] *gadA* etc. when there is the separation by [a sound denoted by] *aṬ* (i.e., all vowels, *h*, semivowels except *l*).

[Bhāṣya:] The addition should be made that [the substitution takes place] in [the *upasarga*] *ni* [used] before [the verbal roots] *gadA* etc. when there is the separation by [a sound denoted by] *aṬ* (i.e., all vowels, *h*, semivowels except *l*). [For example,] *praṇyagadat* and *pariṇyagadat* ('he declared', 3rd sg. impf.). And it should be mentioned that [the substitution takes place even when there is the separation] by [the particle] *āṄ*. [For example,] *praṇyāgadat* ('he declared', 3rd sg. impf.).
[Objection:] But this [infix] *aṬ* being a part of [the verbal roots] *gad* etc. will be understood from mentioning [the very verbal roots] *gad* etc.
[Answer:] It is not achieved [in such a way]. [The infix] *aṬ* is said [to be a part] of an *aṅga* stem and this *aṅga* stem ends in an infix; this very [infix] is a part of a collection. In such a way then [the expression] "when there is the separation by *aṬ*" continues.
[Question:] Where was it first mentioned?

[Answer:] [It is the *sūtra*] A. 8.4.2. Here, therefore, the meaning is this: the qualifier of an element on which an operation is to be performed (*kāryin*) (i.e., the sound *n*) [is understood] by the specification of a cause [of an operation]. In that case there is the specification of a cause as well.

{Explanation:
The term *ghu* used in the *sūtra* refers to the forms *dā* and *dhā* on the basis of the rule A. 1.1.20 *dādhā ghv adāp*.[512] Thus, it refers to the verbal stems *ḌUdāÑ* ('to give', DhP III:3), *ḌUdhāÑ* ('to hold', DhP III:10), *do* ('to break into pieces', DhP IV:40), *dāṆ* ('to give', DhP I:977), *deṄ* ('to protect', DhP I:1011), and *dheṬ* ('to drink, suck', DhP I:951). The verbal stems excluded are *dāP* ('to cut', DhP II:50) and *daiP* ('to purify', DhP I:971).
In the case of the form *mā* mentioned in the *sūtra*, there can be two verbal roots *māṄ* ('to measure', DhP IV:34) and *meṄ* ('to give', DhP I:1010); but this form does not refer to verbal roots where *mā* is achieved through substitution by A. 6.1.50 *mīnātiminotidīṅāṃ lyapi ca*.[513]
The infix *aṬ* is suggested to constitute the whole with the verbal stems enlisted with the *sūtra*. It is, however, not so because it is added to an *aṅga* stem, that is, the verbal root to which the *vikaraṇa*, depending on the particular class it belongs to, has been added.[514] If we consider the example *praṇyagadat*, we notice that the infix comes after the consonant *n* that is subject to substitution and the consonant *r* which causes this substitution. So, the question arises as to where the separation in question is; it is not apparently between the *nimitta* and *nimittin* of the operation. Kaiyaṭa explains (VMBh_2: V.500) that the verbal roots *gad* etc. are the cause in here. The separation does not mean the situation when the *nimittin* follows the element separating it from the *nimitta*. It may also mean the situation when the cause follows the separation, as in *praṇyagadat*.}

{A. 8.4.18 *śeṣe vibhāṣā 'kakhādāv aṣānta upadeśe*
[The retroflex sound *ṇ*] optionally [comes in place of the sound *n* of the *upasarga ni* used] before remaining [verbal roots] not beginning with [the sounds] *k* or *kh* or ending in *ṣ* in original enunciation [occurring after the *upasarga* containing the sounds *r* or *ṣ* even when there is the separation by a

---

[512] A. 1.1.20 *dādhā ghv adāp* || ("[The technical term] *ghu* denotes [the verbal stems of the form] *dā* and *dhā* except those which have the shape of *dā* marked with *P*.")

[513] A. 6.1.50 *mīnātiminotidīṅāṃ lyapi ca* || ("[The substitute vowel *ā* comes in place of the vowel of the verbal roots] *mīÑ* ('to injure', DhP IX:4), *ḌUmiÑ* ('to scatter', DhP V:4) and *dīṄ* ('to decay, perish', DhP IV: 26) before [the substitute absolutive suffix] *LyaP* as well as [the suffixes marked with *Ś*].")

[514] A. 6.4.71 *luṅlaṅlṛṅkṣv aḍudāttaḥ* || ("[The initial augment] *aṬ udātta* accented comes [at the beginning of an *aṅga* stem] before [the *l*-substitutes of] aorist (*lUṄ*), imperfect (*lAṄ*) and conditional (*lṚṄ*).")

sound denoted by *aṬ* (i.e., all vowels, *h*, semivowels except *l*), a sound belonging to the group *kU* or *pU*, the particle *āṄ* or the infix *nUM* in close proximity].} *This *sūtra* was not commented upon by Patañjali.

A. 8.4.19 *aniteḥ*
[The retroflex sound *ṇ* comes in place of the sound *n*] of [the verbal root] *anA* ('to breathe', DhP II:61) [after the *upasarga* containing the sounds *r* or *ṣ* even when there is the separation by a sound denoted by *aṬ* (i.e., all vowels, *h*, semivowels except *l*), a sound belonging to the group *kU* or *pU*, the particle *āṄ* or the infix *nUM* in close proximity].
A. 8.4.20 *antaḥ*
[The retroflex sound *ṇ* comes in place of the sound *n*] occurring as a *pada* final [of the verbal root *anA* ('to breathe', DhP II:61) after the *upasarga* containing the sounds *r* or *ṣ* even when there is the separation by a sound denoted by *aṬ* (i.e., all vowels, *h*, semivowels except *l*), a sound belonging to the group *kU* or *pU*, the particle *āṄ* or the infix *nUM* in close proximity].

VMBh_1: III.459.11-15; VMBh_2: V.500.10-13

[Question:] What is the purpose [in using] the expression *antaḥ*?

1) [The expression] "a *pada* final of the verbal root *an*" [is used] for the sake of the vocative.

[Answer:] [The expression] "a *pada* final of the verbal root *an*" [is used] for the sake of the vocative. [For example,] *he prāṇ* ('Oh, breath!').

{**Explanation:**
The derivation of the form *prāṇ* is as follows.

(1) *pra* + *anA* (DhP II:61) + *KviP* + *sU* (A. 3.2.76 *kvip ca*, A. 4.1.2 *svaujasamauṭśasṭābhyāmbhisṅebhyāmbhyasṅasibhyāmbhyasṅasisāmṅyossup*)
(2) *pra* + *an* + 0 + *s* (A. 6.1.67 *ver apṛktasya*)
(3) *pra* + *an* + (*s* → 0) (A. 6.1.68 *halṅyābbhyo dīrghāt sutisy apṛktam hal*)
(4) *pr* (*a* + *a* → *ā*) *n* (A. 6.1.87 *ād guṇaḥ*)
(5) *prā* (*n* → *ṇ*) (A. 8.4.20 *antaḥ*)
prāṇ

The consonant *n* in the above form terminates a nominal stem so it would be subject to deletion by A. 8.2.7 *nalopaḥ prātipadikāntasya*, which is blocked by A. 8.2.8 *na ṅisambuddhyoḥ*. However, the correct result could easily be achieved by the previous *sūtra*, so the question which remains is why we need two separate rules.}

VMBh_1: III.459.16-17; VMBh_2: V.500.14-16

[Bhāṣya:] Another one says: [the expression] "The final [sound] of the verbal root *an*" [is stated in order to block the prohibition of substitution of the sound *n*] which is the final [sound] of a *pada*. [The expression] "the final [sound] of the verbal root *an*" is used; by [the *sūtra*] A. 8.4.37 the prohibition would result, this [rule] is for the sake of blocking that [prohibition].

{**Explanation:**
The *sūtra* A. 8.4.37 *padāntasya* prohibits the *ṇ*-substitute when *n* appears at the end of a *pada*, which would block it in the example *prāṇ*. For the sake of blocking that prohibition the rule A. 8.4.20 is formed. The word *anta* should be, consequently, interpreted as *padānta* 'the final of a *pada*'. In the above example, the vocative ending is deleted by the general term *lopa*, which allows A. 1.1.62 *pratyayalope pratyayalakṣaṇam* to apply. So, despite the deletion of the suffix, the stem can still be termed *pada* and operations pertaining to a *pada* can take place.
According to Nārāyaṇa (MPV X.470), these two rules have to be separate. If they formed one rule *aniter antaḥ*, the *ṇ*-substitution could not take place in the forms such as *prāṇiti* because the consonant *ṇ* does not constitute the final sound of a *pada*.}

VMBh_1: III.459.18-22; VMBh_2: V.500.17-501.4

2) Alternatively, [it means that] which is nearest to that.

[Bhāṣya:] Alternatively, this word *anta* expresses a part only. Just like [in these examples,] *vastrānta* or *vasanānta* ('the end of garnment, i.e., a part of it'). It is used in the sense of 'in the vicinity'. Just like [in these examples,] *udakāntaṃ gataḥ* ('he went to the water'). It is understood as 'he went in the vicinity of water'. Therefore, its meaning is 'that which is in the vicinity'. [The substitution] of [the sound] *n* should take place after such a sound *r* which is in the vicinity of [the sound *n*] of [the verbal root] *an*. [For example,] *prāṇiti* ('he breathes'). Here it must not be: *paryaniti* ('he breathes').

{**Explanation:**
The word *anta* can also be interpreted as *samīpya* 'proximity'. This interpretation would allow for the *ṇ*-substitution when the consonants *r* or *ṣ* and *n* are separated by one sound, as in *prāṇiti*. On the other hand, it would block the substitution in

the form *paryaniti* where there are more sounds separating the *nimitta* and *nimittin*. Accepting this view requires the repetition of the word *anta* so that the forms such as *prāṇ* were possible. In such a way one *anta* would be used with the meaning of 'proximity' and the other with the meaning of 'the final of a *pada*'.}

A. 8.4.21 *ubhau sābhyāsasya*
[The retroflex sound *ṇ* comes in place of] both [sounds *n* of the verbal root *anA* ('to breathe', DhP II:61)] with a reduplicated syllable [after the *upasarga* containing the sounds *r* or *ṣ* even when there is the separation by a sound denoted by *aṬ* (i.e., all vowels, *h*, semivowels except *l*), a sound belonging to the group *kU* or *pU*, the particle *āṄ* or the infix *nUM* in close proximity].

VMBh_1: III.460.1-3; VMBh_2: V.501.5-7

1) It is required [that the substitution replaces] two [sounds *n* of the verbal root] with a reduplicated syllable.

[Bhāṣya:] It is required that the *ṇ*-substitute [replaced] two [sounds *n* of the verbal root] with a reduplicated syllable. [For example,] *prāṇiṇiṣati* ('he wishes to breathe', 3rd sg. desid.).

{**Explanation:**
The use of *ubha* in the *sūtra* might be cosidered superfluous, as the *ṇ*-substitution in the reduplicated syllable could be the result of the preceding rule, and the *ṇ*-substitution in the verbal root could result from the application of the present one. According to Kaiyaṭa (VMBh_2: V.501.14-18), however, this interpretation would hold true when there is an intervention between the *nimitta* and *nimittin*. The examples when there is no such separation would not be covered based on the application of the *takrakauṇḍinya* maxim; which says that Brahmins are to get yoghurt and Kauṇḍinya buttermilk. Even though Kauṇḍinya is a Brahmin, he will get only buttermilk and not both. With reference to the *sūtra*, the *ṇ*-substitute will not apply when there is no intervention between the cause and the caused. When the context of separation between the two has been specified, the substitution cannot apply in any other context. This is the purpose of the term *ubha*.
As for the example of *prāṇiṇiṣati*, the problem arises during the derivation, which is as follows.

(1) *pra* + *anA* (DhP II:61) + *saN* + *ŚaP* + *tiP* (A. 3.1.7 *dhātoḥ karmaṇaḥ samānakartṛkād icchāyāṃ vā*, A. 3.1.68 *kartari śap*, A. 3.4.78 *tiptasjhisipthasthamibvasmastātāmjhathāsāthāmdhvamiḍvahimahiṅ*)
(2) *pra* + *an* + *iṬ* + *sa* + *a* + *ti* (A. 7.2.35 *ārdhadhātukasyeḍ valādeḥ*)
(3) *pra* + *a* + (*n* → *ṇ*) *i* + *sa* + *a* + *ti* (A. 8.4.21 *ubhau sābhyāsasya*)

(4) *pra* + *a* + *ṇi* + *ṇi* + *sa* + *a* + *ti* (A. 6.1.9 *sanyaṅoḥ*, A. 6.1.2 *ajāder dvitīyasya*)
(5) *pr* (*a* + *a* → *ā*) + *ṇi* + *ṇi* + *sa* + *a* + *ti* (A. 6.1.87 *ād gunaḥ*)
(6) *prā* + *ṇi* + *ṇi* + *s* (*a* + *a* → *a*) + *ti* (A. 6.1.97 *ato guṇe*)
(7) *prā* + *ṇi* + *ṇi* + (*s* → *ṣ*) *a* + *ti* (A. 8.3.59 *ādeśapratyayayoḥ*)
prāṇiṇiṣati

The reduplication is prescribed by the rule A. 6.1.9 and the *ṇ*-substitution by the rule in the *pūrvatrāsiddha* section which makes the latter suspended. We should apply the reduplication first followed by the *ṇ*-substitution. However, after the substitution has applied to the consonant *n* of the reduplicated syllable, it prevents the *n* of the verbal root from undergoing the substitution. So it must be concluded that the *ṇ*-substitution takes precedence over the reduplication and, consequently, it is the syllable with the retroflex *ṇ* that is reduplicated. The commentators say that it is indeed so on the basis of the *paribhāṣā*: *pūrvatrāsiddhīyam advitve* ("[An operation] which by A. 8.2.1 would be considered *asiddha* [with respect to the preceding rule] is not considered *asiddha* when [the preceding rule prescribes] the reduplication").[515]
However, I believe there is a simple solution to the interpretation of this *sūtra*. Commentators explain that the term *ubha* is used for the sake of covering both the examples where we find the separation between the *nimitta* and *nimittin* and those without the separation. For that reason, they have to resort to the mentioned *paribhāṣā*. If, on the other hand, we were to assume that the term *ubha* refers to two sounds *n* that undergo the substitution at the same time, the problem would be solved in a much simpler way. There would be no need to invoke a new interpretative tool, particularly that it is considered *anitya* – not universal. The mere existence of this *sūtra* is to prove that this *paribhāṣā* cannot apply universally. In my opinion, it is an *ad hoc paribhāṣā* which can be dispensed with if a more straightforward understanding of the rule were accepted.}

A. 8.4.22 *hanter atpūrvasya*
[The retroflex sound *ṇ* comes in place of the sound *n*] preceded by the vowel *a* of [the verbal root] *hanA* ('to kill', DhP II:2) [after the *upasarga* containing the sounds *r* or *ṣ* even when there is the separation by a sound denoted by *aṬ* (i.e., all vowels, *h*, semivowels except *l*), a sound belonging to the group *kU* or *pU*, the particle *āṄ* or the infix *nUM* in close proximity].

VMBh_1: III.460.4-7; VMBh_2: V.501.8-11

[Question:] What is the purpose [in saying] "preceded by the vowel *a*"?

[515] PŚ 117, vol. I:110-111, vol. II:510-511.

[Answer:] [The forms] *praghnanti* or *parighnanti* ('they kill').

1) It has been mentioned in the rule [that the substitution takes place] in [the verbal root] *hanA* [when the sound *n*] is preceded by the vowel *a*.

[Question:] What has been mentioned?
[Answer:] When [a sound belonging to the group] *kU* intervenes, prohibition [should be mentioned] with respect to the substitution of [the verbal root] *hanA* (*vt*. 4 on A. 8.4.2).

{**Explanation:**
The purpose of the condition *atpūrvasya* is discussed. If this condition were not specified, we would get the *ṇ*-substitution in the forms such as *praghnanti* or *parighnanti*. The derivation of *praghnanti* is as follows:

(1) *pra* + *hanA* (DhP II:2) + *jhi* (A. 3.4.78 *tiptasjhisipthasthamibvasmastātāmjhathāsāthāmdhvamiḍvahimahiṅ*)
(2) *pra* + *han* + (*jh* → *ant*) *i* (A. 7.1.3 *jho 'ntaḥ*)
(3) *pra* + *h* (*a* → 0) *n* + *anti* (A. 6.4.98 *gamahanajanakhanaghasāṃ lopaḥ kṅity anaṅi*)
(4) *pra* + (*h* → *gh*) *n* + *anti* (A. 7.3.54 *ho hanter ñṇitneṣu*)
praghnanti

The *ṇ*-substitute does not apply here due to the deletion of the penultimate *a* of the verbal stem at the stage (3). The *vārttika* points, however, that such examples were stated before, in the *sūtra* A. 8.4.2. The *vt*s 4 and 5 on that rule state and explain the prohibition of the *ṇ*-substitution in cases where the consonant *n* is not preceded by *a*. By referring to those *vārttika*s, and accepting them as valid, Patañjali implies that the condition *atpūrvasya* is not necessary. They allow for the derivation of the forms such as *prāghāni* ('let me kill', 1st sg. impv. from *prāhan*) where *n* is preceded by *ā* and where the substitution is blocked. The derivation of the form *prāghāni* is as follows:

(1) *pra* + *hanA* (DhP II:2) + *lUṄ*
(2) *pra* + *han* + *Cli* + *tha* (A. 3.1.43 *cli luṅi*, A. 3.4.78 *tiptasjhisipthasthamibvasmastātāmjhathāsāthāmdhvamiḍvahimahiṅ*)
(3) *pra* + *han* + *Cli* + (*tha* → *ta*) (A. 3.4.101 *tasthasthamipāṃ tāntantāmaḥ*)
(4) *pra* + *han* + *CiṆ* + *ta* (A. 3.1.66 *ciṇ bhāvakarmaṇoḥ*)
(5) *pra* + *aṬ* + *han* + *CiṆ* + *ta* (A. 6.4.71 *luṅlaṅlṛṅkṣv aḍudāttaḥ*)
(6) *pra* + *a* + (*h* → *gh*) *an* + *i* + *ta* (A. 7.3.54 *ho hanter ñṇitneṣu*)
(7) *pr* (*a* + *a* → *ā*) + *ghan* + *i* + *ta* (A. 6.1.101 *akaḥ savarṇe dīrghaḥ*)
(8) *prā* + *gh* (*a* → *ā*) *n* + *i* + *ta* (A. 7.2.116 *ata upadhāyāḥ*)

(9) *prā* + *ghān* + *i* + (*ta* → 0) (A. 6.4.104 *ciṇo luk*)
prāghāni}

{A. 8.4.23 *vamor vā*
[The retroflex sound *ṇ*] usually [comes in place of the sound *n* preceded by the vowel *a* of the verbal root *hanA* ('to kill', DhP II:2) after an *upasarga* containing the sounds *r* or *ṣ* even when there is the separation by a sound denoted by *aṬ* (i.e., all vowels, *h*, semivowels except *l*), a sound belonging to the group *kU* or *pU*, the particle *āṄ* or the infix *nUM*] before [the sounds] *v* or *m* [in close proximity].
A. 8.4.24 *antar adeśe*
[The retroflex sound *ṇ* comes in place of the sound *n* preceded by the vowel *a* of [the verbal root *hanA* ('to kill', DhP II:2)] after [the particle] *antar* ('inside') [in close proximity] when it does not denote a place.
A. 8.4.25 *ayanaṃ ca*
[The retroflex sound *ṇ*] also [comes in place of the sound *n*] of [the nominal stem] *ayana* ('going') [after the particle *antar* ('inside') in close proximity when it does not denote a place].
A. 8.4.26 *chandasy ṛdavagrahāt*
In Vedic [the retroflex sound *ṇ* comes in place of the sound *n* of a posterior member of a compound occurring after a prior member of a compound ending in] the vowel *ṛ* separated (in *padapāṭha*) by an *avagraha* [in close proximity].
A. 8.4.27 *naś ca dhātusthoruṣubhyaḥ*
[In Vedic the retroflex sound *ṇ*] also [comes in place of the sound *n* of a pronominal substitute of *asmad* ('we')] *nas* occurring after a verbal *pada* [containing the sounds *r* or *ṣ* even when there is the separation by a sound denoted by *aṬ* (i.e., all vowels, *h*, semivowels except *l*), a sound belonging to the group *kU* or *pU*, the particle *āṄ*, the infix *nUM*] or *uru* ('wide, broad'), or *ṣu* (=*su*) [in close proximity].} *These *sūtra*s were not commented upon by Patañjali.

A. 8.4.28 *upasargād anotparaḥ*
[The retroflex sound *ṇ* comes in place of the sound *n* of a pronominal substitute of *asmad* ('we')] *nas* occurring after an *upasarga* [containing the sounds *r* or *ṣ* even when there is the separation by a sound denoted by *aṬ* (i.e., all vowels, *h*, semivowels except *l*), a sound belonging to the group *kU* or *pU*, the particle *āṄ*, the infix *nUM* in close proximity] when it is not followed by the vowel *o*.

VMBh_1: III.460.8-16; VMBh_2: V.502.1-11

[Question:] How is this understood? [Should it be understood as] *otparaḥ* [meaning] "following the vowel *o*"; [hence,] *anotparaḥ* [would mean] "not following the vowel *o*"? Or [should it be understood as] *otparaḥ* [meaning] "this which is after that which the vowel *o* follows"; [hence,] *anotparaḥ* [would mean] "not followed by the vowel *o*".
[Question:] What of it?
[Objection:] If it were understood as *otparaḥ* [meaning] "following the vowel *o*"; [therefore] *anotparaḥ* [would mean] "not following the vowel *o*", in this case – *pra no muñcatam* ("Set us free")[516] – [the substitution] would result as well. But if it were understood as *otparaḥ* [meaning] "this which is after that which the vowel *o* follows"; [hence,] *anotparaḥ* [would mean] "not followed by the vowel *o*", in this case – *pra ṇo vanir devakṛtā* ("The wish has been granted to us by the gods")[517] – [the substitution] would not result.
[Answer:] And in both cases there is the problem in the recitation of Veda (*prakrama*). [See:] *pra naḥ muñcatam pra no muñcatam* and *pra u naḥ pro naḥ*.

But it is not required "when there is the vowel *o*".

[Answer:] But the *ṇ*-substitute is not required when there is the vowel *o*. Therefore, it should be said: "[the substitution] takes place variously after an *upasarga*".

{**Explanation:**
An amendment is proposed in this *sūtra* to include *bahulam* ('variously'), which would allow it to apply in all instances. The problem appears because the expression *anotparaḥ* could be understood as either "not following the vowel *o*" or "not followed by the vowel *o*". In either case there are some undesired results as specified by Patañjali. The reference is made to the Vedic types of recitation where the vowel *o* sometimes appears, as in *saṃhitapāṭha*, or disappears, as in *padapāṭha* or *kramapāṭha*, where the sandhi rules are omitted. The last example *pra u naḥ* → *pronaḥ* shows that when the word is divided into parts, the vowel *o* disappears; therefore the *ṇ*-substitution would not be possible. As Kaiyaṭa says (VMBh_2: V.502), the secondary meaning cannot be taken into consideration when the primary is possible. Thus, the amendment has to be made in order to allow for the substitution even in such cases where the vowel *o* is the result of the application of sandhi. The reason is that in Vedic we find both forms, with and without the substitution.

---

[516] ṚgV 6.74.4.
[517] AV 5.7.3.

In VMBh_2 edition of the *Mahābhāṣya* there is a *kārikā*, which Kielhorn does not quote. It gathers the *vārttika*s from the *sūtras* A. 8.4.19/20, A. 8.4.21 and A. 8.4.28. It reads:

[The expression] "the final [sound] of the verbal root *an*" [is stated in order to block prohibition of the substitution of the sound *n*] which is the final [sound] of a *pada*; or [it means that] which is nearest to that.
It is required [that the substitution comes in place] of two [sounds *n* of the verbal root] with a reduplicated syllable. But it is not required "when there will be the vowel *o*".}

A. 8.4.29 *kṛty acaḥ*
[The retroflex sound *ṇ* comes in place of the sound *n*] occurring after a vowel in a primary suffix (*kṛt*) [introduced after a verbal root occurring with an *upasarga* containing the sounds *r* or *ṣ* even when there is the separation by a sound denoted by *aṬ* (i.e., all vowels, *h*, semivowels except *l*), a sound belonging to the group *kU* or *pU*, the particle *āṄ*, the infix *nUM* in close proximity].

VMBh_1: III.460.17-19; VMBh_2: V.503.1-4

1) The addition [should be made] when the *ṇ*-substitute takes place, with respect to [the sound *n*] being a part of a primary suffix after [the verb] *nirvid* ('to depress').

[Bhāṣya:] The addition should be made when the *ṇ*-substitute takes place, with respect to [the sound *n*] being a part of a primary suffix after [the verb] *nirvid* ('to depress'). [For example,] *nirviṇṇo 'ham anena vāsena* ("I'm depressed by living here").

{Explanation:
The derivation of the form *nirviṇṇa* is as follows:

(1) *nir + vid + Kta* (A. 3.2.102 *niṣṭhā*, A. 1.1.26 *ktaktavatū niṣṭhā*)
(2) *nir + vi (d → n) + (t → n) a* (A. 8.2.42 *radābhyāṃ niṣṭhāto naḥ pūrvasya tu daḥ*)
(3) *nir + vin + (n → ṇ) a* (A. 8.4.29 *kṛty acaḥ*)
(4) *nir + vi (n → ṇ) + ṇa* (A. 8.4.41 *ṣṭunā ṣṭuḥ*)
nirviṇṇa

The condition for the substitution is that the consonant *n* follows a vowel. In the case of *nirviṇṇa* only the first *n* follows a vowel and it is a part of the verbal stem, not the *kṛt* suffix. As the substitution needs to take place in the suffix first, we require the *vārttika*.}

A. 8.4.30 *ṇer vibhāṣā*
[The retroflex sound *ṇ*] rarely [comes in place of the sound *n* of a primary suffix (*kṛt*) introduced after a verbal stem] ending in the causative suffix *ṆiC* [occurring with an *upasarga* containing the sounds *r* or *ṣ* even when there is the separation by a sound denoted by *aṬ* (i.e., all vowels, *h*, semivowels except *l*), a sound belonging to the group *kU* or *pU*, the particle *āṄ*, the infix *nUM* in close proximity].

VMBh_1: III.461.1-3; VMBh_2: V.503.5-8

1) The addition [should be made] that [the substitution in a primary suffix introduced after a verbal stem ending] in the causative suffix *ṆiC* optionally takes place when there is the separation by an infix.

[Bhāṣya:] The addition [should be made] that [the substitution in a primary suffix introduced after a verbal stem ending] in the causative suffix *ṆiC* usually takes place when there is the separation by an infix. [For example,] *prāpyamāṇa* or *prāpyamāna* ('to be reached').

{**Explanation:**
The ablative case of the form *ṇer* indicates that the suffix *ṆiC* should be directly followed by the primary suffix. Therefore, the *vārttika* is proposed which allows for the substitution even if another element intervenes between the causative suffix *ṆiC* and the *kṛt* suffix. The derivation of *prāpyamāṇa*, with the optional *ṇ*-substitution, is as follows:

(1) *pra* + *āpḶ* (DhP X:295) + *ṆiC* + *yaK* + *lAṬ* (A. 3.1.26 *hetumati ca*, A. 3.1.67 *sārvadhātuke yak*)
(2) *pra* + *āp* + *ṆiC* + *ya* + *ŚānaC* (A. 3.2.124 *laṭaḥ śatṛśānacāv aprathamāsamānādhikaraṇe*)
(3) *pra* + *āp* + 0 + *ya* + *āna* (A. 6.4.51 *ṇer aniṭi*)
(4) *pra* + *āp* + *ya* + *mUK* + *āna* (A. 7.2.82 *āne muk*)
(5) *pr* (*a* + *ā* → *ā*) *p* + *ya* + *m* + *āna* (A. 6.1.101 *akaḥ savarṇe dīrghaḥ*)
(6) *prāp* + *ya* + *m* + *ā* (*n* → *ṇ*) *a* (A. 8.4.30 *kṛty acaḥ*)
prāpyamāṇa

The *vārttika* uses the term *sādhana* which Kaiyaṭa (VMBh_2: V.503) understands as and infix of *vikaraṇa* type; it might include the verbal class suffixes but also the suffix *yaK*.}

VMBh_1: III.461.4-5; VMBh_2: V.503.9-10

2) It has been achieved by the prescription.

[Bhāṣya:] The word *Ṇi* [is used] as a qualifier to what is prescribed. [It means] "that which is prescribed after that which ends in [the suffix] *ṆiC*".

{Explanation:
Kaiyaṭa explains that the suffix *kṛt* is added to the stem ending the suffix *ṆiC* but it can be supplemented with other elements. Thus, the primary suffix does not have to follow *ṆiC* directly but can be separated from it. Another solution is proposed in the following *vārttika*. It can be assumed that the governing expression *aḍvyavāye* ("when there is the separation by *aṬ*") continues in the present rule from A. 8.4.2. Therefore the *ṇ*-substitution of *n* being a part of the suffix *kṛt* will also take place when there is the separation between the primary suffix and the causative suffix *ṆiC*.}

VMBh_1: III.461.6-7; VMBh_2: V.503.11-12

3) Alternatively, [it is achieved] thanks to the governing term *aṬ*.

[Bhāṣya:] [The expression] "when there is the separation by *aṬ*" continues.

{A. 8.4.31 *halaś cejupadhāt*
[The retroflex sound *ṇ* usually comes in place of the sound *n* of a primary suffix (*kṛt*) introduced after a verbal stem] beginning with a consonant and having a penultimate vowel other than *a* (*iC*) [occurring with an *upasarga* containing the sounds *r* or *ṣ* even when there is the separation by a sound denoted by *aṬ* (i.e., all vowels, *h*, semivowels except *l*), a sound belonging to the group *kU* or *pU*, the particle *āṄ*, the infix *nUM* in close proximity].}
*This *sūtra* was not commented upon by Patañjali.

A. 8.4.32 *ijādeḥ sanumaḥ*
[The retroflex sound *ṇ* usually comes in place of the sound *n* of a primary suffix (*kṛt*) introduced after a verbal stem] with the infix *nUM*, [ending in a consonant] and beginning with vowel other than *a* (*iC*) [occurring with an *upasarga* containing the sound *r* or *ṣ* even when there is the separation by a sound denoted by *aṬ* (i.e., all vowels, *h*, semivowels except *l*), a sound belonging to the group *kU* or *pU*, the particle *āṄ*, the infix *nUM* in close proximity].

VMBh_1: III.461.8-15; VMBh_2: V.503.13-504.5

[Question:] Why is this said? Is it not achieved by [the *sūtra*] A. 8.4.29?
[Answer:] The purpose is to start a restriction. [The substitution] applies to such a root used with the *nUM* infix which begins with a vowel other than *a*, and not any other root used with the *nUM* infix.
[Question:] Where must it not be?
[Answer:] [For example,] *pramaṅkanam* and *parimaṅkanam* ('immersing').

1) In the case of the *ṇ*-substitute with respect to [verbal stems] with the infix *nUM* the restriction is not obtained because there is [something] to be prescribed.

[Bhāṣya:] In the case of the *ṇ*-substitute with respect to [verbal stems] with the infix *nUM* the restriction is not obtained.
[Question:] What is the reason?
[Answer:] Because there is [something] to be prescribed.
[Question:] Why is it a restriction? Nothing is prescribed – [thus] has been done.
[Answer:] Here there is also something to be prescribed.
[Question:] What?
[Answer:] The option [of the *ṇ*-subsitute] results [for the verbs] ending in [the suffix] *ṆiC* (by the *sūtra* A. 8.4.30); therefore, the *ṇ*-substitute should be prescribed as obligatory.
[Proposition:] In that case let it be a rule prescribing something that was not prescribed before [or] let it be a restriction.
[Answer:] It will be a rule prescribing something that was not prescribed before, not a restriction.

{**Explanation:**
The above discussion regards the interpretation of this *sūtra* as either a *niyama* or a *vidhi* rule. Kaiyaṭa states (VMBh_2: V.504.20 ff) that in the case of a *niyama* there is prohibition of the operation stated before and there is a problem with the repetition due to acceptance of what has already been stated. The previous rule, namely A. 8.4.30, establishes the *ṇ*-substitute only optionally, while the present one would make it obligatory. This is what commentators mean by using the term repetition (*anuvāda*). In the case of a *niyama* we also limit the application of this *sūtra* to only those verbal stems that are used with the infix *nUM*, the others are excluded. If, on the other hand, we were to accept the rule as a *vidhi*, the problems with repetition and blocking of what was stated before does not arise. Out of these two possibilities, Kaiyaṭa favours the *vidhi* interpretation.}

VMBh_1: III.461.16-19; VMBh_2: V.504.6-9

2) But it has been achieved in the governing domain of prohibition due to the use of [the expression] "with [the infix] *nUM*".

[Objection:] It has been achieved.
[Question:] How?
[Answer:] Due to the use of [the expression] "with [the infix] *nUM*" in the governing domain of prohibition. [The expression] "with [the infix] *nUM*" should be used in the governing domain of prohibition; [in the *sūtra*] A. 8.4.34.
[Objection:] In this case, it would not result here either: *preṅgaṇa* or *preṅgaṇīya* ('shaking' and 'to be shaken' respectively).

{**Explanation:**
The proposal is made to include the expression *sanumaḥ* in the prohibitive *sūtra* A. 8.4.34. In such a way, the forms such as *pramaṅkana* could not undergo the *ṇ*-substitution, even though they would be excluded by the condition *ijādeḥ*, because the verbal root in this example does not begin with the mentioned vowel. Kaiyaṭa further explains that the inclusion of the expression *sanumaḥ* in A. 8.4.34 would make the negation applicable everywhere. In such a case, the present rule could be a *vidhi* rule.
The derivation of *preṅgana* is as follows:

(1) *pra* + *igI* (DhP I:163) + *LyuṬ* (A. 3.3.115 *lyuṭ ca*)
(2) *pra* + *ig* + (*yu* → *ana*) (A. 7.1.1 *yuvor anākau*)
(3) *pra* + *i* + *nUM* + *g* + *ana* (A. 7.1.58 *idito num dhātoḥ*)
(4) *pr* (*a* + *i* → *e*) *ng* + *ana* (A. 6.1.87 *ād guṇaḥ*)
(5) *pre* + (*n* → *ṃ*) *g* + *ana* (A. 8.3.24 *naś cāpadāntasya jhali*)
(6) *pre* + (*ṃ* → *ṅ*) *g* + *ana* (A. 8.4.58 *anusvārasya yāyi parasavarṇaḥ*)
(7) *pre* + *ṅg* + *a* (*n* → *ṇ*) *a* (A. 8.4.32 *ijādeḥ sanumaḥ*)
preṅgaṇa

The infix *nUM* is inserted because the verbal root *ig* ('to move', DhP I:163) appears in the *Dhātupāṭha* with the marker *I*. In the above example the consonant *n* of *nUM* is replaced at the stage (5) by the *anusvāra* that is further replaced by the sound homogenous with the following sound at the stage (6). However, the *sūtra* A. 8.4.58 should be considered suspended with respect to the *ṇ*-substitution prescribed by A. 8.4.32, which leaves us with the *anusvāra*. The condition of the present rule states *nUM* explicitly, not its *anusvāra* substitute. Therefore, we must resort to *sthānivadbhāva*, which is what will allow us to see the consonant *n* rather than the *anusvāra* and will enable the *ṇ*-substitution to take place. We also could reverse the order of rule application and apply the *ṇ*-substitution first. The rule A. 8.3.24 is placed earlier in the treatise so the substitution would be considered suspended, but it would not affect the conditions for *n*→*ṃ* substitution in any way.}

VMBh_1: III.461.20-462.6; VMBh_2: V.504.10-19

3) This *sūtra* (*ijādeḥ sanumaḥ*) [should be] used when the *ṇ*-substitute [comes in place of the sound *n*] which is a part of a primary suffix.

[Bhāṣya:] This *sūtra* (*ijādeḥ sanumaḥ*) should be used when the *ṇ*-substitute [comes in place of the sound *n*] which is a part of a primary suffix. What is achieved then is that the *sūtra* is divided.
[Answer:] Let it be just according to the text of the *sūtra*.
[Objection:] But has it not been said that "in the case of the *ṇ*-substitute with respect to [verbal stems] with the infix *nUM*, the restriction is not obtained because there is [something] to be prescribed"?
[Answer:] This is not a fault. [The expression] "[ending] in a consonant" continues.
[Question:] Where is the context?
[Answer:] [In the *sūtra*] A. 8.4.31. The meaning here is really this: "specifying the beginning [is done] by specifying the end".
[Question:] But how is this uderstood – "specifying the beginning there"?
[Answer:] It is said "after [the verbal root] having a penultimate vowel other than *a*", therefore the meaning is not "by specifying the end". What is in that case specifying the beginning, in this case will be specifying the end.
[Question:] How?
[Answer:] It is said "after [the verbal root] beginning with a vowel other than *a*", therefore the meaning is not "by specifying the beginning". Alternatively, in [the *sūtra*] A. 8.4.32 [the *sūtra*] A. 8.4.30 will continue.

{Explanation:
Reference is made to the rule A. 8.4.31 which prescribed the *ṇ*-substitute in the case of verbal roots beginning with a consonant and having the vowel other than *a* as penultimate. The term *haL* in the previous rule could not be taken to mean "that which ends in a consonant" because all the verbal roots with a vowel denoted by *iC* end in a consonant. In the present rule, however, such an interpretation is not possible due to the condition *ijādeḥ*. The verbal root must begin with a vowel so, obviously, it cannot begin with a consonant as well. Thus, this expression, which specifies the beginning in the previous rule, specifies the end in the present one.
Another solution is also proposed, that A. 8.4.30 is read together with the present *sūtra*. In such a way, it could serve as a restrictive rule because verbal roots ending in the causative suffix *ṆiC* do not end in a consonant but a vowel; which

would make the optional *ṇ*-substitution prescribed by A. 8.4.30 restricted here. The conclusion is that the *sūtra* prescribes the consonant *ṇ* in place of *n* being a part of a primary suffix added to such a verbal stem beginning with a vowel denoted by *iC* and ending in a consonant, which contains the infix *nUM*, and appears after an *upasarga* containing *r* or *ṣ* as the cause for the substitution.}

{A. 8.4.33 *vā niṃsanikṣanindām*
[The retroflex sound *ṇ*] usually [comes in place of the sound *n*] of [verbal stems] *ṇisI* ('to touch closely, kiss', DhP II:15), *ṇikṣA* ('to kiss', DhP I:689) and *ṇidI* ('to censure, blame', DhP I:66) [occurring with an *upasarga* containing the sounds *r* or *ṣ* even when there is the separation by a sound denoted by *aṬ* (i.e., all vowels, *h*, semivowels except *l*), a sound belonging to the group *kU* or *pU*, the particle *āṄ*, the infix *nUM* in close proximity].} *This *sūtra* was not commented upon by Patañjali.

A. 8.4.34 *na bhābhūpūkamigamipyāyīvepām*
[The retroflex sound *ṇ*] does not come [in place of the sound *n* occurring after a vowel in a primary suffix (*kṛt*) introduced after verbal roots] *bhā* ('to shine', DhP II:42), *bhū* ('to become', DhP I:1), *pūÑ* ('to purify', DhP IX:12), *kamU* ('to love', DhP I:470), *gamḶ* ('to go', DhP I:1031), *Opyāyī* ('to swell, increase', DhP I:517) and *ṬUvepṚ* ('to tremble', DhP I:391) [occurring with an *upasarga* containing the sounds *r* or *ṣ* even when there is the separation by a sound denoted by *aṬ* (i.e., all vowels, *h*, semivowels except *l*), a sound belonging to the group *kU* or *pU*, the particle *āṄ*, the infix *nUM* in close proximity].

VMBh_1: III.462.7-9; VMBh_2: V.505.1-3

1) In [the list of verbal roots] *bhā* etc. [the verbal root] *pūÑ* [should be understood].

[Bhāṣya:] In [the list of verbal roots] *bhā* etc. [the verbal root] *pūÑ* should be [understood]. In this case [the rule] must not apply: *prapavaṇam somasya* ('the purification of Soma').

{Explanation:
In the *Dhātupāṭha* there are two stems *pū*, both meaning 'to clean, purify'. The one that is meant in the present rule belongs to the 9th class and is marked with *Ñ*. The other one belongs to the 1st class (DhP I:1015) and is marked with *Ṅ*. They differ, because the root *pūÑ* has the marker *svarita* accented and the root *puṄ* is used with *atmanepada* endings and is *udātta* accented.}

VMBh_1: III.462.10-12; VMBh_2: V.505.3-6

2) And the addition [should be made] that [prohibition of the substitution refers to verbal roots] ending in [the causative suffix] *ṆiC*.

[Bhāṣya:] And the addition should be made that [prohibition of the substitution refers to verbal roots] ending in [the causative suffix] *ṆiC*.
[Question:] Is it only in the case of [the verbal root] *pūÑ*?
[Answer:] He says 'no'. Without specification. [For example,] *prabhāpana* or *paribhāpana* ('causing to shine').

{**Explanation:**
The verbal root to which the suffix *ṆiC* is added is also treated as a verbal root on the basis of A. 3.1.32 *sanādyantā dhātavaḥ*.[518] Due to absence of this specification in the text of the *sūtra*, the *vārttika* has to be made.
The derivation of *prabhāpana* is as follows:

(1) *pra* + *bhā* (DhP II:42) + *ṆiC* + *LyuṬ* (A. 3.1.26 *hetumati ca*, A. 3.3.115 *lyuṭ ca*)
(2) *pra* + *bhā* + *ṆiC* + (*yu* → *ana*) (A. 7.1.1 *yuvor anākau*)
(3) *pra* + *bhā* + *pUK* + *ṆiC* + *ana* (A. 7.3.36 *artihrīvlīrīknūyīkṣmāyyātāṃ puṅ ṇau*)
(4) *pra* + *bhā* + *p* + 0 + *ana* (A. 6.4.51 *ṇer aniṭi*)
prabhāpana}

A. 8.4.35 *ṣāt padāntāt*
[The retroflex sound *ṇ* does not come in place of the sound *n* occurring] after a *pada* ending in [the sound] *ṣ* [even when there is the separation by a sound denoted by *aṬ* (i.e., all vowels, *h*, semivowels except *l*), a sound belonging to the group *kU* or *pU*, the particle *āṄ*, the infix *nUM* in close proximity].

VMBh_1: III.462.13-17; VMBh_2: V.505.7-12

1) It [should be mentioned that prohibition of the substitution refers to such a sound *n* which] follows [the sound] *ṣ* followed by the beginning of a *pada*.

[Bhāṣya:] It should be mentioned that [prohibition of the substitution refers to a sound *n* which] follows [the sound] *ṣ* followed by the beginning of a *pada*. Just as in these cases it should be: *niṣpāna* and *duṣpāna* ('drinking up' and 'difficult

---

[518] A. 3.1.32 *sanādyantā dhātavaḥ* || ("[The technical term] *dhātu* ('a verbal root') denotes all items ending in [the suffixes] *saN* etc.")

to drink' respectively). Here [prohibition] must not apply: *sasarpiṣkeṇa* and *sayajuṣkeṇa* ('the one that has clarified butter' and 'the one who has a Yajus formula' respectively). It should it be mentioned then.
[Answer:] It should not be mentioned. [The compound] *padānta* is not understood in this way – "the end of a *pada*", [hence,] "after the end of a *pada*".
[Question:] How then?
[Answer:] [It is understood thus:] *padānta* [means] "the final in a *pada*", [hence,] "after the final in a *pada*".

{Explanation:
The *vārttika* proposes that the consonant *n* subject to prohibition of the present *sūtra* should follow *ṣ* that precedes the beginning of a *pada*, as in the example *niṣpāna* where the substitution does not take place. However, we can avoid formulating the *vārttika* by adopting the change in the interpretation of *padāntāt* from the rule itself; instead of treating it as a genitive *tatpuruṣa* compound meaning "the end of a *pada*", we should consider it a locative *tatpuruṣa* meaning "the final in a *pada*". It indicates that the rule applies to the compounds where we find two *pada*s combined. This is why prohibition of the *ṇ*-substitute will not apply in the case of the form *sasarpiṣkeṇa*. To the *pada sasarpis* the suffix *kaP* is added by A. 5.4.154 *śeṣād vibhāṣā*[519] due to it being a *bahuvrīhi* compound. The *ṣ*-substitute applies by A. 8.3.39 *iṇaḥ ṣaḥ*. So, the consonant *ṣ* appears at the end of a *pada* but is not followed by another *pada*, only a suffix. Therefore the *ṇ*-substitute applies on the basis of the general rule A. 8.4.1 as the conditions for the prohibition are not met.}

A. 8.4.36 *naśeḥ ṣāntasya*
[The retroflex sound *ṇ* does not come in place of the sound *n*] of [the verbal root] *ṇaśA* ('to disappear', DhP IV:85) ending in the sound *ṣ* [occurring with an *upasarga* containing the sounds *r* or *ṣ* even when there is the separation by a sound denoted by *aṬ* (i.e., all vowels, *h*, semivowels except *l*), a sound belonging to the group *kU* or *pU*, the particle *āṄ*, the infix *nUM* in close proximity].

VMBh_1: III.462.18-22; VMBh_2: V.505.13-18

1) [It should be mentioned that the substitution] does not take place in [the verbal root] *naś* ending in [the sound] *ś*.

---

[519] A. 5.4.154 *śeṣād vibhāṣā* || ("[The *taddhita samāsānta* suffix *kaP*] is rarely introduced after [the nominal stems occurring at the end of a *bahuvrīhi* compound] not covered by the above rules.")

[Bhāṣya:] It should be mentioned that [the substitution] does not take place in [the verbal root] *naś* ending in [the sound] *ś*. Just as in this case it should be: *pranaṅkṣyati* and *parinaṅkṣyati* ('will get destroyed').
[Question:] Should it be mentioned then?
[Answer:] It should not be mentioned. It is achieved here by [stating] so much as *naśeḥ ṣaḥ*. When this is thus achieved, he uses the expression *anta* and its purpose should be so that [prohibition of the *ṇ*-substitute took place] also when the sound *ṣ* was at the end [of the verbal root] *naś* previously.

{**Explanation:**
The *vārttika* is proposed to make the *sūtra* more general, so that prohibition of the substitution also applied to such forms that have the verbal stem ending in sounds other than *ṣ*; prohibition should be made with respect to all those not ending in *ś*. The *vārttika* is rejected, though, because the term *anta* used in the rule indicates that it also applies in cases where the consonant *ṣ* appeared in the derivational process and was later replaced by another sound. The derivation of *pranaṅkṣyati* is as follows:

(1) *pra* + *naśA* (DhP IV:85) + *sya* + *tiP* (A. 3.1.33 *syatāsī lṛluṭoḥ*, A. 3.4.78 *tiptasjhisipthasthamibvasmastātāmjhathāsāthāmdhvamiḍvahimahiṅ*)
(2) *pra* + *na* + *nUM* + *ś* + *sya* + *ti* (A. 7.1.60 *masjinaśor jhali*)
(3) *pra* + *na* + *n* + (*ś* → *ṣ*) + *sya* + *ti* (A. 8.2.36 *vraścabhraśjasṛjamṛjayajarājabhrājachaśāṃ ṣaḥ*)
(4) *pra* + *na* + *n* + (*ṣ* → *k*) + *sya* + *ti* (A. 8.2.41 *ṣaḍhoḥ kaḥ si*)
(5) *pra* + *na* + (*n* → *ṃ*) + *k* + *sya* + *ti* (A. 8.3.24 *naś cāpadāntasya jhali*)
(6) *pra* + *na* + *ṃ* + *k* + (*s* → *ṣ*) *ya* + *ti* (A. 8.3.59 *ādeśapratyayayoḥ*)
(7) *pra* + *na* + (*ṃ* → *ṅ*) + *k* + *ṣya* + *ti* (A. 8.4.58 *anusvārasya yāyi parasavarṇaḥ*)
pranaṅkṣyati}

{**A. 8.4.37** ***padāntasya***
[The retroflex sound *ṇ* does not come in place of the sound *n*] which is at the end of a *pada* [occurring after the sounds *r* or *ṣ* even when there is the separation by a sound denoted by *aṬ* (i.e., all vowels, *h*, semivowels except *l*), a sound belonging to the group *kU* or *pU*, the particle *āṄ*, the infix *nUM* in close proximity].} *This *sūtra* was not commented upon by Patañjali.

A. 8.4.38 ***padavyavāye 'pi***
[The retroflex sound *ṇ* does not come in place of the sound *n*] also when separated [from preceding sounds *r* or *ṣ*] by a *pada* [in close proximity].

VMBh_1: III.463.1-5; VMBh_2: V.506.1-6

1) [It should be mentioned that prohibition] does not apply when the separating *pada* is a *taddhita* formation.

[Bhāṣya:] It should be mentioned [that prohibition] does not apply when the separating *pada* is a *taddhita* formation. Here it must not be: *ārdragomayeṇa* or *śuṣkagomayeṇa* ('by wet cow-dung' and 'by dry cow-dung' respectively).
[Question:] Should it be mentioned then?
[Answer:] It should not be mentioned. [The expression] *padavyavāya* is not understood in this way: "when there is the separation by a *pada*".
[Question:] How then?
[Answer:] [The expression] *padavyavāya* [is understood as:] "the separation before a *pada*", [hence,] "when there is the separation before a *pada*".

{**Explanation:**
The *sūtra* states that there is no substitution if an intervening element between the cause and the caused is a *pada*. The *vārttika*, which proposes to block the prohibition in the case of *taddhita* formations, is ultimately rejected for a change in the interpretation of *padavyavāya* is suggested; instead of considering it a compound with an instrumental *pada*, it should be treated as the locative. Thus, Patañjali implies that prohibition may apply only in the case of compounds where one *pada* follows another. This is not the case with the *taddhita* examples. We find three elements there: *ārdra*, *go* and *maya*, of which the third is only a suffix and therefore does not get the designation *pada*. The word *go* can be termed *pada* in this case on the basis of the rule A. 1.4.17 *svādiṣv asarvanāmasthāne*. Thus, all the elements before the *taddhita* suffixes are designated *pada*. The *taddhita* suffix *mayaṬ* is added by A. 4.3.145 *goś ca pūrīṣe*.[520]
If we accept the locative interpretation rather than the instrumental one, we do not need a *vārttika*. The word *go* does not appear before another *pada*, but before the suffix. Observed separation is not between two *pada*s but only between one *pada* and a suffix. This situation would not fall under the scope of application of this *sūtra* then and the *ṇ*-substitution would take place.
All the later commentators, however, disagree with Patañjali and accept the *vārttika* instead, interpreting the expression *padavyavāya* as *padena vyavāyaḥ*.}

A. 8.4.39 *kṣubhnādiṣu ca*
[The retroflex sound *ṇ* does not come in place of the sound *n* preceded by the sounds *r* or *ṣ* even when there is the separation by a sound denoted by *aṬ* (i.e., all vowels, *h*, semivowels except *l*), a sound belonging to the group *kU*

---

[520] A. 4.3.145 *goś ca pūrīṣe* || ("[The *taddhita* suffix *mayaṬ*] is also introduced after [the nominal stem] *go* ('a cow') [to denote its modification] to mean 'cow-dung'.")

or *pU*, the particle *āṄ*, the infix *nUM*] in [the expressions] *kṣubhnā* (from *kṣubh* 'to tremble') etc. [in close proximity].

VMBh_1: III.463.6-7; VMBh_2: V.506.7-8

[Bhāṣya:] Prohibition in the case of *kṣubhnā* etc. should be seen as an unprescribed rule.

{**Explanation:**
This rule covers all the other examples where the *ṇ*-substitution is not required and which were not covered by the previous rules starting from A. 8.4.34. It is an open group of words (*ākṛtigaṇa*). The word *kṣubhnā* in the text of the *sūtra* refers to the form itself – the verbal root *kṣubh* together with the *vikaraṇa Śnā* as this verb belongs to the 9th class. It does not refer to the verb generally, so the forms such as *kṣobhaṇa* ('disturbing') will not have the *ṇ*-substitution blocked.}

A. 8.4.40 *stoḥ ścunā ścuḥ*
[The palatal sounds (sibilant and stop respectively)] *ś* and *cU* come in place of [the dental sounds (sibilant and stop respectively) *s* and *tU* when [the sounds] *ś* and *cU* occur [in close proximity].

VMBh_1: III.463.8-11; VMBh_2: V.506.9-12

[Question:] Why is the third case (instrumental) mentioned? Why is it not said: "before [the sounds] *ś* and *cU*"?
[Answer:] The palatalisation should take place only in immediate sequence. [For example,] *yajñaḥ* ('a sacrifice'), *rājñaḥ* ('of/from the king'), *yācñā* ('begging').
[Question:] Why then is it not applied due to the number?
[Answer:] The teacher's use indicates that the application due to the number does not take place in this case, just as he orders prohibition [of the substitution] after [the sound] *ś*.

{**Explanation:**
The substitution prescribed by the present rule works both ways – it can apply to what precedes the cause of an operation and what follows. This is why the instrumental *ścunā* is used rather than the locative *ścoḥ*. In the examples given by Patañjali, *yajñaḥ*, *rājñaḥ* and *yācñā*, the consonants *j* and *c* cause the change of the following *n* into *ñ*. The example derivation is as follows:

(1) *ṬUyācṚ* (DhP I:916) + *naṄ* (A. 3.3.90 *yajayācayatavicchapraccharakṣo naṅ*)
(2) *yāc* + *na* + *ṬāP* (A. 4.1.4 *ajādyataṣ ṭāp*)
(3) *yāc* + *n* (*a* + *ā* → *ā*) (A. 6.1.101 *akaḥ savarṇe dīrghaḥ*)

(4) *yāc* (*n* → *ñ*) *ā* (A. 8.4.40 *stoḥ ścunā ścuḥ*)
yācñā

The question arises whether A. 1.3.10 *yathāsaṃkhyam anudeśaḥ samānam*[521] applies here because we have two elements to be replaced and two substitutes. It does not, however, because the substitution does not take place when the consonant *s* is next to *ś* and the sounds belonging to the class *tU* next to *cU*. In other words, the consonant *s* will become *ś* also when it appears next to the sounds belonging to the class *cU*. Moreover, if A. 1.3.10 were to apply, Pāṇini would not have to state A. 8.4.44 that prohibits the substitution of the sounds denoted by *tU* when they appear after *ś*. The formulation of A. 8.4.44 indicates that A. 1.3.10 has no scope in the present rule.}

A. 8.4.41 *ṣṭunā ṣṭuḥ*
[The retroflex sounds (sibilant and stop respectively)] *ṣ* and *ṭU* [come in place of the dental sounds (sibilant and stop respectively) *s* and *tU*] when [the sounds] *ṣ* and *ṭU* occur [in close proximity].

VMBh_1: III.463.12-15; VMBh_2: V.506.13-507.2

[Question:] Why is the third case (instrumental) mentioned? Why is it not said: "before [the sounds] *ṣ* and *ṭU*"?
[Answer:] The cerebralisation should take place only in immediate sequence. [For example,] *peṣṭā* ('the one that pounds') and *leḍhā* ('licker').
[Question:] Why then is it not applied due to the number?
[Answer:] The teacher's use indicates that the application due to the number does not take place in this case, just as he orders prohibition [of the substitution] before [the sound] *ṣ*.

{**Explanation:**
The discussion from the previous rule repeats here; the only difference being the *sūtra* of reference, which is in this case A. 8.4.43 prohibiting the retroflex substitution of the sounds belonging to the class *tU* before *ṣ* when the dental stop appears at the end of a *pada*.
The example *peṣṭā* is derived as follows:

(1) *piṣḶ* (DhP VII:15) + *tṛC* + *sU* (A. 3.1.133 *ṇvultṛcau*, A. 4.1.2 *svaujasamauṭ-śasṭābhyāmbhisṅebhyāmbhyasṅasibhyāmbhyasṅasosāmṅyossup*)

---

[521] A. 1.3.10 *yathāsaṃkhyam anudeśaḥ samānām* || ("[When two sequences of elements] which have the same number of members are stated in rules, [the elements of the subsequent sequence] are related to the former in a one-to-one order.")

(2) *p* (*i* → *e*) *ṣ* + *tṛ* + *sU* (A. 7.3.84 *sārvadhātukārdhadhātukayoḥ*)
(3) *peṣ* + *t* (*ṛ* → *an*) + *sU* (A. 7.1.94 *ṛduśanaspurudaṃśonehasāṃ ca*)
(4) *peṣ* + *tan* + 0 (A. 6.1.68 *halṅyābbhyo dīrghāt sutisy apṛktam hal*)
(5) *peṣ* + *t* (*a* → *ā*) *n* (A. 6.4.8 *sarvanāmāsthāne cāsambuddhau*)
(6) *peṣ* + *tā* (*n* → 0) (A. 8.2.7 *nalopaḥ prātipadikāntasya*)
peṣṭā}

A. 8.4.42 *na padāntaṭ ṭor anām*
[The retroflex stop] *ṭU* does not come in place of [the dental sibilant and stops occurring] after a *pada* final retroflex stop apart from [the genitive plural ending] (*nām*) [in close proximity].

VMBh_1: III.463.16-18; VMBh_2: V.507.3-6

[Question:] Why [is it said] "apart from [the genitive plural ending] *nām*"?
[Answer:] [Because we have:] *ṣaṇṇāṃ bhavati kaśyapaḥ* ("Kaśyapa is of six [mothers]"[522]).
[Bhāṣya:] It is too little to say "apart from [the genitive plural ending] *nām*". It should also be mentioned "apart from *nām*, *navati* ('ninety') and *nagarī* ('a city')". [For example,] *ṣaṇṇām* ('of the six'), *ṣaṇṇavatiḥ* ('ninety-six') and *ṣaṇṇagarī* ('six cities').

{**Explanation:**
This *sūtra* was not commented on by either of the commentators. The exclusion from prohibition is made for the genitive ending *nām* as in the form *ṣaṇṇām* whose derivation is as follows:

(1) *ṣaṣ* + *ām* (A. 4.1.2 *svaujasamauṭśasṭābhyāmbhisṅebhyāmbhyasṅasibhyāmbhyasṅasosāmṅyossup*)
(2) *ṣaṣ* + *nUṬ* + *ām* (A. 7.1.55 *ṣaṭcaturbhyaś ca*)
(3) *ṣa* (*ṣ* → *ḍ*) + *nām* (A. 8.2.39 *jhalāṃ jaśo 'nte*)
(4) *ṣaḍ* + (*n* → *ṇ*) *ām* (A. 8.4.42 *na padāntāṭ ṭor anām*)
(5) *ṣa* (*ḍ* → *ṇ*) + *ṇām* (A. 8.4.45 *yaro 'nunāsike 'anunāsiko vā*)
ṣaṇṇām}

{**A. 8.4.43 *toḥ ṣi***
[The retroflex stop *ṭU* does not come in place] of a *pada* final dental stop before the [the retroflex sibilant] *ṣ* [in close proximity].
A. 8.4.44 *śāt*

[522] AVP 4.40.6.

[The palatal stop does not come in place of the dental stop occurring] after [the palatal sibilant] *ś* [in close proximity].} *These *sūtra*s were not commented upon by Patañjali.

A. 8.4.45 *yaro 'nunāsike 'nunāsiko vā*
The nasal stop (*anunāsika*) usually comes in place of [a *pada* final sound denoted by] *yaR* (i.e., semivowels, stops and sibilants) before the nasal stop (*anunāsika*) [in close proximity].

VMBh_1: III.464.1-4; VMBh_2: V.507.7-10

1) [The substitution should be] mentioned as obligatory in the case of [a *pada* final sound denoted by] *yaR* (i.e., semivowels, stops and sibilants) being followed by a nasal stop of a suffix in common language.

[Bhāṣya:] And [the substitution] should be mentioned as obligatory in the case of [a *pada* final sound denoted by] *yaR* (i.e., semivowels, stops and sibilants) being followed by a nasal stop of a suffix in common language. [For example,] *vāṅmayam* ('relating to speech') and *tvaṅmayam* ('made of skin').

{**Explanation:**
The expression *padāntāt* continues in the present rule but it is changed into *padāntasya*, because the substitution should refer to the sound at the end of a *pada*. Therefore, in such examples as *vedmi* ('I know', 1st sg. praes.) or *kṣubhnāti* ('he disturbs, trembles', 3rd sg. praes.) there is no substitution even though the stops *d* and *bh* appear before nasal consonants, because they are not *pada* finals. The *vārttika* stating the obligatory character of the substitution in certain cases is accepted by Patañjali, which enables us to derive the forms such as *vāṅmaya*.

(1) *vāc* + *mayaṬ* (A. 4.3.144 *nityaṃ vṛddhaśarādibhyaḥ*)
(2) *vā* (*c* → *k*) + *maya* (A. 8.2.30 *coḥ kuḥ*)
(3)*vā* (*k* → *g*) + *maya* (A. 8.2.39 *jhalāṃ jaśo 'nte*)
(4) *vā* (*g* → *ṅ*) + *maya* (A. 8.4.45 *yaro 'nunāsike 'nunāsiko vā*)
vāṅmaya

The *Kāśikā* points out (KV VI.651) that these examples can be accepted as a fixed option (*vyavasthitavibhāṣā*) as well.}

{A. 8.4.46 *aco rahābhyāṃ dve*
[The sound denoted by *yaR* (i.e., semivowels, stops and sibilants) occurring] after [the sounds *r* or *h* preceded by a vowel (*aC*) [is usually replaced by] two [sounds in close proximity].} *This *sūtra* was not commented upon by Patañjali.

A. 8.4.47 *anaci ca*
[The sound denoted by *yaR* (i.e., semivowels, stops and sibilants) occurring after a vowel is usually replaced by two sounds] also when it is not before a vowel [in close proximity].

VMBh_1: III.464.5-9; VMBh_2: V.507.11-15

1) In the case of reduplication [a sound denoted by] *maY* (i.e., all stops except *ñ*) after [a sound denoted by] *yaṆ* (i.e., semivowels) / [a sound denoted by] *yaṆ* (i.e., semivowels) after [a sound denoted by] *maY* (i.e., all stops except *ñ*) [should be included].

[Bhāṣya:] It should be mentioned that in the case of reduplication [a sound denoted by] *maY* (i.e., all stops except *ñ*) after [a sound denoted by] *yaṆ* (i.e semivowels) / [a sound denoted by] *yaṆ* (i.e., semivowels) after [a sound denoted by] *maY* (i.e., all stops except *ñ*) [should be included].
[Question:] What are the examples?
[Answer:] If [the expression] *yaṇaḥ* [is interpreted as] the ablative and [the expression] *mayaḥ* as the genitive, the examples are: *ulkkā* ('a fiery phenomenon in the sky') and *vālmmīka* ('belonging to Valmīki'). But if [the expression] *mayaḥ* [is interpreted as] the ablative and [the expression] *yaṇaḥ* as the genitive, the examples are: *dadhyy atra* ("Here's yoghurt") and *madhvv atra* ("Here's honey").

{**Explanation:**
There are two ways of interpreting this *vārttika*. According to the first view, the reduplication takes place when a sound denoted by *maY* follows a sound denoted by *yaṆ*, which gives us such examples as *ulkkā* and *vālmmīka* where the consonants *k* and *m* respectively are doubled because they appear after the semivowel *l*. If, on the other hand, we accept the view that the reduplication takes place of a sound denoted by *yaṆ* that follows the one denoted by *maY*, we achieve such forms as *dadhyy atra* and *madhvv atra* where the semivowels *y* and *v* respectively follow the stop *dh*. The commentators do not decide which version is acceptable; they apparently accept both of them.}

VMBh_1: III.464.10-13; VMBh_2: V.507.16-19

2) [In the case of reduplication a sound denoted by] *śaR* (i.e., sibilants) after [a sound denoted by] *khaY* (i.e., voiceless stops) / [a sound denoted by] *khaY* (i.e., voiceless stops) after [a sound denoted by] *śaR* (i.e., sibilants) [should be included].

[Bhāṣya:] It should be mentioned that in the case of reduplication [a sound denoted by] *śaR* (i.e., sibilants) after [a sound denoted by] *khaY* (i.e., voiceless stops) / [a sound denoted by] *khaY* (i.e., voiceless stops) after [a sound denoted by] *śaR* (i.e., sibilants) [should be included].
[Question:] What are the examples?
[Answer:] If [the expression] *śaraḥ* [is interpreted as] the ablative and [the expression] *khayaḥ* as the genitive, the examples are: *stthālī* ('possessing a vessel') and *stthātā* ('a driver'). But if [the expression] *khayaḥ* [is interpreted as] the ablative and [the expression] *śaraḥ* as the genitive, the examples are: *vatssaḥ* ('a child'), *kṣṣīram* ('milk') and *apssarā* ('a nymph').

{**Explanation:**
As previously, there are two ways of interpreting this *vārttika*. According to the first view, the reduplication takes place when a sound denoted by *kyaY* follows a sound denoted by *śaR*, which gives us such examples as *stthālī* and *stthātā* where the consonant *th* is doubled because it appears after the sibilant *s*. Further, one *th* is replaced by *t* by A. 8.4.55. If, on the other hand, we accept the view that the reduplication takes place of a sibilant (*śaR*) that follows a sound denoted by *khaY*, we achieve such forms as *vatssa*, *kṣṣīra* and *apssarā* where the sibilants *s* and *ṣ* follow the stops *t*, *k* and *p* respectively. Again in this case the commentators do not decide which version is acceptable.}

VMBh_1: III.464.14-17; VMBh_2: V.507.20-508.2

3) [It should] also [be mentioned that the reduplication takes place] before a pause.

[Bhāṣya:] It should also be mentioned that the reduplication takes place before a pause. [For example,] *vākk*, *vāk* ('speech'), *tvakk*, *tvak* ('skin') or *srukk*, *sruk* ('wooden laddle').
[Question:] Should it be mentioned then?
[Answer:] It should not be mentioned. This is not *prasajyapratiṣedha* [meaning] "when not before a vowel".
[Question:] What then?
[Answer:] This is *paryudāsapratiṣedha* [meaning] "something else than a vowel".

{**Explanation:**
The above discussion refers to two types of negation in Pāṇini's grammar: *paryudāsa* and *prasajya*. The former negates the condition, that is the reduplication of a sound denoted by *yaR* (i.e., semivowels, stops and sibilants) takes

place when this sound appears before something else than *aC* (i.e., a vowel). The latter, on the other hand, negates the operation, that is the reduplication does not take place when the vowel follows. Kaiyaṭa points out (VMBh_2: V.507) that there must be a mistake in the text and two types should be reversed. He states that the *paryudāsapratiṣedha* specifies that something similar to the vowel, but also different from it, should follow the sound in question. In the case of a pause there is no sound following so the reduplication would not result. Kaiyaṭa further explains that the *prasajyapratiṣedha* interpretation would infer the injunction that the reduplication always takes place when a sound denoted by *yaR* follows a vowel, and this is why we need a prohibition in the case when it appears before another vowel. In such a way, it could also take place in a pause due to reduplication being without any definite cause. It could also be possible to continue the option from A. 8.4.45 to achieve such forms. As Patañjali apparently accepts the forms with the reduplicated consonants at the end of a *pada* in a pause, the *vārttika* is not necessary and he goes with the *prasajyapratiṣedha* interpretation.}

A. 8.4.48 *nādiny ākrośe putrasya*
[Two sounds] do not come in place of [the sound *t*] of [the nominal stem] *putra* ('a son') occurring before [the word] *ādin* ('eater') when it denotes 'scolding, abuse' [in close proximity].

VMBh_1: III.464.18-22; VMBh_2: V.508.3-7

1) [It should be mentioned that prohibition is prescribed] when [the nominal stem] *putra* is followed by [the word] *ādin*, to denote anger, and also when it is followed by the same (i.e., *putra*, so it is separated from the word *ādin* by another word *putra*).

[Bhāṣya:] It should be mentioned [that prohibition is prescribed] when [the nominal stem] *putra* is followed by [the word] *ādin*, to denote anger, and also when it is followed by the same, i.e., in the case of [the compound] *putraputrādin* ('eater of a grandson').

2) [Prohibition of reduplication should be] optional when [the nominal stem *putra*] is followed by [the words] *hata* ('killed') or *jagdha* ('eaten').

[Bhāṣya:] [Prohibition of reduplication] should be mentioned as optional when [the nominal stem *putra*] is followed by [the words] *hata* ('killed') or *jagdha* ('eaten'). [For example,] *putrahatī* or *puttrahatī* ('the woman whose son got killed') and *putrajagdhī* or *puttrajagdhī* ('the woman whose son got eaten').

{Explanation:

Kaiyaṭa explains (VMBh_2: V.508.16 ff) that the *bahuvrīhi* compound *putrahatī* is formed with the help of the feminine suffix *ṄīṢ* by A. 4.1.53 *asvāṅgapūrvapadād vā* ॥ ("[The suffix *ṄīṢ*] is optionally introduced after [a nominal stem consisting of a *bahuvrīhi* compound ending in the suffix *Kta* and a high-pitched final accent] preceded by a prior member not denoting a member of one's body [to derive a feminine nominal stem]"). He also mentions that the compound *hatajagdhapare* in the *vārttika* is an attributive compound where the word *para* is placed irregularly at the end by A. 2.2.31 *rājadantādiṣu param* ॥ ("In the class of [compounds] *rājadanta* ('principal tooth') etc. [the *upasarjana*] occurs as a posterior member").}

VMBh_1: III.465.1-3; VMBh_2: V.508.8-10

3) [A sound denoted by] *caY* (i.e., voiceless unaspirated stops) [is replaced by] a second [sound of the same group] before [a sound denoted by] *śaR* (i.e., sibilants) according to Pauṣkarasādi.

[Bhāṣya:] According to the teacher Pauṣkarasādi, [a sound denoted by] *caY* (i.e., voiceless unaspirated stops) [is replaced by] a second [sound of the same group] before [a sound denoted by] *śaR* (i.e., sibilants). [For example,] *vathsaḥ* ('a child'), *khṣīram* ('milk'), *aphsarāḥ* ('a nymph').

{A. 8.4.49 *śaro 'ci*
[Two sounds do not come] in place of [a sound denoted by] *śaR* (i.e., sibilants) [occurring after the sounds *r* or *h* preceded by a vowel] before a vowel [in close proximity].
A. 8.4.50 *triprabhṛtiṣu śākaṭāyanasya*
[The reduplication does not take place] in a cluster of three or more [consonants denoted by *yaR* (i.e., semivowels, stops and sibilants) in close proximity] according to Śākaṭāyana.
A. 8.4.51 *sarvatra śākalyasya*
[The reduplication does not take place] anywhere according to Śākalya.
A. 8.4.52 *dīrghād ācāryāṇām*
[The reduplication does not take place] after a long vowel [in close proximity] according to all teachers.
A. 8.4.53 *jhalāṃ jaś jhaśi*
[A sound denoted by] *jaŚ* (i.e., voiced unaspirated stops) comes in place of [a sound denoted by] *jhaL* (i.e., non-nasal stops and fricatives) before [a sound denoted by] *jhaŚ* (i.e., voiced stops) [in close proximity].
A. 8.4.54 *abhyāse car ca*
[A sound denoted by] *caR* (i.e., voiceless unaspirated stops and sibilants) as well as [a sound denoted by *jaŚ* (i.e., voiced unaspirated stops) come in place

of a sound denoted by *jhaL* (i.e., non-nasal stops and fricatives)] occurring in a reduplicated syllable [in close proximity].
A. 8.4.55 *khari ca*
[A sound denoted by *caR* (i.e., voiceless unaspirated stops and sibilants)] also [comes in place of a sound denoted by *jhaL* (i.e., non-nasal stops and fricatives)] before [a sound denoted by] *khaR* (i.e., all voiceless consonants) [in close proximity].
A. 8.4.56 *vāvasāne*
[A sound denoted by *caR* (i.e., voiceless unaspirated stops and sibilants)] usually [comes in place of a sound denoted by *jhaL* (i.e., non-nasal stops and fricatives)] in a pause.
A. 8.4.57 *aṇo 'pragṛhyasyānunāsikaḥ*
The nasalised vowel (*anunāsika*) [usually] comes in a place of [a sound denoted by] *aṆ* (i.e., *a*, *i*, *u*) but not the one termed *pragṛhya* [in a pause].
A. 8.4.58 *anusvārasya yayi parasavarṇaḥ*
The substitute sound homogenous with the following [sound denoted by] *yaY* (i.e., semivowels and stops) comes in place of an *anusvāra* [in close proximity].
A. 8.4.59 *vā padāntasya*
[The substitute sound homogenous with the following sound denoted by *yaY* (i.e., semivowels and stops)] usually comes in place of a *pada* final [*anusvāra* in close proximity].
A. 8.4.60 *tor li*
[The substitute homogenous with the following sound] *l* comes in place of [the dental stop belonging to the group] *tU* before [the sound] *l* [in close proximity].} *These *sūtra*s were not commented upon by Patañjali.

{Explanation:
Kielhorn's edition does not include Patañjali's commentary on the *sūtra* A. 8.4.54 which is found in VMBh_2: V.508.11-13. The text reads:

[Bhāṣya:] A sound denoted by *caR* (i.e., voiceless unaspirated stops and sibilants), which is originally in a word, remains. [For example,] *cicīṣati* ('he wants to collect', 3rd sg. desid.). A sound denoted by *jaŚ* (i.e., voiced unaspirated stops), which is originally in a word, remains. [For example,] *jijanīṣati* ('he wants to produce', 3rd sg. desid.), *bubudhe* ('he woke up', 3rd sg. perf.), *dadau* ('he gave', 3rd sg. perf.).

The *sūtra* is formulated in this way for the sake of brevity. It must, however, be understood that the substitution takes place in this way: voiced unaspirated stops (*jaŚ*) come in place of voiced aspirated stops (*jhaṢ*), and unvoiced unaspirated stops (*caR*) come in place of unvoiced aspirated stops (*khaR*). Other combinations are not possible.}

A. 8.4.61 *udaḥ sthāstambhoḥ pūrvasya*
[The substitute sound homogenous with] the preceding one comes in place of [the initial sounds] of [the verbal roots] *ṣṭhā* ('to stand', DhP I:975) and *stambhU* ('to support, sustain', DhP IX:7) occurring after [the *upasarga*] *ud* [in close proximity].

VMBh_1: III.465.4-7; VMBh_2: V.509.1-4

1) [It should be] added that in Vedic [the substitution should take place] in [the verbal root] *skandIR* ('to leap, jump', DhP I:1028) preceded by [the *upasarga*] *ud*.

[Bhāṣya:] It should be added that in Vedic [the substitution should take place] in [the verbal root] *skandIR* ('to leap, jump', DhP:1028) preceded by [the *upasarga*] *ud*. [For example,] *aghnye duram utkanda* ("O Agni, jump far away!").

[Bhāṣya:] It should also be mentioned in the case of 'an affliction'. [For example,] *utkandako rogaḥ* (a type of disease).

{Explanation:
The derivation of the the form *utthātum* ('to stand'), which can be the example of this rule, is as follows:

(1) *ud* + *ṣṭhā* (DhP I:975) + *tumUN* (A. 3.3.10 *tumunṇvulau kriyāyāṃ kriyārthāyām*)
(2) *ud* + (*ṣ* → *s*) *ṭhā* + *tum* (A. 6.1.64 *dhātvādeḥ ṣaḥ saḥ*)
(3) *u* (*d* → *t*) + *sthā* + *tum* (A.8.4.55 *khari ca*)
(4) *ut* + (*s* → *t*) *thā* + *tum* (A. 8.4.61 *udaḥ sthāstambhoḥ pūrvasya*)
(5) *ut* + (*t* → 0) *thā* + *tum* (A. 8.4.65 *jharo jhari savarṇe*)
utthātum

As the deletion of the consonant *t* at the last stage of the derivation is optional, we might as well get the form *uttthātum* without it. The verbal root *sthā* appears with *ṣ* in the *Dhātupāṭha*, therefore the rule A. 6.1.64 applies that prescribes the *ṣ* → *s* substitution.}

{A. 8.4.62 *jhayo ho 'nyatarasyām*
[The substitute sound homogenous with the preceding one] optionally comes in place of [the sound] *h* occurring after [a sound denoted by] *jhaY* (i.e., non-

nasal stops) [in close proximity].} *This *sūtra* was not commented upon by Patañjali.

A. 8.4.63 *śaś cho 'ṭi*

[The sound] *ch* [optionally] comes in place of [the sound] *ś* [occurring after a sound denoted by *jhaY* (i.e., non-nasal stops)] before [a sound denoted by] *aṬ* (i.e., vowels and semivowels *y*, *r*, *v*) [in close proximity].

VMBh_1: III.465.8-10; VMBh_2: V.509.5-7

1) The *ch*-substitute [should be said to take place] before [a sound denoted by] *aM* (i.e., vowels, semivowels and nasals) in order [to allow forms] *tacchlokena* ('with this verse') and *tacchmaśruṇā* ('with this beard').

[Bhāṣya:] The *ch*-substitute should be said to take place before [a sound denoted by] *aM* (i.e., vowels, semivowels and nasals).
[Question:] What is the purpose?
[Answer:] [The forms:] *tacchlokena* ('with this verse') and *tacchmaśruṇā* ('with this beard').

{**Explanation:**
This rule might be connected with the rules A. 8.4.40 and A. 8.4.55. It is placed last of the three because it is considered suspended with respect to the prior ones. The optional *ch*-substitution then takes place after other substitutions have applied. In the example *tacchlokeṇa* the stems joined are *tat* and *ślokena*. The final consonant *t* undergoes the *c*-substitution by A. 8.4.40 due to the consonant *ś* following. Then, A. 8.4.63 applies changing *ś* into *ch*. As the substitution is optional, we can also have the form *tac ślokena*.}

{A. 8.4.64 *halo yamāṃ yami lopaḥ*

[A sound denoted by] *yaM* (i.e., semivowels and nasal stops) occurring after a consonant is [optionally] deleted before [a sound denoted by] *yaM* [in close proximity].} *This *sūtra* was not commented upon by Patañjali.

A. 8.4.65 *jharo jhari savarṇe*

[A sound denoted by] *jhaR* (i.e., all non-nasal stops and sibilants) [occurring after a consonant is optionally deleted] before the homogenous sound [denoted by] *jhaR* [in close proximity].

VMBh_1: III.465.11-15; VMBh_2: V.509.8-12

[Question:] What is the purpose [in using] the term 'homogenous'?

1) [In the case of the deletion] of [a sound denoted by] *jhaR* (i.e., all non-nasal stops and sibilants) before [a sound denoted by] *jhaR*, the term 'homogenous' [is used] in order to prohibit [the assignment] of equivalency in the order of elements (A. 1.3.10).

[Answer:] [In the case of the deletion] of [a sound denoted by] *jhaR* (i.e., all non-nasal stops and sibilants) before [a sound denoted by] *jhaR*, the term 'homogenous' is used in order to prohibit [the assignment] of equivalency in the order of elements. [The *sūtra*] A. 1.3.10 must not apply.
[Question:] What should be then?
[Answer:] Here [the rule] would not apply: *śiṇḍhi* ('Leave!') and *piṇḍhi* ('Grind!').

{**Explanation:**
The above discussion refers to the term *savarṇa* used in the *sūtra*. The question arises whether it is necessary and perhaps it would be sufficient to only state *jharo jhari*. The omission of the term *savarṇa*, however, would lead to the application of A. 1.3.10 *yathāsaṃkhyam anudeśaḥ samānam*, according to which the consonant could be deleted only when appearing before the same consonant. Consequently, the forms such as *śiṇḍhi* and *piṇḍhi* could not be derived. The derivation of *śiṇḍhi* is as follows:

(1) *śiṣL̥* (DhP VII:14) + *si* (A. 3.4.78 *tiptasjhisipthasthamibvasmastātāmjhathās-āthāmdhvamiḍvahimahiṅ*)
(2) *śi* + *ŚnaM* + *ṣ* + *si* (A. 3.1.78 *rudhādibhyaḥ śnam*)
(3) *śi* + *na* + *ṣ* + (*si* → *hi*) (A. 3.4.87 *ser hyapic ca*)
(4) *śi* + *n* (*a* → 0) + *ṣ* + *hi* (A. 6.4.111 *śnāsor allopaḥ*)
(5) *śi* + *n* + *ṣ* + (*hi* → *dhi*) (A. 6.4.101 *hujhalbhyo her dhiḥ*)
(6) *śi* + *n* + *ṣ* + (*dh* → *ḍh*) *i* (A. 8.4.41 *ṣṭunā ṣṭuḥ*)
(7) *śi* + *n* + (*ṣ* → *ḍ*) + *ḍhi* (A. 8.4.53 *jhalāṃ jaś jhaśi*)
(8) *śi* + *n* + (*ḍ* → 0) + *ḍhi* (A. 8.4.65 *jharo jhari savarṇe*)
(9) *śi* + (*n* → *ṃ*) + *ḍhi* (A. 8.3.24 *naś cāpadāntasya jhali*)
(10) *śi* + (*ṃ* → *ṇ*) + *ḍhi* (A. 8.4.58 *anusvārasya yayi parasavarṇaḥ*)
śiṇḍhi

The *n* → *ṃ* substitution could take place at an earlier stage of the derivation because it applies before a sound denoted by *jhaL* (i.e., a non-nasal consonant or a fricative). It cannot happen before the *a*-deletion. The *ṃ* → *ṇ* substitution could also take place earlier but as these two operations do not affect the others, it does not seem to be of great importance.}

{A. 8.4.66 *udāttād anudāttasya svaritaḥ*
The *svarita* accent comes in place of the *anudātta* accent occurring after the *udātta* accent [in close proximity].
8.4.67 *nodāttasvaritodayam agārgyakāśyapagālavanām*
[The *svarita* accent] does not [come in place of the *anudātta* accent occurring after the *udātta accent* when it is followed by the *udātta* or *svarita* accent [in close proximity] according to the teachers other than Gārgya, Kāśyapa and Gālava.} *These *sūtra*s were not commented upon by Patañjali.

A. 8.4.68 *a a*
The vowel *a*, [which was treated as an open one,] is replaced by the vowel *a* [which is a closed one in close proximity].

VMBh_1: III.465.16-18; VMBh_2: V.509.13-15

[Question:] Why is this said?
[Answer:] The vowel *a* is taught in the collection of sounds (*akṣarasamāmnāya*) as an open one, [here] it is made closed again.

{Explanation:
The vowel *a* is taught as an open one only in the science of grammar for technical purposes, as is explained later on. Normally, in usage, be it Vedic or classical Sanskrit, we find that the pronunciation of *a* is a closed one. The purpose then is to return to the natural pronunciation and to show that the vowel *a* is open only for the sake of grammar.
Kaiyaṭa (VMBh_2: V.509) refers to Patañjali's discussion on the *pratyāhāra sūtra*: *aiuṇ*; he mentions two first *vārttika*s: *akārasya vivṛtopadeśa ākāragrahaṇārthaḥ* ǁ ("The vowel *a* is taught as open in grammar for the sake of the vowel *ā*.") and *tasya vivṛtopadeśād anyatrāpi vivṛtopadeśaḥ savarṇārthaḥ* ǁ ("Due to it being taught as open, in other places it is also taught as open for the sake of homogeneity."). The distiction is made between the first enunciation, that is, in the *akṣarasamāmnāya* (a collection of sounds) where the sounds are enumerated, and the appearance of the vowel *a* in such elements as a verbal root, a nominal stem or a suffix. In this second case the issue in question is homogeneity, which is discussed below.}

VMBh_1: III.465.18-466.7; VMBh_2: V.509.15-510.7

[Question:] What is the reason that [the vowel *a*] is taught as an open one?

The vowel *a* is taught as open one for the sake of substitution and homogeneity.

So that the short [vowel *a*] came in place of the vowel *ā*; for the sake of that there is the Pāṇini's [rule] A. 8.4.68.

[Answer:] So for the sake of substitution: *vrkṣābhyām* (inst./dat./abl. du. of *vṛkṣa* 'a tree'), *devadattā3* ('Oh, Devadatta!'). Due to closeness, the open vowels *ā* and *ā3* should come in place of an open [vowel]. And for the sake of homogeneity: the vowel *a* on the basis of the term 'homogenous' should be understood as the sound *ā* as well. So that the short one was like the vowel *ā*. And in the same way in [the forms] *atikhaṭvaḥ* ('who has violated the nuptial bed') and *atimālaḥ* ('excelling a necklace') the short [vowel *a*] will come in place of the vowel *ā*, and will be open. It should be closed and this is how the [proper] meaning is restored [by the present rule]. This is the purpose.

{**Explanation:**
The first part of the *śloka* refers to the *vārttika* 1 on the *pratyāhārasūtra* 1. When Patañjali says that the vowel *a* is treated as open for the sake of *ā*, what he means is that it is so done for the sake of substitution. The examples given are *vṛkṣābhyām* and *devadattā3*. In the former, the vowel *ā* comes in place of *a* when it appears at the end of an *aṅga* nominal stem before the case ending beginning with a semivowel, nasal or the consonant *bh* (A. 7.3.102 *supi ca*[523]). The second form is an example of the prolated *ā3* substitution of the syllable beginning with the last vowel of an utterance (A. 8.2.82 *vākyasya ṭeḥ pluta udāttaḥ*). As the vowels *ā* and *ā3* cannot be considered closed, the vowel *a* should be considered open for these substitutions to take place. The problem that arises with *a*, *ā* and *ā3* is that *a* is nowhere known as open whereas *ā* and *ā3* are nowhere known as closed.
In the above *śloka* Patañjali states yet another purpose of considering the short vowel *a* in grammar as open, and this is for the sake of the forms *atikhaṭvaḥ* and *atimālaḥ* where the long *ā* of *khaṭvā* and *mālā* respectively is replaced by its short counterpart by A. 1.2.48 *gostriyor upasarjanasya*[524] before a case ending. It would not be possible if the vowels *a* and *ā* were not homogeneous.}

VMBh_1: III.466.7-11; VMBh_2: V.510.7-11

[Question:] What then?

---

[523] A. 7.3.102 *supi ca* || ("[A long vowel comes in place of the final vowel *a* of an *aṅga* stem] before a case ending [beginning with the consonant denoted by *yaÑ* (i.e., semivowels, nasals or *bh*)].")

[524] A. 1.2.48 *gostriyor upasarjanasya* || ("[A short vowel] comes in place of [the final vowel of the nominal stem] *go* ('a cow') occurring as an *upasarjana* and of an *upasarjana* ending in a feminine suffix.")

1) When the vowel *a* has been restored, there is prohibition of *ā*.

[Objection:] When the vowel *a* has been restored, prohibition of *ā* should be mentioned. [For example,] *khaṭvā* ('a bedstead') and *mālā* ('a garland').
[Answer:] This is not a fault. Just as the term 'homogeneous' refers to the base, in the same way it should be done with the substitute; therefore, due to close relation, a short vowel will come in place of a short one and a long vowel will come in place of a long one.

{**Explanation:**
Commentators explain that the first *a* in this *sūtra* should be viewed as the substituend and the second as the substitute. The closed *a* always comes in place of the open one; but due to absence of the marker *T* after the vowel *a*, the long and prolated version would be included as well. The argument is that if the *sūtra* were formulated as *ad a*, then only the short *a* would be taken into consideration. The absence of *T* allows us to include the long and prolated vowels as well. Therefore, the vowels *ā* and *ā3* would be taken as substituends and would be replaced by the closed *a*, which is not desired. Hence the *vārttika* prohibiting it. Patañjali says that the substitution is made on the basis of the closest relation which can be of different sorts: the place of articulation, the meaning, the quality and prosodial value. Thus the short closed *a* cannot replace either *ā* or *ā3* in the *sūtra*.}

VMBh_1: III.466.12-14; VMBh_2: V.510.12-14

2) But there is no homogeneity because the substitute is not a part of [the abbreviation] *aṆ*.

[Objection:] The homogeneous vowels would not result because the substitute is not a part of [the abbreviation] *aṆ*.
[Question:] What [homogenous vowels]?
[Answer:] [Those marked with] *udātta*, *anudātta* or *svarita* accents, or nasal ones.

{**Explanation:**
The meaning of this *vārttika* is this – the closed vowel *a* cannot be included in the abbreviatory term *aṆ* (i.e., *a*, *i*, *u*) so there would be no homogeneity with vowels marked with different accents as well as nasal ones. The inclusion in the term *aṆ* does not take place due to the substitution of the open *a* with the closed one. Reference is probably made here to the *paribhāṣā*: *bhāvyamānena savarṇānāṃ grahaṇaṃ na* ("[A letter] which is to be taught [in a rule] does not

denote [the letters] homogeneous with it").[525] As the substitute closed vowel *a* is pronounced with certain qualities such as the accent, these very qualities would apply to all three variants: *a*, *ā* and *ā3* which is not desired. In the case of the short *a* possessed of the qualities such as *udātta* etc., restoration of a vowel possessed of these qualities and of a duration of one mora only is desired, which is not possible due to the lack of homogeneity.}

VMBh_1: III.466.15-25; VMBh_2: V.511.1-11

3) But it has been achieved on the basis of the marker *T* following.

[Objection:] It has been achieved.
[Question:] How?
[Answer:] On the basis of the marker *T* following. The instruction regarding the marker *T* following should be done (see A. 1.1.70[526]), [the rule should read] *ad a*.
[Bhāṣya:] Another one says: When the vowel *a* has been restored, there is prohibition of *ā*. When the vowel *a* has been restored, prohibition of *ā* should be mentioned. [For example,] *khaṭvā* ('a bedstead') and *mālā* ('a garland').
[Answer:] This is not a fault. By force of pronouncing a long vowel there will not be [prohibition]. This is the purpose then: *vṛkṣābhyām* and *plakṣābhyām* (inst./dat./abl. du. of *vṛkṣa* 'a tree' and *plakṣa* 'a fig tree' respectively). In this case, by force of mentioning a long vowel, it will not be either; so then: *api kākaḥ śyenāyate* (see A. 7.4.25 *akṛtsārvadhātukayor dīrghaḥ*[527]).
[Question:] But in this case will it not be due to mentioning a long vowel as well?
[Answer:] There is another purpose in mentioning a long vowel.
[Question:] What?
[Answer:] [The forms] *dadhīyati* and *madhūyati* ('he likes milk' and 'he likes honey' respectively). In this case it is really a fault [to say] that "the homogenous vowels would not result because the substitute is not a part of [the abbreviation] *aṆ*."
[Question:] What [homogenous vowels]?
[Answer:] [Those marked with] *udātta*, *anudātta* or *svarita* accents, or nasal ones.

---

[525] PŚ 19, I.19, II.148-149. See also WUJASTYK 1993: vol. I:34-35, vol. II:132-133. Wujastyk quotes the *paribhāṣā* differently: *bhāvyamāno 'ṇ savarṇān na gṛhṇāti* || ("A vowel or semi-vowel which is being generated does not include letters homorganic with it.")

[526] A. 1.1.70 *taparas tatkālasya* || ("A sound followed or preceded by the marker *T* denotes homogeneous sounds of its time duration.")

[527] A. 7.4.25 *akṛtsārvadhātukayor dīrghaḥ* || ("The long vowel comes in place of [the final vowel of an *aṅga* verbal stem] before [the suffix beginning with *y* and marked with *K* or *Ṅ*] excluding [the suffixes] *kṛt* and *sārvadhātuka*.")

[Objection:] But it has been achieved on the basis of the marker *T* following. It has been achieved.
[Question:] How?
[Answer:] On the basis of the marker *T* following. The instruction regarding the following *T* should be done, [the rule should be] *ad at*.

{**Explanation:**
Kaiyaṭa (VMBh_2: V.511) explains that the expression *atparaḥ* can be interpreted in two ways: "that after which *T*" occurs and "that which occurs after *T*". The former interpretation allows us to exclude the vowels *ā* and *ā3* as it refers to the vowel *a* that is the substituend, namely the open *a*. And as its long and prolated counterparts are characterised by different length, they are not to be taken into consideration here. The substitute, however, the closed *a*, will be understood as possessed of its proper time and qualities such as accent and nasalisation.
Annaṃbhaṭṭa (MPV X.477) refers to the rule A. 1.1.70 *taparas tatkālasya* and says that there are two views regarding that *sūtra*: the *jātipakṣa* and the *vyaktipakṣa*. According to the former, where the genus is the denotation of the word, it is formulated for the sake of restriction. The second view is that A. 1.1.70 is formulated for the sake of stating the particular length of the vowel.
Yet others claim that two markers *T* should be used after both vowels *a* in the text of the *sūtra*.}

VMBh_1: III.467.1-3; VMBh_2: V.512.1-3

4) Alternatively, the division of vowels is achieved by lord Pāṇini by stating one remaining instead of many.

[Bhāṣya:] Alternatively, the division of vowels is achieved by lord Pāṇini by stating one remaining instead of many. It is the instruction of [stating] one remaining instead of many. [It should be formulated thus] *a a a*.

{**Explanation:**
There are six vowels *a*, being substituends, with the duration of one mora, that are established here, that is *udātta*, *anudātta* and *svarita* accented and thus accented but nasalised as well. In the same way there are six substitutes. This is why the principle of *ekaśeṣa* is thought to be used here, where many elements are replaced by just one, the principle that Pāṇini formulated first in A. 1.2.64 *sarūpāṇām ekaśeṣa ekavibhaktau* || ("When there is the single occurrence of a single case ending, only one of a series of repeated morpheme stems remain in use"). He adds that specifying six substituends excludes the long and prolated vowels of the class *a* from being subject to the replacement. What is desired then is the substitution of six open vowels with six closed vowels *a*.}

This was the first *āhnika* of the fourth *pada* of the eighth *adhyāya* in the *Vyākaraṇamahābhāṣya* composed by Patañjali. This is the end of a *pada*.

This is the end of the eighth *adhyāya*.

6. Patañjali and *asiddhatva*

It has been commonly accepted that in the Sanskrit tradition *asiddhatva* and *asiddhavattva* are identical and function in the same way. The accepted interpretation always reads *asiddha* with the suffix *vatI*, whether it is actually present, as in A. 6.4.22, or merely implied as in A. 6.1.86 and A. 8.2.1. Despite that fact, Patañjali never uses the term *asiddhavat*. Naturally, we might assume that it is implied, but I do not believe that this assumption is supported by evidence; I think we can safely say that what Patañjali in fact meant when he wrote *asiddha* was indeed *asiddha*. This would lead to the conclusion that at the earliest stage of the development of the Sanskrit grammatical tradition the identification of both terms – *asiddha* and *asiddhavat* – was not accepted, or simply conceived. Only in the *Kāśikāvṛtti* do we find this equation *asiddha=asiddhavat* for the first time. It is Kaiyaṭa who tries to explain the usage of the suffix *vatI* in A. 6.4.22. It seems that this is a problem that did not concern Patañjali. But it does mean that he viewed both terms as synonymous, similarly to Kātyāyana.

Bronkhorst in his article,[528] while discussing Kātyāyana's *vārttika* on A. 6.1.86 explaining the purpose of *asiddhatva*, states that the explanation Kātyāyana proposes would be more suitable to interpret the principle of *asiddhavattva* rather than *asiddhatva*; or to be more precise, it would be more appropriate if the rule A. 6.1.86 read *asiddhavat* instead of *asiddha*. When we consider the examples from the *Ābhīya* section and compare them to those from the *Tripādī* that cannot be explained via *asiddhavattva*, we cannot but agree. It does not mean, however, that despite the fact that neither Kātyāyana nor Patañjali use the term *asiddhavat* they both understand it indeed as *asiddhavat*. What follows is a short summary of Patañjali's interpretation of the *asiddhatva* principle as presented in the *Tripādī* section, whose detailed translation and explanation was presented in Chapter 5.

In the opening *sūtra* Patañjali discusses the problem of technical terms (*saṃjñā*) and rules of interpretation (*paribhāṣā*), concluding that they must apply along with described operations. He is a supporter of the *kāryakālapakṣa*; he also agrees that the *sūtra* A. 8.2.1 has to be an *adhikāra* because otherwise suspension within the *Tripādī* section would not be possible. We would only be able to talk about suspension of sections, namely the entire *asiddhatva* section would be suspended with respect to the entire preceding part of the *Aṣṭādhyāyī*. Patañjali accepts Kātyāyana's *vārttika* on A. 6.1.86 prescribing the two-fold purpose of *asiddhatva*: *utsargalakṣaṇabhāva* (allowing the application of a rule conditioned by a substituend) and *ādeśalakṣaṇapratiṣedha* (prohibiting the application of a rule conditioned by a substitute).

---

528 BROKNHORST 1980.

6.1. The lack of suspension

6.1.1. Exceptions and negations following the natural order

It was mentioned in previous chapters that the *utsarga-apavāda* relation also holds true in the *Tripādī* section. Pāṇini usually proceeds from the most general rules to the most detailed ones, which means that first a general operation is described, followed by its exceptions and finally optional forms, negation and irregularities, of course within one domain. Following Kātyāyana, Patañjali also agrees with an *apavāda* always prevailing over the general rule even though it might be, and often is, placed later in the *Tripādī* than the general *sūtra*. Kātyāyana's *vārttika* reads: *apavādo vacanaprāmāṇyāt* || ("An exception [applies] by force of the statement itself"), which means that the mere existence of exceptions indicates their application prior to general rules. Otherwise, they would be *anavakāśa* (without the scope of application), particularly if the domain of an exception is completely included in the domain of a general rule.

Prohibitive *sūtras* that disallow an operation under certain circumstances are usually placed after the general rule. We have the example of the rule A. 8.2.8, which negates the *n*-deletion (prescribed by A. 8.2.7) before some case endings.

In the *vārttika* 6 under the *sūtra* A. 8.2.6 Kātyāyana states that the rule A. 8.2.29 *skoḥ saṃyogādyor ante ca* should be said unsuspended with respect to A. 8.2.23 *saṃyogāntasya lopaḥ*. Patañjali rightly rejects this statement, as the former rule is an exception to the latter. Its domain is wholly included in the domain of A. 8.2.23, so even though they are not two consecutive rules, they still refer to the same domain.

The *sūtras* A. 8.2.68 *ahan* and A. 8.2.69 *ro 'supi* prescribe the *rU* and *r*-substitution of the final sound of the stem *ahan*. Theoretically the final *n* could be subject to deletion by A. 8.2.7 *nalopaḥ prātipadikāntasya*, which is not the case due to the use of the form *ahan* in A. 8.2.68. It is an indication that the deletion cannot take place.

These few examples show that the relation between *utsarga* and *apavāda* in the *Aṣṭādhyāyī* is on the one hand straightforward, but at the same time operates on various levels. Let us evoke Kātyāyana's opinion on the purpose of *asiddhatva*, namely the prohibition of an operation based on a subsititute and allowing an operation based on a substitutend. This purpose is the reversal of the natural order within Pāṇini's treatise. A similarly natural order is the one between a general rule and an exception; it seems commonplace to introduce general prescriptions before their specifications, and therefore restrictions, are made. This rule, also based on our every day experience, has to be preserved in the domain of suspension in the *Aṣṭādhyāyī*; it is the principle that needs to transgress purely theoretical and formal devices to allow the correct description of the language.

This is why the *utsarga-apavāda* relationship has to operate within the *Tripādī* section; it cannot be suspended in a certain domain, so to speak. At the same time, certain measures had to be undertaken by Pāṇini to ensure that the principal of *utsarga-apavāda* does not clash with *asiddhatva*, and one way to do that (albeit not the only one as we will see below) is blocking, that is operating on the level of groups rather than individual rules. Patañjali uses the expression *na yoge yogo 'siddhaḥ* / *prakaraṇe prakaraṇam asiddham* || ("It is not the rule that is suspended with respect to another rule. It is the context that is suspended with respect to another context"). So, topical domains are like bubbles within which the standard principles function; this is the situation often refered to within the *Tripādī*; there is no suspension within the bubbles.

6.1.2. Exceptions and negations preceding the general rule

There are examples, however, where an exception or a negative *sūtra* precedes a more general rule in the *Tripādī* section. As Cardona points out, the purpose is to limit certain operations.[529] The *sūtra* A. 8.2.2 *nalopaḥ supsvara-saṃjñātugvidhiṣu kṛti* prescribes the suspension of the *n*-deletion, established by the rule A. 8.2.7, with respect to certain operations. In other cases, which are not enlisted in A. 8.2.2., the suspension does not take place. The following *sūtra* A. 8.2.3 *na mu ne* negates the suspension of the *mu*-substitution prescribed by A. 8.2.80 *adaso 'ser dād u do maḥ* in the stem *adas* before the case ending *Ṅā*, so that the correct form *amunā* can be derived. The reason why these two rules precede the ones to which they are the exceptions is that they limit or negate the suspension itself, not merely the elements that are subject to suspension.

6.1.3. Indications

There are also *sūtras* in the *Tripādī* that cannot be considered suspended with respect to prior rules. This lack of suspension, however, has not been stated openly by Pāṇini but merely indicated. In such cases Patañjali sometimes uses the expression *āśrayāt* ('because it is dependent [on it]'). The reason why these *sūtras* are not suspended is that other rules, preceding them either in the *Tripādī* or *Sapadasaptādhyāyī* section, are contingent on the application, and output, of the suspended rules. Otherwise they become without the scope of application.

In the *sūtra* A. 8.2.4 *udāttasvaritayor yaṇaḥ svarito 'nudāttasya* the accent of the *yaṆ*-substitute should be considered unsuspended with respect to the *yaṆ*-substitution itself that is prescribed by the rule A. 6.1.77 *iko yaṇ aci*.[530] The

---

[529] CARDONA 2012:124ff.

[530] A. 6.1.77 *iko yaṇ aci* || ("The semivowels (*yaṆ*) come in place of the vowels *i*, *u*, *ṛ* and *ḷ* respectively before a vowel [in continuous utterance].")

examples given by Patañjali under this rule show that suspension of the accent would result in the wrong accent altogether for the expression in question. It seems, however, that Patañjali is not in favour of such a solution as he proposes the division of the *sūtra* instead. A similar situation occurs with the rule A. 8.2.5 *ekādeśa udāttenodāttaḥ*, also prescribing accent, which he does not comment upon but refers to in the commentary on the following *sūtra*. These accentual rules cannot be analysed separately from other phonological and morphological operations they serve.

The *vārttika* 3 on A. 8.2.6 *svarito vānudātte padādau* states that the rule A. 8.2.23 *saṃyogāntasya lopaḥ* should be unsuspended with respect to A. 6.1.114 *haśi ca*[531] for the sake of the expression *harivo medinaṃ tvā*.[532] This *vārttika* seems to be accepted by Patañjali, or at least it is not rejected, but it also seems unnecessary. As the *rU*-substitution prescribed by A. 8.3.1 *matuvaso ru sambuddhau chandasi* has to be considered unsuspended with respect to the rule A. 6.1.114 due to the latter otherwise being without the scope of application, so must be A. 8.2.23 because A. 8.3.1 is the result of the application of A. 8.2.23. Besides, the rule A. 6.1.114 comes into play only before another *pada* following, in this case *medinam*. It can be assumed that before we apply the rules applicable to the combination of *pada*s, we derive the *pada*s in question themselves. It can be deduced on the basis of Pāṇini's own statements, additional *vārttikas* are not necessary. The following *vārttika* presents a similar situation, where the prolation (on basis of A. 8.2.84 *dūrād dhūte ca*) is decided unsuspended with respect to A. 6.1.113 *ato ror aplutād aplute*.[533] I find that Patañjali is wrong in this case as well and does not read between the lines where this unsuspension is implied.

Yet the next *vārttika* provides for the unsuspension of the *sIC* deletion of the rule A. 8.2.28 *iṭa īṭi* with respect to the single substitution by A. 6.1.101 *akaḥ savarṇe dīrghaḥ*.[534] Patañjali accepts it even though it is not necessary either. The indication of the lack of suspension in the case of A. 8.2.28 is slightly more complex but it can still be deduced. The suffix *sIC* in the examples given is preceded by the infix *iṬ*. The rule A. 8.2.28 solely prescribes the deletion of the sound *s*, but as the suffix is marked with C, which indicates that the vowel it is attached to bears an *udātta* accent. This is done for the sake of the application of A. 8.2.5 *ekādeśa udāttenodāttaḥ*, which in turn requires that the single substitution be performed by A. 6.1.101.[535]

---

[531] A. 6.1.114 *haśi ca* || ("[The sound *u* comes in place of *rU* when it is preceded by the sound *a*] also before a voiced consonant (*haŚ*) [in continuous utterance].")

[532] For the detailed derivation see the relevant *sūtra*.

[533] A. 6.1.113 *ato ror aplutād aplute* || ("[The sound *u*] comes in place of *rU* (A. 8.2.66) when it is preceded and followed by a non-prolated sound *a* [in continuous utterance].")

[534] A. 6.1.101 *akaḥ savarṇe dīrghaḥ* || ("A long vowel comes in place of [both the sound denoted by] *aK* (i.e., *a*, *i*, *u*, *r̥*, *l̥*) and the following homogenous vowel [in continuous utterance].")

[535] See as well CARDONA 2012:147-148.

The *vārttikas* 9 and 10 on the *sūtra* A. 8.2.6 *svarito vānudātte padādau* are a very interesting example of Patañjali's attitude to the tradition preceding him. The former states that the rule A. 8.2.81 *eta īd bahuvacane* prescribing the *mī*-substitution of the element *de* of the pronoun *adas* to derive the expression *amī atra* should be unsuspended with respect to the rule A. 6.1.78 *eco 'yavāyāvaḥ*.[536] Otherwise we would get the incorrect form *ade atra* → **adayatra*. Kātyāyana in the following *vārttika* states that such an ending (i.e., *ī*) would be called *pragṛhya*, because it is a dual ending, which defeats the purpose of the restriction; as a *pragṛhya* ending it would not be subject to sandhi regardless of whether the ending would be *e* or *ī*. Besides, Pāṇini refers to the stem *adas* with the substitution performed in the rule A. 1.1.12 *adaso māt*,[537] which indicates that the suspension does not take place. Patañjali, interestingly enough, does not reject these two *vārttikas*, but states that as they were uttered one by one, they stay there and cannot be removed. These *vārttikas* are obviously not necessary, yet still Patañjali keeps them.

The *vārttika* 11 prescribes the unsuspension of prolation (A. 8.2.107 *eco 'pragṛhyasyādūrād dhūte pūrvasyārdhasyād uttarasyedutau*) with respect to the infix *tuK* (A. 6.1.73 *che ca*[538]) so that we could derive the form *agnā3i cchattram*. However, here again the second *pada* is added when the first one has been formed so there seems no need for the *vārttika*. Patañjali does not acknowledge this. The situation repeats itself with the *vārttika* 15, prescribing the unsuspension of a number of rules from the *Tripādī* with respect to the reduplication by A. 8.1.1 *sarvasya dve*.[539] If we consider the words subject to reduplication as finished entities, the *vārttika* in not necessary and the correct result can still be achieved.

The *sūtra* A. 8.2.38 *dadhas tathoś ca* allows for the substitution *d* → *dh* in the verbal root *dhā*. For the application of this rule, the *jaŚ*-substitution in the reduplicated syllable (i.e., *dh* → *d*) prescribed by A. 8.4.53 *jhalāṃ jaś jhaśi* should be considered unsuspended. Otherwise, the correct results would not be possible. Patañjali proposes the solution that the *jaŚ*-substitution is unsuspended with respect to the reduplication. This seems completely unnecessary because the rule A. 8.2.38 includes the form *dadhas*, the reduplicated stem of the verbal root *dhā*, and through such an inclusion Pāṇini indicates that the substitution *dh* → *d* has to take place before the application of this rule.

---

536 A. 6.1.78 *eco 'yavāyāvaḥ* ॥ ("[The substitutes] *ay*, *av*, *āy* and *āv* come in place of [the vowels denoted by] *eC* (i.e., *e*, *o*, *ai*, *au*) respectively [before a vowel in continuous utterance].")

537 A. 1.1.12 *adaso māt* ॥ ("[The technical term *pragṛhya* denotes the vowels *ī*, *ū* and *e* occurring] after [the sound] *m* being a part of [the pronominal stem] *adas* ('that').")

538 A. 6.1.73 *che ca* ॥ ("[The final infix *tUK* comes at the end of a short vowel] before [the sound] *cha* [in continuous utterance].")

539 A. 8.1.1 *sarvasya dve* ॥ ("Two [expressions] come in place of the whole [sequence].")

The section of rules prescribing prolation and accent beginning with A. 8.2.82 *vākyasya ṭeḥ pluta udāttaḥ* should also most probably be considered unsuspended with respect to the part of the *Aṣṭādhyāyī* preceding the *Tripādī*. In the *sūtra* A. 8.2.108 *tayor yvāv aci saṃhitāyām* the substitution with *y* and *v* is taught with respect to such sounds as *i* and *u* respectively that form a part of a prolated diphthong. The inclusion of the term *pluta* in the *sūtra* A. 6.1.125 *plutapragṛhyā aci nityam*[540] indicates that the *pluta* itself cannot be suspended. However, this substitution could be also achieved by the *sūtra* A. 6.1.77 *iko yaṇ aci*, which in turn would result in the application of accent based on A. 8.2.5 *ekādeśa udāttenodāttaḥ*. As this is not a desired outcome, A. 8.2.108 was formulated. The discussion that follows introduces two reasons for the creation of that rule: the prohibition of lengthening (A. 6.1.101 *akaḥ savarṇe dīrghaḥ*[541]) and the *śākala* operations (A. 6.1.127 *iko 'savarṇe śākalyasya hrasvaṃ ca*).[542] This purpose is rejected by Patañjali, as he accepts the *vārttikas* under the rule A. 6.1.77: 1) "And the *yaṆ*-substitution [takes place of the vowels *i* and *u* that are] preceded by a prolated vowel"; 2) "It serves to prohibit the substitution with a long vowel and *śākala* operations."[543] Their acceptance is not necessary, however, because the same can be deduced from Pāṇini's own formulations of rules. Thus Patañjali prefers to accept the additional solutions proposed by Kātyāyana instead of a wider interpretation of the rule A. 8.2.108.

The *sūtra* A. 8.3.13 *ḍho ḍhe lopaḥ* is yet another example of Patañjali not understanding the indications Pāṇini makes. The example in question is the form *līḍha* (past passive participle of the verb *lih* – 'to lick') whose relevant stages of derivation look thus:

liḍh + (*dh* → *ḍh*) *a* (A. 8.4.41 *ṣṭunā ṣṭuḥ*)
li (*ḍh* → 0) + *ḍha* (A. 8.3.13 *ḍho ḍhe lopaḥ*)
l (*i* → *ī*) + *ḍha* (A. 6.3.111 *ḍhralope pūrvasya dīrgho 'ṇaḥ*[544])

---

[540] See A. 6.1.125 *plutapragṛhyā aci nityam* || ("Prolated vowels and *pragṛhya* vowels obligatory [retain their original form] before vowels [in close proximity].")

[541] A. 6.1.101 *akaḥ savarṇe dīrghaḥ* || ("A long vowel comes in place of [both the sound denoted by] *aK* (i.e., *a*, *i*, *u*, *ṛ*, *ḷ*) and the following homogenous vowel [in continuous utterance].")

[542] The operation called *śākala* is the one prescribed by Śākalya. He was an ancient grammarian whose name is mentioned in the treatise a few times. He stated that the vowels *i*, *u*, *ṛ* and *ḷ* remain without phonetical combination or they are shortened when long: e.g., A. 6.1.127 *iko 'savarṇe śākalyasya hrasvaś ca* || ("According to Śākalya [the final vowel] *iK* (i.e., *i*, *u*, *ṛ*, *ḷ*) [of a *pada* retains its form] before non-homogenous [vowels] and [is replaced by] a [corresponding] short vowel.")

[543] See *vārttikas* 1 and 2 under A. 6.1.77: 1) *yaṇādeśaḥ plutapūrvasya ca* 2) *dīrghaśākala-pratiṣedhārtham*.

[544] A. 6.3.111 *ḍhralope pūrvasya dīrgho 'ṇaḥ* || ("A long vowel comes in place of a vowel denoted by *aṆ* (i.e., *a*, *i*, *u*) before a deleted [substitute] of [sounds] *ḍh* or *r* when it immediately precedes it.")

The dependence of these rules can be easily seen. The *sūtra* A. 8.3.13 depends on the substitution prescribed by A. 8.4.41 *ṣṭunā ṣṭuḥ*, which is even stated in the text itself. The expression *ḍhe* ('before *ḍh*') shows that the *ḍh*-substitution, which must take place on the basis of A. 8.4.41, has already taken place. Consequently, it cannot be suspended because A. 8.3.13 would have no scope of application. Similarly, A. 6.3.111 whose formulation mentioning *ḍh-lopa* indicates that A. 8.3.13 must have applied. Patañjali resorts to different and more complex solutions instead of noticing a straightforward indication made by Pāṇini.

6.2. The use of *sthānivadbhāva*

Both Patañjali and later commentators employ *sthānivadbhāva* in their search for the correct interpretation of Pāṇinian rules and the solution to various problems; although this principle is referred to only a few times by Patañjali himself, and slightly more often by Kaiyaṭa in a much later period. When the reference is made, Patañjali often resorts to solutions originally found under A. 1.1.58 *na padāntadvirvacanavareyalopasvarasavarṇānusvāradīrghajaścarvidhiṣu*, which actually prohibits *sthānivadbhāva*: *vārttika* 3 *pūrvatrāsiddhe ca* ("Also in the *pūrvatrāsiddha* section") openly forbids the operation of this principle in the *Tripādī*, and *vārttika* 10 *tasya doṣaḥ saṃyogādilopalatvaṇatveṣu* ("There is a fault in [forbidding *sthānivadbhāva* in the cases of] the deletion of the initial [sound] of a cluster (A. 8.2.29), the *l*-substitute (A. 8.2.18 etc.) and the *ṇ*-substitute"), on the other hand, describes some exceptions. As mentioned in chapter 4, this rule is considered by some scholars to be a later addition because it formulates a negation in between other positive rules describing the conditions for *sthānivadbhāva*. If it were the case, it would have had to have been added very early on, already at or before the time of Kātyāyana as he extensively comments on it. This would also suggest that the commentators in the first century following Pāṇini, whose work has not come down to us but who must have existed, greatly misunderstood one of the most important features of Pāṇini's grammar. The summary of the *sthānivadbhāva* references is presented below.

The rule A. 8.2.23 *saṃyogāntasya lopaḥ* employs both solutions to derive correct forms: *sthānivadbhāva* as well as the *antaraṅga-bahiraṅga* principle. The problematic formations, potentially subject to sound deletion, are those where we find the *yaṆ*-substitution between *pada*s. In the example *kākyartham/vāsyartham* Patañjali employs *sthānivadbhāva* to avoid the deletion of the sounds *k* and *s* forming the initial of the cluster. This is direct reference to the *vārttika* 10 on A. 1.1.58. The same set of arguments, quoting both *vārttika*s 3 and 10 on A. 1.1.58, and thus establishing his support for *sthānivadbhāva* in this case, can be found in A. 8.4.15 *hinumīnā*. The rule prescribes the *ṇ*-substitution in the case of two verbal roots which are specified in the *sūtra* in a particular form. In order to ensure that the substitution is not limited to these forms only, the *vārttika* is specified; it is followed by another in which Kātyāyana directly refers to *sthānivadbhāva* as a solution, and at the same a rejection of the *vārttika* number 1.

The abovementioned *vārttika* 10 is not referred to, however, in A. 8.2.38 *dadhas tathoś ca* where the problem with the form *dadh* arises. This is clearly not the original verbal root but the form which has already undergone reduplication and some phonological substitutions. The reference to *sthānivadbhāva* is made so that we could derive forms such as *dadhāsi* to prevent the deletion of the root *ā*. In this case, however, *sthānivadbhāva* is dismissed based on the *vārttika* 3 on 1.1.58 and an additional *vārttika* on A. 8.2.38 is proposed instead; the reason for such a solution might be the fact that the *bhaṢ*-substitution is not included in the exemption list of *vt* 10 on A. 1.1.58.

It seems that Patañjali accepts *sthānivadbhāva* suggested in A. 8.2.78 *upadhyāyāṃ ca*, where it is evoked to prevent undesired lengthening in certain forms. In this case the reference is made to the *vārttika* 1 on A. 1.1.58, which reads *pratiṣedhe svaradīrgayalopeṣu lopājādeśo na sthānivat* ("With reference to the prohibition [of *sthānivadbhāva*, it should be said that] the vowel substitute in the form of deletion is not treated like the substituend with respect to [the rules prescribing] accent, the substitution with a long vowel and the deletion of [the sound] *y*"). This restrictive interpretation of the prohibition in the application of *sthānivadbhāva* is suggested as the solution. However, Patañjali seems to side with an additional *vārttika* prescribing prohibition in the case of *Uṇādi* suffixes, due to their underivable character.

This last case, the rule A. 8.3.17 *bhobhagoaghoapūrvasya yo 'śi* is an interesting example because *sthānivadbhāva* is ultimately rejected but not for reasons of its inapplicability within the *Tripādī*. The discussion is centred around the necessity of using the condition *aŚ* and it comes down to the doubt whether the replacement *rU* can be treated as a single sound similar to the substitution with *r*, devoid of a marker. This discussion is interesting because it refers to the general condition stated in A. 1.1.56 *sthānivad ādeśo 'nalvidhau*, which prevents *sthānivadbhāva* when the rules depend on individual sounds.

6.3. The *antaraṅga-bahiraṅga* principle

Patañjali, as well as Kātyāyana, makes use of the *antaraṅga-bahiraṅga* principle in the *Tripādī* section in various places. In the *sūtra* A. 8.2.23 *saṃyogāntasya lopaḥ* the problem arises with examples such as *dadhy atra* where the sound *y*, being the final of a *pada*, should be deleted. One of the solutions proposed is the reference to the *antaraṅga-bahiraṅga* relation as *y* being the result of the *yaṆ*-substitution is conditioned by the following *pada atra*. This makes it externally conditioned and as such suspended with respect to the deletion, which depends on one *pada* only and is internally conditioned. However, another solution proposed in the *vārttika* 2 seems more interesting, that is reading into the rule A. 8.2.23 the expression *jhalaḥ* from the *sūtra* A. 8.2.26. It would allow for the prohibition of deletion, as the sound *y* is not included in the abbreviation *jhaL*. This is unacceptable because the rule A. 8.2.26 is suspended, but it might indicate that Patañjali followed Kātyāyana in preferring to read *asiddha* as *asiddhavat*. If the later *sūtras* are only 'as if suspended', the problem with the *anuvṛtti* from the following rule is far more acceptable than in the case of *asiddha* proper.

In the rule A. 8.2.42 *radābhyāṃ niṣṭhāto naḥ pūrvasya ca daḥ* prescribing the *t* → *n* substitution of the *niṣṭhā* suffix the prohibition is proposed with respect to such stems that contain a *vṛddhi* vowel. The conclusion Patañjali reaches is that the *vṛddhi* vowel is the result of the externally conditioned operation and consequently suspended with respect to the substitution. And it is only after the vowel is raised to the *vṛddhi* grade that the substitution could be performed.

A very interesting discussion takes place in the commentary on the *sūtra* A. 8.3.15 *kharavasānayor visarjanīyaḥ*. The *vārttika* 1 proposes the prohibition of the *visarjanīya* in examples such as *nārkuṭa* and *nārpatya*, and the following one suggests that we can resort to the *antaraṅga-bahiraṅga* relation to derive correct results. The sound *r*, that is subject to *ḥ*-substitution by A. 8.3.15, in these examples is the result of *vṛddhi* of the vowel *ṛ* in stems *nṛkuṭī* and *nṛpati* respectively. As this operation is conditioned by a secondary suffix, it is considered externally conditioned and as such suspended with respect to the *visarjanīya*, which is internally conditioned. Patañjali, interestingly, rejects this solution because he states that the *ḥ*-substitution is placed in the *Tripādī* section so with respect to the *vṛddhi* substitution prescribed by the *sūtra* A. 7.2.117 *taddhiteṣv acām ādeḥ*[545] it is suspended. It indicates that the *antaraṅga-bahiraṅga* solution should not be accepted in the *Tripādī* at all if the reference is made to the *Sapādasaptādhyāyī*.

The problem with the application of the *paribhāṣā*: *asiddhaṃ bahiraṅgam antaraṅge*, prescribing the suspension of externally conditioned operations with respect to those internally conditioned, is that it evokes the principle of suspension. If an internally conditioned operation is placed in the *Tripādī*, and an externally conditioned operation precedes it (that means is placed in the *Sapādasaptādhyāyī*) both of them could be considered suspended on different grounds. It would make them mutually exclusive. We would have to choose which suspension takes precedence. It seems reasonable to assume that

545 A. 7.2.117 *taddhiteṣv acām ādeḥ* ‖ ("[A substitute *vṛddhi* vowel] comes in place of the first vowel [of the *aṅga* nominal stem] before the *taddhita* [suffixes marked with Ñ or Ṇ].")

even though there are a number of underlying principles in the *Aṣṭādhyāyī* that have to be implied while not mentioned by Pāṇini, those which were explicitly stated in the treatise should take precedence in the case of conflict. Consequently, when the conflict between *asiddhatva* and *antaraṅga-bahiraṅga* arises, the former should be followed rather than the one that was imposed by the later tradition. Moreover, the *antaraṅga-bahiraṅga* principle should be evoked in the case of conflict; in other words, when both operations are potentially applicable at the same time. There are numerous examples discussed by Patañjali where this is not the case. An externally conditioned operation would create the conditions for the *Tripādī* rule to apply yielding the incorrect result.

6.4. Conclusions

The principle of suspension that governs *sūtra*s within the *Tripādī* section is one of the most important devices used by Pāṇini to determine the order of rule application in the *Aṣṭādhyāyī*. It does not mean, however, that all of them are always *asiddha* with respect to all possible rules preceding them. There are cases where suspension must not operate, amongst which some are stated by Pāṇini explicitly and some are merely indicated in a more or less straightforward manner. In the summary of Patañjali's comments referring solely to the *asiddhatva* principle it has been shown that he does not always read the indications provided by Pāṇini. He tries to solve disputable and difficult cases with the help of other principles that were not of Pāṇini's making, even though some of them might have been accepted by him, though not stated. He sometimes preferred to accept additional statements in the form of *vārttika*s proposed by Kātyāyana rather than the *sūtra*s themselves.

Patañjali does not comment on all the *sūtras* in the *Tripādī* section although he often refers to them in other comments. It is impossible to determine the reasons that stood behind the choices he made. What can be inferred on the basis of the *sūtra*s he comments upon is that he discussed problematic issues regarding individual operations or wording of the *sūtras*. The discussion at times focuses on the split interpretation of single rules, which might indicate that at the time of Patañjali the text of the *Aṣṭādhyāyi* was still recited and passed on in a continuous manner. Consequently, it created problems with the correct interpretation.

It seems that Patañjali was not convinced as to the character of the *asiddha* section. He proposes solutions, some of them summarised above and others in Chapter 5 in the translation, that go against Pāṇini's intentions. He was not interested in the analysis of the term *asiddha* itself, which seems rather surprising, particularly in view of the attempts undertaken by later tradition to properly understand the term itself. It already appears that at the very beginning of the centuries-long tradition the *Aṣṭādhyāyī* was not entirely understood. The lack of distinction between the sections *Tripādī* and *Ābhīya*, regardless of the accepted interpretation of either *asiddhatva* or *asiddhavattva*, shows that both of them were treated in the same manner.

Even though immense research has already been conducted with respect to the principles of ordering in Pāṇini's *Aṣṭādhyāyī*, the lack of unanimity between scholars should impel further analysis on this subject, primarily based on the text of the *Aṣṭādhyāyī* itself.

Appendix

Additional *sūtras*

Adhyāya 1

A. 1.1.11 *īdūded dvivacanaṃ pragṛhyam* || ("[The technical term] *pragṛhya* denotes [the final vowels] *ī*, *ū* and *e* of dual endings.")
A. 1.1.12 *adaso māt* || ("[The technical term *pragṛhya* denotes the vowels *ī*, *ū* and *e* occurring] after *m* being a part of [the pronominal stem] *adas* ('that').")
A. 1.1.14 *nipāta ekāj anāṅ* || ("[The technical term *pragṛhya* denotes] a particle consisting of a single vowel with the exception of [the particle] *āṄ*.")
A. 1.1.17 *uñaḥ* || ("[According to Śākalya, the particle] *uÑ* [is termed *pragṛhya* before a non-Vedic *iti*].")
A. 1.1.18 *ūm̐* || ("[According to Śākalya, the technical term *pragṛhya* denotes the particle] *ūm̐* [which replaces *uÑ*].")
A. 1.1.20 *dādhā ghv adāp* || ("[The technical term] *ghu* denotes [the verbal stems of the form] *dā* and *dhā* except those which have the shape of *dā* marked with *P*.")
A. 1.1.22 *taraptamapau ghaḥ* || ("[The technical term] *gha* denotes [the suffixes] *taraP* and *tamaP*.")
A. 1.1.24 *ṣṇāntā ṣaṭ* || ("[The technical term] *ṣaṭ* denotes [a subclass of numbers] ending in *ṣ* or *n*.")
A. 1.1.27 *sarvādīni sarvanāmāni* || ("[The words] *sarva* ('whole') etc. [are termed] pronouns.")
A. 1.1.26 *ktaktavatū niṣṭhā* || ("[The technical term] *niṣṭhā* denotes [the suffixes] *Kta* and *KtavatŪ*.")
A. 1.1.46 *ādyantau ṭakitau* || ("[An infix] marked with *Ṭ* constitutes the initial [of the unit to which it is added, and one] marked with *K* constitutes the final.")
A. 1.1.47 *mid aco 'ntyāt paraḥ* || ("[The infix] marked with *M* is inserted after the last vowel of the expression to which it is added.")
A. 1.1.50 *sthāne 'ntaratamaḥ* || ("[A substitute which is to replace a substituend must be] the closest in place of articulation.")
A. 1.1.51 *ur aṇ raparaḥ* || ("[A vowel denoted by] *aṆ* (i.e., *a*, *i*, *u*) [which comes] in place of [the sound] *ṛ* [and *ḷ*] is followed by [the sound] *r* [and *l* respectively].")
A. 1.1.52 *alo 'ntyasya* || ("[The substitute ordered in the genitive comes] in place of the final sound.")
A. 1.1.55 *anekāl śit sarvasya* || ("[A substitute ordered for an element in genitive] comes in place of the whole [element when the substitute consists of] more than one sound (*aL*) or is marked with *Ś*.")

A. 1.1.57 *acaḥ parasmin pūrvavidhau* ǁ ("A vowel [substitute conditioned] by the following [element is treated like the original vowel] with respect to an operation on what precedes it.")
A. 1.1.58 *na padāntadvirvacanavareyalopasvarasavarṇānusvāradīrghajaścar-vidhiṣu* ǁ ("[The substitute of a vowel] is not [treated like the substituend] with respect to the operations concerning: the final [sound] of a *pada*, reduplication, the deletion before [the suffixes] *varaC* and *ya*, the accent [of what precedes], homogeneous [sounds], *anusvāra* [substitution of what precedes], lengthening [of what precedes], the *jaŚ* and *caR* substitutions [of what precedes].")
A. 1.1.62 *pratyayalope pratyayalakṣaṇam* ǁ ("When a suffix is deleted, operations conditioned by it still operate [as if the suffix was still present].")
A. 1.1.63 *na lumatāṅgasya* ǁ ("[When the deletion of a suffix is conditioned] by [the use of technical terms] containing *lu* (i.e., *luK*, *Ślu* or *luP*, [operations conditioned by this suffix] on the *aṅga* stem do not take place.")
A. 1.1.64 *aco 'ntyādi ṭi* ǁ ("[That part] of [an item] which begins with its last vowel is called *Ṭi*.")
A. 1.1.67 *tasmād ity uttarasya* ǁ ("A form stated in the ablative denotes an element that follows [which is subject to grammatical operations].")
A. 1.1.68 *svaṃ rūpaṃ śabdasyāśabdasaṃjñā* ǁ ("An expression denotes itself unless it is the name of a linguistic technical term.")
A. 1.1.70 *taparas tatkālasya* ǁ ("A sound followed or preceded by the marker *T* denotes homogeneous sounds of its time duration.")
A. 1.1.72 *yena vidhis tadantasya* ǁ ("When an operation is stated by means of a unit X which is a part of a larger unit which it qualifies, that X denotes the element ending in it [as well as itself].")
A. 1.2.5 *asaṃyogāl liṭ kit* ǁ ("[Substitutes ending of] *lIṬ* (perfect tense) function like those marked with *K* [when introduced after a vebal stem] not ending in a consonant cluster.")
A. 1.2.8 *rudavidamuṣagrahisvapipracchaḥ sañ ca* ǁ ("[The suffix *Ktvā*] and [the suffix] *saN* introduced after [the verbal roots] *rudA* ('to cry', DhP II:58), *vidA* ('to know', DhP II:51), *muṣA* ('to steal', DhP IX:58), *grahI* ('to grasp', DhP IX:61), *ÑIṣvapA* ('to sleep', DhP II:59) and *prachA* ('to ask', DhP VI:120) [funtion like suffixes marked with *K*].")
A. 1.2.27 *ūkālo 'j hrasvadīrghaplutaḥ* ǁ ("[The technical terms] *hrasva* ('short'), *dīrgha* ('long') and *pluta* ('prolated') denote vowels having the duration of *u*, *ū* and *ū3* [respectively].")
A. 1.2.28 *acaḥ* ǁ ("[A replacement which is specified by *hrasva*, *dīrgha* and *pluta* comes] in place of a vowel (*aC*).")
A. 1.2.32 *tasyādita udāttam ardhahrasvam* ǁ ("The first part of that (*svarita* accented vowel) which is half a short vowel is *udātta* accented [and the other half is *anudātta* accented].")

A. 1.2.33 *ekaśruti dūrāt sambuddhau* || ("When calling someone from a distance, [the utterance is articulated as] monotone.")
A. 1.2.41 *apṛkta ekāl pratyayaḥ* || ("[The technical term] *apṛkta* [denotes] a suffix [consisting of] a single sound.")
A. 1.2.45 *arthavad adhātur apratyayaḥ prātipadikam* || ("[The technical term] *prātipadika* denotes a meaningful unit other than a verbal stem or a suffix.")
A. 1.2.48 *gostriyor upasarjanasya* || ("[A short vowel] comes in place of [the final vowel of the nominal stem] *go* ('a cow') occurring as an *upasarjana* and of an *upasarjana* ending in a feminine suffix.")
A. 1.3.10 *yathāsaṃkhyam anudeśaḥ samānām* || ("[When two sequences of elements] which have the same number of members are stated in rules, [the elements of the subsequent sequence] are related to the former in a one-to-one order.")
A. 1.3.14 *kartari karmavyatihāre* || ("[The *ātmanepada* *l*-substitutes are introduced after a verbal stem] when the agent with reciprocity of an action is to be expressed.")
A. 1.3.17 *ner viśaḥ* || ("[The *ātmanepada* *l*-substitutes] come after [the verbal root] *viśA* ('to enter', DhP VI:130) with [the *upasarga*] *ni*.")
A.1.3.18 *parivyavebhyaḥ kriyaḥ* || ("[The *ātmanepada* *l*-substitutes] come after [the verbal root] *ḌUkrīÑ* ('to buy', DhP IX:1) with [the *upasargas*] *pari*, *vi* and *ava*.")
A. 1.3.19 *viparābhyāṃ jeḥ* || ("[The *ātmanepada* *l*-substitutes] come after [the verbal root] *ji* ('to win, conquer', DhP I:593, 993) with [the *upasargas*] *vi* and *parā*.")
A. 1.4.1 *ākaḍārād ekā saṃjñā* || ("[In this section] up to A. 2.2.38 one technical term [applies to one element].")
A. 1.4.15 *naḥ kye* || ("[The technical term *pada* denotes an element] ending in [the sound] *n* before [the suffixes] *Kya* (i.e, *KyaṄ*, *KyaC* and *KyaṢ*).")
A. 1.4.17 *svādiṣv asarvanāmasthāne* ("[The technical term *pada*] denotes an item before the class of suffixes *sU* etc. excluding those termed *sarvanāmasthāna*.")
A. 1.4.18 *yaci bham* || ("[The technical term] *bha* denotes [an element] before [the suffix beginning with] a semivowel *y* or a vowel.")
A. 1.4.20 *ayasmayādīni chandasi* || ("In Vedic literature [the technical term *bha* denotes the class of expressions] *ayasmaya* ('made of metal') etc. [before the suffix].")
A. 1.4.102 *tāny ekavacanadvivacanabahuvacanāny ekaśaḥ* || ("Those [three and three triplets of verbal endings] taken one by one [are termed] *ekavacana* 'singular', *dvivacana* 'dual' and *bahuvacana* 'plural' [to denote them respectively].")
A. 1.4.103 *supaḥ* || ("[The triplets of the suffixes] *sUP* (i.e., case endings) [taken one by one are termed *ekavacana* 'singular', *dvivacana* 'dual' and *bahuvacana* 'plural' to denote them respectively].")

A. 1.4.110 *virāmo 'vasānam* II ("[The term] *avasāna* means pause.")

Adhyāya 2

A. 2.2.18 *kugatiprādayaḥ* II ("[The indeclinable *pada*] *ku* ('bad'), [particles termed] *gati* and *pra* etc. [form *tatpuruṣa* compounds with nominal *pada*s].")
A. 2.2.19 *upapadam atiṅ* II ("An *upapada* which does not terminate in a verbal personal ending [necessarily combines with a syntactically connected nominal *pada* to form a *tatpuruṣa* compound].")
A. 2.3.37 *yasya ca bhāvena bhāvalakṣaṇam* II ("[The locative ending is introduced after a nominal stem] denoting an action which serves to characterise another action.")
A. 2.4.37 *luṅsanor ghasḷ* II ("[The substitute] *ghasḶ* comes in place of [the whole verbal stem *adA* ('to eat', DhP II:1)] before [*ārdhadhātuka* substitutes of] *lUṄ* and [the desiderative suffix] *saN*.")
A. 2.4.38 *ghañapoś ca* II ("[The substitute *ghasḶ* comes in place of the whole verbal stem *adA* ('to eat', DhP II:1)] also before [*ārdhadhātuka* suffixes] *GHaÑ* and *aP*.")
A. 2.4.39 *bahulaṃ chandasi* II ("In Vedic literature [the substitute *ghasḶ*] variously [comes in place of the verbal stem *adA* ('to eat', DhP II:1)].")
A. 2.4.40 *liṭy anyatarasyām* II ("[The substitute *ghasḶ*] optionally [comes in place of the whole verbal stem *adA* ('to eat', DhP II:1)] before [*ārdhadhātuka* substitutes of] *lIṬ* (perfect tense).")
A. 2.4.47 *sani ca* II ("Also before [the desiderative suffix] *saN* [the substitute *gam* comes in place of the verbal stem *iṆ* when it does not signify 'understanding'].")
A. 2.4.71 *supo dhātuprātipadikayoḥ* II ("The case ending of [a *pada* consisting of] a verbal or a nominal root [is deleted by *luK*].")
A. 2.4.72 *adiprabhṛtibhyaḥ śapaḥ* II ("[The suffix] *ŚaP* [introduced] after [the verbal roots] *adA* ('to eat', DhP II:1) etc. [is deleted by *luK*].")
A. 2.4.75 *juhotyādibhyaḥ śluḥ* II ("[The suffix *ŚaP* introduced] after [the verbal roots] *hu* ('to offer an oblation', DhP III:1) etc. is deleted by *Ślu*.")
A. 2.4.82 *avyayād āpsupaḥ* II ("[The feminine suffixes covered by] *āP* (i.e., *CāP*, *ṬāP*, *ḌāP*) and case endings [are deleted by *luK*] after the indeclinable [nominal stems].")

Adhyāya 3

A. 3.1.3 *ādyudāttaś ca* II ("And [the suffix which follows the nominal or verbal root is marked with] an *udātta* accent on the first syllable.")
A. 3.1.4 *anudāttau suppitau* II ("Case endings and [suffixes] marked with *P* have vowels *anudātta* accented.")

A. 3.1.5 *guptijkidbhyaḥ saN* || ("The suffix *saN* is added after [the verbs] *gupA* ('to hide', DhP X:231), *tijA* ('to sharpen', DhP I:1020) and *kitA* ('to know, perceive', DhP I:1042).")

A. 3.1.7 *dhātoḥ karmaṇaḥ samānakartṛkād icchāyāṃ vā* || ("[The suffix *saN*] optionally comes after a verbal stem, the action denoted by which is the object of a verbal stem expressing desire and both actions have the same agent.")

A. 3.1.8 *supa ātmanaḥ kyac* || ("[The suffix] *KyaC* [optionally] comes after a nominal stem ending in *sUP* [when it is the object of a verbal stem expressing desire which the agent desires] for himself.")

A. 3.1.9 *kāmyac ca* || ("[The suffix] *kāmyaC* also [optionally comes after a nominal stem ending in case ending when it is the object of a verbal stem expressing desire and which the agent desires for himself].")

A. 3.1.22 *dhātor ekāco halādeḥ kriyāsamabhihāre yaṅ* || ("[The suffix] *yaṄ* [optionally comes] after a monosyllabic verbal stem beginning with a consonant when that action is performed repeatedly or intensely.")

A. 3.1.25 *satyāpapāśarūpavīṇatūlaślokasenālomatvacavarmavarṇacūrṇa-curādibhyo ṇic* || ("[The suffix] *ṆiC* comes after [nominal stems] *satyāpa* ('truth'), *pāśa* ('a fetter'), *rūpa* ('a form'), *vīṇa* ('a lute'), *tūla* ('cotton'), *śloka* ('a verse'), *senā* ('army'), *loman* ('hair'), *tvaca* ('skin'), *varman* ('a coat of mail'), *varṇa* ('a colour'), *cūrṇa* ('flour') and [the class of verbal stems] *curA* ('to steal', DhP X:1) etc..")

A. 3.1.26 *hetumati ca* || ("[The suffix *ṆiC*] is also introduced [after a verbal stem] to denote a casual agent.")

A. 3.1.32 *sanādyantā dhātavaḥ* || ("[The technical term] *dhātu* ('a verbal root') denotes all items ending in [the suffixes] *saN* etc.")

A. 3.1.33 *syatāsī lṛluṭoḥ* || ("[The suffixes] *sya* and *tāsi* are respectively introduced [after a verbal stem] before [the *l*-substitutes of] *lṚ* (i.e., *lṚṬ* and *lṚṄ*, sigmatic future and conditional respectively) and *lUṬ* (periphrastic future).")

A. 3.1.34 *sib bahulaṃ leṭi* || ("[The suffix] *sIP* is variously introduced [after a verbal stem] before [the *l*-substitutes of] *lEṬ* (Vedic subjunctive).")

A. 3.1.43 *cli luṅi* || ("[The suffix] *Cli* [comes after a verbal root] before the *l*-substitutes of *lUṄ* (aorist).")

A. 3.1.44 *cleḥ sic* || ("[The aorist suffix] *sIC* comes in place of [the suffix] *Cli* [before the *l*-substitutes of *lUṄ* (aorist)].")

A. 3.1.48 *ṇiśridrusrubhyaḥ kartari caṅ* || ("[The substitute aorist suffix] *CaṄ* [comes in place of *Cli*] after [verbal stems ending in] *ṆiC* and [the verbal stems] *śriÑ* ('to serve', DhP I:945), *dru* ('to run', DhP I:92), *sru* ('to flow', DhP I:987) [when the *l*-substitutes of *lUṄ*] denote an agent.")

A. 3.1.66 *ciṇ bhāvakarmaṇoḥ* || ("[The substitute aorist suffix] *CiṆ* [comes in place of *Cli* after a verbal stem before *lUṄ* substitute *ta*] when denoting the action itself or the object.")

A. 3.1.67 *sārvadhātuke yak* || ("[The suffix] *yaK* comes [after a verbal stem] before *sārvadhātuka* [suffixes when denoting the action itself or the object].")
A. 3.1.68 *kartari śap* || ("[The suffix] *ŚaP* comes [after the verbal stem before *sārvadhātuka l*-substitutes] to denote an agent.")
A. 3.1.77 *tudādibhyaḥ śa* || ("[The suffix] *Śa* comes after [the verbal roots] *tudA* ('to hit', DhP VI:1) etc. [before *sārvadhātuka l*-substitutes to denote the agent].")
A. 3.1.78 *rudhādibhyaḥ śnam* || ("[The suffix] *ŚnaM* comes after [the class of verbal stems] *rudhIR* ('to obstruct', DhP VII:1) etc. [before the *sārvadhātuka l*-substitutes to denote an agent].")
A. 3.1.81 *kryādibhyaḥ śnā* || ("[The suffix] *Śnā* is introduced after [the verbal roots] *ḌUkrīÑ* ('to buy', DhP IX:1) etc. [before the *sārvadhātuka l*-substitutes to denote the agent].")
A. 3.1.82 *stanbhustunbhuskanbhuskunbhuskuñbhyaḥ śnuś ca* || ("[The suffixes *Śnā*] and *Śnu* come after [the verbal stems] *stanbhU*, *stunbhU* ('to support', DhP IX:7), *skanbhU*, *skunbhU* ('to support, fix', DhP IX:8), and *skuÑ* ('cover, conceal', DhP IX:6) [before the *sārvadhātuka l*-substitutes to denote an agent].")
A. 3.1.133 *ṇvultṛcau* || ("[The *kṛt* suffixes] *ṆvuL* and *tṛC* [are introduced after all verbal stems].")
A. 3.1.134 *nandigrahipacādibhyo lyuṇinyacaḥ* || ("[The *kṛt* suffixes] *Lyu*, *Ṇini* and *aC* [respectively] come after [the verbal roots] *TUnadI* ('to be glad, rejoice', DhP I:67) etc., *grahA* ('to seize', DhP IX:61) etc. and *ḌUpacAṢ* ('to cook', DhP I:1045) etc. [to denote the agent].")
A. 3.1.135 *igupadhajñāprīkiraḥ kaḥ* || ("[The *kṛt* suffix] *Ka* comes after [the verbal roots containing the sound denoted by] *iK* (i.e., *i*, *u*, *r*, *l*) as penultimate or [the roots] *jñā* ('to know', DhP IX:36), *prīÑ* ('to please', DhP IX:2) and *kṝ* ('to scatter', DhP VI:116) [to denote the agent].")
A. 3.2.1 *karmaṇy aṇ* || ("[The primary suffix] *aṆ* [comes after a verbal root occurring with a nominal *pada*] functioning as a direct object.")
A. 3.2.58 *spṛśo 'nudake kvin* || ("[The suffix] *KviN* comes after [the verbal root] *spṛśA* ('to touch', DhP VI:128) [co-ocurring with a nominal *pada*] other than *udaka* ('water') [to denote an agent].")
A. 3.2.59 *ṛtvijdadhṛksragdiguṣṇigañcuyujikruñcāṃ ca* || ("[The forms] *ṛtvij* ('a priest'), *dadhṛṣ* ('audacious'), *sraj* ('a garland'), *diś* ('a direction'), *uṣṇih* (the name of a metre) [are formed in an irregular way with the suffix *KviN* which is] also [added after verbal roots] *añcU* ('to worship, go', DhP I:203), *yujIR* ('to join', DhP VII:7) and *kruñcA* ('be crooked', DhP I:201).")
A. 3.2.61 *satsūdviṣadruhaduhayujavidabhidacchidajinīrājām upasarge 'pi kvip* || ("[The *kṛt* suffix] *KviP* comes after [the verbal stems] *sadḶ* ('to sit down', DhP I: 907), *ṣūṄ* ('to produce', DhP II: 21), *dviṣA* ('to hate', DhP II: 3), *druhA* ('to hurt', DhP IV: 88), *duhA* ('to milk', DhP II: 4), *yujA* ('to join', DhP IV: 68), *vidA* ('to know', DhP II: 55), *bhidIR* ('to break', DhP VII: 2), *chidIR* ('to split', DhP

VII: 3), *ji* ('to win, conquer', DhP I: 593), *ṇīÑ* ('to lead', DhP I: 950) and *rājṚ* ('to shine', DhP I: 874) also with an *upasarga* [and with nominal *padas*].")
A. 3.2.63 *chandasi sahaḥ* || ("In Vedic [the suffix *Ṇvi* comes] after [the verbal stem] *ṣahA* ('to endure', DhP I:905) [co-occurring with a nominal *pada*].")
A. 3.2.67 *janasanakhanakramagamo viṭ* || ("[In Vedic the *kṛt* suffix] *vIṬ* comes after [the verbal stems] *janA* ('to be born', DhP III: 24, IV: 41), *ṣanU* ('to obtain as a gift', DhP VIII: 2), *khanU* ('to dig', DhP I: 927, *kramU* ('to march', DhP I: 502) and *gamḶ* ('to go', DhP I 1031) [co-occurring with nominal *padas* and with or without *upasargas*].")
A. 3.2.74 *āto maninkvanibvanipaś ca* || ("[In Vedic the primary suffixes *viC*,] *maniN*, *KvaniP* and *vaniP* come after [a verbal stem ending in] the vowel *ā* [occurring with a nominal *pada* and with or without the *upasarga*].")
A. 3.2.75 *anyebhyo 'pi dṛśyate* || ("[The suffixes *manIN*, *KvanIP* and *vanIP* together with *vIC*] are also seen after other [verbal roots].")
A. 3.2.76 *kvip ca* || ("[The primary suffix] *KviP* also comes [after verbal roots occurring with or without nominal *padas* or *upasargas*, in Vedic literature or elsewhere].")
A. 3.2.87 *brahmabhrūṇavṛtreṣu kvip* || ("[The primary suffix] *KvIP* comes [after the verbal root *han* ('to kill', DhP II:2) preceded by nominal *padas*] *brahman* ('a brahmin'), *bhrūṇa* ('an embryo') and *vṛtra* (name of a demon) [being its direct object to denote general past tense].")
A. 3.2.90 *some suñaḥ* || ("[The suffix *KviP* comes] after [the verbal root] *ṣuÑ* ('to press Soma', DhP V:1) [occurring with the nominal *pada*] *soma* [functioning as its object to denote general past tense].")
A. 3.2.102 *niṣṭhā* || ("[The suffixes termed] *niṣṭhā* [are introduced after verbal stems to denote the general past tense].")
A. 3.2.124 *laṭaḥ śatṛśānacāv aprathamāsamānādhikaraṇe* || ("[The *kṛt* suffixes] *ŚatṚ* and *ŚānaC* replace [the *l*-substitutes of] *lAṬ* when it has the same reference [with a nominal *pada*] ending in [a *sUP* triplet] other than the first.")
A. 3.2.134 *ākves tacchīlataddharmatadsādhukāriṣu* || ("Up to and including the *sūtra* A. 3.2.177 [the *kṛt* suffixes introduced after verbal stems] are meant to denote that the agent performs the action as a part of his habitual disposition, as his duty or efficiently.")
A. 3.2.154 *laṣapatapadasthābhūvṛṣahanakamagamaśṝbhya ukañ* || ("[The *kṛt* suffix] *ukaÑ* comes after [the verbal roots] *laṣA* ('to desire', DhP I:937), *patḶ* ('to fall, fly', DhP I:898), *padA* ('to walk', DhP IV:60), *ṣṭhā* ('to stand', DhP I:975), *bhū* ('to be, exist', DhP I:1), *vṛṣU* ('to rain', DhP I:738), *hanA* ('to kill', DhP II:2), *kamU* ('to love', DhP I:470), *gamḶ* ('to go', DhP I: 1031), *śṝ* ('to destroy', DhP IX:18) [to denote the agent's habitual disposition, duty or excellence].")

A. 3.2.172 *svapitṛṣor najiṅ* ("[The suffix] *najiṄ* comes after [the verbal stems] *ÑIṣvapA* ('to sleep', DhP II:59) and *ÑItṛṣA* ('to be thirsty', DhP IV:118) [to denote the agent's habitual disposition, duty or excellence].")
A. 3.2.178 *anyebhyo 'pi dṛśyate* || ("[The *kṛt* suffix] *KviP* is also seen as [introduced after] other [verbal roots to denote agent's habitual disposition, duty or excellence].")
A. 3.3.1 *uṇādayo bahulam* || ("[The suffixes] *uṆ* etc. [are introduced] variously [after verbal stems when the action refers to the present time to form the names].")
A. 3.3.10 *tumunṇvulau kriyāyāṃ kriyārthāyām* || ("[When an action refers to the general future time, the *kṛt* suffixes] *tumUN* and *ṆvuL* are introduced [after a verbal root] co-ocurring with another action which is performed in order to perform this action.")
A. 3.3.19 *akartari ca kārake saṃjñāyām* || ("[The *kṛt* suffix *GHaÑ* comes after a verbal root] to derive forms denoting *kāraka*s other than the agent when the derivative as a proper name.")
A. 3.3.90 *yajayācayatavicchapraccharakṣo naṅ* || ("[The *kṛt* suffix] *naṄ* is introduced after [the verbal stems] *yajA* ('to sacrifice', DhP I:1051), *ṬUyācṚ* ('to beg', DhP I:916), *yatĪ* ('to exert', DhP I:30), *vichA* ('to move', DhP VI:129), *prachA* ('to ask', DhP VI:120) and *rakṣA* ('to protect', DhP I:688) [to form action nouns or denote a *kāraka* other than agent].")
A. 3.3.94 *striyāṃ ktin* || ("[The *kṛt* suffix] *KtiN* [is introduced after a verbal stem to form an action noun or denote a *kāraka* other than agent] in feminine.")
A. 3.3.115 *lyuṭ ca* || ("[The *kṛt* suffixes *Kta*] as well as *LyuṬ* [are introduced after a verbal stem to form a neuter action noun].")
A. 3.3.121 *halaś ca* || ("[The suffix *GHaÑ*] comes also after [a verbal root ending in] a consonant [to form a masculine noun denoting a name signifying an instrument or place].")
A. 3.3.175 *māṅi luṅ* || ("[The *l*-substitutes of] *lUṄ* (aorist) come [after verbal roots co-ocurring] with [the privative particle] *māṄ*.")
A. 3.4.108 *jher jus* || ("[The substitute suffix] *Jus* comes in place of [the *l*-substitute] *jhi* [of *l*-member *lIṄ*].")
A. 3.4.21 *samānakartṛkayoḥ pūrvakāle* || ("[The suffix *Ktvā* is introduced] after that one of two [verbal roots] having the same agent whose action precedes that of the other.")
A. 3.4.78 *tiptasjhisipthasthamibvasmastātāmjhathāsāthāmdhvamiḍvahimahiṅ* || ("[The substitute suffixes] *tiP* etc. [come in place of the *l*-members introduced after a verbal root].")
A. 3.4.79 *ṭita ātmanepadānāṃ ṭer e* || ("[The vowel] *e* comes in place of the syllable beginning with the last vowel of the *ātmanepada* [*l*-substitutes of the *l*-members] with marker *Ṭ* (i.e., *lAṬ*, *lIṬ*, *lUṬ*, *lṚṬ*, *lEṬ* and *lOṬ*).")

A. 3.4.80 *thāsaḥ se* || ("[The suffix] *se* comes in place of [the whole suffix] *thās* [of *l*-members with marker *Ṭ* introduced after the verbal stem].")
A. 3.4.82 *parasmaipadānāṃ ṇalatususthalatusaṇalvamāḥ* || ("[The suffixes] *ṆaL*, *atus*, *us*, *thaL*, *atus*, *a*, *ṆaL*, *va* and *ma* come in place of *parasmaipada* [*l*-substitutes *tiP*, *tas*, *jhi*, *siP*, *thas*, *tha*, *miP*, *vas* and *mas* of *lIṬ*].")
A. 3.4.85 *loṭo laṅvat* || ("[The *l*-substitutes] of *lOṬ* (imperative) are like those of *lAṄ* (imperfect).")
A. 3.4.87 *ser hyapic ca* || ("[The suffix] *hi* without the marker *P* comes in place of [the ending] *siP* [of the *l*-substitutes of the imperative mood introduced after a verbal root].")
A. 3.4.89 *mer niḥ* || ("[The substitute suffix] *ni* comes in place of [the whole of *l*-substitute of *lOṬ* (imperative)] *miP* [introduced after the verbal stem].")
A. 3.4.92 *āḍ uttamasya pic ca* || ("[The initial augment] *āṬ* comes at the beginning of [the *l*-substitutes of] the first person [of *l*-member *lOṬ* (imperative)] and it functions as if it was marked with *P*.")
A. 3.4.94 *leṭo aḍāḍau* || ("[The initial infixes] *aṬ* and *āṬ* [are inserted at the beginning of *l*-substitutes] of *lEṬ* (Vedic subjunctive).")
A. 3.4.97 *itaś ca lopaḥ parasmaipadeṣu* || ("The vowel *i* of the *parasmaipada* [*l*-substitutes of *lEṬ* (Vedic subjunctive) is optionally deleted.")
A. 3.4.100 *itaś ca* || ("[The sound] *i* [of the *parasmaipada* *l*-substitutes of *l*-members marked with *Ṅ*] is also deleted.")
A. 3.4.101 *tasthasthamipāṃ tāntantāmaḥ* || ("[The suffixes] *tām*, *tam*, *ta* and *am* come in place of [the *l*-substitutes] *tas*, *thas*, *tha* and *miP* [respectively of *parasmaipada* endings of *l*-members marked with *Ṅ*].")
A. 3.4.103 *yāsuṭ parasmaipadeṣv udātto ṅic ca* || ("[The initial infix] *yāsUṬ* with high-pitched accent [constitutes the beginning of] *parasmaipada* [*l*-substitutes of *l*-member *lIṄ*] and functions as marked with *Ṅ*.")
A. 3.4.104 *liṅaḥ sīyuṭ* || ("[The initial infix] *sīyUṬ* [constitutes the beginning of *l*-members] of *lIṄ* (optative/potential mood).")

Adhyāya 4

A. 4.1.2 *svaujasamauṭśasṭābhyāmbhisṅebhyāmbhyasṅasibhyāmbhyasṅasosāmṅyossup* || ("[The suffixes] *sU* etc. [are introduced after expressions ending in feminine suffixes or other nominal stems].")
A. 4.1.4 *ajādyataṣ ṭāp* || ("[The suffix] *ṬāP* comes after [the nominal stems] *aja* ('a goat') etc. and those ending in the vowel *a* [to derive feminine stems].")
4.1.5 *ṛnnebhyo ṅīp* || ("[The suffix] *ṄīP* comes after [nominal stems ending in the sounds] *ṛ* or *n* [to derive a feminine nominal stem].")
A. 4.1.6 *ugitaś ca* || ("[The suffix *ṄīP*] also comes after [a nominal stem ending in a suffix] with a marker *U*, *Ṛ* or *Ḷ* [to derive a feminine stem].")

A. 4.1.20 *vayasi prathame* || ("[The suffix *ṄīP* comes after a nominal stem] denoting the first part of life [to derive feminine].")
A. 4.1.95 *ata iñ* || ("[The *taddhita* suffix] *iÑ* is introduced after [nominal stems ending in the vowel] *a* [to denote the meaning 'his offspring'].")
A. 4.1.99 *naḍādibhyaḥ phak* || ("[The *taddhita* suffix] *phaK* comes after [the nominal stems] *naḍa* etc. [to denote the meaning 'his descendant'].")
A. 4.1.135 *catuṣpādbhyo ḍhañ* || ("[The *taddhita* suffix] *ḍhaÑ* comes after [nominal stems] designating quadrupeds [ending in genitive to denote an offspring].")
A. 4.1.162 *apatyaṃ pautraprabhṛti gotram* || ("[The technical term] *gotra* denotes a descendant beginning with a grandson.")
A. 4.2.85 *nadyāṃ matup* || ("[The *taddhita* suffix] *matUP* comes after [the nominal stems to denote the meanings 'it is in this place', 'completed by him', 'his abode' and 'situated not far from it'] when they mean a river.")
A. 4.3.53 *tatra bhavaḥ* || ("[The *taddhita* suffixes introduced from A. 4.1.83 onwards come after a nominal stem ending in] the locative ending to denote 'being there'.")
A. 4.3.73 *aṇ ṛgayanādibhyaḥ* || ("[The *taddhita* suffix] *aṆ* comes after [nominal stems] *ṛgayana* etc. [to denote a commentary or 'found therein'].")
A. 4.3.120 *tasyedam* || ("[The *taddhita* suffix as was prescribed comes after the nominal stem ending in genitive to denote] 'it is his'.")
A. 4.3.144 *nityaṃ vṛddhaśarādibhyaḥ* || ("[The *taddhita* suffix *mayaṬ*] is necessarily introduced after [nominal stems belonging to] the *vṛddha* type and *śara* ('reed') etc. [ending in the sixth *sUP* triplet to denote their modification or limb, excluding food or clothing, in colloquial speech].")
A. 4.3.145 *goś ca pūrīṣe* || ("[The *taddhita* suffix *mayaṬ*] is also introduced after [the nominal stem] *go* ('a cow') [to denote its modification] to mean 'cow-dung'.")
A. 4.4.7 *naudvyacaṣ ṭhan* || ("[The *taddhita* suffix] *ṭhaN* comes after [the nominal stem] *nau* ('a boat') and those containing two syllables [to denote 'crosses with it'].")
A. 4.4.77 *dhuro yaḍḍhakau* || ("[The *taddhita* suffixes] *yaT* and *ḍhaK* come after [the nominal stem] *dhur* ('burden, load') [ending in the accusative to denote 'he bears or carries it'].")

Adhyāya 5

A. 5.1.130 *hāyanāntayuvādibhyo 'ṇ* || ("[The *taddhita* suffix] *aṆ* comes after [the nominal stems] ending in *hāyana* ('year') as well as *yuvan* ('youth') etc. [ending in the genitive to denote its essential condition or state, its function or duty.")

A. 5.2.94 *tad asyāsty asminn iti matup* || ("[The *taddhita* suffix] *matUP* [comes after a nominal stem ending in] the nominative case to denote 'belongs to this' or 'exists in this'.")
A. 5.2.107 *vt.* 2 *nagapāṃsupāṇḍubhyaś ca* || ("[The suffix *ra* should be added] also after [the nominal stems] *naga* ('a mountain, snake'), *pāṃsu* ('dust, sand') and *pāṇḍu* ('white').")
A. 5.3.47 *yāpye pāśap* || ("[The *taddhita* suffix] *pāśaP* comes [after a nominal stem pleonastically] to denote something unimportant.")
A. 5.3.56 *tiṅaś ca* || ("[The *taddhita* suffixes *tamaP* and *iṣṭhaN*] come also after [the verbal stems ending in] personal endings.")
A. 5.3.57 *dvivacanavibhajyopapade tarabīyasunau* || ("[The *taddhita* suffixes] *taraP* and *īyasuN* [come after nominal and verbal stems ending in personal endings] to express a comparison between two objects or that from which something is to be distinguished].")
A. 5.3.60 *praśasyasya śraḥ* || ("[The element] *śra* comes in place of [the element] *praśasya* ('praiseworthy') [before a *taddhita* suffixes beginning with a vowel (i.e., *īyasUN* and *iṣṭhaN*)].")
A. 5.3.65 *vinmator luk* || ("[The *taddhita* suffixes] *vin* and *matUP* [introduced after nominal stems and before the *taddhita* suffixes beginning with a vowel (i.e., *iṣṭhaN* and *īyasuN*)] are deleted (by *luK*).")
A. 5.3.67 *īṣadasamāptau kalpabdeśyadeśīyaraḥ* || ("[The *taddhita* suffixes] *kalpaP*, *deśya* and *deśīyaR* come [after a nominal stem] to denote 'not quite fully'.")
A. 5.3.70 *prāg ivāt kaḥ* || ("In the section beginning here up to A. 5.3.96 [the *taddhita* suffix] *ka* comes [after a nominal stem to denote the meaning listed in this section].")
A. 5.4.11 *kimettiṅavyayaghād āmv adravyaprakarṣe* || ("[The *taddhita* suffix] *āmU* comes after [nominal stems] *kim* ('who, what, which'), [expressions ending in the vowel] *e*, [verbal stems ending in] personal endings and indeclinables, [all the above] ending in [the suffixes] *gha* (i.e., *taraP* and *tamaP*) when they do not refer to the excellence of the object itself.")
A. 5.4.17 *saṃkhyāyāḥ kriyābhyāvṛttigaṇane kṛtvasuc* || ("[The suffix] *kṛtvasUC* comes after numbers to denote the counting of the repetition of an action.")
A. 5.4.18 *dvitricaturbhyāṃ suc* || ("[The *taddhita* suffix] *suC* comes after [the nominal stems] *dvi* ('two'), *tri* ('three') and *catur* ('four') [to denote the counting of the repetition of an action].")
A. 5.4.87 *ahaḥsarvaikadeśasaṃkhyātapuṇyāc ca rātreḥ* || ("[The *taddhita samāsānta* suffix *aC*] comes after [the nominal stem] *rātri* ('a night') preceded by *ahan* ('a day'), *sarva* ('whole, all'), [expressions signifying] *ekadeśa* ('a portion'), *saṃkhyāta* ('counted') and *puṇya* ('auspicious') as well as [with numerals and indeclinables in a *tatpuruṣa* compound].")

A. 5.4.88 *ahno ahna etebhyaḥ* ǁ ("[The morpheme] *ahna* comes in place of [the whole nominal stem] *ahan* ('a day') [as the last member of a compound] after these [i.e., *sarva* ('whole'), expressions meaning 'a portion' (*ekadeśa*), 'enumerated' (*saṃkhyāta*) and 'auspicious' (*puṇya*) as well as numbers and indeclinables].")
A. 5.4.91 *rājāhaḥsakhibhyaṣ ṭac* ǁ ("[The *taddhita samāsānta* suffix] *ṬaC* is introduced after [the nominal stems] *rājan* ('a king'), *ahan* ('a day') and *sakhi* ('a friend') [occurring at the end of a compound].")
A. 5.4.154 *śeṣād vibhāṣā* ǁ ("[The *taddhita samāsānta* suffix *kaP*] is rarely introduced after [the nominal stems occurring at the end of a *bahuvrīhi* compound] not covered by the above rules.")

Adhyāya 6

A. 6.1.2 *ajāder dvitīyasya* ǁ ("[Two syllables] come in place of the second [syllable] of [a verbal stem] beginning with a vowel [containing two or more syllables].")
A. 6.1.3 *na ndrāḥ saṃyogādayaḥ* ǁ ("[The sounds] *n*, *d* and *r*, occurring at the beginning of a consonant cluster [and forming a part of the second syllable of a polysyllabic verbal root beginning with a vowel,] are not [reduplicated].")
A. 6.1.8 *liṭi dhātor anabhyāsasya* ǁ ("[Two syllables come in place of one of a monosyllabic verbal root or the second of a polysyllabic one beginning with a vowel] if the root does not contain a reduplicated syllable before [the *l*-substitutes of] *lIṬ* (perfect).")
A. 6.1.9 *sanyaṅoḥ* ǁ ("[Two syllables come in place of a monosyllabic verbal stem or the second one of the pollysyllabic verbal stem beginning with a vowel, if the stem does not contain a reduplicated syllable] before [the suffixes] *saN* and *yaṄ*.")
A. 6.1.10 *ślau* ǁ ("[Two syllables come in place of the first syllable of a monosyllabic verbal stem or the second of the polysyllabic one beginning with a vowel when the stem does not already contain a reduplicated syllable,] before [the substitute] *Ślu* [of the suffix *ŚaP*].")
A. 6.1.11 *caṅi* ǁ ("[Two syllables come in place of a monosyllabic verbal stem or the second syllable of a polysyllabic verbal stem beginning with a vowel, when the stem does not already contain a reduplicated syllable] before [the substitute aorist suffix] *CaṄ*.")
A. 6.1.15 *vacisvapiyajādīnāṃ kiti* ǁ ("[Vocalisation replaces the semivowels] of [the verbal stems] *vacI* ('to speak', DhP II:54), *svapI* ('to sleep', DhP II:59) and *yajA* etc. ('to sacrifice', DhP I:1051-59) before [the suffixes] marked with *K*.")
A. 6.1.16 *grahijyāvayivyadhivaṣṭivicativṛścatipṛcchatibhṛjjatīnāṃ ṅiti ca* ǁ ("[Vocalisation comes in place of semivowels] of [the verbal stems] *grahA* ('to seize', DhP IX:61), *jyā* ('to grow old', DhP IX:29), *vay* (the substitute of veÑ 'to

weave', DhP I:1055), *vyadhA* ('to pierce', DhP IV:72), *vaśA* ('to desire', DhP II:70), *vyacA* ('to deceive', DhP VI:12), *OvraścŪ* ('to cut', DhP VI:11), *prachA* ('to ask', DhP VI:120) and *bhrasjA* ('to roast', DhP VI:4) before [the suffixes] with the marker *Ṅ* as well as [*K*].")

6.1.17 *liṭy abhyāsasyobhayeṣām* || ("Before [the *l*-substitutes of] *lIṬ* (perfect) [vocalisation of semivowels] of a reduplicated [syllable] of both classes of verbal roots – A. 6.1.15-16 – takes place].")

A. 6.1.19 *svapisyamivyeñāṃ yaṅi* || ("Before [the intensive suffix] *yaṄ* [vocalisation comes in place of the semivowels] of [the verbal stems] *svapI* ('to sleep', DhP II: 59), *syamI* ('to cry', DhP I: 878) and *vyeÑ* ('to cover', DhP I: 1056).")

A. 6.1.37 *vt.* 6 *rayer mato bahulam* || ("[In Vedic literature vocalisation] variously takes place [of the semivowel] of [the stem] *rayi* ('property, wealth') before [the suffix] *matUP*.")

A. 6.1.45 *ād eca upadeśe 'śiti* || ("[The vowel] *ā* comes in place of [the final sound denoted by] *eC* (i.e., *e*, *o*, *ai*, *au*) [of the verbal stem] in original enunciation before [the suffixes] not marked with *Ś*.")

A. 6.1.58 *sṛjidṛśor jhaly am akiti* || ("[The infix] *aM* comes [after the last vowel of the verbal roots] *sṛjA* ('to let go, discharge', DhP VI:121) and *dṛśIR* ('to see', DhP I:1037) before [the suffixes beginning with the sound denoted by] *jhaL* (i.e., non-nasal consonants) excluding those marked with *K*.")

A. 6.1.64 *dhātvādeḥ ṣaḥ saḥ* || ("[The sound] *s* comes in place of [the sound] *ṣ* being the initial [sound] of a verbal stem.")

A. 6.1.66 *lopo vyor vali* || ("[The sounds] *v* and *y* are deleted before [a sound denoted by] *vaL*.")

A. 6.1.67 *ver apṛktasya* || ("A single sound suffix *vi* [is deleted].")

A. 6.1.68 *halṅyābbhyo dīrghāt sutisy apṛktam hal* || ("A single consonantal suffix *sU* [introduced] after [the nominal stems ending in] a consonant or a long vowel [of the feminine suffixes] *Ṅī* or *āP* as well as [the suffixes] *ti* and *si* [introduced after a verbal root] ending in a consonant, [are deleted].")

A. 6.1.69 *eṅhrasvāt sambuddheḥ* || ("[The consonant] of the vocative singular [suffix introduced after a nominal stem ending] in [the sound denoted by] *eṄ* or a short vowel is deleted.")

A. 6.1.71 *hrasvasya piti kṛti tuk* ("[The infix] *tUK* is inserted [at the end of a verbal stem] before a *kṛt* [suffix] marked with *P* when [the preceding stem ends] in a short vowel.")

A. 6.1.73 *che ca* || ("[The final infix *tUK* comes at the end of a short vowel] before [the sound] *cha* [in close proximity].")

A. 6.1.76 *padāntād vā* || ('[The infix *tUK*] usually comes [after the long vowel] at the end of a *pada* [before the sound *ch* in close proximity].")

A. 6.1.77 *iko yaṇ aci* || ("The semivowels (*yaṆ*) come in place of the vowels *i*, *u*, *ṛ* and *ḷ* respectively before a vowel [in close proximity].")

A. 6.1.78 *eco 'yavāyāvaḥ* || ("[The substitutes] *ay*, *av*, *āy* and *āv* come in place of [the vowels denoted by] *eC* (i.e., *e*, *o*, *ai*, *au*) respectively [before a vowel in close proximity].")
A. 6.1.87 *ād guṇaḥ* || ("[A single sound denoted by] *guṇa* (i.e., *a*, *e*, *o*) comes in place of [both the vowel following] the vowel *a* as well as the vowel [preceding that vowel in close proximity].")
A. 6.1.88 *vṛddhir eci* || ("[A single substitute denoted by] *vṛddhi* [comes in place of both the vowel following the vowel class *a*] represented by *eC* (i.e., *e*, *o*, *ai*, *au*) [and the vowel class *a* preceding it in close proximity].")
A. 6.1.90 *āṭaś ca* || ("[A single *vṛddhi* substitute comes in place of both the vowel denoted by *aC* occurring after the initial augment] *āṬ* and [preceding] *āṬ* [in close proximity].")
A. 6.1.93 *auto 'mśasoḥ* || ("[The single substitute] *ā* comes in place of [both the stem final sound] *o* [and the following initial vowel of the suffix] *am* and *Śas* [in close proximity].")
A. 6.1.96 *usy apadāntāt* || ("[A single substitute consisting of the second of two continuous sound comes in place of] a non-*pada* final [sound class *a*] preceding [the substitute suffix] *us* [and the initial vowel of *us* following it in close proximity].")
A. 6.1.97 *ato guṇe* || ("[A single substitute consisting of the second of the sounds] comes in place of [a non-*pada* final] vowel *a* before a *guṇa* vowel [in close proximity].")
A. 6.1.101 *akaḥ savarṇe dīrghaḥ* || ("A long vowel comes in place of [both] a vowel denoted by *aK* (i.e., *a*, *i*, *u*, *ṛ* and *ḷ*) and the following homogenous vowel [in close proximity].")
A. 6.1.102 *prathamayoḥ pūrvasavarṇaḥ* || ("[A single substitute long vowel] homogenous to the first [of the two vowels denote by *aK* (i.e., *a*, *i*, *u*, *ṛ*, *ḷ*)] comes in place of [both the nominal stem-final vowel denoted by *aK* (i.e., *a*, *i*, *u*, *ṛ*, *ḷ*) and the initial vowel of the suffix] of the first and second *sUP* triplet.")
A. 6.1.108 *samprasāraṇāc ca* || ("[A single substitute vowel homogenous to the first of two vowels] also comes in place of [both] the vocalised semivowel (*saṃprasārana*, *iK*) [and the vowel following it in close proximity].")
A. 6.1.109 *eṅaḥ padāntād ati* || ("[A single substitute homogenous to the first of two vowels denoted by] *eṄ* (i.e., *e* and *o*) comes in place of [both] the *pada* final [sound denote by] *eṄ* and [the following vowel] *a* [of the following *pada* in close proximity.")
A. 6.1.111 *ṛta ut* || ("[A single substitute vowel] *u* comes in place of [both the stem final vowel] *ṛ* [and the following initial vowel *a* of the ablative and genitive singular suffixes in close proximity].")
A. 6.1.113 *ato ror aplutād aplute* || ("[The vowel *u*] comes in place of [the sound] *rU* preceded by and followed by a non-prolated vowel *a* [in close proximity].")

A. 6.1.114 *haśi ca* || ("[The sound *u* comes in place of *rU* when it is preceded by the sound *a*] also before a voiced consonant (*haŚ*) [in close proximity].")
A. 6.1.125 *plutapragṛhyā aci nityam* || ("Prolated vowels and *pragṛhya* vowels compulsorily [retain their original form] before vowels [in close proximity].")
A. 6.1.127 *iko 'savarṇe śākalyasya hrasvaṃ ca* || ("According to Śākalya [the final vowel denoted by] *iK* (i.e., *i*, *u*, *ṛ*, *ḷ*) [of a *pada* retains its form] before non-homogenous [vowels] and [is replaced by] a [corresponding] short vowel.")
A. 6.1.137 *samparyupebhyaḥ karotau bhūṣaṇe* || ("[The initial infix *suṬ* comes before the sound *k*] of [the verbal stem] *karoti* ('is doing') after [the *upasarga*s] *sam*, *pari* and *upa* to denote 'to adorn, beautify' [even with the intervention of *aṬ* or the reduplicated syllable in close proximity].")
A. 6.1.50 *mīnātiminotidīṅāṃ lyapi ca* || ("[The substitute vowel *ā* comes in place of the vowel of the verbal roots] *mīÑ* ('to injure', DhP IX:4), *ḌUmiÑ* ('to scatter', DhP V:4) and *dīṄ* ('to decay, perish', DhP IV: 26) before [the substitute absolutive suffix] *LyaP* as well as [the suffixes marked with *Ś*].")
A. 6.1.158 *anudāttaṃ padam ekavarjam* || ("A *pada* is *anudātta* accented with the exception of one [syllable which bears an *udātta* or a *svarita* accent].")
A. 6.1.161 *anudāttasya ca yatrodāttalopaḥ* || ("[The *udātta* accent] comes in place of the *anudātta* syllable when the preceding *udātta* syllable has been deleted.")
A. 6.1.162 *dhātoḥ* || ("[The final syllable] of the verbal root [bears the *udātta* accent].")
A. 6.1.186 *tāsyanudātteṅnidadupadeśāl lasārvadhātukam anudāttam ahnviṅoḥ* || ("A *sārvadhātuka* [suffix replacing the] *l*-member (i.e., verbal endings and the suffixes *ŚatṚ* and *ŚanaC*) bears the *anudātta* accent when introduced after [the tense marker] *tāsI*, verbal roots with an *anudātta* or *Ṅ* marker, apart from [the verbal root] *hnuṄ* ('to hide', DhP II:72) and *iṄ* [with *adhi*] ('to study', DhP II:37) and the vowel *a* introduced as such in first enunciation.")
A. 6.1.173 *śatur anumo nady ajādi* || ("The feminine (*nadī*) [suffix *ṄīP* introduced] after [nominal stems ending in the suffix] *ŚatṚ* without the infix *nUM* [and bearing the *udātta* accent on the final] as well as [case endings excluding those denoted by the term *sarvanāmasthāna*] beginning with a vowel [bear the *udātta* accent].")
A. 6.1.174 *udāttayaṇo halpūrvāt* || ("[The feminine *ṄīP* suffix as well as case endings excluding those termed *sarvanāmasthāna* beginning with a vowel bear an *udātta* accent when introduced after a nominal stem] whose final *udātta* vowel is replaced by a semivowel preceded by a consonant.")
A. 6.1.175 *noṅdhātvoḥ* || ("[Case endings excluding those termed *sarvanāmasthāna* beginning with a vowel introduced after a nominal stem whose final *udātta* vowel of the feminine suffix] *ūṄ* or of a verbal root [is replaced by a semivowel preceded by a consonant] do not [bear an *udātta* accent].")

A. 6.1.197 *ñnity ādir nityam* || ("Before [the suffix] marked with *Ñ* or *N* the initial [syllable] necessarily [bears the *udātta* accent].")
A. 6.1.198 *āmantritasya ca* || ("[The initial syllable] of the vocative also [bears an *udātta* accent].")
A. 6.1.205 *niṣṭhā ca dvyaj anāt* || ("[The initial syllable] of a dissyllabic [stem ending in the suffixes termed] *niṣṭhā*, excluding those having *ā* [in the first syllable, when denoting a name, bears an *udātta* accent].")
A. 6.1.220 *anto 'vatyāḥ* || ("The final [of the stem] ending in *avatī* [is marked with an *udātta* accent when it denotes a name].")
A. 6.1.221 *īvatyāḥ* || ("[The final of the stem] ending in *īvatī* [is marked with an *udātta* accent when it denotes a name].")
A. 6.2.2 *tatpuruṣe tulyārthatṛtīyāsaptamyupamānāvyayadvitīyākṛtyāḥ* || ("In a *tatpuruṣa* compound [the prior member retains its original accent] if it consists of synonyms of *tulya* ('similar, comparable') or [ends in] the instrumental or the locative, or [serves as] an object of comparison, is an indeclinable or [ends in] the accusative or is a *kṛtya* [suffix].")
A. 6.2.49 *gatir anantaraḥ* || ("A *gati* particle [being the first member of a compound retains its original accent before the nominal stem ending in the suffix *Kta* added to denote an object] without intervention.")
A. 6.2.139 *gatikārakopapadāt kṛt* || ("[In a *tatpuruṣa* compound the final member ending] in a primary suffix [retains its original accent when occurring] after a *gati* [particle], *kāraka* or an *upapada*.")
A. 6.2.143 *antaḥ* || ("[From this *sūtra* up to the end of the *pāda*] the final [syllable of the final member of a compound bears the *udātta* accent].")
A. 6.2.144 *thāthaghañktājapitrakāṇām* || ("[The final syllable of the last member of a compound ending in the suffixes] *tha*, *atha*, *GHaÑ*, *Kta*, *aC*, *aP*, *itra* and *Ka* [is *udātta* accented when occurring after a *gati* particle, a *kāraka* or a subordinate word (*upapada*)].")
A. 6.2.189 *anor apradhānakanīyasī* || ("[In a compound the final syllable of the last member] which is not the main one and [of the nominal stem] *kanīyasī* ('a younger female') [bears an *udātta* accent when occurring] after [the *upasarga*] *anu*.")
A. 6.3.22 *putre 'nyatarasyām* || ("Before [the final member of a compound] *putra* ('a son'), [the deletion *luK* does not come in place of the genitive ending introduced after the first member of a compound] optionally [to denote an insult].")
A. 6.3.23 *ṛto vidyāyonisambandhebhyaḥ* || ("[The genitive singular suffix introduced] after [the first member of a compound ending in the sound] *ṛ* and expressing kinship through knowledge or blood [is not deleted].")
A. 6.3.27 *īd agneḥ somavaruṇayoḥ* || ("[The substitute vowel] *ī* comes in place of [the final sound of] *agni* ('Agni') before [the posterior member of a compound] *soma* ('Soma') or *varuṇa* ('Varuṇa') [in a *devatādvandva* compound].")

A. 6.3.84 *samānasya chandasy amūrdhaprabhṛtyudarkeṣu* || ("In Vedic literature [the element *sa* comes in place of the whole] of [the nominal stem] *samāna* ('the same, common') [before a final member of a compound] excluding [the nominal stems] *mūrdhan* ('a head'), *prabhṛti* ('commencement') and *udarka* ('consequence').")

A. 6.3.92 *viśvagdevayoś ca ṭer adryañcatau vapratyaye* || ("[The form] *adri* [comes] in place of [the element] *Ṭi* of [the words] *viśvañc* ('all-pervading') and *deva* ('a god'), and [a *sarvanāman*] before [the verbal root] *añcU* ('to move towards') ending in the suffix *vA* (i.e., *KviN*).")

A. 6.3.111 *ḍhralope pūrvasya dīrgho 'ṇaḥ* || ("[There is a substitution] of a vowel denoted by *aṆ* by its long counterpart when there follows a sound before which *ḍh* or *r* is deleted.")

A. 6.3.112 *sahivahor od avarṇasya* || ("[The vowel] *o* comes in place of the vowel *a* [of the verbal stems] *ṣahA* ('to endure', DhP I:905) and *vahA* ('to carry', DhP I:1053) [before the deleted consonant *ḍh*].")

A. 6.3.120 *śarādīnāṃ ca* || ("[Before the *taddhita* suffix *matUP* the long vowel comes in place of the final vowel of an *aṅga* stem of] *śara* ('reed') etc. [to derive proper names in close proximity].")

A. 6.3.132 *oṣadheś ca vibhaktāv aprathamāyām* || ("[In the mantra section of the *Veda* a long vowel comes in place of the final vowel of the nominal stem] *oṣadhi* ('a plant') before *vibhakti* [suffixes] excluding nominative [in close proximity].")

A. 6.3.137 *anyeṣām api dṛśyate* || ("[A substitute long vowel] is also seen [to replace the vowel *a*] of other [*padas*].")

A. 6.4.2 *halaḥ* || ("[A long vowel comes in place of the final *saṃprasāraṇa* vowel (denoted by *aṆ*) of the *aṅga* verbal stem when this vowel] follows the consonant.")

A. 6.4.3 *nāmi* || ("[A long vowel comes in place of the final vowel of the *aṅga* stem] before [the genitive plural ending] *nām*.")

A. 6.4.8 *sarvanāmasthāne cāsambuddhau* || ("[A long vowel comes in place of a penultimate short one of an *aṅga* stem ending in *n*] before strong case endings (*sarvanāmasthāna*), excluding the voc. sg.")

A. 6.4.10 *sāntamahataḥ saṃyogasya* || ("[The substitute long vowel comes in place of a penultimate vowel preceding] the final *s* forming a cluster [with the sound *n*] as well as [the penultimate sound of the stem] *mahat* ('great') [before the strong case endings excluding the vocative].")

A. 6.4.14 *atvasantasya cādhātoḥ* || ("[Before a non-vocative *sUP* triplet *sU* a long vowel comes in place of a penultimate vowel of an *aṅga* stem] other than a verbal root ending in *atU* or *as*.")

A. 6.4.16 *ajhanagamāṃ sani* || ("[A substitute long vowel replaces the final vowel of the *aṅga* verbal stem ending in] a vowel or of *hanA* ('to kill', DhP II:2) and *gamḶ* ('to go', DhP I:1031) before [the desiderative suffix] *saN*].")

A. 6.4.19 *cchvoḥ śūṭh anunāsike ca* || ("[The elements] *ś* and *ūṬH* [respectively] come in place of [the sounds] *c-ch* and *v* [of an *aṅga* stem before the suffixes beginning with a non-nasal consonant marked with *K* or *Ṅ*] as well as before a nasal consonant.")
A. 6.4.24 *aniditāṃ hala upadhyāyāḥ kṅiti* || ("The penultimate [sound *n* of an *aṅga* verbal stem] not marked with *I* [and ending in] a consonant [is deleted before the suffixes] marked with *K* or *Ṅ*.")
A. 6.4.30 *nāñceḥ pūjāyām* || ("[The sound *n*] of [the verbal root] *añcU* ('to move, honour', DhP I:203) is not [deleted before the suffixes marked with *K* or *Ṅ* and beginning with a consonant] when [the verbal root denotes] 'honour'.")
A. 6.4.41 *viḍvanor anunāsikasyāt* || ("[The vowel] *ā* comes in place of [the final sound of the *aṅga* stem ending in] a nasal stop before [the suffixes] *vIṬ* or *vanIP*.")
A. 6.4.48 *ato lopaḥ* || ("[The final vowel] *a* [of the *aṅga* stem] is deleted [before *ārdhadhātuka* suffixes].")
A. 6.4.49 *yasya halaḥ* || ("[The *aṅga* final syllable] *ya* [is deleted] after a consonant [and before an *ārdhadhātuka* suffix].")
A. 6.4.51 *ṇer aniṭi* || ("[The vowel *i* of the verbal stem formed with the affix] *ṆiC* [is deleted before an *ārdhadhātuka* suffix which] does not take [the infix] *iṬ*.")
A. 6.4.60 *niṣṭhāyām aṇyadarthe* || ("[A long vowel comes in place of the final vowel of the verbal stem *kṣi* ('to decay', DhP I:255)] before [the suffixes termed] *niṣṭhā* when the meaning is not the one of [the suffix] *ṆyaT*.")
A. 6.4.63 *dīṅo yuḍ aci kṅiti* || ("[The augment] *yuṬ* [is inserted at the beginning of an *ārdhadhātuka* suffix] before a vowel with a marker *K* or *Ṅ* after [the verbal root] *dīṄ* ('to perish', DhP IV:26).")
A. 6.4.64 *āto lopa iṭi ca* || ("[The final vowel] *ā* [of the *aṅga* stem] is deleted before [the infix] *iṬ* and [the *ārdhadhātuka* suffixes beginning with a vowel and marked with *K* or *Ṅ*].")
A. 6.4.71 *luṅlaṅlṛṅkṣv aḍudāttaḥ* || ("[The initial augment] *aṬ udātta*-accented comes [at the beginning of an *aṅga* stem] before [the *l*-substitutes of] aorist (*lUṄ*), imperfect (*lAṄ*) and conditional (*lṚṄ*).")
A. 6.4.74 *na māṅyoge* || ("[The initial augments *aṬ* and *āṬ*] are not [inserted at the beginning of the verbal *aṅga* stem before the *l*-substitutes of *lUṄ*, *lAṄ* and *lṚṄ*] when co-ocurring with the prohibitive particle *māṄ*.")
A. 6.4.77 *aci śnudhātubhruvāṃ yvor iyaṅuvaṅau* || ("[The elements] *iyAṄ* and *uvAṄ* come in place of [the vowels] *i* and *u* [respectively] before [the suffix beginning with] a vowel [when they are the final sounds of an *aṅga* stem ending in the infix] *Śnu* or of a verbal root or of [the nominal stem] *bhrū* ('a brow').")
A. 6.4.83 *oḥ supi* || ("[The semivowel substitute *v* of *yaṆ*] comes in place of [the final vowel] *u* [of an *aṅga* stem of a polysyllabic verbal stem, not preceded by a consonant cluster] before *sUP* [triplets beginning with a vowel].")

A. 6.4.98 *gamahanajanakhanaghasāṃ lopaḥ kṅity anaṅi* || ("[The penultimate vowel of the *aṅga* stem of the verbal stems] *gamḶ* ('to go', DhP I:1031), *hanA* ('to kill', DhP II:2), *janA* ('to be born', DhP III:24), *khanU* ('to dig', DhP I:927) and *ghasḶ* ('to eat', DhP I:747) is deleted before [the suffixes] marked with *K* or *Ṅ* excluding *aṄ*.")
A. 6.4.100 *ghasibhasor hali ca* || ("[In Vedic literature the penultimate vowel of an *aṅga* stem] of [the verbal roots] *ghasḶ* ('to eat', DhP I:747) and *bhasA* ('to shine', DhP III:18) [is deleted] before [the suffixes beginning with] a consonant as well as [with vowels and with markers *K* or *Ṅ*].")
A. 6.4.101 *hujhalbhyo her dhiḥ* || ("[The element] *dhi* comes in place of [whole of the substitute] *hi* (of *siP*) [introduced] after [a verbal root] *hu* ('to sarifice', DhP III:1) and those ending in [the sounds denoted by] *jhaL* (i.e., all consonants apart from nasals and semivowels).")
A. 6.4.104 *ciṇo luk* || ("[The suffix introduced] after [the aorist suffix] *CiṆ* is deleted.")
A. 6.4.111 *śnāsor allopaḥ* || ("The vowel *a* of [the present marker] *ŚnaM* and [the verbal root] *asA* ('to be', DhP II:56) is deleted [before *sārvadhātuka* suffixes marked with *K* or *Ṅ*].")
A. 6.4.112 *śnābhyastayor ātaḥ* || ("The vowel *ā* of the class infix *Śnā* or [the final sound of the *aṅga* stem of] the reduplicated [verbal stem is deleted before *sārvadhātuka* suffixes marked with *K* or *Ṅ*].")
A. 6.4.113 *ī haly aghoḥ* || ("[The vowel] *ī* comes in place of [the vowel *ā* occurring in the suffix *Śnā* or as the *aṅga* final of a reduplicated verbal stem] excluding those termed *ghu* (A. 1.1.20) [before the *sārvadhātuka* suffixes] beginning with a consonant [marked with *K* or *Ṅ*].")
A. 6.4.120 *ata ekahalmadhye 'nādeśāder liṭi* || ("The vowel *e*] comes in place of the vowel *a* between single consonants [in a verbal *aṅga* stem] where the initial was not replaced [in a reduplicated syllable] before [the *l*-substitutes of] *lIṬ* (perfect) [with marker *K* or *Ṅ* and deleted reduplicated syllable].")
A. 6.4.122 *tṝphalabhajatrapaś ca* || ("[The vowel *e* comes in place of the vowel *a* of the verbal *aṅga* stem of] *tṝ* ('to cross, traverse', DhP I:1018), *phalA* ('to be fruitful, DhP I:563), *bhajA* ('to serve', DhP I:1047) and *trapŪṢ* ('to be ashamed', DhP I:399) [before the *l*-substitutes of *lIṬ* (perfect) with marker *K* or *Ṅ* as well as before the *lIṬ* substitute *thaL* occurring with the initial infix *iṬ*].")
A. 6.4.134 *allopo 'naḥ* || ("[The vowel *a* [of the final syllable] *an* [of the *aṅga* stem termed *bha*] is deleted.")
A. 6.4.144 *nas taddhite* || ("[There is the deletion of the *Ṭi* element of the *aṅga* stem termed *bha* ending in] *n* before a *taddhita* [suffix].")
A. 6.4.147 *ḍhe lopo 'kadrvāḥ* || ("There is the deletion of [the final sound of an *aṅga* stem termed *bha* ending in the vowel *u*] before [the *taddhita* suffix] *ḍha* excluding [the nominal stem] *kadru*.")

A. 6.4.148 *yasyeti ca* || ("[The final sounds] *i* or *a* [of a *bha* stem are deleted] before the vowel *ī* as well as [*taddhita* suffixes beginning with a vowel or the consonant *y*].")
A. 6.4.155 *ṭeḥ* || ("The *Ṭi* part [of an *aṅga* stem termed *bha* is deleted when the suffixes *iṣṭhaN*, *imanIC* and *īyasUN* follow.")
A. 6.4.155 *vt.* 1 *ṇāv iṣthāvat prātipadikasya* || ("When a nominal stem is followed by [the suffix] *ṆiC*, it goes through similar operations as when it is followed by *iṣṭha*.")

Adhyāya 7

A. 7.1.1 *yuvor anākau* || ("[The substitutes elements] *ana* and *aka* come in place of [the elements] *yu* and *vu* respectively [of the suffixes].")
A. 7.1.2 *āyaneyīnīyiyaḥ phaḍhakhachaghāṃ pratyayādīnām* || ("[The elements] *āyan*, *ey*, *īn*, *īy* and *iy* come in place of the initial sounds *ph*, *ḍh*, *kh*, *ch* and *gh* of suffixes, respectively.")
A. 7.1.3 *jho 'ntaḥ* || ("[The element] *ant* comes in place of [the element] *jh* [occurring as initial of the suffix].")
A. 7.1.17 *jasaḥ śī* || ("[The element] *Śī* comes in place of [the case ending] *Jas* [introduced after pronominal stems ending in the vowel *a*].")
A. 7.1.20 *jaśśasoḥ śi* || ("[The element] *Śi* comes in place of [the whole endings] *Jas* and *Śas* [introduced after neuter *aṅga* stem].")
A. 7.1.22 *ṣaḍbhyo luk* || ("There is the *luK* deletion [of the endings *Jas* and *Śas* (nom., acc. pl.) introduced] after [numbers denoted by the term] *ṣaṭ*.")
A. 7.1.23 *svamor napuṃsakāt* || ("[The case endings] *sU* (nom. sg.) and *am* (acc. sg.) [introduced] after the neuter [*aṅga* stem are deleted by *luK*].")
A. 7.1.34 *āta au ṇalaḥ* || ("[The substitute] *au* comes in place of [the *l*-substitute of *lIṬ*] *ṆaL* [introduced after a verbal stem ending in] the vowel *ā*.")
A. 7.1.37 *samāse 'nañpūrve ktvo lyap* || ("[The element] *LyaP* comes in place of [the suffix] *Ktvā* [occurring after a verbal *aṅga* stem being a final member] in a compound, excluding *naÑ* as the first [member].")
A. 7.1.39 *supāṃ sulukpūrvasavarṇātśeyāḍāḍyāyājālaḥ* || ("[In Vedic literature the substitutes] *sU*, *luK*, a long vowel corresponding to the preceding one, *ā*, *āt*, *Śe*, *yā*, Ḍā, *Ḍyā*, *yāC* and *āL* come in place of case endings [introduced after an *aṅga* stem].")
A. 7.1.55 *ṣaṭcaturbhyaś ca* || ("[The initial infix *nUṬ*] is also [inserted at the head of the sixth triplet *ām*, introduced after nominal *aṅga* stems indicating numbers] comprised by the technical term *ṣaṭ* and *catur* ('four').")
A. 7.1.58 *idito num dhātoḥ* || ("The infix *nUM* [comes after the last vowel] of a verbal root marked with *I* [in the first enunciation].")
A. 7.1.60 *masjinaśor jhali* || ("[The infix *nUM* comes after the last vowel of the *aṅga* stem] *ṬUmasjO* ('to sink, plunge', DhP VI:122) and *ṇaśA* ('to disappear',

DhP IV:85) before [the suffixes beginning with a sound denoted by the term] *jhaL* (i.e., non-nasal stops and fricatives.")

A. 7.1.70 *ugidacāṃ sarvanāmasthāna 'dhātoḥ* || ("[The infix *nUM* comes after the last vowel of a nominal *aṅga* stem] marked with *uK* (i.e., *U*, *Ṛ* or *Ḷ*) or one ending in [such a suffix] excluding verbal stems and the verbal stem *ac* (=*añc*) before the strong *sUP* triplets.")

A. 7.1.72 *napuṃsakasya jhalacaḥ* || ("[The infix *nUM* comes after the last vowel of] a neuter [*aṅga* stem ending in a sound denoted by] *jhaL* (i.e., non-nasal consonants] or a vowel (*aC*).")

A. 7.1.76 *chandasy api dṛśyate* || ("In Vedic literature, [the substitute *anAṄ*] is also seen [to come in place of the final sound of an *aṅga* stem of the nominal stems *asthi* ('a bone'), *dadhi* ('curd'), *sakthi* ('a thigh') and *akṣi* ('an eye')].")

A. 7.1.82 *sav anaḍuhaḥ* || ("[The infix *nUM* comes after the last vowel of the *aṅga* stem] *anaḍuh* ('an ox') before [the suffix] *sU*.")

A. 7.1.90 *goto ṇit* || ("[The strong *sUP* suffixes introduced] after [the *aṅga* stem] *go* ('a cow, bull') [are treated as] having a marker *Ṇ*.")

A. 7.1.94 *ṛduśanaspurudaṃśonehasāṃ ca* || ("[The substitute element *anaṄ*] also [comes in place of the final sound of the *aṅga* stems ending in] *ṛ* and *uśanas*, *purudaṃśas* ('abounding in mighty deeds') and *anehas* ('unrivaled') [before the *sUP* triplet *sU* excluding the vocative singular].")

A. 7.1.98 *caturanaḍuhor ām udāttaḥ* || ("[The infix] *āM*, which is *udātta* accented, comes [after the last vowel of a nominal *aṅga* stem] *catur* ('four') or *anaḍuh* ('an ox') [before the strong case endings].")

A. 7.1.100 *ṝta iddhātoḥ* || ("[The vowel] *i* comes in place of [the final sound of the *aṅga*] verbal stem [ending in] *ṝ*.")

A. 7.2.1 *sici vṛddhiḥ parasmaipadeṣu* || ("[The vowels termed] *vṛddhi* [come in place of the final sound denoted by *iK* (i.e., *i*, *u*, *ṛ*, *ḷ*) of an *aṅga* stem of a verbal root] before [the aorist suffix] *sIC* before *parasmaipada l*-substitutes.")

A. 7.2.3 *vadavrajahalantasyācaḥ* || ("[The *vṛddhi* vowel] comes in place of the vowel of [the verbal *aṅga* stems] *vadA* ('to speak', DhP I:1058), *vrajA* ('to walk', DhP I:272) and those ending in a consonant (*haL*) [before the aorist suffix *siC* co-occurring with *parasmaipada l*-substitutes].")

A. 7.2.8 *neḍ vaśi kṛti* || ("[The initial infix] *iṬ* does not come at the beginning of a *kṛt* [suffix beginning with semivowels and] voiced stops (*vaŚ*) excluding [the consonant] *y*.")

A. 7.2.14 *śvīdito niṣṭhāyām* || ("[The initial infix *iṬ* does not come at the beginning of] a *niṣṭhā* [suffix introduced] after [the verbal roots] *ṬUOśvi* ('to swell', DhP I:1059) and those marked with *Ī* [in the first enunciation].")

A. 7.2.35 *ārdhadhātukasyeḍ valādeḥ* || ("[The infix] *iṬ* comes at the beginning of an *ārdhadhātuka* [suffix] beginning with [the sounds denoted by] *vaL* (i.e., semivowels and consonants apart from *y*).")

A. 7.2.46 *niraḥ kuṣaḥ* || ("[The initial infix *iṬ* is optionally inserted at the beginning of the *ārdhadhātuka* suffixes beginning with semivowels or consonants excluding *y*] after [the verbal root] *kuṣA* ('to hurt', DhP IX:46) occurring with [the *upasarga*] *nir*.")

A. 7.2.79 *liṅaḥ salopo'nantyasya* || ("The non final sound *s* of [the *sārvadhātuka*] *lIṄ* [suffixes *yāsUṬ* and *sīyUṬ*, and *sUṬ*] is deleted.")

A. 7.2.82 *āne muk* || ("[The final infix] *mUK* is inserted [after a verbal *aṅga* stem ending in *a*] before [the suffix] *ŚānaC*.")

A. 7.2.102 *tyadādīnām aḥ* || ("[The vowel] *a* comes in place of [the final sound of the *aṅga* stem of pronominal roots] *tyad* ('that') etc. [before a case ending].")

A. 7.2.103 *kimaḥ kaḥ* || ("[The element] *ka* comes in place of [the element] *kim* ('who, what, which') [before case endings].")

A. 7.2.106 *tadoḥ saḥ sāvanantyayoḥ* || ("[The consonant] *s* comes in place of a non-final *t* or *d* [of the pronominal stem *tyad* ('that') etc.] before *sU*.")

A. 7.2.114 *mṛjer vṛddhiḥ* || ("[The substitute sound denoted by] *vṛddhi* comes in place of [the *aṅga* stem final denoted by *iK*] of the [verbal stem] *mṛjŪ* ('to wash, purify', DhP II:57) [before *vibhakti l*-substitutes of *l*-members].")

A. 7.2.115 *aco ñṇiti* || ("[A substitute *vṛddhi* vowel] comes in place of the [final] vowel [of the *aṅga* stem] before [the suffixes] marked with *Ñ* or *Ṇ*.")

A. 7.2.116 *ata upadhāyāḥ* || ("[The vowel *ā*] comes in place of the penultimate vowel *a* [before suffixes marked with *Ñ* or *Ṇ*].")

A. 7.2.117 *taddhiteṣv acām ādeḥ* || ("[A *vṛddhi* vowel comes in place] of the first vowel [of the *aṅga* stem] before *taddhita* [suffixes marked with *Ṇ* or *Ñ*].")

A. 7.3.36 *artihrīvlīrīknūyīkṣmāyyātāṃ puṅ ṇau* || ("[The infix] *pUK* [is inserted at the end of the verbal *aṅga* stems] *ṛ* ('to go', DhP I:983, III:16), *hrī* ('to feel shy', DhP III:3), *vlī* ('to crush', DhP IX:32), *rī* ('to let go, flow', DhP IX:30), *knūyĪ* ('to make a creaky noise', DhP I:514), *kṣmāyĪ* ('to shake', DhP I:515) and those ending in [the vowel] *ā* before [the causative suffix] *ṆiC*.")

A. 7.3.50 *ṭhasyekaḥ* || ("[The element] *ik* comes in place of [the element] *ṭh* [of a suffix introduced after an *aṅga* stem].")

A. 7.3.52 *cajoḥ ku ghiṇṇyatoḥ* || ("[A sound denoted by] *kU* come in place of [the sounds] *c* or *j* [of an *aṅga* stem] before [the suffixes] marked with *GH* or [the suffix] *ṆyaT*.")

A. 7.3.54 *ho hanter ñṇitneṣu* || ("[A substitute velar stop] comes in place of the sound *h* of [the verbal root] *hanA* ('to kill', DhP II:2) before [the suffix] marked with *Ñ* or *Ṇ*, or the sound *n* [when the penultimate vowel is deleted by A. 6.4.98.")

A. 7.3.61 *bhujanyubjau pāṇyupatāpayoḥ* || ("[The words] *bhuja* and *nyubja* [are formed in an irregular way without velar substitute of the consonant *j* before the suffix *GHaÑ* (A. 7.3.52)] to denote 'a hand' and 'heat, pain' respectively.")

A. 7.3.84 *sārvadhātukārdhadhātukayoḥ* || ("[The substitute *guṇa* vowel comes in place of the final vowel of an *aṅga* verbal stem ending in a vowel denoted by *iK* (i.e., *i*, u, *ṛ* and *ḷ*)] before *sārvadhātuka* and *ārdhdhātuka* [suffixes].")
A. 7.3.86 *pugantalaghūpadhasya ca* || ("[A *guṇa* vowel] comes in place of the penultimate vowel [of an *aṅga* stem] ending in [the infix] *pUK* or containing a short [penultimate] vowel [denoted by *iK* (i.e., *i*, *u*, *ṛ*, *ḷ*), before *sārvadhātuka* and *ārdhadhātuka* suffixes].")
A. 7.3.96 *astisico 'pṛkte* || ("[The infix *īṬ* comes at the beginning of a *sārvadhātuka* suffix] consisting of a single sound (*apṛkta*) [consonant introduced after the verbal root] *asA* ('to be', DhP II:56) and [the aorist suffix] *sIC*.")
A. 7.3.102 *supi ca* || ("[A long vowel comes in place of the final vowel *a* of an *aṅga* stem] before a case ending [beginning with the consonant denoted by *yaÑ* (i.e., semivowels, nasals or *bh*)].")
A. 7.3.103 *bahuvacane jhaly et* || ("The vowel *e* [comes in place of the final *a* of an *aṅga* stem] before [a case ending] beginning with [a sound denoted by] *jhaL* (i.e., non-nasal consonants) denoting plural.")
A. 7.3.105 *āṅi cāpaḥ* || ("[The substitute vowel *e*] comes also in place of [the final vowel of an *aṅga* stem ending in the feminine suffixes] *āP* (i.e., *CāP*, *ṬāP*, *ḌāP*) before [the case ending] *āṄ* (= *Ṭā*) [as well as *os*].")
A.7.3.108 *hrasvasya guṇaḥ* || ("A substitute *guṇa* vowel comes in place of [the final vowel of an *aṅga* stem ending in] a short vowel denoted by *iK* (i.e., *i*, *u*, *ṛ*, *ḷ*) before the vocative singular ending *sUP*].")
A. 7.3.111 *gher ṅiti* || ("[The substitute *guṇa* vowel comes in place of the final vowel denoted by *iK* (i.e., *i*, *u*, *ṛ* and *ḷ*) of the *aṅga* stem termed] *ghi* before [case endings] marked with *Ṅ*.")
A. 7.3.112 *āṇ nadyāḥ* || ("[The initial augment] *āṬ* comes [in front of case endings with marker *Ṅ* introduced] after [nominal stems termed] *nadī*.")
A. 7.3.120 *āṅo nāstriyām* || ("[The morpheme] *nā* comes in place of [the instrumental singular suffix] *āṄ* [introduced after a stem termed *ghi*] excluding feminine [stems].")
A. 7.4.25 *akṛtsārvadhātukayor dīrghaḥ* || ("The long vowel comes in place of [the final vowel of an *aṅga* verbal stem] before [the suffix beginning with *y* and marked with *K* or *Ṅ*] excluding [the suffixes] *kṛt* and *sārvadhātuka*.")
A. 7.4.33 *kyaci ca* || ("[The long vowel *ī*] also comes in place of [the final *a* of the *aṅga* stem] before [the suffix] *KyaC*.")
A. 7.4.59 *hrasvaḥ* || ("A short vowel [comes in place of the vowel of the reduplicated syllable].")
A. 7.4.60 *halādiḥ śeṣaḥ* || ("The first consonant [of a reduplicated syllable] remains [and all the remaining ones are deleted].")
A. 7.4.61 *śarpūrvāḥ khayaḥ* || ("Unvoiced stops (*khaY*) preceded by sibilants (*śaR*) [of a reduplicated syllable remain and the sibilants are deleted].")

A. 7.4.61 *vt*. 1 *kharpūrvāḥ khayaḥ* || ("Unvoiced stops preceded by unvoiced consonants [of the reduplicated syllable remain and the preceded consonant is deleted].")
A. 7.4.79 *sany ataḥ* || ("[The substitute vowel *i*] comes in place of the vowel *a* [of the reduplicated syllable of the *aṅga* stem of a verbal stem] before [the desiderative suffix] *saN*.")
A. 7.4.82 *guṇo yaṅlukoḥ* || ("A substitute *guṇa* vowel [somes in place of the vowel denoted by *iK* (i.e., *i*, *u*, *ṛ*, *ḷ*) of the reduplicated syllable] before [the suffixes] *yaṄ* and *yaṄ-luK*.")
A. 7.4.89 *ti ca* || ("[The substitute vowel *u* comes in place of the vowel *a* of the *aṅga* stem of the verbal stems *carA* ('to move', DhP I:591) and *phalA* ('to bear fruit', DhP I:563)] before [the suffix beginning with the consonant] *t*.")
A. 7.4.90 *rīg ṛdupadhasya ca* || ("[There is the infix] *rīK* after [the reduplication of the *aṅga* stem] which has [the sound] *ṛ* as the penultimate [before the suffix *yaṄ* or its deletion by *luK*].")
A. 7.4.94 *dīrgho laghoḥ* || ("A long vowel comes in place of a short vowel [of the reduplicated syllable of the *aṅga* stem of the verbal stem before the causative suffix *ṆiC* co-occurring with the aorist suffix *CaṄ*, without the deletion of the final vowel before *ṆiC*].")

Adhyāya 8

A. 8.1.1 *sarvasya dve* || ("Two [expressions] come in place of the whole [sequence].")
A. 8.1.4 *nityavīpsayoḥ* || ("[Two expression come in place of a whole] to denote 'over and over again, continually' or 'pervasion of a thing by property and action.")
A. 8.1.8 *vākyāder āmantritasyāsūyāsammatikopakutsanabhartsaneṣu* || ("[Two come] in place of a vocative (*āmantrita*) occurring at the beginning of an utterance when the meaning is *asūyā* ('envy, jealousy'), *sammati* ('sameness of opinion'), *kopa* ('anger'), *kutsana* ('abuse, reproach') and *bhartsana* ('threat').")
A. 8.1.16 *padasya* || ("[In the section beginning here and extending up to and inclusive of A. 8.3.54 all operations are introduced] to a *pada*.")
A. 8.1.17 *padāt* || ("[All the operations are introduced] after a *pada*.")
A. 8.1.28 *tiṅ atiṅaḥ* || ("After a non verbal [*pada*], a verbal *pada* [is marked with an *anudātta* accent].")
A. 8.1.55 *āma ekāntaram āmantritam anantike* || ("The vocative [is not all *anudātta* accented when co-occurring with] *ām*, but separated from it by a single [*pada*] except when following it.")
A. 8.1.69 *kutsane ca supy agotrādau* || ("[A verbal *pada* occurring with or without a *gati* becomes *anudātta* accented] before a *sUP* [suffix] except for [a group of words] *gotra* etc. to mean 'reproach, abuse'].")

A. 8.1.71 *tiṅi codāttavati* || ("[A *gati* co-ocurring] with a verbal *pada* containing the *udātta* accent [becomes *anudātta* accented].")

BIBLIOGRAPHY:

A = *Aṣṭādhyāyī of Pāṇini*: (1) Sumitra M. Katre (tr.), Motilal Banarsidass, New Delhi, 1989. (2) Śrīśa Chandra Vasu (ed.&tr.), vol. I&II, Motilal Banarsidass, New Delhi, 1997 (1st edition: Allahabad, 1891). (3) Sharma, Rama Nath (tr.), vol. I-VI, Munshiram Manoharlal, New Delhi, 2002 (1st edition: New Delhi, 1987).

ABHYANKAR 1986 = Abhyankar, K. V.: *A Dictionary of Sanskrit Grammar*. Oriental Institute, Baroda 1986.

AKLUJKAR 1978 = Aklujkar, Ashok: 'The Concluding Verses of Bhartṛhari's *Vākya-kāṇḍa*' [in:] Dandekar, R.N. (ed.) *Annals of the Bhandarkar Oriental Research Institute* (Diamond Jubilee Volume), pp. 9-26. Pune 1978.

AKLUJKAR 1991 = Aklujkar, Ashok: 'Interpreting Vākyapadīya 2.486 historically (part 3)' [in:] Deshpande, Madhav and Bhate, Saroja (eds.) *Pāṇinian Studies – Professors S. D. Joshi Felicitation Volume*, pp. 1-49. Centre for South and Southeast Asian Studies no. 37, University of Michigan 1991.

AKLUJKAR 2008a = Aklujkar, Ashok: 'Patañjali's Mahābhāṣya as a Key to Happy Kashmir' [in:] Aklujkar, Ashok and Kaul, Mrinal (eds.) *Linguistic traditions of Kashmir – Essays in Memory of Pandid Dinannath Yaksha*, pp. 41-87. D.K. Printworld (P) Ltd., New Delhi 2008.

AKLUJKAR 2008b = Aklujkar, Ashok: 'Gonardīya, Goṇikā-putra, Patañjali and Gonandīya' [in:] Aklujkar, Ashok and Kaul, Mrinal (eds.) *Linguistic traditions of Kashmir – Essays in Memory of Pandid Dinannath Yaksha*, pp. 88-172. D.K. Printworld (P) Ltd., New Delhi 2008.

AKLUJKAR 2008c = Aklujkar, Ashok: 'Patañjali – a Kashmirian' [in:] Aklujkar, Ashok and Kaul, Mrinal (eds.) *Linguistic traditions of Kashmir – Essays in Memory of Pandid Dinannath Yaksha*, pp. 173-205. D.K. Printworld (P) Ltd., New Delhi 2008.

BANERJEE 1984 = Banerjee, Rabi Shankar: *Concept of asiddhatva in Pāṇini (Along with a connected*

History of Grammatical studies in Ancient India). Sanskrit Pustak Bhandar, Calcutta 1984.

BELVARKAR 1997 = Belvarkar, Shripad Krishna: *Systems of Sanskrit Grammar*. The Bharatiya Book Corporation, New Delhi 1997 (First edition: 1909).

BHATE 2004 = Bhate, Saroja: 'Patañjali, The Bhāṣyakāra' [in:] Ray, Bidyut Lata (ed.) *Pāṇini to Patañjali – A Grammatical March*, pp. 128-142. D.K. Printworld (P) Ltd., New Delhi 2004.

BLOCH 1961 = Bloch, Jules: *The grammatical structure of Dravidian languages*. Deccan College, Pune 1961.

BRONKHORST 1980 = Bronkhorst, Johannes: '*Asiddha* in the *Aṣṭādhyāyī* – a misunderstanding among the traditional commentators?'. *Journal of Indian Philosophy* 8 (1980), pp. 69-85.

BRONKHORST 1981 = Bronkhorst, Johannes: 'Meaning entries in Pāṇini's Dhātupāṭha'. *Journal of India Philosophy* 9 (1981), pp. 335-357.

BRONKHORST 1983 = Bronkhorst, Johannes: 'On the history of Pāṇinian grammar in the early centuries following Patañjali'. *Journal of Indian Philosophy* 11 (1983), pp. 357-412.

BRONKHORST 1984 = Bronkhorst, Johannes: 'Review of: Paul Kiparsky *Some theoretical problems in Pāṇini's grammar*, pp. 77-121. (Professor K.V. Abhyankar Memorial Lectures [Second Series]), BORI 16, Bhandarkar Oriental Research Institute, Pune 1982'. *Indo-Iranian Journal* 27 (1984), pp. 309-314.

BRONKHORST 1987 = Bronkhorst, Johannes: *Three problems pertaining to the Mahābhāṣya* (Pandit Shripad Shastri Deodhar Memorial Lectures [Third Series]), BORI 30 (I: The first vārttikas in the Mahābhāṣya [1-13], II: The text history of the Mahābhāṣya [14-42], The Mahābhāṣya and the development of Indian philosophy [43-71]), Bhandarkar Oriental Research Institute, Pune 1987.

BRONKHORST 1989 = Bronkhorst, Johannes: 'What is asiddha?' *Annals of the Bhandarkar Oriental Research Institute*. Vol. LXX, pp. 309-311, Pune 1989.

BRONKHORST 1998a = Bronkhorst, Johannes: 'Language, Indian theories of' [in:] *Routledge Encyclopedia of Philosophy*, Craig, Edward (ed.). Vol. 5, pp. 379-384, London 1998.

BRONKHORST 1998b = Bronkhorst, Johannes: 'Patañjali (*c*. 2nd century BC)' [in:] *Routledge Encyclopedia of Philosophy*, Craig, Edward (ed.). Vol. 7, pp. 248-250, London 1998.

BRONKHORST 2002a = Bronkhorst, Johannes: 'The Cāndra-vyākaraṇa: Some questions' [in:] Deshpande, Madhav and Hook, Peter (eds.) *Indian Linguistic Studies Festschrift in Honor of George Cardona*, pp. 182-201. Motilal Banarsidass Publishers Pvt. Ltd., New Delhi 2002.

BRONKHORST 2002b = Bronkhorst, Johannes: 'Patañjali and the Buddhists' [in:] *Buddhist and Indian Studies in Honour of Professor Sodo Mori*, pp. 485-491. Kokusai Bukkyoto Kyokai (International Buddhist Association), Hamamatsu 2002.

BRONKHORST 2008 = Broknhorst, Johannes: 'A note on Kashmir and ortodox Pāṇinian grammar' [in:] Aklujkar, Ashok and Kaul, Mrinal (eds.) *Linguistic traditions of Kashmir – Essays in Memory of Pandid Dinannath Yaksha*, pp. 271-280. D.K. Printworld (P) Ltd., New Delhi 2008.

BUISKOOL 1939 = Buiskool, H.E.: *The Tripādī – being an abridged English recast of Pūrvatrāsiddham (an analytical-synthetical inquiry into the system of last three chapters of Pāṇini's Aṣṭādhyāyī)*. E.J. Brill, Leiden 1939.

CARDONA 1978 = Cardona, George: 'Still again on the History of Mahābhāṣya' [in:] Dandekar, R.N. (ed.) *Annals of the Bhandarkar Oriental Research Institute* (Diamond Jubilee Volume), pp. 79-99, Pune 1978.

CARDONA 1989 = Cardona, George: 'Pāṇinian Studies' [in:] Jha, V. N. (ed.) *New Horizons of Research in Indology* (Silver Jubilee Volume), pp. 49-84,

Centre of Advanced Study in Sanskrit, Class E no. 10, University of Poona 1989.

CARDONA 1997a = Cardona, George: *Pāṇini – A Survey of Research*. Motilal Banarsidass Publishers Pvt. Ltd., New Delhi 1997.

CARDONA 1997b = Cardona, George: *Pāṇini – His Work and Its Tradition*. Vol. I: *Background and Introduction*. Motilal Banarsidass Publishers Pvt. Ltd., New Delhi 1997.

CARDONA 2004 = Cardona, George: *Recent Research in Pāṇinian Studies*. Motilal Banarsidass Publishers Pvt. Ltd., New Delhi 2004 (1st edition: 1999).

CARDONA 2012 = Cardona, George: '*pūrvatrāsiddham* and *āśrayāt siddham*' [in:] Cardona, George; Aklujkar, Ashok and Ogawa, Hideyo (eds.) *Studies in Sanskrit Grammars (Proceedings of Vyākaraṇa Section of the 14th World Sanskrit Conference)*, pp. 123-162, D. K. Printworld (P) Ltd., New Delhi 2012.

CARDONA&JAIN 2017 = George Cardona and Dhanesh Jain (eds.) *The Indo-Aryan Languages*. Routledge, London 2017 [First edition: London 2003].

DVIVEDI 1978 = Dvivedi, H. P.: *Studies in Pāṇini: technical terms in the Aṣṭādhyāyī*. Inter-India Publications, New Delhi 1978.

EIP = Harold G. Coward and K. Kunjunni Raja (eds.) *Encyclopedia of Indian Philosophies*. Vol. V: *The Philosophy of The Grammarians*, Motilal Banarsidass Publishers Pvt. Ltd., New Delhi 2001 [First edition: New Delhi 1990].

FILLIOZAT 1991 = Filliozat, Pierre: *An Introduction to commentaries on Patañjali's Mahābhāṣya* (Professor K.V. Abhyankar Memorial Lectures [Fourth Series]), BORI 35 (I: Patañjali and his commentators [1-32], II: Patañjali's definition of *śabda* [33-85]), Bhandarkar Oriental Research Institute, Pune 1991.

FRESCHI &PONTILLO 2013 = Freschi, Elisa and Pontillo, Tiziana: 'When One Thing Applies More Than Once: *tantra* and *prasaṅga* in Śrautasūtra, Mīmāṃsā and

Grammar.' [in:] Pontillo, Tiziana and Candotti, Maria Piera (eds.) *Signless Signification in Ancient India and Beyond*, Anthem Press, 2013.

JOSHI 1965 = Joshi, S. D.: *Two methods of interpreting Pāṇini*. Publications of the Centre of Advanced Study in Sanskrit, class A no. 5, University of Pune 1965.

JOSHI 1968 = Joshi, S. D.: *Patañjali's Vyākaraṇa-mahābhāṣya – samarthāhnika (P. 2.1.1)*, Publications of the Centre of Advanced Study in Sanskrit, class C no. 3, University of Pune 1968.

JOSHI 1978 = Joshi, S. D.: 'The Ordering of the Rules in Pāṇini's Grammar' [in:] Dandekar, R.N. (ed.) *Annals of the Bhandarkar Oriental Research Institute* (Diamond Jubilee Volume), pp. 667-674, Pune 1978.

JOSHI 1981 = Joshi, S. D.: 'The Functions of Asiddhatva and Sthānivadbhāva in Pāṇini's Aṣṭādhyāyī' [in:] Centre of Advanced Study in Sanskrit Studies no. 6, pp. 153-168. University of Pune 1981.

JOSHI&KIPARSKY 1979 = Joshi, S. D. and Kiparsky, Paul: 'Siddha and Asiddha in Pāṇinian Phonology' [in:] *Current Approaches to Phonological Theory*, Dinnsen, Daniel A. (ed.), Indiana University Press, pp. 223-250, Bloomington 1979.

JOSHI&KIPARSKY 2006 = Joshi, S. D. and Kiparsky, Paul: 'The extended siddha-principle' *Annals of the Bhandarkar Oriental Research Institute*, pp. 1-26, Pune 2006.

JOSHI &ROODBERGEN 1986 = Joshi, S. D. and Roodbergen, J. A. F.: *Patañjali's Vyākaraṇa-mahābhaṣya – paspaśānika*, Publications of the Centre of Advanced Study in Sanskrit, class C no. 15, University of Pune 1986.

JOSHI &ROODBERGEN 1987 = Joshi, S. D. and Roodbergen, J. A. F.: 'On siddha, asiddha and sthānivad'. *Annals of Bhadarkar Oriental Research Institute*, vol. LXVIII (Ramakrishna Gopal Bhandarkar 150th Birth-Anniversary Volume) Palsule, G. B. and Dandekar, R. N. (eds.), pp. 541-549. Pune 1987.

JOSHI &ROODBERGEN 1990 = Joshi, S. D. and Roodbergen, J. A. F.: *Patañjali's Vyākaraṇa-mahābhaṣya – sthānivadbhāvānika*, Bhadarkar Oriental Research Institute, Pune 1990.

JOSHI &ROODBERGEN 1993 = Joshi, S. D. and Roodbergen, J. A. F.: *The Aṣṭādhyāyī of Pāṇini with Translation and Explanatory Notes, Volume II (1.2.1-1.2.73)*. Sahitya Akademi, New Delhi 1993.

KIPARSKY 1980 Kiparsky, Paul: *Pāṇini as a variationist*. Publications of Centre of Advanced Study in Sanskrit, class B no. 6, University of Pune 1980.

KIPARSKY 1982 = Kiparsky, Paul: 'The ordering of rules in Pāṇini's grammar' [in:] *Some theoretical problems in Pāṇini's grammar*, pp. 77-121. (Professor K.V. Abhyankar Memorial Lectures [Second Series]), BORI 16 (I: Case, Control and Ellipsis [1-54], II: The Vedic and Pāṇinian accent systems [55-76], III: The ordering of rules in Pāṇini's grammar [77-121]), Bhandarkar Oriental Research Institute, Pune 1982.

KIPARSKY 1987 = Kiparsky, Paul: 'What is siddha?'. *Annals of the Bhandarkar Oriental Research Institute*, vol. LXVIII (Ramakrishna Gopal Bhandarkar 150th Birth-Anniversary Volume) Palsule, G. B. and Dandekar, R. N. (eds.), pp. 295-303. Pune 1987.

KOBAYASHI 2006 = Kobayashi, Masato: 'Pāṇini's Phonological Rules and Vedic: Aṣṭādhyāyī 8.2'. *Journal of Indological Studies* 18 (2006).

KV = *Kāśikā-vṛtti of Jayāditya-Vāmana along with Commentaries Vivaraṇa-pañcikā – Nyāsa of Jinendrabuddhi and Padamañjarī of Haradatta Miśra*, Ed. Śrīnārāyaṇa Miśra, vol. I-VI, Ratna Publications, Varanasi, 1985.

MISHRA 2004 = Mishra, Jatindramohan: 'Date of Patañjali: A Review' [in:] Ray, Bidyut Lata (ed.) *Pāṇini to Patañjali – A Grammatical March*, pp. 143-157. D.K. Printworld (P) Ltd., New Delhi 2004.

MPV = M. S. Narasimhacharya (ed.) *Mahābhāṣya-pradīpa-vyākhyānāni*. Vol. X: *Adhyāya 7 et 8*, Institut Français d'Indologie, Pondichéry 1983.

MW = Monier-Williams, Monier: *The Sanskrit-English Dictionary*. Munshiram Manoharlal Publishers Pvt. Ltd., New Delhi 1999.

Nir = *The Nighaṇṭu and The Nirukta – The Oldest Indian Treatise on Etymology, Philology and Semantics*. Sarup, Lakshman (ed. and tr.), Motilal Banarsidass, New Delhi 1998 (1st edition: New Delhi 1920-1927).

PhS = *The Phiṭ-sūtras*, in *The Siddhānta-Kaumudī*, Ed. and tr. Śrīśa Chandra Vasu, vol. III pp. 112-125, Motilal Banarsidass, Delhi, 1995 (1st edition: Allahabad, 1906).

PŚ = *The Paribhāṣenduśekhara of Nāgoji Bhaṭṭa*. Kielhorn, F. (ed.), Part I: The Sanskrit text and various readings; Part II: Translation and notes, Indu-Prakash Press, Mumbai 1868.

RAU 1985 = Rau, Wilhelm: *Die vedischen Zitate im Vyākaraṇa-mahābhāṣya*. Akademie der Wissenschaften und der Literatur, Mainz 1985.

RAY 2004 = Ray, Bidyut Lata: 'Prolegomenon' [in:] Ray, Bidyut Lata (ed.) *Pāṇini to Patañjali – A Grammatical March*, pp. 1-40. D.K. Printworld (P) Ltd., New Delhi 2004.

SCHARF 2012 = Scharf, Peter M.: ''Rule selection in the Aṣṭādhyāyī' or 'Is Pāṇini's Grammar Mechanistic?'' [in:] Cardona, George; Aklujkar, Ashok and Ogawa, Hideyo (eds.) *Studies in Sanskrit Grammars (Proceedings of Vyāraṇa Section of the 14th World Sanskrit Conference)*, pp. 319-350, D. K. Printworld (P) Ltd., New Delhi 2012.

SCHARFE 1977 = Scharfe, Hartmut: *Grammatical Literature*. Otto Harrassowitz, Wiesbaden 1997.

SULICH-COWLEY 2016 = Sulich-Cowley, Małgorzata: 'Alternative Solutions to the Problem of A. 8.2.3 *na mu ne* in Pāṇini's Aṣṭādhyāyī' [in:] Cardona, George and Ogawa, Hideyo (eds.) *Vyākaraṇaparipṛcchā: Proceedings of the Vyākaraṇa section of the 16th World Sanskrit Conference*, pp. 321-336, DK Publishers Distributors, New Delhi 2016.

US = *The Uṇādi affixes*, in *The Siddhānta-Kaumudī*, Ed. and tr. Śrīśa Chandra Vasu, vol. II pp. 147-

333, Motilal Banarsidass, Delhi, 1995 (1st edition: Allahabad, 1906).

VMBh_1 = *The Vyākaraṇa-mahābhaṣya of Patañjali*, Ed. F. Kielhorn, vol. I, II&III, Bhandarkar Oriental Research Institute, Pune, 1986 (1st edition: Pune, 1880).

VMBh_2 = *Vyākaraṇa-mahābhāṣya of Patañjali with the commentary Bhāṣya-pradīpa of Kaiyaṭa and the super commentary Bhāṣya-pradīpoddyota of Nāgeśa Bhāṭṭa*, Ed. Vedavrata, vol. I-V, Haryāṇā Sāhitya Saṃsthāna, Gurukula Jhajjar (Rohatak), 1962-63.

WITZEL 1986 = Witzel, Michael: 'On the archetype of Patañjali's Mahābhaṣya'. *Indo-Iranian Journal* 29 (1986) pp. 249-259, D. Reidel Publishing Company 1986.

WIELIŃSKA 1998 = Wielińska, Małgorzata: 'Zarys fonetyki sanskrytu i jej odbicie w piśmie', Studia Indologiczne 1998 (5), pp. 13-22.

WUJASTYK 1993 = Wujastyk, Dominik: *Metarules of Pāṇinian Grammar – Vyāḍi's Paribhāṣāvṛtti*. Vol. I&II, Egbert Forsten, Groningen 1993.

YAGI 1992 = Yagi, Toru: 'The asiddha/asiddhavat reconsidered' [in:] *Wiener Zeitschrift für die Kunde Süd- und Ostasiens und Archiv für indische Philosophie* 36, pp. 49-58, Wienna 1992.

INDEX OF NAMES AND TERMS

INDEX OF SŪTRAS